The Pharmaceutical Regulatory Process

AF734705

DRUGS AND THE PHARMACEUTICAL SCIENCES
A Series of Textbooks and Monographs

Executive Editor
James Swarbrick
PharmaceuTech, Inc.
Pinehurst, North Carolina

Advisory Board

Larry L. Augsburger
University of Maryland
Baltimore, Maryland

Jennifer B. Dressman
University of Frankfurt Institute of Pharmaceutical Technology
Frankfurt, Germany

Anthony J. Hickey
University of North Carolina School of Pharmacy
Chapel Hill, North Carolina

Ajaz Hussain
Sandoz
Princeton, New Jersey

Joseph W. Polli
GlaxoSmithKline Research Triangle Park
North Carolina

Stephen G. Schulman
University of Florida
Gainesville, Florida

Yuichi Sugiyama
University of Tokyo, Tokyo, Japan

Geoffrey T. Tucker
University of Sheffield
Royal Hallamshire Hospital
Sheffield, United Kingdom

Harry G. Brittain
Center for Pharmaceutical Physics
Milford, New Jersey

Robert Gurny
Universite de Geneve
Geneve, Switzerland

Jeffrey A. Hughes
University of Florida College of Pharmacy
Gainesville, Florida

Vincent H. L. Lee
US FDA Center for Drug Evaluation and Research
Los Angeles, California

Kinam Park
Purdue University
West Lafayette, Indiana

Jerome P. Skelly
Alexandria, Virginia

Elizabeth M. Topp
University of Kansas
Lawrence, Kansas

Peter York
University of Bradford School of Pharmacy
Bradford, United Kingdom

1. Pharmacokinetics, Milo Gibaldi and Donald Perrier
2. Good Manufacturing Practices for Pharmaceuticals: A Plan for Total Quality Control, Sidney H. Willig, Murray M. Tuckerman, and William S. Hitchings IV
3. Microencapsulation, edited by J. R. Nixon
4. Drug Metabolism: Chemical and Biochemical Aspects, Bernard Testa and Peter Jenner
5. New Drugs: Discovery and Development, edited by Alan A. Rubin
6. Sustained and Controlled Release Drug Delivery Systems, edited by Joseph R. Robinson
7. Modern Pharmaceutics, edited by Gilbert S. Banker and Christopher T. Rhodes
8. Prescription Drugs in Short Supply: Case Histories, Michael A. Schwartz
9. Activated Charcoal: Antidotal and Other Medical Uses, David O. Cooney
10. Concepts in Drug Metabolism (in two parts), edited by Peter Jenner and Bernard Testa
11. Pharmaceutical Analysis: Modern Methods (in two parts), edited by James W. Munson
12. Techniques of Solubilization of Drugs, edited by Samuel H. Yalkowsky
13. Orphan Drugs, edited by Fred E. Karch
14. Novel Drug Delivery Systems: Fundamentals, Developmental Concepts, Biomedical Assessments, Yie W. Chien
15. Pharmacokinetics: Second Edition, Revised and Expanded, Milo Gibaldi and Donald Perrier
16. Good Manufacturing Practices for Pharmaceuticals: A Plan for Total Quality Control, Second Edition, Revised and Expanded, Sidney H. Willig, Murray M. Tuckerman, and William S. Hitchings IV
17. Formulation of Veterinary Dosage Forms, edited by Jack Blodinger
18. Dermatological Formulations: Percutaneous Absorption, Brian W. Barry
19. The Clinical Research Process in the Pharmaceutical Industry, edited by Gary M. Matoren
20. Microencapsulation and Related Drug Processes, Patrick B. Deasy
21. Drugs and Nutrients: The Interactive Effects, edited by Daphne A. Roe and T. Colin Campbell
22. Biotechnology of Industrial Antibiotics, Erick J. Vandamme
23. Pharmaceutical Process Validation, edited by Bernard T. Loftus and Robert A. Nash
24. Anticancer and Interferon Agents: Synthesis and Properties, edited by Raphael M. Ottenbrite and George B. Butler
25. Pharmaceutical Statistics: Practical and Clinical Applications, Sanford Bolton
26. Drug Dynamics for Analytical, Clinical, and Biological Chemists, Benjamin J. Gudzinowicz, Burrows T. Younkin, Jr., and Michael J. Gudzinowicz
27. Modern Analysis of Antibiotics, edited by Adjoran Aszalos

28. Solubility and Related Properties, Kenneth C. James
29. Controlled Drug Delivery: Fundamentals and Applications, Second Edition, Revised and Expanded, edited by Joseph R. Robinson and Vincent H. Lee
30. New Drug Approval Process: Clinical and Regulatory Management, edited by Richard A. Guarino
31. Transdermal Controlled Systemic Medications, edited by Yie W. Chien
32. Drug Delivery Devices: Fundamentals and Applications, edited by Praveen Tyle
33. Pharmacokinetics: Regulatory • Industrial • Academic Perspectives, edited by Peter G. Welling and Francis L.S. Tse
34. Clinical Drug Trials and Tribulations, edited by Allen E. Cato
35. Transdermal Drug Delivery: Developmental Issues and Research Initiatives, edited by Jonathan Hadgraft and Richard H. Guy
36. Aqueous Polymeric Coatings for Pharmaceutical Dosage Forms, edited by James W. McGinity
37. Pharmaceutical Pelletization Technology, edited by Isaac Ghebre-Sellassie
38. Good Laboratory Practice Regulations, edited by Allen F. Hirsch
39. Nasal Systemic Drug Delivery, Yie W. Chien, Kenneth S. E. Su, and Shyi-Feu Chang
40. Modern Pharmaceutics: Second Edition, Revised and Expanded, edited by Gilbert S. Banker and Christopher T. Rhodes
41. Specialized Drug Delivery Systems: Manufacturing and Production Technology, edited by Praveen Tyle
42. Topical Drug Delivery Formulations, edited by David W. Osborne and Anton H. Amann
43. Drug Stability: Principles and Practices, Jens T. Carstensen
44. Pharmaceutical Statistics: Practical and Clinical Applications, Second Edition, Revised and Expanded, Sanford Bolton
45. Biodegradable Polymers as Drug Delivery Systems, edited by Mark Chasin and Robert Langer
46. Preclinical Drug Disposition: A Laboratory Handbook, Francis L.S. Tse and James J. Jaffe
47. HPLC in the Pharmaceutical Industry, edited by Godwin W. Fong and Stanley K. Lam
48. Pharmaceutical Bioequivalence, edited by Peter G. Welling, Francis L.S. Tse, and Shrikant V. Dinghe
49. Pharmaceutical Dissolution Testing, Umesh V. Banakar
50. Novel Drug Delivery Systems: Second Edition, Revised and Expanded, Yie W. Chien
51. Managing the Clinical Drug Development Process, David M. Cocchetto and Ronald V. Nardi
52. Good Manufacturing Practices for Pharmaceuticals: A Plan for Total Quality Control, Third Edition, edited by Sidney H. Willig and James R. Stoker

53. Prodrugs: Topical and Ocular Drug Delivery, edited by Kenneth B. Sloan
54. Pharmaceutical Inhalation Aerosol Technology, edited by Anthony J. Hickey
55. Radiopharmaceuticals: Chemistry and Pharmacology, edited by Adrian D. Nunn
56. New Drug Approval Process: Second Edition, Revised and Expanded, edited by Richard A. Guarino
57. Pharmaceutical Process Validation: Second Edition, Revised and Expanded, edited by Ira R. Berry and Robert A. Nash
58. Ophthalmic Drug Delivery Systems, edited by Ashim K. Mitra
59. Pharmaceutical Skin Penetration Enhancement, edited by Kenneth A. Walters and Jonathan Hadgraft
60. Colonic Drug Absorption and Metabolism, edited by Peter R. Bieck
61. Pharmaceutical Particulate Carriers: Therapeutic Applications, edited by Alain Rolland
62. Drug Permeation Enhancement: Theory and Applications, edited by Dean S. Hsieh
63. Glycopeptide Antibiotics, edited by Ramakrishnan Nagarajan
64. Achieving Sterility in Medical and Pharmaceutical Products, Nigel A. Halls
65. Multiparticulate Oral Drug Delivery, edited by Isaac Ghebre-Sellassie
66. Colloidal Drug Delivery Systems, edited by Jörg Kreuter
67. Pharmacokinetics: Regulatory • Industrial • Academic Perspectives, Second Edition, edited by Peter G. Welling and Francis L. S. Tse
68. Drug Stability: Principles and Practices, Second Edition, Revised and Expanded, Jens T. Carstensen
69. Good Laboratory Practice Regulations: Second Edition, Revised and Expanded, edited by Sandy Weinberg
70. Physical Characterization of Pharmaceutical Solids, edited by Harry G. Brittain
71. Pharmaceutical Powder Compaction Technology, edited by Göran Alderborn and Christer Nyström
72. Modern Pharmaceutics: Third Edition, Revised and Expanded, edited by Gilbert S. Banker and Christopher T. Rhodes
73. Microencapsulation: Methods and Industrial Applications, edited by Simon Benita
74. Oral Mucosal Drug Delivery, edited by Michael J. Rathbone
75. Clinical Research in Pharmaceutical Development, edited by Barry Bleidt and Michael Montagne
76. The Drug Development Process: Increasing Efficiency and Cost Effectiveness, edited by Peter G. Welling, Louis Lasagna, and Umesh V. Banakar
77. Microparticulate Systems for the Delivery of Proteins and Vaccines, edited by Smadar Cohen and Howard Bernstein
78. Good Manufacturing Practices for Pharmaceuticals: A Plan for Total Quality Control, Fourth Edition, Revised and Expanded, Sidney H. Willig and James R. Stoker

79. Aqueous Polymeric Coatings for Pharmaceutical Dosage Forms: Second Edition, Revised and Expanded, edited by James W. McGinity
80. Pharmaceutical Statistics: Practical and Clinical Applications, Third Edition, Sanford Bolton
81. Handbook of Pharmaceutical Granulation Technology, edited by Dilip M. Parikh
82. Biotechnology of Antibiotics: Second Edition, Revised and Expanded, edited by William R. Strohl
83. Mechanisms of Transdermal Drug Delivery, edited by Russell O. Potts and Richard H. Guy
84. Pharmaceutical Enzymes, edited by Albert Lauwers and Simon Scharpé
85. Development of Biopharmaceutical Parenteral Dosage Forms, edited by John A. Bontempo
86. Pharmaceutical Project Management, edited by Tony Kennedy
87. Drug Products for Clinical Trials: An International Guide to Formulation • Production • Quality Control, edited by Donald C. Monkhouse and Christopher T. Rhodes
88. Development and Formulation of Veterinary Dosage Forms: Second Edition, Revised and Expanded, edited by Gregory E. Hardee and J. Desmond Baggot
89. Receptor-Based Drug Design, edited by Paul Leff
90. Automation and Validation of Information in Pharmaceutical Processing, edited by Joseph F. deSpautz
91. Dermal Absorption and Toxicity Assessment, edited by Michael S. Roberts and Kenneth A. Walters
92. Pharmaceutical Experimental Design, Gareth A. Lewis, Didier Mathieu, and Roger Phan-Tan-Luu
93. Preparing for FDA Pre-Approval Inspections, edited by Martin D. Hynes III
94. Pharmaceutical Excipients: Characterization by IR, Raman, and NMR Spectroscopy, David E. Bugay and W. Paul Findlay
95. Polymorphism in Pharmaceutical Solids, edited by Harry G. Brittain
96. Freeze-Drying/Lyophilization of Pharmaceutical and Biological Products, edited by Louis Rey and Joan C.May
97. Percutaneous Absorption: Drugs–Cosmetics–Mechanisms–Methodology, Third Edition, Revised and Expanded, edited by Robert L. Bronaugh and Howard I. Maibach
98. Bioadhesive Drug Delivery Systems: Fundamentals, Novel Approaches, and Development, edited by Edith Mathiowitz, Donald E. Chickering III, and Claus-Michael Lehr
99. Protein Formulation and Delivery, edited by Eugene J. McNally
100. New Drug Approval Process: Third Edition, The Global Challenge, edited by Richard A. Guarino
101. Peptide and Protein Drug Analysis, edited by Ronald E. Reid

102. Transport Processes in Pharmaceutical Systems, edited by Gordon L. Amidon, Ping I. Lee, and Elizabeth M. Topp
103. Excipient Toxicity and Safety, edited by Myra L. Weiner and Lois A. Kotkoskie
104. The Clinical Audit in Pharmaceutical Development, edited by Michael R. Hamrell
105. Pharmaceutical Emulsions and Suspensions, edited by Francoise Nielloud and Gilberte Marti-Mestres
106. Oral Drug Absorption: Prediction and Assessment, edited by Jennifer B. Dressman and Hans Lennernäs
107. Drug Stability: Principles and Practices, Third Edition, Revised and Expanded, edited by Jens T. Carstensen and C. T. Rhodes
108. Containment in the Pharmaceutical Industry, edited by James P. Wood
109. Good Manufacturing Practices for Pharmaceuticals: A Plan for Total Quality Control from Manufacturer to Consumer, Fifth Edition, Revised and Expanded, Sidney H. Willig
110. Advanced Pharmaceutical Solids, Jens T. Carstensen
111. Endotoxins: Pyrogens, LAL Testing, and Depyrogenation, Second Edition, Revised and Expanded, Kevin L. Williams
112. Pharmaceutical Process Engineering, Anthony J. Hickey and David Ganderton
113. Pharmacogenomics, edited by Werner Kalow, Urs A. Meyer and Rachel F. Tyndale
114. Handbook of Drug Screening, edited by Ramakrishna Seethala and Prabhavathi B. Fernandes
115. Drug Targeting Technology: Physical • Chemical • Biological Methods, edited by Hans Schreier
116. Drug–Drug Interactions, edited by A. David Rodrigues
117. Handbook of Pharmaceutical Analysis, edited by Lena Ohannesian and Anthony J. Streeter
118. Pharmaceutical Process Scale-Up, edited by Michael Levin
119. Dermatological and Transdermal Formulations, edited by Kenneth A. Walters
120. Clinical Drug Trials and Tribulations: Second Edition, Revised and Expanded, edited by Allen Cato, Lynda Sutton, and Allen Cato III
121. Modern Pharmaceutics: Fourth Edition, Revised and Expanded, edited by Gilbert S. Banker and Christopher T. Rhodes
122. Surfactants and Polymers in Drug Delivery, Martin Malmsten
123. Transdermal Drug Delivery: Second Edition, Revised and Expanded, edited by Richard H. Guy and Jonathan Hadgraft
124. Good Laboratory Practice Regulations: Second Edition, Revised and Expanded, edited by Sandy Weinberg
125. Parenteral Quality Control: Sterility, Pyrogen, Particulate, and Package Integrity Testing: Third Edition, Revised and Expanded, Michael J. Akers, Daniel S. Larrimore, and Dana Morton Guazzo

126. Modified-Release Drug Delivery Technology, edited by Michael J. Rathbone, Jonathan Hadgraft, and Michael S. Roberts
127. Simulation for Designing Clinical Trials: A Pharmacokinetic-Pharmacodynamic Modeling Perspective, edited by Hui C. Kimko and Stephen B. Duffull
128. Affinity Capillary Electrophoresis in Pharmaceutics and Biopharmaceutics, edited by Reinhard H. H. Neubert and Hans-Hermann Rüttinger
129. Pharmaceutical Process Validation: An International Third Edition, Revised and Expanded, edited by Robert A. Nash and Alfred H. Wachter
130. Ophthalmic Drug Delivery Systems: Second Edition, Revised and Expanded, edited by Ashim K. Mitra
131. Pharmaceutical Gene Delivery Systems, edited by Alain Rolland and Sean M. Sullivan
132. Biomarkers in Clinical Drug Development, edited by John C. Bloom and Robert A. Dean
133. Pharmaceutical Extrusion Technology, edited by Isaac Ghebre-Sellassie and Charles Martin
134. Pharmaceutical Inhalation Aerosol Technology: Second Edition, Revised and Expanded, edited by Anthony J. Hickey
135. Pharmaceutical Statistics: Practical and Clinical Applications, Fourth Edition, Sanford Bolton and Charles Bon
136. Compliance Handbook for Pharmaceuticals, Medical Devices, and Biologics, edited by Carmen Medina
137. Freeze-Drying/Lyophilization of Pharmaceutical and Biological Products: Second Edition, Revised and Expanded, edited by Louis Rey and
138. Supercritical Fluid Technology for Drug Product Development, edited by Peter York, Uday B. Kompella, and Boris Y. Shekunov
139. New Drug Approval Process: Fourth Edition, Accelerating Global Registrations, edited by Richard A. Guarino
140. Microbial Contamination Control in Parenteral Manufacturing, edited by Kevin L. Williams
141. New Drug Development: Regulatory Paradigms for Clinical Pharmacology and Biopharmaceutics, edited by Chandrahas G. Sahajwalla
142. Microbial Contamination Control in the Pharmaceutical Industry, edited by Luis Jimenez
143. Generic Drug Product Development: Solid Oral Dosage Forms, edited by Leon Shargel and Isadore Kanfer
144. Introduction to the Pharmaceutical Regulatory Process, edited by Ira R. Berry
145. Drug Delivery to the Oral Cavity: Molecules to Market, edited by Tapash K. Ghosh and William R. Pfister
146. Good Design Practices for GMP Pharmaceutical Facilities, edited by Andrew Signore and Terry Jacobs
147. Drug Products for Clinical Trials, Second Edition, edited by Donald Monkhouse, Charles Carney, and Jim Clark

148. Polymeric Drug Delivery Systems, edited by Glen S. Kwon
149. Injectable Dispersed Systems: Formulation, Processing, and Performance, edited by Diane J. Burgess
150. Laboratory Auditing for Quality and Regulatory Compliance, Donald Singer, Raluca- Ioana Stefan, and Jacobus van Staden
151. Active Pharmaceutical Ingredients: Development, Manufacturing, and Regulation, edited by Stanley Nusim
152. Preclinical Drug Development, edited by Mark C. Rogge and David R. Taft
153. Pharmaceutical Stress Testing: Predicting Drug Degradation, edited by Steven W. Baertschi
154. Handbook of Pharmaceutical Granulation Technology: Second Edition, edited by Dilip M. Parikh
155. Percutaneous Absorption: Drugs–Cosmetics–Mechanisms–Methodology, Fourth Edition, edited by Robert L. Bronaugh and Howard I. Maibach
156. Pharmacogenomics: Second Edition, edited by Werner Kalow, Urs A. Meyer and Rachel F. Tyndale
157. Pharmaceutical Process Scale-Up, Second Edition, edited by Michael Levin
158. Microencapsulation: Methods and Industrial Applications, Second Edition, edited by Simon Benita
159. Nanoparticle Technology for Drug Delivery, edited by Ram B. Gupta and Uday B. Kompella
160. Spectroscopy of Pharmaceutical Solids, edited by Harry G. Brittain
161. Dose Optimization in Drug Development, edited by Rajesh Krishna
162. Herbal Supplements-Drug Interactions: Scientific and Regulatory Perspectives, edited by Y. W. Francis Lam, Shiew-Mei Huang, and Stephen D. Hall
163. Pharmaceutical Photostability and Stabilization Technology, edited by Joseph T. Piechocki and Karl Thoma
164. Environmental Monitoring for Cleanrooms and Controlled Environments, edited by Anne Marie Dixon
165. Pharmaceutical Product Development: In Vitro-In Vivo Correlation, edited by Dakshina Murthy Chilukuri, Gangadhar Sunkara, and David Young
166. Nanoparticulate Drug Delivery Systems, edited by Deepak Thassu, Michel Deleers, and Yashwant Pathak
167. Endotoxins: Pyrogens, LAL Testing and Depyrogenation, Third Edition, edited by Kevin L. Williams
168. Good Laboratory Practice Regulations, Fourth Edition, edited by Anne Sandy Weinberg
169. Good Manufacturing Practices for Pharmaceuticals, Sixth Edition, edited by Joseph D. Nally
170. Oral-Lipid Based Formulations: Enhancing the Bioavailability of Poorly Water-soluble Drugs, edited by David J. Hauss
171. Handbook of Bioequivalence Testing, edited by Sarfaraz K. Niazi

172. Advanced Drug Formulation Design to Optimize Therapeutic Outcomes, edited by Robert O. Williams III, David R. Taft, and Jason T. McConville
173. Clean-in-Place for Biopharmaceutical Processes, edited by Dale A. Seiberling
174. Filtration and Purification in the Biopharmaceutical Industry, Second Edition, edited by Maik W. Jornitz and Theodore H. Meltzer
175. Protein Formulation and Delivery, Second Edition, edited by Eugene J. McNally and Jayne E. Hastedt
176. Aqueous Polymeric Coatings for Pharmaceutical Dosage Forms, Third Edition, edited by James McGinity and Linda A. Felton
177. Dermal Absorption and Toxicity Assessment, Second Edition, edited by Michael S. Roberts and Kenneth A. Walters
178. Preformulation Solid Dosage Form Development, edited by Moji C. Adeyeye and Harry G. Brittain
179. Drug-Drug Interactions, Second Edition, edited by A. David Rodrigues
180. Generic Drug Product Development: Bioequivalence Issues, edited by Isadore Kanfer and Leon Shargel
181. Pharmaceutical Pre-Approval Inspections: A Guide to Regulatory Success, Second Edition, edited by Martin D. Hynes III
182. Pharmaceutical Project Management, Second Edition, edited by Anthony Kennedy
183. Modified Release Drug Delivery Technology, Second Edition, Volume 1, edited by Michael J. Rathbone, Jonathan Hadgraft, Michael S. Roberts, and Majella E. Lane
184. Modified-Release Drug Delivery Technology, Second Edition, Volume 2, edited by Michael J. Rathbone, Jonathan Hadgraft, Michael S. Roberts, and Majella E. Lane
185. The Pharmaceutical Regulatory Process, Second Edition, edited by Ira R. Berry and Robert P. Martin

The Pharmaceutical Regulatory Process
Second Edition

edited by
Ira R. Berry
International Regulatory Business Consultants, LLC
Freehold, New Jersey, USA

Robert P. Martin
RPMartin Consulting
Lebanon, Pennsylvania, USA.

CRC Press
Taylor & Francis Group
Boca Raton London New York

CRC Press is an imprint of the
Taylor & Francis Group, an **informa** business

CRC Press
Taylor & Francis Group
6000 Broken Sound Parkway NW, Suite 300
Boca Raton, FL 33487-2742

First issued in paperback 2019

© 2008 by Taylor & Francis Group, LLC
CRC Press is an imprint of Taylor & Francis Group, an Informa business

No claim to original U.S. Government works

ISBN-13: 978-0-4200-7042-2 (hbk)
ISBN-13: 978-1-138-38128-5 (pbk)

This book contains information obtained from authentic and highly regarded sources. While all reasonable efforts have been made to publish reliable data and information, neither the author[s] nor the publisher can accept any legal responsibility or liability for any errors or omissions that may be made. The publishers wish to make clear that any views or opinions expressed in this book by individual editors, authors or contributors are personal to them and do not neces sarily reflect the views/opinions of the publishers. The information or guidance contained in this book is intended for use by medical, scientific or health-care professionals and is provided strictly as a supplement to the medical or other professional's own judgement, their knowledge of the patient's medical history, relevant manufacturer's instructions and the appropriate best practice guidelines. Because of the rapid advances in medical science, any information or advice on dosages, procedures or diagnoses should be independently verified. The reader is strongly urged to consult the relevant national drug formulary and the drug companies' and device or material manufacturers' printed instructions, and their websites, before administering or utilizing any of the drugs, devices or materials mentioned in this book. This book does not indicate whether a particular treatment is appropriate or suitable for a particular individual. Ultimately it is the sole responsibility of the medical professional to make his or her own professional judgements, so as to advise and treat patients appropriately. The authors and publishers have also attempted to trace the copyright holders of all material reproduced in this publication and apologize to copyright holders if permission to publish in this form has not been obtained. If any copyright material has not been acknowledged please write and let us know so we may rectify in any future reprint.

Except as permitted under U.S. Copyright Law, no part of this book may be reprinted, reproduced, transmitted, or utilized in any form by any electronic, mechanical, or other means, now known or hereafter invented, including photocopying, microfilming, and recording, or in any information storage or retrieval system, without written permission from the publishers.

For permission to photocopy or use material electronically from this work, please access www.copyright.com (http://www.copyright.com/) or contact the Copyright Clearance Center, Inc. (CCC), 222 Rosewood Drive, Danvers, MA 01923, 978-750-8400. CCC is a not-for-profit organization that provides licenses and registration for a variety of users. For organizations that have been granted a photocopy license by the CCC, a separate system of payment has been arranged.

Trademark Notice: Product or corporate names may be trademarks or registered trademarks, and are used only for identification and explanation without intent to infringe.

Library of Congress Cataloging-in-Publication Data

The pharmaceutical regulatory process / edited by Ira R. Berry, Robert P. Martin. – 2nd ed.
p. cm. – (Drugs and the pharmaceutical sciences ; v. 185)
Includes bibliographical references and index.
ISBN-13: 978-1-4200-7042-2 (hardcover : alk. paper)
ISBN-10: 1-4200-7042-8 (hardcover : alk. paper) 1. Pharmacy–Law and legislation–United States. 2. Drugs–Law and legislation–United States. I. Berry, Ira R., 1942– II. Martin, Robert P. (Robert Paul) III. Series.
[DNLM: 1. Legislation, Drug–United States. 2. Guideline Adherence–legislation & jurisprudence–United States. 3. Pharmaceutical Preparations–standards–United States. W1 DR893B v.185 2008 / QV 33 AA1 P5365 2008]
KF2036.D7P47 2008
344.7304'233–dc22 2008042661

Visit the Taylor & Francis Web site at
http://www.taylorandfrancis.com

and the CRC Press Web site at
http://www.crcpress.com

Preface

This book is a follow-up to the First Edition that described the regulatory process by which sponsors of pharmaceutical products receive approval to market—especially for the U.S. market and through the approval by the U.S. Food and Drug Administration (FDA). The First Edition provided a history of pharmaceutical regulations, policies, and guidances. This Second Edition, now several years later, describes the many changes that have taken place such that terminology is different, updated requirements are based on stricter scientific standards and with some product registrations and industry practices facing basic changes in a constantly changing regulatory environment. This Second Edition contains the subject matter from the First Edition, but with in-depth, updated, and reformed requirements. New additions cover the need for established drug safety standards for post-approval marketed products, marketing drugs that have not required regulatory approval, and the increased supply of APIs and drug products from foreign countries. Just as for the First Edition, this Second Edition is intended to provide an understanding of the requirements to obtain regulatory approval to market a pharmaceutical product and also the policies and procedures needed by pharmaceutical companies to create and implement regulatory compliance postapproval. This book provides the most current information available from industry professionals, practicing attorneys, and FDA regulators—to be used by students, industry professionals, and any person needing to understand the mechanisms and means to establish regulatory compliance for pharmaceutical products and company practices.

The first section of the book includes chapters that describe the legal requirements needed to obtain regulatory approval of pharmaceutical products and remain in regulatory compliance. The first chapter describes the history, "Pharmaceutical Regulations Before and After the Food, Drug, and Cosmetic Act." From the drug approval system that was revised in 1984 and updated in the 1990s, there have been significant changes in order to create a more reasonable and practical regulatory scheme. The chapter "Modernizing the Food and Drug Administration" reviews the substantive legal changes that have been made to FDA and the regulatory process. "The New Drug Approval Process—Before and After 1962" chapter contains the basic requirements for a sponsor to obtain approval of a New Drug. The next chapter focuses on the "Generic Drug Approval Process: Hatch-Waxman Update." The importance of generic drugs to reduce health-care costs is ever more important and this chapter is focused on these issues. The regulation of biological products and the debate regarding creation of a legislative scheme for "follow-on biologics" continue to present many medical, scientific, and regulatory issues that are covered in the chapter "FDA Regulation of Biological Products." The next chapter, "FDA's Antibiotic Regulatory Scheme: Then and Now," addresses the current requirements for regulatory approval of an antibiotic product. The chapter "Generic Drugs in a Changing Intellectual Property Landscape" describes current patent issues relating to the relationship between New Drugs and Generic Drugs. "The Influence of the Prescription Drug User Fee Act on the Approval Process" chapter has been updated with major legislative revisions that impact the requirements for drug safety reviews, product regulatory approvals, and marketing practices. The next chapter, "Clinical Research Requirements for New Drug Applications," provides an update to the clinical testing requirements for pharmaceutical products. "The Post-Approval Marketing Practices Regarding Drug Safety and Pharmacovigilance" the chapter describes the requirement for a pharmacovigilance program that should be designed to document and prevent widespread safety issues related to a pharmaceutical product postapproval. The next chapter describes the history and current programs for "Drugs Marketed Without FDA Approval." Approval from FDA is not required prior to marketing all pharmaceutical products; however, this issue has been receiving a good amount of attention from FDA—and industry has been focused on working with FDA to keep these products in regulatory compliance following current standards. The issues are complex and the chapter provides an excellent review and explanation. The chapter "FDA Regulation of Foreign Drug Imports, the Need for Improvement" follows and describes the current problems and issues that have arisen from the expanded scope of the importation of pharmaceuticals from foreign countries.

The second section of the book deals with updated specific regulatory requirements for product applications for approval and also postmarketing practices. The first chapter describes the role of "Active Pharmaceutical Ingredients" in regulatory approval of a drug product. It is common for an API to be produced by a different manufacturer from the dosage form manufacturer such that the regulatory requirements must be clear. The next three chapters describe the industry's current views for "Obtaining Approval of NDAs and ANDAs from a Chemistry, Manufacturing and Controls Perspective," "Obtaining Approval of a Generic Drug: Pre-1984 to the Present," and "New Developments in the Approval and Marketing of Nonprescription or OTC Drugs." Emphasis is given to the Common Technical Document format. Along with these three chapters, the next chapter should be followed alongside—"Current Good Manufacturing Practice and the Drug Approval Process," which is a critical part of the process for pharmaceutical product regulatory approvals. The next chapter, "The Influence of the USP on the Drug Approval Process," continues to be necessary for registration of pharmaceuticals as compliance with this compendium on pharmaceutical standards is required. The chapter "Ways, Means and Evolving Trends in the U.S. Registration of Drug Products from Foreign Countries" describes current issues related to the registration and marketing of drugs produced in foreign countries such as drug safety, the critical path to develop new drugs, and evidence needed to establish efficacy. The chapter "Impact of Government Regulation on Prescription Drug Marketing and Promotion" addresses the continually increased depth and enforcement taken by FDA in marketing and advertising practices. The next chapter addresses "CMC Post-Approval Regulatory Affairs: Constantly Managing Change." This continues to be a critically important practice that needs to be followed postapproval so that change for improvement can be implemented. The last chapter, "Living with 21 CFR Part 11 Compliance," covers the significant changes that have occurred for electronic documentation, with a discussion of computer validation.

This Second Edition provides an update to the significant changes that have occurred in the regulation of pharmaceutical products since the First Edition was published. These changes have made the First Edition a basic history book in government regulations and requirements in many respects. This new edition provides invaluable information—just as the First Edition—to the newcomer working in the pharmaceutical industry as well as to students. The world of regulations for the pharmaceutical industry is constantly changing—the basics remain the same as a foundation—but the science, interpretation, and implementation expand as technology increases.

Ira R. Berry
Robert P. Martin

Contents

Contributors

Lorien Armour Armour CMC Regulatory Consulting, LLC, Durham, North Carolina, U.S.A.

Jane Baluss Foley & Lardner LLP, Washington, D.C., U.S.A.

Ann M. Begley, Esq. K. & L. Gates LLP, Washington, D.C., U.S.A.

Ira R. Berry International Regulatory Business Consultants, LLC, Freehold, New Jersey, U.S.A.

Marie C. Boyd Covington & Burling LLP, Washington, D.C., U.S.A.

Paul A. Braier, Esq. Greenblum & Bernstein, P.L.C., Reston, Virginia, U.S.A.

Richard L. Burcham BPI Technologies, Corp., Irving, Texas, U.S.A.

Krista Hessler Carver Covington & Burling LLP, Washington, D.C., U.S.A.

Edward M. Cohen EMC Consulting Services, Newtown, Connecticut, U.S.A.

Benjamin L. England Benjamin L. England & Associates, LLC, FDAImports.com, Inc., Columbia, Maryland, U.S.A.

Michael J. Fink, Esq. Greenblum & Bernstein, P.L.C., Reston, Virginia, U.S.A.

Loren Gelber RRI Consulting Inc., Lake Wylie, South Carolina, U.S.A.

Daniel Glassman Medimetriks Pharmaceuticals, Inc., Fairfield, New Jersey, U.S.A.

Gene Goldberg Medimetriks Pharmaceuticals, Inc., Fairfield, New Jersey, U.S.A.

Neil F. Greenblum, Esq. Greenblum & Bernstein, P.L.C., Reston, Virginia, U.S.A.

Alberto Grignolo PAREXEL International Corporation, Waltham, Massachusetts, U.S.A.

Marc S. Gross Darby & Darby, P.C., New York, New York, U.S.A.

Michael S. Labson Covington & Burling LLP, Washington, D.C., U.S.A.

Max S. Lazar FDA Regulatory Compliance Consulting, Surprise, Arizona, U.S.A.

Jay Lessler Darby & Darby, P.C., New York, New York, U.S.A.

Leo J. Lucisano GlaxoSmithKline, Research Triangle Park, North Carolina, U.S.A.

S. Peter Ludwig Darby & Darby, P.C., New York, New York, U.S.A.

Robert P. Martin RP Martin Consulting, Lebanon, P.A., U.S.A.

William J. Mead Consultant, Rowayton, Connecticut, U.S.A.

Kevin A. Miller GlaxoSmithKline, Research Triangle Park, North Carolina, U.S.A.

Sean Myers-Payne, Esq. Greenblum & Bernstein, P.L.C., Reston, Virginia, U.S.A.

P. Branko Pejic, Esq. Greenblum & Bernstein, P.L.C., Reston, Virginia, U.S.A.

Michael P. Peskoe Edwards Angell Palmer & Dodge LLP, Boston, Massachusetts, U.S.A.

David Rosen Foley & Lardner LLP, Washington, D.C., U.S.A.

Stephen M. Roylance, Esq. Greenblum & Bernstein, P.L.C., Reston, Virginia, U.S.A.

Marc J. Scheineson, Esq. Alston & Bird LLP, Washington, D.C., U.S.A.

Dhiren N. Shah Aventis Pharmaceuticals, Kansas City, Missouri, U.S.A.

Barbara Spallitta Reckitt Benckiser, Inc., Parsippany, New Jersey, U.S.A.

John P. Swann FDA History Office, Rockville, Maryland, U.S.A.

Arthur Y. Tsien, Esq. Olsson Frank Weeda Terman Bode Matz PC, Washington, D.C., U.S.A.

Amanda L. Vaught Darby & Darby, P.C., New York, New York, U.S.A.

Irving L. Wiesen, Esq. Law Offices of Irving L. Wiesen, Esq., New York, New York, U.S.A.

Gary L. Yingling, Esq. K. & L. Gates LLP, Washington, D.C., U.S.A.

1 Pharmaceutical Regulation Before and After the Food, Drug, and Cosmetic Act

John P. Swann
FDA History Office, Rockville, Maryland, U.S.A.

INTRODUCTION: 19TH-CENTURY BACKGROUND TO DRUG REGULATION IN THE UNITED STATES

Federal drug regulation in 19th-century America was a fleeting phenomenon, limited in part by a lack of both scientific capacity and sustained political exigency. Citizens stood a better chance of being safeguarded by their own states, although the legislation and enforcement varied widely in this period. By the turn of the 20th century, Connecticut, Georgia, Illinois, Iowa, the Oklahoma territory, California, and most other states had outlawed drug adulteration and/or failure to label a medicine that had morphine, cocaine, digitalis, nux vomica, chloroform, cantharides, strychnine, ergot, or a host of other substances (1,2). Typically, violations were considered as misdemeanors and were penalized accordingly. But absent a federal proscription, it was all the protection a citizen might hope for.

Still, there were some notable though short-lived developments at the national level. Baltimore physician James Smith, inspired by the marketing of spurious smallpox vaccine, convinced Congress to pass a law in 1813 to ensure the provision of reliable vaccine. Under this law, the president appointed a so-called vaccine agent (Smith) "to preserve the genuine vaccine matter, and to furnish the same to any citizen of the United States, whenever it may be applied for, through the medium of the post office." The blame for a smallpox outbreak in North Carolina in 1822 was assigned to vaccine supplied by the vaccine agent, although this was never proven. The impact of the event led to repeal of the vaccine act and restoration to states of the responsibility for pure and effective smallpox vaccine (3).

The publication of the *The Pharmacopeia of the United States of America* in 1820 was a milestone in the history of drug regulation because it established a national compendium of drug standards to help respond to what medical and pharmaceutical professionals observed to be an increasingly corrupt drug supply. Ultimately, it would prove to be unique among most legally recognized publications of this kind in the world because it was, and still is, a private venture. There had been occasional local compilations of standard drugs and their preparation, the first of which was the *Lititz Pharmacopeia* of 1778. But the convention that assumed responsibility for a national collection of drug standards and their preparation had something broader in mind.

Led by New Hampshire native Lyman Spalding, 11 physician delegates from medical societies and schools across the country, representing four districts, met in Washington in January 1820 to discuss drafts and recommendations from district proceedings and what would and would not be included in the USP. The first USP aimed "to select from among substances which possess medical power, those, the utility of which is most fully established and best understood; and to form from them preparations and compositions, in which their powers may be exerted to the greatest advantage" (4). The USP thus endeavored to elevate the pharmaceutical armamentarium in a way that would make both the practice of medicine and the practice of pharmacy more reliable (5–8).

The first federal law that addressed pharmaceuticals in general invoked the USP as well as other pharmacopeias. Lewis Caleb Beck's 1846 publication, *Adulteration of Various Substances Used in Medicine and the Arts, with the Means of Detecting Them: Intended as a Manual for the Physician, the Apothecary, and the Artisan,* revealed an American marketplace rife with adulterated medicines. Opium, one of the most valued medicines, was most frequently subjected to fraud, mixed with all manner of deceptive ingredients, such as gum arabic, sand, and lead. Beck identified many other drugs commonly adulterated, including tartar emetic, quinine, and rhubarb. It was a state of affairs perhaps best captured by British statesman and pharmacist Jacob Bell, who related the widespread belief abroad that drugs rendered unsuitable by decay or fraud were still "good enough for America" (9).

If Beck's book provided the scientific evidence why the United States needed a law to protect the drug supply, then the Mexican–American War (1846–1848) provided the political impetus. Many in Congress blamed adulterated drugs for the massive wartime deaths. In truth, considering the drugs then available, it would have made little difference whether or not the drugs were pure. Squalid camps, inadequate nutrition, and an understaffed medical corps were largely responsible for deaths due to disease—about 10% of the total fighting force each year, a rate seven times the mortality rate due to combat (10). The continuing prevalence of drug adulteration in the 1840s, particularly evident in the ports, produced, as James Harvey Young observed, "a sense of outrage." Senator John Davis of Massachusetts believed that, "If we can stop the importation of the spurious drug from abroad, we shall know how to deal with those who may choose to go into their adulteration in the United States" (11). Such sentiments, combined with Congress's conception of pharmaceutical fraud in the Mexican–American conflict and the documentation supplied by Beck, helped shape a law that attempted to bring some order to the chaos.

The Drug Import Law, signed by President James K. Polk on June 26, 1848, required the examination of all drugs that came into the ports of New York, Boston, Philadelphia, Baltimore, Charleston, and New Orleans for "quality, purity, and fitness for medical purposes." The law identified the USP as well as the pharmacopeias and dispensatories of Edinburgh, London, France, and Germany as the source of standards used by the port examiners in their appraisals. Drugs had to be labeled with the name of the manufacturer and the place of preparation. The Secretary of the Treasury was authorized to appoint suitably qualified personnel at each of these ports. Any drug so adulterated or deteriorated to fall short of the standard of purity or strength as established by these compendia would not pass the customhouse. The owner or consignee could request a reexamination by an analytical chemist endorsed by the medical profession and the local school of medicine or pharmacy. But if that analysis upheld the port examiner, the violative drug would be either removed by the owner or destroyed by the port (12).

Initially, the law was enforced vigorously by those appointed by Secretary of the Treasury Robert J. Walker. In the first few months, the New York port was reported to have turned away over 90,000 pounds of drugs. Some even hoped, like

Senator Davis, that it might be possible to address the problem of domestic traffic in problematical drugs. However, the impact of the law soon diminished. In part, this was due to inadequately developed methods of analysis, a problem that pharmacists, in particular, tried to rectify. But the problem also rested in the appointment of unqualified individuals to special examiner positions, appointments which began to be awarded more on the basis of political debts than the suitable qualifications as stated in the law. By 1860, Edward Squibb announced that the law was barely enforced any more, and that remained the case despite the efforts of some physicians and pharmacists for the remainder of the century (13–15).

EARLY REGULATION OF BIOLOGICAL THERAPIES

The next significant milestone in the history of regulating therapeutic products in the United States followed a major advancement in biological therapeutics. In 1890, Emil von Behring and Shibasaburo Kitasato, working at the Robert Koch Institute in Berlin, announced that they had successfully treated diphtheria by injecting patients with blood serum of animals immunized against the pathogen. The last two decades of the 19th century witnessed the identification of nearly two dozen microorganisms responsible for disease, and the work of von Behring, Kitasato, Louis Pasteur, Emile Roux, and others applied these discoveries to develop and refine biological treatments for these diseases (16,17).

State and local public health laboratories and a few commercial concerns soon began producing their own diphtheria antitoxin once European scientists perfected the production methodology. On the eve of this milieu, Joseph Kinyoun, head of the Hygienic Laboratory of the U.S. Marine Hospital Service (later renamed the Public Health Service), warned the Surgeon General in November 1894 of "... what will evidently ensue in our country. Many persons will, during the ensuing year, commence to prepare the (antidiphtheria) serum as a business enterprise, and there will, without a doubt, be many worthless articles called antitoxin thrown upon the market. All the serum intended for sale should be made or tested by competent persons. The testing, in fact, should be done by disinterested parties. The danger with us is perhaps greater than could exist here (in Germany) under any circumstances" (18). Early in 1895, the Hygienic Laboratory developed a standard diphtheria antitoxin for distribution (19–21). Businesses, as Kinyoun suspected, indeed took up production, but it was the antitoxin manufactured by a municipal public health laboratory that launched a movement for regulatory intervention (Fig. 1).

In October 1901, the St. Louis Health Department produced a batch of antitoxin that killed 13 children being treated for diphtheria; the cause of death in each case was tetanus. An investigation led by the city council and the health department revealed that the consulting bacteriologist who had produced the antitoxin had used a horse that contracted and later died of tetanus. The bacteriologist allegedly was aware of the horse's condition but failed to destroy the product or otherwise prevent its distribution. Although he was unaware of the tainted source of the antitoxin, the janitor in the laboratory had responsibility for bottling the product; he complicated recovery of the antitoxin by initially claiming that the antitoxin had been destroyed. The incident in St. Louis was not an isolated one. There were other accidents also involving biological medicines, such as about 100 cases of postvaccination tetanus that occurred in Camden, New Jersey, in the Fall of 1901, where nine children died.

FIGURE 1 This cartoon from *Puck*, 1880, deftly captures the fear of vaccination with unreliable vaccine matter. *Source*: Courtesy of William Helfand.

But it was the St. Louis disaster that was specifically invoked (22) in the hearings on a bill that proposed bringing production of biologics under federal control. Introduced on April 5, 1902, President Theodore Roosevelt signed the Biologics Control Act on July 1, 1902, virtual light speed compared to the quarter-century it took for the admittedly more comprehensive and much more hotly contested Food and Drugs Act of 1906 (23). The Hygienic Laboratory was responsible for enforcement of the 1902 legislation.

Drawing upon extant legislation in Europe, this law required manufacturers of any biological medicine or analogous product to be licensed annually by the government, and licensure was predicated on a satisfactory and unannounced inspection of the establishment. All aspects of production could be examined, including records. Samples of licensed products were obtained on the open market and tested at the Hygienic Laboratory for purity and potency. Licenses could be suspended pending correction of a manufacturing or product defect, and violation of the law was subject to a fine of up to $500 and/or imprisonment for up to 1 year. While there certainly were cases of license suspensions, there appears to be little evidence that the Hygienic Laboratory pursued fines or imprisonment under the law until the early 1960s (24–26). The number of licenses issued by the Hygienic Laboratory grew quickly, from 13 concerns licensed to produce mostly diphtheria antitoxin and smallpox vaccine in 1904, to two dozen operations producing about 20 different medicines in 1908, to 41 establishments licensed for over 100 biologics in 1921 (27–30).

FEDERAL AND PRIVATE REGULATION OF DRUGS IN THE EARLY 20TH CENTURY

Other federal agencies offered limited regulation over pharmaceuticals beginning in the early 20th century. The Post Office Department, for example, was able to prosecute some products that were otherwise beyond the reach of the government under the postal fraud laws of 1872 and 1895 (31,32). These laws prohibited the use of mail to collect money under fraudulent pretenses. Violations resulted in a fraud order, wherein the offending mail was intercepted and returned to the sender. Thus in 1928 the Post Office secured a fraud order, upheld on appeal, against Tuberclecide, a worthless treatment for tuberculosis, and years earlier against Habitina, an alleged drug addiction cure that contained both morphine and heroin (33,34). The Federal Trade Commission (FTC) exercised its jurisdiction over drug advertising from time to time following its establishment in 1914. For example, it attempted to regulate Marmola, a hazardous thyroid preparation intended for weight reduction, on two occasions in the 1920s and 1930s (35). The Wheeler-Lea Amendment of 1938 clarified FTC's unique authority over all drug advertising, although jurisdiction over prescription drug advertising was transferred to the U.S. Food and Drug Administration (FDA) in 1962 (36–38).

Ironically, probably the most significant effort to regulate prescription drugs prior to 1938 was a private venture that was voluntary, under the American Medical Association (AMA). Shortly after the turn of the century, the AMA and the American Pharmaceutical Association (APA) combined resources to press for the establishment of a federal authority that would certify drugs—and thus help rid the landscape of patent medicines. These not only posed a threat to the public health but they also represented some competition for physicians. Nostrums certainly played an important role in the retail business of many pharmacists, but others in the profession excoriated their sale. The AMA abandoned the idea of federal certification and instead formed its own Council on Pharmacy and Chemistry in 1905, a 15-member group that included physicians, pharmacists, pharmacologists, chemists, and government representatives. The AMA Board of Trustees charged the council to publish an annual volume of proprietary pharmaceuticals approved by the council that were not, according to pharmacopeial rules, permitted in the USP (39–41).

Manufacturers submitted to the council evidence to support any claims made for the drug and a proposed name, and the council relied heavily on the advice of outside consultants to evaluate these data. An accepted drug would be included in its compendium, *New and Nonofficial Remedies* (NNR), which entitled the firm to label its drug with the council's "accepted" seal. But under the council's rules, no pharmaceutical would be admitted to NNR if it had "unwarranted, exaggerated or misleading statements as to therapeutic value." Moreover, a drug would not be accepted if its firm derived substantial earnings from products not listed in NNR. But rejection by the council meant more than just failure to appear in NNR or enhance its label. Unaccepted drugs were denied the right to advertise in the family of AMA journals (42–45).

The council terminated its acceptance program in 1955, largely due to the AMA's depletion of cash reserves and a growing apathy for the program within the association, according to one informed observer (46). However, the council continued to publish its compendium of drugs for reference use of the profession. With the proscriptive element of the program inactivated, the possibility existed in which a drug might be advertised in the *Journal of the American Medical Association* (*JAMA*) for an indication not supported in NNR (47). Moreover, firms were less compelled to submit the sort of evidence to the council that they had in the past, such that the council's consultants had to search for supplemental data on NNR candidates elsewhere. Still, NNR included comparative assessments of a drug's efficacy, something FDA did not do when the efficacy statutes were passed (48–50).

THE DRUG MARKETPLACE AT THE TURN OF THE CENTURY

Federal regulation over the bulk of the drug supply was still nonexistent at the turn of the 20th century. It was a menacing marketplace. Despite the existence of several comprehensive drug compendia—including the USP—there were no legally required standards of identity for drugs, whether the pharmaceuticals were prescribed by a physician and dispensed by a pharmacist (so-called ethical drugs) or purchased directly by the consumer for self-medication. Some of the manufacturers of the former by this time had quality-control procedures in place and produced standardized drugs of predictable therapeutic response. Parke-Davis was the first firm to subscribe to this approach, introducing 20 chemically assayed fluidextracts of botanicals by 1883 (51,52). Parke-Davis and Mulford were the early leaders in the production of biologicals, a venture that by definition and by law required the institutionalization of science. Incorporating science was, as Jonathan Liebenau points out, good business for drug manufacturers even at this early stage. And they made sure their clientele knew it (53).

But science was still very much in its infancy for most of the American pharmaceutical industry at the turn of the century. It was an expensive proposition, and many company chiefs remained to be convinced that more (or any) science and research necessarily meant more business (54). To be sure, even the ethical industry had its share of scientifically questionable products. One of Eli Lilly and Company's best sellers at this time was Succus Alterans, a blood purifier and treatment for rheumatism, syphilis, and a variety of skin diseases that Lilly supposedly derived from a Creek Indian remedy (55). In 1889, Smith Kline & French purchased the D. B. Hand Company and then manufactured and distributed the Hand line of products, still under the Hand brand. This inventory consisted of teething lotions, colic cures, croup and cough medicine, worm elixir, and other preparations advertised for infants and children. Like so many other pediatric products of other firms

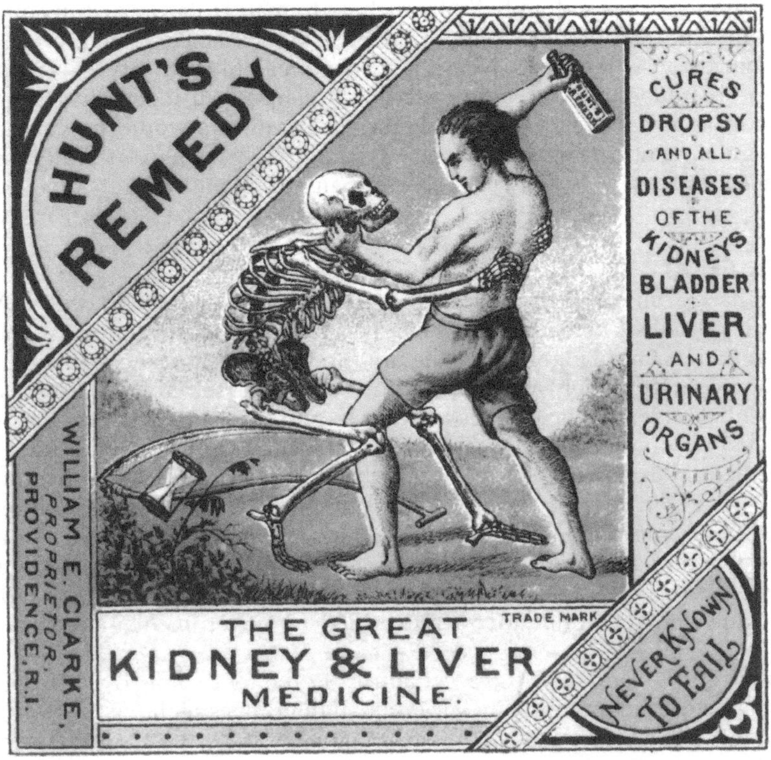

FIGURE 2 Hunt's Remedy, manufactured since 1850, illustrates the unrestricted claims and eye-catching advertising imagery that characterized many patent medicines at the turn of the 20th century. This particular advertisement was used for the design of a 1998 U.S. postage stamp to commemorate the 1906 Food and Drugs Act.

at this time, these Hand medicines typically contained alcohol, opium, and chloral hydrate (56–58).

But regardless of the extent to which the ethical industry marketed nostrums, it paled next to the patent medicine industry, those who vended William Radam's Microbe Killer, Mrs. Winslow's Soothing Syrup, Swaim's Panacea, Benjamin Bye's Soothing Balmy Oils to cure cancer, Dr. Hollick's Aphrodisiac Remedy, and on and on (59). Nostrums were omnipresent in late 19th-century America, and their rise, not coincidentally, was paralleling that of advertising. Products appealed to exotica, the medical knowledge of Native Americans, death, religion, patriotism, mythology, and eventually new developments in science. Nothing but the size of the bottle prevented patent medicines makers from claiming anything and putting anything in their products (Fig. 2). At the same time, the biomedical sciences awaited elaboration, leaving medicine ill equipped to deal with most diseases. If there were a demand for cancer and arthritis cures, baldness remedies, bust developers, and manhood restorers, a cure could be supplied. And if there were not a demand, that too could be manufactured.

The nostrum industry undoubtedly knew how to market its wares, but companies also promoted their interests in more surreptitious ways. For example, they subdued any curiosity in the press with their economic strength. By the 1890s, patent medicine manufacturers used so-called "red clauses" in their advertising contracts to muzzle newspapers and magazines. The contracts would be voided if a state law regulating nostrums were passed. Thus, not only were many editorials silent on the need for such laws, they actively campaigned against them.

THE FEDERAL FOOD AND DRUGS ACT OF 1906

Such was the pharmaceutical landscape in America as the 20th century began. A few muckraking journalists helped reveal the red clauses, the false testimonials, the nostrums laden with harmful ingredients, the unfounded cures for cancer, tuberculosis, syphilis, narcotic addiction, and other serious as well as self-limited diseases. The most influential patent medicine exposé was a 10-part series entitled "The Great American Fraud," by Samuel Hopkins Adams, which began in *Collier's* on October 7, 1905, and ended the following February. A subsequent series by Adams examined doctors who advertised fake clinics. That same month saw the publication of another work that, more than any other single event, spurred on passage of a comprehensive federal law. Socialist writer Upton Sinclair published *The Jungle*, a fact-based novel about immigrant life and the meatpacking industry of Chicago. Sinclair's shocking and revolting story was verified by government undercover investigators.

The search for a federal law to correct abuses in the food and drug marketplace began long before Adams and Sinclair initiated their investigations. Congress received the first bill to address these concerns in January 1879, although that version addressed only foods; some months later another bill, this time encompassing drugs as well as foods, was introduced in the House. Every session of Congress for the next 25 years considered at least one sweeping food and drug control bill (60). Those who believed they would be adversely affected by an omnibus law managed to thwart passage of the dozens of bills that were introduced during this span. But their opponents obviously were equal to the task—or at least persistent.

Many championed a food and drug law, but one person more than any other was responsible for keeping the need for such a law squarely in front of both the Congress and the people. Harvey Washington Wiley was a chemist on the faculty of Purdue University when he came to Washington in 1883 to become the fourth chief chemist in the Department of Agriculture. From the time of his arrival in the capital, Wiley was an enthusiastic, infectious, and effective champion for remedial legislation. When he was not stumping for a law, he was publishing extensively on the proliferation of food adulteration (61). His forceful personality and commitment to reform brought together important but disparate groups to help lobby Capitol Hill, including state food and drug officials, the General Federation of Women's Clubs, the APA, and the AMA (62–64).

On June 30, 1906, President Roosevelt signed the Food and Drugs Act into law (65), nearly 4 years to the day after he signed the Biologics Control Act. The law prohibited interstate commerce in adulterated or misbranded foods and drugs. It was unlawful to add an ingredient to a food that would represent a health hazard, result in a filthy or decomposed product, conceal damage, or substitute for the food itself. If the manufacturer chose to label the weight or measure of the food, that had to be done accurately. A food or drug label could not be false or misleading in any particular.

A drug under the act was any substance intended for the cure, mitigation, or prevention of disease in humans or animals. It could not be sold in any condition of purity, strength, or quality other than that stated in the USP or the *National Formulary*, unless the specific variation from that standard was stated on the label. The presence and amount of 11 dangerous ingredients, including heroin, morphine, cocaine, and alcohol, had to be labeled on all drugs (and foods). Violative goods were subject to seizure and, if upheld by the court, destruction. Infractions were considered misdemeanors, and those behind the offense could be fined up to $500 and imprisoned for up to one year. The Bureau of Chemistry of the Department of Agriculture, the home of more chemists than anywhere else in the U.S. government (66), was assigned to enforce the law and promulgate regulations (67).

APPLYING THE NEW LAW TO DRUGS

One immediate impact of the law was to persuade many patent medicine manufacturers to remove ingredients from their preparations that were subject to labeling. Therapeutic claims, however, were another story. The Bureau of Chemistry quickly applied the law to products that bore false therapeutic claims, based on a charge of misbranding. About 100 such cases were made in 5 years (68). However, when the bureau tried to move against Dr. Johnson's Mild Combination Treatment for Cancer, the firm prevailed over the bureau in court. The case reached the Supreme Court in 1911, which ruled in a 6–3 decision against the government. The majority believed that the 1906 act pertained only to the identity of ingredients in a product. Moreover, the Court believed that the Bureau of Chemistry was capable of making an informed judgment about a drug's contents, "but hardly so as to medical effects." Finally, based on an earlier case involving the Post Office, the court argued that ideas about therapeutics were still too far ranging to come to definitive conclusions (69).

President William Howard Taft asked Congress to develop a legislative solution for the 150 pending drug misbranding cases, as well as those yet to come. Among these cases, according to the president, were "some of the rankest frauds by which the American people were ever deceived" (70). Congress responded in 1912 with the Sherley Amendment, couched as severely as members believed possible without infringing on expressions of opinion. The new law prohibited statements about a product's ingredients or its curative or therapeutic effect that were false and fraudulent (71,72). However, to establish fraud meant that the bureau of chemistry had to show that the manufacturer knew the product was worthless—that there was intent to defraud the consumer. This proved to be difficult in many cases.

For example, Lee Barlett, a former shirt salesman from Pittsburgh, promoted a medicine called Banbar, an extract of the horsetail weed, as an effective treatment for diabetes. Barlett sold Banbar for $12 a pint, a hefty price in the 1920s, but it allowed diabetics to take their medicine orally rather than administering injections of insulin, which Frederick Banting and his colleagues at the University of Toronto had introduced in 1923. The government took Barlett to court for selling a misbranded drug. Elliott P. Joslin, the internationally recognized authority on diabetes, was the plaintiff's principal witness. On the basis of the 12,000 diabetic patients he saw every year, Joslin testified that insulin—combined with diet and exercise—was

FIGURE 3 Pharmacologists in the Bureau of Chemistry employed biological assays to develop the first reference standards issued to industry to promote compliance with the testing requirements for select pharmaceuticals in USP X (1926).

the only effective treatment for this disease. The defense offered hundreds of testimonial letters on behalf of Banbar. The jury found in favor of the defense, despite the fact that the government presented death certificates—attributed to diabetes—for individuals who had submitted these testimonials (73).

Under Wiley, enforcement of the Food and Drugs Act weighed heavily toward foods. Of the first 1000 actions taken by the bureau up to 1911, fewer than one quarter dealt with drugs. And those drug actions typically addressed patent medicines; as seen earlier, false therapeutic claims were a driving force for action. Official drugs such as belladonna and asafetida were the subjects of fewer than 100 of these actions. Most defendants did not challenge the bureau, but rather paid their fines, adjusted their labeling, and continued to advertise as before, since the latter was beyond the reach of the 1906 law (74).

Carl Alsberg followed Wiley as chief chemist in 1912, and he continued to favor foods. But he also focused more attention on ethical drugs. To address these, the bureau developed new analyses for crude drugs, and by the 1920s bureau scientists pioneered biological assays for ergot, digitalis, and other drugs, which were adopted by the USP (75) (Fig. 3). The bureau also monitored drugs dispensed by pharmacists in the District of Columbia (believing state pharmacy boards were the more appropriate monitor elsewhere) beginning in the 1910s and found substantial deviations from official standards. By the early 1930s, FDA and the APA reached an agreement as to what would be considered reasonable tolerances for dispensed drugs (76).

When Walter Campbell succeeded Alsberg in 1921, he revitalized the drug regulatory effort, beginning with the appointment of George Hoover, a physician and chemist, to head drug regulation. The bureau consequently expanded its interests from crude drugs to tablets, discovering fairly wide variations from official standards. But by this time, when the Republicans came to power and the policy was made to be more cooperative with business, court action began to be superseded by negotiation. Hoover met with the pharmaceutical industry's trade associations, the American Drug Manufacturers Association and the American Pharmaceutical Manufacturers Association, which in turn formed so-called contact committees to investigate the tablet problems in cooperation with the bureau. The committees helped improve tableting technologies and negotiated with the bureau over allowable deviations from the labeled amount of active ingredient. But in the New Deal era, drug regulation took a less collaborative tone with industry (77).

TOWARD THE 1938 FOOD, DRUG, AND COSMETIC ACT

The 1906 act was arguably the pinnacle of Progressive Era legislation, but the difficulty of prosecuting medicines with false therapeutic claims was just one of many shortcomings of the 1906 act. Foods did not have standards, cosmetics and medical devices were unregulated, the penalties imposed by the law were paltry relative to the crime, with the exception of the 11 ingredients there was no required listing of drug ingredients, factory inspections—although interpreted and executed by the bureau as warranted under the law—were not explicitly authorized, and although the law prohibited a food that was made to be unsafe, there was no similar protection for drugs. By the 1920s, and increasing considerably after Franklin Roosevelt became president in 1932, FDA began to publicize rather creatively the more egregious examples of deceptive and hazardous products that were on the market and perfectly within the law, an argument for a new comprehensive law (78). Indeed, shortly after FDR's inauguration, Congress began considering bills that would replace the Food and Drugs Act and plug the holes left in consumer protection legislation (79).

The public's vulnerability became dramatically clear in October 1937. Months after the introduction of the wonder drug sulfanilamide, the S. E. Massengill Company of Bristol, Tennessee, began investigating a liquid dosage form for the drug. Their investigation consisted of finding a solvent in which the drug would dissolve (sulfanilamide was known to be stubbornly insoluble) and flavoring and coloring the preparation so as to be especially useful for children and others not inclined toward tablets. Quality control amounted to little more than an organoleptic appraisal. Harold Watkins, the company chemist, selected diethylene glycol as the vehicle for the sulfa without testing the solvent or even examining the medical literature. Had he at least bothered to look, the latter certainly attested to the glycol's poisonous nature. He did not bother testing it himself, he claimed, because glycols were related to glycerin, which had long been used in medicines. The company thus began shipping its Elixir Sulfanilamide from Tennessee and its Kansas City office in early September.

On October 11, a representative from the Tulsa County Medical Society contacted the AMA to inform them that several deaths in the Oklahoma county appeared to be associated with the Massengill product. The physician wanted to know what the AMA's Council on Pharmacy and Chemistry could tell them about the preparation. Neither Elixir Sulfanilamide nor any Massengill product had ever been accepted by the Council. The FDA heard about the suspicious deaths 3 days after the AMA from a New York physician with ties to Massengill. FDA learned that the Elixir was involved in all the Tulsa fatalities, at which point the agency dispatched its chief medical officer and one of its finest field investigators to Bristol to investigate. They learned that proprietor Samuel E. Massengill issued an inadequate recall notice and that 240 gallons remained unaccounted for.

FDA dedicated virtually its entire field force to tracking down the remaining product—although forced to rely on a technical error for legal cause. Nothing in the 1906 act prohibited unsafe drugs. Rather, FDA was allowed to seize Elixir Sulfanilamide because it was misbranded; an elixir, by definition, had to employ alcohol, and the Massengill medicine of course had none. Most physicians and pharmacists encountered by FDA investigators during the frantic recovery effort were helpful, but some were uncooperative and even obstructive, no doubt to deflect personal responsibility and liability. Much was recovered from warehouses, pharmacy shelves, and medicine cabinets, but overall, Elixir Sulfanilamide killed at least 107, mostly in the South.

Many were children, such as the 6-year-old girl from Tulsa who perished in this ordeal (Fig. 4). Her mother, Marie Nidiffer, wrote to President Roosevelt on November 9: "Tonight Mr. Roosevelt that little voice is stilled. The first time I ever had occasion to call in a doctor for her and she was given the Elixir of Sulfanilamide. Tonight our little home is bleak and full of despair. . . . Even the memory of her is mixed with sorrow for we can see her little body turning to and fro and hear that little voice screaming with pain and it seems as though it drives me insane. . . . Tonight President Roosevelt as you enjoy your little grandchildren of whom we read about, it is my plea that you will take steps to prevent such sales of drugs that will take little lives and leave such suffering behind. . . ." (80–82).

The bills to correct the gaps in the 1906 act had been delayed and diluted over the previous 5 years. However, the impact of the Elixir Sulfanilamide tragedy was to strengthen the drug provisions of the latest bills and in fact propel passage of the law itself. Roosevelt signed the bill on June 25, 1938 (83). The Food, Drug, and Cosmetic Act brought medical devices and cosmetics under regulation, provided for standards of identity for foods, prohibited once and for all false therapeutic claims on drug labeling, required that drugs be labeled with adequate directions for use, authorized factory inspections (which had been executed anyway under the bureau's interpretation of the old law), instituted court injunctions for violative products, corrected abuses in the quality and packaging of foods, instituted adequate drug manufacturing controls (84), and, most important from the standpoint of the history of drug regulation, mandated that all new drugs had to be shown by the manufacturer to be safe before they could be marketed—the birth of the new drug application (NDA). The premarket provision, inspired by the fear of another Elixir Sulfanilamide disaster, had an immediate impact, with over 6000 new drug applications filed in the first 9 years and 13,000 by 1962 (85).

DRUG REGULATION AND THE POSTWAR CHEMOTHERAPEUTIC REVOLUTION

One early development under the drug provisions of the 1938 act concerned self-medication. The law called for adequate directions for use by the patient, and by

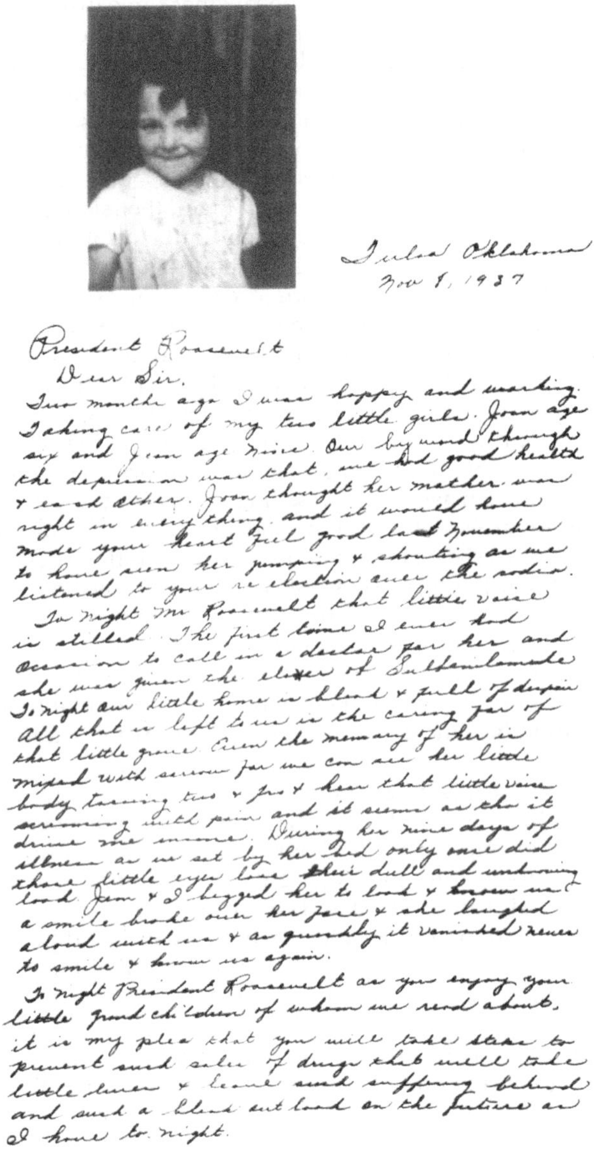
Tulsa Oklahoma
Nov 8, 1937

President Roosevelt
Dear Sir,
Two months ago I was happy and working taking care of my two little girls, Joan age six and Jean age nine. Our byword through the depression was that we had good health & each other. Joan thought her mother was right in everything and it would have made your heart feel good last November to have seen her jumping & shouting as we listened to your re election over the radio.
To night Mr Roosevelt that little voice is stilled. The first time I ever had occasion to call in a doctor for her and she was given the elixir of Sulfanilamide. To night our little home is bleak & full of despair. All that is left to us is the caring for of that little grave. Even the memory of her is mixed with sorrow for we can see her little body turning to & fro & hear that little voice screaming with pain and it seems as tho it drive me insane. During her nine days of illness as we sat by her bed only once did those little eyes lose their dull and unknowing look. Jean & I begged her to look & know us & a smile broke over her face & she laughed aloud with us & as quickly it vanished never to smile & know us again.
To night President Roosevelt as you enjoy your little grand children of whom we read about, it is my plea that you will take steps to prevent such sales of drugs that will take little lives & leave such suffering behind and such a bleak out look on the future as I have to night.

FIGURE 4 The face of a drug disaster. This excerpt from a moving letter to President Roosevelt from Mrs. J. Nidiffer of Tulsa describes her anguish and helplessness over the loss of her 6-year-old daughter, Joan Marlar. Ironically, sulfanilamide saved the life of FDR's son just 1 year earlier, not long after American clinicians got their hands on the drug.

1940 FDA issued nearly 30 detailed warning statements to be labeled on a variety of drugs. For example, bromides were labeled with the following: "Warning: Frequent or continued use may lead to mental derangement, skin eruptions or other serious effects. Do not take more than the dosage recommended. Not to be taken by those suffering from kidney disease" (86).

However, it was FDA's opinion within weeks of the law that some drugs simply could not be labeled with adequate directions. For example, the use of a sulfa drug in a venereal disease was hardly routine, complicated as it was by both the adverse reactions that many of the early sulfas produced and the identification and progress of the disease. In other words, FDA ruled that in some cases medical expertise had to be involved in the medication process for the drug to be safe. The agency identified an increasing number of drugs that had to be labeled for dispensing only on the order of a physician or dentist; the birth of another standard of modern medicine, the prescription drug (87–90). This created confusion about how a drug would be categorized—prescription or nonprescription—and who would have primary responsibility for that designation. The absence of statutory direction was resolved in 1951 when the Durham–Humphrey Amendment was passed. That law established broad parameters for deciding which drugs merited designation as prescription legend status and which could be available over the counter (91).

The illegal sale of two groups of prescription drugs, amphetamines and barbiturates, took up more of FDA's drug enforcement time in the 1940s, 1950s, and 1960s than all other drug violations under the 1938 act combined. At first the agency focused on pharmacies, some of which were either selling these drugs over the counter without a prescription or incessantly refilling old prescriptions that did not authorize any refills. By the mid-1950s, FDA's attention turned to the trucking industry, a major source of traffic in these pharmaceuticals, where some spectacular and highly publicized highway crashes were directly connected to the use of amphetamines and barbiturates (92). Eventually many other drugs prone to abuse, such as hallucinogens, were consolidated for special interdiction by FDA under the Drug Abuse Control Amendments of 1965 (93,94). However, 3 years later that function was transferred to what would become the Drug Enforcement Administration (DEA).

The introduction of the sulfa drugs, beginning with sulfanilamide in 1935, launched a revolution in chemotherapy. Statutes and regulations did their best to keep track of new therapies. For example, literally hours before expiration of the patent on insulin (and the University of Toronto's oversight of quality control in the production of the hormone) in 1941, Congress passed the Insulin Amendment to require FDA to test every batch of insulin produced for strength, quality, and purity to ensure its safety and effectiveness (95). A similar law in 1945 provided for FDA certification of batches of penicillin—a service carried out by FDA beginning in 1943 for the War Production Board's supply of penicillin headed for troops. As additional antibiotics were discovered, laws were passed to accommodate them (96–98).

As mentioned earlier, companies flooded FDA with drug applications at the outset. The agency received an average of over 100 NDAs monthly from 1938 to 1941 because sponsors were apparently unsure of what constituted a new drug. NDA 1596, received on August 30, 1939 and approved on September 20, 1939, was for 4-H Household Cough Syrup, consisting of horehound, molasses, and vinegar. The Aiellos Ped-Vale Company submitted NDA 407 on January 12, 1939, for Aiellos Foot Remedy Powder, made up solely of boric acid; FDA approved the application on April 1 of that year. During this period, seven firms and one physician submitted NDAs for aspirin that were approved by FDA. Interestingly, in January 1945 the agency ruled that the indications for aspirin were so well known to consumers that directions for use were not required. Aspirin lollipops, though, were a different matter, requiring a physician's prescription (99–102).

The application submission rate slowed during World War II and the early postwar years to about 350 annually. However, it picked up again in the 1950s to approximately 400 each year, when research funds flooded laboratories almost as fast as pathbreaking new medicines flooded the marketplace. Upon the end of hostilities in Europe, the Committee on Medical Research of the Office of Scientific Research and Development disbursed remaining wartime research funds to the National Institutes of Health (NIH). This source of funding, together with strong congressional support, launched in full force the modern era of autonomously peer-reviewed extramural funding of biomedical research at NIH (103).

In addition, the pharmaceutical industry accelerated a trend that began in the period between the wars, pouring more and more revenue into research and development (104,105). That decision might have been made a little easier by the success of their wartime experience with penicillin, synthetic anti-infective agents, and other drugs. Thus, a host of antibiotics, diuretics, ataractics, corticosteroids, antispasmodics, and other classes of drugs proliferated during that decade (106,107). Of course, the number of supplements grew as the base number of NDAs increased. And then there were some drugs that yielded scores or even hundreds of NDAs, such as diethylstilbestrol and rauwolfia serpentina. David Cavers reports that the latter led to applications from 319 different firms and was included in 2500 different medicines (108).

COMING TO GRIPS WITH EFFICACY BEFORE 1962

Another drug regulation policy was growing increasingly important in the 1950s—the relationship between drug safety and drug efficacy. The idea of federally mandated effectiveness in medicines was nothing new at this time. For example, regulations issued by the National Institutes of Health (formerly the Hygienic Laboratory) in 1934 required that biologics had to work: "[A] license for new products shall not be granted without satisfactory evidence of therapeutic or prophylactic efficiency" (109). This formalized a policy that had been in place for years.

In the late 1930s, FDA promulgated a rule requiring manufacturers of oral or otherwise inert ovary, suprarenal, pituitary, prostate, pineal, and mammary extracts to label their products with a statement that such an article "does not contain any known therapeutically useful constituent of the glands mentioned." Of course, even under the 1906 act, actions taken against patent medicines that made false therapeutic claims were implicitly driven by efficacy considerations (considerations that the Supreme Court believed were ahead of their time). The Insulin Amendment, Penicillin Amendment, and the other antibiotic amendments literally invoked efficacy as a prerequisite for certification by FDA. Reviews of certain NDAs that claimed to treat serious diseases such as pneumonia certainly took efficacy into account (110). The concept that in certain cases a drug could not be safe without being effective was employed but never pressed forward as an official policy—until Hepasyn® came along.

The Hepasyn story began in the early 1930s, when various researchers observed that cancerous tissue bore a high concentration of the amino acid, arginine, which appeared to promote cell division in tumors. Some tried to exploit this observation by applying the liver enzyme arginase, which helps to hydrolyze arginine, as a possible treatment to control tumor growth. Success was fleeting for most. However, dentist Wesley G. Irons, working as an anatomist at the Schools of

Pharmacy and Dentistry at the University of California at San Francisco in the 1940s, claimed to have success treating animal tumors with arginase. When his funding fell through at the university, Irons was offered funding and laboratory space at the San Francisco College of Mortuary Science, a source for cadavers in Irons's classes.

The mortuary school reserved commercial rights to Irons's work and served as the manufacturing establishment for Hepasyn, the name they gave to arginase. In November 1950, the school arranged with a Hollywood clinician to test arginase, and within a year 100 patients had received the substance. Eventually, the Hollywood physician began treating other cancer patients on an ambulatory basis once a week at the mortuary school. The story became even more curious after Irons and the school parted company, but the San Francisco school submitted an NDA late in 1953. FDA inspectors visited the mortuary school and found serious production problems, such as organoleptic sterility testing. The NDA contained results for only 10 patients, although the sponsors claimed to have data on 175 patients. FDA, not surprisingly, considered the application incomplete and requested more data. As problematical as the manufacturing operation was, FDA chose to focus on the clinical evidence submitted by the college (Fig. 5).

By October 1955, the application was deemed complete enough for a review. The agency's strategy was made clear to a medical officer in San Francisco: "We have given considerable thought to the proper handling of this application and have decided in conjunction with (General Counsel William) Goodrich that since this preparation is ineffective in the treatment of malignant disease its use is not safe in such situations. In other words, while section 505 does not refer to efficacy we are going to try and take the position that efficacy is so intimately bound up in the use of this material that the lack of efficacy will make it unsafe for use" (111). The Hepasyn review thus was not going to be just another NDA evaluation. Rather, it was to be a blatant stand on therapeutics and the law. FDA's expectation or hope was that the San Francisco College of Mortuary Science, its application denied on the basis of lack of efficacy, would appeal the decision in an administrative hearing.

In late December of that year, FDA Commissioner George Larrick informed the college that its NDA was denied because of misleading statements and omissions, because of inadequate manufacturing and control procedures, and because "safety has not been proven because of lack of proof of efficacy in diseases that are invariably fatal unless treated with adequate efficacious means" (112). While there was not a surfeit of bona fide treatments for the cancers Hepasyn claimed to benefit, there certainly were some. An approved yet ineffective Hepasyn, the reasoning went, would lead some patients to delay or possibly avoid treatment with established effective treatments. Larrick informed the mortuary school that if the NDA were not withdrawn, a hearing notice—as provided in the 1938 act to sponsors who wished to petition adverse NDA decisions by FDA—would be issued next month. Led by medical officer Barbara Moulton, FDA continued to assemble its case for a hearing. Medical director Albert Holland observed that this case "may well be a precedent-establishing case no matter which way the courts decide it." But in the end the courts would not have the opportunity, as the San Francisco school withdrew the application rather than face the hearing (113).

FDA had another chance to press the safety-efficacy policy a few years later, and this time the drug firm was more accommodating. On September 9, 1959, FDA approved Eaton Laboratories' application for Altafur (furaltadone), a systemic antibacterial agent. However, FDA's reevaluation of the NDA as a rising number of neurological and other adverse reactions came to light led the agency to question

FIGURE 5 The San Francisco College of Mortuary Science served as the manufacturer, ambulatory clinic, and new drug application sponsor for a cancer treatment. FDA used this opportunity to press for a formalized policy mandating an efficacy requirement in some drugs. *Source*: Courtesy of the San Francisco History Center, San Francisco Public Library.

the efficacy of Altafur (114). Among other issues, FDA believed there were insufficient reports in the application from experts in the treatment of infectious diseases, and certain claims would have required unattainable plasma levels even at triple the recommended dosage. The agency did not explain why these issues were not apparent at the time of the application.

Eaton Laboratories submitted additional data, but FDA said that evaluation of those data should be done in the venue of a formal hearing over suspension of the Altafur NDA; its lack of effectiveness did not justify its toxicity. The hearing began in January 1961 and lasted several weeks. The hearing examiner was persuaded by the testimony of Maxwell Finland of Harvard, George Jackson of Illinois, and other experts on infectious diseases who disputed Altafur's claim of therapeutic value. The examiner decided that efficacy was indeed relevant to Altafur's safety considering the diseases treated—diseases amenable to effective treatment by other, less toxic drugs on the market. The NDA for Altafur was suspended in August 1962, less than 2 months before Congress passed the Kefauver–Harris Drug Amendments (115,116).

KEFAUVER, KEVADON, AND A NEW APPROACH TO DRUG REGULATION

Estes Kefauver of Tennessee was not the first senator to voice concern about the increasing cost of drugs. Fellow Democrat Warren Magnuson of Washington had heard complaints from constituents and also learned about the rising cost of drugs in America as a member of the Labor, Health, Education, and Welfare Subcommittee. But Kefauver, chairman of the Subcommittee on Antitrust and Monopoly since January 1957, was in a position to explore this development in depth. Thus, in December 1959, following an extensive investigation by his staff that began the previous year, Kefauver initiated hearings into administered prices in the pharmaceutical industry. The early testimony provided some headline-grabbing statistics into how the pharmaceutical industry arrived at drug prices. For example, the committee learned that the German firm Schering had purchased bulk estradiol progynon (for symptoms associated with menopause) from Roussell of France for resale in the United States. When the committee compared the cost of the bulk product and what Schering charged for tablets produced therefrom, they discerned a markup of 7000% (117). The Schering president objected that such a hyperbolic figure ignored the costs of manufacturing, advertising, distribution, and research on this drug. Kefauver replied that Schering would have incurred no research costs for this Roussell drug itself.

When the hearings shifted into a study of drug costs as a function of research expenses in the industry, A. Dale Console, a former medical director at Squibb, testified that research indeed leads to many failures, but that "the problem arises out of the fact that (firms) market so many of their failures" (118). The hearings thus took on another dimension by investigating advertising practices of the pharmaceutical industry and the delivery of information about their drugs to doctors. Records subpoenaed by Kefauver from the 22 largest firms revealed that in 1958 they expended an average of one-fourth of their gross income on advertising. Investment in detail men represented a considerable portion of that expense, as estimates for the same year indicated a detail force for the industry of 15,000, or one for every 10 doctors (119).

The committee also heard about the relationship between FDA and the pharmaceutical industry. Former FDA medical officer Barbara Moulton described an acquiescent agency, frequently and inappropriately deferring to the wishes of firms. The committee's inquiry into Henry Welch, director of the Antibiotic Division at FDA who developed a lucrative business in medical reprint sales with drug companies, revealed a high-ranking regulatory official who was, at minimum, far too cozy with regulated interests (120). After 10 months of hearings, Kefauver's committee had raised a number of concerns, concerns that soon would be reflected in proposed legislation, introduced by Kefauver on April 12, 1961 (121–124).

Kefauver first addressed patents in his bill, severely curtailing the monopoly that drug companies would have on their products (an outgrowth of another facet of the hearings). The bill also gave FDA increased authority over drug production, distribution, and advertising. Food and Drug's inspection authority would be enhanced to uphold stronger quality-control standards in a system reminiscent of that applied to biologics. Advertising would include explicit and prominent warnings, again responding to problematical issues during the hearings. The law would extend FDA's role for batch certification of selected antibiotics to all such drugs, not just those covered by the amendments up to the early 1950s. The drug clearance provision of the 1938 act, in which a drug application became effective after 60 days unless prevented by specific FDA action, would be ended under this bill. Finally, sponsors would have to show drugs to be effective as well as safe (125).

Opposition emerged quickly. The AMA, for example, came out strenuously opposed to the effectiveness requirement, arguing that only the physician can make a determination if a drug works or not. The industry, operating in part through its trade association, the Pharmaceutical Manufacturers Association, worked vehemently against elements of the bill that would affect its profits and force firms to advertise a drug's adverse reactions as well as its indications. The support of the White House was tepid at best (126). The process of negotiation, dilution, and revision ensued once Kefauver's bill cleared his subcommittee, proceeded to a parent committee, and then to the full Senate. However, unbeknownst to Kefauver and his colleagues, at this time a drug disaster was developing that would have an impact on Kefauver's law analogous to the legislative effect of the Elixir Sulfanilamide tragedy.

On September 12, 1960, the William S. Merrell Company of Cincinnati submitted an application for Kevadon, known generically as thalidomide. Merrell was the U.S. licensee for the German firm Chemie Grünenthal, which introduced this sedative in Europe in 1956. The application was routed to Frances Kelsey, who had replaced Barbara Moulton. Kelsey's superiors believed that this apparently straightforward NDA would be appropriate for a newcomer. However, Kelsey found the chronic toxicity data inadequate to support the safety of the drug and the labeling unsuitable. Merrell continued to append data to the application, which Kelsey continued to find inadequate to the task. The contacts between Merrell and Kelsey or her superiors thereafter occurred almost weekly until the spring, as the firm was rushing to make March 1 launch date for Kevadon. At this time, Kelsey also was deeply involved in FDA's administrative hearing with Eaton Laboratories over Altafur.

But crucial news emerged in February 1961, when the medical officer read a report in the December 1960 issue of the *British Medical Journal* that associated long-term use of thalidomide with peripheral neuritis. When representatives from Merrell met with Kelsey in May to discuss this revelation (which Merrell believed rather inconsequential, assuming the effects were reversible), Kelsey requested evidence that Kevadon would be safe in pregnancy. Although the request was based on a theoretical consideration stemming from the neurological side effect, it was consistent with Kelsey's own training as a pharmacologist at the University of Chicago, and it was shared by her medical officer colleagues at FDA. Merrell and outside clinical investigators representing the company continued to argue that Kevadon was effective and safe relative to the barbiturates, the firm now hoping to meet a November 1961 launch in time for the holidays.

On the last day of that month, Merrell reported to Kelsey that thalidomide had been withdrawn from Germany, where use of the drug had been correlated with severe congenital abnormalities. On March 8, 1962, Merrell withdrew its NDA for Kevadon. The United States narrowly escaped the fate of many other countries. But the agency learned in April for the first time the true scale of Merrell's investigation. Over 1100 doctors received Kevadon (the agency had assumed from three to six dozen investigators were involved), and the investigation involved about 20,000 patients, 624 of whom were pregnant. Despite assurances by Merrell that a recall had been completed, field investigators discovered that over 25,000 doses were still unaccounted for in August, prompting an Elixir Sulfanilamide–like national search for outstanding samples of the drug. Seventeen cases of thalidomide-induced phocomelia occurred in the United States, seven of which were documented to be caused by thalidomide obtained outside the Merrell study (127–129).

The shock of what might have happened with thalidomide wrested the drug regulation reform bill from congressional inertia, and President Kennedy, surrounded by Kefauver, Kelsey, and others, signed the bill into law on October 10, 1962 (130) (Fig. 6). Although much had changed in the bill Kefauver introduced, still some elements remained. Attempts to cut costs via patent adjustments were long gone, as was the biologics-like system of licensing (although firms had to register). Manufacturers had to prove that their drugs were effective as well as safe—not just drugs introduced from that point forward, but all new drugs introduced since 1938. FDA's control over the clinical investigation of drugs was clarified and strengthened, and a surprise provision required experimental subjects to give informed consent. Safety, effectiveness, and reliability of a drug would be further provided for by requiring that production adhere to current good manufacturing practice, although that provision was made clear in FDA regulations as far back as the early 1940s (131). New drug clearance would no longer be based on an application becoming effective automatically after 60 days unless FDA action indicated otherwise; a new drug now could be marketed only with FDA's assent. Oversight of prescription drug advertising was transferred from FTC to FDA. And finally, drug inspectors

FIGURE 6 President Kennedy hands Senator Kefauver one of the pens used to sign the 1962 Drug Amendments. Among those looking on is Frances Kelsey, standing second from left.

would have enhanced access to establishment records other than financial or personnel documents (132).

CONCLUSION

The 1962 law was a landmark in the history of drug regulation, and no law since then has been as sweeping in its coverage of the pharmaceutical enterprise. But subsequent laws and regulations stand out, too, for many reasons. For example, the rise in the consumer movement certainly had an impact on drug regulation. The issuance of one of the first patient package inserts in 1970 for oral contraceptives followed pointed protest by women's health advocates against AMA's opposition to this precedent in patient education (133). The Vitamins and Minerals Amendment (Proxmire Amendment) of 1976, which prevented FDA from limiting potency of supplements or regulating them as drugs, was due in no small part by organized efforts of consumers to inundate their members of Congress and FDA with letters of protest on a scale unheard of at that time (134,135). The National Organization for Rare Disorders led the effort behind the Orphan Drug Act of 1983 to persuade pharmaceutical companies to develop drugs, otherwise unprofitable, for diseases with small patient populations (136,137).

In the same year, as part of an overall revision of investigational new drug (IND) procedures (the IND rewrite), FDA proposed so-called treatment-use INDs, expanding physician and patient access to experimental drugs for therapeutic rather than investigational purposes in patients "with serious diseases or conditions, for whom alternative therapies do not exist or cannot be used" (138–140). However, there were several restrictions to treatment INDs, such as the need to have a firm request treatment IND status, to be treated by a physician skilled in therapy of that disease, and to have no other therapies available. Activists representing HIV and AIDS victims, families, and friends engaged FDA directly on this issue and helped not only to relax these restrictions but also to refocus the overall drug development and evaluation process. FDA thereafter would consult with sponsors to plan more efficient clinical studies of drugs for life-threatening and severely debilitating diseases, modeled on the testing and evaluation of AZT (zidovudine approved in 1987 for patients with HIV) (141,142). Moreover, continuing pressure by AIDS activists for expedited access to experimental therapies figured in a policy announced by FDA Commissioner Frank Young in July 1988. Individuals would be allowed to return to the country with a 3-month supply of any drug desired as long as the agency ensured that the product was not fraudulent, counterfeit, or harmful, and if the traveler presented the name and address of the physician responsible for the treatment. The volleying over IND and NDA policies between FDA and the AIDS community continued into the 1990s (143).

The history of drug regulation has come full circle, from the second decade of the 19th century, when a Maryland physician persuaded Congress to pass a law to ensure genuine smallpox vaccine, to the first decade of the 21st century, when the United States again faced smallpox vaccination as a policy issue. In between we have witnessed a vast array of stimuli to changes in the way drugs are regulated. Therapeutic disaster and concomitant outrage, of course, are perhaps the most visible sources for tectonic shifts in policy. But political upheaval, organized social action, institutionalization of professional authority, the political and economic strength of the drug industry, the will and whims of all three branches of government, the manner in which the fourth estate captures and conveys regulatory issues, and basic shifts in therapeutics itself all have had an impact on the way this country regulates drugs. FDA often refers to itself as a science-based regulatory agency, but the context for drug regulation over the past 200 years has been and will always be much broader than science and law.

REFERENCES AND NOTES

1. Wedderburn AJ. A Compilation of the Pharmacy and Drug Laws of the Several States and Territories. Bulletin 42, Division of Chemistry, U.S. Department of Agriculture. Washington, DC: GPO, 1894, *passim*.
2. Sonnedecker G, Urdang G. Legalization of drug standards under state laws in the United States of America. Food Drug Cosmetic Law J 1953; 8:741–760.
3. Hutt PB, Merrill RA. Food and Drug Law: Cases and Materials. 2nd ed. Westbury, NY: Foundation Press, 1991:660–661 (quote from p. 660).
4. Pharmacopoeia of the United States of America. Boston, MA: Charles Ewer, 1820:17.
5. Sonnedecker G. The founding period of the U.S. pharmacopeia: I. European antecedents. Pharm Hist 1993; 35:151–162.
6. Sonnedecker G. The founding period of the U.S. pharmacopeia: II. A national movement emerges. Pharm Hist 1994; 36:3–25.
7. Sonnedecker G. The founding period of the U.S. pharmacopeia: III. The first edition. Pharm Hist 1994; 36:103–122.
8. Anderson L, Higby GJ. The Spirit of Voluntarism, A Legacy of Commitment and Contribution: The United States Pharmacopeia. Rockville, MD: USP, 1995:7–25.
9. Quoted in Ridgway C. Good Enough for America! The Drug Import Law of 1848. Madison, WI: Seminar paper, University of Wisconsin, Madison, WI, 1986. Cited in: Young JH. Pure Food: Securing the Federal Food and Drugs Act of 1906. Princeton, NJ: Princeton University Press, 1989:7.
10. Young. Pure Food, pp. 6–7.
11. Congressional Globe. 30th Cong., 1st sess., December 1, 1847 – August 15, 1848, p. 858.
12. Drug Import Act. Pub L No. [30–45]. 9 U.S. Stat 237, June 26, 1848 (quote is from Sec 1).
13. Young. Pure Food, pp. 14–17.
14. Okun M. Fair Play in the Marketplace: The First Battle for Pure Food and Drugs. DeKalb, IL: Northern Illinois University Press, 1986:14–15.
15. Sonnedecker G. Contributions of the pharmaceutical profession toward controlling the quality of drugs in the nineteenth century. In: Blake JB, ed. Safeguarding the Public: Historical Aspects of Medicinal Drug Control. Baltimore, MD: Johns Hopkins University Press, 1970:105–111.
16. Dowling HF. Fighting Infection: Conquests of the Twentieth Century. Cambridge, MA: Harvard University Press, 1977.
17. Lechevalier HA, Solotorovsky M. Three Centuries of Microbiology. New York, NY: McGraw-Hill, 1965; New York, NY: Dover, 1974.
18. Treasury Department, Marine Hospital Service. Annual Report of the Supervising Surgeon-General of the Marine-Hospital Service of the United States for the Fiscal Year 1895. Washington, DC: GPO, 1896:327.
19. Treasury Department, Marine Hospital Service. Annual Report of 1895, 1896:329–335.
20. Kondratas RA. Biologics control act of 1902. In: The Early Years of Federal Food and Drug Control. Madison,WI: American Institute of the History of Pharmacy, 1982:11.
21. The laboratory notebook that documents the Hygienic Laboratory's work (in the possession of the Center for Biologics Evaluation and Research, Food and Drug Administration, Bethesda, Maryland) and a sample of the standard itself (in the possession of the Division

of Science, Medicine, and Society, National Museum of American History, Smithsonian Institution, Washington, DC) were incorporated as part of an exhibit, "Safety for Millions: The Biologics Control Act of 1902 Centennial," National Museum of American History, Smithsonian Institution, Washington, DC, September 2002.
22. U.S. Congress, House. Sale of Viruses, Etc., in the District of Columbia. Report No. 2713, to Accompany H R 15289, 57th Cong., 1st sess., June 27, 1902, pp. 6–7 (testimony of George M. Kober, Acting Chairman, Medical Society of the District of Columbia, Washington, DC, April 16, 1902). Reproduced in: Legislative History of the Regulation of Biological Products. N. p.: Division of Biologics Standards, National Institutes of Health, Department of Health, Education, and Welfare, 1967.
23. Biologics Control Act. Pub L No. 57–244. 32 U.S. Stat 728, July 1, 1902.
24. Perhaps it is more accurate to say that any charges brought under the 1902 act or under its consolidation in the 1944 Public Health Service Act were not contested. The suit brought by the government against John P. Calise and the Westchester Blood Bank in 1962 for altering expiration dates appears to be the first litigated case of any kind under the 1902 Biologics Act.
25. Solomon JM. Legislation and regulation in blood banking. In: Schaeffer M, ed. Federal Legislation and the Clinical Laboratory. Boston, MA: G. K. Hall, 1981:150.
26. Hutt PB, personal communication, September 12, 2002, who suspects that Calise might have been the first case.
27. Kondratas. Biologics Control Act of 1902.
28. Treasury Department, Public Health and Marine-Hospital Service. Annual Report of the Surgeon-General of the U.S. Public Health and Marine-Hospital Service of the United States for the Fiscal Year 1904. Washington, DC: GPO, 1904:372.
29. Treasury Department, Public Health and Marine-Hospital Service. Annual Report of the Surgeon-General of the U.S. Public Health and Marine-Hospital Service of the United States for the Fiscal Year 1908. Washington, DC: GPO, 1909:44.
30. Center for Biologics Evaluation and Research, Food and Drug Administration. Science and the Regulation of Biological Products: From a Rich History to a Challenging Future. N. p.: [CBER], 2002.
31. 17 U.S. Stat 322–323, June 18, 1872.
32. 28 U.S. Stat 963, March 2,1895.
33. Young JH. The Medical Messiahs: A Social History of Health Quackery in Twentieth-Century America. Princeton, NJ: Princeton University Press, 1967; rev. ed., 1992:66 ff., 86–87.
34. Kebler LF. Public health conserved through the enforcement of postal fraud laws. Am J Public Health 1922; 12:678–683.
35. Young. Medical Messiahs, pp. 122–128.
36. Young. Medical Messiahs, pp. 296–315.
37. Wheeler-Lea Amendments. Pub L No. 75–447. 52 U.S. Stat 111, March 21, 1938.
38. Handler M. The control of false advertising under the Wheeler-Lea act. Law Contemp Problems 1939; 6:91–110.
39. Fishbein M. A History of the American Medical Association. Philadelphia, PA: W.B. Saunders, 1947:226–227, 235–236.
40. Smith A. The council on pharmacy and chemistry and the chemical laboratory. In: Fishbein. American Medical Association, pp. 876–877, 884–885.
41. Burrow JG. The prescription drug policies of the American Medical Association. In: Blake. Safeguarding the Public, pp. 113–114.
42. Starr P. The Social Transformation of American Medicine. New York, NY: Basic Books, 1982:133.
43. Marks H. The Progress of Experiment: Science and Therapeutic Reform in the United States, 1900–1990. Cambridge MA: Cambridge University Press, 1997:23–41.
44. Smith. Council on pharmacy and chemistry and the chemical laboratory, pp. 870 ff.
45. Smith AE. The council on pharmacy and chemistry. J Am Med Assoc 1944; 124:434 ff.
46. Dowling HF. Medicines for Man: The Development, Regulation, and Use of Prescription Drugs. New York, NY: Alfred A. Knopf, 1970:170–177.

47. It was more than a possibility; see the case of Clarin (heparin potassium), as discussed in U.S. Congress, Senate, Subcommittee on Antitrust and Monopoly of the Committee on the Judiciary. Drug Industry Antitrust Act. Hearings pursuant to S. Res. 52 on S. 1552, 87th Cong., 1st sess., September 13 and 15, 1961 and December 12–13, 18–29, 1961, Part 5. Washington, DC: GPO, 1962, pp. 2587–2588. Reproduced in: A Legislative History of the Federal Food, Drug, and Cosmetic Act and Its Amendments 20: 329–330.
48. Bishop J. Drug evaluation programs of the AMA, 1905–1966. J Am Med Assoc 1966; 196:122–123.
49. New program of operation for evaluation of drugs. J Am Med Assoc 1955; 158:1170–1171.
50. Dowling HF. The impact of the new drug laws on the council on drugs of the American Medical Association. Clin Res 1965; 13:162–165.
51. Weikel MK. Research as a Function of Pharmaceutical Industry: The American Formative Period. M. S. thesis, Madison, WI: University of Wisconsin, 1962:29–36.
52. Cowen DL. The role of the pharmaceutical industry. In: Blake. Safeguarding the Public, p. 73.
53. Liebenau J. Medical Science and Medical Industry: The Formation of the American Pharmaceutical Industry. Baltimore, MD: Johns Hopkins University Press, 1987, *passim*, but especially, pp. 57–78.
54. Swann JP. Academic Scientists and the Pharmaceutical Industry: Cooperative Research in Twentieth-Century America. Baltimore, MD: Johns Hopkins University Press, 1988:9–23.
55. Madison JH. Eli Lilly: A Life, 1885–1977. Indianapolis: Indiana Historical Society, 1989:27, 52.
56. Young JH. "Even to a sucking infant": Nostrums and children. In: American Health Quackery: Collected Essays by James Harvey Young. Princeton, NJ: Princeton University Press, 1992:135, 138.
57. Nelson GL, ed. Pharmaceutical Company Histories. Bismarck, ND: Woodbine, 1983; 1:161.
58. Liebenau J. A case unresolved: Mrs. George vs. Dr. Hand and his colic cure. Pharm Hist 1989; 31:135–138.
59. The best source on the history of patent medicines remains Young JH. The Toadstool Millionaires: A Social History of Patent Medicines in America before Federal Regulation. Princeton, NJ: Princeton University Press, 1961. Young's Medical Messiahs and his American Health Quackery also address this subject.
60. Young. Pure Food, pp. 50–51.
61. Wiley typically emphasized the problem of food adulteration as a more serious public health issue than drug adulteration, perhaps in part because of his scientific interests.
62. On Wiley and his time, see Wiley HW. An Autobiography. Indianapolis: Bobbs-Merrill, 1930.
63. Anderson OE. The Health of a Nation: Harvey W. Wiley and the Fight for Pure Food. Chicago, IL: University of Chicago Press, 1958.
64. Young. Pure Food.
65. Food and Drugs Act of 1906. Pub L No. 59–384. 34 U.S. Stat 768, June 30, 1906.
66. Thackray A, et al. Chemistry in America, 1876–1976: Historical Indicators. Dordrecht: D. Reidel, 1985:126–131.
67. For bibliographic information on the variety of regulations issued by the bureau at this time, see A Guide to Resources on the History of the Food and Drug Administration: Published Primary Sources: Sources on Regulation and Enforcement. ≤http://www.fda.gov/oc/history/resourceguide/ sources.html≥, January 18, 2002.
68. Sellers A, Grundstein ND. Administrative Procedure and Practice in the Department of Agriculture under the Federal Food, Drug, and Cosmetic Act of 1938. 308-page typescript in 2 parts. Part I: 12 (files, FDA History Office, Rockville, MD).
69. White MG, Gates OH. Decisions of Courts in Cases under the Federal Food and Drugs Act. Washington, DC: GPO, 1934:267–269 (quote is from p. 268).
70. Quoted in Young, "Drugs and the 1906 Law". In: Blake. Safeguarding the public, p. 149.
71. Sellers, Grundstein. Administrative Procedure and Practice. 1: 14–15, n. 31.

72. Sherley Amendment of 1912. Pub L No. 62–301. 37 U.S. Stat 416, August 23, 1912.
73. Lamb RdeF. American Chamber of Horrors. New York, NY: Farrar and Rinehart, 1936:64–68.
74. Young: Drugs and the 1906 Law, pp. 147–152.
75. Young: Drugs and the 1906 Law, pp. 149–152.
76. Swann JP. FDA and the practice of pharmacy: prescription drug regulation to 1951. Pharm Hist 36: 57–59, 1994.
77. Young. Drugs and the 1906 Law, pp. 153–156.
78. On the effort by FDA to promote the need for a new law, see Kay G. Healthy public relations: The FDA's 1930s legislative campaign. Bull Hist Med 2001; 75:446–487.
79. The standard source on the construction of the 1938 Food, Drug, and Cosmetic Act is Jackson CO. Food and Drug Legislation in the New Deal. Princeton, NJ: Princeton University Press, 1970.
80. An excellent source on the Elixir Sulfanilamide disaster is Young JH. Sulfanilamide and diethylene glycol. In: Parascandola J, Whorton JC, eds. Chemistry and Modern Society: Historical Essays in Honor of Aaron J. Ihde. American Chemical Society Symposium Series 228. Washington, DC: American Chemical Society, 1983:105–125.
81. Elixir of Death. RubinTarrant Productions, History Channel, December 11, 2003.
82. The letter quoted is reproduced in the files, FDA History Office, Rockville, MD.
83. Food, Drug, and Cosmetic Act. Pub L No. 75–717. 52 U.S. Stat 1040, June 25, 1938.
84. A recent article has shed light on this provision of the act, largely forgotten by those who would believe a requirement for good manufacturing practices began in 1962 (or even later). Cooper DE. Adequate controls for new drugs: Good manufacturing practice and the 1938 federal food, drug, and cosmetic act. Pharm Hist 2002; 44:12–23.
85. Cavers DF. The evolution of the contemporary system of drug regulation under the 1938 Act. In: Blake. Safeguarding the Public, pp. 167–168.
86. Warning Statements for Drug Preparations. TC-14, November 1, 1940. Reproduced in: Kleinfeld VA, Dunn CW. Federal Food, Drug, and Cosmetic Act: Judicial and Administrative Record, 1938–1949. Chicago, IL: Commerce Clearing House, c. 1949:574–578; quote is from p. 577.
87. Marks HM. Revisiting "the origins of compulsory drug prescriptions." Am J Public Health 1995; 85:109–115.
88. Swann. FDA and the practice of pharmacy.
89. To Distributors of Sulfanilamide and Related Drugs. TC-1, August 26, 1938. Reproduced in: Kleinfeld, Dunn. Federal Food, Drug, and Cosmetic Act, p. 561.
90. The generalization about prescription drugs applies, of course, only to nonnarcotic drugs. Narcotics could be dispensed only under a doctor's authorization under the Harrison Narcotic Act of 1914.
91. An Act to Amend the Federal Food, Drug, and Cosmetic Act. Pub L No. 82–215. 65 U.S. Stat 648, October 26, 1951.
92. The illegal trade in amphetamines and barbiturates in the trucking industry received dramatic treatment on television in the early 1960s: 330 Independence SW. The Dick Powell Theater, NBC, March 20, 1962.
93. Drug Abuse Control Amendments of 1965. Pub L No. 89–74. 79 U.S. Stat 226, July 15, 1965.
94. Swann JP. Drug abuse control under FDA, 1938–1968. Public Health Rep 1997; 112:83–86.
95. Insulin Amendment of 1941. Pub L No. 77–366. 55 U.S. Stat 851, December 22, 1941.
96. Penicillin Amendment of 1945. Pub L No. 79–139. 59 U.S. Stat 462, July 6, 1945.
97. Streptomycin Amendment. Pub L No. 80–16. 61 U.S. Stat 11, March 10, 1947.
98. Aureomycin Amendment of 1949. Pub L No. 81–164. 63 U.S. Stat 409, July 13, 1949, which accounted for chlortetracycline, chloramphenicol, and bacitracin.
99. Cavers. Drug regulation under the 1938 act, p. 167.
100. Directions for Use. TC-426, January 22, 1945. Reproduced in: Kleinfeld, Dunn. Federal Food, Drug, and Cosmetic Act, p. 746.
101. Lollipops Containing Aspirin. TC-130, March 7, 1940. Reproduced in: Kleinfeld, Dunn. Federal Food, Drug, and Cosmetic Act, p. 620.

102. Specific NDAs were collected from NDA summary data, files, FDA History Office, Rockville, MD.
103. Mandel RH. A Half Century of Peer Review, 1946–1996. Bethesda, MD: Division of Research Grants, National Institutes of Health, 1996, especially pp. 16 ff. Year-by-year drug application data can be found in "New Drug Application Approvals and Receipts, Including New Molecular Entities, 1938 to Present," http://www.fda.gov/oc/history/NDAapprovals.html, 2007.
104. Swann. Academic Scientists and the Pharmaceutical Industry.
105. Landau R, Achilladelis B, Scriabine A. Pharmaceutical Innovation: Revolutionizing Human Health. Philadelphia, PA: Chemical Heritage Press, 1999:72 ff.
106. de Haen P. Compilation of new drugs, 1940 thru 1975. Pharm. Times 1976; 42(3):40–75.
107. de Haen P. New Drug Parade: A Historical Minireview, 1954–1982. Poster Exhibit Presentation. Drug Information Association Annual Meeting, Washington, D. C., July 28, 1983. Englewood, CO: Paul de Haen International, 1983.
108. Cavers. Drug regulation under the 1938 act, pp. 164 (rauwolfia), 167 (NDA submission rates).
109. U.S. Department of the Treasury, Public Health Service. Regulations for the Sale of Viruses, Serums, Toxins and Analogous Products in the District of Columbia and in Interstate Traffic. Misc. Publication No. 10, Approved March 13, 1934. Washington, DC: GPO, 1934:3.
110. Swann JP. Sure cure: Public policy on drug efficacy before 1962. In Higby GJ, Stroud EC, ed. The Inside Story of Medicines: A Symposium. Madison, WI: American Institute of the History of Pharmacy, 1997:228–232, 235–237.
111. Granger GA to Weilerstein RW. October 14, 1955, NDA 9214, Misc. File IV, FDA Records, Rockville, MD.
112. Quoted in Swann. Sure cure, p. 244.
113. The Hepasyn case is drawn from Swann. Sure cure, pp. 237–246 (Holland quote is from p. 244).
114. Around the same time, an HEW-requested review of antibiotic decisions made by FDA in the wake of the Henry Welch affair, conducted by the National Research Council, led to a similar conclusion. See Swann. Sure cure, p. 248.
115. Mintz M. The Therapeutic Nightmare. Boston, MA: Houghton Mifflin, 1965:54–56.
116. Swann. Sure cure, pp. 246–250.
117. Harris R. The Real Voice. New York, NY: Macmillan, 1964:59–64.
118. Quoted in Harris. The Real Voice, pp. 78–79.
119. Harris. The Real Voice, pp. 88–91. Greene JA. Prescribing by Numbers: Drugs and the Definition of Disease (Baltimore, MD: Johns Hopkins University Press, 2007), offers an in-depth analysis of pharmaceutical advertising that includes this period.
120. McFadyen RE. FDA's regulation and control of antibiotics in the 1950s: The Henry Welch Scandal, Félix Martí-Ibáñez, and Charles Pfizer and Co. Bull Hist Med. 1979; 53(2):159–169.
121. Harris. The Real Voice, captures the hearings succinctly, though weighted toward Kefauver's perspective; the preceding description draws from pp. 5–116.
122. McFadyen RE. Estes Kefauver and the Drug Industry. Ph.D. dissertation, Atlanta, GA: Emory University, 1973.
123. The complete hearings are reproduced in A Legislative History of the Federal Food, Drug, and Cosmetic Act and Its Amendments 17:178–558 (Report No. 448, pursuant to S. Res. 52, a study of administered prices in the drug industry, June 27, 1961); 17:559–807 (Hearings, Part 1; July 5, 6, 18–21, 25, 1961); 18:1–212 (Hearings, Part 1; cont.); 18:213–944 (Hearings, Part 2; exhibits and appendices); 19:1– 799 (Hearings, Part 3; October 16–18, 31, 1961 and November 1, 9, 1961); 19:800–899 (Hearings, Part 4; December 7–9, 1961); 20:1–313 (Hearings, Part 4; cont.); 20:314–797 (Hearings, Part 5; September 13, 15, 1961, December 12–13 and 18–20, 1961). In addition, the hearings before the Committee on Interstate and Foreign Commerce in the House of Representatives on the Drug Industry Act of 1962 (H R 11581 and 11582), under Chairman Oren Harris of Arkansas, June 19–22,

1962 and August 20–23, 1962, are reproduced in A Legislative History of the Federal Food, Drug, and Cosmetic Act and Its Amendments 21:170–883.
124. On Kefauver in general, see Fontenay CL. Estes Kefauver: A Biography. Knoxville, TN: University of Tennessee Press, 1980.
125. U.S. Congress, Senate. S 1552. A bill to amend and supplement the antitrust laws with respect to the manufacture and distribution of drugs, and for other purposes, 87th Cong., 1st sess., April 12, 1961. Reproduced in: A Legislative History of the Federal Food, Drug, and Cosmetic Act and Its Amendments 17:121–144.
126. Harris. The Real Voice, pp. 123–153.
127. The preceding account is drawn from U.S. Congress, Senate, Subcommittee on Reorganization and International Organizations of the Committee on Government Operations. Interagency Coordination in Drug Research and Regulation. Hearings pursuant to S. Res. 276, 87th Cong., 2nd sess., August 1, 9, 1962, Part 1 of 2. Washington, DC: GPO, 1963:75 ff.
128. McFadyen RE. Thalidomide in America: A brush with tragedy. Clio Med 1976; 11:79–86.
129. Knightley P, et al. Suffer the Children: The Story of Thalidomide. New York, NY: Viking Press, 1979, which provides the most detail to this story.
130. Two months earlier Kennedy conferred on Kelsey the President's Award for Distinguished Federal Civilian Service (the highest award for federal civilian service) for work that "... prevented a major tragedy of birth deformities in the United States ...;" Presentation of The President's Award for Distinguished Federal Civilian Service. Program, the White House, August 7, 1962, files, FDA History Office. See the report that made public Kelsey's role in the Kevadon review: M Mintz. "Heroine" of FDA Keeps Bad Drug Off Market. Washington Post, July 15, 1962.
131. Swann JP. The 1941 sulfathiazole disaster and the birth of good manufacturing practices. PDA J Pharmaceut Sci Technol 1999; 53:148–153.
132. Drug Amendments of 1962. Pub L No. 87–781. 76 U.S. Stat 780, October 10, 1962.
133. See Marks LV. Sexual Chemistry: A History of the Contraceptive Pill. New Haven, CT: Yale University Press, 2001:150–152.
134. Health Research and Health Services Amendments of 1976. Pub L No. 94–278. 90 U.S. Stat 401, April 22, 1976.
135. Apple RD. Vitamania: Vitamins in American Culture. New Brunswick, NJ: Rutgers University Press, 1996.
136. Orphan Drug Act. Pub L No. 97–414. 96 U.S. Stat 2049, January 4, 1983.
137. Basara LR, Montagne M. Searching for Magic Bullets: Orphan Drugs, Consumer Activism, and Pharmaceutical Development. New York: Haworth Press, Pharmaceutical Products Press, 1994:143 ff.
138. 48 Fed Reg 26721,26728–26730, 26742–26743, June 9, 1983.
139. Cf. 52 Fed Reg 8850–8857, March 19, 1987.
140. 52 Fed Reg 19466–19477, May 22, 1987, which reproposed and then finalized the proposal—after 4 years. This citation itemized several diseases as illustrations of those normally considered immediately life-threatening, including advanced AIDS cases, advanced congestive heart failure, and severe combined immunodeficiency syndrome, as well as examples of serious diseases, such as Alzheimer's disease, advanced Parkinson's disease, and active advanced lupus. Treatment INDs would not apply to those suffering the latter group of serious diseases (p. 19467).
141. 53 Fed Reg 41516–41524, 44144.
142. The President's Task Force on Regulatory Relief certainly had a significant role as well in this reappraisal of the drug approval process.
143. For a summary of investigational drug revisions and the role of AIDS activists, see Young JH. AIDS and the FDA. In: Hannaway C, Harden V, Parascandola J, eds. AIDS and the Public Debate. Amsterdam: IOS Press, 1995:54–66; see also Arthur A. Daemmrich, Pharmacopolitics: Drug Regulation in the United States and Germany. Chapel Hill, NC: University of North Carolina Press, 2004:96 ff.

2 Modernizing the Food and Drug Administration

Arthur Y. Tsien, Esq.

Olsson Frank Weeda Terman Bode Matz PC, Washington, D.C., U.S.A.

INTRODUCTION AND OVERVIEW

In recent years, Congress has enacted and the president has signed into law a number of significant changes to the Federal Food, Drug, and Cosmetic Act (FDC Act) to modernize the Food and Drug Administration's (FDA) regulation of drugs and biological products. This chapter summarizes the significant changes.

These legislative changes began with the Prescription Drug User Fee Act of 2002 (PDUFA) (1), enacted in October 2002. PDUFA imposed user fees and other fees related to the review of new drug applications. In exchange for paying user fees, drug sponsors got the benefit of substantially shortened review times in the form of "performance goals." PDUFA has been enhanced and reauthorized three times since its inception, so that the current program is authorized until 2012. The major impact of PDUFA on FDA's drug review process is discussed in chapter 8.

The Food and Drug Administration Modernization Act (FDAMA) (2), enacted in November 1997, made substantial changes to FDA's practices and procedures. FDAMA was discussed in detail in chapter 6 of the first edition of this book.

The Best Pharmaceuticals for Children Act (BPCA) (3), enacted in January 2002, revised and reauthorized the 6-month pediatric exclusivity provisions added to the FDC Act by FDAMA. These changes are discussed in section "Pediatric Studies Exclusivity" of this chapter.

The Public Health Security and Bioterrorism Preparedness and Response Act of 2002 (commonly called the Bioterrorism Act) (4), enacted in June 2002, provided for the accelerated approval of drugs and biologicals to be used in the event of a bioterrorism attack or similar public health emergency. These provisions are discussed in section "Accelerated Approval of Priority Countermeasures" of this chapter. It also required public disclosure of a drug or biological sponsor's failure to fulfill its commitment to conduct postmarketing studies. These provisions are discussed in section "Reports of Postmarketing Approval Studies" of this chapter.

The Pediatric Research Equity Act (5), enacted in December 2003, gave FDA the statutory authority to require sponsors of applications for drugs and biologicals to conduct clinical studies to assess the safety and effectiveness of their products in children. These provisions are discussed in section "Mandatory Pediatric Assessment" of this chapter.

The Medicare Prescription Drug, Improvement, and Modernization Act of 2003 (MMA) (6), enacted in December 2003, made fundamental changes to 180-day exclusivity for abbreviated new drug applications (ANDAs), including circumstances under which 180-day exclusivity is forfeited. The MMA also revised statutory provisions regarding the timing of the notice of a Paragraph IV certification given to the patent owner and the holder of new drug application (NDA) referenced in an ANDA or 505(b)(2) NDA, the provisions regarding the filing of a declaratory judgment action by an ANDA or 505(b)(2) NDA sponsor to obtain patent certainty, and the 30-month delay of final approval for an ANDA or 505(b)(2) NDA. These provisions are discussed in chapter 4.

The Dietary Supplement and Nonprescription Drug Consumer Protection Act (7), enacted in December 2006, amended the FDC Act to impose adverse event reporting requirements on manufacturers and distributors of nonprescription drugs that are marketed outside of FDA's premarket approval system. These provisions are discussed in section "Adverse Event Reporting for Nonprescription Drugs" of this chapter.

The Food and Drug Administration Amendments Act of 2007 (FDAAA) (8), was enacted on September 27, 2007. FDAAA's changes relevant to drugs and biologicals include the following:

- Prescription drug user fees were reauthorized for another 5 years (now expiring in 2012). A new voluntary user fee program for FDA review of direct-to-consumer television advertisements for prescription drugs was authorized. These changes are discussed in chapter 8.
- Substantial new requirements regarding postmarketing studies and safety of marketed prescription drugs and biologicals were added. These provisions are discussed in chapter 10.
- Provisions of existing law that requires most sponsors of drug and biological applications to assess the safety and effectiveness of their products in pediatric populations were reauthorized (now expiring in 2012) and expanded. Provisions concerning 6-month pediatric exclusivity were also reauthorized (now expiring in 2012) and expanded. These changes are discussed in sections "Mandatory Pediatric Assessment" and "Pediatric Studies Exclusivity" of this chapter.
- Provisions of the Public Health Service Act requiring the establishment of "data banks" regarding clinical trials and experimental treatments were substantially expanded. These changes are discussed in section "Clinical Trial Registry and Results Database" of this chapter.
- New limitations on citizen petitions that seek to block or delay the final approval of ANDAs and 505(b)(2) NDAs were added to the FDC Act. These changes are discussed in section "Citizen Petitions Affecting Generic Drug Approvals" of this chapter.

PEDIATRIC STUDIES

Mandatory Pediatric Assessment

As discussed in section 2.2 of chapter 6 of the first edition of this book, in 1999 FDA adopted a final rule that required that sponsors of certain newly approved and marketed drugs and biologicals conduct clinical studies to provide adequate labeling for the use of their products in children. That rule was challenged in federal district court, and FDA was barred from enforcing it because the court concluded that FDA did not have the statutory authority to issue the rule. In response to that decision, the Pediatric Research Equity Act was enacted into law in 2003. Those provisions had a sunset date of October 1, 2007.

Section 402 of FDAAA amended section 505B of the FDC Act (9) to reauthorize these requirements through October 1, 2012.

Section 402 of FDAAA also made some changes to the pediatric study requirements in section 505B of the FDC Act. As amended, section 505B of the FDC Act requires that an application (or supplement) for a new active ingredient, new indication, new dosage form, new dosing regimen, or new route of administration for a drug or biological include a pediatric assessment, unless the requirement is waived or deferred. The pediatric assessment must:

> contain data, gathered using appropriate formulations for each age group for which the assessment is required, that are adequate (i) to assess the safety and effectiveness of the drug or the biological product for the claimed indications in all relevant pediatric subpopulations, and (ii) to support dosing and administration for each pediatric subpopulation for which the drug or the biological product is safe and effective.

Where appropriate, FDA may conclude that pediatric effectiveness can be extrapolated from studies of the drug or biological in adults, or that extrapolation between different pediatric age groups is appropriate. FDA may defer submission of some or all required pediatric assessments until a specified date after product approval or licensure. If the submission of the pediatric assessment is deferred, the applicant must report to FDA on an annual basis regarding progress made in meeting the assessment requirement.

FDA is authorized to grant partial or full waivers of the pediatric assessment based on a number of criteria, including findings by FDA that the necessary studies are impossible or highly impracticable, that there is evidence strongly suggesting that the product would be ineffective or unsafe in all pediatric age groups, or that the product does not represent a meaningful therapeutic benefit over existing therapies and is not likely to be used by a significant number of pediatric patients. Where appropriate, the basis for FDA's decision to grant a waiver must be included in the labeling of the drug or biological.

Similar provisions apply to approved, marketed drugs and biologicals. FDA is authorized to require applicants to submit pediatric assessments by a specified date. FDA can also grant partial and full waivers.

The failure to submit a required pediatric assessment is, expressly, not a basis for withdrawal of approval of a drug or revocation of the license of a biological. However, the drug or biological may be considered "misbranded" and subject to seizure or injunction.

Where appropriate, FDA may require a drug or biological sponsor to include labeling information regarding the results of a pediatric assessment, and regarding whether the assessment does or does not demonstrate that the product is safe and effective in pediatric populations or subpopulations. If a product sponsor and FDA cannot agree on labeling changes, the dispute is to be referred to FDA's Pediatric Advisory Committee. FDA may deem a drug or biological to be misbranded if the sponsor does not agree to make a labeling change requested by FDA.

During the first year, following a labeling change based on a pediatric assessment, all adverse event reports regarding the drug or biological must be referred to FDA's Office of Pediatric Therapeutics. That office must provide the adverse event reports for review by the Pediatric Advisory Committee and obtain the recommendations of that advisory committee. FDA may, if appropriate, follow this process in subsequent years.

Unless FDA requires otherwise by regulation, the requirements for pediatric assessments do not apply to orphan drugs. However, the pediatric assessment requirements do apply to ANDAs and 505(b)(2) NDAs. Thus, for example, the sponsor of an ANDA submitted pursuant to an approved ANDA suitability petition (see chap. 4) for a new dosage form (e.g., liquid, where the reference product is a tablet or a capsule) will find itself having to conduct a pediatric assessment or seeking a waiver.

FDA is required to make publicly available data regarding its processing of pediatric assessments, waivers, and deferrals; the internal FDA medical, statistical, and clinical pharmacology reviews of pediatric assessments; and a study and report to Congress to be conducted by the Institute of Medicine.

Section 402(b) of FDAAA provides that, with minor exceptions, the revised requirements of section 505B of the FDC Act apply to pediatric assessments that were pending or deferred on September 27, 2007.

Section 403 of FDAAA added new section 505C of the FDC Act (10) that requires FDA to establish an internal pediatric review committee, consisting of FDA employees. Under section 505B(f) of the FDC Act (11), among other functions, the internal committee is required to consult with drug and biological revision divisions regarding pediatric plans and assessments, and to review all requests for assessments, deferrals, and waivers. The internal committee is required to conduct a retrospective review and analysis of a representative sample of pediatric assessments submitted and referrals and waivers granted by September 27, 2008. Based on that review, FDA is required to issue recommendations to drug and biological review divisions and guidance to industry related to pediatric studies. FDA, in consultation with the internal committee, is required to track and make available to the public information regarding pediatric assessments and related topics.

Pediatric Studies Exclusivity

As discussed in section 2.1 of chapter 6 of the first edition of this book, FDAMA added new section 505A of the FDC Act (12) to provide 6 months of extra-market exclusivity, if the sponsor of a drug application conducted pediatric studies in response to FDA's "written request" for such studies. In 2002, the BPCA reauthorized and revised these provisions. Section 502 of FDAAA further amended section 505A of the FDC Act to reauthorize this provision, so that it now sunsets on October 1, 2012.

FDAAA also made a number of substantive changes to section 505A. Most importantly, pediatric exclusivity must now be awarded at least 9 months before the expiration of the underlying nonpatent 3-, 5-, or 7-year exclusivity period or Orange Book patent that is to be extended. Under prior law, a qualifying study could be submitted at any time before expiration of the underlying exclusivity period or patent. FDA then had up to 90 days to determine whether the study qualified for an additional 6 months of exclusivity. During that 90-day time period, final approval of ANDAs and 505(b)(2) NDAs was blocked, giving the innovator drug sponsor a de facto exclusivity period. (In practice, however, the de facto exclusivity period did not work to the disadvantage of ANDA and 505(b)(2) NDA sponsors, as FDA has granted pediatric exclusivity in essentially all instances.)

Among other changes to section 505A of the FDC Act made by the FDAAA, qualifying studies may include, where deemed appropriate by FDA, preclinical studies (such as animal studies). FDA's written request for a pediatric study may now encompass both approved and unapproved uses, a change from prior FDA policy. At the time of submission of a pediatric study pursuant to a written request, the applicant is required to submit all postmarketing adverse event reports. An NDA or supplemental NDA with proposed labeling or proposed labeling revisions based on new pediatric information resulting from studies conducted pursuant to FDA's written request will get the benefit of priority review by FDA. FDA now has 180 days to review a submitted pediatric study to determine whether it complies with FDA's written request, compared with 60 days under prior law.

If FDA determines that a pediatric study does or does not demonstrate that the studied drug is safe and effective in pediatric populations or subpopulations, product labeling is required to include information about the results of the study and FDA's conclusions (including a conclusion that the study results are inconclusive, if this is the case).

Sponsors of studies that result in labeling changes are required to distribute to physicians and other health-care providers, at least annually (or more frequently, if FDA determines that it would be beneficial), information about labeling changes related to pediatric use. With some minor exceptions, the new provisions apply to pediatric written requests issued on or after September 27, 2007.

CLINICAL TRIAL REGISTRY AND RESULTS DATABASE

As discussed in section 4.1 of chapter 6 of the first edition of this book, FDAMA added new subsection (j) to section 402 of the Public Health Service Act (PHS Act) (13). Section 402(j) of the PHS Act required the National Institutes of Health (NIH), in cooperation with FDA and others, to establish a "data bank" consisting of a registry of clinical trials and information regarding experimental treatments that may be available. In brief, as established by FDAMA, the data bank was required only to list clinical trials and experimental treatments for "serious or life-threatening diseases and conditions."

Section 801 of FDAAA substantially expanded the clinical trial registry requirement so that it applies to all clinical trials (except phase I trials) for all diseases and conditions. The "responsible party" (defined as the trial sponsor or the principal investigator, if so designated by the trial sponsor) for a clinical trial is required to submit to NIH information describing the trial, recruitment information, contact information, and administrative data. For unapproved drugs or unlicensed biological products, the information submitted is required to include whether there is an expanded access program for those who do not qualify for enrollment in the clinical trial. In general, the information must be submitted within 21 days after the first patient is enrolled in the trial. Data regarding trials that were ongoing as of September 27, 2007 must be submitted by December 25, 2007, except the data regarding a then-ongoing trial that is not for a serious or life-threatening disease or condition must be submitted by September 27, 2008.

NIH is required to post data into the data bank within 30 days after submission, regardless of whether the product is approved or not approved. The data bank must be in a format that is searchable by keyword and by a number of specified criteria.

Over time, the clinical trials registry database will expand to include links for accessing information on the results of clinical trials:

- By December 25, 2007, NIH is required to include information regarding the clinical trials that form the primary basis of an efficacy claim and regarding postapproval trials, including links to FDA summaries presented to an advisory committee, FDA summaries of pediatric studies, FDA public health advisories, FDA drug approval packages, MedLine citations to any publications regarding the clinical trial, and the entry for the drug in the National Library of Medicine database of structured product labels.

- By September 27, 2008, NIH is required to include information regarding the "basic results" of trials for approved drugs and licensed biologicals, including demographic and baseline characteristics of the patient sample, primary and secondary outcomes, a point of contact for scientific information, and disclosure of any agreements that restrict the principal investigator's ability to discuss the trial results or to publish information concerning the trial results.
- By March 27, 2009, FDA is required to determine, through rulemaking, the best method for including information regarding serious adverse and frequent adverse events in a manner and form that is useful and not misleading to patients, physicians, and scientists.
- By September 27, 2010, FDA is required to adopt regulations to expand the database to include a summary of each clinical trial and its results written in nontechnical, understandable language for patients (if possible), as well as information regarding the protocol. The regulations must encompass all approved drugs and licensed biologicals. FDA is authorized to, but need not, extend the database to unapproved or unlicensed products.

Premarket approval applications for drugs and biologicals must include a certification that all applicable clinical trial data bank requirements have been satisfied. Among other remedies, civil money penalties are available for violations (14).

Finally, section 801(d) of FDAAA preempts state or local requirements for the registration of clinical trials. It also provides a rule of construction that submitted clinical trial information concerning an unapproved use of a drug or biological is not to be taken as evidence of the drug's or biological's "intended use."

PREAPPROVAL ISSUES

Combination Products

Section 503(g) of the FDC Act (15) has long addressed the regulation of combination products that are typically the combination of a device and a drug or the combination of a device and a biological. The Medical Device User Fee and Modernization Act of 2002 (16) amended section 503(g) to require FDA to establish, within the Office of the Commissioner, a new office to ensure the prompt assignment of applications for combination products to the appropriate agency centers, to ensure timely and effective premarket review, to ensure consistent postmarketing regulation of like products to the extent permitted by law, and to resolve disputes among FDA Centers. The office is required to be staffed with employees with appropriate scientific and medical expertise.

Critical Path Initiative

FDA launched its Critical Path Initiative in March 2004 (17). The Critical Path Initiative is FDA's effort to stimulate and facilitate a national effort to modernize the sciences through which drugs, biologicals, and other FDA-regulated products are developed, evaluated, approved, and manufactured.

FDAAA added three new sections to the FDC Act to further FDA's Critical Path Initiative.

First, section 601 of FDAAA amended the FDC Act by adding new section 770 (18) to establish the "Reagan-Udall Foundation for the Food and Drug Administration," a nonprofit corporation whose purpose is "to advance the mission of the Food and Drug Administration to modernize medical, veterinary, food, food ingredient, and cosmetic product development, accelerate innovation, and enhance product safety."

The Foundation's Board of Directors is to consist of four ex officio members, the FDA Commissioner, the Director of the National Institutes of Health, the Director of the Centers for Disease Control and Prevention, and the Director of the Agency for Healthcare Research and Policy, with 14 voting members appointed for staggered 4-year terms by the four ex officio government members from industry, professional groups, academia, consumer or patient organizations, and health-care providers. As required, the four ex officio members met in October 2007 and in November 2007, appointed the remaining members of the Foundation Board (19). Federal employees are not eligible to serve as appointed members of the Foundation Board, but may serve on committees that advise the Foundation or be detailed to assist the Foundation.

FDA is required to fund the Foundation at an annual level of between $500,000 and $1,250,000 from its appropriated funds; the Foundation may also accept funding from other sources, including private sources.

Second, new section 771 of the FDC Act (20), also added by FDAAA section 601, requires the Foundation to be located in the metropolitan Washington, D.C. area.

Third, new section 772 of the FDC Act (21), also added by FDAAA section 601, requires FDA to report to Congress on an annual basis regarding the activities of the Reagan-Udall Foundation.

Fourth, new section 910 of the FDC Act (22). added by section 602 of FDAAA, established the Office of the Chief Scientist within the Office of the FDA Commissioner. The new office is charged with overseeing FDA's own research programs, and ensuring that there is no duplication of research efforts supported by the Reagan-Udall Foundation.

Finally, section 603 of FDAAA added new section 566 to the FDC Act (23) that authorizes FDA to enter into public–private partnerships with institutions of higher learning or tax-exempt charitable institutions to help FDA implement the Critical Path Initiative, including fostering the development of drugs and biologicals.

Accelerated Approval of Priority Countermeasures

Section 122 of the Public Health Security and Bioterrorism Preparedness and Response Act of 2002, enacted in June 2002 in response to the 9/11 terrorist attacks, added new section 506A of the FDC Act (24). This provision authorizes FDA to designate drugs, biologicals, and medical devices that are potential "priority countermeasures" for responding to a bioterrorism attack (or similar public health emergency) as eligible for "fast-track" review under section 506 of the FDC Act (25). FDA is permitted to grant approval based on evidence of effectiveness derived from animal studies.

As mandated by statute, FDA issued a final rule regarding the use of animal trials to establish effectiveness of drugs and biologicals when clinical trials in humans cannot be conducted ethically (26).

Priority Review to Encourage Treatments for Tropical Diseases

Section 1102 of FDAAA added new section 524 to the FDC Act (27) to establish a "priority review" system for drugs and biologicals for preventing or treating a tropical disease. Tropical disease is defined as any of 16 listed diseases (including well-known diseases such as tuberculosis, malaria, cholera, and leprosy), or any other infectious disease for which there is no significant market in developed countries and that disproportionately affects poor and marginalized populations. A drug or biological that is eligible for priority review is to be reviewed by FDA under a 6-month "review clock," rather than FDA's standard review clock.

To receive the benefit of priority review, a prospective drug or biological sponsor must notify FDA at least 1 year before the submission of its application. That notification must include a binding commitment to pay a special priority review user fee, in addition to the usual PDUFA drug application user fee (see chap. 8). The amount of the special priority review user fee is to be determined by FDA. Unlike other user fees, there are no waivers, exemptions, reductions, or refunds of the priority review user fee. However, a sponsor paying the priority review user fee receives a "priority review voucher," which may be sold for use by another sponsor.

FDA may issue priority review vouchers starting September 27, 2008, for applications to be submitted starting September 27, 2009.

Antibiotic Drugs

Section 911 of FDAAA added new section 511 to the FDC Act (28). The new provision requires FDA to issue, by September 27, 2008, guidance concerning the conduct of clinical trials for antibiotic drugs, including specifically antimicrobials that treat acute bacterial sinusitis, acute bacterial otitis media, and acute bacterial exacerbation of chronic bronchitis. The guidance is required to address appropriate models and valid surrogate markers. FDA is also required to review and update the guidance by September 2012. The purpose of the new provision is to address the so-called "moving target" with regard to clinical trials to support approval of antibiotics, particularly with regard to the specified diseases or conditions.

In addition, section 1111 of FDAAA requires FDA to identify (where such information is reasonably available) and publicly update "clinically susceptible concentrations," which is defined as "specific values that characterize bacteria as clinically susceptible, intermediate, or resistant to the drug (or drugs) being tested." FDA is required to make this information publicly available on the internet within 30 days after it becomes available. This provision is expressly not to be construed to restrict the prescribing of antibiotics by physicians or to limit the practice of medicine.

Finally, section 1112 of FDAAA requires FDA to convene a public meeting regarding which serious and life-threatening infectious diseases, such as diseases due to gram-negative bacteria and other diseases due to antibiotic-resistant bacteria, potentially qualify for orphan drug grants or other incentives.

Advisory Committee Referral

Section 918 of FDAAA added new subsection (s) to section 505 of the FDC Act (29). The new subsection (s) requires FDA to refer an application for a new active ingredient (including a biological product) to the appropriate FDA advisory committee for review. If FDA does not refer the application to an advisory committee for review, it must provide a summary of the reasons why the agency did not do so in its action letter on the application.

This new provision was effective upon enactment. It seems unlikely that this new provision will change prevailing FDA practice, as FDA almost always refers applications for products with new active ingredients to an advisory committee before approval.

Single-Enantiomer Exclusivity

Section 1113 of FDAAA added new subsection (u) to section 505 of the FDC Act (30) to provide an optional exclusivity period for certain drugs containing single enantiomers.

FDA's longstanding interpretation is that a single enantiomer of a previously approved racemic mixture is not regarded as a "new chemical entity" (NCE) that is eligible for 5-year NCE exclusivity (31). New section 505(u) does not change that interpretation. Rather, the new provision creates an optional exception, under which a sponsor can elect for a single enantiomer to "not be considered the same active ingredient as that contained in the approved racemic drug"—that is, the sponsor can elect for the enantiomer to be considered a new active moiety that is eligible for 5-year NCE exclusivity—if all of the following conditions are met:

- The single enantiomer has not been previously approved except in the approved racemic drug.
- The application for the enantiomer includes full reports of clinical studies (other than bioavailability studies) necessary to support the approval, which studies were sponsored by the applicant, i.e., it is a "full" 505(b)(1) NDA.
- The application does not rely on any studies that support the approval of the racemic drug.
- The enantiomer is not intended for a use that is in a "therapeutic category" for which the racemic drug has been approved, or for which any other enantiomer of the racemic drug has been approved. Therapeutic category is defined by the USPs list for purposes of the Medicare Part D prescription drug benefit; FDA is authorized to revise the categories through rulemaking.

A qualifying sponsor must elect to receive the benefit of this provision. The election may only be made in an NDA submitted after September 27, 2007, and before October 1, 2012. If the sponsor elects to use this provision, FDA is prohibited from approving the enantiomer for any condition of use in the therapeutic category in which the racemic drug has been approved for 10 years. The labeling of the enantiomer would have to include a statement that it has not been approved for any condition of use for the racemic drug.

POSTAPPROVAL ISSUES

Reports of Postmarketing Approval Studies

The provisions of section 506B of the FDC Act (32), added by FDAMA in 1997, are discussed in section 3.5 of chapter 6 of the first edition of this book. In brief, section 506B provided FDA with additional authority for monitoring the progress of postmarketing studies that drug and biological applicants had agreed to conduct, including the submission of annual reports to FDA until each study is completed or terminated.

In 2002, the Bioterrorism Act added new subsections (d) and (e) to section 506B of the FDC Act to require FDA to publish a statement on the agency's internet site if studies were not submitted to FDA in timely fashion, including (if appropriate) the reasons why the failure to complete the study were not deemed acceptable by FDA. FDA also may (but need not) require a drug or biological sponsor to notify health-care practitioners of the failure to complete a study and the questions of clinical benefit or safety that remain unanswered as a result of that failure.

FDA has issued a guidance document regarding the implementation of these requirements for drugs and biologicals (33).

Prescription Drug Safety Information for Patients and Providers

Section 915 of FDAAA added new subsection (r) to section 505 of the FDC Act (34) to address postmarketing drug safety information for patients and providers. The purpose of the new provision is to improve the transparency of information about prescription drugs and improve the access of patients and health-care providers to drug information.

By September 27, 2008, FDA is required to make available, via a single internet Web site, easily searchable drug safety information that is currently found on a variety of federal government Web sites. The information is required to include patient labeling and patient package inserts, medication guides, a link to the clinical trials registry and results data bank (discussed in section "Clinical Trial Registry and Results Database" of this chapter), recent and current FDA safety information and alerts (such as information about product recalls, Warning Letters, and import alerts), publicly available information about implemented RiskMAPs and risk evaluation and mitigation strategies, and guidance documents and regulations relevant to drug safety. The Web site also must provide access to data summaries regarding surveillance related to known and serious side effects (see chap. 10).

Eighteen months after approval or after use of the drug by 10,000 individuals, whichever is later, the Web site must include a summary analysis of adverse drug reaction reports received by FDA. The Web site must enable patients, health-care providers, and drug sponsors to submit adverse event reports.

Within 21 days after initial approval or after the approval of a supplemental application that results in a labeling change, FDA is required to post approved professional labeling and any required patient labeling on the Web site.

Public Availability of Drug Approval Package

Under a longstanding FDA regulation, a summary of the safety and effectiveness data and information that support a drug approval are "immediately" available for public disclosure after approval, with very limited exceptions (35). In practice, however, the public availability of a data summary, often referred to as "summary basis of approval" (SBA), varies widely. In some cases, information is available on FDA's Web site within days of a drug approval. In other cases, the information is not in fact publicly available for months or even years, despite the submission of multiple requests for such information pursuant to the Freedom of Information Act.

FDAAA section 916 amended section 505(l) of the FDC Act (36) to address this situation. As amended, FDA is now required to post the "action package" for approval of an NDA drug or a biological on its Web site within 30 days after approval if the approval involves a new active ingredient, and within 30 days after the third Freedom of Information Act request for the documents for any other NDA drug or biological. While 505(b)(2) NDAs are within the scope of the new provision, the new provision does not affect the public availability of information regarding the approval of ANDAs.

The action package includes documents generated by FDA related to review of the application, labeling, a "summary review" that documents the agency's review process (including any critical issues and disagreements with the drug sponsor and within the FDA review team and how they were resolved), the "decision document" of the Division Director and Office Director, and identification of each FDA employee who participated in the approval decision and who consents to have his or her name included in the package. In addition to making the action package available, FDA is required to post on its internet site a "summary review that documents the agency's review process, including critical issues and disagreements with the applicant and within the FDA review team, within 48 hours after approval, unless FDA needs additional time for the redaction of nondisclosable information.

To preserve the integrity of the review process, section 505(l) of the FDC Act provides that a "scientific review" is considered the work of the reviewer and may not be altered by either the reviewer or management once final.

The new provision was effective upon enactment.

Prescription Drug Distribution

Section 913 of FDAAA added new section 505D to the FDC Act (37). The new provision requires FDA to develop, by March 2010, a "standardized numerical identifier" to be applied to a prescription drug at the point of manufacture and repackaging at the "package or pallet level." The purpose of the identifier is "to facilitate the identification, validation, authentication, and tracking and tracing of the prescription drug" through the supply chain. In developing the standard, FDA is required to consult with other federal agencies, manufacturers, distributors, pharmacies, and other stakeholders in the pharmaceutical supply chain. To the extent practicable, the standard developed is to be harmonized with international consensus standards and is to take into account appropriate technologies, such as radio frequency identification. The underlying purpose is to provide technology to help secure the prescription drug supply chain against counterfeit, diverted, expired, or otherwise substandard drugs.

Other than requiring FDA to engage in standards development, FDAAA did not impose any requirements in this area. However, further federal legislative developments seem likely, possibly in response to conflicting state requirements. At the time of this writing, California law will require that most prescription drugs have an electronic record (known as a "pedigree") that tracks each package size distributed by a manufacturer through the supply chain to the pharmacy, health-care provider, or other person authorized to dispense or administer the prescription drug. Each package is required to have a unique identification number established at the point of manufacture (38). The assignment of a unique identifier to each package of a prescription drug is commonly known in the industry as "serialization," while the ability to trace the distribution history of any particular package of a prescription drug is known as "track and trace."

OTHER ISSUES

Importation of Prescription Drugs

In general, foreign versions of drugs and biologicals that are not FDA approved for sale in the United States may not be lawfully imported into the United States, as the foreign versions are regarded as unapproved drugs or unlicensed biologicals. In 2003, section 1121 of the MMA added section 804 of the FDC Act (39) to create an exception for imports from Canada, if certain conditions are met. Among other requirements, a licensed pharmacist or a licensed prescription drug wholesale distributor can be authorized to import from Canada prescription drugs, other than controlled substances, biologicals, intravenous or parenteral drugs, infused drugs, and drugs inhaled during surgery. FDA is required to adopt regulations regarding detailed submissions to be made to FDA by prospective importers, including laboratory testing to ensure that the drug complies with all established standards and specifications. FDA is directed to exercise its enforcement discretion to permit individuals to make importations for personal use.

Importantly, section 804 does not go into effect unless the Secretary of Health and Human Services certifies to Congress that implementation of section 804 will pose "no additional risk to the public's health and safety," and will result in a "significant reduction in the cost of covered products to the American consumer." To date, that certification has not been made, so section 804 has not gone into effect. Similarly, previous versions of section 804 enacted in 1990 and 1993 never went into effect because no HHS Secretary was willing to make similar required certifications (40).

Adverse Event Reporting for Nonprescription Drugs

The Dietary Supplement and Non-Prescription Drug Consumer Protection Act (DSNPDCPA) (41), enacted in December 2006, added new section 760 to the FDC Act (42), to require manufacturers, packers, and distributors of certain nonprescription drugs to report serious adverse events to FDA. Serious adverse events are defined as adverse events that result in death, a life-threatening experience, inpatient hospitalization, a persistent or significant disability or incapacity, or a congenital anomaly or birth defect, or adverse events that require medical intervention to prevent one of those outcomes. The manufacturer, packer, or distributor identified on the label is required to submit to FDA any report received regarding a serious adverse event within 15 business days after receipt, using the MedWatch form. In addition, the responsible manufacturer, packer, or distributor must submit to FDA, within 15 business days after receipt, any new medical information related to a submitted serious adverse event report received within 1 year of the initial report. The responsible manufacturer, packer, or distributor is required to maintain records of all adverse events (not just serious adverse events) received for 6 years that are subject to routine FDA inspection.

Section 760 of the FDC Act includes a rule of construction, under which the submission of any adverse event report is not to be construed as an admission that the nonprescription drug involved caused or contributed to the adverse event.

Under section 760, inconsistent or additional state and local requirements for mandatory adverse event reporting are preempted. FDA is authorized to provide adverse event reports and information to its state and local counterparts under memoranda of understanding. However, state and local officials are expressly prohibited from making personally identifiable information publicly available without the written consent of FDA and the person submitting the information. State and local officials are also prohibited from using any safety report received from FDA in a manner inconsistent with federal law.

New subsection (x) of section 502 of the FDC Act (43) deems a drug subject to the new requirements to be misbranded, if its label does not provide a domestic address or a domestic phone number for consumers to report adverse events.

Section 760 of the FDC Act applies only to nonprescription drugs that are not the subject of an NDA or ANDA approval. Covered drugs consist of products marketed under an "OTC monograph," as well as other products marketed on the basis of the manufacturer's or distributor's view that the product is exempt from FDA's premarket approval requirements. Products that are the subject of an approved NDA or ANDA are already subject to a variety of reporting requirements, including, but not limited to, the reporting of adverse events (44).

In October 2007, FDA issued a draft guidance to assist manufacturers and distributors in complying with the new adverse event reporting requirements (45).

The DSNPDCPA also added essentially identical requirements that apply to dietary supplements in new section 761 of the FDC Act (46).

The new provisions became effective in December 2007.

Toll-Free Number for Adverse Event Reporting

Section 17 of the BPCA, enacted in January 2002, required FDA to adopt a regulation requiring that the labeling of each drug that is the subject of an approved NDA or ANDA include a toll-free number maintained by FDA for the purpose of receiving reports of adverse events only, but not for purposes of receiving medical advice (47).

FDA has implemented this requirement, in part, by means of its new requirements for the labeling of human prescription drugs and biologicals (48). These requirements are being phased in, and apply initially to newly approved products and products with newly approved efficacy supplements (49).

Citizen Petitions Affecting Generic Drug Approvals

Section 914 of FDAAA added new subsection (q) to section 505 of the FDC Act (50), to address citizen petitions and other efforts to block or delay the approval of an ANDA or a 505(b)(2) NDA. The new provision is intended to address widely held concerns of the generic drug industry and others that citizen petitions are sometimes used solely for the purpose of prolonging the innovator firm's monopoly.

FDA is prohibited from delaying the approval of a pending ANDA or 505(b)(2) NDA unless the request is in the form of a citizen petition, and FDA determines that "a delay is necessary to protect the public health." If FDA determines that a delay is necessary, FDA must so notify the sponsor of the pending application within 30 days after making its determination that a delay is necessary. The notification must include a brief summary of the specific substantive issues raised that form the basis of the determination that a delay is necessary and, if applicable, a description of any additional information that the applicant needs to submit to permit the agency to review the petition promptly. FDA may provide the notification either in writing or during a meeting. Information conveyed to the applicant is considered to be part of the application and subject to the usual public disclosure rules applicable to pending applications.

If FDA determines that a petition was submitted with the primary purpose of delay and the petition does not on its face raise "valid scientific or regulatory issues," FDA may summarily deny the petition. FDA may (but need not) issue guidance regarding the factors that the agency will take into consideration in deciding whether a petition was submitted primarily for purposes of delay.

FDA is required to make a final decision on a petition related to an ANDA or 505(b)(2) NDA final approval within 180 days, and this time period cannot be extended for any reason.

If the final approval of an ANDA that has 180-day exclusivity rights is delayed because of a petition, the 30-month period for obtaining tentative approval to avoid forfeiture of the 180-day exclusivity rights (see chap. 7) is extended by the period during which the petition was pending before FDA.

Citizen petitions and comments on petitions are required to contain a new, detailed certification or verification, under penalty of perjury. The certification or verification must disclose the date on which information regarding the action requested first became known to the party on whose behalf the petition or comment is submitted. In addition, the petition or comment must disclose the identity of any persons or organizations from whom the submitter of the comment has received, or expects to receive, compensation. Thus, "blind" petitions and comments submitted by law firms, consultants, and experts will no longer be possible, if such petitions or comments relate to the final approval of an ANDA or 505(b)(2) NDA.

If FDA fails to issue a final decision within 180 days after submission, FDA's failure to act is deemed to be final agency action for judicial review purposes. (This does not mean that a court will automatically consider a challenge to a petition. For example, a court could refuse to consider a lawsuit on the basis that the matter is not considered "ripe" for judicial determination.) If a lawsuit is filed against FDA with regard to any issue raised in a petition before FDA has issued a final decision or 180 days has passed without FDA action, the court is required to dismiss the lawsuit without prejudice on the basis that administrative remedies were not exhausted.

Citizen petitions that relate solely to the timing of ANDA final approval as a result of 180-day exclusivity are excluded from the new provisions. Similarly, a petition submitted by the sponsor of an application that relates solely to that sponsor's application is outside the scope of the new provisions.

This new provision became effective upon enactment.

Prohibition Against Food with Added Drugs or Biological Products

Section 912 of FDAAA established a new "prohibited act" in section 301(ll) of the FDC Act (51). The commission of a prohibited act can result in federal court legal action, including product seizure (52), injunction (53), or criminal prosecution of business entities and individuals (54).

The new provision prohibits the addition to food of any approved drug, licensed biological, or other drug or biological that is the subject of completed or ongoing "substantial" publicly disclosed clinical studies. The new provision includes four exceptions:

- The drug or biological was marketed in food before approval, licensure, or before substantial clinical investigations were started.
- FDA has approved use of the drug or biological in food by means of notice-and-comment rulemaking.

- The drug or biological enhances the safety of the food and does not have an independent biological or therapeutic effect on humans. In addition, the use either conforms to a food additive regulation, a "generally recognized as safe" regulation, a premarket notification that has not been disputed by FDA, an effective food contact substance notification, or the drug or biological was marketed for smoking cessation before September 27, 2007.
- The drug is an approved animal drug.

The new provision is self-executing and became effective upon enactment.

Pharmacy Compounding

FDA's recent efforts to regulate pharmacy compounding are described in section 5.5 of chapter 6 of the first edition of this book. In brief, section 503A of the FDC Act (55), added by FDAMA, was declared invalid in its entirety in 2001 by the U.S. Court of Appeals for the Ninth Circuit on the basis that the restrictions on the advertising of compounded drugs were unconstitutional. The U.S. Supreme Court upheld the Ninth Circuit's decision that the advertising restrictions were unconstitutional, but did not expressly address the Ninth Circuit's conclusion that the statutory advertising restrictions could not be severed from the remaining provisions of section 503A of the FDC Act.

In light of these court decisions, FDA issued a Compliance Policy Guide to set forth its enforcement policy on pharmacy compounding (56). FDA assumed that all of section 503A of the FDC Act is invalid.

In August 2006, a Texas federal district court reached a different conclusion regarding the severability of section 503A of the FDC Act. That court concluded that the unconstitutional prohibitions on the advertising of compounded drugs could be severed from the remainder of section 503A, meaning that the remaining provisions remain in effect (57). The district court concluded that the remaining provisions of section 503A demonstrate that Congress recognized that compounding is an approved and lawful practice. Specifically, the district court held that compounded drugs, when created for an individual patient pursuant to a prescription from a licensed practitioner, are exempt from the FDC Act's premarket approval provisions. As of this writing, FDA's appeal of that decision is pending (58). Pending a decision on appeal, FDA is taking the position that the district court decision applies only in the Western District of Texas.

The case also concerned the compounding of drugs from bulk ingredients for nonfood animals. The court concluded that drugs compounded from legal bulk ingredients by pharmacists do not require premarket approval.

Cast in simple terms, the underlying controversy in this area is the dividing line between drug manufacturing, which is subject to active FDA regulation, including but not limited to premarket approval, and pharmacy compounding, which is not subject to FDA active regulation and is generally regulated by the states in connection with the practice of pharmacy.

REFERENCES

1. Pub L No. 107–188.
2. Pub L No. 105–115.
3. Pub L No. 107–109.
4. Pub L No. 107–188.

5. Pub L No. 108–155.
6. Pub L No. 108–173.
7. Pub L No. 109–462.
8. Pub L No. 110–85.
9. 21 USC §355c.
10. 21 USC §355d.
11. 21 USC §355c(f).
12. 21 USC §355a.
13. 42 USC §282(j).
14. FDC Act sections 301(jj) and 303(f)(3), 21 USC §§331(jj) and 333(f)(3).
15. 21 USC §353(g).
16. Pub L No. 107–250.
17. General information is available at: http://www.fda.gov/oc/initiatives/criticalpath.
18. 21 USC §379dd.
19. See 72 Fed Reg 56362 (Oct. 3, 2007) (seeking nominations).
20. 21 USC §379dd-1.
21. 21 USC §379dd-2.
22. 21 USC §399a.
23. 21 USC §360bbb-5.
24. 21 USC §356-1.
25. 21 USC §356.
26. 21 CFR §314.600 et seq. and §601.90 et seq.
27. 21 USC §360n.
28. 21 USC §360a.
29. 21 USC §355(s).
30. 21 USC §355(u).
31. See 54 Fed Reg 28872, 28898 (July 10, 1989) and 62 Fed Reg 2167 (Jan. 15, 1997).
32. 21 USC §356b.
33. Available at http://www.fda.gov/cder/guidance/5569fnl.pdf; announced in 71 Fed Reg 8307 (Feb. 16, 2006).
34. 21 USC §355(r).
35. 21 CFR §314.430(e)(2).
36. 21 USC §355(l).
37. 21 USC §355e.
38. Cal. Bus. & Prof. Code §4034.
39. 21 USC §384.
40. Congressional Research Service Report for Congress: Importing Prescription Drugs: Objectives, Options, and Outlook (Jan. 26, 2007) at 6, 7.
41. Pub L No. 109–462.
42. 21 USC §379aa.
43. 21 USC §352(x).
44. See 21 CFR §314.80.
45. Available at http://www.fda.gov/cder/guidance/7950dft.pdf; announced in 72 Fed Reg 58313 (Oct. 15, 2007).
46. 21 USC §379aa-1.
47. 21 USC §355b.
48. 21 CFR §201.57(a)(11).
49. See 21 CFR §201.57 and § 201.56(c).
50. 21 USC §355(q).
51. 21 USC §331(ll).
52. FDC Act section 304, 21 USC §334.
53. FDC Act section 302, 21 USC §332.
54. FDC Act section 303, 21 USC §333.
55. 21 USC §353a.
56. CPG 460.200, available at www.fda.gov/ora/compliance_ref/cpg/cpgdrg/cpg460–200.html; announced in 67 Fed Reg 39409 (June 7, 2002).
57. *Medical Center Pharmacy v. Gonzales*, 451 F. Supp. 2d 854 (WD Tex. 2006).
58. Appeal No. 06–51583 (5th Cir).

3 The New Drug–Approval Process—Before and After 1962

Michael P. Peskoe

Edwards Angell Palmer & Dodge LLP, Boston, Massachusetts, U.S.A.

INTRODUCTION

The history of the regulation of pharmaceuticals in the United States has been an evolving one, shaped by both historical events and perceptions of medical need. It has also been affected significantly by the ongoing tensions between the various societal components involved either directly or indirectly in the process: what are now commonly known as "stakeholders." These include the pharmaceutical industry, the government [mostly as represented by the U.S. Food and Drug Administration (FDA) and its predecessor agencies], the consuming public (either represented by proxy by the government or by self-appointed consumer groups, but rarely by consumers themselves), and the medical profession. It has also been shaped, in part, by the general evolution of administrative and regulatory practice during the past 40 years. Although the regulation of pharmaceuticals predates significantly the regulation of the subject matter of many other modern regulatory agencies, such as the Environmental Protection Agency (EPA), the Federal Aviation Administration (FAA), the National Traffic and Motor Vehicle Safety Agency (NHTSA), the Consumer Protection Safety Commission (CPSC), and the Federal Trade Commission (FTC), its recent evolution has been affected by the development of modern tenets of American administrative law and practice.

While the need for federal government approval of pharmaceuticals prior to their marketing has been a fundamental part of the regulatory landscape for more than 60 years, it was not always so. Notwithstanding the greatly diminished controversy over this policy that exists today, particularly with respect to government's prior approval of drug effectiveness, pressures continue to be applied to the approval system. These pressures result from both external events and market forces. As a consequence, the country's drug approval regulatory system still presents an interesting study of the evolution of a regulatory system almost 100 years old, yet still fluid and subject to continuing change.

THE FEDERAL FOOD AND DRUGS ACT OF 1906

Known as the Wiley Act, in honor of Henry A. Wiley, the first director of the government's Office of Chemistry in the Department of Agriculture, and also as the Pure Food and Drugs Act, this first foray into actual government regulation of drugs embodies concepts that still remain in the current legislation, although in a secondary role. The act proscribed the manufacture and interstate shipment in the United States of adulterated or misbranded drugs (or foods), making both criminal (a misdemeanor).

1. "Adulterated" and "misbranded" were defined in the law, in a manner more limited than today. The former was defined essentially as noncompliance with

the United States Pharmacopeia or National Formulary, or generally if strength or purity fell below the "professional standard or quality" under which the drug was sold.
2. The latter proscribed any statement in either the package or the label of a drug regarding the article or its ingredients that was false or misleading in any particular, or if the drug were an imitation of another drug, or if the packaging were removed, or failed to contain a statement on the label of the quantity of any alcohol or other named potentially toxic substances.
3. No prior approval requirements were contained in the statute, nor was there any suggestion that they were entertained. Rather, the act was essentially a truth-in-labeling statute, directed in part at controlling the manufacture and sale of worthless and potentially dangerous patent medicines and requiring the government to find illegal conduct after the fact if it wished to prosecute.

THE 1912 SHIRLEY AMENDMENT

In a 1911 Supreme Court decision, *United States v. Johnson* (4), involving a criminal indictment for the interstate shipment of medicine falsely labeled as a cure for cancer, the court found that the proscription in the 1906 law against the misbranding of drugs dealt only with false statements as to characteristics of identity, such as strength, quality, or purity, but not with claims of effectiveness. As a result, in 1912 Congress added language to the misbranding provisions that proscribed, in the case of drugs, "any statement regarding curative or therapeutic effect, which is false and fraudulent" (5). Although extending the statute's enforcement reach to fraudulent claims of efficacy, the amendment gave FDA no premarket approval power over drugs or related products.

1938 FEDERAL FOOD, DRUG, AND COSMETIC ACT

Statutory Drug–Approval Provisions

In 1933, Congress began a 5-year effort at amending the 1906 act that would ultimately create the framework of human drug regulation that exists today. Between the initiation of congressional debate and passage, over 100 children died from taking a drug called Elixir Sulfanilamide, in which a manufacturer placed a well-known and accepted drug, sulfanilamide, into a new vehicle, diethylene glycol (now used in antifreeze), that was unfortunately fatally toxic to those who took it.

As enacted, the new Federal Food, Drug, and Cosmetic Act of 1938 added the first requirements for premarket approval of drugs. It defined both "drugs" and "new drugs" in a manner still utilized today: the former to encompass the wide range of medicants sold or likely to be sold to alleviate human disease, and the latter in a manner that would effectively subject to prior approval every new drug entity and product and, after the agency's lawyers were through interpreting the law, older ones as well.

As enacted in 1938, "new drug" was defined as follows (6):

> Sec. 201 . . .
> (p) The term "new drug" means—
> (1) Any drug the composition of which is such that such drug is not generally recognized, among experts qualified by scientific and experience to evaluate

> the safety of drugs, as safe for use under the conditions prescribed, recommended, or suggested in the labeling thereof, except that such a drug not so recognized shall not be deemed to be a "new drug" if at any time prior to enactment it was subject to the Food and Drugs Act of 1906, as amended, and if at such time its labeling contained the same representations concerning the conditions of its use; or
> (2) Any drug the composition of which is such that such drug, as a result of investigations to determine its safety for use under such conditions, has become so recognized, but which has not, otherwise than in such investigations, been used to a material extent or for a material time under such conditions.

At the same time that it defined "new drug," the new law prohibited the introduction or delivery for introduction into interstate commerce of any new drug unless an application filed pursuant to the new act was "effective with respect to such drug" (7). This was the initial premarket approval requirement for drugs.

A new drug application (NDA) was required to contain "full reports of investigations which have been made to show whether or not such drug is safe for use" (8), as well as articles used as components, a full statement of composition, methods used in and facilities and controls used for manufacturing, processing and packing the drug, samples of the drug as required by the secretary, and specimens of labeling (9).

An application would become effective on the sixtieth day after filing, unless the effective date was postponed in writing to such time, not to exceed 180 days, as the agency determined necessary "to study and investigate the application" (10). In other words, an application would become effective without further action by the agency within 60 days unless the agency stopped it from becoming so. The agency's ability to so forestall an application from becoming effective was limited to 180 days (11). Provisions were also included establishing requirements for the agency's decision not to approve an application (12). These included provisions that the investigations did not include adequate tests by all methods reasonably applicable to show whether or not the drug was safe for use under the conditions set forth in labeling; that such tests show that the drug is unsafe for use under those conditions; that the methods for manufacture, processing or packing are inadequate to preserve identity, strength, quality, and purity; or whether the information submitted in the application or on the basis of any other information was insufficient to determine whether the drug was unsafe for use. However, the agency was required, in reaching any such conclusion, to provide both notice and an opportunity for hearing to any applicant whose application was determined not worthy of approval (13).

The new statute also empowered the agency, specifically, to suspend the effectiveness of an approved application, again following notice and opportunity for hearing, if it found that clinical experience, new test methods, or even methods not thought applicable at the time of approval showed the drug to be unsafe for use under its labeled indications or that the application was found to contain any untrue statement of material fact (14).

Should a manufacturer contest the agency's order suspending the effectiveness of an application, its recourse would be filing an action in federal district court (15). In keeping with what are now modern tenets of administrative law, any new factual matters were required to be presented to the agency before any adjudication by the court. The agency conclusions as to any findings of fact were deemed conclusive (16). Finally, the new law imposed an obligation on the agency to develop regulations exempting drugs solely for investigational use from the above restrictions (17).

The statutory framework enacted in 1938 is still the model in use today, with additions and modifications as outlined in the remainder of this chapter up to 1997. In establishing global criteria for premarket approval contained in the concept of "new drug," the new law all but assured from that time forward that government would now evaluate drugs prior to their marketing. Definitions were written broadly: not only "new drug" but the definition of "drug" itself was written to be inclusive (18). Moreover, by including within the new drug definition the concept of "general recognition," requiring that a determination of safety be recognized based on the views of experts, Congress gave the agency power to establish high barriers to market entry. On the other hand, the new law gave significant credence to an approval earned under the statute; withdrawal of an application, once approved, was not made particularly easy for the government to accomplish.

The 1938 "Grandfather" Provisions and "Old Drug" Status

Two provisions deserve special comment. The statute did exempt or "grandfather" certain drugs from the new drug requirements. This exemption included any drug marketed under the 1906 act whose labeling had not changed (19). Thus, at least in this respect, the law did not portend to reach backward unless an existing drug's labeling had at some point been changed. The second exemption concerned those drugs that might be determined to be "not new," that is, where "general recognition" of safety might already exist. In that the exemption from "new drug" status was obviously desirable to drug manufacturers, this would be a future area of contention.

Finally, the "new drug" definition also seemed to create a situation in which "new drug" status was fluid, in which a drug that might be "new" today would at some point no longer be so and would no longer be subject to the myriad requirements applicable only to new drugs. This was contained in the second "new drug" definition, which stated, in essence, that a drug recognized by experts as safe for labeled conditions on the basis of tests conducted to establish safety, but not otherwise, and not used to a "material extent" or for a "material time" under such conditions, would nonetheless still be a new drug (20). The converse of this, that such a drug used for a material extent or for a material time would no longer be a "new drug," suggests that such a drug might ultimately graduate to a post–"new drug" status. To date, no post-1938 prescription drug has done so.

Regulation of Antibiotics and Insulin

In 1941, Congress added new special approval provisions to the 1938 act regarding drugs composed wholly or partly of insulin. Unlike the existing provisions, section 506 required that, prior to distribution, insulin be batch certified by the agency "if such drug has such characteristics identity . . . strength, quality and purity . . . as necessary to insure safety and efficacy of use" (21). This was essentially a requirement that the agency itself test a sample of each batch of insulin prior to release by the manufacturer and stemmed from concern that insulin manufactured from live organisms required further protections compared to other drugs.

Similarly, in 1945 batch-certification requirements for penicillin were added in a new section 507 and were modeled after the insulin requirements (22). Over the next several years, the requirements were extended to additional antibiotics, culminating in an extension to all antibiotics in 1962 (23). The added requirements stemmed from the fact that antibiotics were derived from microorganisms, resulting in a concern that actual batch testing by the government should be required as a condition of marketing. Although these sections included a specific requirement for effectiveness, it was assumed as part of the certification process that appropriate proof of identity, strength, quality, and purity would necessarily permit a conclusion regarding effectiveness. Ultimately, due to the added expense to the agency of supporting a batch-certification laboratory and growing confidence in the manufacturing processes of both insulin and antibiotics, both products were exempted from certification. Later, as part of legislation adopted in 1997, both sections were repealed (24). Insulin and antibiotics are now regulated like other new drugs.

THE DRUG EFFECTIVENESS AMENDMENTS OF 1962

Approval Provisions

The modern era of drug regulation begins with the drug effectiveness amendments of 1962. These amendments added the requirement that all new drugs be proven effective as well as safe and far more detailed requirements for the safety testing of new drugs prior to marketing, the latter as a direct result of the thalidomide tragedy that occurred in Europe (and almost in the United States) in the latter 1950s and early 1960s. The addition of an effectiveness requirement was made exceedingly complicated by the added requirement that all drugs whose safety and effectiveness were established between 1938 and 1962 would be made retroactively subject to the new effectiveness standard.

The 1962 amendments accomplished these objectives in several ways. Initially, the statutory definition of "new drug" in section 201(p) of the act was amended by adding the words "and effectiveness" following "safety" where it appeared in the section (25). Thus, any drug whose effectiveness was not a matter of "general recognition" by experts qualified by scientific training and experience to evaluate effectiveness would be a new drug for that additional reason and subject to premarket approval requirements for effectiveness as well as safety.

The requirement for general recognition of effectiveness has been the cornerstone of the agency's now generally accepted interpretation of the section that once a new drug, always a new drug. As noted earlier, section 201(p)(2) of the act provided an alternative new drug definition: a drug's safety or effectiveness could be recognized (as opposed to "generally recognized") on the basis of investigations, but the drug would still be a new drug if it had not been used to a material extent or for a material time. This suggested a possibility that new drugs ultimately could "graduate" from new drug status over time, ending their need to be subject to an effective NDA and similarly ending their obligation to comply with numerous requirements applicable to new drugs, but not to "not new drugs." It is this potential statutory movement from new drug to not new drug status that has not been acknowledged by FDA; nor sought by manufacturers, at least for the past three decades; and nor has the issue been given publicity in the numerous statutory amendments to the act that have occurred during the past 15 years.

Other significant changes in the FDA approval process were also implemented by the 1962 amendments. Perhaps most importantly, the amendments replaced the "passive approval" mechanism of the 1938 act, which permitted an NDA to become effective automatically after a 60-day period, with an active approval scheme. Section 505(c) of the act provided that (20):

> Within one-hundred and eighty days after the filing of an application under subsection (b), or such additional period as may be agreed upon by the Secretary, and the applicant, the Secretary shall either—(A) approve the application if he then finds that none of the grounds for denying approval... applies, or (B) give the applicant notice of an opportunity for hearing before the Secretary... on the question whether such application is approvable.

The new legislation also expanded significantly the provisions of the 1938 act regarding the statutory bases for refusing to approve a submitted application [section 505(d)] and for withdrawing approval of an approved application [section 505(e)].

With respect to the refusal to approve an application, the statute left the existing provisions regarding lack of safety intact, but added to them the following proscription regarding the new effectiveness requirement (27):

> If the Secretary finds that, evaluated on the basis of the information submitted to him as part of the application and any other information before him with respect to such drug, there is a lack of substantial evidence that the drug will have the effect it purports or is represented to have under the conditions of use prescribed, recommended, or suggested in the proposed labeling thereof... he shall issue an order refusing to approve the application.... As used in this subsection... the term "substantial evidence" means evidence consisting of adequate and well-controlled investigations, including clinical investigations, by experts qualified by scientific training and experience to evaluate the effectiveness of the drug involved, on the basis of which it could fairly and responsibly be concluded by such experts that the drug will have the effect it purports or is represented to have under the conditions of use prescribed, recommended, or suggested in the labeling or proposed labeling thereof.

Thus, unlike the statutory safety test, which required simply that studies demonstrate safety, the statutory test of effectiveness, set forth ironically in the statutory section containing criteria for withholding approval, was legislated as one of "substantial evidence" requiring "adequate and well-controlled investigations, including clinical investigations by experts qualified... to evaluate the effectiveness of the drug involved" (28). This requirement of substantial evidence of effectiveness would play a paramount role in the decades following the 1962 enactment in enabling FDA to set the bar high before approving a drug as safe and effective (29).

With respect to those provisions concerning the withdrawal of an approved (i.e., effective) application, the amendments added provisions for the withdrawal of an application should there be new information, evaluated together with the evidence available when the application was approved, that there was a lack of substantial evidence that the drug would have the effect it was represented to have according to its labeling (30). The amendments also added new provisions for the immediate suspension of the effectiveness of an application should the secretary find an imminent hazard to the public health. The authority to implement this section was reserved to the secretary, and was not delegable to the FDA (31).

In response to the then recent thalidomide episode, Congress also greatly expanded the statutory provisions regarding the investigation of drugs. While the 1938 act had simply authorized the promulgation of regulations exempting such drugs from the prohibition against interstate shipment of unapproved new drugs, the 1962 amendments directed that the regulations consider including the submission to FDA, before the undertaking of any clinical tests using such a drug; reports of preclinical tests (including animal tests) to justify the proposed clinical tests (32) signed agreements between investigators and sponsors of investigations that patients to whom the drug administered will be under the investigator's direct or indirect supervision (33); and the establishment and maintenance of records obtained as a result of the investigational use that will enable the secretary to evaluate the safety and effectiveness of the drug in the event of the filing of an NDA (34).

What was not optional under the amendments, however, was that any such clinical trial exemption be conditioned on the requirement that investigators certify to sponsors that any study subjects be informed that the drugs were investigational and obtain their consent (except where not feasible or contrary to the best interests of the study subjects) (35). As a result of these provisions and the regulations that followed, and notwithstanding the regulatory provision that such an exemption will become effective automatically after 30 days unless delayed by the agency (36), there is no area of FDA regulation where the agency has more unrestricted power than in its oversight of clinical investigations.

The 1962 Grandfather Clause

The amended new drug definition also extended the category of drugs not subject to the new drug provisions, that is, those considered "grandfathered." First, in section 201(p), it essentially extended the 1938 grandfather clause through the 1962 enactment so that a drug that was subject to the 1938 clause (because it was subject to the 1906 act and its labeling had not been changed) and exempt thereby from the new drug provisions would continue to be exempt, now from the new effectiveness requirement as well, if its labeling had continued to remain unchanged. The number of drugs that continue to meet these criteria has never been fully documented; it is safe to say that FDA views the category as an anachronism and, to the extent that it is required to focus on any such drugs as part of a regulatory event, it has had little difficulty arguing successfully that grandfather status is no longer applicable.

A new grandfather provision was enacted in 1962 that would, when the criteria were met, exempt such a drug from the effectiveness but not the safety provisions of the act. Section 107(c)(4) of the 1962 amendments specified a four-part test: on the day immediately preceding the enactment date, October 10, 1962, the drug was commercially sold in the United States, was not a new drug as defined by then in effect section 201(p) (meaning that it was generally recognized as safe on that date), was not subject to an NDA on that date (meaning under the 1938 act), and was intended for use solely for its labeled indications as they existed on that day (in short, its labeling could not have changed).

The DESI Review and the Imposition of Effectiveness on Pre-1962 Drugs

The addition of an effectiveness requirement in 1962 was made more complicated for the agency by the added requirement that all new drugs approved solely for safety under the 1938 act be subject to the new effectiveness standard unless grandfathered (see earlier).

"Transitional amendments" enacted as section 107(c) implemented this legislative scheme in the following manner (37). First, any NDA that was "effective" on the day before the new amendments were enacted (the enactment date) was deemed approved as of the enactment date (38), the new effectiveness amendments did not apply to any such "deemed approved" application as long as the application was not withdrawn or suspended when intended solely for use under its preenactment date indications (but not as to any changed indications) (39), and the provision permitting withdrawal of an approved application for a lack of substantial evidence of effectiveness as to existing uses was determined not to apply until one of the following events occurred: the expiration of a 2-year period beginning on the enactment date or the withdrawal or suspension of the application (40).

These provisions effectively applied the new effectiveness standard on October 10, 1964, to all drugs approved under the 1938 act and permitted their withdrawal if effectiveness had not been established. All post-1938-approved applications had been simply "deemed" approved under the 1962 amendments for a 2-year grace period (41). While withdrawal for lack of effectiveness was not automatic, first requiring the agency to initiate and conduct withdrawal proceedings under section 505(e), the premarket approval requirements of the statute permitted the agency to allege that effectiveness had not been established, shifting the burden on pre-1962 applicants to then produce the necessary information to demonstrate substantial evidence of effectiveness in order to prevent withdrawal.

Due to administrative difficulties attendant to implementation of this section, FDA ultimately contracted with outside groups, notably the National Academy of Sciences and National Research Council, to review the available data, usually as compiled by manufacturers, on all pre-1962-approved drugs, and to make recommendations to FDA on whether there existed for those drugs the substantial evidence of effectiveness now required by the statute. This process became known as the Drug Efficacy Review Implementation, or "DESI" Review, and took the better part of 25 years, until the mid-1980s, to complete, although even to this day certain drugs remain on the market in a state of regulatory limbo, with no final determinations having been made as to their effectiveness under the 1962 standard (42).

Important Legal Developments Regarding the 1962 Amendments

The 1962 amendments to the drug-approval process, particularly the increased burdens for prior approval for "new drugs," generated significant efforts by various components of the pharmaceutical industry to avoid the added regulation imposed by the new amendments, particularly insofar as they rewrote the rules applicable to drugs already on the market. This also resulted from the significant procedural protections written into the earlier law, and continued in the new law, for applications that had already become "effective." Over the next two decades, certain disagreements involving the agency's interpretation of the amended new drug, "grandfather," and effectiveness provisions of the statute wound their way through the courts, culminating in several court decisions that ultimately both supported the agency's strict "high bar" and inclusive interpretation of the new amendments and set the tone of the agency's review policies for the next several decades.

In USV *Pharmaceutical Corp. v. Weinberger* (43), decided in 1973, the issues were the scope of the grandfather and transitional amendments enacted in 1962. This manufacturer had products containing the same active ingredient, some of which were covered by pre-1962 NDAs, and some of which were not. Of the criteria found in the 1962 grandfather exemption, one was that the drug not be covered by an effective application on the effective date. The court found that, while NDAs were intended and applied to individual products, in this instance it would consider none of the products to be lawfully subject to the exemption even though they were literally not subject to an NDA at the time, as the exemption was intended to treat all products whether or not of different manufacturers containing the same active ingredient the same, that is, as either new or not new. The court also found that a manufacturer was not capable of deactivating an existing NDA so as to also avail himself of the exemption. The net effect of the opinion was to include any drug that had at any time been subject to the new drug provisions enacted in 1938 to also be subject to the effectiveness requirements enacted in 1962.

In *Weinberger v. Bentex Pharmaceuticals, Inc.* (44), decided at the same time as USV, the court squarely faced the question of who decided what constituted general recognition of effectiveness—FDA or the courts. In this case, the court interpreted the act as authorizing FDA, subject to judicial review, as the locus of jurisdiction on the new drug question for both individual drugs and classes of drugs, determining that such questions were to be administratively determined by the agency, and not de novo in the courts.

In *Ciba Corp. v. Weinberger* (45), again decided at the same time as USV and Bentex, the court further established FDA, in the context of its withdrawal of pre-1962 NDAs for the manufacturer's failure to establish effectiveness, as the administrative agency responsible for making new drug determinations in an administrative setting, reviewable in the Court of Appeals, but not subject to having the new drug issue litigated in other court proceedings.

Finally, in the last and probably the most important case, *Weinberger v. Hynson, Westcott & Dunning* (46), also decided with the other cases noted, the court reviewed the withdrawal of the NDA of a drug subject to the transitional amendments of the 1962 act, that is, one approved under the 1938 act for safety but ostensibly lacking substantial evidence of effectiveness, and thus subject to proceedings for NDA withdrawal. In so doing, it sustained the validity of FDA's then new Summary Judgment regulations, which permitted the agency, following publication of a Notice of Opportunity for Hearing, to then deny a hearing and summarily withdraw the NDA when the applicant did not tender information in response sufficient to make a prima facie showing that it could demonstrate substantial evidence of effectiveness through the statutory standard requiring adequate and well-controlled clinical investigations. In addition, the court also sustained FDA's view that whether a drug's effectiveness was supported by substantial evidence was part of the new drug determination, and not simply requirements that must be met following a new drug determination. This case and the others decided with it effectively made all post-1938 drugs new drugs subject to NDA requirements for effectiveness and largely closed the door on the efforts of companies to avoid the requirements for adequate and well-controlled studies by claiming "not-new-drug" status under the "new-drug" definition.

This 1973 "grand slam" for FDA in the U.S. Supreme Court regarding the scope of the 1962 amendments was the beginning of a multidecade trend in which the agency seemed relatively invincible in its efforts to expand the statute, in both its old and new drug provisions, particularly regarding the effectiveness requirements of the act (47). Under the rubric of "protecting the public health," FDA was able to establish and maintain through several significant court victories its expansionist view of its mandate to control the new drug process at both the macro and micro levels. Other cases decided in the next several years further solidified that mind-set.

In 1975, the Supreme Court decided *United States v. Park* (48). While involving a criminal prosecution of a senior manager of a national food company for sanitation failures, it affirmed earlier cases establishing strict criminal liability for senior company managers for violations of the act, including, theoretically, violations involving the drug provisions of the act.

In 1979, in *United States v. Rutherford* (49), the Supreme Court held that drugs for terminally ill patients whose safety or effectiveness were unproven were subject to the new drug provisions of the act. In this case, notwithstanding that all parties conceded that the cancer patients involved were surely to die from their disease, and that no other remedies were available, the court refused to allow the sale of laetrile, an unproven cancer remedy, by finding an implied exception to the safety and effectiveness requirements.

In 1983, in *United States v. Generix Drug Corp.* (50), the court resolved the additional question of the application of the new drug definition to generic versions of approved drugs. While innovator drugs were subject to NDAs, generic versions were not, and the question before the court was whether the "new drug" definition applied to them. Specifically, did the new drug definition apply only to the active ingredient, potentially exempting generic products from new drug regulation, or each specific product, both innovator and generic, thereby subjecting all versions of the drug to the new drug provisions. Again, the court sustained FDA's expansive reading of the new drug definition, concluding that the new drug–licensing provisions were applicable to individual products, including each separate generic product, and not merely the active ingredient. It relied in its opinion on the fact that each generic product would be different, at least in inactive ingredients or excipients, from the innovator, raising issues of safety and effectiveness warranting premarket review.

By the time the Generix case was decided, FDA's view of the regulatory world of new drugs was essentially institutionalized. The new drug provisions were seen to apply to all prescription drug products, both brand and generic, and once applied to a drug product, were attached indefinitely. Little attention was paid then, or has been paid since, to the notion that drugs in new drug status could evolve to a post-, nonregulated, old drug status, notwithstanding inferences both in the new drug definition as well as in several court opinions that such was Congress's original intent.

THE POST-1962 ERA

The two decades after 1962 were not ones of substantial legislative attention to the new drug–approval process. Other issues were more prominent. The growth in public financing of drug purchases under Medicaid caused a revolution in the public's perception of the value of generic drugs. While industry complained continuously about delays in getting drugs through FDA's approval mechanism, Congress did not engage the issue. Efforts to rewrite the Federal Food, Drug, and Cosmetic Act that were initiated in the late 1970s came to naught, while FDA revised its own IND and NDA regulations in a manner that, while clarifying certain concepts such as compassionate INDs and drug adverse event reporting, embraced the notion that FDA's requirements for proof of safety and effectiveness would not be relaxed in order to promote innovation or for drugs for use in treating serious and fatal diseases, notwithstanding the lack of alternatives for either patients or doctors.

The Orphan Drug Act of 1983

In 1982, recognizing that certain diseases involved only small numbers of patients and were thus being largely ignored by pharmaceutical companies due to the lack of financial incentives to development, Congress initiated legislation specifically directed at this problem. The Orphan Drug Act of 1983 provided federal financial incentives for drug development heretofore unavailable and also presaged other significant legislative developments that would come years later (51).

As enacted, the Orphan Drug Act applied to drugs for any disease or condition "which occurs so infrequently in the United States that there is no reasonable expectation that the cost of developing and making available in the United States a drug for such disease or condition will be recovered from sales in the United States for such drug." It provided two major financial incentives to companies that would undertake to develop these products. First, the act provided a tax credit based on clinical trial expenses. Second, it provided a 7-year "exclusivity" for any nonpatentable drug, during which time FDA would be unable to approve an NDA or biological product license for the same drug for the same disease or condition. On a nonfinancial level, and to some extent foretelling later legislative developments, FDA was mandated to provide prospective orphan drug candidate applicants with "written recommendations for the non-clinical and clinical investigations" that the agency believed would be necessary for approval. This provision dented, perhaps for the first time, FDA's view that manufacturers were entirely responsible for the development of the studies required for approval, and that it was not FDA's role to prejudge trial design, and by inference data produced from such design, prior to submission of the data for approval (52).

In 1984 and 1985, Congress further amended the act to make its enticement provisions more appealing. To reduce complexity regarding qualifications for orphan drug exclusivity, the test was made far more objective and inclusive: an orphan disease was defined as any disease or condition that affected fewer than 200,000 persons in the United States, or that affected more than 200,000 persons but for which there was still no reasonable expectation that development costs could be recovered from sales (53). Second, the exclusivity provision was changed to no longer be contingent on the availability of patent protection; all orphan drugs approved would receive a 7-year exclusivity under which FDA would not be permitted to approve the same drug for the same disease or condition (54). At the same time, FDA took the position that, while it would assist in the development of appropriate trials for approval, and while the law did provide incentives previously unavailable to development initiatives, it did not in any way reduce the scientific burden on manufacturers to establish effectiveness based on adequate and well-controlled clinical trials (55).

The Era of Shifting Priorities

Two events merged in the latter years of the 1980s and continued through the early 1990s that, together, significantly altered the FDA's implementation of the requirements for investigation and approval of new drugs. The AIDS crisis was one; while FDA was able to fend off the demands of cancer patients in the 1970s and 1980s who desired access to unproven cancer drugs, it was not able to curtail access to unproven AIDS therapies by patients afflicted with an unexpected, and unremittingly lethal, new disease. The second event was more subtle. For years, the industry had relentlessly criticized the agency for what it perceived as the delay in getting it to act on pending applications. Review and approval times could stretch into years, for no apparent reason, despite a long-standing legislative provision requiring agency action on pending NDAs within 180 days of filing. Comparisons were frequently made during this period to approval times in other developed countries, mostly the United Kingdom, where it was often said drug-approval times were substantially less for the same drugs than in the United States—a so-called drug lag—with no apparent loss in safety.

Unlike the cancer population, AIDS victims were young people who were suffering egregiously before invariably losing their lives in their prime, rather than, as with most cancer patients, if not in old, than at least in middle age. They also shared other characteristics. Many were homosexual males from middle-class families living in the same neighborhoods in major urban areas and were able to coalesce into an active political force, no doubt enhanced by the support of their healthy, or at least not-yet-sick, colleagues. A further distinction from the cancer patients of the previous decade was the position of the medical establishment, always a force in FDA decisions and policy, if not always an apparent force. Unlike the cancer scenario, where doctors at least had some drugs and procedures to offer, for AIDS they had none that were remotely promising, leaving them as hopeless as their patients.

FDA's adherence to the regulatory system that had served well for two decades, a reliance on scientific proof of safety and effectiveness prior to permitting the marketing of any drug no matter how serious the disease or the availability of alternative therapies, did not play well to an audience of suffering and dying young men and their frustrated physicians. FDA relied initially on its traditional safety valve for making available unproven drugs, the "compassionate IND," under which drugs under investigation could be made available with the sponsor's consent to individual practitioners for individual patients outside of study protocols. This, however, was woefully insufficient in scope to deal with a growing national epidemic, and FDA's initial reliance became problematic. The combination of pressures from constant criticism based on supposed drug lag together with the agency's inability to handle the AIDS crisis fostered two reform movements that have altered its approval processes, perhaps permanently.

On the issue of drug lag, and to respond to agency representations that at least some of that issue was based on limited resources, Congress undertook to impose, against the agency's will, at least initially, "user fees." These fees, common elsewhere in government, are simply the government's charging for the performance of its services—in this particular case, its licensing function. Resisted initially by FDA as a potential intrusion of its independence, it has now become an accepted part of the new medical product landscape, providing funds to the agency to enhance its approval performance, although at some cost to the traditional opaqueness of the approval processes that had previously existed. While not necessarily impacting the actual requirements for approval, the user fee legislation (56) did tacitly recognize, if not validate, the industry's dissatisfaction with the approval process, and essentially required FDA, in return for its new funding source, to make the process more responsive to industry desires in two fundamental ways—the time required for agency action on applications, and providing industry with more awareness of the status of applications and access to the agency during the process.

The User Fee Act of 1992

The Prescription Drug User Fee Act of 1992 (PDUFA), beginning with fiscal year 1993 and continuing for 5 years, required set fees for each NDA (and biological product licenser supplement containing clinical data, though not bioequivalence data), to be paid in part at the time of submission and prior to approval. These fees were not insignificant, set at the outset in 1993 at $100,000 for a full NDA, and half that for a supplement, to $233,000 in 1997. Certain exemptions, such as one for certain small businesses, were included. It also required certain establishment fees and product fees.

Documentation on the concessions (euphemistically referred to as "performance goals") made by FDA in 1992 is not readily available; however, documentation provided with the renewal of user fees in 1997 indicates that both review times and more transparency in the approval process were uppermost in the minds of reformers. Action was expected on 90% of "standard" applications within 12 months, and on "priority" applications, those for serious diseases, within 6 months. Actual approval was not necessarily expected but, rather, FDA's initial review of the application and the issuance of an action letter. Other measurements involved 12-month review of standard efficacy supplements, 6-month review of priority efficacy supplements, and 6-month review of manufacturing supplements. These criteria were made more restrictive in the years following 1997. Other actions involved responses to requests for meetings, scheduling meeting dates, issuance of minutes following meetings, responding to sponsor clinical hold responses, dispute resolution, study protocol assessments, and simplifying action letters, all of which were designed to give manufacturers a more reliable sense of the agency's actions on pending applications, as well as make it more difficult for the agency to modify its views or position on such applications (57).

The dynamic of the user fee legislation seems to be universally seen as positive. Similar legislation has now been enacted for both animal drugs and medical devices. For detailed information on the effects of this legislation and for subsequent changes in the approval requirements resulting from the AIDS epidemic, see the chapters in this book regarding PDUFA and the FDA Modernization Act of 1997.

REFERENCES AND NOTES

1. Wiley Act, Pub L No. 59–384, 34 Stat 768 (1906), sec 1, 2.
2. Wiley Act, sec 7.
3. Wiley Act, sec 8.
4. 221 U.S. 488 (1911).
5. 37 Stat 416 (1912).
6. 1938 act, Pub L No. 75–717, 52 Stat 1040 (1938), sec 201(p).
7. 1938 act, sec 505(a).
8. 1938 act, sec 505(b)(1)(A).
9. 1938 act, secs 505(b)(1)(B)–505(b)(1)(F).
10. 1938 act, sec 505(c).
11. *Id.*
12. 1938 act, sec 505(d).
13. *Id.*
14. 1938 act, sec 505(e).
15. 1938 act, sec 505(h).

16. *Id.*
17. 1938 act, sec 505(i).
18. 1938 act, sec 201(g).
19. 1938 act, sec 201(p).
20. 1938 act, sec 201(p)(2).
21. 55 Stat 851 (1941).
22. 59 Stat 463(1945).
23. 76 Stat 780, 785(1962). See Hutt and Merrill, Food and Drug Law, Cases and Materials, Foundation Press, 1991; 521–522.
24. Pub L No. 105–115 (1997).
25. Federal Food, Drug and Cosmetic Act, (FDCA) sec 201(p)(1), sec 201(p)(2), 21 USC 321(p)(1), (p)(2); Pub L No. 87–781 (1962).
26. FDCA, sec 505(c); 21 USC 355(c).
27. FDCA, sec 505(d); 21 USC 355(d).
28. *Id.*
29. As with the 1938 act, the act provided significant procedural protections to manufacturers whose applications were not deemed worthy of approval, including notice, and opportunity for hearing, which, if granted, was contemplated to be a full administrative hearing.
30. The requirement for "new information" is considered by the agency to include a reevaluation of existing information, rather than requiring wholly new information as a prerequisite for withdrawal.
31. FDCA, sec 505(e), 21 USC 355(e). See, also, 21 CFR.
32. FDCA, sec 505(i)(1), 21 USC 355(i)(1).
33. FDCA, sec 505(i)(2), 21 USC 355(i)(2).
34. FDCA, sec 505(i)(3), 21 USC 355(i)(3).
35. FDCA, sec 505(i), 21 USC 355(i).
36. See 21 CFR 312.40.
37. Sec 107(c), Pub L No. 87–781 (1962).
38. Sec 107(c)(2).
39. Sec 107(c)(3).
40. Sec 107(c)(3)(B).
41. Secs 107(c)(2) and 107(c)(3)(B).
42. A "News Along the Pike" publication of FDA dated December 3, 2003, reports that, under the DESI review, FDA evaluated 3443 drugs having 16,000 claims, removing 1099 of them from the market.
43. 412 U.S. 655 (1973).
44. 412 U.S. 645 (1973).
45. 412 U.S. 640 (1973).
46. 412 U.S. 609 (1973).
47. FDA did not win every case. Nor does this discussion begin to discuss the judicial history. Rather, it includes the two cases that best reflect the agency's success at persuading the court, under the mantra of protecting the public health, to read the new drug definition expansively. One significant loss by the agency involved its efforts, through regulation, to control the distribution of the drug methadone. FDA believed that "safe" under section 505 included the potential for possible misuse, rather than simply inherent safety, and could thus regulate postapproval distribution of a new drug. In *American Pharmaceutical Ass'n. v. Weinberger*, 530 F2d 1054 (DC Cir1976); affirming 377 F Supp 824 (DC DC, 1974), the courts disagreed, interpreting safety to mean inherent safety for the uses in labeling, thus invalidating postapproval distribution restrictions. Regardless of this opinion, FDA has successfully controlled postapproval distribution of certain potentially toxic drugs through "voluntary" arrangements with manufacturers reached during the approval process.
48. 421 U.S. 658 (1975).
49. 442 U.S. 544 (1979).
50. 460 U.S. 453 (1983).

51. 96 Stat 2049 (1983). The diseases used as examples were not necessarily obscure. Muscular distrophy, for example, widely known through annual telethons, was a principal example, and was particularly noteworthy in that a well-known actor, Jack Klugman, whose brother suffered from the disease, used his then significant celebrity status to promote the legislation and enhance its passage. Another example, amyotrophic lateral sclerosis, was also well known as Lou Gherig's disease. The orphan drug provisions are codified at sects 525–528 of the FDCA, 21 USC 360 aa–360 dd.
52. In providing for tax credits and exclusivity, this legislation presaged similar, but far more controversial provisions in the 1984 Drug Price Competition and Patent Term Restoration Act, and later in the Pediatric Exclusivity Act. It appears that such provisions are now routinely considered appropriate to entice and reward manufacturers to develop new drugs or new uses for existing drugs.
53. 98 Stat 2815 (1984).
54. 99 Stat 387 (1985).
55. In an attempt to provide some additional level of competition, FDA has taken the position that it will not consider orphan drugs to be the same, despite similarities, if a second manufacturer can show "clinical benefit," and will thereby permit such a manufacturer to break the 7-year exclusivity. See 21 CFR 316.
56. Pub L No. 102–571 (1992).
57. See letter from Donna Shalala to Thomas Bliley, November 12, 1977.

4 Generic Drug-Approval Process: Hatch–Waxman Update

Marc S. Gross, Jay Lessler, S. Peter Ludwig, and Amanda L. Vaught
Darby & Darby, P.C., New York, New York, U.S.A.

OVERVIEW OF GENERIC DRUG-APPROVAL PROCESS UNDER HATCH–WAXMAN

The regulatory scheme for approval of generic drugs changed in April 1984 with enactment of the Drug Price Competition and Patent Term Restoration Act of 1984, commonly known as the "Hatch-Waxman" or "Waxman-Hatch" Act (1). The act was intended to balance the interests of consumers, the brand-name (innovator) pharmaceutical industry, and the generic drug industry to "make available more low cost generic drugs [and] to create a new incentive for increased expenditures for research and development of certain products which are subject to pre-market approval" (2). Since enactment of the statute, generic drugs have increased from 19% of prescriptions in 1984 to 67% in 2007 and, in 1998, accounted for savings to consumers of $8 to 10 billion (3).

Breaking new ground, Title I of Hatch–Waxman authorized the marketing of generic drugs upon approval of Abbreviated New Drug Applications (ANDAs) (4). Under the Act, an ANDA can be approved upon submission of evidence that the active ingredient of the generic drug is the "bioequivalent" of a drug previously approved by the Food and Drug Administration (FDA) after submission of a full New Drug Application (NDA), without having to submit studies establishing the safety and efficacy of the drug (5). Hatch–Waxman contains similar provisions respecting ANDAs and so-called "505(b)(2) applications" or "paper NDAs," which rely on safety and/or efficacy data submitted in a prior NDA (6).

Title II of Hatch–Waxman provided for specific extensions of patents covering drugs (and other products) subject to "regulatory review" by FDA and other governmental agencies (7). This provision was intended to balance the benefits of ANDA practice by providing brand-name drug companies with the restoration of portions of the terms of their drug patents lost during the testing period required for approval of the drugs. Patent term extensions under 35 USC §156 (Section 156 extensions), as well as patent extensions implemented 10 years after enactment of Hatch–Waxman pursuant to the Uruguay Round of Negotiations under the General Agreement on Tariffs and Trade (8), authorized extended drug patent terms to brand-name companies.

The Hatch–Waxman statutory scheme incorporates several provisions relating to the submission and approval of both ANDAs and 505(b)(2) applications subject to certain patent and other marketing exclusivities for drugs granted to brand-name companies. The act also specifically provides a "safe harbor" for companies seeking approval of generic drugs, that is, the statute specifies that it is not an act of patent infringement to use a patented invention "solely for uses reasonably related to the development and submission of information" for FDA or other governmental approval (9). On the other hand, Hatch–Waxman provides that an applicant for an ANDA or a 505(b)(2) applicant must make an appropriate certification respecting marketing of the generic drug vis-à-vis any patents for the same drug that are listed by the brand-name NDA holder in FDA's list of "Approved Drug Products With Therapeutic Equivalence Evaluations" (commonly referred to as the "Orange Book") (10).

Where the generic applicant certifies that there are no patents listed in the *Orange Book* (a "Paragraph I Certification") or that any listed patents have previously expired (a "Paragraph II Certification"), the drug may enter the marketplace immediately upon FDA approval. Where the applicant certifies that any listed patent has not yet expired but will expire on a particular date and that it will not enter the market until after that date (a "Paragraph III Certification"), FDA may approve the ANDA and make it effective as of the patent expiration date.

Where the applicant for generic approval intends to market the drug prior to expiration of any patent(s) listed in the *Orange Book*, the applicant makes a certification that, in its opinion, the patent(s) are not infringed or are invalid (a "Paragraph IV Certification"), and it notifies the NDA holder and patent owner accordingly (11). In such instance, the statute provides that the NDA holder/patent owner may then initiate a patent infringement action against the applicant for generic approval and FDA must suspend approval of the ANDA or 505(b)(2) application for up to 30 months (the "30-month stay"), subject to the earlier of a court determination or the expiration of the listed patent(s) (12).

In an effort to encourage generic drug entry into the pharmaceutical market, the Hatch–Waxman Act provides a commercial incentive to those generic companies who are the first to file ANDAs incorporating Paragraph IV Certifications challenging infringement or validity of *Orange Book*–listed brand-name pharmaceutical patents. Thus, in the event the listed brand-name patent(s) are adjudged to be invalid or not infringed prior to their normal expiration date(s); the first generic filer(s) entitled to approval of their ANDAs receive a 180-day exclusivity period during which no other ANDA can be approved for the same product (13). In such circumstances, the first entity or entities to file an ANDA can be the only generic marketer(s) for 180 days.

In addition, Hatch–Waxman incorporates several provisions limiting the filing or approval of ANDAs and 505(b)(2) applications in view of marketing "exclusivities" previously obtained by a brand-name NDA holder. Chief among such limitations is a 5-year bar on submitting an application for generic drug approval following approval of an NDA on a "new chemical entity" (NCE) (14), and a 3-year bar on obtaining approval of a generic drug application following approval of an NDA based on new clinical investigations respecting a previously approved drug (15). There is also a 7-year bar on obtaining approval of any drug application following approval of an orphan drug for the same indication (16). Finally, pediatric exclusivity, which is granted upon completion of pediatric studies requested by FDA, prevents generic drug approval for an additional 6 months after expiration of any pertinent patent listed in the *Orange Book*. Pediatric exclusivity also extends the 3-year, 5-year, and 7-year exclusivities by 6 months (17).

FDA's approval scheme for ANDAs containing Paragraph I, II, III, or IV Certifications is illustrated in Figures 1 and 2 (18).

Since enactment of Hatch–Waxman, several amendments have been made to enhance and prevent abuse of the Hatch–Waxman scheme. For instance, changes

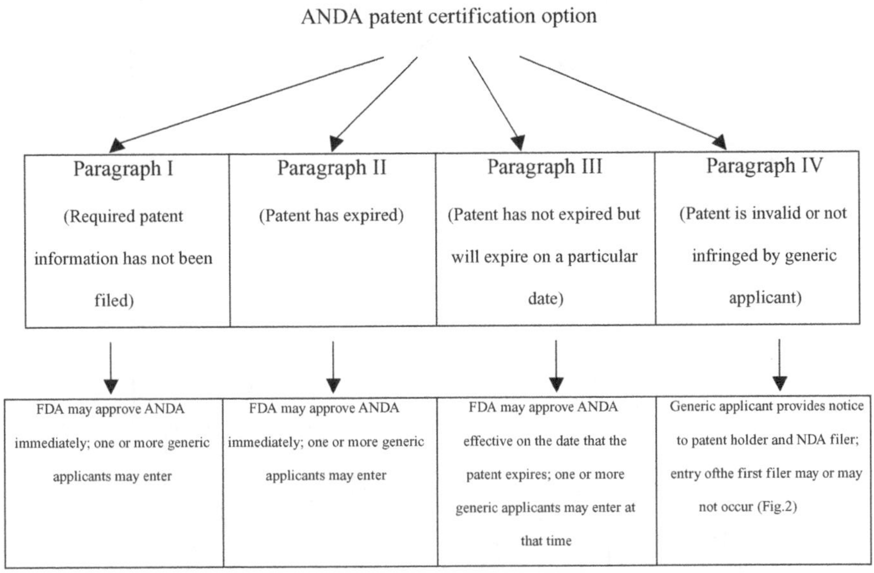

FIGURE 1 ANDA Patent Certifications.

made to Hatch–Waxman in the Medicare Prescription Drug Improvement, and Modernization Act of 2003 (hereinafter "the 2003 Statutory Changes") were designed to limit brand-name companies to the opportunity to obtain a single 30-month stay of approval of ANDA or 505(b)(2) applications for the resolution of patent infringement litigation respecting listed drug patents. More recently, the Food and Drug Administration Amendments Act of 2007 (FDAAA) provided that optically pure enantiomers of previously approved drugs may be considered new chemical entities and thus receive 5 years of market exclusivity if certain conditions are met. FDAAA also prevents delay of generic approval based on a third-party submission of citizen petitions suggesting that generic applications should not be approved, unless delay is necessary to protect public health.

LISTING PATENTS IN THE *ORANGE BOOK*

Requirements

In 1984, for the first time, Hatch–Waxman required each NDA applicant to identify any patent which claims the drug for which the NDA was submitted or a method of using such drug which the applicant believed could reasonably be asserted against potential generic infringers (19). The patent information must be submitted during the pendency of the NDA. On the other hand, if a patent eligible for listing in the *Orange Book* is granted after approval of the NDA (or even after the filing of an ANDA seeking approval of a generic equivalent of the listed product), then the patent information must be submitted within 30 days after grant of the patent (20). The information submitted during pendency of an NDA must be set forth in FDA Form 3542a, while information for listing submitted after approval of an NDA must

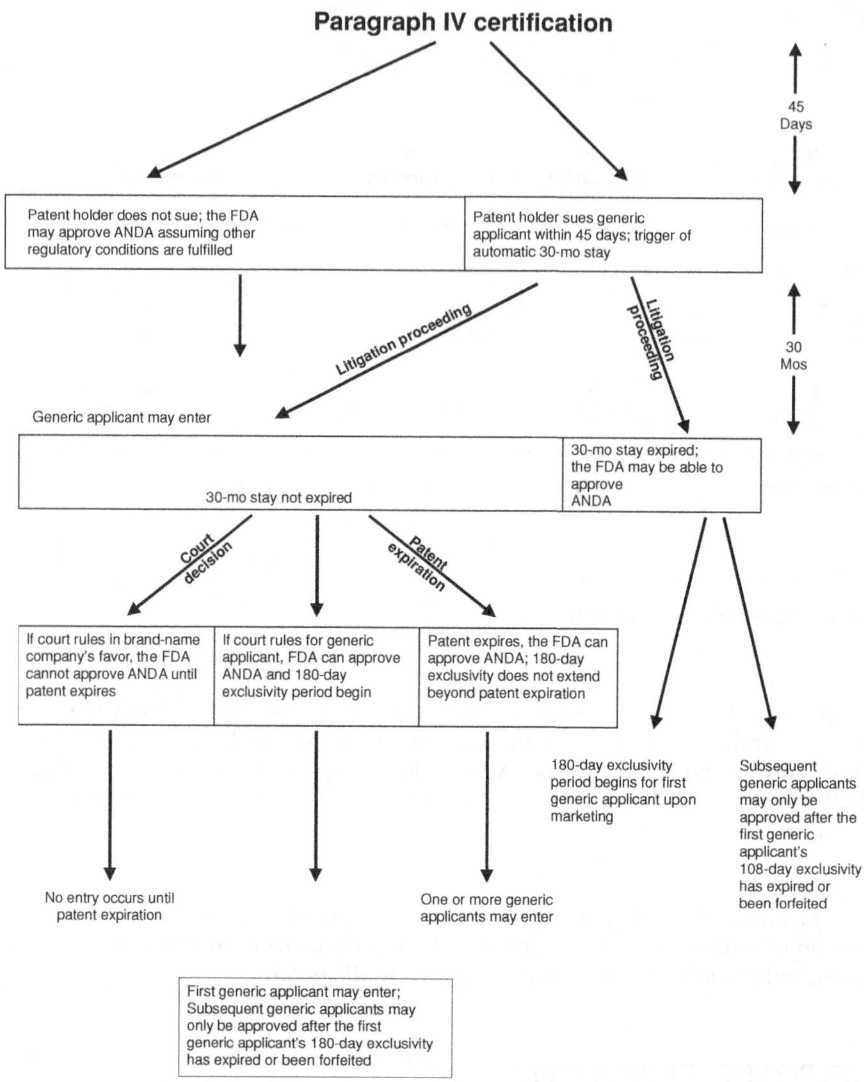

FIGURE 2 Paragraph IV Certifications.

be incorporated in FDA Form 3542 (21). Under Hatch–Waxman, the generic applicant must make a patent certification as to each such listed patent (22), and if the patent is not listed until after filing of the ANDA, amend its application accordingly (23).

On the other hand, if the brand-name company fails to submit the patent information for listing in the *Orange Book* within the 30-day period after the grant of the patent, the generic applicant need not submit an amended certification and the patent owner may not initiate an infringement suit under 35 USC §271(e)(2) (24).

Further, a brand-name company cannot obtain a 30-month stay of generic approval based on the listing of a patent after the filing of the ANDA (25).

In one recent case, *Eisai*, the NDA holder, owned a patent which claimed the active pharmaceutical ingredient donepezil hydrochloride in its commercial drug products Aricept® and Aricept ODT® (26). While Eisai properly submitted the forms to list its patent for Aricept in 1996, Eisai failed "by ... repeated oversights" to submit the proper forms and information to FDA for Orange Book listing of the patent for Aricept ODT, which was approved in 2005 (27). Accordingly, FDA did not list the patent until more than 5 months after the generic party filed its ANDA (28). By reason of such error, which the district court characterized as "more than merely 'clerical,'" (29) the ANDA applicant did not have to submit a Paragraph IV certification, and Eisai was not entitled to the 30-month stay of approval of the ANDA that the prompt commencement of suit would have achieved. Additionally, the district court dismissed the lawsuit for lack of subject matter jurisdiction due, in part, to the ANDA applicant's failure to submit a Paragraph IV certification.

The patents for which information must be submitted in connection with an NDA include those directed to the drug substance (active ingredient), the drug product (formulation or composition), and methods of use (indications) approved for the listed drug product (30). The patents thus submitted to FDA are listed in the *Orange Book* (31), and are the "listed patents" or "Orange Book patents".

Since enactment of Hatch–Waxman, brand-name companies have submitted patents for listing in the *Orange Book* directed to a wide range of subject matter, which include different forms of an active drug substance, for example, anhydrous or hydrated forms, salts, enantiomers or crystal forms of the active substance, different formulations of the drug, metabolites formed in patients after administration of the drug, and methods of use of the drug whether or not previously approved by FDA (32). The listing of multiple patents in the *Orange Book* has compelled ANDA and 505(b)(2) applicants to make multiple patent certifications and, in some instances, resulted in the imposition of multiple 30-month stays of generic product approvals, with consequent delays of generic entry into the market.

FDA does not review the propriety of patents submitted by NDA holders for listing in the *Orange Book* because FDA "does not have the expertise to review patent information" (33). Rather, if the accuracy or relevance of patent information submitted for listing in the *Orange Book* is disputed by an ANDA or 505(b)(2) applicant it must notify FDA. The agency will then ask the NDA holder to confirm the correctness of the patent information, and unless the NDA holder withdraws or amends its patent information, FDA "will not change the patent information in the" *Orange Book* (34). The agency's failure to review patent listings in the *Orange Book* for possible delisting provoked criticism, and prompted proposals for reform.

In response to such criticisms, FDA implemented several rule changes in 2003 (hereafter "the 2003 Rule Changes"). Under those regulations, drug substances that are the same active ingredients as the subject of NDAs, but in different physical forms, that is, polymorphs (35), must be submitted for listing in the *Orange Book*. An NDA holder or patent owner must, however, establish that a polymorph claimed in a patent will "perform the same as the drug product described in the NDA with respect to such characteristics as dissolution, solubility, and bioavailability" for listing (36). To establish such "sameness" for a polymorph, the NDA holder or patent owner must submit detailed test data in five different categories, using forms specified in the 2003 Rule Changes (37).

Further in accordance with the 2003 Rule Changes, the listing of product-by-process patents is permitted (38), provided, however, that to be submitted for listing "the product-by-process patent must claim the drug product that is the subject of the NDA" and the drug product must be novel (39).

On the other hand, when "the drug that is the subject of [a new drug] application contains an antibiotic drug and the antibiotic drug was the subject of any application" received by FDA on or before November 20, 1997, the *Orange Book* listing requirements of the Hatch–Waxman Act do not apply (40).

Finally, patents for products approved pursuant to a biologics license application are not subject to the listing requirement and, therefore, are not listed in the *Orange Book*.

In addition, the 2003 Rule Changes prohibit submitting patents for listing which claim packaging, metabolites, or intermediates [in addition to the previous prohibition against the submission of process patents claiming methods of making drug substances (active ingredients)] (41). Packaging is distinct from finished dosage forms for approved drug products, which must be submitted for listing (42). A metabolite is defined by FDA as a "chemical compound that results after the active ingredient of the drug has broken down inside the body"; metabolites may not be submitted for listing since they are not the active ingredients described in NDAs (43). Finally, intermediates, "materials that are produced during preparation of the active ingredient and are not present in the finished drug product," may not be submitted for listing (44). FDA considers intermediates as "in-process materials" as distinguished from drug substances or components in a finished drug product (45).

Challenges to Listing

In several cases, ANDA applicants sought to compel FDA to delist patents improperly listed in the *Orange Book*. Those efforts were without success; the Court of Appeals for the Federal Circuit held that delisting is a private right of action both barred by the FDCA and not a recognized defense to a claim of patent infringement (46). While the Federal Circuit held out the possibility that a generic company might secure federal jurisdiction on some other basis (47) (e. g., by an action against the listing company in a counterclaim to a patent infringement suit), any attempt by a generic company to seek delisting would involve substantial additional delays during which it would be barred from the market by reason of the continued patent listing in the *Orange Book*.

In its 2003 Rule Changes, FDA declined to create any administrative procedures for challenging patent listings or for delisting patents. Instead, it affirmed its long-standing view that it has only a ministerial role in overseeing *Orange Book* listings (48). However, in an effort to "reduce confusion and help curb attempts to take advantage of this process (the Hatch–Waxman administrative scheme)" (49), the agency restricted the types of patents and supporting evidence required for listing (see Section "Requirements" of this chapter).

The 2003 Statutory Changes made no alterations to the requirements for the types of patents which must be submitted for listing in the *Orange Book*. The amendments, however, provided a remedy for improper listings. In the event a patent infringement action is commenced based on the filing of an ANDA or 505(b)(2) application, the applicant may assert a counterclaim to correct or delete the patent listing if the patent does not claim the approved drug or an approved method of use (50). The counterclaim may not seek damages. To date, there has not been a successful action for improper listing without a patent infringement lawsuit being filed by the patent owner or NDA holder.

Delisting and Relisting

FDA does not normally take affirmative action to delist a patent, rather, it allows the patent to expire, terminating the effect of listing. When requested by the NDA holder for the listed patent, however, FDA will delist the patent. This can lead to unusual situations where, for example, an ANDA filer having 180-day marketing exclusivity may seek relisting of a patent to preserve its exclusivity vis-à-vis other generic filers (51). In the cited case, Mylan had obtained 180-day generic market exclusivity until September 2007, in view of the March 25, 2007, expiration of the applicable Pfizer patent and subsequent 6-month pediatric exclusivity (52). On Pfizer's request, FDA delisted the Pfizer patent on June 22, 2007, and held that Mylan's exclusivity did not survive the March expiration date of the patent (53). Notwithstanding Mylan's repeated efforts to enjoin the agency's action (and thus delay generic competition for up to 3 months, by eight other ANDA filers), the courts held FDA's interpretation of the law as reasonable and refused to grant mandatory injunctive relief to Mylan (54).

ABBREVIATED NEW DRUG APPLICATIONS

The "Listed" Drug

Under Section 505(j) of Hatch–Waxman, an ANDA may be filed for a generic version of any "listed drug" (55). FDA deems any drug for which an NDA has previously been approved a listed drug and lists the drug in the *Orange Book* (56). Both drugs, previously approved under ANDAs (57), and antibiotics (58) are regarded as listed drugs.

An ANDA must include all of the information required in an NDA except, significantly, full reports of investigations demonstrating that the drug is safe and effective in use. Additionally, the ANDA must show (*i*) the labeling of the drug for which the ANDA is sought is the same as the approved labeling for the listed drug; (*ii*) the generic drug, its route of administration, dosage form, and strength are the same as the listed drug, or supply such information respecting any differences as FDA may require; and (*iii*) the generic drug is bioequivalent to the listed drug; and also (*iv*) supply information regarding the status of any *Orange Book*–listed patents on the approved drug (59).

Establishing Equivalence to the Listed Drug

Initially, an ANDA filer must show that the conditions of use identified in its proposed labeling have been previously approved for the listed drug on which the ANDA is based (60). According to the statute, the ANDA must incorporate the same labeling as that previously approved for the listed drug, except for any changes required because of differences approved on the basis of a suitability petition (see Section "Suitability Petitions for Drugs That Differ From Listed Drug" of this chapter) or because the generic drug and the listed drug are "produced or distributed by different manufacturers" (61). Changes in the proposed labeling, which may be approved under FDA regulations, include the listing of differences in expiration date, formulation, bioavailability, pharmacokinetics, or revisions made to comply with current FDA labeling guidelines (62). Consistent with the case law, the current regulation also specifically authorizes the "omission of an indication or other aspect of labeling protected by patent or accorded exclusivity under section 505(j)(4)(D) of the act" (63).

This provision, coupled with a "Section (viii) Statement" (see Section "Section VIII Statement of Listed Use Patents Which Do Not Cover Indications for Which Approval Is Sought" of this chapter), provides a mechanism for avoiding infringement of listed method-of-use patents for indications for which generic applicants do not seek approval

An ANDA applicant must establish that the active ingredient(s) in its prospective generic product are the same as those in the listed drug (64). In case one of the active ingredients is different, the ANDA applicant must demonstrate both: (1) that FDA approved a suitability petition for the new drug and (2) that the different active ingredient is either an active ingredient of a different listed drug, or is not a "new drug" within the meaning of Hatch–Waxman (65).

Finally, the ANDA must show that the new drug is "bioequivalent" to the listed drug (66). As defined by statute, a generic drug is bioequivalent to a listed drug if

(a) the rate and extent of absorption of the respective drugs do not significantly differ from one another, or
(b) there is no significant difference in the extent of absorption of the respective drugs and the difference in the rate of absorption of the respective drugs is intentional, reflected in the proposed labeling of the generic drug, not essential to achieving effective concentrations and considered medically insignificant. (67)

FDA may exercise discretion in determining whether the evidence submitted to show bioequivalence is adequate (68), and FDA has discretion to waive the requirement for proof of bioequivalence (69).

Additional Requirements

Although FDA does not require safety testing data in support of an ANDA, it may consider safety questions associated with the identity or concentrations of the inactive ingredients of the generic drug. Thus, approval of an ANDA may be denied if the agency finds that the inactive ingredients are unsafe under the conditions set forth in the proposed labeling for the drug, or the composition of the drug is unsafe because of the type or quantity of the inactive ingredients in the composition (70). The regulations specify a number of changes in the inactive ingredients of a generic product on which the agency may predicate a "reasonable basis to conclude that one or more of the inactive ingredients of the proposed drug or its composition raises serious questions of safety" (71) and may refuse approval. FDA has considerable latitude in determining whether the identity or amounts of inactive ingredients in a generic drug may adversely affect the safety of the drug.

Suitability Petitions for Drugs That Differ From Listed Drug

If a party wants to submit an ANDA for a new drug which differs in specific respects from the listed drug to which the ANDA refers, it may submit a suitability petition to FDA seeking permission to file such an application (72). Such petitions may be filed where the new drug has (*i*) a different active ingredient, (*ii*) a different route of administration, (*iii*) a different dosage form, or (*iv*) a different strength from the listed drug (73). Any different active ingredient must be within the "same pharmacological or therapeutic class" as the active ingredient in the listed drug, and the modified drug must be expected to have "the same therapeutic effect" as the listed drug (74). When the party filing a suitability petition seeks approval to incorporate a different active ingredient than a listed drug having more than one active ingredient, it must establish (*i*) the other active ingredients of the new drug are the same as the active ingredients of the listed drug, and (*ii*) the different active ingredient is an active ingredient of a different listed drug, or that the different active ingredient is an active ingredient of a drug which is not a "new drug" under the FDCA (75).

Consistent with the statutory provisions, FDA should grant a suitability petition unless it finds that investigations must be conducted to show:

1. the safety and efficacy of the modified drug or of any of (*i*) its active ingredients, (*ii*) route of administration, (*iii*) dosage form or (*iv*) strength, which differ from the listed drug; or
2. that the drug may not be adequately evaluated for approval as safe and effective on the basis of the information required in an ANDA. (76)

The procedure for submitting a suitability petition is set forth in FDA regulations (77). The petition must identify the listed drug, incorporate a copy of the proposed labeling for the generic product (as well as a copy of the approved labeling for the listed drug), and make the several specific showings outlined in the regulation.

By statute, FDA must either approve or disapprove a suitability petition within 90 days of the date of the petition's submission (78).

Removal of *Orange Book* Listing of a Drug

Hatch–Waxman specifies that listing of a drug in the *Orange Book* will be terminated if either its approval is withdrawn or suspended, or the drug is withdrawn from sale for safety or efficacy reasons (79). FDA will not approve an ANDA when the approval of the corresponding NDA for the listed drug has been withdrawn or suspended and FDA has "published a notice of opportunity for hearing to withdraw approval of the listed drug," or when the secretary has determined that the listed drug has been withdrawn from sale for safety or efficacy reasons (80).

Withdrawal of approval of a listed drug may occur where, after due notice and opportunity for hearing, FDA finds (*i*) that the drug is unsafe for use under the conditions for which it was approved, (*ii*) that there is a lack of substantial evidence that the drug is effective under the conditions set forth in the product labeling, or (*iii*) that the NDA contained any untrue statement of material fact (81). An ANDA holder may submit written comments in response to the notice of opportunity for hearing issued on the proposed withdrawal of the related listed drug. In the event of a hearing, the ANDA holder may join as a nonparty participant (82). If the Secretary of Health and Human Services finds that continued use of the drug presents "an imminent hazard to the public health" (83), then the ANDA will be withdrawn when FDA enters a final decision withdrawing approval of the listed drug (84).

APPROVAL OF GENERIC DRUGS UNDER SECTION 505(B)(2)

This section of Hatch–Waxman provides for approval of certain drugs without full safety and efficacy investigations, whereas NDAs require such information under Section 505(b)(1). 505(b)(2) applications may apply when the applicant has not obtained a "right of reference or use" from the party for which the full safety and efficacy investigations were previously conducted (85).

FDA interprets the provisions of Section 505(b)(2) to sanction reliance by a generic applicant on the safety and/or efficacy data submitted in a prior NDA for the related listed drug (86). Hence, the "paper NDA" denomination has been used because the applicant relies on laboratory and clinical data from a third party. A number of 505(b)(2) applications have been filed for approval of salts differing from the NDA-approved salts of the same active ingredients, where the generic applicants rely on data previously submitted to FDA by the NDA holders (87). In one such instance, the NDA holder/patent owner unsuccessfully challenged the foregoing FDA interpretation by a citizen petition (88).

As noted later, 505(b)(2) applicants must make patent certifications and comply with patent notice provisions analogous to those required for ANDA applicants (89). Because of the similar requirements, FDA may refuse to accept 505(b)(2) applications for drugs which are duplicates of listed drugs and are eligible for approval of ANDAs under Section 505(j) (90).

Reliance Upon Literature

Investigations relied upon by a 505(b)(2) applicant may include both studies which it owns and reports from studies owned by third parties. Such studies may include both clinical and animal safety and efficacy tests. FDA views all such tests submitted in a 505(b)(2) application as having been "relied upon" by the 505(b)(2) applicant (91).

Variants of Listed Drugs

505(b)(2) applications are necessary for new generic drugs which sufficiently differ from the prior listed drugs that suitability petitions for filing ANDAs would not be approved. For example, this is the case where the listed drug has only one active ingredient (92). Accordingly, as indicated earlier, the filing of a 505(b)(2) application is appropriate where, for example, the generic drug for which approval is sought is a different salt of the listed drug (72).

FDA ACTION ON ANDAS AND 505(B)(2) APPLICATIONS

An ANDA or 505(b)(2) application may not be submitted within 5 years after the approval of an NDA for an NCE, unless the application contains a Paragraph IV Certification, in which case the application may be submitted on the fourth anniversary of the approval of the NDA (93).

Under Hatch–Waxman, FDA must approve an ANDA unless it finds that the methods and facilities of the applicant are inadequate to assure the identity, strength, quality, and purity of the drug, or the information submitted in the application is insufficient to meet the other statutory requirements (94). On the other hand, since a 505(b)(2) application is basically an NDA, it must meet each of the requirements for an NDA save that it may rely upon investigations of safety and efficacy which were not conducted by the applicant and for which it has not obtained a right of reference (91).

The statute provides the agency must complete its review of the sufficiency of an ANDA or 505(b)(2) application within 180 days of initial receipt of the application (95). During the review period, FDA may either approve or disapprove the application. If it disapproves the application, it must give the applicant notice (a "not approvable letter") and provide it with the opportunity to amend the application, withdraw it, or request a hearing to challenge the agency's grounds for denying approval (96). The opportunity to request a hearing is designed to provide the applicant with the opportunity to contest the grounds asserted by the agency for denying approval of the application (97).

Alternatively, if FDA approves the ANDA or 505(b)(2) application, the effective date of approval may be delayed (14) on any of the various grounds indicated later, or revoked based upon subsequent court order (98).

PATENT CERTIFICATIONS

Types of Certifications

An applicant for an ANDA or a 505(b)(2) application must certify to FDA that, in its opinion and to the best of its knowledge, with respect to each listed patent which claims the drug or a use of the drug for which the applicant is seeking approval, that:

1. The patent information which the NDA holder is required to file (including the identification of any listed patent) has not in fact been filed (a Paragraph I Certification),
2. The listed patent has expired (a Paragraph II Certification),
3. The listed patent will expire on some specified date and the ANDA or 505(b)(2) applicant does not intend to commence marketing the drug for which it seeks approval until after that date (a Paragraph III Certification), or
4. The listed patent is invalid or will not be infringed by the manufacture, use, or sale of the drug for which the ANDA or 505(b)(2) application is submitted (99).

FDA regulations provide that a Paragraph IV Certification may be based on the asserted unenforceability of the listed patent as well as noninfringement or invalidity thereof (100).

Content of Certifications

The Paragraph I Certification simply permits the ANDA or 505(b)(2) applicant to inform FDA that the NDA holder has not listed any patents, which might affect the agency's approval of the application (101). Similarly, the Paragraph II Certification serves to inform FDA that a previously listed *Orange Book* patent has expired, and would not have any effect on approval by the agency. In like manner, a Paragraph III Certification informs FDA when a listed patent will expire, thus providing notice to the agency to delay approval of the ANDA or 505(b)(2) application until that date. (Fig. 2).

The Paragraph IV Certification, on the other hand, imposes certain obligations on each of (*i*) the ANDA or 505(b)(2) applicant, (*ii*) the owner of the listed patent, and (*iii*) FDA. The initial obligation is imposed on the applicant, who must include a statement in its application that it will provide notice of its application and the basis for its position to the owner of each challenged listed patent and the holder of the NDA for the listed drug, or the representatives thereof (102).

NOTICE TO PATENT OWNER AND HOLDER OF NDA ACCOMPANYING PARAGRAPH IV CERTIFICATION

The notice required of the ANDA or 505(b)(2) applicant making a Paragraph IV Certification must state that an application for approval has been submitted to FDA (103). The notice states applicant's intent to engage in the commercial manufacture, use, or sale of the listed drug before the expiration of the patent as to which the certification has been made (104). The notice must include, inter alia, a "detailed statement of the factual and legal basis of the applicant's opinion that the patent is not valid or will not be infringed" (105).

FDA regulations provide that the notice of "factual and legal basis" must set forth a detailed statement for each claim of the listed patent for which a Paragraph IV Certification is submitted and provide a "full and detailed explanation of why the claim is not infringed" and/or such an explanation of the grounds supporting the allegation of invalidity (or, alternatively, unenforceability) of each such claim (106). The regulations further require that the notice given by the ANDA applicant must identify the ANDA number; the established name, if any, of the proposed drug product; the active ingredient, strength, and dosage form of the proposed drug product; and the patent number and expiration date of each of the listed patents believed to be invalid, unenforceable, or not infringed (107).

When the Paragraph IV Certification is in the ANDA or 505(b)(2) application, the notice of the factual and legal basis for the certification must be given to the patent owner/NDA holder (104) no later than 20 days after the postmark date on the notice from FDA of filing of the application (108). When the certification is in an amendment or supplement to the generic application, the notice must be given at the same time as the submission of the amendment or supplement (109).

Assuming compliance with the procedural requirements, FDA presumes the notice to be effective upon receipt by the patent owner and NDA holder, and counts the day following the date of receipt as the first day of the 45-day period provided in Hatch–Waxman for possible commencement of infringement litigation, as described later (110).

Brand-name companies have asserted in some infringement actions (predicated on Paragraph IV Certifications) that ANDA applicants have not satisfied the requirement to provide a sufficient notice of the factual and legal basis for asserting noninfringement or invalidity of listed patents, and sought court orders remedying allegedly deficient notices. To date, no such orders have been issued (111).

Section VIII Statement of Listed Use Patents Which Do Not Cover Indications for Which Approval Is Sought

Hatch–Waxman provides that Paragraph IV Certifications need not be made in ANDAs or 505(b)(2) applications for *Orange Book*–listed use patents that do not claim a use for which the applicant seeks approval. In this instance, the statute (and

FDA rules) provides that the applicant may file a statement that the use patent does not claim such a use (112). A "Section viii Statement" is significant since it may avoid the necessity to submit a Paragraph IV Certification and thus preclude the patent owner from commencing an infringement suit and invoking the 30-month stay of approval of the generic drug.

FDA has disclaimed any role in assessing whether a use patent covers an indication for which an ANDA or 505(b)(2) applicant seeks approval (113). Moreover, it has taken the position that it must accept the representations by the NDA holder as to the scope of the use patent. In a number of instances, FDA held a Section viii Statement improper and instead required a Paragraph IV Certification (114). FDA's approach has been specifically endorsed by the courts (115). In another case, however, a trial court ordered FDA to accept an ANDA applicant's Section viii Statement in lieu of a Paragraph IV Certification (116). The court did not take issue with FDA's policy of "deference to NDA holders' characterizations of the scope of use patents" but found, on the specific facts of the case, that the patent owner had consistently distinguished the use claimed in the method patent in question from the indication for which the ANDA applicant sought approval.

In *Aventis Pharma Deutschland GMBH v. Cobalt Pharmaceuticals, Inc.*, Cobalt contended in their Section viii Statement that they would not market generic ramipril for treating heart failure (117). Rather, Cobalt intended to market ramipril "solely for treating hypertension and reducing the risk of heart attack, stroke, and death from cardiovascular causes" (118). Cobalt's knowledge that some physicians may prescribe generic ramipril for treating heart failure was considered to be "'legally irrelevant' to an active inducement analysis" (119).

In order to refine its treatment of Section viii Statements, FDA, in its 2003 Rule Changes, modified the declaration required of an NDA holder for listing of a method-of-use patent. It now requires that the declarant must

> ... describe each individual method of use [and identify the related patent claim(s)] for which a patent is submitted for listing, and identify the corresponding language found in the labeling of the approved NDA that corresponds to that method of use. (120)

By requiring greater particularity in the declaration, FDA may take more of a substantive role in evaluating the propriety of Paragraph IV Certifications vis-à-vis Section viii Statements.

Amending ANDAs or 505(b)(2) Applications to Make Paragraph IV Certifications

When an ANDA or 505(b)(2) applicant amends its application to make a Paragraph IV Certification, the statute requires notification of the listed patent owner and NDA holder (121). The generic applicant may meet this requirement by amending a Paragraph III Certification to a Paragraph IV Certification. The applicant can also add a Paragraph IV Certification for a newly listed patent during the pendency of the application (122). A notice of the factual and legal basis for the Paragraph IV Certification must be sent "at the same time that the amendment... is submitted to FDA" (123). FDA regulations do not require an ANDA or 505(b)(2) applicant to amend its prior certifications if either the NDA holder failed to provide the requisite patent information within 30 days after patent issuance, or if the application originally contained appropriate patent certifications (124).

An ANDA or 505(b)(2) applicant who amends the application to add a Paragraph IV Certification need only to provide notice to the NDA holder and patent owner if:

1. The application did not already contain a Paragraph IV Certification with respect to the same patent, or
2. There was not a full opportunity for the NDA holder to obtain a 30-month stay (125).

As pointed out earlier, the statute still requires notice of amended or supplemental Paragraph IV Certifications. The 2003 act provided, however, for only a 30-month stay of FDA approval upon the initiation of an infringement suit based on patents listed in the *Orange Book* prior to the filing of an ANDA or 505(b)(2) application—not the amendment or supplementation—of such an application. (See Section "The 30-Month Stay" later.)

THE SAFE HARBOR EXEMPTION FROM PATENT INFRINGEMENT

As part of the effort to balance the rights of brand-name and generic pharmaceutical manufacturers, the Hatch–Waxman Act provided that the development of information by or for generic drug companies for the purpose of preparing ANDAs or 505(b)(2) applications does not constitute patent infringement. Thus, Hatch–Waxman amended the patent statute to provide that "[i]t shall not be an act of infringement to make, use, offer to sell, or sell . . . a patented invention . . . solely for uses reasonably related to the development and submission of information under a Federal law which regulates the manufacture, use, or sale of drugs" (126).

In the recent *Integra* case, the Supreme Court illuminated both the breadth and depth of the safe harbor (127). The court held that research results that were not intended to be submitted to FDA but which may lead to data suitable for such purpose were within the safe harbor.

Integra owned five patents relating to Arginine- Glycine-Aspartic acid (RGD) peptides (128). While the patents were in force, Merck collaborated with the Scripps Research Institute on research to reverse tumor growth. The process required an RGD peptide to inhibit angiogenesis. As part of their collaboration, Merck funded research at Scripps to investigate RGD peptides produced by Merck as potential drug candidates. Once Scripps identified a primary candidate, Merck performed the "toxicology tests necessary for FDA approval to proceed with clinical trials." Ultimately, Merck investigated several RGD peptides, but only initiated a project to "guide one of its RGD peptides through the regulatory process in the United States" (129).

Integra filed suit against Merck and Scripps for infringing its patents relating to RGD peptides. The district court found for Integra, and explained that "'any connection between the infringing Scripps experiments and FDA review was insufficiently direct to qualify for the [§271(e)(1) exemption]'" (130). On appeal, the Federal Circuit found the safe harbor inapplicable as Merck's sponsorship of Scripps's research work "'was not clinical testing to supply information to FDA, but only general biomedical research to identify new pharmaceutical compounds'" (131).

The Supreme Court reversed the Federal Circuit, stating the text of the statute "provides a wide berth for the use of patented drugs in activities related to the federal regulatory process" (132). The court went on: "[w]e think it apparent from the statutory text that §271(e)(1)'s exemption from infringement extends to all uses of patented inventions that are reasonably related to the development and submission of any information under the FDCA" (133). The language of the statute leaves no room for "excluding certain information from the exemption on the basis of the phase of research in which it is developed or the particular submission in which it could be included" (134). Thus, while Merck did not ultimately submit all of its research on RGD peptides to FDA, Merck had a "reasonable basis for believing that the experiments [would] produce 'the types of information that are relevant to an IND or NDA'" (135).

The safe harbor, then, supplies protection for research into potential drug candidates that may reasonably produce data relevant for submission to FDA:

Properly construed, §271(e)(1) leaves adequate space for experimentation and failure on the road to regulatory approval: At least where a drugmaker has a reasonable basis for believing that a patented compound may work, through a particular biological process, to produce a particular physiological effect, and uses the compound in research that, if successful, would be appropriate to include in a submission to the FDA, that use is "reasonably related" to the "development and submission of information under . . . Federal law" (136).

On remand, the Federal Circuit applied the Supreme Court's interpretation of the safe harbor provision and reversed the district court's finding of infringement (137). The court highlighted the fact that the accused experiments occurred after discovery of the underlying "physiological effect"—the angiogenesis-inhibiting properties of the RGD peptides (138). In addition, the experiments produced information relevant to "efficacy, mechanism of action, pharmacology, or pharmacokinetics" of Integra's claimed compounds (139). Thus Merck's research activities met the court's criterion of being "reasonably related to research that, if successful, would be appropriate to include in a submission to the FDA" (140).

The Supreme Court further indicated that its decision had no bearing on "whether, or to what extent, §271(e)(1) exempts from infringement the use of 'research tools' in the development of information for the regulatory process" (141). On remand, the Federal Circuit noted that Integra was not an appropriate case "to make new law on the issue of whether patent claims to research tools (however that term may be defined) are excluded from the ambit of Section 271(e)(1)" (142). Such a case is yet to occur.

The safe harbor also applies to International Trade Commission (ITC) proceedings where a party alleges the unlawful importation of products made abroad by a patented process (143).

SUBMISSION OF AN ANDA OR 505(B)(2) APPLICATION AS AN ACT OF PATENT INFRINGEMENT

To balance the safe harbor rights of generic applicants to develop information for ANDA or 505(b)(2) filings, Hatch–Waxman provided that the submission of an ANDA or 505(b)(2) application may be treated as (what the Supreme Court has characterized as) an "artificial act of infringement" for a drug claimed in a patent or the use of which is claimed in a patent (144). Thus, the patent statute was amended to specify that "[i]t shall be an act of infringement to submit . . . [an ANDA or 505(b)(2) application] . . . if the purpose of such submission is to obtain [FDA] approval ... to engage in the commercial manufacture, use, or sale of a drug ... claimed in a patent before the expiration of such patent" (145). The question of whether a Paragraph IV certification must be included in the ANDA or 505(b)(2) application to establish the statutory tort has been at issue in several cases (146).

In two separate cases (*Teva v. Abbott* and *Glaxo v. Apotex*), a Northern District of Illinois court held that the submission of an ANDA without a Paragraph IV certification was sufficient to be considered an artificial act of infringement and to establish subject matter jurisdiction (147). In so holding, the court relied on the language of §271(e)(2), which mentions neither patent certifications nor any other limitation on the type of ANDA that would suffice to establish infringement. Both of these cases involved antibiotics approved by FDA before November 21, 1997, which are exempt from *Orange Book* listing requirements (148).

However, in the recent Eisai litigation, a different district court, citing a number of prior interpretations of the statute by the Supreme Court and the Federal Circuit (149), read §271(e)(2) to require that an ANDA or 505(b)(2) application must contain a Paragraph IV certification to constitute an act of infringement (150). Based on that interpretation, the Eisai court dismissed Eisai's infringement suit since the allegedly infringed patent "was not listed in the Orange Book for the drug at issue [when the ANDA was filed] and the ANDA contained no Paragraph IV certification against the patent" (151).

Hatch–Waxman provides that a patent owner has 45 days after receiving notice of a Paragraph IV Certification to sue the ANDA [or 505(b)(2)] applicant for infringement (152). The applicant is required to notify FDA "immediately" upon the filing of suit within the 45-day period (153). If the patentee does not file an infringement action within the 45-day period, FDA may immediately approve the ANDA or 505(b)(2) application. If, on the other hand, the patent owner initiates suit, FDA cannot approve the application until the expiration of the 30-month stay for resolution of the litigation, as more fully set forth later (12).

Accordingly, upon receipt of notice of Paragraph IV Certifications, brand-name pharmaceutical companies frequently sue ANDA and 505(b)(2) applicants during the 45-day notice period, which forestalls generic competition in the marketplace for the 30-month period(s) sanctioned by Hatch–Waxman (154).

Scope and Jurisdiction of Infringement Actions Commenced Under 35 USC §271(e)(2)

The artificial act of infringement under 35 USC §271(e)(2) is limited to indications for which approval is sought. It is not an act of infringement under §271(e)(2) to submit an ANDA to market a listed drug for a different indication than an unapproved indication covered by a listed use patent (155).

NDA holders are authorized to list patents in the *Orange Book* which they believe "could reasonably be asserted ... [against an unlicensed party] engaged in the manufacture, use or sale of the drug" (156). In the past, ANDA or 505(b)(2) applicants could not seek patent delisting in infringement suits based on *Orange Book*–listed patents (157). A number of antitrust suits were commenced; however, they were predicated on the mala fides of *Orange Book* listings (158). Moreover, as indicated in Section "Challenges to Listing" earlier, an ANDA or 505(b)(2) filer sued on the basis of a Paragraph IV Certification may counterclaim for an order requiring the NDA holder to correct or delete the listing (50).

With respect to personal jurisdiction, it has been held that U.S. subsidiaries of foreign generic manufacturers actively involved in ANDA filings are subject to jurisdiction under §271(e)(2) (159). On the other hand, actions under that provision for infringement by third-party manufacturers that supply the active ingredients of generic drugs in issue in ANDAs have been dismissed (160).

Right of ANDA or 505(b)(2) Applicants to Seek Declaratory Judgments

Hatch–Waxman precludes an ANDA or 505(b)(2) applicant from initiating a declaratory judgment action for noninfringement or invalidity of a listed patent within the 45-day period after receipt of its notice of the factual and legal basis for its Paragraph IV Certification (161). This provision facilitates initial commencement of a patent infringement suit and the consequent 30-month stay in accordance with the statutory scheme.

On the other hand, it has been held that an ANDA or 505(b)(2) applicant may seek a declaratory judgment during the 45-day period on other grounds, or file a counterclaim in the infringement suit for a declaratory judgment that it is not infringing other, unlisted patents (162). In either instance, it need only be shown that there is an actual controversy between the parties.

The 2003 statutory changes further sanctioned the commencement of an action for declaratory judgment of noninfringement of a patent for which a Paragraph IV Certification has been made, provided that:

a) the NDA holder or patent owner did not file an infringement suit within 45 days after receiving notice of such certification; (163) and
b) in any case in which the notice from the ANDA or 505(b)(2) applicant asserts non-infringement, and the notice is accompanied by a document offering confidential access to the ANDA or 505(b)(2) application for the sole purpose of determining whether an infringement action should be brought (164). The document offering confidential access must contain such restrictions as to persons entitled to access, and the use and disposition of any information accessed as would apply had a protective order been entered to protect trade secrets and confidential business information. A request for access under an offer of confidential access is considered an acceptance of the terms and restrictions in the offer and creates an enforceable contract.

Any ANDA or 505(b)(2) application to which confidential access is provided may be redacted by the applicant to remove information not relevant to any issue of patent infringement.

Any action for declaratory judgment brought subject to the foregoing provisions must meet the case or controversy requirements of 28 USC §2201 (165), and can only be commenced in the judicial district in which the defendant has its principal place of business or a regular and established place of business (166).

The Congressional intent was to make a claim for declaratory judgment of noninfringement subject to the constitutional requirement for determining whether a "case or controversy" is presented sufficient to support jurisdiction. That test has been furthered by the Federal Circuit decision in *Teva v. Novartis* (167), applying the recent landmark Supreme Court decision in *MedImmune v. Genentech* (168).

In *Teva*, the court reversed the dismissal of a declaratory judgment action commenced by Teva, which had filed an ANDA certifying noninfringement of five *Orange Book*–listed Novartis patents and been sued for infringement of only one of those patents. Teva sought a declaratory judgment of noninfringement for the remaining four patents to establish "patent certainty." The Federal Circuit, relying on *MedImmune*, pointed out that:

> In *MedImmune*, the Supreme Court in a detailed footnote stated that our two-prong "reasonable apprehension of suit" test "conflicts" and would "contradict" several cases in which the Supreme Court found that a declaratory judgment plaintiff had a justiciable controversy. *127 S. Ct. at 774 n.11*. In *MedImmune*, the Court disagreed with our "reasonable apprehension of imminent suit" test and re-affirmed that the "actual controversy" requirement in the Declaratory Judgment Act is the same as the "Cases" and "Controversies" requirement in Article III. *Id. at 771*. The Court further re-affirmed that an "actual controversy" requires only that a dispute be "'definite and concrete, touching the legal relations of parties having adverse legal interests'; and that it be 'real and substantial' and 'admi[t] of specific relief through a decree of a conclusive character, as distinguished from an opinion advising what the law would be upon a hypothetical set of facts.'" (169)

Based thereon, the court reasoned that:

> Allowing Teva's declaratory judgment action is consistent with the "controversy" requirement in Article III and the Declaratory Judgment Act because the suit will achieve a final determination that resolves the entire dispute between Teva and Novartis. Teva has experienced real and actual injury. Consequently, Teva's injuries are traceable to Novartis' conduct and those injuries can be redressed by a favorable judicial decision. Therefore, Teva has established standing and an actual controversy sufficient to confer jurisdiction under the Declaratory judgment Act. (170)

The Teva court concluded:

> [A] declaratory judgment plaintiff is only required to satisfy Article III, which includes standing and ripeness, by showing under "all the circumstances" an actual or imminent injury caused by the defendant that can be redressed by judicial relief and that is of "sufficient immediacy and reality to warrant the issuance of a declaratory judgment." (171)

Accordingly, under the *Teva* case an ANDA filer may seek a declaratory judgment as to noninfringement of an *Orange Book*–listed patent which has not been asserted against it so long as it can establish a real and immediate dispute between it and the NDA holder/patent owner affecting its legal rights.

In *Pfizer v. Ranbaxy*, a district court granted, based on a covenant not to sue, a motion to dismiss a declaratory judgment action by the ANDA-filer Ranbaxy (172). The court found no valid patent to enforce due to the pending reissue patent (173). The court had no jurisdiction Hatch–Waxman because "(1) Pfizer cannot enforce a pending reissue application against Ranbaxy; (2) any reissued patent has not been listed in the FDA Orange Book and cannot be until it has issued, 21

USC §355(c)(2); and (3) Ranbaxy has not had to certify against a reissued patent" (174).

More recently, the Federal Circuit found a "substantial controversy" justifying declaratory judgment jurisdiction for an ANDA filer even where the NDA holder had granted the generic company a covenant not to sue on an *Orange Book*–listed patent (175). The Caraco case is instructive as to the complexity which may occur in Hatch–Waxman litigations. In Caraco, the first ANDA filer, Ivax, had been held to infringe one of Forest's two *Orange Book*–listed patents (the '712 patent). Forest did not sue Ivax for infringement of the other listed patent (the '941 patent), and Ivax had not sought declaratory relief as to noninfringement or invalidity of that patent (176). The court held that since Ivax could not trigger its 180-day exclusivity period before the expiration of both the '712 and '941 patents, subsequent Paragraph IV filers (including Caraco) could not trigger the exclusivity period (and thus expedite their own market entry) until both patents were held not infringed or invalid (177). Accordingly, notwithstanding Forest's covenant not to sue Caraco on the '941 patent, since Caraco's market entry was dependent on the conclusion of Ivax's exclusivity period, the court, citing *MedImmune,* held Caraco and Forest had a substantial legal controversy "of sufficient immediacy and reality to warrant the issuance of a declaratory judgment" (178).

Right of Patent Owners to Seek Declaratory Judgments

The courts have recognized that the *MedImmune* decision also affects the scope of a patent owner's right to seek declaratory relief in the face of imminent infringement, but have yet to define the "outer boundaries" of such jurisdiction (179). In activities outside the Hatch–Waxman sphere, the Federal Circuit has held that "where a patentee asserts rights under a patent based on certain identified ongoing or planned activity of another party, and where that party contends that it has the right to engage in the accused activity without license, an Article III case or controversy will arise" (180).

Where the safe harbor exemption under §271(e)(1) is in issue, however, the patent owners' rights are more limited. Thus, in *Eisai* the district court dismissed the patentees' declaratory judgment claim (181), holding that "activities protected by the safe harbor provision cannot serve as the basis for a declaratory judgment of actual future infringement" (182). The court dismissed the claim notwithstanding the ANDA applicant's assertion that it might launch the generic product at risk upon FDA approval and stipulation that it would provide Eisai with 45-day notice before commencing marketing (183). The court concluded that the "parties' stipulation allows sufficient time to resolve certain issues by way of an infringement action and a potential motion for preliminary relief, if Eisai so chooses" (184). How the court would have ruled in the absence of the stipulation is subject to conjecture.

DELAYS IN THE APPROVAL OF ANDAS AND 505(B)(2) APPLICATIONS

Patent-Related Delays

Delays Attributable to Patent Term Extensions

Delays in approval of ANDAs or 505(b)(2) applications may be prolonged because of extensions of the listed patents on which Paragraph IV Certifications must be made. Such extensions may result from patent term extensions under 35 USC §156 or because of the 20-year term provisions under the URAA.

Section 156 Term Adjustments

To be eligible for a term extension under Section 156, a patent relating to a drug product:

1. Must be in force when the application for term extension is filed in the U.S. Patent and Trademark Office, (185)
2. The term of the patent must not have been previously extended (186),
3. An application for the extension must be filed by the patent owner or its agent and must meet certain formal requirements, (187)
4. The drug product covered by the patent must have been subject to an FDA review period before its commercial marketing or use, (188) and
5. FDA approval for commercial marketing or use after such review period must be the first commercial marketing or use of the drug product (189).

The scope of any drug product patent extended under Section 156 shall, during the extension period, be limited to any "use approved for the product"

1. under FDA law (190) and
2. on or after the expiration of the review period on which the extension was based (191).

The period of term extension may not exceed 5 years (192), but may be shorter depending upon the delay in obtaining regulatory approval as determined by a specific calculation (193). Under this provision, the period of the extension is reduced by any delays in the regulatory review procedure attributable to the NDA applicant (194). In any case, the patent term may not be extended beyond 14 years from the date of approval of the NDA for the drug product (195).

The scope of a patent claiming a drug product is limited during the period of term extension to any FDA-approved use(s) and to drug products containing the approved active ingredient and salts and esters thereof (196).

URAA Extensions

The URAA conformed U.S. patent law with foreign law by providing that the term of a U.S. patent issued on or after June 8, 1995, extends 20 years from its effective filing date, rather than 17 years from its issue date. Thus, a patent issuing after June 8, 1995, claiming an effective U.S. filing date less than 3 years before its issue date is entitled to a term of 20 years from the effective filing date. On the other hand, a patent issued on an application filed after June 8, 1995, but claiming an effective filing date more than 3 years before its issue date, is entitled to the 20-year term from the effective filing date (and will thus be in force less than the original 17-year patent term from the issue date) (197). Accordingly, the effect of a prior listed patent on an ANDA or 505(b)(2) application may depend on its term under the URAA provisions.

The 30-Month Stay

When an ANDA or 505(b)(2) applicant certifies that the patent or patents listed in the *Orange Book* respecting the drug would not be infringed by the proposed generic drug product or that the patent or patents are invalid or unenforceable (a Paragraph

IV Certification), FDA will, if an infringement action is commenced by the patent owner or NDA holder within the 45-day notice period, defer approval for the 30-month stay period, as discussed later (12).

By delaying approval of an ANDA or 505(b)(2) application under which a generic applicant seeks to enter the market prior to expiration of a listed patent or patents, the stay provision protects the brand-name company's exclusive market-pending completion of the infringement litigation. At the same time, the 30-month stay enables the generic applicant to obtain a judicial determination of infringement and validity of any listed patents without incurring the liability it might otherwise risk were it marketing the generic drug and facing a possible award of damages based on the patent owner's lost profits. (In some cases, this potential liability could be more than the generic company's total revenue from the sales of its drug, in view of the typical differences in the prices and profits of brand-name and generic products.)

The "30-month stay" is in fact somewhat of a misnomer. Hatch–Waxman provides that if an infringement action is initiated during the 45-day notice period, approval of an ANDA or 505(b)(2) application is delayed until the earlier of expiration of the 30-month period, or the date of a district court decision holding the patent(s) invalid or not infringed (198). The 30-month stay may be modified, if before the expiration of that period the court hearing the infringement action determines that the patent is valid and infringed and grants an injunction (199), or determines that one of the parties has not reasonably cooperated in expediting the action (200).

If the ANDA or 505(b)(2) application is filed between the fourth and fifth years after approval of a drug product which received NCE exclusivity, the 30-month stay is extended to $7^1/_2$ years from the date of approval of the brand-name company's NDA (201).

Additionally, the 30-month stay is extended by 6 months where the drug product has received pediatric exclusivity (202).

The 2003 Statutory Changes simplified and restricted the grant of the 30-month stay. Thus, the stay may only be obtained with respect to patents listed in the *Orange Book* prior to the filing of the ANDA or 505(b)(2) application; no 30-month stay will be triggered as to any patents which are listed after the filing date of the ANDA or 505(b)(2) application (12).

180-Day Marketing Exclusivity for ANDAs

Hatch–Waxman provides a specific incentive to generic drug companies to file ANDAs seeking approval to market generic forms of listed drugs prior to expiration of brand-name companies' patents for such drugs, namely the right to 180-days of marketing exclusivity vis-à-vis later ANDA filers (13). There is no comparable exclusivity accorded a 505(b)(2) applicant who may successfully challenge the validity or infringement of an asserted listed patent. Interpretation of the 180-day exclusivity provision led to considerable controversy (and changes in agency positions), as discussed later.

Separate Exclusivity Periods for Different Dosage Forms and Different Listed Patents

Before the 2003 Statutory Changes, the Hatch–Waxman Act did not specify whether separate 180-day exclusivities would be accorded to independent ANDA applicants who may first make Paragraph IV Certifications for different dosage forms of the same listed drug, or to those independent Paragraph IV filers who may be the first to certify as to different listed patents for the same listed drug (203). FDA thus fashioned individual regulatory policies as to each of these situations.

Initially, the agency awarded separate 180-day exclusivity periods to different ANDA filers based upon the priority of their Paragraph IV Certifications respecting different strengths of the same listed drug. That policy was challenged and upheld as a reasonable exercise of the agency's discretion under the Administrative Procedures Act (APA) (204).

Similarly, neither the statute nor FDA regulations specifically provided for single or multiple exclusivities based upon priority of Paragraph IV Certifications as to multiple listed patents relating to a single drug. In one case, the agency interpreted its regulations to warrant separate exclusivity awards to two different generic applicants based on the priority of their Paragraph IV Certifications respecting two different listed patents (205). In a subsequent proceeding involving twelve listed patents, FDA decided that the award of independent exclusivity periods to either of two Paragraph IV filers would result in a blocking situation where neither party could be given approval until the other party's exclusivity as to certain patents had run. The agency decided that any 180-day exclusivity award would be shared between the two applicants (206). In yet another more recent case, FDA refused to provide any shared exclusivity where there was no possibility of blocking exclusivities (207).

The 2003 Statutory Changes eliminated the possibility of independent exclusivity periods for different generic applicants based on different listed patents. Only one 180-day exclusivity period may be obtained for a listed drug and that period is based on patents for which a Paragraph IV Certification is first made by any generic applicant (208). Under the amendments to the statute, multiple "first applicants" who submit substantially complete ANDAs with Paragraph IV Certifications on the same day and subsequently obtain approval of their applications are eligible for 180-day exclusivity (209). Pursuant to these amendments, multiple generic applicants frequently file ANDAs on the same day (210). These "first applicants" may obtain shared exclusivity during the one 180-day exclusivity period. FDA grants the 180-day exclusivity independently for each approved dosage form.

Commercial Marketing of the Generic Drug by a First Applicant Triggers the 180-Day Exclusivity

Prior to enactment of the 2003 Statutory Changes, Hatch–Waxman provided that the 180-day exclusivity provision would be triggered, inter alia, on the date FDA received notice of the first commercial marketing by any first ANDA applicant (211). This could occur (*i*) in the relatively rare instance in which an ANDA applicant commenced marketing after the 30-month stay and prior to a court decision in an infringement action predicated on its filing, (*ii*) where the owner of the listed patent had not sued for infringement, or (*iii*) where the ANDA applicant had agreed to market the listed drug pursuant to a settlement of infringement litigation (212). In one case relating to the last-mentioned situation, FDA had interpreted the statutory reference to "commercial marketing of the drug under the previous application" as embracing marketing by the ANDA applicant under license from the NDA holder after settlement of its litigation. Since more than 180 days had passed after commencement of such use, the agency concluded that the 180-day period had run and that other generic manufacturers could commence marketing. Upon attack under the APA, the court held that FDA's interpretation of the statutory language was reasonable and denied a preliminary injunction to the first filer (213).

The 180-day exclusivity period is only triggered by commercial marketing of the listed drug by any first ANDA applicant(s) (214). As pointed out in the next section, the decision of a court (on either the district court or appellate court level) does not directly trigger the 180-day exclusivity period, but may be the precursor of a "forfeiture event" for which the exclusivity period may be forfeited by the first applicant.

The Effect of a "Court Decision" on Approval of an ANDA and Triggering of the 180-Day Exclusivity

Prior to enactment of the 2003 Statutory Changes, the 180-day exclusivity could be effective, inter alia, on the "date of a decision of a court" in an infringement action based on a Paragraph IV Certification (215). FDA initially interpreted the date of the court decision as the date on which "the court ... enters final judgment from which no appeal can be or has been taken" (216). Subsequently, in response to a number of adverse court decisions the agency amended its rules to provide that with respect to ANDAs containing Paragraph IV Certifications filed after March 2000, a decision of a trial court would trigger the 180-day exclusivity (217). In later litigation in which a trial court held a patent invalid and the patent owner and generic applicant had subsequently entered into a settlement agreement, it was held that the 180-day exclusivity period was triggered by the trial court decision (218).

In yet another case, a court held that the 180-day exclusivity period would commence as of the date of a decision dismissing a declaratory judgment action for lack of subject matter jurisdiction where the plaintiff generic company lacked reasonable apprehension of a patent infringement suit (219). Such holding was inconsistent with a previously proposed FDA rule and caused the agency to withdraw the prior regulation (220). In its subsequently published notice, FDA was constrained to indicate that it would continue "to make 180-day exclusivity decisions on an issue-by-issue basis ... [and] will also carefully evaluate possible options for future rule making addressing 180-day exclusivity and the timing of ANDA approvals" (221).

Under the 2003 Statutory Changes, approval of an ANDA or 505(b)(2) application may be made effective on the date on which a district court enters a judgment holding the listed patent invalid or not infringed, permitting (but not requiring) subsequent commercial marketing. Based on such marketing, the 180-day exclusivity period may commence (222). However, FDA does not have power to enforce the 180-day exclusivity period (223).

The First ANDA Applicant(s) Making a Paragraph IV Certification is Awarded Exclusivity

Prior to enactment of the 2003 Statutory Changes, FDA regarded only the first applicant making a Paragraph IV Certification to be entitled to the 180-day exclusivity. In the event of an adverse decision in an infringement suit against the Paragraph IV applicant, FDA regulations provide that the applicant must amend its certification to a Paragraph III Certification indicating that it will not seek approval to market the generic product until the expiration of the listed patent (224). In its subsequently withdrawn August 1999 proposed rule, FDA suggested that only the first Paragraph IV filer could be eligible for the 180-day exclusivity and would lose such award if it amended its certification to a Paragraph III certification for any reason (225).

In one case in which the first filer amended its certification to a Paragraph III Certification after settlement with the patent holder, FDA asserted that the first filer retained its exclusivity, but the court found this "'best of all worlds'" interpretation in favor of the first filer to be "inconsistent with [the] purpose of Hatch-Waxman," and that the first filer's 180-day exclusivity period had already run (226). In a subsequent case, the first Paragraph IV filer settled its litigation with the patent holder, but did not amend its certification to a Paragraph III Certification. FDA concluded that it should treat the Paragraph IV Certification as though it had been changed to a Paragraph III Certification. The court disagreed, finding such construction unreasonable under the APA. The court did not reach the rights of the later filer because it found that the exclusivity period had run after the first filer had settled with the patent owner and commenced commercial marketing under the NDA.

In a further example of a disputed interpretation of the 180-day exclusivity provisions, FDA initially concluded that exclusivity could only be awarded to a Paragraph IV filer that had successfully prevailed in its litigation with the patent owner (227). Following multiple adverse court decisions, the agency issued a Guidance indicating that it would no longer enforce this "successful defense" requirement (228), and thereafter issued an interim rule removing the requirement (229). Further, it has been held that the first Paragraph IV filer may obtain exclusivity even when it is not sued based on the certification (230).

Under the 2003 Statutory Changes, the amendment by a first applicant of the Paragraph IV Certification for all of the patents for which it has submitted such a certification is a forfeiture event for which the first applicant will forfeit its 180-day exclusivity period (231).

Transfer or Waiver of Exclusivity

Prior to the 2003 Statutory Changes, the Hatch–Waxman Act did not provide that the 180-day exclusivity may be transferred from one Paragraph IV filer to another, or waived in favor of a subsequent filer. Nevertheless, FDA permitted transfer or waiver in particularly, complex factual contexts. Thus, the agency permitted a first Paragraph IV filer to waive its marketing exclusivity in favor of a subsequent filer where the exclusivity period had commenced and the first filer had not yet obtained agency approval and thus could not obtain the benefit of exclusivity (232).

More recently, FDA interpreted the statute to permit sharing the potential 180-day exclusivity where two Paragraph IV filers had differing priorities with respect to the multiple listed patents asserted by the prior NDA holder/patent owner (233). Subsequently, when the trial court held that the sharing applicants infringed various of the listed patents, FDA permitted waiver of the exclusivity in favor of a third filer whose generic product was held not to infringe the patents in question (234).

Forfeiture of Exclusivity

The 2003 Statutory Changes expressly provide that 180-day exclusivity may be forfeited based upon any of a number of distinct "forfeiture event(s)," and that in the event of such forfeiture no subsequent filer will be eligible for a 180-day exclusivity period (235).

The forfeiture provisions were adopted by Congress in an effort to halt the widespread practice of "ANDA parking" among innovators and first to file generics. In a typical "parking" arrangement, a first-to-file generic would agree with the innovator to delay entering the market until some time in the future, in effect "parking" the 180-day period of exclusivity. Such a "parking" agreement would not only delay market entry by the first-to-file generic, but also by any subsequent ANDA filer until after the exclusivity period, expiration of the patent, or a subsequent ANDA filer obtains a favorable appellate decision. "Parking" was particularly troublesome when the litigation between the first-to-file generic company and the innovator was settled without a court decision on the merits and the innovator did not commence litigation against subsequent ANDA filers.

The events defined in the 2003 Statutory Changes for which the first applicant may forfeit the 180-day exclusivity period include:

(I) The later of

(aa) its failure to market the drug 75 days after approval of its application (AA), or 30 months after filing of the application (BB), whichever is earlier; or

(bb) as to the first applicant or any other applicant that has received tentative approval of its application, at least one of the following has occurred:
75 days after a final decision or order in an infringement or declaratory judgment action holding the patent invalid or not infringed (AA);
a court has signed a settlement order or consent decree entering a final judgment that the patent is invalid or not infringed (BB); or the patent has been withdrawn from listing by the NDA holder (CC); (236)

(II) Its withdrawal of the application, or if FDA considers the application to have been withdrawn as a result of an administrative determination that the application did not meet the requirements for approval; (237)

(III) It amends or withdraws its Paragraph IV Certification; (238)

(IV) It fails to obtain tentative approval of its application within 30 months after filing; (239)

(V) It enters into an agreement with another ANDA applicant, the NDA holder, or the patent owner, which has been held in a final decision in an action brought by the Federal Trade Commission or Attorney General to violate the antitrust laws; (240) or

(VI) All of the patents as to which the ANDA filer had filed a Paragraph IV Certification have expired (241).

As provided in (I) earlier, forfeiture of the 180-day exclusivity period cannot be premised on the failure of the first applicant to market the drug within the 75-day period after its effective approval date or after 30 months of its application date, unless there has previously been, inter alia, a final decision that the patent is invalid or not infringed.

As noted earlier, in the event of any such forfeiture, no subsequent ANDA filer will be eligible for any 180-day exclusivity (234).

The impact of these antiparking provisions has been diluted by a 2008 FDA decision that Teva Parenteral Medicines had not forfeited its 180-day exclusivity period by failing to market the product at issue (granisetron) within 30 months of filing its ANDA because there had been no court decision or court-signed settlement order or consent decree adverse to the patent, and the patent had not been delisted from the *Orange Book* (242). The decision (in the form of a letter ruling from FDA dated January 17, 2008) provided that

> 180 day exclusivity is not forfeited for failure to market when an event under subpart (aa) has occurred, but—as in this case—none of the events in subpart (bb) has occurred. The 'failure to market' provision results in forfeiture when there are two dates on the basis of which FDA may identify the 'later' event as described in section 505(j)(5)(D)(i)(I). The provision does not affect a forfeiture when an event under subpart (aa) has occurred, but no event under subpart (bb) has yet occurred. (243)

Under this FDA ruling, the first filer will not forfeit its 180-day exclusivity period (even if 30 months have elapsed since the ANDA was filed with FDA by that filer), if there has not been an appellate court decision against the patent or the patent has not been removed from the *Orange Book*. This issue may be taken up by Congress and the courts in an effort to strengthen the exclusivity forfeiture provisions.

Delays in ANDA or 505(b)(2) Approvals Based on Marketing/Data Exclusivities

Hatch–Waxman contains several other exclusivity provisions which delay approval of ANDAs and 505(b)(2) applications. Of principal interest is the 5-year marketing exclusivity for NCEs (244), the 3-year marketing exclusivity for new or supplemental NDAs supported by new clinical investigations (245), and the 6-month exclusivity for pediatric studies.

With the exception of the pediatric exclusivity provisions, each of these marketing exclusivities was added to Hatch–Waxman in 1984 in last minute negotiations with a group of brand-name drug companies that objected to the terms originally negotiated prior to enactment of the legislation. These provisions were thus added to provide additional protection for the brand-name companies in the form of additional delays in the approval of generic drugs.

15-Year Exclusivity for New Chemical Entities

The 5-year NCE exclusivity applies to drugs which do not contain any active ingredient, including any ester or salt thereof, which has been approved in any prior NDA after the 1984 enactment of Hatch–Waxman.

The NCE exclusivity differs from the other marketing exclusivities in that it prohibits the submission of an ANDA or 505(b)(2) application—not merely its approval—prior to expiration of the exclusivity period (246). In view of the period required to obtain approval of the ANDA or 505(b)(2) application, this provision effectively extends NCE exclusivity beyond 5 years.

An ANDA or 505(b)(2) application incorporating a Paragraph IV Certification may be submitted 4 years after approval of an NDA entitled to NCE exclusivity. However, if an infringement action is commenced within the fifth year of the NCE exclusivity, the statute provides that the 30-month stay pending the patent infringement proceeding will be extended, if necessary, so that the period after approval of the application entitled to NCE exclusivity totals $7^1/_2$ years, equal to the sum of the 5-year marketing exclusivity and the 30-month stay (247). Thus, an ANDA or 505(b)(2) application incorporating a Paragraph IV Certification may be filed within the fifth year of an NCE marketing exclusivity, but may not be approved until $7^1/_2$ years after the grant of the application entitled to NCE exclusivity, if the brand-name patent holder initiates an infringement suit as discussed earlier.

FDA interprets the term NCE as referring to the "active moiety" of the previously approved NDA, that is, the molecule or ion (excluding the groups which form an ester or salt or other noncovalent derivative of the molecule) which is responsible for the physiological or pharmacological action of the drug (248). According to FDA, a prodrug which is not a salt or ester of a previously approved product is an NCE and entitled to 5-year exclusivity (249). Similarly, FDA has considered metabolites, which are not salts or esters of previously approved drugs as NCEs (250).

For many years, optically pure enantiomers (251) of previously approved racemates (252) could qualify only for 3-year exclusivities for new clinical investigations of previously approved active drug moieties, and not for 5-year NCE exclusivities (253). However, under the Food and Drug Administration Amendments Act of 2007 (FDAAA), an applicant for an NDA for an enantiomer of a previously approved racemate (or an ester or salt thereof) may obtain an NCE exclusivity for the enantiomer under certain specified conditions.

First, the applicant for the enantiomer NDA must "elect to have the single enantiomer not be considered the same active ingredient as that contained in the approved racemic drug" (254). Further, the enantiomer NDA must not be for a use (*i*) in a therapeutic category in which the approved racemic drug has been approved, or (*ii*) for which any other enantiomer of the racemic drug has been approved (255).

Where the enantiomer NDA holder receives exclusivity, FDA may not approve the enantiomer for use in the therapeutic category in which the racemate was approved until 10 years after approving the enantiomer NDA (256).

Under the new provision, an ANDA applicant may thus be subject to both a 5-year delay in obtaining approval for use of the enantiomer in the distinct therapeutic category in which the enantiomer NCE has been approved and a 10-year delay in obtaining approval of the enantiomer in the therapeutic category in which the racemate NCE was originally approved. Future litigation relating to this provision is likely.

This provision of the FDAAA is effective as to enantiomer NDAs filed between September 27, 2007 and October 1, 2012 (257).

3-Year Exclusivities for NDAs or Supplemental NDAs Based on New Clinical Investigations

The 3-year exclusivity provisions prohibit approval—not submission—of an ANDA or a 505(b)(2) application for 3 years after approval of an NDA or supplemental NDA approved on the basis of "reports of new clinical investigations (other than bioavailability studies) essential to the approval . . . and conducted or sponsored by the person submitting the NDA or supplemental NDA" (258).

Pediatric Exclusivity

In 1997, 2002, and again in 2007, the FDCA was amended to provide a 6-month exclusivity period for conducting pediatric studies of listed drugs (259). The pediatric exclusivity delays the approval of ANDAs and 505(b)(2) applications for an additional 6 months after expiration of any pertinent listed patents, and extends the 5-year and 3-year marketing exclusivities for 6 months (260). The pediatric exclusivity was originally effective as to NDAs filed before January 1, 2002, and, as of this writing, has been extended to NDAs submitted prior to October 1, 2012 (261).

Pediatric exclusivity applies both to previously approved drugs and drugs which are the subject of pending NDAs. The procedures for obtaining pediatric exclusivity are described elsewhere in this text.

If a 6-month pediatric exclusivity has been accorded to a particular drug, an additional 6-month exclusivity may be added to the 3-year exclusivity for a supplemental NDA (262). A second 6-month pediatric exclusivity may not, however, further delay ANDA approvals subject to patent certifications (263). The omission of any approved pediatric indication from the labeling for an ANDA will not further delay approval of the generic drug (264).

The immense financial consequences of the expiration of marketing exclusivities to both brand-name and generic drug companies accounts for the complexity and intensity of recent confrontations respecting the right to market major drug products. These were no more evident than in the disputes respecting the final days of pediatric exclusivities on AstraZeneca's omeprazole proton pump inhibitor (Prilosec) and Pfizer's amlodipine besylate antihypertensive (Norvasc).

The Revocation of Approval to Market Apotex's Generic Omeprazole

In litigation involving Apotex, FDA revoked the prior approval of Apotex's generic omeprazole based on AstraZeneca's pediatric exclusivity, notwithstanding Apotex's more than 3 years prior marketing of the generic drug product (265). The pertinent facts were as follows:

December 5, 2002	Apotex filed an ANDA
October 6, 2003	FDA granted final approval of Apotex's ANDA
October 6, 2003	Apotex commenced marketing its generic product
April 20, 2007	Astra's patents for Prilosec expired
June 14, 2007	District court held the Apotex product infringed AstraZeneca's patents and that pediatric exclusivity applied, until October 20, 2007
June 28, 2007	FDA revoked Apotex's final approval of its ANDA
June 28–October 20, 2007	Apotex precluded from marketing

Notwithstanding Apotex's prior marketing of its generic omeprazole product and the district court's holding of infringement after expiration of the AstraZeneca patents, Apotex was precluded from marketing for 4 months because of the pediatric exclusivity.

Mylan's 180-Day Exclusivity to Market Generic Amlodipine

In a complex series of events Mylan extended its generic exclusivity on amlodipine besylate vis-à-vis Apotex and other generic marketers based on Pfizer's pediatric exclusivity, notwithstanding Apotex's success in invalidating the Pfizer patent. The unique chronology respecting Mylan's and Apotex's ANDAs was as follows:

Date	Mylan	Apotex
11/27/01	Pediatric exclusivity for Norvasc granted	
5/02	ANDA filed with Paragraph IV Certification (first Filer)	
9/20/02	Infringement suit filed (30-mo stay inapplicable) (266)	
4/13/03		ANDA filed
7/30/03		Infringement suit filed
10/3/05	ANDA approved	
1/24/06		D.Ct. held patent valid and infringed (267)
3/16/07	D.Ct. held patent valid and infringed, and enjoined approval of ANDA until after patent expiration (268)	
3/22/07		Fed Cir Reversed D.Ct., holding Pfizer patent invalid (269)
3/23/07	Fed Cir stayed injunction, Mylan began marketing its product and asserted that 180-day exclusivity commenced (270)	
3/25/07	Patent expired	
4/18/07	FDA held Mylan's 180-day marketing exclusivity expired when patent expired; Apotex's ANDA blocked by pediatric exclusivity until mandate issued on Fed Cir decision (271)	
5/21/07	Fed Cir mandate issued; generic marketing possible	
5/23/07		ANDA approved
6/22/07	FDA delists Pfizer's patent for Norvasc (272)	

The above are but a few of the multiple legal proceedings initiated in efforts to obtain or maintain exclusive marketing rights in amlodipine besylate. Mylan was the first to file a paragraph IV ANDA, which normally would reserve the 180-day exclusivity period for Mylan. The district court, however, found the Pfizer patent valid and infringed. Apotex, meanwhile, had filed suit to obtain approval of its ANDA and also lost at the district court. On Apotex's appeal to the Federal Circuit, the court invalidated Pfizer's patent.

Although Apotex was the successful party, Mylan received de facto exclusivity because it was the first to file its ANDA. Apotex's ANDA remained blocked by Pfizer's pediatric exclusivity until the Federal Circuit issued its mandate.

The above table illustrates the application and limitations of the patent and 180-day and pediatric marketing exclusivities. Before FDA delisted Pfizer's patent from the *Orange Book* on June 22, Mylan and Apotex had the only approved ANDAs for generic Norvasc. Subsequent to June 22, numerous generics received FDA approval and entered the market.

FDA Procedures for Resolving Marketing Exclusivity Issues

Beginning in 2007, FDA began soliciting public comments on a case-by-case basis for marketing exclusivity issues that it was unprepared to resolve (273). After expiration of the public comment period, FDA issues a written decision available with the comments submitted by third parties on a public docket (274).

In the case of amlodipine besylate, Mylan sued FDA before it determined whether Mylan was entitled to a 180-day exclusivity period. FDA informed the court that it proposed to seek public comments from interested parties and subsequently issue a determination. The court agreed to FDA's proposal and enjoined FDA from approving any ANDAs until a few days after FDA's determination to provide the court with sufficient time to review the determination (275).

WITHDRAWAL OF APPROVAL OF AN ANDA

As indicated in Section "Removal of *Orange Book* Listing of a Drug" earlier, FDA may withdraw or suspend approval of an ANDA when the approval of the listed drug on which the ANDA relies is either withdrawn or suspended. Further, approval of an ANDA or a 505(b)(2) application may be withdrawn on the basis of evidence showing that the drug is unsafe for use or ineffective, or that the ANDA or 505(b)(2) application contains any untrue statement of material fact (81). A further provision sanctioning the withdrawal of approval of ANDAs was added by the Generic Drug Enforcement Act of 1992. That amendment specifically provides that FDA must withdraw approval of an ANDA if it finds that the approval "was obtained, expedited, or otherwise facilitated through bribery, payment of an illegal gratuity, or fraud or material false statement" (276), or may withdraw approval of an ANDA if it finds that the applicant has "repeatedly demonstrated a lack of ability to produce the drug . . . and has introduced, or attempted to introduce, such adulterated or misbranded drug into commerce" (277).

CITIZEN PETITIONS

FDA states that the appropriate procedure for challenging any of its actions is the filing of a "citizen petition," a written request that FDA take specific action (278) in accordance with its regulations (279).

Citizen petitions frequently urge FDA to impose additional requirements for the approval of ANDAs and 505(b)(2) applications. In the past, FDA delays in deciding such petitions have resulted in corresponding delays in ANDA and 505(b)(2) approvals and consequent generic competition. For a number of years assertions were made that a number of citizen petitions had been filed for frivolous purposes and were an abuse of the administrative process, prompting proposed FDA action (280).

The recent FDAAA addresses possible abuses of the citizen petition process, providing that citizen petitions will not delay approval of a pending ANDA or 505(b)(2) application unless FDA determines that a delay is necessary to protect public health (281).

Citizen petitions submitted to FDA must include a certification substantiating the bona fides of the petition, including an identification of the date the petitioner became aware of the basis for the petition and the persons from whom any consideration was or would be received respecting the petition (282).

Under FDAAA, the agency must take final action on all citizen petitions within 180 days after their submission (283). The petition may be denied if FDA determines it "was submitted with the primary purpose of delaying the approval of an application and the petition does not on its face raise valid scientific or regulatory issues" (284). Alternatively, if FDA determines that public health concerns necessitate delay of generic drug approval, then FDA must provide its reasons to the generic applicant within 30 days of making such a determination. Specifically, FDA must provide a brief summary of the substantive issues raised in the petition that form the basis of its determination and, if applicable, any clarification or additional data that the generic applicant should submit to expedite FDA's review of the citizen petition (285).

Where the approval of an ANDA filed by a first applicant eligible for 180-day exclusivity is delayed as the result of a citizen petition covered under the FDAAA, the deadline for obtaining approval or tentative approval of the ANDA to avoid forfeiture of the 180-day exclusivity is extended. The period of the extension is "equal to the period beginning on the date on which [FDA] received the petition and ending on the date of final agency action on the petition (inclusive of such beginning and ending dates), without regard to whether [FDA] grants, in whole or in part, or denies, in whole or in part, the petition." (287). Thus, a first applicant whose ANDA is delayed as a result of a petition will not automatically forfeit eligibility for 180-day exclusivity if tentative approval is not obtained within 30 months after the date on which the application is filed (288).

A party dissatisfied with FDA's action on a citizen petition may seek judicial review in district court. FDA contends that the petitioner must first obtain a final decision on a citizen petition before it seeks judicial relief, and will raise the exhaustion of administrative remedies defense in any lawsuit not preceded by the determination of a citizen petition (289).

REFERENCES AND NOTES

1. Pub L No. 98–417, 98 Stat. 1585, Federal Food, Drug, and Cosmetic Act (FDCA), Human Drug Approval Provisions, FDCA §505, 21 USC §355. Provisions similar to those discussed herein have been enacted for the approval of animal drugs in the Generic Animal Drug and Patent Term Restoration Act of 1988, Pub L No. 100–670, 102 Stat. 3971 (1988). The animal drug approval provisions are outside the scope of this discussion.
2. *Glaxo, Inc. v. Novopharm, Ltd.*, 110 F3d 1562, 1568 (Fed Cir 1997) (quoting H R Rep. No. 98–857 (I), at 14–15 (1984), reprinted in 1984 U.S.C.C.A.N. 2647, 2647–48).
3. IMS 2007 U.S. Pharmaceutical Market Performance Review, http://www.imshealth.com/ims/portal/front articleC/027776599_3665_83470499,00.html (last viewed Apr. 8, 2008); July 2002 U.S. Federal Trade Commission (FTC) Report, "Generic Drug Entry Prior to Patent Expiration: An FTC Study" (the July 2002 FTC Report), page i and 9 [citing "How Increased Competition from Generic Drugs Has Affected Prices and Returns in the Pharmaceutical Industry," Congressional Budget Office (July 1998) at 31].
4. FDCA §505(j), codified at 21 USC §355(j). For convenience, 21 USC §355, et seq. are referred to herein by the appropriate FDCA sections, namely §§505 et seq.
5. A generic drug is "bioequivalent" to a previously approved drug if the extent and rate of absorption of the respective drugs do not differ significantly from one another. FDCA §505(j)(8)(B).
6. FDCA §505(b)(2).
7. Pub L No. 98–417, Title II (1984), and Pub L No. 100–670, Title II (1988) (creating 35 USC §156, and amending 35 USC. §§271 and 282).
8. Pub L No. 103–465, 108 Stat. 4809 (1994), the Uruguay Round Agreements Act (URAA).

9. 35 USC §271(e)(1). In its latest interpretation of the scope of the exemption, the Federal Circuit has held that §271(e)(1) does not preclude patent infringement by drug development activities "far beyond those necessary to acquire information for FDA approval of a patented pioneer drug already on the market." *Integra Life Sciences I, Ltd. v. Merck KGaA*, 331 F3d 860, 867 (Fed Cir June 6, 2003).
10. FDCA §505(j)(2)(A)(vii), (viii), [ANDAs]; and §505(b)(2)(A)(iv) [§505(b)(2) applications]. The "Orange Book" was so named because it was published by the FDA with orange covers.
11. FDCA §505(j)(2)(A)(vii)(IV) [ANDAs]; 21 Code of Federal Regulations ("CFR") 314.94(a)(12)(i)(A)(4), [ANDAs]; and FDCA §505(b)(2)(A)(iv) [§505(b)(2) applications]. Under the FDA's 2003 modified regulations (the "2003 Rule Changes" herein) discussed later, the notice requirements were not required for all Paragraph IV certifications, in order to provide only a single 30-month stay per listed drug product (see Section 10.1.2 later). The regulatory changes were nullified in this respect in the 2003 statutory amendment to 21 USC §355 under the Medicare Prescription Drug Improvement and Modernization Act of 2003 ("MPDIMA"), Title XI Access to Affordable Pharmaceuticals (the "2003 Statutory Changes" herein). The amended statute requires the notice with all Paragraph IV Certifications, whether made in generic drug applications or in amendments or supplements to such applications. For convenience, the amended statutory sections, 21 USC §355, et seq. are referred to herein by the appropriate FDCA Sections, namely §505, et seq., and by their proposed MPDIMA Sections.
12. FDCA §505(j)(5)(B)(iii); amended by MPDIMA §1101(a)(2)(A) [ANDAs]; and §505(c)(3)(C) amended by MPDIMA §1101(b)(2)(B) [§505(b)(2) applications].
13. FDCA §505(j)(5)(B)(iv) [ANDAs] amended by MPDIMA §1102(a) (1)(iv)(I); there is no comparable exclusivity period for the first filer of a section 505(b)(2) application.
14. FDCA §505(j)(5)(D)(ii) amended by MPDIMA §1101(a)(2)(B) [ANDAs]; and §505(c)(3)(D)(ii) amended by MPDIMA §1101(b)(2)(C) [section 505(b)(2) applications].
15. FDCA §505(j)(5)(D)(iii) and (iv) amended by MPDIMA §1101(a)(2)(B) [ANDAs]; and §505(c)(3)(D)(iii) amended by MPDIMA §1101(b)(2)(C) [section 505(b)(2) applications].
16. 21 USC §360bb and §360 cc(a).
17. FDCA §505(a), (b), and (c).
18. July 2002 FTC Report, pp. 6, 8.
19. FDCA §§505(b)(1) and (c)(2).
20. FDCA §§505(b)(1) and (c)(2); and 21 CFR §314.94(a)(12)(B)(vi).
21. 21 CFR §314.53 (c)(2)(i), (ii).
22. FDCA §505(j)(2)(A)(vii) [ANDAs]; and §505(b)(2)(A) [505(b)(2) applications].
23. 21 CFR §314.94(a)(12)(B)(vi) [ANDAs]; and 21 CFR §314.52(d) [505(b)(2) applications]. Under the 2003 Statutory Changes an ANDA or 505(b)(2) applicant must give notice to the patent holder within 20 days from the date the FDA acknowledges filing of the ANDA or 505(b)(2) application, or at the time at which the applicant submits an amendment or supplement to the application. FDCA §(j)(2)(B)(ii) amended by §1101 (a)(1)(A)[ANDAs]; and FDCA §505(b)(3)(B) amended by MPDIMA §1101(b)(1)(A) [505(b)(2) applications].
24. 21 CFR 314.94(a)(12)(B)(vi); *Abbott Labs., Inc. v. Zenith Labs., Inc.*, 35 U.S.P.Q.2 d 1161 (N.D. Ill. 1995) (dismissing claim for patent infringement where plaintiff failed to list patent within 30-day period after issuance of patent).
25. FDCA §505(c)(3)(C); FDCA §505(j)(5)(B)(iii).
26. *Eisai Co., Ltd. v. Mutual Pharmaceutical Co., Inc.*, 2007 U.S. Dist. LEXIS 93585 (D.N.J. Dec. 20, 2007) (Not for Publication).
27. *Id.* at *12.
28. *Id.* at *15–18.
29. *Id.* at *15.
30. 21 CFR §314.53(b).
31. 21 CFR §§314.53(e) and 314.3(b).
32. See October 24, 2002 proposed FDA rulemaking, "Applications for FDA Approval to Market a New Drug: Patent Listing Requirements and Application of 30-Month Stays on

Approval of Abbreviated New Drug Applications Certifying That a Patent Claiming a Drug is Invalid or Will Not Be Infringed," 21 CFR Part 314 [Docket No. 02N-0417], RIN 0910-AC48 section II A.

33. 59 Fed Reg 50338, 50343 (Oct. 3, 1994) ("The agency believes that its scarce resources would be better utilized in reviewing applications rather than reviewing patent claims.").
34. 21 CFR §314.53(f); Abbreviated New Drug Application Regulations, 54 Fed Reg 28872, 28910 (July 10, 1989) ("In deciding whether a claim of patent infringement could reasonably be asserted ... the agency will defer to the information submitted by the NDA applicant."); see also *AaiPharma v. Thompson*, 296 F3d 227 (4th Cir 2000); and *Watson Pharms., Inc. v. Henney*, 194 F Supp 2d 442, 445 (D.Md. 2001).
35. 21 CFR §314.53(b) (2003). As used in the rule, polymorphs "include chemicals with different crystalline structures, different waters of hydration, solvates, and amorphous forms." 68 Fed Reg 36676, 36678 (June 18, 2003).
36. 68 Fed Reg 36676, 36678 (June 18, 2003).
37. 21 CFR §314.53(b), (c) (2003). The categories include:

    (i) a full description of the polymorphic form, including its physical and chemical characteristics and stability; its synthesis; the process controls used during manufacture and packaging; and such specifications and analytical methods as necessary to assure its identity, strength, quality and, purity;
    (ii) the executed batch record for a drug product containing the polymorph and documentation that the batch was manufactured under GMP conditions;
    (iii) demonstration of bioequivalence between the executed batch of the drug product containing the polymorph and the drug product described in the NDA;
    (iv) a list of all components used in the manufacture of the polymorph-containing drug product and a statement of the composition of the drug product; a statement of the specifications and analytical methods for each component as are necessary to demonstrate pharmaceutical equivalence and comparable product stability; and
    (v) comparative in vitro dissolution testing on 12 dosage units, the executed test batch and NDA product. 68 Fed. Reg. 36676, 36679 (June 18, 2003).

38. As used in the rules, a product-by-process patent is one which "claims a product by describing or listing process steps to wholly or partially define the claimed product." 68 Fed Reg 36676, 36679 (June 18, 2003). Under U.S. patent law, a product-by-process patent claim is directed to the product, i.e., is a "product claim" but defines the product by reference to the steps used to make the product.
39. 68 Fed Reg 36676, 36680 (June 18, 2003).
40. The Food and Drug Modernization Act of 1997, Pub L No. 105–115, 111 Stat. 2296, §125(d)(2)(ii); *Proposed Rule: Marketing Exclusivity and Patent Provisions for Certain Antibiotic Drugs*, 65 Fed Reg 3623, 3624 (Jan. 24, 2000); *Guidance for Industry and Reviewers: Repeal of Section 507 of the Federal Food, Drug, and Cosmetic Act*, revised May 1998, p. 2.
41. 21 CFR §314.53(b) (2003).
42. The FDA lists current dosage forms which may be listed as including metered aerosols, capsules, metered sprays, gels, and prefilled drug delivery systems. 68 Fed Reg 36676, 36680 (June 18, 2003).
43. 68 Fed Reg 36676, 36680 (June 18, 2003).
44. *Id.*
45. *Id.*
46. See *Mylan Pharms., Inc. v. Thompson*, 268 F3d 1323 (Fed Cir 2001), *cert. denied*, 123 S. Ct. 340 (2002); and *Andrx v. Biovail Corp.*, 276 F3d 1368 (Fed Cir 2002).
47. See *Mylan*, 268 F3d at 1329 and 1333, n. 3; and *Andrx*, 276 F3d at 1379, n. 8. Subsequently, in *AaiPharma v. Thompson*, 296 F3d at 235–43, the Court of Appeals for the Fourth Circuit held that FDA's "purely ministerial approach" to *Orange Book* listing was not arbitrary and capricious under the Administrative Procedure Act (APA), but approved of antitrust actions brought against NDA holders who use improper *Orange Book* listings to extend monopoly power. 296 F3d at 243.
48. 68 Fed Reg 36676, 36684 (June 18, 2003).

49. 68 Fed Reg 36676 (June 18, 2003).
50. MPDIMA §1101(a)(2)(C)(ii)[ANDAs]; and MPDIMA §1101(b)(2)(D)(ii)[505(b)(2) applications].
51. *Mylan Laboratories v. Leavitt*, 495 F Supp 2d 43 (D.D. C. 2007).
52. *Id.* at 45.
53. *Id.* at 46.
54. *Id.* at 49.
55. FDCA §505(j)(2) and (4).
56. FDCA §505(j)(7).
57. FDCA §505(j)(7)(A)(ii).
58. 54 Fed Reg 28872 (July 10, 1989).
59. FDCA §505(j)(2)(A).
60. FDCA §505(j)(2)(A)(i).
61. FDCA §505(j)(2)(A)(v).
62. 21 CFR §314.70.
63. 21 CFR §314.94(a)(8)(iv). See *Bristol-Myers Squibb Co. v. Shalala*, 91 F3d 1493, 1496 (DC Cir 1996). (Bristol-Myers Squibb's complaint seeking to enjoin the FDA from approving an ANDA for captopril which omitted an approved indication for treating diabetic nephropathy was remanded to the trial court with instructions to dismiss.)
64. FDCA §505(j)(2)(A)(ii)(I).
65. FDCA §505(j)(2)(A)(ii)(I), (II), and (III).
66. FDCA §505(j)(2)(A)(iv).
67. FDCA §505(j)(8)(B).
68. FDCA §505(j)(8)(A)(ii) amended by MPDIMA §1103(a)(1); FDCA §505(j)(8)(c) amended by MPDIMA §1103(a)(2); *Schering Corp. v. Sullivan*, 782 F Supp 645 (D.D. C. 1992), vacated for mootness, 995 F2d 1103 (DC Cir 1993); *Schering Corp. v. FDA*, 51 F3d 390 (3rd Cir 1995); and *Fisons Corp. v. Shalala*, 860 F Supp 859 (D.D. C. 1994).
69. In Fisons, 860 F Supp at 866, the court approved an FDA regulation permitting the waiver of a specific type of in vivo testing for categories of drugs where in vivo bioequivalence was self-evident based on other bioequivalence data in the application.
70. FDCA §505(j)(4)(H).
71. 21 CFR §314.127(a)(8)(ii)(A)(1)-(7) (1997).
72. FDCA §505(j)(2)(C).
73. FDCA §505(j)(2(C)(i).
74. FDCA §505(j)(2)(A)(iv).
75. FDCA §505(j)(2)(A)(ii).
76. FDCA §505(j)(2)(C)(i) and (ii).
77. 21 CFR §314.93.
78. FDCA §505(j)(2)(C); and 21 CFR §314.93(e).
79. FDCA §505(j)(7)(C).
80. FDCA §505(j)(4)(I); and 21 CFR §314.127(a)(9) and (a)(11) (1997).
81. FDCA §505(e).
82. 21 CFR §314.151(b)(2).
83. 21 CFR §314.151(c)(7); and 21 CFR §314.150(a)(1).
84. 21 CFR §314.150(c)(7).
85. FDCA §505(b)(2); the "Right of Reference or Use" simply refers to approval by the prior party, generally the NDA holder, to the generic applicant to refer to or use its prior safety or efficacy investigations. 21 CFR 314.3(b). When such a "Right of Reference or Use" is relied upon by a 505(b)(2) applicant, it is required to provide in its application a written statement by the owner of the data from each such investigation that the applicant may rely on such data in support of the application and that it will provide the FDA access to the underlying raw data supporting the report of the investigation. 21 CFR 314.50(g)(3).
86. Draft Guidance For Industry Applications Covered by §505(b)(2), Center for Drug Evaluation and Research, October 1999.
87. For example,505(b)(2) Application No. 021–435 filed by Dr. Reddy's Laboratories for approval of amlodipine maleate, relying on data submitted by Pfizer in its NDA for amlodipine besylate (NORVASC®).

88. Citizen petition by Pfizer Inc. and Pharmacia Corporation, No. 01P-0323 (filed July 27, 2001), and Amendment to Citizen Petition (Apr. 4, 2002); and Pfizer Inc. Citizen petition dated October 11, 2002.
89. FDCA §505(b)(2)(A) and (3).
90. 21 CFR §314.101(d)(9).
91. 21 CFR §314.3.
92. FDCA §505(j)(4)(C)(i).
93. See Note (14), supra; and 21 §CFR 314.108(b)(2).
94. FDCA §505(j)(4)(A) [ANDAs]; and §505(d)(1) [505(b)(2) applications].
95. FDCA §505(j)(5)(A) [ANDAs]; and §505(c)(1) [505(b)(2) applications].
96. 21 CFR §314.127 [ANDAs]; and 21 CFR 314.125 [505(b)(2) applications]. Notwithstanding the theoretical opportunity for a hearing, the FDA may deny a hearing if it concludes there are no material factual issues to be determined.
97. FDCA §505(j)(5)(C) amended by MPDIMA §1101(a)(2)(B) [ANDAs]; and §505(c)(1) [505(b)(2) applications].
98. *Apotex, Inc. v. FDA*, 508 F Supp 2d 78 (D.D. C. Sept. 17, 2007).
99. FDCA §505(b)(2)(A); FDCA §505(j)(2)(A)(vii).
100. See *Merck & Co., Inc. v. Danbury Pharmacal, Inc.*, 694 F Supp 1 (D. Del. 1988), *aff'd*, 873 F2d 1418 (Fed Cir 1989); 21 CFR §314.94 (a)(12)(i)(A)(4).
101. 21 CFR §314.94(a)(12)(ii); the regulations specify that this certification be in the following form: In the opinion and to the best knowledge of (name of applicant), there are no patents that claim the listed drug referred to in this application or that claim a use of the listed drug.A certification to substantially the same effect is required with respect to 505(b)(2) applications. 21 CFR 314.50(i)(1)(i)(B)(ii).
102. FDCA §505(j)(2)(B)(i) amended by MPDIMA §1101(a)(1)(A) [ANDAs]; and §505(b)(3) amended by MPDIMA §1101(b)(1)(A) [505(b)(2) applications]; 21 CFR §314.95(a)(1).
103. 21 CFR §§314.52(c)(1) and 314.95(c)(1).
104. FDCA §505(j)(2)(B)(ii) amended by MPDIMA §1101(a)(1)(A) [ANDAs]; FDCA §505(b)(3)(B) amended by MPDIMA §1101(b)(1)(A) [505(b)(2) applications].
105. FDCA §505(j)(2)(B)(iv)(II); FDCA §505(b)(3)(D)(ii).
106. 21 CFR §314.95(c)(6) and (i); and 21 CFR §314.94 (a)(12)(i)(A)(4).
107. 21 CFR §314.95(c)(2)-(5).
108. FDCA §505(j)(2)(B), amended by MPDIMA, §1101(a)(1)(A) [ANDAs], and FDCA §505(b)(3)(B) amended by MPDIMA §1101(b)(1)(A) [505(b)(2) applications].
109. FDCA §505(j)(2)(B)(ii) amended by MPDIMA §1101(a)(1)(A) [ANDAs], and FDCA §505(b)(3)(B), amended by MPDIMA §1101 (b)(1)(A)[505(b)(2) applications]. The prior law had no time limit. This raised issues as to the effective filing date of an ANDA, Paragraph IV, and who was the first to file for the purpose of awarding 180 days of market exclusivity. In a suit filed by Purepac against FDA on October 29, 2003 in the District of Columbia, Purepac alleged that it was entitled to first-to-file status because a Paragraph IV certification in an original ANDA is deemed effectively submitted on the date it is received by the FDA and that the date of notification to the patent holder is irrelevant. "The Pink Sheet," Vol. 65, No. 46, p. 12 (Nov. 17, 2003). In this instance, FDA awarded first-to-file status to Ivax based upon its original ANDA with a Paragraph IV certification, submitted one day prior to Purepac's notice to the NDA holder of its amended ANDA with a Paragraph IV certification. "The Pink Sheet," Vol. 65, No. 46, p. 12 (Nov. 17, 2003). Purepac later withdrew its action against the FDA and agreed to share 180-day exclusivity with Ivax. "The Pink Sheet," Vol. 65, No. 48, p. 17 (Dec. 1, 2003).
110. 21 CFR §314.95(f); and FDCA §505(j)(5)(B)(iii). FDA requires the ANDA applicant to provide it with a return receipt or other evidence of the date of receipt of the notice by the patent owner and NDA holder. 21 CFR §314.95(e).
111. In *AstraZeneca AB v. Mutual Pharm. Co.*, 221 F Supp 2d 528 (E.D.Pa. 2002), the court denied such relief, holding that the ANDA applicant's notice was sufficient in that it alerted the patent owner to the applicant's claim of noninfringement. However, in three other cases courts have held that insufficient notices could ultimately be relied upon in litigation in support of an award of attorney's fees for willful infringement. *Yamanouchi Pharm. Co. Ltd. v. Danbury Pharmacal, Inc.*, 231 F3d 1339, 1347–48 (Fed Cir 2000); *Eli*

Lilly & Co. v. Zenith Goldline Pharms., Inc., 2001 WL 1397304, at *25–26 (S.D. Ind. Oct. 29, 2001); *Takeda Chem. Indus., Ltd. v. Mylan Labs., Inc.*, 459 F Supp 2d 227 (S.D. N.Y. 2006).

112. FDCA §505(j)(2)(A)(viii) [ANDAs]; FDCA §505(b)(2)(B) [505(b)(2) applications]; and 21 CFR 314.94(a)(12)(iii).
113. See Patent Provisions Rulemaking, 59 Fed Reg 50338, 50345 (Oct. 3, 1994) ("FDA does not have the resources to review patent information for its accuracy and relevance to an NDA."); Proposed ANDA Rules, 54 Fed Reg 28872, 28909 (July 10, 1989) ("because the FDA has no experience in the field of patents, the agency has no basis for determining whether a use patent covers the use sought by the generic applicant").
114. See Proposed ANDA Rules, 54 Fed Reg 28872, 28909 (July 10, 1989) ("The agency believes that [this] approach more fairly implements Congress' intent that patent owners receive pre-approval notice of potentially infringing patents.").
115. See *AaiPharm, Inc. v. Thompson,* 296 F3d 227, 241 (4th Cir 2002) ("[T]he whole point of the Act's [P]aragraph IV [C]ertification scheme is to let private parties sort out their respective intellectual property rights through patent infringement suits while the FDA focuses on its primary task of ensuring the drugs are safe and effective. This division of labor is appropriate because the FDA has no expertise in making patent law judgment."); *Watson Pharm., Inc. v. Henney*, 194 F Supp 2d 442, 445 (D. Md. 2001) ("[the FDA] has no expertise—much less any statutory franchise—to determine matters of substantive patent law. In making its decision to list a patent, therefore it is entirely appropriate and reasonable for the FDA to rely on the patentee's declaration as to coverage, and to let the patent infringement issues play out in other, proper arenas . . .").
116. *Purepac Pharm. Co. v. Thompson*, 238 F Supp 2d 191 (D.D. C. 2002), affirmed, *Torpharm, Inc. v. Purepac Pharm. Co.*, 2004 U.S. App. LEXIS 767 (C.A. D.C. Jan. 20, 2004). (Warner-Lambert, the patent owner, had consistently represented to the FDA that the patent in question claimed the use of the drug gabapentin to treat neurodegenerative diseases—not epilepsy—the only approved indication for the drug, the prior patent for the epilepsy use having expired. Purepac sought only approval for the epilepsy indication. Based upon the specific record, the district court ordered the FDA to vacate its decision not to approve Purepac's ANDA because it did not include a Paragraph IV Certification respecting the indication for the treatment of neurodegenerative disease for which Purepac did not seek approval (and which had not been previously approved by the agency). In view of the court's decision, the FDA subsequently delisted the patent and required that the applicants with pending ANDAs for gabapentin products withdraw any prior certifications or Section viii Statements as to that patent. See January 28, 2003 letter from Gary Buehler, Director Office of Generic Drugs, FDA to "ANDA Applicant for Gabapentin" (Jan. 28, 2003 Buehler letter) (available at http://www.fda.gov/cder/ogd/75350.479pat.pdf). The Court of Appeals affirmed. 2004 U.S. App. LEXIS 767 *23–24.

    In a subsequent decision, the court found that the FDA had acted within its discretion in precluding another generic applicant (Torpharm) from maintaining a Paragraph IV Certification as to the patent in question and asserting 180-day exclusivity based on that patent. *Torpharm v. Thompson*, 260 F Supp 2d 69 (D.D. C. Apr. 25, 2003), affirmed 2004 U.S. App. LEXIS 767*32.

117. 355 F Supp 2d 586, 590 (D. Mass. 2005).
118. *Id.*
119. *Id.* at 599.
120. 68 Fed Reg 36676, 36682 (June 18, 2003).
121. FDCA §505(j)(2)(B)(ii)(II); FDCA §505(b)(3)(B)(ii); 21 CFR §314.95(d); In the *Torpharm* case, the court held that it was within the discretion of the FDA to hold that the operative date (assuming proper notice) for the filing of an amended Paragraph IV Certification was the date of receipt of the certification (260 F Supp 2d at 81–82) and that the penalty for an applicant's failure to provide notice at the same time as its amended certification was postponement of the effective date of the certification to the date of transmission of the notice of the amendment (260 F Supp 2d at 78–79).

122. *Id.*
123. *Id.*
124. 21 C.F.R. §314.94(a)(12)(vi); 68 Fed Reg 36676, 36684 (June 18, 2003).
125. 21 CFR §§314.52(a)(3) and 314.95(a)(3) (2003).
126. 35 USC §271(e)(1).
127. *Merck KGaA v. Integra Lifesciences I, Ltd.*, 545 U.S. 193 (2005).
128. *Merck* at 197 [*quoting Integra Lifesciences I, Ltd. v. Merck KGaA*, 331 F3d 860, 866 (Fed Cir 2003)].
129. *Merck* at 197–199.
130. *Integra Lifesciences I, Ltd. v. Merck KGaA*, Civ. Action No. 96 CV-1307 JMF (S.D. Ca., Mar. 6, 2001), App. To Pef. For Cert. 49 a.
131. *Integra Lifesciences I, Ltd. v. Merck KGaA*, 331 F3d 860, 866 (Fed Cir 2003).
132. *Merck* at 202.
133. *Id.*
134. *Id.*
135. *Merck* at 208 (quoting Brief of the United States as amicus.)
136. *Merck* at 207 (quoting §271(e)(i)).
137. *Integra Lifesciences I Ltd. v. Merck KGaA*, 496 F3d 1334, 1348 (Fed Cir 2007) (*Integra*).
138. *Id.* at 1339.
139. *Id.*
140. *Id.* at 1348.
141. *Merck* at 205, n. 7. The court noted that the RGD peptides were not used at Scripps as a research tool, noting Judge Newman's statement in dissent in the prior Federal Circuit decisions that "[u]se of an existing tool in one's research is quite different from study of the tool itself." 331 F3d at 878.
142. *Integra* at 1348; the court cited an N.I.H. regulation defining research tools as "tools that scientists use in the laboratory including cell lines, monoclonal antibodies, reagents, animal models, growth factors, combinational chemistry and DNA libraries, clones and cloning tools (such as PCR), methods, laboratory equipment and machines." 64 Fed Reg. 72090, 72092 n. 1 (Dec. 23, 1999).
143. *Amgen, Inc. v. U.S. International Trade Commission*, slip no. 2007–1014, 2008 U.S. App. LEXIS 5751 (Fed Cir Mar. 19, 2008).
144. 35 USC §271(e)(2); *Eli Lilly & Co. v. Medtronic, Inc.*, 496 U.S. 661, 678 (1990).
145. 35 USC §271(e)(2).
146. *Eisai Co., Ltd. v. Mutual Pharmaceutical Co., Inc.*, 2007 U.S. Dist. LEXIS 93585, *8 et seq. (D. N. J. Dec. 20, 2007); *Teva Pharm. USA Inc. v. Abbott Labs.*, 301 F Supp 2d 819 (N.D. Ill. 2004); *Glaxo Group Ltd. v. Apotex, Inc.*, 272 F Supp 2d 772 (N.D. Ill. 2003).
147. *Teva Pharm.* at 829–30; *Glaxo Group* at 775.
148. When the Hatch–Waxman Act was enacted in 1984, the *Orange Book* listing requirement only applied to drugs approved under 21 USC §355 and therefore did not apply to antibiotic drugs which were approved under a different statute, 21 USC §357. See Proposed Rule: Marketing Exclusivity and Patent Provisions for Certain Antibiotic Drugs, 65 Fed Reg 3623, 3624 (Jan. 24, 2000). In 1997, Congress adopted the Food and Drug Administration Modernization Act of 1997 (FDAMA) which repealed §357 and required all new drug applications for antibiotic drugs be submitted under §355 (FDAMA, Pub L No. 105–115, 111 Stat. 2296). FDAMA, however, provided that products containing an old antibiotic drug, i.e., an antibiotic drug approved by FDA on or before the enactment of FDAMA (Nov. 21, 1997), would remain exempt from the *Orange Book* listing requirements of the Hatch–Waxman Act.
149. *Eisai* at *9–11 [citing *Eli Lilly & Co. v. Medtronic, Inc.*, 496 U.S. 661 (1990); *Bristol-Myers Squibb Co. v. Royce Labs Inc.*, 69 F3d 1130 (Fed Cir 1995); *aaiPharma Inc. v. Thompson*, 296 F3d 227 (Fed Cir 2002); and *Allergan, Inc. v. Alcon Labs, Inc.*, 324 F3d 1322 (Fed Cir 2003)].
150. *Eisai* at *12.
151. *Id.* at *13.
152. FDCA §505(c)(3)(C).
153. 21 CFR §314.107(f)(2).

154. See July 2002 FTC Report, p. 14 ["The data revealed 75 drug products, out of a total of 104 NDAs (72 percent), in which the brand-name company sued the first generic applicant."].
155. *Warner-Lambert Co. v. Apotex Corp.*, 316 F3d 1348 (Fed Cir 2003). [In another case involving the drug gabapentin (see references 101 and 102 above) the court held that Warner-Lambert could not assert infringement of the patent directed to the unapproved use for treating neurodegenerative diseases, where both the patent on the listed products and the approved indication (the treatment of epilepsy) had previously expired. Although Apotex had submitted a Paragraph IV Certification, the court noted that it was effectively a Section viii Statement of a nonapplicable use patent.]; see also *Allergan, Inc. v. Alcon Labs*, 324 F3d 1322 (Fed Cir Mar. 28, 2003); *cert. denied*, 2003 U.S. Lexis 8602 (Dec. 1, 2003).
156. 21 C.F.R. §314.53.
157. See *Mylan Pharms.*, 268 F3d at 1331 (Fed Cir 2001) ("A review of the amendments shows no explicit provisions allowing an accused infringer to defend against infringement by challenging the propriety of the Orange Book listing of the patent.").
158. See *In re Buspirone Anti-Trust Litig.*, 185 F Supp 2d 363 (S.D. N.Y. 2002), in which the district court held that the brand-name defendant was not entitled to Noerr-Pennington immunity against claims arising out of its allegedly fraudulent listing of an *Orange Book* patent. As of this writing, this case is on appeal.
159. *Wyeth v. Lupin Ltd.*, 505 F Supp 2d 303, 306–307 (D.Md. 2007); and *Aventis Pharma Deutschland GMBH v. Lupin Ltd.*, 403 F Supp 2d 484, 494 (E.D. Va. 2005).
160. *SmithKline Beecham Corp. v. Geneva Pharms., Inc.*, 287 F Supp 2d 576 (E.D.Pa. 2002); *SmithKline Beecham Corp. v. Pentech Pharms., Inc.*, 2001 U.S. Dist. LEXIS 1935 (N.D. Ill. 2001).
161. FDCA §505(j)(5)(C)(i)(I)(aa) amended by MPDIMA §1101 (a)(2)(C) [ANDA]; FDCA §505(c)(3)(D)(i)(I)(aa) amended by MPDIMA §1101(b)(2)(D) [505(b)(2) applications].
162. *Kos Pharmaceuticals, Inc. v. Barr Laboratories, Inc.*, 242 F Supp 2d 311 (S.D. N.Y. 2003).
163. FDCA §505(j)(5)(C)(i)(I)(bb) amended by MPDIMA §1101(a)(2)(C) [ANDAs}; FDCA §505(c)(3)(D)(i)(I)(bb) amended by MPDIMA §1101(b)(2)(D) [505(b)(2) applications].
164. FDCA §(j)(5)(C)(i)(I)(cc) amended by MPDIMA §1101(a)(2)(c) [ANDAs]; FDCA §355(c)(3)(D)(i)(cc) amended by MPDIMA §1101(b)(2)(D) [505(b)(2) applications].
165. 35 USC 271(e)(5), created by MPDIMA §1101(d).
166. FDCA §355(j)(5)(C)(i)(II) amended by MPDIMA §1101(a)(2)(C) [ANDAs]; FDCA §355 (c)(3)(D)(i)(II) amended by MPDIMA §1101(b)(2)(D).
167. *Teva Pharmaceuticals USA, Inc. v. Novartis Pharmaceuticals Corp.*, 482 F3d 1330 (Fed Cir 2007).
168. *MedImmune, Inc., Petitioner v. Genentech, Inc.*, 127 S.Ct. 764 (Jan. 9, 2007).
169. *Teva* at 1339.
170. *Id.* at 1346.
171. *Id.* at 1338, quoting *MedImmune*, 127 S.Ct. at 771.
172. *Pfizer, Inc. v. Ranbaxy Laboratories Ltd.*, 525 F Supp 2d 680 (D. Del. Nov. 29, 2007).
173. *Id.* at 686.
174. *Id.* at 687 (citing *Teva*, 482 F3d at 1344).
175. *Caraco Pharmaceutical Laboratories Ltd. v. Forest Laboratories*, 2008 U.S. App. LEXIS 6838 (Fed Cir Apr. 1, 2008); see also *Merck & Co, Inc. v. Watson Labs., Inc.*, 2006 U.S. Dist. LEXIS 36026 (D. Del. June 2, 2006); cf. *Janssen Pharmaceutica v. Apotex, Inc.*, 2007 U.S. Dist. LEXIS 75967 (D.N.J. Oct. 11, 2007), *Merck & Co., Inc. v. Apotex, Inc.*, 488 F Supp 2d 418 (May 21, 2007).
176. *Adenta GmbH v. OrthoArm, Inc.*, 501 F3d 1364 (Fed Cir 2007); *Maxwell v. Stanley Works, Inc.*, 2008 U.S. App. LEXIS 323 (Fed Cir Jan. 8, 2008); *Micron Tech., Inc. v. Mosaid Techs., Inc.*, 518 F3d 897 (Fed Cir 2008); *Caraco Pharm. Labs., Ltd. v. Forest Labs., Ltd.*, 2008 U.S. App. LEXIS 6838 (Fed Cir Apr. 1, 2008).
177. *Caraco.*
178. *Id.* at *27–28.
179. *Sony Elecs., Inc. v. Guardian Media Techs., Ltd.*, 497 F3d 1271, 1284 (Fed Cir 2007); see also *Adenta GmbH v. OrthoArm, Inc.*, 501 F3d 1364 (Fed Cir 2007), *Maxwell v. Stanley Works, Inc.*, 2008 U.S. App. LEXIS 323 (Fed Cir Jan. 8, 2008), *Micron Tech., Inc. v. Mosaid Techs.,*

Inc., 518 F3d 897 (Fed Cir 2008), *Caraco Pharm. Labs., Ltd. v. Forest Labs., Ltd.*, 2008 U.S. App. LEXIS 6838 (Fed Cir Apr. 1, 2008)].
180. *SanDisk Corp. v. STMicroelectronics, Inc.*, 480 F3d 1372, 1381 (Fed Cir 2007).
181. *Eisai* at *13.
182. *Id.* at *15.
183. *Id.*
184. *Id.* at *18.
185. 35 USC §156(a)(1).
186. 35 USC §156(a)(2).
187. 35 USC §156(a)(3).
188. 35 USC §156(a)(4).
189. 35 USC §156(a)(5).
190. 35 USC §156(b)(1)(A)(i).
191. 35 USC §156(b)(1)(B).
192. 35 USC §156(g)(6)(A).
193. 37 CFR 1.775.
194. 35 USC §156(c).
195. 35 USC §156(c)(3).
196. 35 USC §156(b)(1).
197. 35 USC §154(a)(2). Under a transitional provision, patents in force on June 8, 1995 (without prior term adjustment) are entitled to a term of 20 years from their effective filing dates or 17 years from their issue dates, whichever is greater.
198. By way of example, a 30-month stay had been reduced for lack of reasonable cooperation by the brand-name company in *Andrx Pharms., Inc. v. Biovail Corp.*, 175 F Supp 2d 1362, 1375 (S.D. Fla. 2001), *rev'd*, 276 F3d 1368, 1376 (Fed Cir 2002), and extended because of failure of a generic company to reasonably cooperate in *Eli Lilly Co. v. Zenith-Goldline Pharms., Inc.*, 2001 WL 238090 (S.D. Ind. Mar. 8, 2001). An extension of the 30-month stay was denied in *Zeneca Ltd. v. Pharmachemie B.V.*, 16 F Supp 2d 112 (D. Mass. 1998).
199. *Ortho-McNeil Pharmaceutical, Inc. v. Mylan Laboratories, Inc.*, 2008 U.S. App. LEXIS 6786 (Fed Cir 2008).
200. GlaxoSmithKline obtained five overlapping 30-month stays, commencing in 1998 and extending to September 2003, by the multiple listing of several patents related to the drug paroxetine, followed by sequential infringement suits against Apotex, one of several generic ANDA applicants. July FTC Report, pp. 51–52 and 33–34. See also *Dey, L.P. v. Ivax Pharmaceuticals, Inc.*, 2005 U.S. Dist. LEXIS 31039 (C.D. Cal. Nov. 4, 2005), *den'd mtn for reconsideration*, 2005 U.S. Dist. LEXIS 39475 (C.D. Cal. Dec. 22, 2005); FDA Proposed Rule on Patent Listing Requirements and 30-Month Stays on ANDAs, 67 Fed Reg 65448, 65454–56 (Oct. 24, 2002).
201. 21 USC §355(j)(5)(F)(ii).
202. 21 USC §355 a(b).
203. The statute and FDA regulations required that ANDAs *may* be separately filed for individual dosage forms of the same listed drug. 21 CFR 314.92(a)(1).
204. *Apotex, Inc. v. Shalala*, 53 F Supp 2d 454 (D.D. C. 1999), *aff'd*, 1999 WL 956686 (DC Cir Oct. 8, 1999). Subsequently, separate 180-day marketing exclusivities were accorded to Barr Laboratories as the first to make a Paragraph IV Certification as to the 10-mg and 20-mg dosage forms of fluoxetine hydrochloride (Eli Lilly's Prozac®), and Dr. Reddy's Laboratories as the first to make such a certification as to the 40-mg dosage form of the same drug, following the court decision holding the last to expire of Lilly's listed patents invalid.
205. August 2,1999 Response to Citizen's Petitions re: cisplatin, Docket No. 99P-1271/PSA 1 and PSA 2.
206. November 16, 2001 letter from Gary Buehler, Director Office of Generic Drugs, FDA, to Andrx Pharmaceuticals and GenPharm, Inc. Re: Omeprazole Delayed-Release Capsules (available at www.fda.gov/cder/ogd/shared_exclusivity.htm). Neither Andrx nor GenPharm was subsequently accorded exclusivity, the courts having held that the listed

patents in question are valid and infringed by their respective dosage forms. *In re Omeprazole Patent Litig.*, 222 F Supp 2d 423 (S.D. N.Y. 2002), affirmed 2003 U.S. App. LEXIS 24899 (Fed Cir 2003), rehearing denied, 2004 U.S. App. LEXIS 2197, 2198 (Fed Cir Jan. 23, 2004).

207. *Torpharm, Inc. v. Food and Drug Administration*, 2004 U.S. Dist. LEXIS 524 (D.C.D.C., Jan. 8, 2004). On February 6, 2004, the FDA and Alphapharm PTY Ltd., the Intervenor-Defendant, appealed to the Court of Appeals for the District of Columbia.
208. FDCA §505(j)(5)(B)(iv)(II)(bb) amended by MPDIMA §1101(a)(1).
209. FDCA §505(j)(5)(B)(iv)(I) (prior to the 2003 Statutory Changes).
210. *Eli Lilly and Co. v. Actavis Elizabeth LLC*, 2:07-cv-03770 (D.N.J.) (DMC/MF) [filers include: (1) Actavis Elizabeth LLC; (2) Apotex, Inc.; (3) Aurobindo; (4) Glenmark Pharmaceuticals Inc., USA; (5) Sun Pharmaceuticals; (6) Synthon Labs, Inc.; (7) Teva Pharmaceuticals; (8) Zydus Pharmaceuticals USA, Inc.; (9) Sandoz, Inc.; and (10) Mylan Pharmaceuticals, Inc.]; *Schering Corp. v Zydus Pharmaceuticals, USA, Inc.*, 3:06-cv-04715 (D.N.J.) (MC/TJB) [filers include: (1) Orgenus Pharma., Inc.; (2) Perrigo, Co.; (3) Geopharma Inc.; (4) Glenmark Pharmaceuticals Inc., USA; (5) Caraco Pharmaceutical Laboratories Ltd. (or Sun Pharmaceutical Laboratories, Ltd.); (6) Belcher Pharmaceuticals, Inc.; (7) Lupin Pharmaceuticals, Inc.; (8) Zydus Pharmaceuticals USA, Inc.; (9) Sandoz, Inc.; (10) Mylan Pharmaceuticals, Inc.; (11) Ranbaxy Inc.; (12) Dr. Reddy's Labs, Inc.; and (13) Watson Pharmaceuticals, Inc.].
211. Generally, ANDA applicants are reluctant to so proceed because of the magnitude of potential damages in the event of an adverse determination in infringement litigation.
212. *Mylan Pharms., Inc. v. Thompson*, 2001 WL 1654781 (N.D. W.Va. 2001).
213. *Id.*
214. FDCA §505(j)(5)(B)(iv)(I) amended by MPDIMA §1102(a)(1).
215. FDCA §505(j)(5)(B)(iv)(II) (prior to the 2003 Statutory Changes).
216. 64 Fed Reg 42873 (Aug. 6, 1999).
217. 65 Fed Reg 43233 (July 13, 2002); Guidance for Industry, "Court Decisions, ANDA Approvals, and 180-Day Exclusivity Under the Hatch-Waxman Amendments to the Federal Food, Drug, and Cosmetic Act (March 2000), published at 65 Fed Reg 16922 (Mar. 30, 2000), citing *TorPharm, Inc. v. Shalala*, 1997 U.S. Dist. LEXIS 21983 (D.D.C. Sept. 15, 1997), appeal withdrawn and remanded, 1998 U.S. App. LEXIS 4681 (DC Cir Feb. 5, 1998), vacated No. 97–1925 (D.D. C. Apr. 9, 1998); *Mova Pharm. Corp. v. Shalala*, 140 F3d 1060 (DC Cir 1998); *Granutec, Inc. v. Shalala*, 46 U.S.P.Q. 2 d 1398 (4th Cir 1998); and *Mylan Pharms., Inc. v. Shalala*, 81 F Supp 2d 30 (D.D.C. 2000).
218. *Mylan Pharms., Inc. v. Henney*, 94F Supp 2d 36, 58 (D.D. C. 2000), vacated as moot sub nom; and *Pharmachemie B.V. v. Barr Labs., Inc.*, 276 F3d 627, 632 (DC Cir 2002).
219. *Teva Pharms., USA, Inc. v. FDA*, 182 F3d 1003 (DC Cir 1999).
220. 67 Fed Reg 66593 (Nov. 1, 2002), "180-Day Generic Drug Exclusivity For Abbreviated New Drug Applications," withdrawing proposed rule published in 64 Fed Reg 42873 (Aug. 6, 1999).
221. 67 Fed Reg 66594 (Nov. 1, 2002).
222. FDCA §505(j)(5)(B)(iii)(I) amended by MPDIMA §1102(a)(1).
223. *Mylan Pharmaceuticals, Inc. v. FDA*, 454 F3d 270 (4th Cir 2006) ("The statute does not grant the FDA the power to prohibit the marketing of authorized generics during the 180-day exclusivity period afforded to a drug company in Myaln's position.").
224. 21 CFR §314.94(a)(12)(viii)(A).
225. 64 Fed Reg 42873 (Aug. 6, 1999).
226. *Mylan Pharms., Inc. v. Henney*, 94 F Supp 2d 36, 41, 57–58 (D.D. C. 2000), vacated as moot sub nom.
227. 21 CFR §314.107(c)(1) (1997), revoked in 63 Fed Reg 59712 (Nov. 5, 1998).
228. FDA, "Guidance for Industry: 180 Day Generic Drug Exclusivity Under the Hatch-Waxman Amendments to Federal Food, Drug and Cosmetic Act," 63 Fed Reg 37890 (July 14, 1998), citing *Mova Pharm. Corp. v. Shalala*, 955 F Supp 128 (D.D. C. 1997), *aff'd*, 140 F3d 1060 (DC Cir 1998); and *Genentech, Inc. v. Shalala*, 1998 WL 153410 (4th Cir 1998); see also *Andrx Pharms., Inc. v. Friedman*, No. 98–0099 (D.D. C. Mar. 30, 1998).
229. 63 Fed Reg 59710 (Nov. 5, 1998).

230. *Purepac Pharm. Co. v. Friedman*, 162 F3d 1201 (DC Cir 1998).
231. FDCA §505(j)(5)(D)(i)(III) amended by MPDIMA §1101(a)(2).
232. In *Boehringer Ingleheim Corp. v. Shalala*, 993 F Supp 1 (D.D. C. 1997), the court denied a temporary restraining order seeking to preclude approval of a waiver by GenPharm Inc. of an exclusive period to market ranitidine hydrochloride in favor of Granutec, Inc.a later filer. The court concluded that the FDA's interpretation of the statute, approving the waiver agreement between GenPharm and Granutec, was not arbitrary and capricious, and an abuse of discretion or otherwise in violation of the APA.
233. November 16, 2001 letter from Gary Buehler, Director Office of Generic Drugs, FDA, to Andrx Pharmaceuticals and GenPharm, Inc. re. Omeprazole Delayed-Release Capsules (available at www.fda.gov/cder/ogd/shared_exclusivity.htm).
234. Andrx and GenPharm were thus able to waive exclusivity in favor of Kremers Urban Development Co. (Kudco) and Schwarz Pharma, Inc. which the trial court had held not to infringe the various omeprazole dosage form patents held valid by the trial court. See *Astra Aktiebolag v. Adnrx Pharms., Inc.*, 222 F Supp 2d 423 (S.D. N.Y. 2002).
235. MPDIMA §1102(a)(2)(D).
236. MPDIMA §1102(a)(2)(D)(i)(I).
237. MPDIMA §1102(a)(2)(D)(i)(II).
238. MPDIMA §1102(a)(2)(D)(i)(III).
239. MPDIMA §1102(a)(2)(D)(i)(IV).
240. MPDIMA §1102(a)(2)(D)(i)(V).
241. MPDIMA §1102(a)(2)(D)(i)(VI).
242. January 17,2008 letter from Gary Buehler, Director Office of Generic Drugs, FDA to Marc A. Goshko of Teva Parenteral Medicines regarding ANDA 77–165 for granisetron hydrochloride injection (1 mg/mL) (available at http://www.fda.gov/ohrms/dockets/DOCKETS/07n0389/07n-0389-let0003.pdf).
243. *Id.* at 5.
244. FDCA §§505(j)(5)(D)(ii); 505(c)(3)(D)(ii).
245. FDCA §§505(j)(5)(D)(iii) and (iv); 505(c)(3)(D)(iii).
246. FDCA §§505(j)(5)(D)(ii); 505(c)(3)(D)(ii).
247. *Id.*
248. 21 CFR §314.108(a).
249. 54 Fed Reg 28872 m 28898 (July 10, 1989).
250. Clarinex® (desloratidine), which is a metabolite of Claritin® (Loratidine), received 5-year exclusivity.
251. Enantiomers are optical isomers of a chiral compound that are mirror images of one another.
252. A racemate is a mixture containing equal amounts of the enantiomers of a chiral compound.
253. 54 Fed Reg at 28898 (July 10, 1989); 59 Fed Reg 50338, 50359 (Oct. 3, 1994); 62 Fed Reg 2167, 2168 (Jan. 15, 1997).
254. Food, Drug, and Cosmetic Act (FDC Act) §505(u)(1), as amended by Food and Drug Administration Amendments Act of 2007 (FDAAA) §1113.
255. *Id.* §505(u)(1)(B), as amended by FDAAA §1113.
256. *Id.* §505(u)(2)(A), as amended by FDAAA §1113. The therapeutic category is identified in accordance with the list developed by the United States Pharmacopeia pursuant to section 1860D–4(b)(3)(C)(ii) of the Social Security Act and as in effect on September 27, 2007. The FDA must publish this list and may amend it by regulation. FDAAA §1113; FDC Act §505(u)(3).
257. FDAAA §1113; FDC Act §505(u)(4).
258. FDCA §§505(j)(5)(D)(iii) and (iv); 505(c)(3)(D)(iii).
259. The Food and Drug Administration Modernization Act of 1997, Pub L No. 105–115 (1997), Section 111; and Best Pharmaceuticals for Children Act, Pub L No. 107–109 (2002), §505 a(b)(2)(B).
260. FDCA §505 a(b)(1) [ANDAs] and FDCA §505 a(c)(1) [505 (b)(2) applications].
261. FDCA §505 a(q).

262. FDCA §505 a(b)(1)(ii) [ANDAs] and (c)(1)(ii) [505(b)(2) applications].
263. FDCA §505 a(g).
264. FDCA §505 a(l).
265. *Apotex v. FDA*, 508 F Supp 2d 78 (D.D. C. Sept. 17, 2007).
266. *Pfizer Inc. v. Mylan Labs Inc.*, No. 02-cv-1628 (W.D. Pa. Feb. 27, 2007).
267. *Pfizer Inc. v. Apotex*, No. 03 C 5289, 2006 U.S. Dist. LEXIS 95778 (N.D. Ill.).
268. *Pfizer Inc. v. Mylan Labs Inc.*, 2007 U.S. Dist. LEXIS 18699 (W.D. Pa.).
269. *Pfizer Inc. v. Apotex, Inc.*, No. 480 F3d 1348 (Fed Cir 2007).
270. *Pfizer Inc. v. Mylan Labs, Inc.*, No. 236 Fed. Appx. 608 (Fed Cir Jun. 5, 2007).
271. April 18, 2007 Letter from Gary Buehler, Director of Office of Generic Drugs, CDER, FDA to ANDA Applicant/Holder for Amlodipine Besylate Tablets.
272. *Mylan Laboratories, Inc. v. Leavitt*, 495 F Supp 2d 43 (D.D. C. Jun. 29, 2007).
273. FDA has solicited comments for resolving marketing exclusivity issues in granisetron hydrochloride (Kytril) (Oct. 11, 2007), ramipril (Altace) (Oct. 3, 2007), midodrine hydrochloride (Proamatine) (Aug. 7, 2007), acrabose (Precose) (Sept. 26, 2007), and amlodipine besylate (Norvasc) (Mar. 28, 2007).
274. Public dockets for specific matters can be found on the FDA Web site (http://www.fda.gov/ohrms/dockets/default.htm).
275. April 18, 2007 Letter from Gary Buehler, Director of Office of Generic Drugs, CDER, FDA to ANDA Applicant/Holder for Amlodipine Besylate Tablets.
276. FDCA §335 c(a)(1).
277. FDCA §335 c(a)(2).
278. 21 CFR §10.30.
279. 21 CFR §§10.25(a), 10.30.
280. Proposed Rule, Citizen Petitions; Actions That Can be Requested by Petition; Denials, Withdrawals, and Referrals for Other Administrative Action, 64 Fed Reg 66822 (Nov. 30, 1999); and Remarks of Sheldon Bradshaw, Chief Counsel, FDA al the Generic Pharmaceutical Association's first annual Policy Conference, (Sept. 19, 2005).
281. FDCA §§505(q)(1)(A) as added by FDAAA §914(a).
282. FDCA §§505(q)(1)(H), (I) as added by FDAAA §914(a).
283. *Id.* §505(q)(1)(F), as amended by FDAAA §914(a).
284. *Id.* §505(q)(1)(E), as amended by FDAAA §914(a).
285. *Id.* §505(q)(1)(B), as amended by FDAAA §914(a).
286. FDCA §505 (j)(5)(D)(i) (IV).
287. FDCA §505 (q)(1)(G), as amended by FDAAA §914 (a).
288. FDCA §505 (j)(5)(D)(i)(IV).
289. 21 CFR §10.45(b), (c).

5 FDA Regulation of Biological Products*

Michael S. Labson, Krista Hessler Carver, and Marie C. Boyd
Covington & Burling LLP, Washington, D.C., U.S.A.

INTRODUCTION

Biologics as a category contain some of the oldest and earliest regulated preventative and therapeutic medicinal products known, as well as the newest and the most novel. The wide array of products regulated as "biologics" has presented regulatory challenges over the years. The Food and Drug Administration (FDA) and its predecessor agencies from time to time have responded to scientific developments by adopting ad hoc approaches to biologics regulation that defy fully coherent and unified explanation. Change within this product category has also caused shifting approaches over the years with respect to the agency component that has chief responsibility for regulating the products, both in terms of which agency within the government and which offices within an agency have principal regulatory responsibility.

In recent years, Congress and FDA have endeavored to harmonize the regulation of biologics, particularly therapeutic biologics, with traditional chemistry-based drugs. At the same time, some unique features of biologics regulation remain, both for historical reasons and because of unique scientific, legal, and regulatory considerations for biologics and special categories of biologics. This theme of harmonizing the regulation of biological products and traditional drug products while retaining unique approaches for biologics is seen in the current active debate in the Congress over whether and how to create of an abbreviated approval scheme for pseudogeneric versions of innovator biologics (known as "follow-on biologics"). It remains to be seen how this new chapter of biologics regulation will be written, as the negotiation of the specific features of this new potential approval pathway unfolds.

In order to understand the important debate around follow-on biologics and the regulation of biologics more generally, it is critical to begin with the history of biologics regulation. We thus begin with that history, and then review the scope of the definition of "biological product," product jurisdiction issues, and regulatory approval requirements for special types of biologics. We conclude by returning to the specific topics under consideration in the ongoing debate on follow-on biologics.

* Michael Labson is a partner and Krista Carver and Marie Boyd are associates at Covington & Burling LLP in Washington, D.C. Marie is admitted to the Maryland bar and not admitted to the bar of the District of Columbia. She is supervised by principals of the firm. The views expressed here are solely those of the authors and do not necessarily reflect the views of the firm or its clients.

HISTORY OF BIOLOGICS REGULATION

Unlike in many other countries, the regulation of biologics and drugs evolved separately in the United States. The earliest biologics law focused on the regulation of the establishments making biologics, whereas initial drug legislation focused on the safety of the drugs themselves. Because most biologics meet the statutory definition of drugs, technically they have been subject to both authorities. As both sets of regulation evolved to require premarket approval or licensure of products, this created a problematic situation of the dual regulation of biologics. It was unclear whether biologics should be approved under the Federal Food, Drug, and Cosmetic Act (FDCA) or licensed under the Public Health Service Act (PHSA), and there was also uncertainty about which agency or later which Center or Division at FDA should review the applications. Over time, the regulation of biologics became consolidated at the FDA, and the FDA developed a series of formal and informal interpretations and agreements to assign pathways and organizational responsibility for product review. In recent years, both Congress and the agency have attempted to harmonize the regulation of biologics and drugs further. Nevertheless, the approval process for biologics continues to involve more searching review of the manufacturing process than in the case of drugs, in recognition of the greater importance of these inquiries to the safety and efficacy of biologic products.

This section provides an overview of the historical development of the biologics laws, the incidents and occurrences that triggered major changes in biologics regulation, the evolution of the dividing line between products subject to licensure and those subject to approval, and the recent harmonization efforts.

The Biologics Control Act of 1902

As has often been the case in the food and drug context, the first major biologics law was enacted in response to tragedy. During a 1901 diphtheria epidemic in St. Louis, 13 children died from receiving a diphtheria antitoxin contaminated with tetanus (1). Also in the fall of 1901, nine children died from administration of contaminated smallpox vaccine in Camden, New Jersey (2). These events spurred prompt congressional action. In the following year, Congress passed with little debate or opposition an untitled act, now commonly known as the Biologics Control Act (3).

The Biologics Control Act created an establishment-licensing scheme for biologics facilities (4). Under this act, manufacturers of "any virus, therapeutic serum, toxin, antitoxin, or analogous product applicable to the prevention and cure of diseases in man" were required to obtain a license from the Secretary of the Treasury before shipping their products in interstate commerce (5). The Biologics Control Act also prohibited false labeling or marking of biologics packages (6). In line with the act's emphasis on establishments rather than products themselves, it authorized the Department of Treasury officials to inspect biologics facilities, and provided that establishment licenses were granted contingent on the manufacturer's consent to such inspections (7). The Hygienic Laboratory of the Public Health and Marine Hospital Service, later renamed the National Institutes of Health (NIH), administered the Act (8).

The Biologics Control Act contained no requirement that biologics themselves be safe, pure, and potent. It also did not impose any product testing or premarket approval requirements. The Act's early focus on facilities rather than products reveals the importance of the manufacturing process to the safety and efficacy of biologics.

The Public Health Service Act

In 1944, the Biologics Control Act was revised and recodified as a new section 351 of the PHSA. To this day, this section of the PHSA provides the basic framework for biologics licensing. The 1944 Act added a product licensure requirement to the existing establishment license requirement and provided that facilities and biologics could not be licensed unless "the establishment and the products for which a license is desired meet standards, designed to insure the continued safety, purity, and potency of such products" (9). Biologics manufacturers were thereafter required to obtain approval of an establishment license application (ELA) and product license application (PLA) before marketing a product.

The 1944 Act also provided that the FDCA, enacted in 1938, applied to biologics (10). Many biologics meet the definition of "drug" under the FDCA because they are intended for use in the diagnosis, cure, mitigation, treatment, or prevention of disease (11). To avoid duplicative approval processes, however, the Public Health Service indicated that biologics regulated under the PHSA would not be subjected to the FDCA's premarket approval provisions (12). It also clarified which products would be subjected to premarket approval under the FDCA and which to premarket licensure under the PHSA. It issued a regulation providing that a product would be "analogous" to a "therapeutic serum,"– and hence regulated under the PHSA– if it was "composed of whole blood or plasma or containing some organic constituent or product other than a hormone or amino acid derived from whole blood, plasma, or serum" (13). Consequently, hormone products such as insulin, somatropin, and conjugated estrogens were first approved under the FDCA, not the PHSA (14).

The Cutter Incident, Continuing Controversy, and Eventual Transfer of Biologics Regulation to FDA

For the years following passage of the Biologics Control Act, the NIH or its predecessor administered the biologics laws. Several transfers of this authority within NIH occurred. Beginning in 1948, the National Microbiological Institute, a unit of NIH, regulated biologics (15). In 1955, tragedy prompted change in the responsible agency component for biologics regulation. In that year, the National Microbiological Institute issued a license for a polio vaccine made by Cutter Laboratories (16). Written protocols for vaccine production and safety testing were the only required conditions for licensure (17). Unfortunately, two of the first batches of the Cutter polio vaccine contained the live virus. It caused 260 cases of polio, 192 of which were paralytic (18). In the ensuing controversy, responsibility for biologics regulation was transferred again to the newly created Division of Biologics Standards (DBS), an independent entity within NIH, and regulations were strengthened to require more thorough testing before licensure (19).

Nevertheless, controversy continued to surround NIH's administration of the biologics laws. In March 1972, J. Anthony Morris, a DBS research scientist, and his coauthor attorney James S. Turner contended that a "major breakdown of scientific integrity" had occurred at DBS, because the division's research function was overshadowing its regulatory function (20). According to Morris and Turner, DBS "lag[ged] so far behind as to be jeopardizing the very concept of vaccine therapy by its scientific mismanagement" (21). In that same month, the General Accounting Office (GAO) published a report describing DBS's failure to enforce its potency standards (22). According to the report, 130 of 221 vaccine lots released between 1966 and 1968 did not meet DBS's potency standards, and the division released lots "even when its tests showed the potency of the vaccines to be as low as 1 percent of the established standards" (23).

In the wake of these publications, the Secretary of the Department of Health, Education, and Welfare re-delegated authority to regulate biological products to both FDA and DBS (24). The notice also required FDA and DBS to "enforce, and apply all applicable provisions of the [FDCA], as amended, with respect to those human drugs that are biological products" (25). Biologics hence became subject to the FDCA's safety and efficacy requirements. Four months later, DBS's authority was fully transferred to FDA, and the Secretary created the Bureau of Biologics to administer that authority (26). FDA promptly proposed a review of the safety, effectiveness, and labeling of all licensed biologics, known as the "Biologics Review" (27). Manufacturers were generally required to produce "substantial evidence" of product effectiveness (28). FDA initiated proceedings to revoke the licenses of biologics that did not adhere to the safety, effectiveness, or labeling standards of the FDCA (29).

The Biotechnology Revolution and Regulation of Recombinant Products

Recombinant DNA and other biotechnology advances may have changed the face of science and medicine, but their development did not result in substantial alterations to the existing FDCA and PHSA schemes for biologics regulation. Following the early development of biotechnology products, FDA issued "Points to Consider" draft documents providing guidance on manufacturing, testing, characterization, and processing of such products (30). Further, in its 1986 "Statement of Policy for Regulation Biotechnology Products," FDA indicated that the regulation of biotechnology products would proceed under existing statutory authorities, "based on the intended use of each product on a case-by-case basis" (31).

This statement essentially resulted in recombinant versions of biologics being regulated under the same statute under which their naturally derived counterparts had been regulated. Indeed, this 1986 statement simply represented a more formal statement of what had already become agency practice. FDA had already approved recombinant insulin under the FDCA, like its naturally derived counterpart (32). This policy did have significance with respect to recombinant products for which there was no naturally derived counterpart, like erythropoietin and interferon. FDA regulated these under the PHSA, because they were deemed analogous to blood-derived products and therapeutic serums in terms of intended use and technological characteristics.

Evolution of the Agency Review Process for Various Biologics

FDA's internal agency policies for review of biologics applications changed in the late 1980s and early 1990s. In 1982, the Bureau of Biologics was merged with the Bureau of Drugs to form the National Center for Drugs and Biologics (NCDB), but just 6 years later NCDB was split into two centers, the Center for Biologics Evaluation and Research (CBER) and the Center for Drug Evaluation and Research (CDER) (33). CBER was assigned primary authority for "licensing of manufacturers to produce biological products" and regulating "biological products under the biological product control provisions of the [PHSA] and applicable provisions of the [FDCA]" (34). CDER, meanwhile, was responsible for "FDA policy with regard to the safety, effectiveness, and labeling of all drug products for human use" and reviewing NDAs (35).

Because most biologics are also drugs, this declaration of jurisdiction was not particularly helpful. As discussed below, Congress directed FDA to review its policies for assignment of review responsibility of particular products in connection with the Safe Medical Devices Act of 1990 (SMDA) (36). FDA responded by releasing three intercenter agreements, one between CDER and CBER, and the others between each of these centers and the Center for Devices and Radiological Health (CDRH). The CDER/CBER intercenter agreement granted CBER primary review authority over "protein, peptide, or carbohydrate products produced by cell culture" (except for those previously derived from human or animal tissue and approved as drugs) and "protein products produced in animal body fluids by genetic alteration of the animal" (37). The agreement also provided that these products were "subject to licensure" under the PHSA (38). In sum, CBER was to review most therapeutic proteins using the PHSA's premarket licensure authorities.

In keeping with historical distinctions, CDER was given primary authority over hormone products without respect to their method of manufacture and specifically including insulin, human growth hormone, and pituitary hormones (39). CDER continued to regulate such hormone products under the FDCA. Further, it received jurisdiction over products "produced by chemical synthesis that are intended to be analogies of cytokines, thrombolytics, or other biologics" (40).

Harmonization of the Drug and Biologics Review Process: PDUFA, FDAMA, and the Transfer of Therapeutic Proteins to CDER

Beginning in 1992, congressional action helped to harmonize the distinct application and review procedures for drugs and biologics. The Prescription Drug User Fee Act of 1992 (PDUFA) commenced this harmonization process at a procedural level. It subjected biologics applications and new drug applications (NDAs) to the same user fees and performance goals (41). Consequently, the entire review timeline for both biologics applications and NDAs is the same. FDA has subsequently taken steps to integrate the content and format of biologics and drug applications and the agency procedures for meeting with sponsors about such applications.

In enacting the Food and Drug Administration Modernization Act of 1997 (FDAMA) (42), Congress took additional steps to harmonize biologics and drug review. FDAMA abolished the requirement that biologics manufacturers obtain separate product and establishment licenses. It replaced the ELA/PLA requirement with one integrated Biologic License Application (BLA) (43). In this regard, the process for biologics applications was made to resemble that for drugs more closely. FDAMA also directed FDA to "take measures to minimize differences in the review and approval" of products requiring BLAs under the PHSA and products requiring NDAs under the FDCA (44). FDAMA codified the agency practice of applying the FDCA to biologics, and exempted biologics with approved BLAs from the requirement to have an approved NDA under the FDCA (45).

Post-FDAMA, FDA has continued harmonization efforts. In 2003, it transferred the review of most therapeutic protein applications from CBER to CDER, thereby giving one center, CDER, primary authority to review the bulk of such applications and further enabling the harmonization of the review for therapeutic protein products licensed under the PHSA and proteins and other drugs approved under the FDCA (46). Specifically, FDA moved review of "[p]roteins intended for therapeutic use, including cytokines (e.g. interferons), enzymes (e.g. thrombolytics), and other novel proteins... includ[ing] therapeutic proteins derived from plants, animals, or microorganisms, and recombinant versions of these products" to CDER (47). Insulin and other hormones remained with CDER. Under the transfer terms, CBER retained jurisdiction over cell and tissue products, blood products, gene and cell therapy products, and therapeutic vaccines (48).

WHAT IS A BIOLOGIC? CURRENT STATUTORY AND REGULATORY DEFINITIONS

Against the backdrop of the history of biologics regulation provided in the previous section, this section provides a brief overview of the statutory and regulatory definitions of the term "biological product." The next section then provides an examination of product jurisdiction.

Section 351 of the PHSA includes a list of the type of products that constitute "biological products." This section provides that a "biological product" is

> a virus, therapeutic serum, toxin, antitoxin, vaccine, blood, blood component or derivative, allergenic product, or analogous product, or arsphenamine or derivative of arsphenamine (or any other trivalent organic arsenic compound), applicable to the prevention, treatment, or cure of a disease or condition of human beings (49).

FDA has defined many of the important terms that comprise this definition of "biological product" by regulation in 21 CFR §600.3(h).

> (1) A *virus* is interpreted to be a product containing the minute living cause of an infectious disease and includes but is not limited to filterable viruses, bacteria, rickettsia, fungi, and protozoa.
> (2) A *therapeutic serum* is a product obtained from blood by removing the clot or clot components and the blood cells.
> (3) A *toxin* is a product containing a soluble substance poisonous to laboratory animals or to man in doses of 1 milliliter or less (or equivalent in weight) of the product, and having the property, following the injection of non-fatal doses into an animal, of causing to be produced therein another soluble substance which specifically neutralizes the poisonous substance and which is demonstrable in the serum of the animal thus immunized.
> (4) An *antitoxin* is a product containing the soluble substance in serum or other body fluid of an immunized animal which specifically neutralizes the toxin against which the animal is immune (50).

Of particular note, in 21 CFR §600.3(h)(5) FDA has specified when a product is analogous to a virus, therapeutic serum, or a toxin or antitoxin.

> A product is analogous:
>
> (i) To a virus if prepared from or with a virus or agent actually or potentially infectious, without regard to the degree of virulence or toxicogenicity of the specific strain used.
> (ii) To a therapeutic serum, if composed of whole blood or plasma or containing some organic constituent or product other than a hormone or an amino acid, derived from whole blood, plasma, or serum.
> (iii) To a toxin or antitoxin, if intended, irrespective of its source of origin, to be applicable to the prevention, treatment, or cure of disease or injuries of man through a specific immune process (51).

In addition, FDA by regulation has defined trivalent organic arsenicals (52) and stated when a product is deemed applicable to the prevention, treatment, or cure of diseases or injuries of man (53). It has also defined the term "radioactive biological product" by regulation (54).

Although the FDCA does not define "biological products," the definitions of "drug" and/or "device" in the act encompass almost all such products as discussed in the following section (55). Accordingly, biological products generally meet not only the definition of biological product under the PHSA, but also the definition of drug or device under the FDCA and thus, except where otherwise provided, are subject to provisions applicable to drugs or devices.

PRODUCT JURISDICTION

As noted, FDA has repeatedly recognized that "biological products are also either drugs or medical devices as defined in the [FDCA]" (56). Although section II shows that FDA has adopted shifting approaches throughout the years to the governing statutory premarket authorities and review center for given biologics, Congress and FDA have taken steps to clarify these points and to assure that biologics are not subject to duplicative approval requirements. Specifically, the SMDA directed FDA to adopt procedures for assigning "primary jurisdiction" for a given product to a particular component of the agency (57), and in the Medical Device User Fee and Modernization Act of 2002 (MDUFMA), Congress obligated FDA to establish an Office of Combination Products (OCP) to oversee product classification and ensure prompt assignment of combination products (58).

OCP's regulations differentiate "drugs," "devices," "biologics," and "combination products." A product is a combination product if it consists of (1) products that are physically or chemically combined to form one entity; (2) products packaged together; (3) a separately packaged approved product and investigational product, if the investigational product is intended for use only with the approved product, both products are needed to achieve the intended use, and the labeling of the approved product must be changed upon approval of the investigational product; and (4) investigational products that are labeled for use only with a specified other investigational product, if both products are necessary to achieve the intended use (59).

OCP resolves jurisdictional issues in two situations. First, it determines appropriate classification, applicable approval authorities, and assignment for a noncombination product where its jurisdiction is "unclear or in dispute" (60). Second, it assigns responsibility for approval of combination products by determining their "primary mode of action" (61). The sponsor may file a "request for designation" and the agency will respond with a letter of designation (62). The following subsections provide an overview of jurisdictional issues at the biologic/drug and biologic/device margins and with respect to combination products featuring a biologic.

Biologic Vs. Drug

FDA's primary jurisdictional tasks for a product that is both a drug and biologic are to determine which statutory approval process is applicable to the given product, and which center at FDA will review it. The latter inquiry is governed by the CBER/CDER agreements discussed above. The former requires more explanation.

Section 351(j) creates a presumption that products meeting both definitions will be subjected to licensure under the PHSA rather than approval under the FDCA. It exempts the sponsor of a product that is both a drug and biologic from the requirement of obtaining an approved NDA before shipping the product in interstate commerce, where the sponsor has an approved BLA covering the product (63). There is no similar provision in the FDCA, and the PHSA forbids shipping of a product meeting the biologic definition without approval of a BLA (64). Thus, if a product falls into one of the listed categories of biologic products in 351(i), or is "analogous" to one of these products, it will be subjected to the PHSA's licensing requirement rather than the NDA requirement under section 505 of the FDCA.

It is relatively simple to determine whether a product falls into one of the explicitly listed categories of 351(i). The challenge comes in determining whether a product is analogous to the listed products such that it qualifies as a biologic. As described above, FDA has promulgated regulations describing when a product is analogous to a listed biologic, including one providing that a product is analogous to a therapeutic serum, and hence regulated under the PHSA, if it was "composed of whole blood or plasma or containing some organic constituent or product *other than a hormone* or amino acid derived from whole blood, plasma, or serum" (65).

However, these regulations do not end the inquiry. For example, erythropoeitins are regulated under the PHSA as analogous to blood products, even though they are technically hormones, and hormones are explicitly excluded from the list of products that are analogous to a therapeutic serum under 21 CFR §600.3 (66). In essence, FDA employs an ad hoc approach to determining which products are subject to the different approval authorities of the FDCA and PHSA. This approach is informed by the history and context of a given product, and constrained by FDA's previous statements concerning the statutory authorities that govern a product, such as those in the 1991 intercenter agreement.

Biologic Vs. Device

The FDCA defines "device" as "an instrument, apparatus, implement, machine, contrivance, implant, in vitro reagent, or other similar or related article" that is intended for diagnostic purposes, for use in the "cure, mitigation, treatment, or prevention of disease, in man or other animals, or for use to "affect the structure or any function of the body," but which does not "achieve its primary intended purposes through chemical action within or on the body," and "which is not dependent upon being metabolized for the achievement of its primary intended purposes" (67). Many products fulfill this definition in addition to that of a "biological product." For example, a reagent might fall within one of the categories that comprises the definition of biological products under the PHSA while also being a device because it is used for diagnostic purposes.

To clarify the appropriate statutory authorities and agency review center for such products, CBER and CDRH, entered into an intercenter agreement in 1991 that describes general principles governing these inquiries. This agreement provides that CDRH will regulate all devices "not assigned categorically or specifically assigned to CBER" (68). CDRH "will use the device authorities of the [FDCA]" and "any other authorities delegated to it, as appropriate" to regulate devices assigned to it (69).

The agreement designates CBER as the lead agency for medical devices "utilized in or indicated for the collection, processing, or administration of biological products to ensure their safety and effectiveness " (70). More specifically, CBER has primary authority over devices used in conjunction with blood products, blood components, and analogous products; clinical laboratory tests associated with blood banking procedures, including in vitro tests for blood donor screening; and in vitro tests for HIV and other retroviruses (71). CBER utilizes the device authorities of the FDCA to regulate medical devices that are used in conjunction with an in vivo licensed biologic or analogous product; in vitro reagents for processing or quality assurance of biologics; devices used for determining tissue type; and devices (other than reagents) used "in preparation of, in conjunction with, or for the quality assurance of" a blood bank–related biologic (72). CBER, instead, applies the PHSA to in vitro reagents subject to licensure and certain combination products (73).

Because many new products present issues not contemplated in formulating the 1991 intercenter agreement, FDA has proceeded via case-by-case regulation of product jurisdiction in recent years. OCP has posted on its Web site redacted letters of designation and a general "Jurisdictional Determinations" publication to provide industry and regulators with guidance about appropriate classification and assignment for various products. A summary of FDA's jurisdictional determinations shows that the vast majority of devices are regulated by CDRH (74).

Combination Products Featuring a Biologic

For combination products, assignment is made based on the product's "primary mode of action"—the "single mode of action . . . that provides that most important therapeutic action of the combination product" (75). The combination product is reviewed by the agency center that regulates products with that primary mode of action (76). When the primary mode of action inquiry is not determinative, a product is assigned to the center that reviews products with similar questions of safety and efficacy, or if there is none, to the agency center with most expertise on the issues that the product presents (77).

The 1991 intercenter agreements between CBER and both CDRH and CDER outline the basic principles governing combination product jurisdiction. CBER has primary jurisdiction in the case of a device–biologic combination when the device is a delivery system for the biologic packaged with the biologic (e.g., an allergen patch), devices that are prefilled with biologics during the manufacturing process, and devices that are in vivo or implanted delivery systems for use with a licensed biologic (78). This center also has primary responsibility for reviewing drug–biologic combinations where the drug enhances the efficacy or ameliorates the toxicity of the biologic (79). In contrast, CDER regulates biologic–drug combinations where the biologic enhances the efficacy or ameliorates the toxicity of the drug (80).

In practice, few combination products are approved through the BLA route. In 2006, for example, FDA received 231 combination product applications (81). Out of the 91 involving premarket approval applications (as opposed to investigational applications), FDA required BLAs for only 2, but called for 12 NDAs and 75 device submissions (82). One of these BLAs was for a convenience kit, and the other was for a prefilled biologic delivery system (83). In large part, these uneven statistics are due to the much larger number of applications for drug–device combination products. Of the 231 applications received in 2006, 66 were for devices coated or impregnated with a drug, and 70 were for prefilled drug delivery systems (84).

REGULATORY PROCESS AND APPROVALS

General Approval and Postapproval Requirements

Section 351 of the PHSA provides the basic framework for the licensure of biologics (85). The FDCA also applies to biologics even if licensed under the PHSA, although biologics with an approved biologics license are not required to have an approved application under section 505 of the FDCA, which governs the NDA and approval processes (86). There are many similarities, however, between the regulation of drugs and biologics. Furthermore, as noted earlier, Congress has directed the FDA to "take measures to minimize differences in the review and approval" of products required to have approved BLAs under section 351 of the PHSA and products required to have approved NDAs under section 505 of the FDCA (87).

The regulation of investigational drugs and investigational biologics is one area in which the regulation of drugs and biologics is similar. The regulations in 21 CFR part 312 apply "to all clinical investigations of products that are subject to section 505 of the Federal Food, Drug, and Cosmetic Act or to the licensing provisions of the Public Health Service Act," except as provided in 21 CFR §312.2 (88). These regulations set forth the procedures and requirements governing the use of investigational new drugs—a term that includes "biological drug[s] . . . used in a clinical investigation" as well as "biological product[s] . . . used in vitro for diagnostic purposes" (89). A biologic for which an investigational new drug application (IND) is in effect under 21 CFR part 312 "is exempt from the premarketing approval requirements that are otherwise applicable and may be shipped lawfully for the purpose of conducting clinical investigations of that drug" (90).

Section 351 of the PHSA prohibits the introduction or delivery for introduction into interstate commerce of any biological product unless a biologics license is in effect for the product, and each package of the product is plainly marked with certain identifying information, including the license number of the manufacturer (91). To obtain a biologics license a manufacturer must submit, among other things, a BLA and data from nonclinical laboratory and clinical studies that demonstrate the manufactured product meets the prescribed requirements (92). The BLA must also include "[a] full description of manufacturing methods" (93). A BLA is approved by the secretary on the basis of a demonstration that "the biological product that is the subject of the application is safe, pure, and potent" and "the facility in which the biological product is manufactured, processed, packed, or held meets standards designed to assure that the biological product continues to be safe, pure, and potent" (94).

The regulations in 21 CFR §600.3 define "safety," "purity," and "potency" (95). The definition of potency—"the specific ability or capacity of the product, as indicated by appropriate laboratory tests or by adequately controlled clinical data obtained through the administration of the product in the manner intended, to effect a given result" (96)—is of particular significance because this term "has long been interpreted to include effectiveness" (97). Thus, the standard for the approval of a BLA is basically the same as that for an NDA, which under section 505 of the FDCA must be shown to be "safe" and "effective" (98). Under section 351, the applicant (or other appropriate person) must also consent to the inspection of the facility that is the subject of the BLA (99).

In addition to providing the basic regulatory framework for BLAs, section 351 of the PHSA prohibits falsely labeling or marking any package or container of any biological product or altering any label or mark so as to falsify it (100). It also contains provisions that provide for the inspection of any establishment for the propagation or manufacture and preparation of any biological product, the recall of products presenting "an imminent or substantial hazard to the public health," and penalties for violations, among other things (101).

Biologics are subject to a variety of regulatory requirements post approval. These requirements include reporting requirements for deviations, adverse events, distribution, and postmarketing study progress, lot release requirements, and labeling standards (102). Manufacturers are required to report postmarketing adverse experiences for biologics to the FDA under 21 CFR §600.80 (103). FDA may require the manufacturer to undertake formal phase IV studies or postmarketing commitments, which are subject to annual reporting requirements under 21 CFR §601.70 (104). In addition, the regulations require manufacturers to test each lot for conformity with applicable standards prior to the release of the product under 21 CFR §610.1 (105). Under 21 CFR §610.2, the FDA may require that samples of any licensed product as well as protocols showing the results of the applicable tests be sent to the agency, and upon notification by the agency not be distributed until the lot is released (106). There are also ongoing requirements for meeting current good manufacturing practices.

An applicant must inform FDA "about each change in the product, production process, quality controls, equipment, facilities, responsible personnel, or labeling established in the approved license application(s)" (107). A major change, i.e., a "change in the product, production process, quality controls, equipment, facilities, or responsible personnel that has a substantial potential to have an adverse effect on the identity, strength, quality, purity, or potency of the product as they may relate to the safety or effectiveness of the product," requires a supplemental submission and approval prior to the distribution of the product (108). A change that has "a *moderate* potential to have an adverse effect" requires a supplemental submission at least 30 days prior to distribution of the product (109). A minor change, i.e., a change that has "a *minimal* potential to have an adverse effect" must be documented in an annual report (110).

Vaccines

Vaccines play an important role in the promotion of public health (111). Vaccines are regulated by the FDA as biologics under the authority of the PHSA and the FDCA (112), and as such are subject to the general regulatory requirements described in the preceding section. The vaccines that the FDA has licensed for immunization and distribution in the United States include vaccines for childhood diseases such as diphtheria, polio, measles, and whooping cough, as well as vaccines for influenza, cervical cancer, and potential bioterrorism agents such as anthrax (113).

In addition to regulating product approval and manufacturing, FDA and other government agencies play a somewhat unique role with respect to vaccines by actively facilitating product development and production (114). This FDA role is illustrated by the seasonal influenza vaccine production process (115). Each year FDA's Vaccines and Related Biological Products Advisory Committee meets to select the influenza virus strains that it recommends comprise the influenza vaccine for use in the upcoming U.S. influenza season as the virus mutates (116). In addition, "[o]nce the strains are selected, the FDA, CDC, or other WHO collaborating centers can produce reference influenza viruses ... [that] are provided to the licensed vaccine manufacturers to generate the 'seed virus' for further manufacturing influenza vaccine" and "CBER produces and provides manufacturers with antiserum, which they use to test vaccine potency for each influenza strain" (117). FDA has issued guidance that "outline[s] the regulatory pathways for the rapid development and approval of [safe and effective influenza vaccines for seasonal use]" (118). In its guidance on the licensure of seasonal inactivated influenza vaccines, FDA discusses the clinical data needed for traditional and accelerated approval of a BLA for a new seasonal inactivated influenza vaccine (119).

Blood

FDA's regulation of blood and blood components seeks to ensure the safety of the nation's blood supply, while not unduly decreasing the availability of these products, which are "used for transfusion or for the manufacture of pharmaceuticals derived from blood and blood components, such as clotting factors" (120). The FDA utilizes five layers of overlapping safeguards to help minimize the transmission of infectious diseases: (*i*) donor screening; (*ii*) donor deferral lists; (*iii*) blood testing; (*iv*) quarantine; and (*v*) investigation, correction, and notification of problems and deficiencies (121).

Blood and blood components and derivatives are specifically listed as biological products in the PHSA and as biologics are subject to the licensing requirements of PHSA (122). FDA heavily regulates these products; there are a number of regulations that establish standards for the manufacturing of these products as well as the products themselves. For example, blood and blood component manufacturers must follow the current Good Manufacturing Practices for blood and blood components set forth in 21 CFR part 606 (123). The current Good Manufacturing Practices for blood and blood components establish standards for organization and personnel, plants and facilities, equipment, production and process controls, finished product control, laboratory controls, and records and reports (124). These quality standards are comparable to those for pharmaceutical manufacturers (125).

FDA generally inspects facilities that manufacture or participate in the manufacture of blood and blood components for human use biennially, although "problem" facilities are inspected more frequently (126). In addition, under 21 CFR part 607 all owners or operators of establishments that engage in the manufacturing of blood and blood products must register with the FDA pursuant to section 510 of the FDCA and submit a list of products to the FDA, unless exempt (127). And 21 CFR parts 630 and 640 set forth general requirements for blood, blood components, and blood derivatives as well as additional standards for blood and blood products, respectively (128). "Whole blood" for example, which "is defined as blood collected from human donòrs for transfusion to human recipients"—is subject to regulations, which in addition to establishing general requirements contain detailed provisions on the suitability of donors, collection of the blood, testing of the blood, and modifications to blood (129). It must be tested for syphilis (130), human immunodeficiency virus (types 1 and 2), hepatitis (types B and C), and human T-lymphotropic virus (types I and II) (131).

In 1997, the FDA initiated the Blood Action Plan (132). The plan, which the FDA is implementing with the Centers for Disease Control, the NIH, and the Centers for Medicare and Medicaid Services (formerly the Health Care Financing Administration), is focused on specific areas of concern, such as updating the blood regulations and developing strategies to address emerging infectious diseases, which may threaten the blood supply (133). Present initiatives of the Blood Action

Plan include, for example, "developing several additional regulations to incorporate existing guidance documents and identified needs" (134).

In addition to regulating blood and blood components and derivatives, FDA "also regulates related products such as cell separation devices, blood collection containers, and HIV screening tests that are used to prepare blood products or to ensure the safety of the blood supply " (135).

Tissue

FDA regulates human cell, tissue, and cellular and tissue-based products (HCT/Ps) under 21 CFR parts 1270 and 1271. While these parts are similar in that they both regulate human tissue, they differ in their coverage and scope. Part 1270 regulates human tissue, which it defines as

> any tissue derived from a human body and recovered before May 25, 2005, which:
>
> (1) Is intended for transplantation to another human for the diagnosis, cure, mitigation, treatment, or prevention of any condition or disease;
> (2) Is recovered, processed, stored, or distributed by methods that do not change tissue function or characteristics; and
> (3) Is not currently regulated as a human drug, biological product, or medical device .... (136).

This definition excludes vascularized human organs, semen and other reproductive tissue, human milk, and bone marrow (137). Part 1270 requires donor screening and testing, written procedures and records, and the inspection of tissue establishments, but its provisions are less comprehensive than those in the more recent part 1271.

In 1997, FDA announced a proposed plan to change its approach to the regulation of human tissue in two documents—"Reinventing the Regulation of Human Tissue" and "Proposed Approach to Regulation of Cellular and Tissue-Based Products" (138). This plan eventually led to a series of rules, which comprise part 1271 (139). This part defines HCT/Ps as "articles containing or consisting of human cells or tissues that are intended for implantation, transplantation, infusion, or transfer into a human recipient" (140). Examples of HCT/Ps include "bone, ligament, skin, dura mater, heart valve, cornea, hematopoietic stem/progenitor cells derived from peripheral and cord blood, manipulated autologous chondrocytes, epithelial cells on a synthetic matrix, and semen or other reproductive tissue" (141). Vascularized human organs for transplantation and whole blood, blood components, and blood derivatives, among other things, are excluded from consideration as HCT/Ps under the regulations (142).

Part 1271 creates a tiered, risk-based approach to the regulation of HCT/Ps. An HCT/P that meets all the criteria of §1271.10 is regulated solely under section 361 of the PHSA and the regulations in part 1271 (143). To meet the criteria of this section an HCT/P must be minimally manipulated, intended for homologous use only, and not involve the combination of the cells or tissues with another article except as permitted by the regulation (144). In addition to meet the criteria of this section, an HCT/P must either (1) not have a systemic effect and not be dependent on the metabolic activity of living cells for its primary function; or (2) have a systemic effect or be dependent on the metabolic activity of living cells for its primary function and be for autologous use, allogenic use in a close blood relative, or reproductive use (145). An HCT/P that does not meet this criteria or qualify for an exception is regulated as drug, device, and/or biological product under the FDCA and/or section 351 of the PHSA, and the applicable regulations in title 21, chapter 1, which require, among other things, that the requirements in subparts B, C, and D of part 1271 are followed (146).

Part 1271 establishes registration and listing procedures for HCT/P establishments, donor eligibility requirements, and current good tissue practice (CGTP) requirements (147). In addition, for HCT/Ps that meet the criteria of §1271.10, part 1271 establishes reporting, labeling, and inspection and enforcement requirements (148). Products regulated as drugs, devices, and/or biological products are not subject to these requirements, because they are already subject to similar requirements (149).

Following FDA's implementation of the HCT/P regulations, there were reports that some tissue recovery establishments were not following the requirements for tissue recovery. In late August 2006, FDA announced that it was forming a Human Tissue Task Force (HTTF) "to assess the effectiveness of the implementation of the new tissue regulations, which went into effect in 2005" (150). In addition, in September 2006 FDA issued a guidance document entitled "Compliance with 21 CFR Part 1271.150(c)(1) – Manufacturing Arrangements" (151). The guidance was motivated at least in part by the fact that then-ongoing "FDA investigations of some recovery establishments under contract, agreement, or other arrangement with processing establishments ... identified significant violations of CGTP requirements" (152). The HTTF released a report in June 2007 that concluded that "there are no significant industry-wide problems in the recovery of human tissues used for transplantation" based on data from inspections of 153 major tissue recovery firms (153).

Cellular and Gene Therapy

Human gene therapy is an emerging technology that uses gene therapy products to introduce genetic material into the body to replace faulty or missing genetic material to treat or cure a disease or abnormal medical condition. This therapy presents significant promise as well as the potential for serious adverse events (154), and accordingly has been subjected to intense public interest and scrutiny. As described below, FDA regulates human gene therapy products, which are biologics. As of September 2000, FDA was overseeing approximately 210 active IND gene therapy studies (155). To date, however, FDA has not approved any gene therapy product for sale (156).

The NIH is also actively involved in the oversight of human gene therapy. NIH "evaluate[s] the quality of the science involved in human gene therapy research, and ... fund[s] the laboratory scientists who invent and refine the tools used for gene transfer clinical studies" (157). And its Recombinant DNA Advisory Committee (RAC), which was established in 1974 "in response to public concerns regarding the safety of manipulating genetic material through the use of recombinant DNA techniques," serves as a "forum for open, public deliberation on the panoply of scientific, ethical, and legal issues raised by recombinant DNA technology," among other things (158).

In 1993 FDA published a notice in the *Federal Register* on the application of existing statutory authorities to human somatic cell and gene therapy products (159). The notice focused on premarket approval issues for this emerging technology (160). FDA indicated that although existing statutory authorities were "enacted prior to the advent of somatic cell and gene therapies, [they] are sufficiently broad in scope to encompass these new products and require that areas such as quality control, safety, potency, and efficacy be thoroughly addressed prior to marketing" (161). In the statement, the FDA defined both somatic cell therapy—"the prevention, treatment, cure, diagnosis, or mitigation of disease or injuries in humans by administration of autologous, allogeneic, or xenogeneic cells that have been manipulated or altered ex vivo"—and gene therapy, "a medical intervention based on modification of the genetic material of living cells" (162). The notice gave examples of these products and how they are regulated. For example, "[c]ellular products intended for use as somatic cell therapy are biological products subject to regulation pursuant to the PHS Act and also fall within the definition of drugs in the [A]ct" (163). Similarly, "[s]ome gene therapy products (e.g., those containing viral vectors) to be administered to humans fall within the definition of biological products and are subject to the licensing provisions of the PHS Act as well as to the drug provisions of the [A]ct" whereas "[o]ther gene therapy products, such as chemically synthesized products, meet the drug definition but not the biological product definition and are regulated under the relevant provisions of the Act only" (164). The FDA has also published a number of guidance, and draft guidance, documents that discuss different aspects of the regulation of human somatic cell and gene therapy, including the 1998 Guidance for Human Somatic Cell Therapy and Gene Therapy (165).

Pharmacogenomic Pairings

Use of genetic or genomic tests in tandem with therapies implicates special regulatory issues. One or both of the components of these pairings may be biologics. FDA has generally regulated these novel products on an ad hoc basis. In some cases, it allows the products to be approved or cleared separately, typically where the products are intended for general uses rather than just for use with one another. In an increasing number of cases, however, FDA will mandate that the products be simultaneously authorized for marketing either through combination product status or as a condition to approval of the therapy.

According to FDA, linked approval may be necessary where "diagnostic testing may prove to be so integral in the use of the new [biologic] that testing will be considered a prerequisite to use," such as when "there is reasonable certainty" that the biologic will work "only in biomarker positive patients" (166). FDA has increasingly indicated a preference for joint approvals in recent years.

Where genetic information is useful but patients have a "reasonable" response to treatment without it, FDA has stated that review of the test "can be subsumed in the general review of the therapeutic and may not require independent credentialing of the assay as a diagnostic test for expected clinical use of the drug" (167). FDA allows separate approval of a biologic and the accompanying diagnostic test (1) where the test is used in patient selection but the therapy is safe and effective in the general population for the indication, and (2) where the test provides information about drug dosing or adverse events (168). The approved labeling of the biologic and pharmacogenomic test may cross-reference the other product in these cases.

FOLLOW-ON BIOLOGICS

Current law provides no abbreviated pathway for approval of follow-on versions of biologics that were licensed under the PHSA (169). Instead, sponsors of biologics subject to licensure must perform full clinical trials and submit a full BLA for such products. There has been a recent push for creation of a regime for follow-on biologics (FOBs). In the first term of the 110th Congress, four bills were introduced on the topic and one—sponsored by Senators Kennedy, Clinton, Hatch, and Enzi—gained some momentum. In the second term, Representative Eshoo introduced a fifth bill, H.R. 5629, which adopts much of the text of the Kennedy bill but incorporates some key differences.

Stakeholders have vigorously debated the appropriate content and structure of FOB legislation, in light of the scientific and regulatory differences between drugs and biologics. Numerous issues must be resolved before FOB legislation can pass. In particular, Congress must make decisions regarding (1) the appropriate scope of products subject to the new pathway; (2) the approval standard and data requirements for FOBs; (3) interchangeability designations for FOBs; (4) naming of FOBs; (5) data exclusivity for innovators; and (6) a scheme for deciding patent issues associated with FOB market entry. This section examines these issues for legislative resolution in more detail, in light of existing proposals.

Scope of Products Eligible for the Pathway

Congress must determine whether the new pathway for FOBs will be available for follow-on versions of PHSA-licensed biologics only, or whether follow-on versions of FDCA proteins will be eligible or required to use this pathway. It also must decide whether it will permit follow-on versions of FOBs and whether it is appropriate to permit certain types of FOBs given the current state of science.

Stakeholders have expressed varying views on these issues. Some believe it is appropriate to leave the FDCA regime unaltered, allow follow-on versions of any type of biologic to be approved in the current state of science, and permit approval of follow-on versions of FOBs themselves. This approach is embodied in H.R. 1038, which creates a pathway for licensure of biologics that are "comparable" to any PHSA-licensed product, including FOBs (170).

However, many others, including those at the Department of Health and Human Services (171), have expressed concern that the current state of science does not permit safe and effective follow-on versions of many products, such as vaccines and blood products. Further, the possibility of "follow-ons of follow-ons" presents additional scientific concerns. Under the proposed FOB regimes, the initial FOB is licensed based on its similarity to the innovator product, which in turn was licensed based on full clinical data. While a subsequent FOB may be similar to the first FOB, it will not necessarily be similar to the innovator product, and hence the available data may not support its safety and efficacy. Finally, many FOBs present the same scientific issues, whether the innovator products were subject to a BLA or NDA. Indeed, FDA's article in *Nature Reviews Drug Discovery* acknowledges this reality by referring to the products at issue as "follow-on protein products" (172).

In light of these scientific issues, S. 1505 and H.R. 1956 preclude follow-on versions of FOBs and limit the initial regime to allowing for approval of follow-on versions of biotechnology-derived therapeutic proteins (173). These bills would also require that such FOBs be licensed under the PHSA rather than approved under sections 505(j) or 505(b)(2) of the FDCA (174). The Kennedy and Eshoo bills require follow-on versions of FDCA proteins to be approved under the new FOB pathway 10 years after enactment (175). They authorize FDA to determine that any product other than a recombinant protein cannot properly serve as a reference product in the current state of science (176). Congress must determine which of these proposals takes the appropriate approach toward the scope of products eligible for the FOB pathway.

Approval Standard and Data Requirements

Stakeholders also hotly contest the appropriate approval and data requirements for FOBs. Debate over this issue derives primarily from the scientific differences between biologics and small molecule drugs. The prospective FOB industry argues that FOBs can be adequately characterized in many cases, and thus clinical data may not be necessary to show such FOBs are safe and effective (177). According to these stakeholders, clinical testing would be expensive and unethical and would simply drive up the price of FOBs.

In contrast, others contend that a pathway like section 505(j) of the FDCA is inappropriate for FOBs. High-ranking FDA staff member Janet Woodcock, has stated that the "current limitations of analytical methods, and the difficulties in manufacturing a consistent product" render a "sameness" analysis inappropriate for biologics (178). The FOB's differences from the reference product could cause it to have significantly different safety and effectiveness than the reference product. *See* Safe and Affordable Biotech Drugs: the Need for a Generic Pathway: Hearing Before the H. Comm. on Oversight and Government Reform, 110th Cong., at 3 (March 26, 2007) (statement of Henry G. Grabowski, Ph.D., Duke University), <http://oversight.house.gov/documents/20070416132526.pdf> (last accessed September 16, 2008) ("Biologicals made with different cell lines or manufacturing facilities can exhibit significantly different efficacy and safety characteristics."). Finally, some also note the possibility of immunogenic adverse events associated with use of biologics —a risk not present in the small molecule context (179)—in finding that generally to assure safe and effective FOBs (180).

The existing proposals reflect that the Hatch–Waxman framework, established in 1984, for the approval of generic versions of traditional drug products cannot be simplistically applied to FOBs. All five proposals require that the FOB be "highly similar" to the innovator product, rather than the "same" as in the small molecule context (181). For example, S. 1695 generally requires the FOB applicant to show its product is "biosimilar" to the reference product by demonstrating, among other things, that the FOB is "highly similar" to the reference product. Further, the four bills generally require nonclinical and clinical testing of FOBs, though FDA is permitted to waive such requirements, if it deems this appropriate under S. 1695, H.R. 5629, and H.R. 1038 (182).

The bills do differ substantially in the explicit scope of testing required. H.R. 1038 mandates submission of "data from chemical, physical, and biological assays, and other nonclinical laboratory studies," as well as data from "any" clinical studies "necessary" to "confirm safety, purity, and potency" of the FOB (183). S. 1695 calls for performance of animal studies and "a clinical study or studies," which include testing of immunogenicity, sufficient to show that the FOB is safe, pure, and potent (184). H.R. 1956 and S. 1505 obligate FOB manufacturers to perform comparative nonclinical tests and comparative clinical trials show that the FOB is similar to the reference product in terms of safety, purity, and potency (185). Legislators will have to choose among the wide range of clinical testing proposals. Scientific and patient safety concerns will strongly influence this decision.

Interchangeability

Because FOBs will at best be highly similar to innovator products, they will not meet the current standard of therapeutic equivalence established for generic drugs. This standard requires the follow-on product to be pharmaceutically equivalent to the innovator product, meaning that the follow-on contains the same active ingredient and is the same dosage form, strength, and route of administration as the innovator product (186). The generic must also be bioequivalent to the innovator product in order to be considered therapeutically equivalent (187). Consequently, stakeholders have debated whether FOBs should be interchangeable with innovator products at all. Given that automatic substitution through pharmacy dispensing largely drives the generic drug market, this issue appears particularly critical to the financial success of FOBs.

Again, the existing proposals take different tacks on these issues. H.R. 1956 and S. 1505 preclude interchangeability determinations for FOBs, reflecting views that FOBs will inevitably have some differences from pioneer products (188). Indeed, FDA's Janet Woodcock expressed doubt about the ability of FOBs to be interchangeable (189). Nonetheless, the other proposals would permit interchangeability determinations under certain circumstances. H.R. 1038 allows interchangeability designations where the FOB and the reference product are "comparable" (lack clinically meaningful differences) and can be "expected to produce the same clinical result as the reference product in any given patient" (190). To be interchangeable under S. 1695 and H.R. 5629, the FOB must be biosimilar to the reference product; must be expected to produce the same clinical result as the reference product in any given patient; and for multiple use products, the risk in terms of the safety or diminished efficacy of switching between the two products may not be greater than the risk of using the reference product without the switch (191). Given the economic significance of the interchangeability determination issue, Congress will likely place particular emphasis on this issue in negotiating final FOB legislation.

Naming of FOBs

Biotechnology stakeholders also debate whether FOBs should have the same nonproprietary names as their relevant innovator products. Prospective follow-on manufacturers contend that these products should have the same names because they will be highly similar and using the same names will foster competition in the biotechnology sphere (192). Others have argued that identical names are inappropriate because they will foil attempts at sound pharmacovigilance, rendering it impossible to determine whether an adverse event was caused by the FOB or pioneer product (193).

The Kennedy bill does not take a position on this issue, but instead opts for silence. H.R. 5629, in contrast, requires unique naming of FOBs (194). Similarly, both Inslee and Gregg mandate that each FOB has a distinct name, either the name selected for it by the United States Adopted Name Council (USAN), if unique, or a distinct official name designated by FDA (195). H.R. 1038 requires FOBs to have the same name as their reference products (196).

Data Exclusivity

One of the most controversial issues on the table for FOB legislation is the appropriate period of data exclusivity for innovators, i.e., the length of time after innovator approval during which no follow-on version of the innovator product may be approved. Follow-on manufacturers contend that data exclusivity postpones the competition that leads to lower prices, and thus should be kept to a minimum (197). Others emphasize the importance of data exclusivity as an incentive to innovate in the first place, particularly in view of the rising cost of bringing a novel biotech product to market (198). Moreover, they contend additional years of exclusivity should be available based on approval of the reference product for new indications, to encourage studying approved biologics for helpful new conditions of use.

The existing proposals also take distinct approaches to data exclusivity. H.R. 1038 provides no data exclusivity period of any kind. S. 1695 provides a 12-year term, but offers no additional exclusivity for new uses (199). Eshoo would grant an initial 12-year term, and also allow innovators to obtain 6 months pediatric exclusivity and/or an additional 2 years of exclusivity if the reference product is approved for a "medically significant" new use (200). S. 1505 and H.R. 1956 both allow for an initial term of 14 years of data exclusivity (201). They also provide for additional exclusivity in the case of new indications with "significant clinical benefit" (202). Congress will need to decide the appropriate length of the initial and supplemental data exclusivity period before FOB legislation can become reality.

Patent Provisions

Many biotechnology stakeholders seek a vastly different scheme for resolution of patent issues than that in the small molecule context, where the innovator must file patent information that FDA then lists in the so-called "*Orange Book*" and generics must certify to these patents when filing their applications (203). Some stakeholders believe that FOB legislation should contain no patent provisions at all, rendering the generally applicable Patent Act the governing framework for resolution of patent issues concerning FOB market entry. The Inslee bill reflects this thinking, as it has no patent provisions.

The other bills provide a scheme for private communication to identify relevant patents, some more complicated than others. S. 1695 sets forth a complex scheme requiring the BLA holder and FOB applicant to identify patents for fast-track litigation through a series of list exchanges and negotiation (204). The scheme enables the FOB manufacturer to dictate the total number of patents that may be subjected to fast-track litigation (205). S. 1505 proposes a simpler framework in which FDA publishes notice of an FOB application; the patent owner may identify patents it believes are implicated by production or sale of the FOB and the FOB manufacturer must provide a written explanation about such patents, which constitutes an act of infringement giving rise to litigation (206). H.R. 1038 permits the FOB applicant to request patent information from the innovator at any time, and then the applicant may optionally provide a notice challenging identified patents, which gives rise to infringement litigation (207). H.R. 5629 provides a private patent identification process triggered by filing of the FOB application, with the FOB applicant being required to challenge relevant patents, if it seeks approval before their expiry (208). It also includes separate provisions to ensure third party patents are identified and litigated (209).

At a basic level, Congress will need to determine whether to include patent provisions in FOB legislation at all. If it does cover patent issues in the FOB legislation, it will need to decide whether to create a public system for identifying relevant patents (like Hatch-Waxman) or a private system, as in the existing proposals. Moreover, Congress will need to assure compliance with free trade agreement requirements, which require pharmaceutical legislation to "link" FDA approval of a biologic to expiry of patent exclusivity (210). Congress will need to grapple with these complicated considerations surrounding the proper patent regime for FOBs to arrive at final legislation.

CONCLUSION

Throughout the last century, biological products themselves and their regulation have ebbed and flowed. Because Congress has been unclear about the appropriate premarket approval regime for biological products, FDA was forced to regulate on an ad hoc basis for many years. As a result, U.S. biologics regulation is distinct in that two frameworks govern rather than one. In recent years, Congress has begun to harmonize the two processes, but manufacturing considerations remain more important for biologics than small molecule drugs. This history and the resulting patchwork approach to regulation at times have added to the complexity of creating an FOB framework. Time marches on nonetheless, and over 100 years after the first biologics regulatory statute, we stand poised on the verge of a new frontier. Time will tell, but the development of an FOB regime presents all indications of being a landmark development for our food and drug laws.

REFERENCES

1. CBER, Centennial Book: From a Rich History to a Challenging Future 13 (2002), available at http://www.fda.gov/Cber/inside/centennial.htm.
2. *Id.*
3. *See id.*; *see also* Peter Barton Hutt, Richard A. Merrill & Lewis A. Grossman, Food and Drug Law: Cases and Materials 877 (Foundation Press 2007).
4. Pub. L. No. 57–244, 32 Stat 728, 728 (1902).
5. *Id.*
6. *Id.* at 728–29.
7. *Id.* at 729.
8. CBER, Centennial Book: From a Rich History to a Challenging Future, *supra* note 1, at 7.
9. Pub. L. No. 78–410, 58 Stat. 682, 702 (1944).
10. *See id.* at 703 ("Nothing contained in this Act shall be construed as in any way affecting, modifying, repealing, or superseding the provision of the [FDCA]"); *see also* Hutt, Merrill & Grossman, *supra* note 3, at 877–78.
11. FDCA §201(g) (1938).
12. 12 Fed Reg 410, 410 (Jan. 21, 1947).
13. *Id.* at 411 (emphasis added).
14. Premarin (conjugated estrogens) Approval Details, NDA No. 04–782 (approved May 8, 1942), http://www.accessdata.fda.gov/scripts/cder/drugsatfda/index.cfm?fuseaction = Search.DrugDetails; FDA, Ever Approved Drug Products Listed by Active Ingredient, at 2291 (printout dated Aug. 2, 1989)(obtained via FOIA request) (insulin approval information); Asellacrin (somatropin) Approval Details, NDA No. 17–726 (July 30, 1976), http://www.accessdata.fda.gov/scripts/cder/drugsatfda/index.cfm?fuseaction = Search.DrugDetails.
15. CBER, Centennial Book: From a Rich History to a Challenging Future, *supra* note 1, at 7.
16. *Id.* at 20.
17. *Id.*
18. *Id.*
19. *Id.*
20. Nicholas Wade. Division of Biologics Standards: Scientific Management Questioned, 175 Science, Mar. 3, 1972; 966;966–67.

21. *Id.* at 966.
22. GAO. Problems Involving the Effectiveness of Vaccines 2 (1972).
23. *Id.*
24. 37 Fed Reg 4004, 4004 (Feb. 25, 1972).
25. *Id.*
26. 37 Fed Reg 12865, 12865 (June 29, 1972).
27. 37 Fed Reg 16679, 16679 (Aug. 18, 1972); Hutt, Merrill & Grossman, *supra* note 3, at 882.
28. 37 Fed Reg at 16679.
29. *See, e.g.*, 42 Fed Reg 62162 (Dec. 9, 1977)(noting opportunity for hearing on intent to revoke certain licenses for bacterial vaccines and bacterial antigens).
30. *E.g.* 49 Fed Reg 1138, 1138 (Jan. 9, 1984); 49 Fed Reg 23456, 23456 (June 6, 1984); 53 Fed Reg 5468, 5468 (Feb. 24, 1988); 54 Fed Reg 46305, 46305 (Nov. 2, 1989).
31. 51 Fed Reg 23309, 23310 (June 26, 1986).
32. Press Release No. 82–50, Department of Health and Human Services (Oct. 29, 1982).
33. CBER, Centennial Book: From a Rich History to a Challenging Future, *supra* note 1, at 7.
34. 52 Fed Reg 38275, 38275 (Oct. 15, 1987).
35. *Id.*
36. *See* Pub. L. No. 101–629 §16, 104 Stat. 4511, 4526 (1990).
37. Intercenter Agreement Between CDER and CBER (effective Oct. 31, 1991) [hereinafter CDER/CBER Intercenter Agreement], §III(B)(1)(f) & (g). FDA also promulgated a regulation vesting all three centers with authority to approve the applications typically handled by other centers. 56 Fed Reg 58758, 58759 (Nov. 21, 1991), issuing 21 CFR §5.33. For example, CBER became authorized to approve new drug applications (NDAs) as well as biologics applications. This regulation was later removed from the Code of Federal Regulations and treated as an internal agency policy. 69 Fed Reg 17285, 17285 (Apr. 2, 2004).
38. CDER/CBER Intercenter Agreement §III(B)(1).
39. *Id.* §III(A)(6).
40. *Id.* §III(A)(5)(a).
41. Pub. L. No. 102–571 §103, 106 Stat. 4491, 4492.
42. Pub. L. No. 105–115, 111 Stat. 2296 (1997).
43. *Id.* §123(a)(2), 111 Stat. at 2323 (codified at 42 USC §262(a)(1)(A)).
44. *Id.* §123(f), 111 Stat. at 2324 (codified at 21 USC §355 note).
45. *Id.* §123(g), 111 Stat. at 2324 (codified at 42 USC §262(j)).
46. 68 Fed Reg 38067, 38068 (June 26, 2003).
47. CBER, Transfer of Therapeutic Products to the Center for Drug Evaluation and Research (2003), http://www.fda.gov/cber/transfer/transfer.htm.
48. *See id.*; 68 Fed Reg at 38068.
49. 42 USC §262(i) (2006).
50. 21 CFR §600.3(h) (emphasis added).
51. 21 CFR §600.3(h)(5).
52. "Trivalent organic arsenicals" are defined as "arsphenamine and its derivatives (or any other trivalent organic arsenic compound) *applicable to the prevention, treatment, or cure of diseases or injuries of man.*" 21 CFR §600.3(i) (emphasis in original).
53. FDA has specified that

    > [a] product is deemed applicable to the prevention, treatment, or cure of diseases or injuries of man irrespective of the mode of administration or application recommended, including use when intended through administration or application to a person as an aid in diagnosis, or in evaluating the degree of susceptibility or immunity possessed by a person, and including also any other use for purposes of diagnosis, if the diagnostic substance so used is prepared from or with the aid of a biological product.

    21 CFR §600.3(j).

54. "Radioactive biological product" is defined as "a biological product which is labeled with a radionuclide or intended solely to be labeled with a radionuclide." 21 CFR §600.3(ee).
55. FDCA §201(g) defines "drugs" as

(A) articles recognized in the official United States Pharmacopeia, official Homoeopathic Pharmacopoeia of the United States, or official National Formulary, or any supplement to any of them; and
(B) articles intended for use in the diagnosis, cure, mitigation, treatment, or prevention of disease in man or other animals; and
(C) articles (other than food) intended to affect the structure or any function of the body of man or other animals; and
(D) articles intended for use as a component of any article specified in clause (A), (B), or (C)....

21 USC §321 (2006). This definition of drugs excludes food and dietary supplements.

56. Intercenter Agreement Between CDER and CBER (effective Oct. 31, 1991), §II.
57. Pub. L. No. 101–629 §16, 104 Stat 4511, 4526 (1990).
58. Pub. L. No. 107–250 §204, 116 Stat 1588, 1611–1612 (2002).
59. 21 CFR §3.2(e).
60. 21 CFR §3.3.
61. *Id.*
62. 21 CFR §§3.7, 3.8.
63. PHSA §351(j).
64. *Id.* §351(a).
65. 21 CFR §600.3(h)(5)(ii) (emphasis added).
66. 21 CFR §600.3(g)(5)(ii).
67. FDCA §201(h).
68. Intercenter Agreement Between CBER and CDRH (effective Oct. 31, 1991), §III.
69. *Id.* §II.
70. *Id.*
71. *Id.* §VI.
72. *Id.* §VI(A).
73. *Id.* §VI(B)(1).
74. FDA, Jurisdictional Determinations, http://www.fda.gov/oc/combination/determinations.html.
75. 21 CFR §§3.2(m), 3.4.
76. 21 CFR §3.4(a).
77. 21 CFR §3.4(b).
78. Intercenter Agreement Between CBER & CDRH (effective Oct. 31, 1991), §VI(B)(2).
79. Intercenter Agreement Between CDER and CBER (effective Oct. 31, 1991), §III(D)(1)(c).
80. *Id.* §III(d)(2)(b).
81. FDA, Report on FY 2006 OCP Requirements, http://www.fda.gov/oc/combination/report2006/requirements.html.
82. *Id.*
83. *Id.*
84. *Id.*
85. 42 USC §262.
86. *Id.* §262(j); *see also* 21 USC §355.
87. Pub. L. No. 105–115, 111 Stat. 2296 (1997).
88. 21 CFR §312.2.
89. *Id.* §312.1, -.3(b).
90. *Id.* §312.1.
91. 42 USC §262(a)(1)(B).
92. 21 CFR §601.
93. *Id.*
94. 42 USC §262(a)(2)(B)(i)–(ii).
95. 21 CFR §600.3(p), (r), (s). Safety is defined as "the relative freedom from harmful effect to persons affected, directly or indirectly, by a product when prudently administered,

taking into consideration the character of the product in relation to the condition of the recipient at the time." 21 CFR §600.3(p). Purity is defined as "relative freedom from extraneous matter in the finished product, whether or not harmful to the recipient or deleterious to the product" and "includes but is not limited to relative freedom from residual moisture or other volatile substances and pyrogenic substances." *Id.* §600.3(r).

96. *Id.* §600.3(s).
97. U.S. Food and Drug Administration, Guidance for Industry: Providing Clinical Evidence of Effectiveness for Human Drugs and Biological Products (May 1998), available at http://www.fda.gov/CBER/gdlns/clineff.pdf.
98. *See* 21 USC §355.
99. 42 USC §262(a)(2)(B)(ii).
100. *Id.* §262(b).
101. *See generally id.* §262.
102. *See* 21 CFR §600.14 (reporting of biological product deviations); 21 CFR §610.1-.2 (release requirements); 21 CFR §600.80 (postmarketing reporting of adverse experiences); 21 CFR §600.81 (distribution reports); 21 CFR §601.70 (postmarketing studies); 21 CFR pt. 610, subpt. G (labeling standards).
103. 21 CFR §600.80.
104. 21 CFR §601.70.
105. 21 CFR §610.1.
106. 21 CFR §610.2.
107. 21 CFR §601.12(a).
108. 21 CFR §601.12(b).
109. 21 CFR §601.12(c) (emphasis added).
110. 21 CFR §601.12(d) (emphasis added).
111. *See* U.S. Food and Drug Administration, Vaccine Frequently Asked Questions, http://www.fda.gov/cber/faq/vacfaq.htm (last visited Feb. 24, 2008) (noting that the number of cases of diphtheria, pertussis, measles, and meningitis, have been decreased by about 96% to 100% because of vaccination); *see also* Hutt, Merrill & Grossman, *supra* note 3, at 894.
112. 42 USC §262(i), (j).
113. U.S. Food and Drug Administration, Vaccines Licensed for Immunization and Distribution in the United States, http://www.fda.gov/cber/vaccine/licvacc.htm (last visited Feb. 24, 2008).
114. Hutt, Merrill & Grossman, *supra* note 3, at 896.
115. *See* Linda Bren, Influenza: Vaccination Still the Best Protection, FDA Consumer Magazine (Sept.–Oct. 2006), available at http://www.fda.gov/fdac/features/2006/506_influenza.html (last visited Mar. 25, 2008); *see generally* U.S. Food and Drug Administration, Influenza Virus Vaccine, http://www.fda.gov/cber/flu/flu.htm (last visited Mar. 25, 2008).
116. Linda Bren, *supra* note 115; *see also* U.S. Food and Drug Administration, Influenza Virus Vaccine, http://www.fda.gov/cber/flu/flu.htm (last visited Mar. 25, 2008) (providing links to information on the influenza virus vaccine for each U.S. influenza season since 1999–2000).
117. Linda Bren, *supra* note 115.
118. U.S. Food and Drug Administration, FDA News, FDA Finalized Guidance for Pandemic and Seasonal Influenza Vaccines (May 31, 2007), available at http://www.fda.gov/bbs/topics/NEWS/2007/NEW01645.html.
119. U.S. Food and Drug Administration, Guidance for Industry: Clinical Data Needed to Support the Licensure of Seasonal Inactivated Influenza Vaccines (May 2007), available at http://www.fda.gov/cber/gdlns/trifluvac.pdf. FDA has also issued guidance on the licensure of pandemic influenza vaccines. U.S. Food and Drug Administration, Guidance for Industry: Clinical Data Needed to Support the Licensure of Pandemic Influenza Vaccines (May 2007), available at http://www.fda.gov/cber/gdlns/panfluvac.pdf.
120. U.S. Food and Drug Administration, Blood, available at http://www.fda.gov/cber/blood.htm (last visited Feb. 23, 2008).

121. U.S. Food and Drug Administration, Have You Given Blood Lately? Consumer Update (Oct. 4, 2007), http://www.fda.gov/consumer/updates/blooddonations100407.html#oversight (last visited Jan. 30, 2008).
122. 42 USC §262(a)(1), (i); Hutt, Merrill & Grossman, *supra* note 3, at 918.
123. 21 CFR pt. 606.
124. *Id.*
125. U.S. Food and Drug Administration, Blood, www.fda.gov/cber/blood.htm (last visited Jan. 29, 2008).
126. *See, e.g.*, U.S. Food and Drug Administration, Compliance Program Guidance Manual, chapter 42: Blood and Blood Products, Inspection of Licensed and Unlicensed Blood Banks, Brokers, Reference Laboratories and Contractors—7342.001, available at http://www.fda.gov/cber/cpg/7342001bld.pdf (last visited Jan. 29, 2008).
127. 21 CFR pt. 607.
128. *Id.* pt. 630 (donor notification); *Id.* pt. 640 (additional standards for blood and blood products).
129. *Id.* pt. 640, subpt. A.
130. *Id.* §640.5(a).
131. *Id.* §640.5(f); *see also id.* §610.40.
132. U.S. Food and Drug Administration, Blood Action Plan, available at http://www.fda.gov/cber/blood/bap.htm (last visited Feb. 24, 2008).
133. *Id.*
134. *Id.*
135. U.S. Food and Drug Administration, Blood, www.fda.gov/cber/blood.htm (last visited Jan. 29, 2008).
136. 21 CFR §1270.3(j).
137. *Id.*
138. U.S. Food and Drug Administration, Reinventing the Regulation of Human Tissue (Feb. 1997), http://www.fda.gov/cber/tissue/rego.htm; U.S. Food and Drug Administration, Proposed Approach to Regulation of Cellular and Tissue-Based Products (Feb. 28, 19997), available at http://www.fda.gov/cber/gdlns/celltissue.pdf.
139. *See, e.g.*, 70 Fed Reg 29949 (May 25, 2006); 69 Fed Reg 68612 (Nov. 24, 2004); 69 Fed Reg 29786 (May 25, 2004); 66 Fed Reg 5447 (Jan. 19, 2001).
140. 21 CFR §1271.3(d).
141. *Id.*
142. *Id.*
143. 21 CFR pt. 1271.
144. *Id.*
145. *Id.*
146. 21 CFR pt. 1271, subpt. A; *see also* 66 Fed Reg at 5449.
147. 21 CFR pt. 1271, subpt. B, C, & D.
148. *Id.* subpt. E & F.
149. 69 Fed Reg at 68614.
150. U.S. Food and Drug Administration, FDA News, FDA Forms Task Force on Human Tissue Safety (Aug. 30, 2006), available at http://www.fda.gov/bbs/topics/NEWS/2006/NEW01440.html.
151. U.S. Food and Drug Administration, Guidance for Industry: Compliance with 21 CFR Part 1271.150(c)(1): Manufacturing Arrangements (Sept. 2006), available at http://www.fda.gov/cber/gdlns/cgtpmanuf.pdf.
152. *Id.*
153. *See* Press Release, U.S. Food and Drug Administration, FDA Releases Human Tissue Task Force Report (June 12, 2007), available at http://www.fda.gov/bbs/topics/NEWS/2007/NEW01650.html (last visited Jan. 25, 2008).
154. *See, e.g.*, Larry Thompson. Human Gene Therapy Harsh Lessons, High Hopes, FDA Consumer Magazine (Sept.–Oct. 2000), available at http://www.fda.gov/fdac/features/2000/500_gene.html (last visited Feb. 22, 2008) (discussing the death of an 18-year-old patient who died from a reaction to a gene therapy treatment); U.S. Food and Drug Administration, FDA Talk Paper, FDA Places Temporary Halt on Gene Therapy

Trials Using Retroviral Vectors in Blood Stem Cells (Jan. 14, 2003), available at http://www.fda.gov/bbs/topics/ANSWERS/2003/ANS01190.html (last visited Feb. 22, 2008) (announcing a temporary halt on gene therapy trials using retroviral vectors in blood stem cells after reports of a second child in a French gene therapy trial developing "a leukemia-like condition").

155. U.S. Food and Drug Administration, Human Gene Therapy and The Role of the Food and Drug Administration (Sept. 2000), http://www.fda.gov/cber/infosheets/genezn.htm (last visited Feb. 22, 2008).
156. U.S. Food and Drug Administration, Cellular and Gene Therapy, http://www.fda.gov/cber/gene.htm (last visited Feb. 22, 2008) (stating that "FDA has not yet approved any human gene therapy product for sale").
157. U.S. Food and Drug Administration, Human Gene Therapy and The Role of the Food and Drug Administration (Sept. 2000), http://www.fda.gov/cber/infosheets/genezn.htm (last visited Feb. 22, 2008).
158. Recombinant DNA Advisory Committee, About RAC, http://www4.od.nih.gov/oba/rac/aboutrdagt.htm (last visited Feb. 23, 2007).
159. 58 Fed Reg 53248 (Oct. 14, 1993).
160. *Id.*
161. *Id.*
162. *Id.* at 53250–53251.
163. *Id.* at 53249 (internal citations omitted).
164. *Id.*
165. U.S. Food and Drug Administration, Guidance for Industry: Guidance for Human Somatic Cell Therapy and Gene Therapy (Mar. 1998), available at http://www.fda.gov/cber/gdlns/somgene.pdf (last visited Feb. 22, 2008).
166. FDA, Drug-Diagnostic Co-Development Concept Paper, at 21 (April 2005).
167. *Id.*, at 21 (April 2005).
168. *See* FDA. Table of Valid Genomic Biomarkers in the Context of Approved Drug Labels, http://www.fda.gov/cder/genomics/genomic_biomarkers_table.htm.
169. Letter of Steven K. Galson, Director, CDER, to Kathleen M. Sanzo, Esq., Morgan, Lewis & Bockius LLP; Stephan E. Lawton, Esq., Biotechnology Industry Organization; and Stephen J. Juelsgaard, Esq., Genentech, Docket Numbers 2004P-0231, 2003P-0176, 2004P-0171, and 2004 N-0355 (May 30, 2006), available at http://www.fda.gov/ohrms/dockets/dockets/04P0231/04P-0231-pdn0001.pdf, at 2 n.7.
170. HR 1038, 110th Cong. §2(a)(1) (2007) (creating new section 351(i)(3) of the PHSA). This bill was also introduced with identical text in the Senate, as S 623. We refer to it for simplicity as HR 1038.
171. Letter of Michael O. Leavitt, Secretary of Health and Human Services, to The Honorable Edward M. Kennedy, Chairman, Senate Committee on Health, Education, Labor and Pensions, at 3 (26 June 2007)("At present, the science does not exist to adequately protect patient safety and ensure product efficacy for an abbreviated follow-on pathway for all biologic products, and questions exist whether some products, such as vaccines or blood products, would ever lend themselves to such a pathway").
172. Janet Woodcock et al. The FDA's assessment of follow-on protein products: A historical perspective, 6 Nature Reviews Drug Discovery Advance Online Publication, at 1–2 (April 13, 2007).
173. HR 1956, 110th Cong. §2(a)(2) (2007)(creating new section 351(k)(1)(B) of the PHSA); S 1505, 110th Cong. §2(a)(2) (2007)(creating new section 351(k)(1)(B)(ii) of the PHSA).
174. HR 1956 §2(a)(2) (creating new section 351(k)(3)(D) of the PHSA); S 1505 §2(a)(2) (creating new section 351(k)(7)(E) of the PHSA).
175. S 1695, 110th Cong. §2(b)(3) (creating new section 351(i)(4) of the PHSA); Id. §2(e)(4) HR 5629, 110th Cong. §101(b).
176. S 1695, 110th Cong. §2(a)(2) (creating new section 351(k)(8)(E) of the PHSA); HR 5629, 110th Cong. §101(a) (creating new section 351(k)(9)(C) of the PHSA).
177. Comments of GPha, Docket No. 2004 N-0355, C9, at 8, 11 (2004), http://www.fda.gov/ohrms/dockets/dockets/04n0355/04n-0355-c000009-vol4.pdf ("If the results [of analytical tests] met appropriate standards of comparability, then the need to conduct

further studies, such as preclinical, pharmacokinetic, pharmacodynamic, or clinical studies could be reduced or even eliminated").

178. Janet Woodcock et al. The FDA's assessment of follow-on protein products: A historical perspective, 6 Nature Reviews Drug Discovery Advance Online Publication, at 1, 7 (April 13, 2007).
179. *See, e.g.*, Daan J. A. Crommelin et al., Shifting paradigms: biopharmaceuticals versus low molecular weight drugs, 266 Int'l J. Pharmaceutics 3, 4 (2003).
180. Safe and Affordable Biotech Drugs: the Need for a Generic Pathway: Hearing Before the H. Comm. on Oversight and Government Reform, 110th Cong., at 11–12 (March 26, 2007) (statement of Janet Woodcock, M.D., Deputy Commissioner and Chief Medical Officer, FDA), <http://oversight.house.gov/documents/20070326104056-22106.pdf> (last accessed September 16, 2008) ("The ability to predict immunogenicity of a protein product, particularly the more complex proteins, is extremely limited. Therefore, some degree of clinical assessment of a new product's immunogenic potential will ordinarily be needed.").
181. *See* S 1695 §2(a)(2) (creating new section 351(k)(2)(A)(i)(I)(aa) of the PHSA); S 1505 §2(a)(2) (creating new section 351(k)(2)(B)(ii)) of the PHSA); HR 1038 §2(a)(2) (creating new section 351(i)(4) of the PHSA); HR 1956 §2(a)(2) (creating new section 351(k)(1) of the PHSA); HR 5629 §101(a) (creating new section 351(k)(2)(a)(i)(I) of the PHSA).
182. S 1695 §2(a)(2) (creating new section 351(k)(2)(A)(i)(I)(bb)-(cc) and 351(k)(2)(A)(ii) of the PHSA); S 1505 §2(a)(2) (creating new section 351(k)(4)(B)(iv) & (v) of the PHSA); HR 1038 §2(a)(2) (creating new section 351(i)(4) of the PHSA); HR 1956 §2(a)(2) (creating new section 351(k)(5)(iv)& (v) of the PHSA).
183. HR 1038 §2(a)(2) (creating new section 351(i)(4) of the PHSA); HR 5629 §101(a) (creating new section 351(k)(2)(a)(i) of the PHSA).
184. S 1695 §2(a)(2) (creating new section 351(k)(2)(A)(i)(I)(bb)-(cc) of the PHSA).
185. S 1505 §2(a)(2) (creating new section 351(k)(4)(B)(iv) & (v) of the PHSA); HR 1956 §2(a)(2) (creating new section 351(k)(5)(iv)& (v) of the PHSA).
186. Approved Drug Products with Therapeutic Equivalence Evaluations, at v–vi (2008).
187. *Id.* at vii–viii.
188. S 1505 §2(a)(2) (creating new section 351(m) of the PHSA); HR 1956 §2(a)(2) (creating new section 351(2)(D) of the PHSA).
189. Safe and Affordable Generic Biotech Drugs: The Need for Generic Pathway. Hearing Before the H. Comm. on Oversight and Government Reform, 110th Cong., at 11–12 (March 26, 2007) (statement of Janet Woodcock, M.D., Deputy Commissioner and Chief Medical Officer, FDA), <http://oversight.house.gov/documents/20070326104056–22106.pdf> (last accessed Feb. 18, 2008).
190. HR 1038 §2(a)(2) (creating new section 351(i)(5) of the PHSA).
191. S 1695 §2(a)(2) (creating new section 351(k)(4) of the PHSA); HR 5629 §101(a) (creating new section 351(k)(4) of the PHSA).
192. *See* GPha, Letter to World Health Organization Regarding the International Nonproprietary Name Programme (Aug. 10, 2006), http://www.gphaonline.org/AM/ Template.cfm?Section = Issues& Template = /CM/ContentDisplay.cfm& ContentID = 2694.
193. *See* Letter of Michael O. Leavitt, Secretary of Health and Human Services, to The Honorable Edward M. Kennedy, Chairman, Senate Committee on Health, Education, Labor and Pensions, at 6 (26 June 2007) ("Therefore, the Administration believes that legislation should recognize the potential impact on pharmacovigilance and prescribing and require that these products be assigned a distinguishable, non-proprietary name for safety purposes.")
194. HR 5629 §101(a) (creating new section 351(k)(10) of the PHSA).
195. HR 1956 §§2(a)(2), 3 (creating new section 351(l) of the PHSA and sections 502(y)& (z) and 503(b)(6) of the FDCA); S 1505 §§2(a)(2), 3 (creating new sections 351(l) of the PHSA and 502(y)& (z) and 503(b)(6) of the FDCA).
196. HR 1038 §3(a)(2) (creating new section 351(k)(6) of the PHSA).
197. *See* GPha, GPhA Statement on Sens. Kennedy-Enzi-Clinton-Hatch Biogenerics Legislation, http://www.gphaonline.org/AM/Template.cfm?Section = Press_Releases& TEMPLATE = /CM/HTMLDisplay.cfm& ContentID = 3560 ("we continue to oppose

the extension of 12 years of market exclusivity that this legislation grants brand biotechnology companies. Such an arbitrary and excessive period of time is not only unprecedented and unwarranted, but more importantly, would unjustifiably delay access to affordable competition and choice for consumers and businesses alike").

198. *E.g.* Safe and Affordable Biotech Drugs: the Need for a Generic Pathway: Hearing Before the H. Comm. on Oversight and Government Reform, 110th Cong., at 12, 14 (March 26, 2007) (statement of Henry G. Grabowski, Ph.D., Duke University), <http://oversight.house.gov/documents/20070416132526.pdf> (last accessed September 16, 2008)
199. S 1695 §2(a)(2) (creating new section 351(k)(7) of the PHSA).
200. HR 5629 §101(a) (creating new section 351(k)(7)& (8) of the PHSA).
201. S 1505 §2(a)(2) (creating new section 351(k)(7) of the PHSA); HR 1956 §2(a)(2) (creating new section 351(k)(3) of the PHSA).
202. S 1505 §2(a)(2) (creating new section 351(k)(7) of the PHSA); HR 1956 §2(a)(2) (creating new section 351(k)(3) of the PHSA).
203. *See* FDCA §505(b), 505(j).
204. S 1695 §2(a)(2) (creating new section 351(l) of the PHSA).
205. *Id.* §2(a)(2) (creating new section 351(l)(5) of the PHSA).
206. S 1505 §2(a)(2) (creating new section 351(k)(8) of the PHSA).
207. HR 1038 §3(a)(2) (creating new section 351(k)(17) of the PHSA)
208. HR 5629 §101(a) (creating new section 351(l)(10) of the PHSA).
209. *Id.* §101(a) (creating new section 351(l)(4)(B) of the PHSA).
210. *See, e.g.*, Free Trade Agreement Between the United States and the Republic of Korea, Article 18.9(5), available at http://www.ustr.gov/assets/Trade_Agreements/Bilateral/Republic_of_Korea_FTA/Final_Text/asset_upload_file273_12717.pdf.

6 FDA's Antibiotic Regulatory Scheme: Then and Now

Irving L. Wiesen, Esq.

Law Offices of Irving L. Wiesen, Esq., New York, New York, U.S.A.

INTRODUCTION

An antibiotic is a drug containing any quantity of any chemical substance produced by a microorganism and which has the capacity to inhibit or destroy microorganisms in dilute solution (1). AQ The history of antibiotic regulation demonstrates the interplay between regulatory schemes, which are artifacts of history, and the scientific/regulatory constraints and marketing conditions in which they operate. Largely an outgrowth of a narrow legislative fix of a scientific and regulatory need, the antibiotic regulatory scheme grew to unwieldy proportions as the market for such drugs increased. Accordingly, the FDA, within the statutory mandate, increasingly revised the regulatory requirements governing antibiotic drugs, gradually eliminating them in successively more radical revamping of its drug approval requirements. This window into FDA rule and policymaking finally closed in 1997, when Congress enacted the Food and Drug Administration Modernization Act, which finally and unambiguously put an end to the particular, and peculiar, requirements for antibiotic drugs.

Antibiotics Regulation: A Brief History

In 1906, Congress passed the first comprehensive scheme of federal law to regulate the marketing of pharmaceutical products. Lacking an approval requirement, however, the Food and Drug Act of 1906 merely proscribed the entry into interstate commerce of drugs, which were "misbranded" or "adulterated." In 1938, Congress passed the Food Drug and Cosmetic Act, which remains the overall federal drug regulatory scheme to this day. The FDCA introduced for the first time a requirement that all drugs marketed in the United States after enactment of the act be reviewed prior to marketing. The criterion of such review, however, was merely for safety; no requirement of effectiveness existed until passage of the Drug Amendments of 1962.

Antibiotics and insulin-containing drugs were added to the regulatory scheme beginning in a series of steps starting in 1941 and culminating in 1945 (2) and were also contained in the 1962 amendments. However, in contrast, the procedures for establishing safety and efficacy which were applicable to other "new drugs," antibiotics were subject to a far different regulatory scheme. This scheme was two-pronged, requiring that antibiotics adhere to a drug "monograph" published by the FDA, and also, that each batch of antibiotic be certified by FDA as conforming to established standards of manufacture and conformity with specifications.

Under the monograph system, FDA issues a set of rules that are given broad applicability to any prospective marketer. Any prospective marketer may market the product in conformity with the rules and specifications contained in the monograph without preclearance of the product per se. In the case of antibiotics, the monographs were developed on the basis of the first product reviewed and approved in the antibiotic class. Thereafter, any prospective marketer merely needed to show it was bioequivalent to the first product on which the monograph was developed, and that it was following the specifications of the monograph.

In this way, the antibiotic approval mechanism paralleled and prefigured the approval mechanism for generic drugs, by which subsequent versions of a drug are approvable based upon standards developed in connection with the first-approved product. Like generic drugs prior to 1962, the first-approved applicant owned no proprietary rights in the information used in approval of the product, which could bar approval of subsequent applicants who relied on the first approval.

Attendant to the monograph system, antibiotics were also subject to a batch certification requirement, which was instituted due to the relative newness of antibiotic manufacturing. Thus, notwithstanding the existence of the monograph, antibiotics were also subject to a requirement that served as a counterpart to the monograph system, which was the requirement of "batch certification." This requirement, enshrined in the FDCA statute (3), required that each batch of antibiotic be certified by FDA to conform to regulations of identity, strength, quality, and purity. To meet this requirement, the antibiotic marketer provided a sample of each batch of the antibiotic to FDA prior to marketing for laboratory testing and certification so that the requirements for marketing set forth by the statute were met. Batches that were found by FDA to meet the required standards were issued an "Antibiotic Certificate," which permitted their shipment in interstate commerce, "Certified by FDA" (4).

Unsurprisingly, the batch certification requirement represented a huge burden on both manufacturers and the FDA. As recounted by its chief, Antibiotic Drug Review Branch of the FDA, the mechanism had long become expensive, time-consuming, and ultimately a bottleneck in drug distribution.

The law required the government to charge fees to manufacturers requesting the required certification tests. Fees in excess of $5 million were collected annually on a user-cost basis to carry on the testing and certification program. The regulated industry's demands on the agency's testing service increased year by year, as the market grew larger and larger. The agency's testing services became slower and slower due to personnel and facilities limitations imposed by the Office of Management Budget. As a result, during the late 1970s, large quantities of antibiotic products were being held in quarantine for many weeks by industry while waiting for FDA's clearance at a time when interest rates were at an all-time high (5).

As a result, FDA increasingly took advantage of its power under the statute (6) to exempt antibiotic products or manufacturers from the batch certification requirement, if the FDA determined that it was not needed to assure the safety and effectiveness of the drug product. FDA took several increasingly significant steps: in October 1980, it indicated to the industry that testing of topical antibiotics would no longer be required. As described by the FDA, this small step was not effective, leading to a cascade of events.

Such limited deregulation (topical antibiotic exemption) was not sufficient to relieve stock buildup. The agency then tried selective testing where certain tests were skipped and certifications granted on the basis of the manufacturer's test results. With less testing, there was less income to support the laboratories' costs and the program headed for a financial deficit (7).

Finally, on September 7, 1982, FDA determined that it was eliminating entirely the batch certification program as unnecessary to assure the safety and effectiveness of antibiotics, whose manufacturing by then had become well understood and whose consistency had proven itself over many years of practice. The new program was made effective on October 1, 1982. Instead of the batch certification procedure, the industry and FDA were now guided by compendial and regulatory specifications—specifically, FDA's monographs setting forth standards of identity, strength, quality, and purity—and by FDA's Good Manufacturing Practice Regulations and Policies applicable to production (8). In 1986, this exemption was extended to over-the-counter antibiotics, which complied with the applicable monograph.

As a result of the FDA's revamping its antibiotic approval process, the way was now cleared for significant new activity by manufacturers and enhanced delivery of antibiotic products to the market. The FDA described the effect of this "deregulatory" effort shortly after in 1986.

At the time batch-by-batch testing of antibiotic products was terminated by FDA, there were approximately 65 domestic and 52 foreign manufacturers having products tested for marketing. Since that phase of deregulation, 25 additional domestic and 8 foreign companies have submitted one or more Form 5/6 applications to enter the U.S. antibiotic market for the first time (9). The FDA analysis concluded, "[a]s deregulation occurs, growth and competition in the industry follows" (10).

The certification regulations remained in effect as a standard of drug quality by which adulteration and misbranding could be gauged. Nevertheless, FDA retained the power to reimpose the requirement for certification, where it determined that a manufacturer or several manufacturers experienced a problem that was believed to pose a significant potential health risk. In such an event, the requirement for certification would be reimposed only on the company or companies in which the problem was evident (11). This process remained in effect until the recent repeal of the entire antibiotic application scheme by Congress in the Food and Drug Modernization Act of 1997, discussed below.

THE CERTIFICATION PROCESS

At the time the antibiotic provisions were enacted in 1945, the only antibiotic product on the market was penicillin. In subsequent years, well over a hundred additional antibiotic products were developed and approved by the FDA. Most of these approvals were under the 1945 regulatory scheme, which used a monograph system in conjunction with batch certification. To receive permission to market a product, the applicant was required to address a request for certification of a batch of an antibiotic drug to the commissioner of the FDA. The application was required to contain information describing the batch, including results of testing required by the regulations, and batch composition. Each batch shipped in interstate commerce was required to adhere to stated standards of identity, strength, quality, and purity. Additionally, batches were required to have results for tests and methods of assay, including sterility tests, biological tests, microbiological assays, chemical tests, and tests for certain antibiotic dosage forms.

In its application, the manufacturer was required to submit actual samples of each batch of antibiotic which FDA would test in its own laboratories. Upon review and confirmation by the FDA that the batch met appropriate requirements, the FDA would certify the batch as safe and effective, and fit for distribution in interstate commerce. These certifications were contained in an "Antibiotic Certificate" issued by the FDA to the applicant. Batches that were released prior to such FDA certification were deemed misbranded under section 502 (1) of the FDCA, and were subject to seizure and other legal sanctions.

Certification was a creature of FDA discretion. FDA was authorized to withhold certification of any batches, which it deemed required a further demonstration of safety and effectiveness. In this respect, FDA could require any additional testing or other information it deemed appropriate, and it did so in cases where new information or other changed circumstances indicated that the standard certification may no longer have been sufficient (12). Moreover, FDA had the power to suspend certification procedures for any person or company that was found to have used fraud, misrepresentation, or concealment in the application for certification, or had otherwise falsified records required by the regulations to be maintained by the company.

The 1962 Drug Amendments added a requirement that drugs demonstrate efficacy, in addition to safety, prior to distribution—a requirement that was equally applicable to antibiotics. Prior to these amendments, the FDA had been authorized to certify certain antibiotics as safe and effective: penicillin, streptomycin, chlortetracycline, chloramphenicol, and bacitracin. Other antibiotics available at the time were either classified as safe and effective or were generally recognized as safe, and therefore did not require a finding of effectiveness prior to marketing. As a result of the 1962 amendments, which now required proof of effectiveness, FDA determined that antibiotics marketed under a pre-1962 New Drug Application (NDA) would be certified or released from certification under the pre-1962 regulatory scheme, despite the fact that the pre-1962 regulatory scheme did not review drugs for efficacy. To address the new efficacy requirements, FDA determined to proceed under the rubric of its Drug Efficacy Study Implementation Program (DESI) to provide appropriate regulations for these antibiotics.

As a result of the 1962 amendments, FDA required the submission for several antibiotics of scientific evidence of "substantial well-controlled clinical studies" demonstrating the effectiveness of the product. Products that failed to provide such evidence had their certifications revoked and the regulations under which they were marketed repealed by the FDA. Legal challenges to this action failed (13). In addition, after review of submissions for other antibiotics, FDA withdrew certification and revoked approval of several antibiotic and antibiotic combination products that did not meet the FDA's standards of substantial scientific evidence (14).

Exemptions from Certification Requirements

Under the FDCA, FDA was permitted to exempt certain products from certification as a requirement for proving safety and efficacy. Accordingly, the FDA exempted antibiotic drugs from the requirements of certification (15). Promulgated by the FDA to relieve the bottleneck in antibiotic approvals, this new regulation exempted from the certification requirements of the FDCA all antibiotic drugs provided there was an approved antibiotic application for each product.

The antibiotic approval process had previously been contained in the FDA's Form FD-1675, rather than in a regulation. This form contained the information required to be submitted by the applicant for approval of the antibiotic, and was also referred to as a "Form 5" and "Form 6" application. Form 5 applications were for antibiotics for which no standards had previously been developed as shown in 21 CFR, Parts 440 to 455; Form 6 applications were for products for which such standards already existed and contained in the regulation.

In 1985, the FDA published new regulations known as the "NDA Rewrite Regulations," which entirely revamped the application procedures for drug products. In these regulations, the FDA dispensed with the previous regulatory scheme of Form 5 and Form 6 for antibiotics, and replaced it with appellations that more closely mirrored those of nonantibiotic drugs. Accordingly, after May 23, 1985, antibiotic applications were classified as either "New Antibiotic Drug Applications" or "Abbreviated Antibiotic Drug Applications" (16). Consonant with the new regulatory framework, applicants, and manufacturers could now make certain changes in their products, without requiring prior FDA approval (17).

FDAMA

In 1997, President Clinton signed into law the Food and Drug Administration Modernization Act of 1997 (FDAMA). This act, which was designed in part to introduce legal mechanisms to permit the speedier and broader introduction of pharmaceutical products to consumers, also addressed a number of prevailing historical anomalies in the FDA's review and approval process. Among those anomalies was the approval mechanism for antibiotics, whose distinction from the general class of pharmaceuticals had long lost any scientific rationale. Accordingly, section 125 of Title I of the Act repealed section 507 of the FDCA, which contained the separate application scheme for antibiotics. Essentially, the import of the repeal is that antibiotics would, with certain exceptions, be reviewed and approved on the same basis as any other pharmaceutical product.

The act specifically provided, moreover, that any full applications (NDA's) approved under FDCA section 597 before the signing into law of FDAMA would be deemed to have been submitted and filed under the general pharmaceutical provisions, section 505(b) of the FDCA, and approved for safety and effectiveness under section 505(c) thereof. In addition, all abbreviated applications (ANDAs) approved under section 507 would be deemed to have been filed and approved under section 505(j) of the act, applicable to ANDAs for general pharmaceutical products.

One consequence of the effective dating of the repeal, however, was that antibiotic applications submitted to the FDA before the date of FDAMA were not subject to the patent listing and notification requirements, as well as the exclusivity attendant thereto.* The inevitable result was that post-FDAMA applications for pre-FDAMA ("old") antibiotics were not required to include patent information and

* Under Section 505 of the FDCA, abbreviated new drug applications are required to certify the status of their product in relation to the patents claimed by the "listed" product in the *Orange Book*. These certifications indicate whether the product infringes the listed product, whether the applicant claims no patents of the listed product apply to the applicant's product, whether listed patents apply, or whether listed patents apply but the patents are invalid. The application itself is deemed a legal infringement of any patents, and therefore may precipitate a patent infringement lawsuit by the owner of the listed drug against the applicant who certifies that listed patents apply, but are invalid. The statute provides a period of exclusivity to the first to file such a certification, in the event of a patent infringement lawsuit by the listed product owner.

were not eligible for the exclusivities of sections 505(c) or 505 (j) of the FD&C Act. This included applications for a new dosage form or new indication for an "old" antibiotic.

FDA's Proposed Rule

In the *Federal Registers* of May 12, 1998, (18) and January 5, 1999, (19) the FDA issued conforming amendments to its regulations to remove provisions that were made obsolete by FDAMA, specifically the provisions that governed certification of antibiotic drugs (20).

Under section 125(d) (1), drugs that had been approved pursuant to section 507 of the act were now to be deemed approved under the standard new drug provisions of the act, and would be considered as NDA drugs. These drugs, having been approved under the previous regulatory scheme, had not been subject to the patent and exclusivity provisions of the act that were enacted under the Drug Price Competition and Patent Restoration Law ("Waxman-Hatch"), enacted in 1984, which were contained in section 505 of the act. Accordingly, FDAMA also exempted antibiotic-related drug applications from the drug exclusivity and patent listing provisions of Waxman-Hatch. As a result, section 125 of FDAMA exempted from the exclusivity and patent listing requirements all applications that contained an antibiotic drug that was the subject of a marketing application received by the FDA under former section 507 of the act and received by the FDA prior to the enactment of FDAMA on November 21, 1997. This included applications that were withdrawn, not filed, or even refused approval under section 507.

In 2000, the FDA published a proposed rulemaking notice in the *Federal Register*, wherein it fleshed out its approach to its regulatory stance on marketing exclusivity and patents for antibiotic drugs (21).

Notwithstanding the relatively bright-line distinctions contained in FDAMA, an issue that was reminiscent of the original enactment of the Waxman-Hatch Amendments, i.e., the definition of the type of drug product included in its strictures, still remained. In the case of FDAMA's section 125 exemption, therefore, it remained unclear what constituted an "antibiotic" exempt from the requirements and benefits of drug exclusivities and patent listing.*

Accordingly, in the *Federal Register* of January 24, 2000, FDA proposed regulations governing the exemption of antibiotic applications from regulatory provisions governing marketing exclusivity and patents (22). In its notice, the FDA noted that under the former section 507 of the act antibiotic drugs were not subject to the patent listing and exclusivity provisions of section 505. Under section 125 of the Modernization Act, however, this distinction is preserved "with an expansive line" (23). Under section 125, applications are exempted which contain an antibiotic drug which was the subject of a marketing application received by FDA under former section 507 prior to the enactment of FDAMA on November 21, 1997. Drugs

* The effect of "drug listing" in the *Orange Book*, for example, is to grant the owner of the Reference Listed Drug ("RLD") an automatic 30-month stay of approval in the event the RLD owner sued a generic applicant for patent infringement following certification by the generic applicant that its product did not infringe the patent of the RLD.

approved and marketed under former section 507 as well as drugs that were the subject of applications, "which may have been withdrawn, not filed, or refused approval under section 507 of the act" were similarly excluded from the patent listing and exclusivity provisions of section 505 (24).

The term "antibiotic drug," the FDA recounted, is defined in section 125 of FDAMA as

> [a]ny drug (except for drugs for use in animals other than humans) composed wholly or partly of any kind of penicillin, streptomycin, chlortetracycline, chloramphenicol, bacitracin, or any other drug intended for human use containing any quantity of any chemical substance which is produced by a micro-organism and which has the capacity to inhibit or destroy micro-organisms in dilute solution (including a chemically synthesized equivalent of any such substance) or any derivative thereof.

21. USC 321(jj) From this definition, the FDA concluded that the term "antibiotic drug" refers not only to the active chemical substance but also to any derivative of the substance, such as a salt or ester of the substance. Accordingly, FDA determined that section 125's applicability applied to any drug that is the subject of a marketing application containing an "active moiety," which could be found in a drug application submitted to the agency prior to the enactment of FDAMA.* In defending its position, FDA noted that it had previously taken the same position for nonantibiotic drugs with regard to patent listing and exclusivity.

In interpreting the exclusivity provisions in the Hatch-Waxman Amendments, the agency concluded that Congress did not intend to confer significant periods of exclusivity on minor variations of previously approved chemical compounds. Therefore, the agency determined that it is appropriate to assess whether the drug seeking exclusivity is a new chemical entity, that is, a drug that does not contain any previously approved active moiety (25).

Having established that the congressional intent was to exempt from patent listing and exclusivity any applications for the same "active moiety" of a prerepeal antibiotic drug, FDA went on to propose a mechanism "[t]o help interested persons determine which drug products [are] exempt from the marketing exclusivity and patent provisions" by maintaining in the Code of Federal Regulations a list of the names of each prerepeal active moiety, in section 314.109(b) of the CFR This list, FDA indicated, is intended to be comprehensive and to provide interested persons a means of determining whether a marketing application would be for a drug that contains a prerepeal antibiotic.† Included with its proposed rule was a list of these active moieties of prerepeal antibiotics, which the FDA considered exempt from patent listing and exclusivity provisions of section 505 of the act (26).

* FDA defined an "active moiety" as the "molecule or ion responsible for physiological or pharmacological action, excluding appended portions that would cause the drug to be an ester, salt, or other noncolvalent derivative of the molecule." 65FR at 3625.

† Although intended to be comprehensive, FDA notably stressed its use as an aid to interested parties, but without legal effect. Thus, if any products were inadvertently omitted from the list, such omissions would not affect the regulatory status of the application; the application would still be exempt from patent listing and exclusivity, notwithstanding inadvertent omission from the list. 65FR at 3625.

FDA'S GUIDANCE

In implementing the repeal, FDA issued a guidance document in which it outlined a new numbering system for applications subject to the old and new regulatory schemes, and in addition, more clearly defined which applications were subject to the respective statutory frameworks (27). The guidance indicated that the section 125 exemption contained in the Modernization Act applicable to "old" antibiotics applied to applications that contained in whole, or in part (i.e., as part of a combination product), an antibiotic drug, as defined in the act (28). Moreover the guidance made clear that the antibiotic contained in the application would need to have been received by the FDA prior to FDAMA, whether or not approved, marketed, marketed and withdrawn by the sponsor for any reason, submitted and withdrawn by the sponsor, and not further submitted. Action letter templates for section 507 drugs would no longer be used, nor would monographs for antibiotics be published or maintained.

With respect to bulk drug applications, prior to FDAMA, FDA had required that bulk antibiotic drug substances be either batch certified or exempted from batch certification via an approved antibiotic drug application. FDA had used an approval mechanism for bulk antibiotics that was similar to the approval mechanism for finished antibiotic applications. Under the new scheme, FDA indicated that it would treat information regarding bulk drug substances as Drug Master Files (DMFs), like their nonantibiotic counterparts. Accordingly, this information would no longer require specific approval, but rather, like DMFs, would merely be filed with the agency and considered as part of the drug application. Like nonantibiotics, antibiotics could also henceforth contain drug substance information in the finished product application itself (29). As a result, all unapproved bulk applications that were pending at the FDA were converted by the FDA into DMFs, and assigned DMF reference numbers.

A RETURN TO THE DEFINITION OF ANTIBIOTIC

This chapter began with a definition of the term "antibiotic"; however, in light of the critical economic consequences of this designation for any particular product as discussed above, it is perhaps not surprising that the courts would have the last word on the subject of what constitutes an antibiotic. This issue came up in the case of *Allergan v. Crawford* (30) litigated in the District Court of Washington, D.C., under the following circumstances.

A product known as "Restasis®" marketed by Allergan, Inc., is a topical ophthalmic emulsion of cyclosporine used to treat an eye condition known as keratoconjunctivities (or dry eye disease). This product was submitted to the FDA in a New Drug Application in 1999 and was approved by the FDA in December 2002. As noted by the court, the issue is that "[t]he distinction between drugs entitled to market exclusivity/patent protection and those not so entitled, depends on whether the drug is classified as an 'antibiotic' that was subject to FDA review prior to 1997." In this case, the FDA classified Restasis as an antibiotic and accordingly denied it Waxman-Hatch exclusivity; Allergan argued that its mechanism of action proved otherwise, i.e., it was not an antibiotic, but rather an immunosuppressive drug and accordingly entitled to exclusivity.

In the course of its application process, Allergan submitted its application to the FDA in 1999 as a nonantibiotic, and it was so approved by the FDA in 2002.

However, in March of the following year, the FDA informed the company that the active ingredient, cyclosporine, was an antibiotic previously approved by the FDA prior to the enactment of FDAMA and its repeal of section 507. Accordingly, it was therefore not eligible for the Waxman-Hatch protections under section 125(d) (2). Interestingly—and crucially, in the eyes of Allergan—Restasis is not approved for any antibiotic use. In fact, the company pointed out the FDA-approved labeling for the product specifically contraindicates its use where an eye infection is present.

It turns out that the issue of the antibiotic status of cyclosporine was itself a prior controversy at the FDA earlier in connection with the drug applications of its innovator, Sandoz Pharmaceuticals, for approval of its Sandimmune® drug product. This product, developed and indicated to suppress organ rejection in transplant patients, was approved by the FDA in 1983 and classified as an antibiotic under section 507. Follow-on applications using the same active ingredient were approved as nonantibiotics in 1994, but then were reversed and reclassified as antibiotics. Sandoz strongly objected to the reclassification, and in fact, the record shows that the decision was itself highly controversial within the FDA. As the court noted, the record showed that "many members in Pilot Drug [FDA] did not agree nor understand why Sandimmune is classified [as] an antibiotic." The company pointed to the statutory language for antibiotics and argued in effect that mere antibiotic activity in vitro, which did not correlate with antibiotic activity in vivo except at unsafely high concentrations, did not cause the product to be classified as an antibiotic given that such antibiotic activity was not relevant to its therapeutic use in humans notwithstanding the existence of such activity.

The FDA effectively agreed with Sandoz, but nevertheless held to its position on narrower grounds. Noting that it agreed that "no credible evidence or rationale was identified that would support the conclusion that cyclosporine has any clinically relevant antibacterial activity," the FDA nevertheless found that "cyclosporine has been shown to possess antifungal activity against 2 relevant human pathogens" in in vitro and animal studies and therefore should remain classified as an antibiotic drug. The FDA applied this antibiotic classification to three approved NDAs and two pending NDAs of Sandoz in 1995.

Allergan cited this and subsequent similar FDA controversies in its attempt to classify its product as a nonantibiotic. At bottom, Allergan argued that its drug was approved for no antibiotic indications and that the FDA as a matter of statutory interpretation should have construed the term "antibiotic drug" in section 125(d) (2) of FDAMA "to mean antibiotic drug product rather than antibiotic active moiety." The former, "product," was dependent on the product as a whole in the context of its indication, whereas the latter, "moiety," related solely to the active drug substance in any of its forms and indications. The FDA determined that the statutory definition related to the drug substance "the definition does not reference a particular quantity of the drug substance, nor a particular indication." Reviewing the scientific study, the FDA noted that cyclosporine in fact has antimicrobial activity against two fungal pathogens at concentrations that are found in plasma following administration of the drug to patients at its recommended doses. Accordingly, it was properly classified as an antibiotic.

The court, noting the plausibility of Allergan's view of the law, nevertheless found that the FDA's action was more consistent with the language of FDAMA. The statute, the court noted, defined "antibiotic" as "any other drug intended for human use containing any quantity of any chemical substance which is produced by a microorganism and which has the capacity to inhibit or destroy microorganisms in dilute solution. . ." 21 USC section 321(jj). Thus, the court found that the language was quite explicit in including in the definition any ingredient in any quantity that destroys microorganisms in dilute solution. Its "intended use" under the statutory language referred, the court held, merely to the fact that it is intended for use in humans, not necessarily for "antimicrobial" use per se, as Allergan argued. Under these criteria, the court found that cyclosporine was clearly included in the class of products defined by the statute as "antibiotic."

Turning to the term "dilute solution," Allergan argued that it clearly referred to the use of the drug and its activity at the levels found in its own product, Restasis, rather than its concentration in the predecessor product, Sandimmune, where it was present in far higher concentrations. The court, adopting the view of the FDA, rejected this contention, by noting that the statutory language did not define "dilute solution" further, and consequently, did not determine what evidence the FDA should consider in determining the antimicrobial character of the ingredient. That it was antimicrobial in concentrations found in Sandimmune, therefore, settled the matter notwithstanding that the amounts in Restasis were not antimicrobial. In other words, its approval at the higher dose in Sandimmune rendered the ingredient an antibiotic, irrespective of the fact that Restasis itself was not antibiotic in effect. At bottom, the FDA's scientific expertise was given great—and decided—deference by the court.

As this case shows, the stakes involved in the classification of a product as antibiotic are quite high, and, as it turns out, a definition believed long-settled has again, in light of the intense economic consequences, come up for renewed debate. The court's decision, however, in so firmly supporting the FDA's scientific expertise and granting it the deference intended by Congress, has in all likelihood settled this issue—at least until another economically weighty set of facts presents yet another angle for intellectual attack.

CONCLUSION

The history and development of antibiotic regulation represents a process of increasing evolution of a particular legislative scheme that had, over time, increasingly outstripped the historical circumstances and needs that were its provenance. Revised by the FDA to take account both of changing scientific standards and regulatory and marketplace realities, the scheme was finally abandoned entirely by the Congress and folded into the standard drug regulations, thereby putting an end to its unique approval mechanism and separate status.

REFERENCES

1. FDCA §507(a), 21 USC 357(a).
2. Pub. L. No. 77–366, 55 Stat 851 (1941); Pub. L. No. 79–139, 59 Stat 463 (1945); codified at 21 USC §356.
3. FDCA §507(a), 21 USC 357.
4. John D. Harrision. Antibiotic Application Requirements. Clin Res Practices & Drug Reg Affairs 1986; 4(4);265, 267.

5. *Id. at 267.*
6. 21 USC §357(a).
7. Harrison. *Id. at 267.*
8. See FDA Proposal, 47FR 19957. May 5, 1982; see also former 21 CFR 314.50, 314.55.
9. Harrison. *Id. at 269.*
10. *Id.*
11. FDA Order, 47 FR 39155. September 7, 1982.
12. See *Barr Laboratories, Inc. v. Harris*, 482 F. Supp. 1183 (DDC 1980).
13. See *Pfizer, Inc. v. Richardson*, 434 F2 d 536 (2 d Cir 1970).
14. See In the Matter of Antibiotic Antifungal Drugs (FDA 1988). 1988–1989n FDC LRept Dev Trans Bind at 38070.
15. 21 CFR 433.1(a) (repealed).
16. See former 21 CFR 314.
17. See former 21 CFR 314.70.
18. 63 FR 26066.
19. 64 FR 396, 64 FR 26657 (May 17, 1999).
20. 21 CFR parts 430–460
21. Marketing Exclusivity and Patent Provisions for Certain Antibiotic Drugs. 65 FR 3623 (Jan. 24, 2000).
22. 65 FR 3623 (Jan. 24, 2000).
23. *Id. at 3624.*
24. *Id.*
25. *Id.*
26. 65 FR at 3625.
27. Guidance for Industry and Reviewers: Repeal of Section 507 of the Federal Food, Drug and Cosmetic Act. FDA Center for Drug Evaluation and Research ("CDER"). May 1998.
28. Section 201(jj) of the FDCA.
29. Guidance for Industry: Drug Master Files for Bulk Antibiotic Drug Substances.FDA Center for Drug Evaluation and Research ("CDER"). November, 1999.
30. Civil Action No. 03–2236 (RMC). U.S. District Court. District of Columbia. (Jan. 19, 2005).

[illegible]

[illegible] Section 507 [illegible]

[illegible]

[illegible]

7

Generic Drugs in a Changing Intellectual Property Landscape

Neil F. Greenblum, Esq., Michael J. Fink, Esq., Stephen M. Roylance, Esq., P. Branko Pejic, Esq., Sean Myers-Payne, Esq., and Paul A. Braier, Esq.

Greenblum & Bernstein, P.L.C., Reston, Virginia, U.S.A.

INTRODUCTION

In almost any industry in the United States, there is no built-in mechanism for detecting patent infringement. Therefore, the typical patent owner would normally be blissfully unaware of any possible infringers unless he or she monitors the marketplace, or unless an allegedly infringing product or process happens by chance to be brought to the patent owner's attention. Nearly always, this will happen only after the alleged infringer is already on the market.

As for the alleged infringer, he or she is under no obligation to search for patents, or to study any allegedly blocking patents (although this would sometimes be advisable). Further, an alleged infringer is under no obligation to bring any finding to the attention of the patent owner.

Due to the highly regulated nature of the drug industry in the United States, however, there is an interplay between patents and drug regulation that is unique among all industries—an interplay that is actually designed to encourage patent litigation and bring generic products to market prior to patent expiration. Details of this interplay are presented in chapter 4, and will not be elaborated upon here. Because of this interplay, however, it is critical for members of the pharmaceutical industry, both branded and generic, to have an understanding of patents and issues that can arise during patent litigation.

This chapter will present an overview of U.S. patent law, and on how patents, litigation, and administrative procedures are strategically employed in the pharmaceutical industry. The section "Life-Cycle Strategies for Branded Products" of this chapter addresses several common strategies—commonly referred to as evergreening—used by the branded pharmaceutical industry to delay generic entry, and to lengthen brand product exclusivity in the market. The section "Current Issues of Importance to the Generic Industry" of this chapter addresses issues commonly raised in patent litigation, including validity, infringement, and enforceability. This section also addresses preliminary injunctions, an issue that is often not sufficiently addressed in Hatch–Waxman litigation. The section "FTC Scrutiny of Agreements with Generics" of this chapter addresses the heightened scrutiny by the Department of Justice and the Federal Trade Commission (FTC) given to agreements between brand companies and generics. Conclusions are presented in the last section of this chapter.

LIFE-CYCLE STRATEGIES FOR BRANDED PRODUCTS

Patent Strategies

Introduction

While the laws and rules that pertain to obtaining a pharmaceutical patent in the United States are the same as for other technologies, many of the underlying strategies will differ considerably. For example, because a pharmaceutical product's entry into the U.S. market is dictated, and in some instances slowed, by the Food and Drug Administration (FDA), managing the timing of patent application filing is particularly important. For this reason as well, multifaceted strategies to maximize the term of the patent are often employed. Still further, understanding who the target potential infringer is, be it an innovator or generic company, is also critical to obtaining a useful patent. These issues and others are presented in the following discussion.

Initial Filing Strategy

The term of a U.S. patent is 20 years from the effective U.S. filing date (1). Thus, for a U.S. utility application having no priority claim, the effective U.S. filing date is the date on which the application is filed in the U.S. Patent and Trademark Office (PTO) and granted a filing date (2). For a U.S. utility application that claims priority to an earlier filed U.S. utility application, the effective filing date is the filing date of the earlier filed U.S. application to which priority is claimed; if there are multiple priority claims, the filing date is the earliest filing date of the applications to which priority is claimed (3). Patent Cooperation Treaty (PCT) international applications have an effective U.S. filing date that is the date the PCT international application is filed (35 USC §365), but if priority of such PCT application is claimed to an earlier filed U.S. application, then the aforementioned rules apply. Finally, U.S. utility applications that claim priority to U.S. provisional applications or foreign applications have as their effective filing date the date of filing the U.S. utility application in the United States (4).

Under most circumstances, the effective U.S. filing date for calculating a patent term is also the U.S. filing date for purposes of considering novelty-defeating art (5). This is not true, however, for applications that claim priority to U.S. provisional applications—in those instances, the effective date for considering novelty-defeating provisions [35 USC §102(b)] is the provisional application filing date (6). Thus, the provisional application provides advantages that are not afforded by foreign priority applications (7).

It is important to keep in mind that priority claims, particularly to U.S. provisional or foreign applications, only serve their intended purpose if the priority application fully describes the invention that is ultimately claimed. In the United States, the priority application will entitle the applicant to its filing date only if it fully supports, as required by 35 USC §112, the invention claimed in the later filed U.S. utility application (8). There is, therefore, little to be gained from filing an ill-conceived or rushed priority application, as such applications often partially, or completely, fail to support the invention that is later claimed.

Other strategic concerns, such as publication of the inventive concept, should be considered. For example, it often serves a business interest on the part of the inventor or the assignee of a patent application to publish a description of the invention in a journal article or similar publication. Such publication will not necessarily bar patentability in the United States if a U.S. provisional or nonprovisional application fully disclosing the invention is filed within 1 year of the publication date of the description of the invention (9). For purposes of determining what date to "docket" for calculating the 1-year anniversary, it is important to consider that many journals electronically prepublish online prior to an actual publication date, and to plan accordingly.

Because a U.S. nonprovisional application will automatically be published, the prior art effect of the application itself should also be considered (10). However, a U.S. application can be filed, under limited circumstances, with a request for nonpublication, which allows the patent applicant to maintain the inventive concept in relative secrecy during the prosecution of the patent (11). If the patent applicant chooses to foreign file the application, perhaps via a PCT application, a request for nonpublication in the United States, cannot be made (or if it has already been made, the applicant must inform the U.S. PTO) (12).

A PCT application, on the other hand, allows applicants to file an application in a language other than English to delay the prior art effect of that application as a pending U.S. application (13). The PCT process also provides to patent applicants the results of an earlier prior art search than would be obtained by filing first in the United States, which allows for the possibility of a more streamlined examination when ultimately entering the United States (14).

Of course, application-filing strategy must be considered in light of the overall patent strategy. For patent applications filed early in the life of a product line, such as those directed to the active ingredient or for a composition, patent term can be critical. Patents that are prosecuted to complement existing patents, however, are often prosecuted with an eye toward rapid issuance, and priority claims may not be favored. Ultimately, a carefully conceived plan for developing an entire portfolio will yield the best results.

Patent Drafting Strategy

As with application filing strategy, strategy for preparing a patent application requires careful consideration of the strategic purpose of the patent. For example, is the patent intended to protect the invention from infringement by innovator companies, which might produce an analogous product with a different active ingredient, or is it intended to stop the generic company, which will produce a bioequivalent product using the same active ingredient? The former requires a patent strategy that will support broad generic claims, while the latter allows for prosecution of claims narrowly tailored to cover only the marketed product. A failure to carefully consider these issues before drafting and filing a patent application can result either in a significant waste of money or in a worthless patent.

Patent strategies aimed at stopping innovator companies can often be made without consideration of the FDA's Approved Drug Products with Therapeutic Equivalence Evaluations (*Orange Book–*) listing strategies. That is, innovator competitors will often enter the market by way of a new drug application process that requires no notice to existing market players. Lawsuits resulting from such market entries occur after entry into the market has already begun, and patents asserted in such lawsuits need not be listed in the *Orange Book*.

Patent strategies aimed at stopping other innovator companies that often focus on obtaining broad generic claims to classes of compounds. While the PTO will grant such patents, they are more difficult to obtain. A patent applicant is entitled to claim that which he has set forth in a manner that demonstrates that he had possession of the claimed invention (35 USC §112, first paragraph, written description), and which he teaches how to make and use (35 USC §112, first paragraph, enablement) (15). Obviously, it is more difficult to demonstrate possession of and to teach how to make and use an entire class of compounds than it is for a single compound. Additionally, even if the production of all of the compounds in a class has been sufficiently described, there is no guarantee that the bioactivity of those compounds will all be the same. While there is no formal requirement, the PTO is increasingly requiring some demonstration of actual possession of the claimed invention, and this adds very significantly to the cost in generating data sufficient to support generic claims.

Because of their generic, and upstream, nature, logic suggests that patents directed to generic processes for making or discovering new drug products, or to precursor compounds used in the production of, a drug product could be quite powerful. However, patents directed to processes for making drug products cannot be listed in the *Orange Book*, which generally renders these patents useful only outside an abbreviated new drug applications (ANDA) context (16). Additionally, the Supreme Court decision in *Merck v. Integra* raised serious questions about the usefulness of patents directed to discovering new drug products, in any context (17).

While patents for stopping innovator companies can be drafted without regard to the FDA-approved product (i.e., the "reference listed drug"), patents for stopping generic companies often cannot. Patents for hindering generic competitors, in most instances, are drafted with the goal of listing the patent in the *Orange Book*. In order to list the patent in the *Orange Book*, at least one claim of the patent must "cover" the *Orange Book* reference listed drug product (18). A patent with claims that cannot be listed in the *Orange Book* may only have value in lawsuits outside the context of ANDA filings, which considerably lessens its value.

Although patents listed in the *Orange Book* must include at least one claim that covers the product, many different types of claims can achieve that purpose. Claims directed to a particular active ingredient, salts, polymorphs, formulations, the active ingredient in combination with other drugs, methods of using the active ingredient, and devices including the active ingredient, can all be listed in the *Orange Book* (19). As noted earlier, patents including only claims for processes, or methods, for making a reference listed drug product cannot be listed in the *Orange Book*, but products made by certain processes (i.e., "product by process" claims) can be listed in the *Orange Book* (20). Thus, where possible, never prosecute a pharmaceutical application with claims limited to methods of making, and always try to include "product by process" claims along with method of making claims.

While claims to a generic class will certainly be more effective in stopping the innovator company, a far narrower claim scope can still effectively stop the generic competitor. That is, because an ANDA can only be filed for the "same" drug [21 USC §355(j)], patent claims that are limited to a specific drug are still quite valuable. Indeed, because ANDA applicants must produce the same active ingredient, arguments for noninfringement of a patent to an active ingredient can seldom be made, and ANDA applicants most often simply wait until the expiration of the "basic compound patent."

Additionally, because an ANDA applicant must demonstrate that its product is bioequivalent to the reference listed product [21 USC §355(j)], patent claims that cover a range of bioequivalence are quite valuable as well. This regulatory requirement for bioequivalence has led innovators to seek patent protection for in vitro dissolution profiles and for in vivo drug plasma levels for their drug products, both of which can be used to demonstrate bioequivalence (*Orange Book* at xii 27th ed. 2007). Patents having claims to both in vitro dissolution profiles and in vivo drug plasma levels are very difficult to avoid infringing by ANDA applicants, and thus, those patents are often challenged on validity grounds. Such challenges are often less than clean cut.

Patents having claims directed to new uses of *Orange Book*–listed products are of more limited value. While such patents can be listed for a product in the *Orange Book* if the claimed use is approved by the FDA (21 CFR §314.53), ANDA applicants can avoid certifying with regard to these patents by simply stating to the FDA that they do not seek approval for that approved use (21). This process, often called a "little eight" certification, renders such late-listed method of use patents of only marginal value.

In conclusion, in drafting and filing a pharmaceutical patent application, it is critical to understand not only the basic invention, but how the patent will be used in the market. A failure to appreciate the business strategy can result in a significant waste in resources.

Patent Prosecution Strategy—Continuing Prosecution

Patent applicants must continue to be mindful of the overall patent strategy throughout prosecution as well. There are numerous pitfalls and traps for the unwary, and strategies that may be beneficial for one market strategy may be useless for others.

For example, for the reasons noted earlier, patent claims directed to methods of making, or to methods of using a drug product, may be of limited value. As the PTO will often restrict claims directed to a basic compound into one application, claims to methods of making into another application, and methods of using into a third application, the potential usefulness of these applications must be evaluated prior to proceeding in their prosecution. However, where the claimed use is the sole approved indication, prosecution of the method of use claims may be the most expedient way to obtain an *Orange Book* listable patent.

Continuation patent applications are frequently used, with considerable success, to develop a significant patent portfolio based on an original well-written patent application. It is often advisable to file a continuation application, where the claims already obtained are of more limited scope or usefulness, or where they exclude certain desired embodiments. It is also frequently advisable to maintain pendency of a family of applications that are deemed by the applicant to be of high value in protecting a product line. However, patent applicants should understand that the longer a patent application remains pending, the greater the opportunity for critical issues to be identified by the PTO. This can be troublesome when litigation on the basic patent is concurrently ongoing. Thus, embarking on a continuation application filing strategy must be made in view of a cost-to-benefit consideration.

Continuation-in-part (CIP) applications (having some "old" and some "new" matter) are viewed by some inexperienced practitioners as a means for supplementing the disclosure of a sparse patent application, or of adding new embodiments discovered after an original filing date. However, such CIP applications should only be filed after a very careful consideration, and complete understanding, of the implications and ramifications of such filings. For example, claims in CIP applications are only entitled to the filing dates of earlier filed applications to the extent that they are *completely* supported by those earlier applications—if even a small portion of a claim is supported only by the new matter, that claim is only entitled to the filing date of the new application (22). Moreover, a CIP's term is 20 years from the filing date of the earliest application to which priority is claimed. These often-misunderstood facts result in the filing and prosecution of many patent applications of marginal value.

Patent Prosecution Strategy—Maximizing and Enhancing Term

To avoid unnecessary costs in the form of extension-of-time fees, it behooves patent applicants in all technology areas to prosecute their patent applications diligently. Additionally, based upon "guarantees" made by the PTO to diligently examine patent applications, the PTO provides for positive patent term adjustments if it fails to diligently examine a patent application. However, the positive adjustments can be offset by an applicants' failure to diligently prosecute the application.

Basically, the PTO provides for a single day of positive patent term adjustment for each day of delay beyond: (*i*) 14 months from filing (a U.S. utility application or national stage of a PCT application) to a first office action on the merits, (*ii*) 4 months for responding to an applicant's reply to an office action or appeal brief, (*iii*) 4 months for acting on a favorable appeal from the Board of Patent Appeals or Court of Appeals for the Federal Circuit, and (*iv*) 4 months to issue a patent after applicant pays the issue fee (23). Additionally, the PTO further provides 1 day of patent term adjustment for each day of pendency beyond 3 years of total pendency, not including the above-noted specific guarantees (24).

But, filing a continuation application will erase any positive adjustment accumulated in a parent application—that is, the accumulated term adjustment will not carry forward (25). Furthermore, positive adjustments will be offset by an applicant's failure to engage in reasonable efforts to prosecute the application, as demonstrated by a failure to respond to any office action within 3 months (26). The PTO will also reduce the positive adjustment if an applicant files an amendment, such as a preliminary amendment, that necessitates a supplemental action by an examiner, or by submitting a nonresponsive or supplemental reply (27). In order to maximize patent term, it is important to understand what actions during prosecution may result in a modification of the term of the patent.

Even after patent issuance, some strategies still exist for obtaining a longer effective patent term. Enacted as a component of the Hatch–Waxman Act, 35 USC §156 provides for patent term extensions for some products in certain situations. This was intended to enable the owners of patents on certain human drugs, food or color additives, medical devices, animal drugs, and veterinary biological products to restore to the terms of their patents some of the time lost while awaiting approval from the FDA (28). Briefly, the extension is available to obtain up to five additional years, provided the enforceable term will not be greater than 14 years from the first FDA approval of the product (even if it has multiple indications) (29). The extension is also only available for one patent, even if multiple patents cover a product (30). The application for extension must be filed by the patentee, with the PTO, within 60 days (not 2 months) from FDA approval of the product; the FDA determines the length of the regulatory approval process; and the PTO determines applicant's eligibility, the length of the extension, and issues a certificate for the extension (31).

Citizen Petitions

On September 27, 2007, the President signed H R 3580, the FDA Amendments Act of 2007 (the Act), which reauthorizes a number of Food and Drug programs including the Prescription Drug User Fee Act (PDUFA) and Medical Device User Fee Act (MDUFA); extends and modifies authorities related to pediatric uses of drugs and medical devices; and expands current authority related to postmarketing surveillance of drugs. As is relevant to this section, the act amended the Federal Food, Drug, and Cosmetic Act (FFDCA) to curb abuses of the citizens petition process, and applies to both ANDAs and new drug approval applications submitted pursuant to section 505(b)(2).

The acts require that a party submitting a citizens petition must provide a certification and verification that the citizens petition is being submitted in good faith and not for the purposes of delaying approval of a pending drug application, and authorizes the FDA to deny a citizens petition if the FDA determines, at any time, that the petition was submitted for purposes of delaying a pending drug application. The act also prohibits the FDA from delaying the approval process, while considering the citizens petition, unless the FDA make a finding that the petition raises issues such that delay is necessary "to protect the public health." The act, however, sets a 180-day limit, which cannot be extended, to take action on a citizens petition.

As early as 2000, the FTC had recognized that, due in part to the unique nature of pharmaceuticals regulation and legislation, citizens petitions were ripe for abuse. Specifically, the FTC noted that:

> Citizen petitions often raise legitimate issues concerning matters before the FDA, and issues raised in citizen petitions have played useful roles in ensuring the safety of various drug products. The FTC staff comment cautioned, however, that regulatory processes can provide an opportunity for anticompetitive abuses, and offered suggestions the FDA may wish to consider to discourage such abuse.
>
> The staff comment noted that, in an industry where entry is regulated, such as those regulated by the FDA (e.g., medical devices, pharmaceuticals, etc.), "to delay competition may be a lucrative strategy for an incumbent," through "improper petitioning." The FTC staff said that its own observation of the pharmaceutical industry shows that existing product holders have an incentive to block generic entrants and may do so by raising concerns about a potential generic entrant's drug application before the FDA. "A competitor may raise these concerns itself or have them raised by independent parties (either individuals or groups) by providing consideration to file a citizen petition raising the issues, so as to disguise the anticompetitive intent behind the petitioning. The effect of such a petition," the staff said, "could be to delay FDA approval of a rival drug application, even if the petition is not ultimately upheld." (32)

The passage of time confirmed the FTC's concerns about the potential for citizens petition abuses, which is illustrated by Gary Buehler's testimony before congress in 2006.

> A high percentage of the petitions OGD reviews are denied. An analysis of petitions answered between calendar years 2001 and 2005, raising issues about

> the approvability of generic products (42 total responses), showed that FDA denied 33, denied three in part, and granted six. It should be noted that when petitions are granted, wholly or in part, it is often because FDA already has the proposed scientific or legal standard in place or is already planning to take the action that the petition requests. While the citizen petition process is a valuable mechanism for the Agency to receive information from the public, it is noteworthy that very few of these petitions on generic drug matters have presented data or analysis that significantly altered FDA's policies. Of the 42 citizen petition responses examined, only three petitions led to a change in Agency policy on the basis of data or information submitted in the petition.

(Statement of Gary Buehler, R.Ph, Director of the Office of Generic Drugs, Center for Drug Evaluation and Research, FDA before U.S. Senate Special Committee on Aging on July 20, 2006). It is against the backdrop of these potential abuses that the act was signed into law.

With respect to the act, it amended section 505 of the FFDCA by adding a new subsection limiting the use of the citizen petition process to delay approval of generic drug applications (33). The amendments apply to both ANDAs submitted pursuant to section 505(j) of the FFDCA and new drug approval applications submitted pursuant to section 505(b)(2) (34).

The amendments require that a party submitting a citizens petition (or any supplement, comment or response thereto) must submit certifications and verifications, with the petition, establishing that it is being submitted in good faith (35). Specifically, the petitioner must provide written certification stating that:

> I certify that, to my best knowledge and belief: (a) this petition includes all information and views upon which the petition relies; (b) this petition includes representative data and/or information known to the petitioner which are unfavorable to the petition; and (c) I have taken reasonable steps to ensure that any representative data and/or information which are unfavorable to the petition were disclosed to me. I further certify that the information upon which I have based the action requested herein first became known to the party on whose behalf this petition is submitted on or about the following date: ________. If I received or expect to receive payments, including cash and other forms of consideration, to file this information or its contents, I received or expect to receive those payments from the following persons or organizations: ________. I verify under penalty of perjury that the foregoing is true and correct as of the date of the submission of this petition (36).

The certification must also contain the date on which such information first became known to such party and the names of such persons or organizations inserted in the first and second blank space, respectively (37). The petitioner must also submit a verification stating that:

> The Secretary shall not accept for review any supplemental information or comments on a petition unless the party submitting such information or comments does so in written form and the subject document is signed and contains the following verification: "I certify that, to my best knowledge and belief: (a) I have not intentionally delayed submission of this document or its contents; and (b) the information upon which I have based the action requested herein first became known to me on or about ________. If I received or expect to receive payments, including cash and other forms of consideration, to file this information or its contents, I received or expect to receive those payments from the following persons or organizations: ________. I verify under penalty of perjury that the foregoing is true and correct as of the date of the submission of this petition." (38)

As with the certification, the verification must contain the date on which such information first became known to the party and the names of such persons or organizations inserted in the first and second blank space, respectively (39).

Absent such certifications and verifications, the FDA is prohibited from accepting a citizens petition. If at any time, the FDA determines that any citizens petition or related submission is being made to delay approval; of an ANDA or section 505(b)(2) application, the FDA may deny the citizens petition (40). The FDA may also deny a citizens petition which it determines on its face does not raise valid scientific or regulatory issues (41).

Upon receiving a properly certified and verified citizens petition, the FDA is prohibited from delaying approval of a pending ANDA or 505(b)(2) application as a result of any request to take action relating to the application either before or during consideration of the request. The amendment establishes the general presumption that a citizens petition should not delay FDA's review of that pending application (42). This presumption, however, may be overcome, and the FDA may delay approval of a pending application, upon a showing that:

1. The request is a written citizen petition submitted pursuant to 21 CFR §10.30 or is a petition seeking an administrative stay of action, and
2. The FDA determines that a delay is necessary "to protect the public health."

The act does not set specific time limits within which the FDA is required to review a citizens petition to make the "public health" determination (43). But, upon making such a determination, the FDA must delay the review of the ANDA or 505(b)(2) application to protect the public health, and the FDA is required to notify the applicant of the delay within 30 days (44). This action is considered to be part of the application itself and is subject to the same confidentiality and disclosure requirements as a pending application (45). In making such a notification, the FDA must provide the following information:

- The fact that the FDA has determined a delay in the application review is necessary to protect the public health as a result of either a citizen petition or a petition for an administrative stay of action.
- Any clarification or additional data the applicant should submit to the docket on the petition to permit FDA to review the petition promptly.
- A brief summary of the specific substantive issues raised in the petition which form the basis of FDA's determination that the delay is necessary to protect the public health (46).

The act also authorizes FDA to issue guidance identifying the factors that it will use to determine when a petition is submitted for the primary purpose of delay. The new subsection further requires that the FDA must take action on a petition within 180 days after submission (47). This 180-day limit may not be extended for any reason, including FDA's determination it is necessary to delay review of the application to protect the public health (48). The act provides that civil action can be brought against the agency for an issue raised in the petition only after the FDA has taken final action (49). Final agency action is defined to include a final decision within the meaning of 21 CFR §10.45(d) or expiration of the 180-day period without a final FDA decision (50).

In addition, prior to the act, a generic first filer could forfeit its 180-day exclusivity by failure to obtain tentative approval (FOTA) within 30 months from when the ANDA was filed. This was problematic when a delay in approval was caused by a citizen petition. As amended by the act, if any citizen petition delays approval of an ANDA, then the 30-month FOTA period for determining forfeiture (unrelated to the 30-month stay of approval) is extended by the amount of time the citizen petition was pending before the FDA (51). The extension of the 30-month FOTA period is granted regardless of whether the citizen petition is ultimately granted or denied (52). This provision helps to protect a first filer from FOTA forfeiture where a delay in approval is caused by a citizen petition.

CURRENT ISSUES OF IMPORTANCE TO THE GENERIC INDUSTRY

Patent Validity Issues

As part of the approval process, an ANDA applicant must make a certification addressing each patent listed in the *Orange Book* that claims the drug (53). The ANDA applicant must certify that (I) no such patent information has been submitted to the FDA; (II) the patent has expired; (III) the patent is set to expire on a certain date; or (IV) the patent is invalid or will not be infringed by the manufacture, use, or sale of the new generic drug for which the ANDA is submitted (54). These are commonly referred to as paragraph I, II, III, and IV certifications.

When an ANDA contains a paragraph IV certification, the ANDA applicant must give notice to the patentee and the NDA holder and provide a detailed basis for its belief that the patent is not infringed, invalid, or unenforceable (55). Further, in order to obtain the 180-day exclusivity afforded by the Hatch–Waxman Amendments, the ANDA applicant generally must prevail on these issues in court.

Accordingly, it is essential that a successful generic competitor have a working understanding of patent validity, unenforceability, and infringement concepts. These concepts are discussed later.

Validity in General

Proving that a patent is invalid (or even unenforceable) is a very difficult challenge. Patent claims are presumed to be valid (56). This presumption can be overcome only by clear and convincing evidence (57).

In order for a court to uphold the validity of a patent claim, the claim must meet the statutory requirements of Title 35 of the United States Code. A patent claim may be held invalid in litigation if the claimed invention fails to satisfy the novelty and/or nonobvious subject matter conditions for patentability set forth in the patent laws, namely 35 USC §§102 and 103 or if it fails to satisfy the requirements of adequacy of description, "enablement," "best mode," or "definiteness" of 35 USC §112.

Patent Claims Are Not Valid If They Are Anticipated Or Obvious

One of the first steps in evaluating a potential generic drug project should be an extensive investigation and review of the development of the technology, which is the context of the particular drug in question. As a first step, a comprehensive prior art "search" should be conducted (as well as a complete investigation of potential "prior art" activities, such as public disclosure, public uses, and the general context of the development of the drug). The goal is to uncover prior art which would potentially render the relevant patent(s) invalid and/or unenforceable by reason, among other things, of "anticipation" or "obviousness." Both of these concepts are, necessarily, legalistic, and are discussed in detail later. Additionally, the patent itself and its history should be thoroughly studied to determine compliance with other requirements, also discussed later.

Anticipation

Anticipation under 35 USC §102 requires the disclosure in a single piece of prior art (this can be a "publication" or an "event") of each and every limitation of a claimed invention (58). If the prior art does not anticipate (exactly disclose) the claimed invention, in a single reference, the question of whether the prior art renders the claimed invention obviously remains. "Obviousness" is discussed in more detail later.

Obviousness

The determination of obviousness under §103 is a question of law (59). Specifically, §103 provides, in pertinent part, that:

> A patent may not be obtained though the invention is not identically disclosed or described as set forth in §102 of this Title, if the differences between the subject matter sought to be patented and the prior art are such that the subject matter as a whole would have been obvious at the time the invention was made to a person having ordinary skill in the art to which the subject matter pertains. Patentability shall not be negatived by the manner in which the invention was made.

The language of §103 requires that the evaluation of obviousness be from the perspective of a *hypothetical* person "of ordinary skill in the art at the time that the invention was made" (60). The proper approach to making a determination of obviousness was first described by the Supreme Court in *Graham v. John Deere Co* (61). Specifically, it was stated that: Under §103, the scope and content of the prior art are to be determined; differences between the prior art and the claims at issue are to be ascertained; and the level of ordinary skill in the pertinent art is to be resolved. Against this background, the obviousness or nonobviousness of the subject matter is determined (62).

Other evidence of nonobviousness such as long-felt but unsolved need, commercial success, failure of others, copying, and unexpected results must also be considered in a determination of obviousness (63).

The Supreme Court has recently elaborated on this approach (64). An obviousness analysis requires "an expansive and flexible approach" with "a broad inquiry [that] invites courts, where appropriate, to look at any secondary considerations that would prove instructive" (65). "The combination of familiar elements according to known methods is likely to be obvious when it does no more than yield predictable results" (66). "[A]ny need or problem known in the field of endeavor at the time of invention and addressed by the patent can provide a reason for combining the elements in the manner claimed" (67). For example, obviousness may be proved by noting that there existed at the time of invention a known problem for which there was an obvious solution encompassed by the patent's claims (obvious to try). Specifically, "[w]hen there is a design need or market pressure to solve a problem and there are a finite number of identified, predictable solutions, a person of ordinary skill has good reason to pursue the known options within his or her technical grasp. If this leads to the anticipated success, it is likely the product not of innovation but of ordinary skill and common sense" (68).

Patent Claims Must Also Satisfy the Requirements of 35 USC §112

35 USC §112, first and second paragraphs, sets forth essentially three requirements for a patent: (*i*) the "written description" and "enablement" requirements, (*ii*) the "best mode" requirement, and (*iii*) the requirement of distinct claiming.

The Written Description Requirement

What is recited in the claims of a patent must be supported by a "written description" thereof in the specification. To fulfill the written description requirement, a patent specification must describe the invention and do so in sufficient detail that one skilled in the art can clearly conclude that "the inventor invented the claimed invention" (69).

Enablement

35 USC §112, first paragraph, requires the patent specification to have an enabling disclosure. Specifically, §112, first paragraph, provides in pertinent part that:

> The specification shall contain a written description of the invention and of the manner and process of making and using it, in such full, clear, concise, and exact terms as to enable any person skilled in the art to which it pertains, or with which it is most nearly connected, to make and use the same....

The specification need only be enabling to a person "skilled in the art to which it pertains, or with which it is most nearly connected" (70). In determining whether a patent has an adequate disclosure, it is necessary to bear in mind that "[p]atents are written for those skilled in the relevant art, and thus, an applicant need to not divulge every piece of information which a lay person would need to operate the invention most effectively" (71). The Federal Circuit has recently determined that the issue of whether a claimed invention is enabled by the specification is a matter of law (72).

In determining whether a disclosure is adequate under 35 USC §112 the question is "whether the disclosure is sufficiently definite to guide those skilled in the art to its successful application ... some experimentation, provided it is not an undue amount, is permissible. However, nothing must be left to speculation or doubt" (73). The specification must provide more than "an invitation to experiment in order to determine *how* to make use of [the inventor's] alleged discovery ... the law requires that the disclosure in the application shall *inform* them *how* to use, not how to find out how to use for themselves" (74).

Best Mode

35 USC §112 requires that the patent applicant set forth the best mode of practicing the invention known to the applicant at the time the application for patent is filed. A best mode analysis has two components: the first inquiry focuses on whether the inventor knew of a mode of practicing his invention at the time he filed his patent application which he considered to be better than any other. If he did have a best mode, the next question is whether the inventor disclosed it and did so adequately to enable one of ordinary skill in the art to practice the best mode (75).

Distinct Claiming

35 USC §112, second paragraph, states that:

> The specification shall conclude with one or more claims particularly pointing out and distinctly claiming the subject matter which the applicant regards as his invention.

Under this statute, the general requirement is that the claims, read in light of the specification, reasonably apprise those skilled in the art of the scope of the invention (76). A decision as to whether a claim is invalid under the second paragraph of §112 requires a determination whether those skilled in the art would understand what is claimed (77).

"Double Patenting" Is Prohibited

An inventor is only entitled to a single patent for a patentable invention. This is reflected in 35 USC §101 which states that:

> Whoever invents or discovers any new and useful process, machine, manufacture, or composition of matter, or any new and useful improvement thereof, may obtain *a patent* therefore. . . .

This prohibition is referred to as "statutory double patenting." In addition to statutory double patenting, the doctrine of "judicially created" or nonstatutory double patenting has been propounded. "[n]on-statutory, or 'obviousness-type,' double patenting is a judicially created doctrine adopted to prevent claims in separate applications or patents that do not recite the 'same' invention, but nonetheless claim inventions so alike that granting both exclusive rights would effectively extend the life of patent protection" (78).

The True Inventors Must Be Named

A patent is invalid if more or fewer than the true inventors are named (79). Because a patent is presumed valid under 35 USC §282, there follows a presumption that the named inventors on a patent are the true and only inventors (80).

When two or more persons jointly invent, they must jointly apply for a patent (81). Coinventors must so apply "even though . . . they did not physically work together or at the same time, . . . each did not make the same type or amount of contribution, or . . . each did not make a contribution to the subject matter of every claim of the patent" (82). Because conception is the touchstone of inventorship, each "joint inventor must contribute in some significant manner to the conception of the invention" (83). "Conception is the formation in the mind of the inventor, of a definite and permanent idea of the complete and operative invention, as it is hereafter to be applied in practice" (84). "An inventor may solicit the assistance of others when perfecting the invention without 'losing' any patent rights" (85).

Because coinventors need not contribute to the subject matter of every claim of the patent, inventorship is determined on a claim-by-claim basis (86).

Practical Application

As a practical matter, an initial goal is often to locate and identify "anticipatory" prior art, as defined earlier. However, such a "smoking gun" is rare, and so resort must be had to other prior art, or other attacks on validity, also outlined earlier.

Thus, it is often necessary to acquire and piece together a mosaic of information which tells the whole story of the context and development of the drug, as well as activities "behind the scenes," which could give rise to meaningful, credible attacks on the patent.

Thus, in the context of the true facts surrounding the development of the drug, the alleged "invention" may be merely an obvious combination of old elements. Or the invention may have been the next (and obvious) progression of ideas which have long existed.

In conducting such an investigation, care should be taken to keep all of the foregoing requirements in mind. Thus, an inventor's (or company's) own patents and publications can be "prior art" with respect to the patent in question. And the award of more than one patent to a particular inventor or company may also give rise to prohibited "double patenting" (discussed earlier), thus invalidating the patent on those grounds.

Other bases for proving invalidity and/or unenforceability, such as failure to comply with the "best mode" requirement, inequitable conduct ("fraud") and inventorship issues are often only developed as a result of the "discovery" process which takes place after litigation has started.

Patent Infringement Issues

In view of requirement that a "paragraph IV" ANDA applicant make the certification discussed earlier (and eventually obtain a judgment of noninfringement and the award of 180-day market exclusivity), it is also essential that a successful generic competitor have a working understanding of patent infringement concepts. These concepts are discussed later.

General Infringement Concepts

Patent infringement involves the violation of the rights of the owner (or licensee) of the patent. Ownership of a patent confers the right to exclude others from making, using, selling, or offering for sale the invention within the United States, or importing the invention into the United States (87). Infringement of a patent is the unauthorized use of a patent owner's exclusive rights as defined by the claims of the patent (88). Thus, acts such as the unauthorized making, using, or selling of the claimed invention, or importing or offering the claimed invention for sale, can constitute infringement.

The claims are the specific part of the patent (found at that portion of the patent with the heading "Claims" or "What is claimed is") that define the patent grant and set its boundaries, that is, they establish the patentee's legal rights (89).

Thus, claims must be construed or interpreted to ascertain what they cover.

Construction of Claims

In determining the meaning and scope of the claims, it is first necessary to analyze the relationship of the claims to the specification and prosecution history of the subject patent (90).

In construing a claim, claim terms are given in their ordinary and accustomed meaning, unless examination of the specification, prosecution history, and other claims indicate that the inventor intended otherwise (91). The best source for interpreting a technical term used in a claim is the specification from which it arose and guided, as needed, by the prosecution history (92). The evolution of restrictions in the claims, during the course of examination in the PTO, reveals how those closest to the patenting process—the inventor and the patent examiner—viewed the subject matter (93).

With regard to scope, in construing a claim, care should be taken to avoid a construction that reads on the prior art. [C]laims should be read in a way that avoids ensnaring prior art if it is possible to do so (94). Also with regard to scope, [w]hether or not claims differ from each other, one cannot interpret a claim to be broader than what is contained in the specification and claims as filed (95).

Moreover, [b]ecause the applicant has the burden to "particularly point out and distinctly claim the subject matter which the applicant regards as his invention" (96), if a claim is susceptible to both a broader and a narrower meaning, and the narrower one is clearly supported by the intrinsic evidence while the broader one raises questions of whether it is "supported," courts will adopt the narrower of the two (97).

Closed, Partially Closed, and Open Terminology

When evaluating the scope of a particular claim, care should be taken to ascertain whether "closed," "partially closed," or "open" terminology is employed in the claim. Such terminology is almost always indicated by the use of certain key terms. In this regard, "consisting of" indicates a "closed claim," the use of "consisting essentially of" indicates a partially closed claim, while the use of "comprising" indicates an open claim. "Closed" claims are not open to the inclusion of additional elements beyond what is recited in the claim. Thus, a "closed" claim reciting a composition "consisting of" components A, B, and C would not be infringed by a composition containing A, B, C, and D. Conversely, an "open" claim reciting a composition "comprising" elements A, B, and C would be infringed by a composition containing A, B, C, and D. The use of "consisting essentially of" presents a gray area. Such claims are open to infringement by matter having an additional element, if the additional element does not alter the "basic and novel" character of the invention.

Infringement

A proper infringement analysis requires that the question of infringement be evaluated both literally and under the doctrine of equivalents.

For literal infringement to exist, an accused product must fall clearly within the literal language of the claim(s) in question (98). Every element of the claim must be present in the accused matter for literal infringement to be properly found (99).

All Elements Rule

A patent claim cannot be infringed if any limitation of the claim, or its substantial equivalent, is not present in the accused matter (100). The claim is compared with the proposed or accused matter on an element-by-element basis (101). However, two physical components of an accused device may be viewed in combination to serve as an equivalent of one element of a claimed invention, as long as no claim limitation is thereby wholly vitiated (102).

Doctrine of Equivalents

Even when a claim is not literally infringed, such a claim may be infringed under the doctrine of equivalents. Infringement under the doctrine of equivalents is appropriately applied in situations in which no literal infringement has taken place, but in which an alleged infringer has only made unimportant and insubstantial changes or substitutions in the patented subject matter which, though adding nothing, would be enough to otherwise evade the reach of law (103).

Although the determination of equivalence involves a determination of whether the accused product embodies only an insubstantial change from the patented invention, the essential inquiry remains: Does the accused product or process contain elements identical or equivalent to each claimed element of the patented invention? (104). Thus, a determination of equivalence needs to be made, as an objective inquiry, and on an element-by-element basis (105).

Prosecution History Estoppel

The prosecution history of the patent is of great importance in interpreting the scope of the claims, because equivalence will not be found if it is limited by prosecution history estoppel or if the equivalent item is in the public domain (106). Prosecution history estoppel applies as a limitation to the doctrine of equivalents after the claims have been properly interpreted and no literal infringement is found (107). As the Court of Appeals for the Federal Circuit has repeatedly held, other players in the marketplace are entitled to rely on the record made in the Patent Office [*sic.*] in determining the meaning and scope of the patent (108).

The US Supreme Court has now stated that, where an applicant does not state a reason for an amendment made to the claims during prosecution, prosecution history estoppel will be presumed (109). Moreover, if a claim element is amended for purposes of patentability, there is no longer a range of equivalency (110). Thus, the prosecution history can limit the interpretation of the patent claims to exclude any interpretation disclaimed or disavowed during the prosecution to secure allowance of the claims (111). Unmistakable assertions made by the applicant to the PTO in support of patentability, whether or not required to secure allowance of the claim, also may operate to preclude the patentee from asserting equivalency (112).

Prior Art Can Limit the Scope of Application of the Doctrine of Equivalents

There are other limitations on the scope of coverage that can be asserted under the doctrine of equivalents. For example, for infringement under the doctrine of equivalents to be properly found, the asserted range of equivalents must not be so broad as to encompass prior art teachings (113). Claims should be construed, if possible, so as to sustain validity. If such construction would result in invalidity of the claims, the appropriate legal conclusion is one of noninfringement, not invalidity (114).

Practical Application

The challenge of avoiding infringement in the *Orange Book* context lies in the fact that the drug which is the subject of the ANDA must be bioequivalent to the listed drug (the listed drug presumably being covered by a listed patent), and the bioequivalence must be proven to the satisfaction of the FDA; all while avoiding the claim(s) of the patent.

Avoiding infringement can often boil down to this question: Is there something that the patent claim requires that can be avoided in designing the drug or dosage form in question? If such a claim requirement is not found in the drug or dosage form in question, either literally or equivalently, then the claim is not infringed.

Accordingly, when choosing or designing a drug product, once a patent of concern is identified (such as a patent listed in the *Orange Book* covering the listed drug), choose or design the product so that one or more "elements" of the claim of the *Orange Book* patent is not present in the product. This can be as simple as avoiding the use of a claimed excipient (or equivalent thereof) in a drug formulation. Ordinarily, the patent specification and the prosecution history of the application for the patent will need to be studied so that one can determine whether certain or various alternatives to claimed elements should be properly considered by a court to be equivalent to the claimed elements.

Of course, the development of noninfringement strategies also can involve considerations that are much more complex than the mere omission of a claim element. Such considerations are beyond the scope of this chapter.

Direct and Indirect Infringement

As noted, 35 USC §271(a) provides that "whoever without authority makes, uses, offers to sell, or sells any patented invention, within the United States or imports into the United States any patented invention during the term of the patent therefore, infringes the patent." These are known as acts of direct infringement.

Other than direct infringement, it is also possible to indirectly infringe a patent through inducement of infringement and contributory infringement. In order to establish induced or contributory infringement, there must be an act of direct infringement (115). In the absence of an act of direct infringement, therefore, there can be no liability for indirect infringement (116).

Inducement usually arises in the context of patents related to methods of treatment and situations wherein the accused product is associated with a package insert containing instructions for administering a drug. Induced infringement is defined in 35 USC §271(b), which provides that "whoever actively induces infringement of a patent shall be liable as an infringer." Although the statute does not specify what constitutes "active inducement," courts have generally held that it requires "proof that the accused infringer knowingly aided and abetted another's direct infringement of the patent" (117). To succeed on the theory of inducement of infringement, a plaintiff must prove that the defendants' actions "induced infringing acts and that they knew or should have known their *actions* would induce actual infringement" (118). However, mere knowledge of possible infringement by others does not amount to inducement; specific intent and action to induce infringement must be proven (119). With respect to intent, obtaining a noninfringement opinion by competent patent counsel may negate the intent element by proving that the alleged infringer did not believe it was infringing the patent (120).

As a practical matter, in the context of pharmaceutical cases, when inducement arises, it often does so in situations involving method claims (such as claims directed to a method of treatment, or a specific blood plasma level profile) and situations wherein an alleged infringer "instructed" others to "infringe" the claims of the patent at issue (such as by means of a package insert or similar administration instructions so as to result in, e.g., the claimed method of treatment or blood plasma level profile). In such cases, it should be noted that package inserts and the language of patent claims rarely comport exactly with each other. Thus, generic companies are advised to scrutinize the differences between the patent claims and the package insert at issue and ascertain what language from the insert can be used without infringing the claims.

A second type of indirect infringement is contributory infringement. Defined in 35 USC §271(c), contributory infringement essentially requires that a material component of a patented invention, having no substantial noninfringing use, is sold, offered for sale, or imported into the United States. However, "[t]he mere sale of a product capable of substantial non-infringing uses does not constitute indirect infringement of a patent" (121). Furthermore, contributory infringement under 35 USC §271(c) requires that the contributory acts must occur in the United States (122).

These issues are discussed in further depth in Indirect Patent Infringement in the U.S.: Points to Consider for Generic and API Manufacturers. Journal of Generic Medicines. 2007; 4:287–292.

Willful Infringement

The patent laws provide that a court may increase the amount of damages assessed for infringement up to three times the amount found or assessed. 35 USC.

§284. This can be based on a determination that the infringement was "willful."

The Court of Appeals for the Federal Circuit in *In re Seagate*, 497 F.3 d 1360 (Fed Cir 2007), addressed the issue of the appropriate standard to determine willful infringement. After over ruling the Court's earlier decision in *Underwater Devices*, which set a lower threshold for willful infringement that was more akin to negligence, the Federal Circuit held that "proof of willful infringement permitting enhanced damages requires at least a showing of objective recklessness"(123). The Federal Circuit also stated that "there is no affirmative obligation to obtain opinion of counsel" and thus abandoning the affirmative duty of care formerly necessary to avoid willful infringement (124).

The standard now required to establish willful infringement is stricter than prior to the *In re Seagate* decision. Objective recklessness requires the "patentee must show with clear and convincing evidence that the infringer acted despite an objectively high likelihood that its actions constituted infringement of a valid patent" (125). The patentee must further show that "this objectively-defined risk... was either known or so obvious that is should have been known to the accused infringer" (126).

In any event is almost always a wise approach to obtain a well-reasoned opinion of noninfringement from competent patent counsel.

Preliminary Injunctions

In patent litigations, generally a patent owner can request the court to issue a preliminary injunction, whereby the court enjoins the alleged infringer(s) from continuing to infringe the patent(s) at issue. In paragraph IV pharmaceutical cases, however, the infringing activity is simply the filing of an Abbreviated New Drug Application (ANDA) with the FDA. As no actual infringing product has been made, used, sold, offered for sale, or imported into the United States without the patent owner's authorization, the automatic 30-month stay eliminates the need to seek a preliminary injunction at the outset of the litigation (127). Furthermore, because the litigation is often completed within the 30 months, preliminary injunctions are often unnecessary. However, if the patentee does not file a paragraph IV litigation within the required 45 days of receiving notice of the filing, or if the 30-month stay in the litigation will expire prior to completion of the litigation, a preliminary injunction may be requested by the patent owner (128).

Requirements

Courts have the statutory authority to grant preliminary injunctions in patent cases (129). A preliminary injunction is not to be routinely granted (130). In determining whether to issue a preliminary injunction, a court will evaluate the following four factors: (*i*) a reasonable likelihood of success on the merits, (*ii*) irreparable harm, (*iii*) that the balance of hardships tips in its favor, and (*iv*) the impact of the injunction on the public interest (131). The court will evaluate and balance the four factors in determining whether to issue a preliminary injunction (132). Although no single factor is dispositive, the patentee must establish the first two factors, that is, likelihood of success on the merits and irreparable harm, otherwise the court will not issue the injunction (133).

Reasonable Likelihood of Success on the Merits

When the court evaluates likelihood of success on the merits, it will take into account all defenses raised by the nonmoving party, for example, validity, enforceability, and infringement. The patent owner must show that it will likely prove that the accused infringer infringes the asserted patent(s) and that the asserted patent claims will likely withstand the challenge to their validity and enforceability. Although patents are statutorily presumed valid (134), a court should not issue a preliminary injunction if the nonmoving party raises one or more defenses which demonstrate a substantial question concerning infringement, validity, and/or enforceability of the patent (135). It is the patent owner's burden to show that the nonmoving party's defenses lack substantial merit (136).

The burdens at the preliminary injunction stage track the burdens at trial (137). Thus, the patent owner must show that it will likely prove that the accused infringer infringes at least one valid and enforceable patent claim (138). Likewise, in order to defeat the injunction based on invalidity or unenforceability defenses, the nonmoving party, as the party bearing the burden of proof on those issues at trial, must establish a substantial question of invalidity or unenforceability, that is, that it is likely to succeed in proving invalidity or unenforceability of the asserted patent(s) (139).

An accused infringer may avoid a preliminary injunction by showing only a substantial question as to invalidity, as opposed to the higher clear and convincing standard required to prevail on the merits (140). Indeed, vulnerability is the issue at the preliminary injunction stage, while validity is the issue at trial. The showing of a substantial question as to invalidity thus requires less proof than the clear and convincing showing necessary to establish invalidity itself (141).

Irreparable Harm

A preliminary injunction is intended to preserve the legal interests of the parties against future infringement, which may have market effects never fully compensable in monetary terms. As such, a patentee must establish that monetary recompense is inadequate (142). However, when the patentee makes a clear showing of likelihood of success on the merits, the patentee is entitled to a presumption of irreparable harm (143). Nevertheless, in some cases a patentee may be denied a preliminary injunction despite establishing a likelihood of success on the merits, such as when the remaining factors are considered and balanced (144). For example, courts have determined that the extent of potential harm suffered by a party can be insufficient to permit an injunction to be granted (145).

Other forms of irreparable harm may be asserted, such as irreversible price erosion, loss of good will, potential layoffs of employees, and the discontinuance of clinical trials that are devoted to other medical uses for the drug.

Once the patent owner has established the showing necessary to raise the presumption of irreparable harm, the nonmoving party must produce evidence sufficient to establish the absence of irreparable harm.

Balance of Hardships

When balancing hardships, the court must balance the harm that will occur to the moving party from the denial of the preliminary injunction with the harm that the nonmoving party will incur if the injunction is granted (146).

Public Interest

There is a public interest in protecting rights secured by valid patents. The general rule has been that where the patents are shown to be valid, the public interest is best served by enforcing them.

However, in pharmaceutical cases, the focus of the public interest analysis should center on whether there exists some critical public interest that would be injured by the grant of preliminary relief. Thus in every pharmaceutical case, the public interest should be carefully evaluated.

In sum, whether a preliminary injunction is granted depends upon the facts of the particular case. When a likelihood of success on the merits can be established, the remaining three factors will usually favor the patent owner, and a preliminary injunction is more likely to be granted.

Inequitable Conduct

A patent may be rendered unenforceable due to inequitable conduct (147). A finding of inequitable conduct results in the permanent unenforceability of the entire patent (148). Inequitable conduct is based upon a breach of the duty of disclosure, candor, and good faith imposed by Rule 1.56 of the U.S. PTO (149):

§1.56 Duty to disclose information material to patentability.

> (a) A patent by its very nature is affected with a public interest. The public interest is best served, and the most effective patent examination occurs when, at the time an application is being examined, the Office is aware of and evaluates the teachings of all information material to patentability. Each individual associated with the filing and prosecution of a patent application has a duty of candor and good faith in dealing with the Office, which includes a duty to disclose to the Office all information known to that individual to be material to patentability as defined in this section. The duty to disclose information exists with respect to each pending claim until the claim is cancelled or withdrawn from consideration, or the application becomes abandoned. [...]. However, no patent will be granted on an application in connection with which fraud on the Office was practiced or attempted or the duty of disclosure was violated through bad faith or intentional misconduct (150).

Noteworthy is that the duty is not only imposed on the inventor(s) but is imposed also on every individual associated with the filing and prosecution of a patent application (151). The duty to disclose information continues from the time the application is filed until the patent is granted (152).

To hold a patent unenforceable due to inequitable conduct, there must be clear and convincing evidence that the applicant (*i*) made an affirmative misrepresentation of material fact, failed to disclose material information, submitted false material information, and (*ii*) intended to deceive the PTO (153).

Information is material to patentability when it is not cumulative to information already of record or being made of record in the application, and:

1. It establishes, by itself or in combination with other information, a *prima facie* case of unpatentability of a claim, or
2. It refutes, or is inconsistent with, a position the applicant takes in:
   a. Opposing an argument of unpatentability relied on by the office, or
   b. Asserting an argument of patentability (154).

A *prima facie* case of unpatentability is established when the information compels a conclusion that a claim is unpatentable under the preponderance of evidence, burden-of-proof standard, giving each term in the claim its broadest reasonable construction consistent with the specification, and before any consideration is given to evidence which may be submitted in an attempt to establish a contrary conclusion of patentability (155).

The intent element of inequitable conduct requires that "the involved conduct, viewed in light of all the evidence, including evidence indicative of good faith, must indicate sufficient culpability to require a finding of intent to deceive" (156). Intent rarely can be, and need not be, proven by direct evidence (157). Instead, an intent to deceive is usually inferred from the facts and circumstances surrounding the conduct at issue (158). Gross negligence alone is insufficient to justify an inference of intent to deceive the PTO (159).

If a court finds that the requirements of materiality and intent have been established by clear and convincing evidence, it must then balance the equities to determine whether the patentee has committed inequitable conduct that warrants holding the patent unenforceable (160). Under the balancing test, "[t]he more material the omission or the misrepresentation, the lower the level of intent required to establish inequitable conduct, and vice versa" (161).

It is inequitable conduct to withhold material information from a patent examiner or submit false material information with the intent to deceive or mislead the examiner into granting a patent (162). Inequitable conduct can be based upon a variety of deceptive conduct, including withholding material prior art (163), withholding translations of foreign prior art publications or submitting only partial translations (164), withholding information about prior sales or use (165), withholding or providing false information regarding inventorship (166), withholding or providing false information regarding enablement or the best mode (167), wrongly making a priority claim to an earlier-filed application that does not provide support (168), misrepresenting material facts to the examiner (169), submitting false affidavits (170), making misrepresentations regarding a prior art search in a petition to make special (171), making a misrepresentation of unintentional abandonment in a petition to revive (172), and wrongly claiming small entity status (173).

A finding of inequitable conduct not only renders the entire patent unenforceable but may in certain instances also infect subsequent related applications, rendering them unenforceable as well (174). Lastly, if a court finds a patent unenforceable for inequitable conduct, the case may be deemed exceptional, and the prevailing party may be entitled to its attorneys' fees (175).

Recent Federal Circuit decisions have shed light on the types of actions in the pharmaceutical industry that would result in findings of inequitable conduct. For example, in *Impax Labs., Inc. v. Aventis Pharm. Inc.*, Aventis was charged with inequitable conduct for withholding certain test data from the examiner during prosecution of the patents-in-suit (176). The district court initially determined that the data withheld was immaterial because it did not produce test results that indicated a level of overall effectiveness, and thus would not have been relevant to the PTO during prosecution (177). In addition, the court pointed out that there was an absence on the part of Aventis of an intent to deceive the PTO (178). The Federal Circuit agreed, pointing out that the data withheld did not refute any position taken or held by Aventis during prosecution of the patent-in-suit (179). Finally, the Federal Circuit noted that there was no evidence that a "reasonable examiner" would have considered the withheld information important in deciding whether to allow the patent (180).

In *Warner-Lambert Co. v. Teva Pharms. USA Inc.*, Teva claimed that Warner had committed inequitable conduct by failing to disclose the existence of Merck's product Vasotec, which Warner had utilized during the testing stage of the patent-in-suit (181). In response, Warner claimed that it had only utilized Vasotec during an initial investigatory stage in order to ascertain information regarding certain pH levels (182). In addition, because the majority of Warner's trials and testing centered around other issues, Warner's scientists determined that its initial use of Vasotec was not material to its application to the PTO (183). In its opinion, the Federal Circuit determined that although it appeared Vasotec did exemplify a high level of materiality, Warner's failure to disclose it did not rise to the level of inequitable conduct (184). The Court noted that Warner had acted in good faith in not disclosing its use of Vasotec because its decision to do so was based on its belief that the product contained no relevance to the application at issue (185). Finally, the court pointed out that because Warner exhibited only "limited familiarity" with the Vasotec formulation, its conduct in withholding disclosure did not rise to the level of inequitable conduct (186).

In *Eli Lilly & Co. v. Zenith Goldline Pharms., Inc.*, Zenith claimed that Lilly had omitted material subject matter from its Information Disclosure Statement, including a relevant patent and a scientific article (187). The district court refused to find inequitable conduct, pointing out that despite its omission of a seemingly relevant patent, Lilly had in fact disclosed a different patent that contained identical technical disclosures to the omitted patent (188). In addition, the court noted that the examiner had found, and relied on the article that Lilly had omitted (189). Thus, in upholding the district court's refusal to find inequitable conduct, the Federal Circuit determined that neither omission was sufficiently material to give rise to a finding of inequitable conduct (190).

Finally, in *In re Metoprolol Succinate Patent Litig.*, the district court determined that inequitable conduct had occurred when Astra failed to disclose to the PTO factual information relating to the actual inventor of metoprolol succinate (191). As a result, the court concluded that due to Astra's actions, the patent-in-suit would have not been entitled to its priority, and thus would have been denied as anticipated by prior art (192). In its decision, the court noted that Astra's motivation not to reveal the dispute over inventorship was great, based on its risk of losing patentability of its invention (193). In reversing the district court's finding, the Federal Circuit determined that the district court had erred by "equating a presence of incentive with an intent to deceive" (194). It thus concluded that whether Astra's actions had risen to the level of inequitable conduct could not be determined solely on its underlying incentives, but required a more factually laden determination (195).

FTC SCRUTINY OF AGREEMENTS WITH GENERICS

Over the past 10 years, FTC scrutiny of the pharmaceutical industry, and settlements including "reverse payments" in Paragraph IV litigations has expanded dramatically (196). All settlement agreements in Paragraph IV litigations must now be filed with the FTC and Department of Justice Antitrust Division (DOJ) for possible review (197). The agreements must be filed within ten (10) business days of execution and prior to commercial marketing of the generic drug (198). After reviewing the agreements, the FTC and/or DOJ may file an antitrust action that may result in civil penalties, forfeiture of the 180-day market exclusivity, and/or an injunction (199).

The FTC's scrutiny of settlement agreements falls into two categories. The first category is settlement agreements under which the generic manufacturer agrees to stay off the market, including voluntary forfeiture of the 180-day market exclusivity, and settlement agreements that cover noninfringing products, that is, those that exceed the scope of the patent(s)-at-issue. The second category is settlement agreements that include so-called reverse payments. Although the FTC has been aware of reverse payment settlements for some time, the agency did not focus on the anticompetitive implications of reverse payments until recently (200).

The courts, however, have not shared the FTC's concern with respect to the second category of settlement agreements. The courts, in private antitrust actions, have sided with the FTC finding that the first category of settlement agreements may violate antitrust laws (201). The courts, however, have yet to find the second category of settlement agreements involving reverse payments in violation of antitrust laws (202). Specifically, the Second and Eleventh Circuit Court of Appeal, in the *Tamoxifen* and *Schering-Plough* case respectively, overturned FTC findings that settlement agreements involving reverse payments violated antitrust laws, and the Supreme Court declined to review the appellate courts' decisions.

History of FTC Scrutiny of Settlement Agreements

In 1999, the FTC ordered 28 brand-name manufacturers and 50 generic manufacturers to submit any agreements relating to an ANDA filing (including any full or partial settlement agreements) the respective companies had entered after December 31, 1994 (203). The results of this survey served as the basis for the FTC's 2002 report entitled Generic Drug Entry Prior to Patent Expiration: An FTC Study ("FTC Study") (204). The study provided, inter alia, a detailed analysis of the settlement agreements and their effect on competition, along with a variety of specific and general recommendations for legislative changes to the Hatch–Waxman Act to address competition concerns identified in the study. Most of the proposed legislative fixes were intended to curtail anticompetitive gaming of the ANDA processes, which in the view of the FTC subverted the legislation's purpose of promoting generic competition (205).

Although the FTC Study discusses a number of settlement agreements involving reverse payments, including some of the earliest Paragraph IV settlements identified in the study, the FTC never opines that reverse payments alone raise antitrust issues, or should be deemed illegal (206). Rather, the study expressly states that it "does not reach any conclusions about the competitive effects of [settlements involving brand payments]" (207).

Specifically, the FTC Study identifies four interim settlement agreements as posing potential antitrust issues, including the agreements which ultimately reached the Eleventh Circuit in *Schering-Plough*, and notes that the FTC had brought enforcement actions against those involved in three of the agreements (208). Incidentally, all of the challenged settlement agreements involved reverse payments, which the study does not address with particularity. The study, instead, discusses the potential forfeiture of the 180-day market exclusivity as the primary focus of the enforcement action (209).

Testimony by FTC commissioners further illustrates the FTC's apparent ambivalence to reverse payments. In a 2000 speech, FTC Commissioner Anthony identified reverse payments as problematic to the extent that such reverse payments occur in connection with settlements that fall into the first category. That is, settlements that include the forfeiture of the 180-day market exclusivity, and/or that exceed the scope of the patent(s) at issue (210).

The FTC's Attention Has Shifted to Reverse Payments

More recently, the FTC has shifted its position on reverse payment settlements, and now advocates holding any settlement agreement involving reverse payments per se illegal. In his April 10, 2007, statements before the FTC, Commissioner J. Thomas Rosch started by discussing the FTC's "efforts to combat what we consider to be illegal 'reverse payments' made by branded drug makers to generic drug makers in patent litigation settlements between branded and generic firms instituted under the Hatch-Waxman Act" (211). Commissioner Rosch then went on to address the Eleventh Circuit's decision in the *Schering-Plough* case that overturned an FTC finding that the reverse payment in that case constituted a violation of the antitrust laws (212). By way of background, the FTC had found that the settlement agreement was tantamount to a market division agreement between a competitor (the branded) and a potential competitor (the generic) (213), which the FTC observed that the Supreme Court has held is illegal (214). The commissioner also addressed the *Tamoxifen* case where, based upon facts similar to *Schering-Plough*, a divided Second Circuit essentially followed the Eleventh Circuit (215). In particular, the commissioner testified that "We [the FTC] believe *Tamoxifen* and *Schering-Plough* are bad law. More specifically, we [the FTC] continue to believe that most, if not all, reverse payments are illegal if they are made at the same time a generic agrees not to compete as soon as it could if it won its challenge to the branded's patent" (216).

Thereafter, on May 2, 2007, Commissioner Jon Leibowitz testified before Congress expressed the support, seeking approval of a bill that would make reverse payments per se illegal (217). "Simply put, we believe that H R 1902 [which is currently pending] is a fundamentally sound approach to eliminate the pay-for-delay settlement tactics employed by the pharmaceutical industry that could cost American consumers (and the federal government) billions of dollars annually" (218).

In describing the FTC's position, Commissioner Leibowitz stated that:

> There is particular urgency to pharmaceutical competition issues today. Recent appellate decisions are making it difficult to challenge so-called exclusion

> payments—or reverse payments; that is, patent settlements in which the brand-name drug firm pays the generic to stay out of the market. If these decisions are allowed to stand, drug companies will enter into more and more of these agreements, and prescription drug costs will continue to rise rapidly. Indeed, in the past year, we have seen a dramatic increase in these types of deals—from none in fiscal year 2004 to more than a dozen in FY 2006.
>
> A legislative approach could provide a swifter and cleaner solution. For that reason, we strongly support legislation to prohibit these anticompetitive payments. Both your approach, Mr. Chairman, and the bipartisan measure reported out of the Senate Judiciary Committee would ensure that consumers continue to have access to low-priced generics. But we also recognize that these issues are complex. So, we want to work with you—and other interested parties—as the bill moves forward (219).

Agreements That Forfeit the 180-day Generic Market Exclusivity or Settlements That Covered Noninfringing Products Are Per Se Violations of Antitrust Laws

FTC Enforcement Action Regarding the Abbott–Geneva Hytrin® and Hoescht–Andrx Cardizem CD® Agreements

The first two reported FTC enforcement actions challenging Paragraph IV settlements were brought against the Abbott–Geneva Hytrin Agreement (220) and the Hoescht–Andrx Cardizem CD Agreement (221). Both FTC complaints alleged that the settlement agreements resulted in voluntary forfeiture of the 180-day market exclusivity, and that the agreements included products that were not covered by the patent, that is, exceeded scope of patent(s)-in-suit (222). The cases resulted in consent orders in 2000 and 2001, respectively, requiring Abbott and Hoechst Marion Roussel to refrain from entering any agreement with terms that would require the generic manufacturer to voluntarily forfeit its 180-day market exclusivity, or that would require the generic manufacturer to forego research or marketing a drug product that is not covered by the patent(s)-at-issue (223). The companies were also required to refrain from entering partial settlement agreements involving reverse payment; however, the consent order was silent as to reverse payments in a final settlement agreement that would terminate the litigation (224).

FTC Enforcement Action Regarding the Bristol-Myers Squibb Agreements

The FTC also brought a complaint against Bristol-Myers Squibb Corporation (BMS) alleging violations of antitrust laws relating, inter alia, to settlement to the BuSpar® litigation and BMS's activities in prosecuting and enforcing the Taxol® patents (225). The FTC complaint alleged that BMS had engaged in a number of anticompetitive acts relating to BuSpar, a medication used to treat anxiety, and two anticancer drugs, Taxol and Platinol, for over 10 years (226). Specifically, the FTC alleged that BMS had improperly settled a lawsuit relating to BuSpar, paying Schein $72.5 million, in order to preserve the validity and enforceability of certain patents while simultaneously keeping generic manufacturers off the market. The FTC also alleged antitrust violations based upon BMS's procurement and listing of a patent covering the active metabolite of BuSpar. On the eve of the expiration date of the patent covering the method for using BuSpar to treat anxiety, BMS filed a continuation application covering the method of using a metabolite of BuSpar. BMS obtained allowance of its patent claim covering the metabolite less than 2 months before expiration of the BuSpar patent. Thereafter, BMS requested and obtained an expedited issuance of its new metabolite patent and subsequently listed this patent in the *Orange Book*. BMS then pursued lawsuits against ANDA filers relating to this new patent, triggering the automatic 30-month stay.

Relating to Taxol, the FTC alleged that BMS had engaged in anticompetitive activities by fraudulently obtaining patents from the U.S. PTO by making false and misleading statements to the PTO and by failing to disclose relevant references, and that BMS then had listed the unenforceable patents in the *Orange Book*. The FTC further alleged that BMS attempted to list a patent obtained under a license agreement with American Bioscience, Inc. that BMS could not reasonably believe was valid.

In its settlement with the FTC, BMS agreed that it would not continue to list its metabolite patent and would discontinue its patent infringement lawsuits. BMS also agreed not to pursue royalties from any license relating to its Taxol patents, or to initiate any 30-month stay relating to either its BuSpar or Taxol products. BMS further agreed not to initiate any 30-month stay relating to certain other categories of patents deemed to be improperly listed in the *Orange Book*. BMS also agreed that it would not enter into cash reverse payment settlements, but also agreed not to enter into reverse payment agreements in which it would provide something of value to the potential generic manufacturer (ANDA filer).

Court Rulings on Agreements That Forfeit the 180-day Generic Market Exclusivity or Settlements that Covered Noninfringing Products Also Finding Them Are Per Se Violations of Antitrust Laws

As noted, the courts have sided with the FTC, in private antitrust actions, in the context of the Abbott–Geneva Hytrin, Hoescht–Andrx Cardizem CD, and BMS BuSpar settlement agreements.

The Abbott–Geneva Settlement Agreement on Hytrin® Private Antitrust Action

The court found the Abbott–Geneva Agreement on Hytrin, a drug prescribed for the treatment of high blood pressure and benign prostatic hyperplasia, to be a horizontal restraint of trade that was a per se violation of the Sherman Act (227).

The agreement provided, inter alia, that Abbott would pay Geneva $4.5 million per month beginning on April 30, 1998. The agreement also provided that in the event of "Final Judgment in Geneva's Favor" (228), Abbott's monthly payments to Geneva would stop and Abbott would pay into escrow $4.5 million per month until the earlier of the "Generic Entry Date," the "Appellate Judgment," or the date of "Final Judgment in Abbott's Favor" (229). The settlement agreement further provided that Geneva would receive the amount in escrow if Geneva prevailed in any appeal. Otherwise, the amount in escrow would be returned to Abbott. Under the agreement, upon a Final Judgment in Abbott's favor, Abbott would have no obligation to make any payment to Geneva. Finally, the agreement provided that Abbott had the option to terminate payments if the Generic Entry Date had not occurred on or before February 18, 2000.

In August 1999, Abbott and Geneva terminated the agreement. As of the date of termination, Abbott had paid a total of $49.5 million into escrow. As part of the termination agreement, $45 million in escrow funds were returned to Abbott. Had Geneva launched on August 13, 1999, without first having terminated the agreement, Abbott would have asserted that Geneva was in breach of the agreement. Geneva launched its generic product on August 13, 1999. Since going to market with a generic form of terazosin hydrochloride in August 1999, Geneva has been an actual competitor of Abbott.

The court found that for purposes of this analysis, the following relevant facts are undisputed and dispositive. It is undisputed that Abbott and Geneva were actual or potential competitors at the time the agreement was executed. It is also undisputed that pursuant to the agreement, Abbott agreed to pay Geneva $4.5 million per month in exchange for Geneva's agreement not to market its generic terazosin hydrochloride products in the United States until a final appellate judgment on the merits of the '207 patent infringement action. The agreement, therefore, guaranteed Abbott that its only potential competitor at the time would, for a substantial price, refrain from marketing its FDA-approved generic version of Hytrin even after an adverse district court ruling as to the validity of '207 patent. This restraint exceeded the scope of the '207 patent, and had the effect of keeping Geneva's generic capsule product, which had already received final FDA approval on March 30, 1998, off the market until August 13, 1999. Further, because of the regulatory framework under Hatch–Waxman, the agreement had the additional effect of delaying the entry of other generic competitors, who could not enter the market until the expiration of Geneva's 180-day period of marketing exclusivity, which Geneva (as stated in the agreement) did not intend to relinquish. As the Sixth Circuit concluded in reviewing a nearly identical agreement, "there is simply no escaping the conclusion that the Agreement . . . was, at its core, a horizontal agreement to eliminate competition" in the domestic market for terazosin hydrochloride drugs, a "classic example" of an output-reducing, naked restraint on trade that qualifies for per se treatment (230).

The Hoechst Marion Roussel and Andrx Settlement Agreement on Cardizem CD® Private Action

Likewise, the court found the settlement agreement between Hoescht Marion Roussel, Inc. (HMR) and Andrx Pharmaceuticals, Inc. relating to Cardizem CD a per se violation of the antitrust laws. Under that settlement agreement Andrx, in exchange for quarterly payments of $10 million, would refrain from marketing its generic version of Cardizem CD even after it had received FDA approval.[231] Andrx would remain off the market until the occurrence of one of the end dates contemplated by the agreement. Although Andrx and HMR terminated the agreement and the payments in June 1999 (before any of the specified end dates occurred.), HMR paid Andrx (between July 1998 and June 1999), $89.83 million, while Andrx kept its generic product off the market. The court found that, "[b]y delaying Andrx's entry into the market, the Agreement also delayed the entry of other generic competitors, who could not enter until the expiration of Andrx's 180-day period of marketing exclusivity, which Andrx had agreed not to relinquish or transfer" (232). The court then, based upon these facts, observed that "[t]here is simply no escaping the conclusion that the Agreement, all of its other conditions and provisions notwithstanding, was, at its core, a horizontal agreement to eliminate competition in the market for Cardizem CD throughout the entire United States, a classic example of a *per se* illegal restraint of trade" (233).

The BuSpar® and Taxol® Private Antitrust Action

In the BuSpar antitrust action, the court, upon BMS's motion to dismiss, ruled that BMS was not entitled to immunity from antitrust liability under the *Noerr–Pennington* doctrine, and that BMS's complained of activities were sufficient to state a claim for violation of the antitrust laws (234). There were also numerous procedural motion filed in the Taxol litigation. Ultimately, however, BMS settled both the BuSpar and Taxol private antitrust actions for $670 million (235).

Courts Rulings Regarding the FTC's Enforcement Actions Against Settlement Agreements Involving Reverse Payments

The FTC has taken the position that any settlement agreement involving reverse payments is a per se violation of the antitrust laws. However, to date, the courts have not shared the FTC view on these settlement agreements.

The Schering-Plough Settlement Agreements With Upsher and ESI

In *Schering-Plough*, the offending payments with respect to Upsher were primarily licensing fees paid under an ancillary licensing agreement. The Schering-Plough/Upsher settlement agreement was a three-part license agreement, under which Schering-Plough paid: (*i*) $60 million in royalty fees; (*ii*) $10 million in milestone royalty payments; and (*iii*) 10 or 15% royalties on sales, and Schering-Plough's board approved of the transaction upon an express finding that the license was valuable to Schering-Plough (236).

In analyzing the settlement agreement and determining to challenge it, the FTC thoroughly analyzed any business justifications for the license agreement, including the negotiations, the market demand, the market value of the licensed products, and Schering-Plough's failure to bring the products to market (237). Based upon this analysis, the FTC concluded that Schering-Plough paid a price inflated above the market value for the licensed products, and that the licensing fees were merely a pretext to delay generic entry (238).

However, on appeal the Eleventh Circuit rejected the FTC's conclusion that the licensing payments were an improper attempt to delay market entry of the generic, and questioned the FTC's analysis. Specifically, the Eleventh Circuit opined that the FTC had not given enough weight to the outcome of the apparent arm's-length negotiations (239). The Eleventh Circuit also noted that, although hindsight indicated that the arrangement had not paid off for Schering-Plough, this was not atypical because pharmaceutical companies often invest large sums of money on compounds that ultimately never make it to the market; and as such, this fact was not indicative of bad faith in reaching the settlement agreement (240). Additionally, the court also cited severe facts as objective indicia of legitimate business negotiation, including the fact that different people negotiated the license agreement and the patent dispute, and Schering-Plough's "long-documented and ongoing interest" in licensing one of the products (241).

In the ESI Lederle, Inc. (ESI) settlement, Schering-Plough and ESI participated in 15 months of court-supervised mediation, which was ultimately fruitless (242). Eventually, Schering-Plough offered to divide the remaining patent life with ESI and allow ESI to enter the market with its product nearly 3 years before the patent's expiration date (243). Although ESI accepted the offer, ESI also demanded payment to settle the case (244). The Judge suggested that Schering-Plough offer to pay ESI $5 million, which was attributed to legal fees, but ESI sought a $10 million payment (245). The Judge and Schering-Plough devised an amicable settlement whereby Schering-Plough would pay ESI up to $10 million should ESI receive FDA approval by a certain date (246). Because it appeared unlikely to Schering-Plough that ESI would receive FDA approval by this date, the Judge intimated that, if Schering-Plough's prediction proved true, it would not have to pay the $10 million. The Judge then oversaw execution of the settlement agreement (247).

In its hearing before the FTC, Schering-Plough sought to justify the payments citing the active involvement and approval of the Judge (248). The FTC acknowledged that Schering was subject to "intense, and perhaps unseemly, judicial pressure" from a "settlement-minded judge," and observed that in view of this pressure the company may well have been concerned about its future litigation prospects, for example, the FTC noted that perhaps the court's pressure to settle could have weakened Schering-Plough's perceived bargaining strength (249). The FTC, however, was not persuaded and faulted Schering-Plough for bowing to the court's pressure, and stated that Schering should have sought out a creative alternative to making payments (250).

On appeal, the Eleventh Circuit was concerned by the FTC's complete discounting of the courts involvement, and likely coercive role, in crafting the settlement terms (251). Specifically, the Eleventh Circuit noted that "[v]eritably, the Commission's opinion would leave settlements, including those endorsed and facilitated by a federal court, with little confidence" (252). After the Eleventh Circuit reversed the FTC's findings, the FTC petitioned for certiorari, but the Supreme Court did not accept the case.

The Tamoxifen Settlement Agreement

The Tamoxifen settlement agreement included, among other things, a so-called "reverse payment" of $21 million from the defendant patent-holders Zeneca, Inc., AstraZeneca Pharmaceuticals LP, and AstraZeneca PLC (collectively "Zeneca") to the defendant generic manufacturer Barr Laboratories, Inc. ("Barr"), and a license from Zeneca to Barr allowing Barr to sell an unbranded version of Zeneca-manufactured tamoxifen. The settlement agreement was contingent on obtaining a vacatur of the judgment of the district court that had heard the infringement action holding the patent to be invalid (253). Thereafter, consumers brought a private antitrust action arguing that the excessive nature of the reverse payments (not the reverse payments alone) was a violation of the antitrust laws, and the district court dismissed the action (254).

The Second Circuit in *Tamoxifen*, specifically, considered and rejected the argument that "excessive" reverse payments could lead to a presumption of antitrust liability (255). The Second Circuit observed that, under certain circumstances, a reverse payment settlement could be illegal, particularly if the settlement is merely a device for circumventing the antitrust laws (256). As an example, the court cited a scenario under which the underlying patent litigation is a "sham," or otherwise objectively baseless, involving a patent that would almost certainly not survive a judicial challenge (257). The Second Circuit, however, opined that, in cases where there "is nothing suspicious about the circumstances of a patent settlement, then to prevent a cloud from being cast over the settlement process a third party should not be permitted to haul the parties to the settlement over the hot coals of antitrust litigation" (258). The court then posited that even if one were to assume that the large reverse payments belied the fact that the patent owner lacked confidence in prevailing in the patent litigation, such a lack of confidence does not amount to an antitrust violation (259).

Based upon these finding, the Second Circuit upheld the district court's dismissal, and the plaintiffs petitioned for certiorari with the FTC joining the request. Again, however, the Supreme Court declined to review the case.

Outlook

The FTC has essentially taken the universal position that in every Paragraph IV litigation, consumers have a vested interest in the litigation based upon the possibility that a successful challenge will lead to lower pharmaceutical costs (260). The FTC argues that any settlement between the parties that improperly benefits the litigating parties at the expense of the consumer is a presumptive violation of the antitrust laws (261).

The FTC, however, appears prepared to allow parties to settle lawsuits by compromising on a marketing date prior to the patent's expiration, without cash payments, because "the resulting settlement presumably would reflect the parties' own assessment of the strength of the patent" (262). The FTC views these "benchmark" settlement terms as consumer and business friendly because they resolve the uncertainty of the litigation early and provide some guaranteed benefit to consumers in proportion to the probability that the patent challenge would succeed (263). By contrast, the FTC generally views any settlement involving reverse payments as anticompetitive, because it fails to provide as much consumer benefit as the so-called "benchmark" agreement (264). The FTC perceives any reverse payment as conclusive indicia of, and a quid pro quo for, delayed generic market entry, on the grounds that were it not for the reverse payment the parties would have either settled on an earlier entry date, or not settled and litigated the case to completion—either scenario benefiting consumers relative to the reverse payment settlement (265). It is important to note that, in the FTC's view, essentially any settlement involving reverse payments is illegal, irrespective of the strength or weakness of the underlying patent case; the FTC's believes that the strength of the underlying patent litigation is only relevant where the cases is objectively baseless or sham patent suit (266).

In addition, it is important to note that pending legislation before the House and Senate would ban certain reverse payment settlements (267). The legislative history of the Senate bill expresses strong support for the FTC's treatment of reverse payment settlements, and criticizes the Eleventh and Second Circuits' *Schering-Plough* and *Tamoxifen* decisions for "revers[ing] the Federal Trade Commission's long-standing position [by upholding the reverse payment settlements challenged in those cases]" (268). The legislation would make it unlawful for any person, in connection with the sale of a drug product, to directly or indirectly be a party to any agreement resolving or settling a patent infringement claim which—(*i*) an ANDA filer receives anything of value; and (*ii*) the ANDA filer agrees not to research, develop, manufacture, market, or sell the ANDA product for any period of time (269).

In conclusion, the FTC and DOJ can be expected to review every patent settlement agreement where the generic manufacturer agrees not to go to market. The FTC will also likely find any settlement agreement that results in a voluntary forfeiture of the 180-day market exclusivity, or which affects products outside the scope of the patent(s)-at-issue, a violation of the antitrust laws. The FTC will also closely scrutinize any settlement agreement including reverse payments, and likely find them in violation of the antitrust laws; however, it is unclear at present what would be the ultimate outcome of any of these situations given the Second and Eleventh Circuit's rulings.

CONCLUSIONS

There is no such thing as a "typical" Hatch–Waxman litigation. The number and type of issues that can be raised makes each litigation unique. Whether one talks of patent or FDA laws and regulations, procedural litigation considerations, or even settlement talks, the number of issues that can be raised, and variations on them, sometimes seems limitless.

The primary aim of this chapter is to provide an overview of the U.S. statutes and regulations that are designed to encourage litigation in order to bring generics to market as early as possible. This system is often described as "a sensitive balance" between the branded and generic industries. There is little doubt that each side of this debate believes that the system is skewed too heavily in favor of the other side, and perhaps this itself indicates the health and vitality of the U.S. system.

REFERENCES AND NOTES

1. U.S. utility applications pending on or prior to June 6, 1995, have a term that is the better of 17 years from issuance, or 20 years from the effective U.S. filing date. 35 USC §154.
2. 35 USC §154.
3. 35 USC §120.
4. 35 USC §119.
5. 35 USC §102.
6. 35 USC §119(e).
7. 35 USC §119(a).
8. 35 USC §119(e).
9. 35 USC §102(b).
10. 35 USC §122.
11. 35 USC §122.
12. 35 USC §122.
13. 35 USC §102(e).
14. PCT Rule 43.
15. 35 USC §112.
16. 21 USC §355.
17. *Merck v. Integra*, 545 U.S. §193 (2005).
18. 21 CFR §314.53.
19. 21 CFR §§314.3 and 314.53; see, e.g., Draft Guidance for Industry: Bioavailability and Bioequivalence Studies for Nasal Aerosols and Nasal Sprays for Local Action (Apr. 2003) at lines 208–211 (recognizing that a formulation together with container is the "drug product").
20. 21 CFR §314.53(c)(2)(L). Note that some courts have ignored process limitations in determining infringement of product by process claims, although others have considered such limitations. See *Scripps Clinic & Research Found. v. Genentech, Inc.*, 927 F2d 1565, 1583 (Fed Cir 1991) (holding that product-by-process claims "are not limited to product prepared by the process set forth in the claims"); *Atl. Thermoplastics Co. v. Faytex Corp.* 970 F2d 834, 846–847 (Fed Cir 1992) (holding that "process terms in product-by-process claims serve as limitations in determining infringement"), *reh'g en banc denied*, 974 F2d 1279 (Fed Cir 1992).
21. 21 USC §355(j)(2)(A)(viii).
22. See 35 USC §120.

23. 35 USC §154(b).
24. 35 USC §154(b).
25. 37 CFR 1.704(c)(11). In addition, filing a Request for Continued Examination tolls the 3-year pendency clock. 37 CFR §1.703.
26. 35 USC §154(b).
27. 37 CFR §1.704.
28. 35 USC §156.
29. 35 USC §156.
30. 35 USC §156.
31. 35 USC §156.
32. FTC Staff Comments on FDA's Proposed Regulations to Improve Efficiency of Citizen Petition Process, March 9, 2000 (www.ftc.gov/opa/2000/03/fdacitpet.shtm).
33. Section(q).
34. Section (q)(1)(A).
35. Sections (q)(1)(H) and (I).
36. Section (q)(1)(H).
37. *Id.*
38. Section (q)(1)(H).
39. *Id.*
40. Section (q)(1)(H).
41. *Id.*
42. Section (q)(1)(A).
43. Section (q)(1)(A).
44. Section (q)(1)(A).
45. *Id.*
46. Section (q)(1)(B)(i–iii).
47. Section (q)(1)(F).
48. *Id.*
49. Section (q)(2(B).
50. Section (2)(A)(i).
51. Section (q)(1)(G).
52. *Id.*
53. 21 USC §355(j)(2)(A)(vii).
54. 21 USC §355(j)(2)(A)(vii)(I–IV).
55. 21 USC § 355(j)(2)(B)(i); 21 CFR §314.95(c)(6).
56. 35 USC §282.
57. *Woodland Trust v. Flowertree Nursery, Inc.*, No. 97-1547 (Fed Cir July 10, 1998); *Hewlett-Packard Co. v. Bausch & Lomb Inc.*, 909 F2d 1464, 1467, 15 U.S.P.Q.2d 1525, 1527 (Fed Cir 1990); *American Hoist & Derrick Co. v. Sowa & Sons*, 725 F2d 1350, 1360, 220 U.S.P.Q. 763, 770–771 (Fed Cir 1984), *cert. denied*, 469 U.S. 821 (1984).
58. *Celeritas Technologies, Ltd. v. Rockwell International Corporation*, Nos. 97-1512, 1542 (Fed Cir, July 20, 1998); *Applied Medical Resources Corporation v. United States Surgical Corporation*, No. 97-1526 (Fed Cir June 30, 1998); *Rockwell International Corporation v. the United States*, Nos. 97-9065, -9068 (June 15, 1998).
59. *Panduit Corp. v. Dennison Manufacturing Co.*, 810 F2d 1561, 1566-68, 1 U.S.P.Q. 1593, 1595–1597 (Fed Cir 1987), *cert. denied*, 481 U.S. 1052 (1987).
60. *Hybritech, Inc. v. Monoclonal Antibodies, Inc.*, 802 F2d at 1379, 231 U.S.P.Q. at 90.
61. *Graham v. John Deere Co.*, 383 U.S. 1, 148 U.S.P.Q. 459 (1966).
62. *Id.*, 383 U.S. at 17, 148 U.S.P.Q. at 467.
63. *Greenwood v. Hattori Seiko Co., Ltd.*, 900 F2d 238, 241, 14 U.S.P.Q.2d 1474, 1476 (Fed Cir 1990); *Graham v. John Deere Co.*, 383 U.S. at 17, 148 U.S.P.Q. at 467.
64. See, e.g., *KSR Int'l Co. v. Teleflex, Inc.*, 550 U.S. __, __, 127 S.Ct. 1727, 1739 (2007) [citing *Graham v. John Deere Co.*, 383, 17-18 U.S. 1 (1966)]; *Akamai Technologies, Inc. v. Cable & Wireless Internet Services, Inc.*, 344 F3d 1186, 1195–1196 (Fed Cir 2003); *McNeil-PPC, Inc. v. L. Perrigo Co.*, 337 F3d 1362, 1367 (Fed Cir 2003).
65. KSR, 127 S.Ct. at 1739.

66. *Id.*
67. *Id.* at 1742.
68. *Id.*
69. *The Regents of the University of California v. Eli Lilly and Company*, 96-1175 (Fed Cir July 22, 1997), quoting *Lockwood v. American Airlines, Inc.* 107 F. 3d 1565, 1572, 41 U.S.P.Q.2d 1961, 1966 (Fed Cir 1997); *In re Gosteli*, 872 F2d 1008, 1012, 10 U.S.P.Q.2d 1614, 1618 (Fed Cir 1989)("The description must clearly allow persons of ordinary skill in the art to recognize that the inventor invented what is claimed").
70. See *DeGeorge v. Bernier*, 768 F2d 1318 (Fed Cir 1985).
71. *Dow Chemical Co. v. American Cyanamid Co.*, 615 F Supp 471 (D.C. La. 1985), *aff'd.*, 816 F2d 617 (Fed Cir 1987).
72. *Amgen v. Chugai Pharmaceutical Co., Ltd.*, 927 F2d 1200, 1212 (Fed Cir 1992).
73. *In re Eltgroth*, 164 U.S.P.Q.221, 223 (CCPA 1970).
74. *In re Gardner*, et. al., 166 U.S.P.Q. 138, 141 (CCPA 1970)(emphasis original).
75. *In re Hayes Microcomputer Products, Inc.*, 982 F2d 1527, 1536–1538 (Fed Cir 1992).
76. See *Hybritech v. Monoclonal Antibodies, Inc.*, 802 F2d 1367, 1385 (Fed Cir 1986).
77. *Amgen, Inc. v. Chugai Pharmaceutical Co., Ltd.*, 927 F2d at 1212 (claims must "reasonably apprise those skilled in the art" as to their scope and be "as precise as the subject matter permits.")
78. *Metoprolol Succinate Patent Litig. v. KV Pharm. Co.*, 494 F3d 1011, 1016 (Fed Cir 2007); *Perricone v. Medicis Pharm. Corp.*, 432 F3d 1368, 1372–1373 (Fed Cir 2005).
79. *Gemstar v. TV Guide International, Inc.*, 383 F3d 1352, 1381 (Fed Cir 2004); *Jamesbury Corp. v. United States*, 518 F2d 1384, 1395 (Ct. Cl. 1975).
80. See *Hess v. Advanced Cardiovascular Sys., Inc.*, 106 F3d 976, 980 (Fed Cir 1997).
81. 35 USC §116.
82. *Id.* §116.
83. *Fina Oil & Chem. Co. v. Ewen*, 123 F3d 1466, 1473 (Fed Cir 1997); see also *Ethicon*, 135 F3d at 1460.
84. *Hybritech Inc. v. Monoclonal Antibodies, Inc.*, 802 F2d 1367, 1376 (Fed Cir 1986) (internal quotation marks omitted).
85. *Trovan, Ltd. v. Sokymat SA*, 299 F3d 1292, 1302 (Fed Cir 2002).
86. *Id.*
87. 35 USC §154.
88. See 35 USC §271 ("[W]hoever without authority makes, uses, offers to sell or sells any patented invention within the United States or imports into the United States any patent invention during the term of the patent therefor, infringes the patent.").
89. *Fromson v. Anitec Printing Plates, Inc.*, 132 F3d 1437, 1441 (Fed Cir 1997).
90. See, e.g., *Kopykake Enterprises, Inc. v. The Lucks Co.*, 264 F3d 1377, 1381 (Fed Cir 2001); *Alpex Computer Corp. v. Nintendo Co. Ltd.*, 102 F3d 1214, 1220 (Fed Cir 1996); *Minnesota Mining & Mfg. Co. v. Johnson & Johnson Orthopaedics, Inc.*, 976 F2d 1559, 1566 (Fed Cir 1992); *SRI Int'l v. Matsushita Electric Corp. of America*, 775 F2d 1107, 1118 (Fed Cir 1985)(en banc).
91. ATD Corporation at 540; *Transmatic, Inc. v. Gulton Indus., Inc.*, 53 F3d 1270, 1277 (Fed Cir 1995).
92. *Multiform Desiccants, Inc. v. Medzam, Ltd.*, 133 F3d 1473, 1478 (Fed Cir 1998).
93. *Id.*
94. *Harris Corp. v. IXYS Corp.*, 114 F3d 1149, 1153 (Fed Cir 1997). Note, however, that the Court of Appeals for the Federal Circuit has held that practicing the prior art is not a defense to per se literal infringement. *Tate Access Floors, Inc. v. Interface Architectural Resources, Inc.*, 279 F3d 1357,. 61 U.S.P.Q.2d 1647 (Fed Cir 2002).
95. *ATD Corp. v. Lydall, Inc.*, 159 F3d 534, 541 (Fed Cir 1998) [quoting *Tandon Corp. v. U.S. International Trade Commission*, 831 F2d 1017, 1024 (Fed Cir 1987)].
96. 35 USC § 112.
97. *Digital Biometrics, Inc. v. Identix, Inc.*, 149 F3d 1335, 1344 (Fed Cir 1998).
98. *Graver Tank & Mfg. Co. v. Linde Air Prods. Co.*, 339 U.S. 605, 607 (1950); see *Warner Jenkinson Co. v. Hilton-Davis Chem. Co.*, 520 U.S. 17, 28–30 (1997).

99. *Warner Jenkinson*, at 20–30; *General American Transportation Corp. v. Cryo-Trans Inc.*, 93 F3d 766, 770 (Fed Cir 1996) [citing *Mannesmann Demag Corp. v. Engineered Metal Products Co.*, 793 F2d 1279, 1282 (Fed Cir 1986)]; *Transmatic* at 1277.
100. *Warner Jenkinson, supra; Hughes Aircraft Co. v. United States*, 140 F3d 1470, 1476–1477 (Fed Cir 1998); *Renishaw PLC v. Marpossa Societa' Per Aziaoni*, 158 F3d 1243 (Fed Cir 1998) (affirming lower court finding of no infringement because accused device lacked claim limitation); *Corning Glass Works v. Sumitomo Electric U.S.A., Inc.*, 868 F2d 1251, 1259 (Fed Cir 1989); *Julien v. Zeringue*, 864 F2d 1569, 1571 (Fed Cir 1989).
101. *Pennwalt Corp. v. Durand-Wayland, Inc.*, 833 F2d 931, 935 (Fed Cir 1987), *Warner Jenkinson, supra.*
102. *Ethicon Endo-Surgery Inc. v. United States Surgical Corp.*, 149 F3d 1309, 1320 (Fed Cir 1998).
103. *Graver Tank*, at 608; *Warner Jenkinson, supra; Insta-Foam Prod. v. Universal Foam Sys., Inc.*, 906 F2d 698, 702 (Fed Cir 1990).
104. *Warner Jenkinson, supra.*
105. *Id.*
106. *Warner Jenkinson*, at 28–30.
107. *Schwarz Pharma, Inc. v. Paddock Labs. Inc.*, 504 F3d 1371, 1375–1376 (Fed Cir 2007).
108. *Vehicular Technologies Corporation, v. Titan Wheel Int'l, Incl.*, 141 F3d 1084, 1091 (Fed Cir 1998)(citing *Lemelson v. General Mills, Inc.*, 968 F2d 1202, 1208 (Fed Cir 1992)).
109. *Festo Corp. v. Shoketsu Kinzoku Kogyo Kabushiki Co., Ltd.*, 535 U.S. 722, 739–740 (2002).
110. *Festo Corp. v. Shoketsu Kinzoku Kabushiki Co.*, 344 F3d 1359, 1367–1370 (Fed Cir 2003).
111. *Jonsson v. Stanley Works*, 903 F2d 812, 817 (Fed Cir 1990).
112. *Texas Instruments Inc. v. United States Int'l Trade Comm'n*, 988 F2d 1165, 1174 (Fed Cir 1993).
113. *Interactive Pictures Corporation v. Infinite Pictures*, 274 F3d 1371, 1380 (Fed Cir 2001); *We Care, Inc. v. Ultra-Mark Int' l Corp.*, 930 F2d 1567, 1570–1571 (Fed Cir 1991); *Wilson Sporting Goods Co. v. David Geoffrey & Assocs.*, 904 F2d 677, 684 (Fed Cir 1990).
114. *Carman Industries, Inc. v. Wahl*, 724 F2d 932, 941 (Fed Cir 1983).
115. *Novartis Pharms Corp. v. Eon Labs Mfg., Inc.*, 363 F3d 1306, 1308 (Fed Cir 2004) (holding that "... it is well settled that there can be no inducement or contributory infringement absent an underlying direct infringement.").
116. *Id.*
117. *Rodime PLC v. Seagate Tech., Inc.*, 174 F3d 1294, 1306 (Fed Cir 1999).
118. *Manville Sales Corp. v. Paramount Sys., Inc.*, 917 F2d 544, 553 (Fed Cir 1990) (emphasis added); *DSU Medical Corp. v. JMS Co., LTD.*, 471 F3d 1293, 1304 (Fed Cir 2006).
119. *Id.* at 1594.
120. *DSU Medical Corp.*, at 1307.
121. *Dynacore Holdings Corp. v. U.S. Philips Corp.*, 363 F3d 1263 (Fed Cir 2004).
122. *DSU Medical Corp.*, at 1303.
123. *Id.* at 1371.
124. *Id.* The Federal Circuit expressly stated that "the reasoning contained in [opinions of counsel] ultimately may preclude a [finding of recklessness]. *In re Seagate.* Although distinction is made between oral and written opinion, the weight given to the type of opinion is based on circumstance. See *Eli Lilly & Co. v. Zenith Goldline Pharmaceuticals, Inc.* 2001 WL 1397304 at *19 (S.D. Ind. 2001) ("Reliance on oral opinions of counsel is not favored ... Oral opinions carry less weight, for example, because they must be proved perhaps years after the event, based only on testimony which may be affected by faded memories and the forces of contemporaneous litigation ... Nevertheless, reliance on an oral opinion is not necessarily unreasonable as a matter of law.") Compare, e.g., *Radio Steel & Mfg. Co. v. MTD Products, Inc.*, 788 F2d 1554, 1558–1559 (Fed Cir 1986) (affirming finding that infringement was not willful where infringer relied on oral opinion of outside patent counsel), with *American Medical Systems, Inc. v. Medical Engineering Corp.*, 6 F3d 1523, 1531 (Fed Cir 1993) (affirming finding of willfulness; oral opinion of invalidity from counsel was not credible, and infringer did not obtain credible written opinion until 20 months after beginning infringement)." (citations omitted).
125. *Id.*

126. *Id.*
127. Technically, the filing of an ANDA necessitates prior production of infringing products, however, products and manufacturing acts for purposes of submitting an ANDA are exempt from patent infringement pursuant to the safe harbor provisions of the Hatch–Waxman Act. See 21 USC §§355 and 360; 35 USC §§156 and 271(e).
128. Although patent holders are free to seek preliminary injunctions after the 30-month stay has expired, they may not be successful. Recently, Altana Pharma and Wyeth sought a preliminary injunction upon the expiration of the 30-month stay. The U.S. District Court for the District of New Jersey determined that an injunction was unnecessary because any harm to the patent holder could be measured and compensated monetarily, and thus was not the type of irreparable harm that would necessitate an injunction. *Altana Pharma AG v. Teva Pharm.*, 2007 U.S. Dist. LEXIS 67285 (D.N.J. 2007).
129. 35 USC §283 (2006).
130. *Nat'l Steel Car, Ltd. v. Canadian Pac. Ry., Ltd.*, 357 F3d 1319, 1324 (Fed Cir 2004) [quoting *Intel Corp. v. ULSI Sys. Tech. Inc.*, 995 F2d 1566, 1568 (Fed Cir 1993)].
131. *Jack Guttman, Inc. v. Kopykake Enters. Inc.*, 302 F3d 1352, 1356 (Fed Cir 2002).
132. *Polymer Techs., Inc. v. Bridwell*, 103 F3d 970, 977 (Fed Cir 1996).
133. *Amazon.com, Inc. v. Barnesandnoble.com, Inc.*, 239 F3d 1343, 1350 (Fed Cir 2001) [quoting *Hybritech, Inc. v. Abbott Labs.*, 849 F2d 1446, 1451 (Fed Cir 1988)].
134. 35 USC §282 (2006).
135. *Abbott Labs. v. Andrx Pharmaceuticals Inc.*, 473 F3d 1196, 1200–1201 (Fed Cir 2007); See *In re Seagate Technology LLC*, 497 F3d 1360, 1374 (Fed Cir 2007).
136. *Abbott Labs.*, at 1200–1201.
137. *See Gonzales v. O Centro Espirita Beneficente Uniao Do Vegetal*, 546 U.S. 418, 428–430 (2006).
138. *Pfizer, Inc. v. Teva Pharmaceuticals, USA, Inc.*, 429 F3d 1364, 1372 (Fed Cir 2005).
139. *Abbott Labs*, at 1200–1201.
140. *In re Seagate Technology*, at 1374.
141. *Amazon.com, Inc.*, 239 F3d at 1359.
142. *Nutrition 21 v. United States*, 930 F2d 867, 871–872 (Fed Cir 1991).
143. *See Smith Int'l, Inc., v. Hughes Tool Co.*, 718 F2d 1573, 1581 (Fed Cir 1983).
144. *In re Seagate Technology LLC*, at 1374.
145. *Serio-US Industries, Inc. v. Plastic Recovery Technologies Corp.*, 267 F Supp 2d 466, 469 (D.Md. 2003); *Reebok Int'l Ltd. v.J. Baker, Inc.*, 32 F3d 1552, 1557–1558 (Fed Cir 1994).
146. *Ortho-Mcneil Pharmaceutical, Inc., v. Mylan Laboratories Inc.*, Nos. CIV.A.04–1689, 06-757, 06-5166, 2007 WL 8695-45 at *1 (D.N.J. Oct. 23, 2006).
147. *McKesson Information Solutions, Inc. v. Bridge Medical, Inc.*, 487 F3d 897, 913 (Fed Cir 2007).
148. See, e.g., *Glaverbel Societe Anonyme v. Northlake Mktg. & Supply, Inc.*, 45 F3d 1550, 1556–1557 (Fed Cir 1995).
149. *See Eli Lilly & Co. v. Zenith Goldline Pharmaceuticals, Inc.*, 471 F3d 1369, 1381 (Fed Cir 2007); *Warner-Lambert Co. v. Teva Pharms. USA, Inc.*, 418 F3d 1326, 1342 (Fed Cir 2005); *Nilssen v. Osram Sylvania, Inc.*, 504 F3d 1223, 1229 (Fed Cir 2007).
150. 37 CFR §1.56 (2006).
151. *Bruno Independent Living Aids, Inc. v. Acorn Mobility Services, Ltd.*, 394 F3d 1348, 1351 (Fed Cir 2005); *Molins PLC v. Textron, Inc.*, 48 F3d 1172, 1178 (Fed Cir 1995).
152. *Fox Indus., Inc. v. Structural Preservation Sys., Inc.*, 922 F2d 801, 803 (Fed Cir 1991); *McKesson* at 917–918.
153. *Impax Labs., Inc. v. Aventis Pharm. Inc.*, 468 F3d 1366, 1374 (Fed Cir 2006); *Nilssen* at 1229.
154. 37 CFR §1.56(b) (2006); *See Agfa Corp. v. Creo Products Inc.*, 451 F3d 1366, 1377 (Fed Cir 2006).
155. See, e.g., *Agfa Corp.* at 1377.
156. *Impax Labs.*, at 1374–1375 [quoting *Kingsdown Med. Consultants, Ltd. v. Hollister Inc.*, 863 F2d 867, 876 (Fed Cir 1988)].
157. *Cargill Inc. v. Canbra Foods, Ltd.*, 476 F3d 1359, 1364 (Fed Cir 2007); *In re Metroprolol Succinate Patent Litig.*, 494 F3d 1011, 1020 (Fed Cir 2007); *Impax Labs*, at 1375.
158. Id.; *Eli Lilly & Co.*, at 1381.

159. *Eli Lilly & Co.*, at 1382; *Kingsdown Med. Consultants, Ltd. v. Hollister, Inc.*, 863 F2d 867, 876 (Fed Cir 1988)
160. See Eli Lilly & Co., at 1381; *Union Pac. Res. Co. v. Chesapeake Energy Corp.*, 236 F3d 684, 693 (Fed Cir 2001).
161. *Critikon, Inc. v. Becton Dickinson Vascular Access, Inc.*, 120 F3d 1253, 1256 (Fed Cir 1997); Cargill at 1364.
162. *Molins* at 1178.
163. See *Labounty Manufacturing Inc. v. United States Int'l Trade Commission*, 958 F2d 1066, 1070–1072, 1076–1077.
164. See, e.g., *Semiconductor Energy Laboratory Co., Ltd. v. Samsung Electronics Co., Ltd.* 204 F3d 1368 (Fed Cir 2000).
165. See *Dippin' Dots, Inc. v. Mosey*, 476 F3d 1337, 1345 (Fed Cir 2007).
166. See *Bellehumeur v. Bonnett*, 127 Fed. Appx. 480, 486 (Fed Cir 2005); *Board of Educ. ex rel Bd. Of Trustees of Florida State University v. American Bioscience, Inc.*, 333 F3d 1330, 1344 (Fed Cir 2003).
167. See *Consolidated Aluminum Corp. v. Foseco Intern. Ltd.*, 910 F2d 804 (Fed Cir 1990).
168. See *Li Second Family Ltd. Partnership v. Toshiba Corp.*, 231 F3d 1373, 1378–1380 (Fed Cir 2000).
169. *Digital Control* at 1318.
170. *Id.* at 1321.
171. See *General Electro Music Corp. v. Samick Music Corp.*, 19 F3d 1405, 1411–1412 (Fed Cir 1994).
172. See *Lumenyte Intern. Corp. v. Cable Lite Corp.*, 1996 U.S. App. LEXIS 16400 *at 3–4, (Fed Cir 1996).
173. See *Nilssen* at 1231.
174. *Nilssen* at 1230.
175. See, e.g., *Agfa Corp.* at 1380; *Bellehumeur* at 486–487.
176. *Impax Labs.* at 1375.
177. *Id.* at 1375–1376.
178. *Id.* at 1376.
179. *Id.* at 1377.
180. *Id.*
181. *Warner-Lambert* at 1343.
182. *Id.*
183. *Id.* at 1343–1344.
184. *Id.* at 1346–1347.
185. *Id.* at 1347.
186. *Id.* at 1348.
187. *Eli Lilly* at 1383.
188. *Id.*
189. *Id.*
190. *Id.*
191. *In re Metoprolol Succinate* at 1020–1021.
192. *Id.*
193. *Id.*
194. *Id.* at 1021.
195. *Id.*
196. See, e.g., FTC, Generic Drug Entry Prior to Patent Expiration: An FTC Study, pp. 24, 25 & nn. 2–3 (2002); http://www.ftc.gov/os/2002/07/genericdrugstudy.pdf ("FTC Study").
197. Medicare Modernization Act of 2003, §1112(a)(1).
198. *Id.* at §1113.
199. *Id.* at §1115.
200. The earliest identified reverse payment settlement in the FTC Study was executed in March 1993. The settlement agreements analyzed in the FTC Study were either executed after December 31, 1994 or were in effect at the time of the 2001 FTC. FTC Study, p. 3.

201. See *In re Terazosin Hydrochloride Antitrust Litig.*, 352 F Supp 2d 1279 (S.D. Fla. 2005); see *In re Cardizem CD Antitrust Litig.*, 332 F3d 896 (6th Cir 2003).
202. *In re Tamoxifen Citrate Antitrust Litig.*, 466 F3d 187 (2d Cir 2006), cert. denied, 127 S. Ct. 3001 (2007); *Schering-Plough Corp. v. FTC*, 402 F3d 1056 (11th Cir 2005), *cert. denied*, 126 S. Ct. 2929 (2006).
203. The FTC sent out special orders pursuant to Section 6(b) of the Federal Trade Commission Act. 15 USC §46(b) (2000). FTC Study, p. 3.
204. See, generally, FTC Study.
205. *Id.* at i–xi.
206. See *id.* at 31 (of the 20 agreements identified, 9 were reverse payment settlements).
207. *Id.* at 25.
208. *Id.* at 25 & n. 3. The FTC Study also reveals that the FTC instituted only 1 enforcement action with respect to 20 identified final Paragraph IV settlement agreements. *Id.* at 25 n. 2.
209. See *id.* at 57–63.
210. Commissioner Sheila F. Anthony Remarks before ABA Antitrust and Intellectual Property Group entitled "Riddles and Lessons from the Prescription Drug Wars: Antitrust Implications of Certain Types of Agreements Involving Intellectual Property," June 1, 2000; http://www.ftc.gov/speeches/anthony/sfip000601.htm.
211. April 10, 2007 Oral Statement of Commissioner J. Thomas Rosch, FTC Oversight Hearing, Committee on Commerce, Science and Transportation, United States Senate, http://www.ftc.gov/speeches/rosch/070410Roschsenatestatment.pdf.
212. Id.
213. *In the Matter of Schering-Plough Corporation*; Docket No. 9297; http://www.ftc.gov/os/adjpro/d9297/index.shtm.
214. *Palmer v. BRG of Georgia, Inc.*, 498 U.S. 46 (1990)(per curiam).
215. *In re Tamoxifen Citrate Antitrust Litig.*, 429 F3d 370 (2d Cir 2005).
216. Oral Statement of Commissioner J. Thomas Rosch, FTC Oversight Hearing, Committee on Commerce, Science and Transportation, United States Senate, April 10, 2007; http://www.ftc.gov/speeches/rosch/070410Roschsenatestatment.pdf.
217. Prepared Statement of the Federal Trade Commission Before the Committee on the Judiciary of the United States Senate on Anticompetitive Patent Settlements in the Pharmaceutical Industry: The Benefits of a Legislative Solution, January 17, 2007; http://www.ftc.gov/speeches/leibowitz/070117anticompetitivepatentsettlements_senate.pdf.
218. *Id.*
219. *Id.*
220. *In the Matter of Abbott Labs.*; Docket No. C-3945; http://www.ftc.gov/os/caselist/c3945.shtm.
221. *In the Matter of Hoechst Marion Roussel, Inc.*; Docket No. 9293; http://www.ftc.gov/os/caselist/d9293.shtm.
222. *In the Matter of Abbott Labs.*; Docket No. C-3945; http://www.ftc.gov/os/caselist/c3945.shtm and *In the Matter of Hoechst Marion Roussel, Inc.*; Docket No. 9293; http://www.ftc.gov/os/caselist/d9293.shtm.
223. *Id.*
224. *Id.*
225. *In the Matter of Bristol-Myers Squibb Company*; Docket No. C-4076, http://www.ftc.gov/os/2003/04/bristolmyerssquibbcmp.pdf.
226. *Id.*
227. See *In re Terazosin Hydrochloride Antitrust Litig.*, 352 F Supp 2d 1279 (S.D. Fla. 2005).
228. The Abbott–Geneva Settlement Agreement defined "Final Judgment in Geneva's Favor" as "the entry pursuant to Federal Rule of Civil Procedure 79(a) by the United States District Court for the Northern District of Illinois in Case No. 96 C 3331 of a final, appealable judgment that Geneva's Terazosin Hydrochloride Products do not infringe or would not infringe any valid and enforceable claim of the '207 patent."
229. "Final Judgment in Abbott's Favor" was defined as "the entry pursuant to the Federal Rule of Civil Procedure 79(a) by the United States District Court for the Northern

District of Illinois in Case No. 96 C 3331 of a final, appealable judgment that Geneva's Terazosin Hydrochloride Products infringed or would infringe any valid and enforceable claim of the '207 patent."
230. See *In re Terazosin Hydrochloride Antitrust Litig.*, 352 F Supp 2d 1279 (S.D. Fla. 2005).
231. See *In re Cardizem CD Antitrust Litig.*, 332 F3d 896 (6th Cir 2003).
232. *Id.* at 907–908.
233. *Id.*
234. See *In re Buspirone Patent Litig.*, 185 F Supp 2d 363 (S.D.N.Y. 2002).
235. BMS settles antitrust litigation—Pharmacy News, Drug Store News, Michael Johnsen, January 20,2003.
236. *Schering-Plough Corp. v. FTC*, 402 F3d 1056 (11th Cir 2005), *cert. denied*, 126 S. Ct. 2929 (2006).
237. *Id.* at 1069–1070.
238. *Id.* at 1070.
239. See *id.* at 1070–1071.
240. *Id.* at 1071.
241. *Id.* at 1069.
242. *Id.* at 1060.
243. *Id.* at 1060–1061.
244. *Id.*
245. *Id.*
246. *Id.*
247. *Id.*
248. In the Matter of Schering-Plough Corporation; Docket No. 9297; http://www.ftc.gov/os/adjpro/d9297/index.shtm.
249. *Id.*
250. *Id.*
251. See *Schering-Plough Corp. v. FTC*, 402 F3d 1056, 1071–1072 (11th Cir 2005), *cert. denied*, 126 S. Ct. 2929 (2006).
252. *Id.* at 1072.
253. *In re Tamoxifen Citrate Antitrust Litig.*, 466 F3d 187 (2d Cir 2006), *cert. denied*, 127 S. Ct. 3001 (2007).
254. *In re Tamoxifen Citrate Antitrust Litig.*, 466 F3d 187 (2d Cir 2006), *cert denied, Joblove v. Barr Labs, Inc.*, 127 S.Ct. 3001 (2007).
255. *Id.* at 208–210.
256. *Id.* at 208.
257. *Id.* at 208.
258. *Id.* at 208.
259. *Id.* at 208.
260. Petition for Writ of Certiorari at 17–18, *FTC v. Schering-Plough Corp.*, http://www.ftc.gov/os/adjpro/d9297/index.shtm.
261. *Id.* at 19.
262. *Id.* at 18.
263. *Id.*
264. *Id.*
265. *Id.*
266. *In the Matter of Schering-Plough Corporation*; Docket No. 9297; http://www.ftc.gov/os/adjpro/d9297/index.shtm.
267. Preserve Access to Affordable Generics Act, S. 316, 110th Cong. (2007); Protecting Consumer Access to Generic Drugs Act, H R 1902, 110th Cong. (2007).
268. S. 316 §2(a)(8).
269. *Id.* §3. and H R 1902.

8 The Influence of the Prescription Drug User Fee Act on the Approval Process

Marc J. Scheineson, Esq.
Alston & Bird LLP, Washington, D.C., U.S.A.

SUMMARY OF THE PRESCRIPTION DRUG USER FEE ACT OF 1992 (PDUFA I) (OCT. 1, 1993, TO SEPT. 30, 1997)

Nature of the Deal

In 1991, when Dr. David Kessler sat in his new desk chair in his downtown Washington, D.C., office, shortly after being nominated and confirmed as the Commissioner of Food and Drugs, he asked himself the recurring question, "How can so few employees with such a limited federal budget perform all the responsibilities expected of us?" At that time, the U.S. Food and Drug Administration (FDA) had fewer than 8000 employees in 25 districts across the United States. Its budget was just over $850 million. Its jurisdiction included inspecting the entire domestic processed food supply, sampling and inspecting imported products under its jurisdiction, reviewing and approving the export of regulated products to foreign countries, inspecting every product manufacturing establishment every 2 years and the country's entire blood supply, reviewing and approving applications and labeling and promotion for new prescription drugs, generic drugs, animal drugs, biologics, vaccines, medical devices, completing over-the-counter drug regulations, conducting surveillance on those approved products, soliciting and investigating adverse reaction reports, supervising the labeling and sale of medical foods, infant formulas, teas, dietary supplements, cosmetics, regulating every product that emits radiation (including light bulbs, cellular telephones, lasers, microwave ovens, television sets), inspecting the kitchens of commercial aircraft and cruise ships, and, with whatever time was left, making sure that product advertising was truthful, fairly balanced, and not false or misleading. This was a relatively paltry budget, especially when compared to the $2 billion budget of the U.S. Department of Agriculture to support hundreds of thousands of employees with a tenth of the jurisdiction. FDA states that it regulates products that comprise $0.25 of every consumer dollar spent. In reality, it regulates nearly one quarter of the American economy. On top of all this pressure, Dr. Kessler was bombarded with industry and congressional pressure to streamline and expedite the review of promising new life-saving prescription drugs and biologics. Those approvals were averaging 2 to 3 years following submission of complete new drug applications (NDAs) and what are now called Biologics Licensing Applications (BLAs). Nonpriority applications for "me-too" drugs could take 5 years or more to preview and approve.

Dr. Kessler convened his policy, legal, and legislative team. Viewing proposals by other agencies to adopt "user fees" to pay the cost of specialized government services that benefited identified categories of Americans, the terms of his offer to industry soon became clear. Would companies be willing to pay for the review of their product applications if it meant faster review? Those additional resources would, in turn, be dedicated to paying the salaries of additional product reviewers. All applications would be assigned to expand agency personnel immediately. They would not wait for months, and sometimes years, until a reviewer was available to pick it up and read it.

Gerald Mossinghoff, president of what was then the Pharmaceutical Manufacturers Association and is now PhRMA, was called in by the commissioner and his team. Mossinghoff, a former commissioner of the Patent and Trademark Office (PTO), was initially skeptical. PTO had made a similar proposal to expedite review of patent applications. Applicants opposed the measure. Then when a nominal fee structure was adopted, all the new money flowed directly into the general federal treasury; it had not been dedicated to supplementing PTO resources. Even if money could be so dedicated, would not HHS budget cutters just reduce FDA's appropriated funds by the amount of revenue from private sources? This would be a zero-sum gain. He also did not believe that companies should have to pay the government to do its job. Was not that what taxes were for?

Finally, an industry committee was formed to work with FDA and the Congress. A creative new proposal was worked out. PhRMA and the Industrial Biotechnology Association (a predecessor of the Biotechnology Industry Association) agreed on behalf of its member companies to support significant fees in the hundreds of thousands of dollars for NDAs, BLAs, and establishment registrations, if the fees met the following criteria. They had to be (*i*) additive to existing FDA baseline appropriations; (*ii*) fully dedicated to the approval of new drugs and biologics; (*iii*) reasonable amounts; (*iv*) based on a long-term government commitment to specific improvements in the approval process; and (*v*) part of performance goals that should be established by the Center for Drug Evaluation and Research (CDER) and the Center for Biologics Evaluation and Research (CBER) to evaluate improvements in the review and approval process.

These parameters were creatively hammered out into specific legislative language in a series of painstakingly long drafting sessions. Meetings were held in the office of the House Legislative Counsel, David Meade, among representatives of FDA's Office of Legislative Affairs, the PhRMA/IBC working group, the Department of Health and Human Services Assistant Secretary for Legislation, Bill Schultz (Rep. Henry Waxman), Mark Childress (Sen. Edward Kennedy), and Anne LaBelle (Sen. Orrin Hatch). Innovative new provisions insured that the industry's fees did not disappear into general government coffers or that direct FDA appropriations were not reduced by the amount of private funds received. FDA's existing fiscal 1992 appropriations became a baseline that had to increase by at least an established cost-of-living adjustment every year or the authority to assess private user fees would terminate. Legal commitments were made that the fees would supplement FDA's direct appropriations. CDER and CBER developed specific plans to hire 600 new full-time equivalent employees. FDA refused to commit to statutory language requiring a specific time frame for application review. It agreed, however, to issue a side letter to congressional committee chairmen containing nonbinding "performance goals." These goals would include a designated percentage of applications that would be reviewed and acted upon within one year of submission for standard applications and within 6 months of submission for priority applications (involving drugs to treat serious and life-threatening illnesses for which no comparable therapy was currently available). The law would expire in 5 years. It would require periodic congressional reauthorization as a mechanism to force FDA to be accountable for these performance goals or risk losing hundreds of millions of user fee funds that would support hundreds of new employees and infrastructure improvements.

Once the deal was reached behind the scenes between industry, FDA, and the Democratic and Republican Committee leadership, legislation was introduced. It was reviewed in cursory hearings and passed in Congress with remarkable speed. On October 29, 1992, the President signed the Prescription Drug User Fee Act of 1992 in the Rose Garden of the White House amid great fanfare and celebration. If CDER's and CBER's detailed action plans could be administered properly, the new law would revolutionize the American drug review process. It would push the industry, and the quality of American health care, ahead of our European counterparts. Drug applications would be reviewed immediately upon completion and filing. Review time would be cut in half. An efficient new system would restore resources and accountability to FDA. Pharmaceutical manufacturers were not buying approvals. The insular FDA Center review structure would not allow that to happen. They were, however, dedicating large sums of money in fees for the opportunity to participate in a more interactive process potentially marketing their new drugs years in advance of the prior system. Patients would no longer be required to wait additional years to gain access to life-saving new therapies. FDA would quantify its progress through written reports to congressional oversight authorities on an annual basis. If the experiment did not work, the parties would pull the plug after the initial 5-year term. The authorization bill creating the user fee program still required separate appropriations legislation to allow the government to fund FDA and collect the private funds. On July 2, 1993, the president signed a supplemental appropriation bill allowing FDA to collect user fees due from October 1, 1992, through September 31, 1993, the government fiscal year (FY).

Type of User Fees

In order for these fees not to be viewed as taxes (and thereby incur the jurisdiction of the congressional taxing committees which did not support the concept of dedicated user fees), the new law was intended to divide the fee burden across existing manufacturers. Segments were created which relied directly on the payment for real FDA services, including (1) the review of drug/biologic applications (application fees), (2) insuring safe manufacturing processes (establishment fees), and (3) monitoring adverse reports, recalls, labeling, etc. (product fees). These three segments insured that a company with a lot of product applications but few products on the market currently or with no existing manufacturing facility would not bear the entire burden of funding FDA review operations. Likewise, if a company marketed many products or maintained numerous facilities, it could afford to sustain FDA's CDER and CBER operations more easily than a new company with few products. Therefore, the fees were divided into three segments, as summarized below.

Application Fees

Who Pays?

Fees are assessed for the submission of certain human drug or biological applications. Human drug applications include new drug applications (NDAs), Pre-Licensing Applications and Establishment Licensing Applications for biologics which have been consolidated into Biological Licensing Applications (BLAs), and initial certification of antibiotic drugs (which became NDAs in the FDA Modernization Act in 1997). Also included are product efficacy and manufacturing supplements. Expressly excluded from application fees, and also from FDA performance commitments, were (*i*) over-the-counter drugs, which commonly do not require advance FDA approval (except for Rx-to-OTC switches, which do commonly contain clinical information and are included), (*ii*) generic drug applications (ANDAs), (*iii*) new animal drug applications (NADAs), (4) blood products, (*iv*) allergenic extracts, (*v*) in vitro diagnostics, and (*vi*) large-volume parenterals.

Fee Schedule

One-third of the total annual revenue was required to come from each fee category. For the term covered by PDUFA I, these fees, which were calculated to meet the total designated income required to hire 600 additional reviewers based on the number of applications actually filed, as well as support staff and computer back-up, included $100,000 per application (FY 1993); $162,000 (FY 1994); $208,000 (FY 1995); $204,000 (FY 1996); and $223,000 (FY 1997). For applications not requiring review of clinical data, fees were reduced by one-half.

Payment Terms

One-half of the fee was due on submission. One-half of the amount submitted was returned, if the application was not accepted for filing by FDA. The remaining payment was due within 30 days of when FDA sent its action letter, or when the applicant withdrew its application.

Drug Establishment Fees

Who Pays?

An Rx drug user fee was due from each person (corporation) that owned an establishment in which at least one Rx drug (or biologic) was manufactured during the relevant fiscal year. If the drugs made in the establishment are all subject to generic competition, no fee would accrue. So that the user fee would not be deemed a tax, the payer had to have at least one application pending for FDA review after September 1, 1992. FDA later interpreted this requirement to mean that if the other establishment fee criteria were met, an original application or supplement (with or without clinical data) that was pending after that date would trigger establishment fees for all qualifying establishments. Contract manufacturers that were not registrants on an FDA application were exempt from this fee.

Prescription Drug Establishment

A separate fee was due on each establishment maintained by the applicant. Both foreign and domestic establishments were subject to a fee, if the products they made were marketed in the United States (1). One or more buildings located within 5 miles of each other were classified as one establishment. The facility had to make one or more Rx drugs manufactured in "finished dosage form," interpreted by FDA to mean in a form approved for administration to a patient without further manufacturing (2). Finally, it had to be under the management of the applicant listed on the NDA or BLA. FDA later interpreted this to mean that the applicant need not be the holder of the approved NDA or BLA for the product manufactured at the establishment.

Fee Schedule

Payment was due annually on each Rx drug establishment, as billed by FDA based on its establishment registration list, and as adjusted at the end of the previous year based on the fees needed to reach the total income amount required by this segment of the user fee. Those amounts were $60,000 (FY 1993), $88,000 (FY 1994); $129,000 (FY 1995); $135,300. (FY 1996); and $138,000 (FY 1997).

Payment Terms

The establishment fee is due on or before January 31 of each calendar year. FDA routinely sends out an invoice based on establishments contained in its establishment registration list. Many of those establishments listed and billed may not conform to the requirements of PDUFA. The initial FDA mailings were overly broad. Therefore, manufacturers should have notified FDA regarding incorrect or unauthorized billing.

Drug Product Fees

A separate annual fee was assessed to each manufacturer based on the number of Rx drug products listed in FDA's product registry.

Who Pays?

The fee is assessed to "each person named as an applicant on a human drug application" for each Rx drug (or biologic) listed on FDA's product registration list. The applicant is required to have at least one application or supplement pending agency review in the year the product fee was assessed (beginning after Sept. 1, 1992). A listed product is exempt from the fee once it has generic competition (3). Innovator antibiotic drug products (approved under §507) are subject to product fees. Generic antibiotic drug products (those that are not the first approval of a particular antibiotic drug) are not subject to product fees (4).

Fee Schedule

The fee for each listed drug included $6000 (FY 1993); $9400 (FY 1994); $12,200 (FY 1995); $12,600 (FY 1996); $14,000 (FY 1997).

Payment Terms

Product fees were due at the time of the first product listing in each calendar year. The product must be listed as required by §510 to be subject to the product fee. FDA considers a product to be listed on the date of receipt of the initial submission of information, whether or not the agency finds that the information submitted was complete or requests additional information (5). A product is considered delisted, and no longer assessed a fee, on the date of the agency's receipt of the submission deleting the product from the Drug Listing. A product is subject to the fee if it is listed under §510, whether or not it is actually marketed or even if it is only marketed abroad. If a product is transferred from one NDA/BLA holder to another during a fiscal year, the first holder will assess the product fee in that fiscal year.

Performance Goals

In negotiating the user fee program, FDA was determined to informally offer nonbinding goals. It refused to include inflexible standards in the language of the statute. In a compromise, industry acquiesced to a side letter sent to the Chairman and the Ranking Member of the House Committee on Energy and Commerce,

Rep. John Dingell (D-MI) and Rep. Norman Lent (R-NY). These goals provided the expectations of regulated industry and the Congress concerning review times that would deem the program successful and allow its reauthorization for successive 5-year terms. PhRMA and BIO reportedly believed that if the resources of its member companies failed to shorten review times in accordance with the written goals included in the letter, it could successfully persuade the Congress to shut down the program.

The letter to the Congress stated the following:

1. The additional user fee revenues would be dedicated to expediting the drug review and approval process.
2. Priority NDAs and BLAs that were complete would be reviewed and acted on (through the issuance of an action letter) within 6 months of submission.
3. Standard NDAs and BLAs that were complete would be reviewed and acted on within 12 months of submission.
4. Priority supplements and amendments (or those not requiring review of clinical data) would be reviewed and acted on within 6 months of submission.
5. Standard supplements and amendments would be reviewed and acted on within 6 months of submission.
6. Applications resubmitted following the receipt of a nonapproval letter would be acted on within 6 months of submission.
7. Application backlogs were to be eliminated within 18 months to 2 years.
8. The goals were to be achieved based on a staggered schedule with 55% compliance with applications received in 1994 moving to 90% compliance in 1997.

Small Business Exception

The law allowed a company to pay one-half of the prescribed application fee, not payable until 1 year following the submission (6), if it maintained fewer than 500 employees (including affiliates) and had no Rx or biologic drug product on the market (7). An affiliate was defined as one business with direct or indirect control of another, one business with the power to control another, or a third party that controls or has the power to control both businesses (8). For these qualifying small businesses, FDA sends an invoice 1 year following the submission for the first installment of the fee, whether or not an action letter was issued. The second installment is due at the same time if an action letter was already issued. The number of an applicant's employees is calculated using the procedures of the Small Business Administration contained in 13 CFR Part 121. The suggested procedure to request the exemption is to submit an application to FDA's Office of the Ombudsman. The written request must contain the details of the applicant and fee for which a waiver or reduction is requested. It must also contain information and analysis showing that the statutory criteria for the waiver or reduction have been met (9). The request for the small business exemption should be submitted approximately 90 days before the application is submitted. It must also contain a statement from a responsible officer of the company that it has fewer than 500 employees, has no Rx drugs on the market and does not intend to introduce any within the next 12 months, and expects to submit an application within 90 days (10). The Office of Ombudsman as waiver officer will review the request, review product listings, and will refer the small business criteria consideration to the SBA. A written acknowledgment of the decision will be made. If the request for exemption is denied, an approval process is available as summarized in FDA's draft interim guidance.

Fee Waiver or Reduction

A fee may be waived or reduced if (*i*) FDA did not spend substantial time or resources in reviewing the application before it was withdrawn, (*ii*) it is necessary to protect the public health, the fee would present a significant barrier to innovation, the fee would exceed the cost incurred in reviewing the application, (*iii*) a competing copy of the drug is not subject to the fee, or (*iv*) the fee was paid previously and the applicant is resubmitting the application (11). These provisions allow FDA to consider the limited resources of the entity when evaluating requests for a fee waiver or reduction. It requests a range of information to evaluate whether user fees present a barrier to an entity's ability to develop or market specific products or otherwise continue to pursue innovative technology. The criteria used by FDA include the following:

Protect Public Health; Significant Barrier to Innovation—FDA believes that the annual establishment fee is the greatest barrier under this category. Therefore, most of the fee waivers or reductions granted for public health or innovation reasons relate to small entities where annual establishment fees would be disproportionate in relation to revenues. FDA requests a certified statement from the entity and its affiliates concerning annual revenues, both domestic and foreign. Commercial and financial information is not releasable to the public under the Freedom of Information Act (12). FDA evaluates the annual cost of user fees versus the entity's gross annual revenues, the resources of the entity's parent, and other major funding sources. Lack of profitability is not considered evidence of limited resources.

Fees paid would exceed cost of FDA review—In order for a government assessment to constitute a true fee for the use of services and not a tax, the law insures that the cost of those services approximates the level of the fee. Therefore, FDA may waive all or a portion of the user fee amount if the fee exceeds the anticipated cost of rendering application review and related services (13). FDA was attempting to quantify the cost of the major elements associated with its review of common applications and supplements (14). Few, if any, fee reductions have been based on this provision, in part because FDA interpreted the provision to determine not just the agency cost of reviewing the one application for which the fee was assessed, but also the cost of reviewing all active applications of that person, including INDs, NDAs, BLAs, supplements, and amendments (15). The agency made it clear, however, that an applicant can apply for such a fee reduction if its application was not accepted for filing and the fee was paid (16).

Reduction because of Paper NDA for Same Product—A fee waiver or reduction request can be made by an NDA sponsor who submitted an application under §505(b)(1) (full-NDA), if assessing such fee would be inequitable because an application or supplement for a product containing the same active ingredient was filed by another person under §505(b)(2) (paper NDA) of the act (17).

Increases and Adjustments

The law provides an annual total amount of user fees that are established each fiscal year by congressional appropriation committees. FDA then sets the level of its specific application, establishment, and product fees in November for the next fiscal year to raise the annual user fee level appropriated by the Congress. FDA's scheduled fee rates are announced by a notice in the *Federal Register.* The application fee rates were set by statute, but are to be adjusted annually for cumulative inflation. Total application fee revenues are structured to increase or decrease each year as the number of fee-paying applications to FDA increases or decreases. Each year, FDA is required to set establishment fees and product fees so that the estimated total fee revenue from each of these two categories will equal the total revenue FDA expects to collect from application fees that year. This procedure continues the arrangement under which one-third of the total user fee revenue is projected to come from each of the three types of fees.

Appropriated Fee Amounts

Each year that user fees are authorized, they must be contained in the annual appropriations legislation for FDA (appropriated by the Agriculture, Rural Development and Related Agencies Subcommittees of Appropriations). In PDUFA I (for the fiscal years Oct. 1, 1993, through Sept. 30, 1997), the appropriated amounts for total Rx drug user fees, as adjusted for the number of applications actually filed, were as follows: $36 million (FY 1993); $56,284,200 (FY 1994); $77,415,000 (FY 195); $79,981,200 (FY 1996); and $84 million (FY 1997).

Effect of Failure to Pay Fees

Under the initial user fee legislation, unless fees were paid timely when assessed, applications would not be accepted for filing or review would be discontinued.

Annual Reports

Two annual reports were required to be prepared by FDA and submitted to the House Energy and Commerce Committee and to the Senate Labor and Human Resources Committee. The first report would quantify FDA's progress in achieving its performance goals and would be filed within 60 days following the end of the first fiscal year (by Nov. 29, 1993). This became known as the "Performance Report" and has been filed annually since. A second report was required to review implementation of FDA's new authorities under the act and how it used the fees collected. This became known as the "Financial Report" and has been filed annually since. This report was due within 120 days after the end of the fiscal year (by Mar. 29, 1994). Annual FDA PDUFA reports are available at www.fda.gov/cder/pdufa/mainpduf.htm

Five-Year Sunset

The act was terminated after 5 years, effective on September 30, 1997. The purpose of this "sunset" was to provide an opportunity for Congress and industry to meet with FDA to assess the program and FDA's progress in expediting application review. Since FDA hired more than 600 FTEs, the agency has enormous pressure to meet its obligations or risk losing significant funding, which sustained that increased workforce. If the program was not reauthorized at the end of that term, FDA would likely be forced to fire its new reviewer workforce. Since enactment of this FDA legislation was considered mandatory every 5 years, its reenactment for two successive 5-year periods has been used as a vehicle to pass other FDA and health-related reforms.

Animal Drug Study

Finally, since manufacturers of animal drugs were not invited to participate in the PDUFA program, the legislative drafters agreed, at the request of industry, to require FDA to prepare a study evaluating whether to impose user fees on new animal drug applications to improve existing review processes. The report was due to Congress by January 4, 1994.

SUMMARY OF FDA MODERNIZATION ACT OF 1997 (PDUFA II) (OCT. 1, 1997, TO SEPT. 30, 2002)

Modifications of Prior Law

Based on FDA's significant progress to reform its review of Rx drug and biologics applications, Congress reauthorized PDUFA as part of broader FDA Reform Act legislation (FDAMA). This new Title 1 of FDAMA (called PDUFA II) amended PDUFA I and extended it through September 30, 2002. In July 1998, FDA released a Five-Year Plan for PDUFA II that presented the major assumptions FDA was making and how it intended to use its additional resources in order to achieve the new goals associated with the amended act.

New Fee Amounts

1. *Application Fees:* $256,846 (applications including data), $128,423 (applications without data and supplements with data) (FY 1998); $272,282 (applications including data), $136,141 (applications without data and supplements with data) (FY 1999); $285,740 (applications including data), $142,870 (applications without data and supplements with data) (FY 2000); $309,647 (applications including data), $154,823 (applications without data and supplements with data) (FY 2001); $313,320 (applications including data), $156,600 (applications without data and supplements with data) (FY 2002).
2. *Establishment Fees:* $141,966 (FY 1998); $128,435 (FY 1999); $141,971 (FY 2000); $145,989 (FY 2001); $140,199 (FY 2002).
3. *Product Fees:* $18,591 (FY 1998); $18,364 (FY 1999); $19,959 (FY 2000); $21,892 (FY 2001); $21,630 (FY 2002).

Performance Goals

As part of the consideration of PDUFA II, FDA again agreed to a series of performance goals against which its performance would be measured when reauthorization of a successive 5-year term was considered in 2002. The goals for CDER and CBER review included the following:

Original NDAs, BLAs, and efficacy supplements	Standard application	Priority application
FY 1998	90% in 12 months	90% in 6 months
FY 1999	30% in 10 months 90% in 12 months	90% in 6 months
FY 2000	50% in 10 months 90% in 12 months	90% in 6 months
FY 2001	70% in 10 months 90% in 12 months	90% in 6 months
FY 2002	90% in 10 months	90% in 6 months

Ninety percent of manufacturing supplements requiring approval were to be reviewed in 6 months, with a sliding scale to be reviewed in 4 months (30% in FY 1999, 50% in FY 2000, 40% in FY 2001, and 90% in FY 2002). Resubmission of original NDAs/BLAs were to be considered in 6 months, with a sliding scale to be considered in 4 months and then 2 months.

Other performance goals unrelated to application reviews were built into the PDUFA II regime. FDA was required to monitor responses to requests for meetings (70% of requests were to be responded to within 14 days moving to 90% by 2001). Type A meetings were to occur within 30 calendar days of the agency receiving the meeting request, Type B meetings within 60 calendar days, and Type C meetings within 75 calendar days. FDA meeting minutes were to be available to the sponsor within 30 calendar days after the meeting. They would clearly outline the important agreements, disagreements, issues for further discussion, and action items from the meeting in bulleted form, and need not be in great detail (18).

Procedures for clinical holds were also carefully delineated. FDA centers would respond to a sponsor's complete response to a clinical hold within 30 days of the agency's receipt of a sponsor's response. Ninety percent of such responses must be timely after FY 1999.

Procedures for major dispute resolution were also quantified. By 2001, 90% of procedural and scientific matters would be responded to within 30 days, which involved drug reviews that could not be resolved at the divisional level and for which a formal dispute resolution petition was filed. A series of conditions was provided, which included (*i*) that the disputes should first be worked through the review chain from the reviewer to the Division Director, (*ii*) that the FDA-timed responses to grant or deny the appeal could be oral (followed by written confirmation within 14 days) or written, and (*iii*) that the reasons for a denial must be provided. Many of these conditions conform to FDA guidance for formal dispute resolution.

Sponsors frequently consult review staff seeking comments on protocol design. The PDUFA II performance standards contain a 45-day time frame and procedural outline for this feedback process. Miscellaneous issues also include using user fee resources to update FDA's information management infrastructure to allow for paperless INDs and human drug applications, use of complete response letters in lieu of action letters, separate information request letters from each discipline reviewing an application, and a definition of terms used in this document.

SUMMARY OF PRESCRIPTION DRUG USER FEE AMENDMENTS OF 2002 (PDUFA III) (OCT. 1, 2002, TO—SEPT. 30, 2007)

Modifications of Prior Law

In 2002, the Prescription Drug User Fee Amendments of 2002 were included as Title 5 of the Public Health Security and Bioterrorism Preparedness and Response Act of 2002. Rx drug user fees were reauthorized for another 5 years until September 30, 2007. The level of fees increased to reflect a decline in the number of applications filed with the agency. In addition, a detailed letter dated June 4, 2002, was prepared for the regulated industry and the Congress under the signature of HHS Secretary Thompson (19). The letter transmitted detailed new performance goals and procedures prepared by the agency (20).

New Fee Amounts

1. *Application fees:* $533,400 (applications including data), $266,700 (applications without data and supplements with data)(FY 2000) (FY 2001) (FY 2003).
2. *Establishment fees:* $209,900 (FY 2003).
3. *Product fees:* $32,400 (FY 2003).

Performance Goals

Application review times maintained the final schedule proposed as part of PDUFA II: original standard applications and efficacy supplements with data—90% within 10 months; original priority applications and efficacy supplements with data—90% within 6 months; class 1 resubmissions—90% within 2 months; class 2 resubmissions—90% within 6 months; and resubmitted efficacy supplements (class 1) reduced from 6 to 2 months for review.

Meeting management goals were refined in the PDUFA III document. CDER and CBER committed to notifying parties requesting meetings, teleconferences, or videoconferences within 14 calendar days of receiving an industry request for a formal meeting with the date, time, place, and expected FDA attendees. Meetings continued to be classified as Type A, B, or C, and detailed procedures for requesting the meetings were provided.

Procedures similar to PDUFA II were provided for clinical hold responses, major dispute resolution, and protocol design review. FDA also agreed to conduct two pilot programs to evaluate the development of a continuous marketing application.

Impact of User Fees on Rx Drug Approvals

There is no question that the enactment and implementation of PDUFA led to the dramatic restructuring of the agency and its industry relationship. Reviewers and their superiors within the FDA product centers were accountable for the pace of their work for the first time. Review time decreased from a median time in excess of 2 years or more to within 1 year for standard applications and 6 months for priority applications. Hundreds of new employees were retained to review data and to interact with the regulatory officials of constituent product sponsors. FDA has consistently reported to the Congress in its annual Performance and Financial Reports that it met and exceeded all its performance goals under PDUFA I, II, and III (for drugs but not biologics). It has noted a trend, however, of fewer original applications and efficacy supplements that pay the largest component of application fees under the act. The number of original new product applications submitted and filed each year increased steadily in the early years, from 88 in FY 1993 to 133 in FY 1997. From FY 1997 to FY 2000, the growth reportedly leveled off, and in FYs 2001 and 2002 application submissions and filings dropped substantially (21). Twenty-five percent fewer applications were filed with FDA in 2001 than in 2000. The number of priority applications was down more than 60% in 2001 from the previous year and was less than half the level of any year since FY 1997 (22). Since priority applications often represent significant therapeutic gains, the Congress commissioned a report by the General Accounting Office (GAO) to evaluate the cause of this decline.

At the same time, FDA continued to report increased productivity. In congressional testimony, FDA Deputy Commissioner Lester Crawford reported approval of 66 new drugs in 2001, 24 of which were new molecular entities (23). Ten of the 66 new drugs (seven of the new molecular entities) received priority review and were reportedly reviewed and approved in the median time of 6 months. CBER reviewed a total of 16 complex BLAs in the median time of 13.8 months and approved them in the median time of 20.3 months. Two priority BLAs were reviewed in the median time of 11.5 months and approved in the median time of 13.2 months.

Finally, FDA reported that 50% of all new drugs worldwide were launched in the United States, and American patients have access to 78% of the world's new drugs within the first few years of their introduction (24). The agency advocated a need to use some PDUFA resources for rigorous safety monitoring of newly approved drugs in the first few years after a product is on the market to quickly detect unanticipated problems outside the application, and a definition of terms used in this document.

SUMMARY OF PRESCRIPTION DRUG USER FEE AMENDMENTS OF 2007 (PDUFA IV) (OCT. 1, 2007 TO –SEPT. 30, 2012)

Modifications of Prior Law

In 2007, the Prescription Drug User Fee Amendments of 2007 were included as Title 1 of the Food and Drug Administration Amendments Act of 2007. Rx drug user fees were reauthorized for another 5 years until September 30, 2012. The level of fees increased to reflect a decline in the number of applications filed with the agency. In addition, a detailed letter dated September 27, 2007, was prepared for the regulated industry and the Congress under the signature of HHS Secretary Leavitt (19). The letter transmitted detailed new performance goals and procedures prepared by the agency (20). Overall, FDA believes that this reauthorization of PDUFA "will provide significant benefits for those who develop medical products, and for those who use them."*

New Fee Amounts

1. *Application fees:* $1,178,000 (applications including data), $589,000 (applications without data and supplements with data)(FY 2008).
2. *Establishment fees:* $392,700 (FY 2008).
3. *Product fees:* $65,030 (FY 2008).

Performance Goals

Application review times maintained the final schedule proposed as part of PDUFA II and III: original standard applications and efficacy supplements with data—90% within 10 months of receipt; original priority applications and efficacy supplements with data—90% within 6 months; class 1 resubmissions (resubmitted after a complete response letter, not approvable or approvable letter that requests limited additional information such as labeling, safety updates, stability, assays, final release testing, etc.)—90% within 2 months; class 2 resubmissions (any other items including presentation to an advisory committee)—90% within 6 months; and resubmitted efficacy supplements (class 1)—90% within 2 months and class 2—90% within 6 months.

* http://www.fda.gov/oc/initiatives/advance/fdaaa.html, Sept. 27, 2007.

Meeting management goals were further refined in the PDUFA IV document. CDER and CBER committed to notifying parties requesting meetings, teleconferences, or videoconferences within 14 calendar days of receiving an industry request for a formal meeting with the date, time, place, and expected FDA attendees. Meetings continued to be classified as Type A, B, or C, and detailed procedures for requesting the meetings were provided.

Procedures similar to PDUFA III were provided for clinical hold responses, major dispute resolution, and special protocol design review. FDA also agreed to amend its regulations and procedures to provide for the issuance of either "approval" or "complete response" letters at the completion of a review cycle for a marketing application. It also agreed to submit deficiencies to a sponsor in the form of a "discipline review" letter on a rolling basis as submitted where comments on the separate parts of the application can be provided more quickly when each discipline finished its initial review of its section of the pending application. This is preferable to waiting longer for all division reviews to be consolidated before any feedback is provided to the applicant.

FDA Drug Safety Enhancement and Modernization

Twenty-five million dollars of total user fees revenue of $459,412,000 was authorized in FY 2008 to fund significant new drug safety initiatives at FDA, with that amount adjusted for inflation and changes in workload in subsequent years through 2012. FDA's written Performance Goals and Procedures details an elaborate program as summarized below.

Development of a 5-Year Plan

FDA will develop and periodically update a 5-year plan describing activities that will lead to enhancing and modernizing FDA's drug safety activities/system. The plan will (*i*) assess current and new methodologies for collecting adverse event information at various points during the product lifecycle; (*ii*) identify epidemiology best practices and develop guidance; (*iii*) expand CBER/CDRH database acquisition; (*iv*) develop and validate risk management and risk communication tools; (*v*) improve postmarket IT systems; and (*vi*) improve coordination among the centers' review offices and surveillance offices.

Review Proprietary Names to Reduce Medication Errors

User fee revenue will be used to create a more predictable system to review proprietary names proposed by sponsors, including reviewing 50% of proprietary name submissions during FY 2009

Within 180 days of receipt; 70% in FY 2010 and 90% in FYs 2011 and 2012; create a process and pilot program where a sponsor can request reconsideration of names found unacceptable by submitting a written rebuttal with supporting data or request a meeting within 60 days; publish a final guidance on the contents of a complete submission package for a proposed proprietary name by the end of FY 2008 and procedure for review in the Manual of Policies and Procedures; and draft guidance on best practices for naming, labeling, and packaging drugs to reduce medication errors.

Streamline First-Cycle Reviews

FDA has committed to communicating with drug sponsors much earlier concerning substantive review issues identified during the initial filing review within 14 calendar days after the 60-day filing date for 90% of applications. FDA will also inform the sponsor of the planned timeline for review of the application and provide greater transparency. Procedure will conform to FDA's Guidance for Review Staff and Industry: Good Review Management Principles and Practices for PDUFA Products.

Improve FDA Operating Efficiencies

FDA has committed to streamline and modernize its existing drug review processes including the issuance of new guidance related to some of its Critical Path priorities including clinical hepatotoxicity (FY 2008), noninferiority trials (FY 2008), adaptive trial designs (FY 2008), use of end of phase-2 meetings (FY 2008), multiple endpoints in clinical trials (FY 2009), imaging standards for use as an endpoint in clinical trials (FY 2011), and will schedule workshops to further science and develop guidance concerning predictive toxicology, biomarker qualification, and evaluation of applications with missing data.

Direct-to-Consumer Television Advertising

PDUFA IV included significant authority to use user fee revenue and assess sponsors additional fees to hire approximately 27 new FTEs, and to tighten regulation of direct-to-consumer broadcast advertising ($6.25 million in 2008 increasing annually). In exchange for significant fees from sponsors seeking preapproval of DTC TV ads, FDA committed to reviewing 75 original submissions within 45 days (50% of 150) in FY 2008, 37 resubmissions (50% of 75 resubmissions); review of 60% rising to 90% of submissions by 2012. The bulk of this program is sponsor funded. It is unclear if drug manufacturers will commit to the level of payment required to ensure continuation of this program (e.g., $41,667 in FY 2008 for each ad review if 150 submissions are "reserved"). Unless the program is sufficiently subscribed to raise a minimum amount of review fees and operating reserve (at least $11.25 million in FY 2008), the program will be discontinued.

Impact of User Fees on Rx Drug Approvals

There is no question that the enactment and implementation of PDUFA led to the dramatic restructuring of the agency and its industry relationship. Reviewers and their superiors within the FDA product centers were accountable for the pace of their work for the first time. Review time decreased from a median time in excess of 2 years or more to within 1 year for standard applications and 6 months for priority applications. Hundreds of new employees were retained to review data and to interact with the regulatory officials of constituent product sponsors. FDA has consistently reported to the Congress in its annual Performance and Financial Reports that it met and exceeded all its performance goals under PDUFA I, II, and III (for drugs but not biologics). It has noted a trend, however, of fewer original applications and efficacy supplements that pay the largest component of application fees under the act. The number of original new product applications submitted and filed each year increased steadily in the early years, from 88 in FY 1993 to 133 in FY 1997. From FY 1997 to FY 2000, the growth reportedly leveled off, and in FYs 2001 and 2002 application submissions and filings dropped substantially (21). Twenty-five percent fewer applications were filed with FDA in 2001 than in 2000. The number of priority applications was down by more than 60% in 2001 from the previous year and was less than half the level of any year since FY 1997 (22). They then began to increase for five consecutive years from FY 2000 to FY 2005 (23), while standard applications continued to decline and manufacturing supplements remained constant.

At the same time, FDA continued to report increased productivity. However, it noted that it has been unable to meet targets for meetings and special protocol assessments. Meeting requests reportedly increased by 46% from FY 2001 to FY 2005 (1662 to 2430) and special protocol requests increased by 200% from 125 to 392 during that same period.

FDA maintains a chart, summarizing the status of the numerous notice, guidance, and rules required to implement FDAAA. That information can be accessed at http://www.fda.gov/oc/initiatives/advance/fdaaa/implementation_chart.html.

EVALUATION OF THE PROGRAM BY THE GENERAL ACCOUNTING OFFICE

In September 2002, the GAO issued a report entitled "Effect of User Fees on Drug Approval Times, Withdrawals, and other Agency Activities" (25). The report concluded that PDUFA has been successful in providing FDA with the funding necessary to hire additional drug reviewers, thereby making new drugs available in the United States more quickly. But while the median approval time for NDAs for standard drugs dropped from 27 months to 14 months from 1993 to 2001, the new priority time for priority drugs remained stable at 6 months after 1997. The median approval times for standard new molecular entities (drugs containing active ingredients that have never been marketed in the United States in any form) increased from 1998 from about 13 months to 20 months. In contrast, median approval times for BLAs have fluctuated since 1993, ranging from a low of 12 months in 1997 to a high of about 32 months in 1995. In 2001 that time had slipped to about 22 months.

FDA reportedly had to increase the amount of its appropriated funds, outside of user fees, to drug and biologics reviews to compensate for the minimum allocation of funds required by PDUFA. FDA also reportedly used user fee proceeds to fund employee pay raises that were generally not covered by annual appropriations. PDUFA II increased reviewer workload by shortening review times and establishing new performance goals to reduce overall drug development times. This resulted in higher attrition rates for drug reviewers than comparable occupations in the federal workforce.

Finally, GAO reported that a higher percentage of drug applications had been withdrawn from the market for safety-related reasons during the most recent term of PDUFA (5.3% from 1997 to 2000) compared to 1.6% in the period immediately after PDUFA implementation (1993–1996). Using 8-year periods before and after enactment of PDUFA, the rate of postapproval drug withdrawals increased from 3.1% to 3.5%. Some drugs were withdrawn because doctors and patients did not use them according to approved labeling, while others were found to have rare side effects that were not detected in clinical trials. GAO recommended that FDA strengthen its postmarket surveillance activities. It plans to spend approximately $71 million in user fees over the next 5 years to better monitor safety and track adverse events. Under PDUFA III, FDA was given the authority for the first time to utilize user fees for these postmarket surveillance and compliance activities. The industry had aggressively resisted the use of its own proceeds to pay for agency compliance activities.

STRATEGIES TO USE PDUFA TO EXPEDITE REVIEW AND APPROVAL

Evaluate Whether the Application will be Subjected to Rx Drug User Fees

These fees, and the performance standards associated with them, generally apply only to original NDAs and BLAs and supplements to those filings. Remember, these are user fees and not taxes for government services. Therefore, FDA has to justify its imposition by utilizing the services of data reviewers hired with the fee proceeds.

Attempt to Negotiate the Lowest Possible Fee

User fees today are substantial; now almost 10 times the rate when the program was adopted originally in 1993. They include a $1,178,000 application fee in FY 2008, a $392,700 fee per manufacturing establishment, and a $65,030 fee per listed product. One half of the application fee is due on submission of the application, and one half is due within 30 days of the date of the action letter (which has become a complete response letter). If the applicant is a small business (fewer than 500 employees with no Rx or biologic product on the market), only half of the fee is owed, and not until 1 year following the date of submission (and only if the application is accepted for filing). A major manufacturer should consider allowing a smaller entity from which it is licensing the product to become the sponsor of the application. Corporate structuring might be possible to save a significant portion of this fee.

An application for fee waiver or reduction might be available under the criteria included in Section 1.5. Specifically, if the fee precludes the application because of an orphan or small market or fewer agency resources are required for a narrow review, the fee might be reduced. In the current budget climate, and with fewer applications, FDA may not give in easily in this regard, but the law might be on your side. Also remember that once a drug has generic competition, or even if a paper NDA is on the horizon, the fee might not be due.

Likewise, the definition of an establishment might be reduced for purposes of the fee. Buildings making multiple drugs might count as a single establishment if they are located within a 5-mile radius. The plant must make finished dosage forms to count. Contract manufacturers or makers of ingredients do not count. Foreign plants only count if their product is imported into the United States.

Finally, product fees can be reduced if a manufacturer limited or aggregated the product listing of multiple dosages or dosage forms of its products. These might be included in one product listing. Antibiotics do not count if they were not approved by NDAs. Once a generic competitor is approved, the innovator product no longer has the fee assessed. Finally, since a drug maker must use the product review services of the agency to owe a fee (remember the law created a user fee and not a product tax), no fee is owed unless the company has at least one application or supplement pending for agency review in the year of the fee assessment.

Create a Priority Application

Performance goals are not legally binding on FDA, but the agency is under great pressure from industry and the Congress to review most priority applications within 6 months of filing. The review divisions have discretion about how they classify new applications. Seek priority designation wherever possible (separate and apart from fast-track review for drugs treating serious or life-threatening illness). This discussion should occur in pre-NDA/BLA meetings with the review staff. If the drug is a new chemical compound, meets an unmet medical need, or treats a debilitating disease, the sponsor should create an organized presentation to the agency to request this designation.

Refer to Agency Performance Goals During the Product Review

The sponsor must create a complete application as quickly in the process as possible, so it is accepted for filing and the FDA clock begins to run. Experienced regulatory lawyers or professionals maintain constant contact and interaction with product reviewers so that reviews progress efficiently. FDA has preserved considerable flexibility to meet its statistical user fee goals while stopping its review clock with informational requests to the sponsor. In order to obtain an approvable letter and avoid a delaying complete response letter that requests additional information, this interaction must be maintained. The company must be responsive and anticipate the need for additional data, analyses, or clarification. The quicker and more lucidly this information is provided, the better the chance of making it under the review goal. FDA must account for meeting its PDUFA goals in annual performance reports to the Congress. Once the FDA clock has shifted back to the sponsor and the performance goal has been met in the first-review cycle, many of the benefits of PDUFA have been lost to the product sponsor. Multiple review cycles delay product approval significantly. Prepare quality applications, anticipate questions or information requests, and do not file the application until "all your ducks are in a row."

Employ Formal Dispute Resolution or Congressional Oversight in Appropriate Circumstances

PDUFA is the product of a delicate compromise between the Congress on behalf of industry and the agency. FDA has become much more interactive in order to relieve last-minute pressures to meet tighter PDUFA performance goals. If scientific differences arise, use the formal dispute resolution guidance that FDA has provided. If policy differences arise, seek congressional oversight and support as appropriate.

REFERENCES

1. If an Rx drug, as defined in PDUFA, was made in a foreign plant for foreign marketing under an approved NDA, the foreign establishment was subjected to establishment fees if it was owned by an NDA/BLA holder that had a pending NDA/BLA or supplement after September. 1, 1992.
2. Thus, for example, if a product is sterilized by filtration and placed into vials by a "contract manufacturer" that has no pending NDAs, BLAs, or supplements after September 1, 1992, then no establishment fee was due for either the contract manufacturer or the facility that performed the rest of the manufacturing steps. Attachment D, "Application,

Product, and Establishment Fees, Common Issues, and their Resolution," revised as of December. 16, 1994.

3. FDA has interpreted the generic exemption narrowly. Therefore, me-too products that are the same as a listed Rx product but were approved under the NDA provision of §505(b)(1) do not qualify for the exclusion. If a listed product has a competitor approved under §505(b)(2)(paper NDA) or (j)(ANDA), that drug is exempt. If the §505(b)(2) or (j) applications have been approved and not withdrawn, the first approved product is excluded from fees even if the generic product is not presently marketed. Tentative approvals of a 505(j) application are not considered approvals. Finally, according to FDA, products listed that were approved by a paper NDA before 1984 when §505(b)(2) was added to the FDCA are not eligible for exclusion from product fees.
4. FDA's interpretation of PDUFA did not allow innovator *anti*biotic drug products to become exempt from the product fee even after subsequent generic antibiotic drug products were approved, when they were approved under §507. However, since 1997 generic antibiotics have been approved under §505(j), and should therefore trigger the exemption of the innovator product. Likewise, bulk antibiotic drugs should not be subjected to product fees because they are not products in finished dosage form.
5. *Id.*
6. The date of submission, according to FDA, is the date the application is received by FDA and stamped as received in the CDER or CBER central document control center. Attachment G, "Draft Interim Guidance Document for Waivers of and Reductions in User Fees," July 16, 1993, 11. This is distinguished from "filing," which occurs after FDA determines that the application is sufficiently complete to permit a substantive review. See 21 CFR §314.101.
7. 21 USC §379h(b)(2). The act did not provide a small business exception for supplement applications.
8. *Id.*
9. *Id.* at 24–32. *This draft guidance document is available* at www.fda.gov/cder/pudfaimainpduf.htm.
10. *Id. at 28*
11. §379h(d).
12. See 5 USC §552, and FDA implementing regulations at 21 CFR Part 20. Supra note 6 at 15.
13. §379(h)(d).
14. Supra note 6 at 18–19.
15. *Id.*
16. Under §379h(a)(1)(D), FDA refunds 50% of the application fee *paid for any application and supplement refused for filing.* That amount actually represents only 25% of the total application fee since only 50% of the total fee is due upon submission. *Id.* at 19.
17. §379 h(d)(4).
18. PDUFA Reauthorization Performance Goals and Procedures; III.C., www.fda.gov/cder/news/pdufagoals.htm.
19. See www.fda.gov/oc/pdufa4/pdufa4goals.html., *September. 27, 2007.*
20. See www.fda.gov/oc/pdufaipdufaHIgoals.html., April 7, 2008.
21. FY 2001 and FY 2002 Performance Reports to Congress, p. 4.
22. *Id.*
23. See www.fda.gov/ope/pdufa/report2005.html
24. Statement of FDA Deputy Commissioner before the House Appropriations Subcommittee on Agriculture Rural Development, FDA and Related Agencies, March 21, 2002, 10, www.fda.gov/o1a/2002/fy2003.html.
25. *Id.* at 20. GAO Report No. 02–958, Report to the Chairman of the Senate Committee on Health, Education, Labor, and Pensions, FDA -Effect of User Fees on Drug Approval Times, Withdrawals, and Other Agency Activities. September 2002.

9 Clinical Research Requirements for New Drug Applications

Gary L. Yingling, Esq. and Ann M. Begley, Esq.
K. & L. Gates, LLP, Washington, D.C., U.S.A.

INTRODUCTION

As the industry is more and more successful in delivering new drugs for a wider array of medical conditions, the need to develop more drugs increases. While the public wants more drugs to cure every illness, it is not really prepared to recognize the risk factors and how difficult it is to evaluate risk, especially at the research stage. The fallout has been more drugs withdrawn from the market with greater fanfare and a Congress that is demanding with one proposed piece of legislation after another to "fix" that which is broken. In the middle of this approval process is the U.S. Food and Drug Administration (FDA) with its current legislative mandate to regulate all drugs manufactured or marketed in the United States. When the agency uses the term "drug," it includes within that definition biologics. The regulation of drugs is basically separated into two categories: those for which preapproval is not required, which includes those that are considered generally recognized as safe and effective, and those that require preapproval in the form of the submission of a new drug application (NDA) or an abbreviated new drug application (ANDA) (1). For those that fall in the category of being under review or generally recognized as safe and effective, which are those subject to the over-the-counter Monograph system, there is no preapproval requirement and, therefore, no submission of information required for the product to enter the marketplace (2). For those drugs that require the submission of a drug application, it is highly likely that the application will be dependent on the submission of clinical data or bioequivalence studies to demonstrate that the product is safe and effective. Just as the submission of the drug application is subject to various statutory, regulatory, and guideline requirements, the clinical or bioequivalence testing necessary for obtaining approval of an NDA or ANDA is covered by a number of statutory, regulatory, and guideline provisions. To fully appreciate the clinical requirements, one needs to recognize that in most cases, for a drug-seeking preapproval, it is a violation of the Federal Food, Drug, and Cosmetic Act (FFDCA) to ship an unapproved new drug in interstate commerce for the purpose of clinical research unless it is the subject of an investigational new drug (IND) application (3). The statute states that, in order to obtain approval, the sponsor or the applicant must submit a drug application under §§505(b)(1), 505(b)(2), or 505(j) of the FFDCA.

When one considers the filing of a §505(b)(1) application, one is looking at submitting an application for a new chemical entity, a novel dosage form, or a very significant labeling change that will require preclinical animal data and clinical studies. The clinical studies will probably be organized into three phases: phase one being basic toxicology studies, phase two being dose range studies, and phase three being the pivotal clinical study or studies that allows that agency to approve the application.

A 505(b)(2) application will, in all likelihood, require less clinical data and could be approved based on a single phase three study or even a bioequivalence study. This is because the 505(b)(2) application relies on the fact that the active pharmaceutical ingredient which is the subject of an approved drug application is well known to the agency so that it is not necessary to obtain the detailed data (e.g., animal studies, phase one and phase two studies) that would be required for a 505(b)(1) application.

If the application is a 505(j), or ANDA, the required data will be a bioequivalence study to demonstrate that the applicant's drug is equivalent to the product already marketed. Under the ANDA regulations, it is possible for the bioequivalence study to be a single dose, crossover, limited patient study looking at blood levels or a 500 or 600 patient clinical study comparing the referenced listed NDA to the proposed abbreviated application. Whatever the form of the application, in all likelihood there will be the necessity to do clinical research and FDA has set forth detailed regulations and guidances controlling clinical and bioequivalence studies that support new drug applications.

SPONSORS

The firm or organization that bears the responsibility for the clinical study is called the sponsor. The sponsor is the organization that will file the drug application, whether it is a complete 505(b)(1), a 505(b)(2), or an abbreviated application. As the sponsor, the organization will be charged with obtaining the data to submit in the NDA or ANDA for the purpose of gaining FDA approval. This undertaking becomes a multistep process, from deciding what drug the firm will file an application on to gathering the supporting scientific data to submit to the agency for the purpose of obtaining approval. For a firm filing a 505(b)(1) application, usually for a new chemical entity, the initial question is what amount of basic research needs to be done before tests can be conducted in humans. This preclinical data stage involves in vitro and animal testing and is normally characterized as the pre-IND stage. The sponsor does not need to notify FDA of its interest in working on the chemical entity, and is under no obligation to update the agency on its development plan at the pre-IND stage. However, once a sponsor decides that it has obtained enough in vitro and animal data to believe there is benefit in conducting human testing, it becomes necessary for a firm to submit an IND application. The IND application is the submission that allows a firm to ship an IND drug for the purpose of conducting clinical research. As noted earlier, it is prohibited to ship a drug that has not been approved unless it is the subject of an IND application (4). The statute specifically provides that the Secretary will promulgate regulations to allow sponsors to conduct studies for the purpose of gathering data so that applications can be submitted for approval.

While the FDA's Code of Federal Regulations (CFR) sets forth the basic requirements for the submission of an IND application and the various requirements that arise from that submission, they are dated and really only provide an overview of the agency's expectations (5). In accordance with the regulations, the sponsor will need to prepare an actual IND application, which will include the animal studies that have been conducted, any data of which the sponsor may be aware concerning studies outside the United States, and the protocol (study plan) for the first studies which the sponsor intends to conduct.

Under the current user fee program, which is designed to create a cooperative working relationship between the agency and the sponsor, the sponsor will normally request a pre-IND meeting to discuss the nonclinical data that has been collected to date, the ingredients being used in the proposed product, and the clinical testing, particularly the studies involved in phase one and early phase two development. The sponsor, in preparing for the pre-IND meeting, will need to prepare a summary of the information that it intends to submit in the IND application. It is to the sponsor's great advantage to provide FDA with a very detailed summary because the first meeting really sets the stage for the drug development program and time spent at this stage can be very beneficial from every perspective, so that the agency does not require testing that may be unnecessary or fail to appreciate if there are data that will suggest an issue. If a pre-IND meeting is held, there is usually a fairly substantial level of agreement between the agency and the sponsor before the actual IND application is submitted. While it is not necessary to request a pre-IND meeting, it has become unusual for firms, particularly if they are seeking 505(b)(2) applications, not to request a pre-IND meeting. The pre-IND meeting allows a firm to obtain a better understanding of what data and information will be necessary to obtain approval.

After receiving an IND application, the agency then has 30 days to review the IND application to determine whether there is enough preclinical data to assure that the product is safe enough to allow the conduct of human clinical studies. There is also a careful review of the clinical study protocols, whether it be one or more protocols, to determine if the study design will result in data that will allow the drug development to move forward. If the proposed phase one study protocol fails to provide enough data and information in its design to move to phase two studies, there is no benefit to subjecting human patients to the drug. Therefore, the agency will carefully look at the proposed protocol. If it is not satisfied with the study design, FDA may notify the sponsor of a clinical hold. A clinical hold means that the sponsor cannot go forward with the study or studies. Clinical holds seldom occur when there have been pre-IND meetings where the agency and sponsor have discussed the study design. Again, it behooves the sponsor to be as detailed as possible regarding the first studies protocols so that the agency has a complete understanding of the preclinical data and proposed design of the studies.

For those sponsors that find themselves in a clinical hold, the agency has created a fairly elaborate review process to assure that the agency's clinical hold decision can be reviewed and that the sponsor will have an adequate opportunity to explain why the proposed protocol is adequate. However, one needs to recognize that FDA's review process is inherently slow and that every effort should be made to avoid this detour by assuring that the protocol design is one that the agency will accept.

After submitting the IND application, a sponsor must comply with a 30-day waiting period before it can initiate the study. If, at the end of the 30 days, the sponsor has not heard from the agency, in theory the sponsor may go forward with the clinical study. However, the sponsor should be very reluctant to go forward with a clinical study at the end of the 30 days if it has not heard from the agency. Under these circumstances, there is a possibility that the agency has some concern that it has not been able to articulate within the 30-day period, and that shortly after the 30-day period expires the agency will notify the sponsor that the study is on clinical hold. If the sponsor has already started the study, both the sponsor and the agency face major problems in that the agency is unhappy with the study design and the sponsor has already enrolled patients. This can be avoided by making contact with the agency shortly after the IND application is submitted to be absolutely sure the agency has received the IND application and that it is being reviewed. Then the sponsor should make contact again, as the 30-day period is winding down, to confirm that the agency will not have problems such that will lead it to consider placing the study on a clinical hold.

While sponsors often identify the clinical investigators at the time they are preparing the study protocols, and will often have the major clinical investigator accompany them to the pre-IND meeting with the agency, it is not necessary to identify up front any or all of the clinical investigators who will participate in the clinical studies. The sponsor does bear the responsibility for the eventual selection of the clinical investigators who will actually do the studies. It is unusual in today's marketplace for a sponsor to have a medical staff capable of doing the studies, or that will even play a major role in overseeing the actual conduct of the study. What is normal for a sponsor is to have numerous contacts in the clinical community and to have identified any number of individuals that they believe are appropriate for the purpose of being clinical investigators in the study.

In today's clinical research environment, sponsors typically have a small, specialized medical staff for the purpose of assisting in study design, reviewing study results, and playing an active role in planning. The actual protocol for the study will probably be prepared by a contract research organization (CRO) or a clinical investigator working with a CRO. There are a number of very large CROs as well as a number of mid-sized and small CRO firms that specialize in clinical studies, and some highly specialized firms that conduct studies on particular organs or disease conditions or patient populations. Therefore, the sponsor often has many options from selecting either a single large CRO, which may have multiple sites at which a study can be done and can therefore increase potential enrollment, to selecting a small CRO for the purpose of going to particular parts of the country or identifying specialized practices.

The sponsor can transfer its study obligations over to a CRO. The FDA's regulations (6) specifically provide for the authority of the sponsor to transfer responsibility for any and all obligations. The transfer, however, must be in writing and as such, it is to the sponsor's advantage to delineate exactly what obligations have been transferred. While the sponsor can transfer its obligations, it is still ultimately responsible for the clinical trial. Therefore, it needs to assure itself that the selected CRO understands the importance of having good investigators, of following the protocol, and of conducting the study in a manner that FDA will find satisfactory. More than one sponsor has entered into a study and become enmeshed in FDA or Congressional oversight for failure to assure that the study is properly conducted (7).

The agency requires that the sponsor monitor the investigators to be sure that the investigators and their staff are conducting the study in accordance with the protocol and with the sponsor's and the agency's expectations. Again, the sponsor can contract with a CRO or a third party for the purpose of monitoring, or it may have monitors of its own. The monitor's role is very important in a clinical study because it is the monitor who visits the study site to determine whether or not the clinical investigator fully understands the protocol and whether the investigator and the investigator's staff are conducting the study in accordance with the sponsor's and the agency's expectations.

In the past, it was not uncommon for the monitor to function mostly as a study promoter, making sure the investigator was actively involved in enrolling patients and in correcting record-keeping errors and oversights of the staff. While monitors today may fulfill some of those roles, FDA's heightened expectations for monitoring to assure quality of data have resulted in monitoring being much more than an important promotion activity. The monitor is the person who is able to identify investigator sites where patients are being entered who fail to meet the study criteria, to identify staff errors and/or malfeasance, and to correct staff and investigator misunderstandings with regard to the protocol and the way the study is being conducted. More and more, when the agency finds problems at a study site, it asks why monitoring did not identify and correct the problem or discontinue the investigation. As the agency becomes more resource conscious, it will turn increasingly to using its enforcement tools to ensure the sponsor compliance with all of the requirements within the IND regulations.

In addition to the monitoring activity required of the sponsor or CRO, there is an expectation that all of the information required to be reported in the case report forms (CRF) or patient medical records (source documents) will be properly recorded (i.e., written down or entered in the computer system). Only information that is actually reported can be used by FDA in its evaluation of the clinical data. The popular phrase is, "If it isn't written down, it didn't happen." The agency is extremely strict with reporting requirements. Efforts by investigators to explain a particular set of events or activities at a later date will be dismissed because there was a failure to record the information properly at the time it should have been recorded. As with all statements that appear to be absolutes, there is a certain level of flexibility in relationship to written records, as long as the reporting is done in the manner required and is corrected in a manner that is appropriate. For instance, a study nurse records the patient's blood pressure as 120/80 in the patient's chart and as 80/140 in the CRF records. Some days later, the study coordinator notes the error and corrects it by drawing a line through it. The correction is recorded, initialed and dated and explained either on the CRF or on a separate memorandum that explains what occurred and why the correction was made. While the agency will accept such corrections, there is an expectation that they will be minimal, and that they will properly be recorded, dated, and signed.

It is understood that neither the sponsor nor the CRO will be doing the actual writing in the patient records or CRF and that, in fact, most of the time the clinical investigator will not be making those recordings either. This task is normally done by study staff. Therefore, monitoring mandates a review of the site's compliance with record-keeping and record-retention requirements. Review of the record is for the purpose of catching the type of error described earlier, or to look for patterns or problems in a clinical study. The record review may be done by the clinical investigator or staff, the CRO, or, in fact, by the sponsor. Today, with many records created and transferred electronically, it is possible for the sponsor or CRO staff to do an almost instantaneous review of records for completeness and to ensure there are no apparent discrepancies. It is the agency's expectation that the records have been reviewed and monitored to assure that the required information is recorded. There is also a record-keeping requirement that the retainer of the records, whether it be the clinical investigator, the CRO, or perhaps even the sponsor, will retain the records for a period of 2 years after the drug is approved or 2 years after the study is completed if there has been a decision that the drug will not be the subject of an application, and FDA has been notified. FDA regulations outline record-retention time frames (8). The sponsor or CRO must be extremely vigilant in relationship to the record-keeping and record-retention requirements.

In addition to the monitoring, reporting requirements, and record review, there is the need to keep track of the actual study drug. The sponsor provides the study drug for the study. Many times in addition to the drug itself, it will be necessary to provide a placebo that is indistinguishable from the drug so that the study can be blinded. To ensure that the study is properly blinded it must be coded. Coding may be the sponsor's responsibility or the CRO's. Once the drug is sent to the clinical investigator, the responsibility for keeping track of the drug falls to the investigator. That which is not dispensed at the end of the study should be sent back to the sponsor so that it can make records of the drug that was manufactured, dispensed, used, and returned. There is one quirk in the process for those manufacturers involved in ANDA Applications: even if they are biostudies that are basically clinical studies in design and length, the retention samples cannot be sent back to the sponsor but must be retained by the clinical investigator, the CRO, or independent third party (9). The failure of the retention samples for an ANDA application to be in the possession of an independent third party can and has resulted in clinical studies being called into question by the agency.

CLINICAL INVESTIGATORS

While sponsors are responsible for the development, monitoring, and submission of clinical studies in an NDA or ANDA, the clinical investigators are responsible for the actual conduct of the study. Prior to allowing the clinical investigator to participate in the clinical study, the sponsor or CRO must obtain a signed form FDA 1572, in which the clinical investigator commits to performance of a number of study-related responsibilities. The clinical investigator is responsible for understanding and complying with the investigational plan, obtaining Institutional Review Board (IRB) approval before beginning the study, protecting the rights and welfare of the participating research subjects, and assuring that legally effective informed consent is obtained from each subject. In addition, prior to commencing the study, the clinical investigator must provide the sponsor with sufficient financial information to allow the sponsor to make complete and accurate certification or disclosure statements under 21 CFR part 54 concerning potential financial conflicts of interest. The clinical investigator must also commit to update this financial information if relevant changes occur during the course of the study and 1 year following the completion of the study.

The lead clinical investigator is usually referred to as the principle investigator (PI), and those clinical investigators who work under the PI's supervision, if any, are referred to as subinvestigators. PIs with significant research practices will likely have a clinical research team composed of a clinical research coordinator, who is generally responsible for managing the research team, one or more subinvestigators, and one or more study nurses to assist in the conduct of the research. While the PI can delegate appropriate research responsibilities to his team members, ultimately, the PI is responsible for supervising all members of the research team, and for assuring that they understand their obligations in conducting the research.

FDA has historically used the inspectional process in part as an educational tool for educating PIs as to their obligations and responsibilities. The agency has also relied on the sponsor or CRO to undertake the educational responsibility. Finally, FDA has on a number of occasions brought criminal charges or sent a warning letter to a PI for engaging in what the agency saw as fraud. Clearly, as to pharmaceutical and device firms, the prosecution of one sends a message to the others that a particular activity is not going to be allowed.

However, with PIs, the reliance on sponsor/CRO educational programs, inspectional 483 observations, and criminal prosecution/warning letters was not working, so FDA turned to what it has done historically and issued a draft guidance in May 2007 titled "Guidance for Industry, Protecting the Rights, Safety, and Welfare of Study Subjects—Supervisory Responsibilities of Investigators" (Guidance) (10). The Guidance is only a draft, and in all likelihood it will never be finalized, but it is instructive. It is the joint effort of Center for Biologics Evaluation and Research (CBER), Center for Drug Evaluation and Research (CDER), and Center for Devices and Radiological Health (CDRH). It starts with an introduction explaining the investigator's obligations. Section II is an overview which contains a Part A for drugs and biologics and a Part B for device clinical trials. The major focus of the Guidance is Part III, which addresses first the issue of supervision of the conduct of the study. The supervision section recognizes that the PI will be delegating tasks, but that the PI remains accountable. The FDA focuses on four major issues regarding the PI delegation of tasks:

1. Individual qualifications of delegate,
2. Adequate training,
3. Adequate supervision, and
4. Oversight of third parties (labs, etc.).

With regards to qualifications, the question is education, training, or experience. The FDA poses the following questions: (*i*) Does the person have the license or certification necessary to perform the task assigned? and (*ii*) Has the PI followed the protocol if the person assigned to a task was not qualified? FDA believes that the PI should maintain a list of appropriately qualified persons to whom tasks are delegated (11).

A second concern is training. Does the PI really know the level of training that the staff has, or is the PI assuming training and experience that may not exist? Clearly, FDA is concerned when the sponsor provides training materials and the PI never assures that the staff is trained.

Of greatest importance is supervision. Many PIs, especially ones who have never done a study before, assume that clinical practice and research are one and the same, but they are not. Research requires meticulous record keeping, and a staff will only understand that if properly supervised. The Guidance recommends several things including routine meetings with staff and procedures for documenting performance. From FDA's perspective, unless a PI is personally engaged in fraud, the major problem for almost every PI who has problems with FDA (lengthy 483 or warning letter) is the actions of the staff because of lack of supervision. The staff either does not know what is expected of them or there may be a lack of motivation to perform the many tasks. The Guidance lists eight items that may adversely impact the ability of a PI to supervise a clinical trial, including inexperienced or overburdened staff, complex clinical trial, and large patient population. The Guidance stresses the need for the PI to create a detailed plan to address these potential issues.

Another significant issue for the PI are any third parties involved in the study who are not employed by the PI. FDA has placed the total burden on the PI not only for their own staff but also for all the data and information coming from a third party. FDA recommends that the PI assure that staff not under the PI's direct employ has adequate training. The agency notes that clinical chemistry testing, radiologic assessments, and electrocardiograms all fall within the area of concern since the work is done by a central independent laboratory that has been retained. The Guidance recommends procedures to assure integrity but does not suggest how that is to be accomplished. At a minimum, the PI should give some consideration to providing test samples or double-checking results with a second laboratory. Of greatest concern is that the PI does not ignore what on first impression appear to be sloppy results.

This section of the Guidance has a second part addressing protections and rights of patients (12). However, the section only addresses the need for the PI to practice good medical care and has little to do with the role of the PI in conducting the study.

Another area that has been of major importance to FDA is that the subject be properly informed of the risk of the research. To accomplish this, one traditionally thinks of informed consent in terms of a document, signed and dated by the participant, setting forth the purpose, benefits, risks, and other study information necessary to allow the participant to make an informed and voluntary decision to participate in the clinical study. In reality, informed consent is a process that applies to each communication with the participant, commencing with the subject recruitment material and the initial telephone screening of potential subjects, through the conclusion of the study. If new information that may affect a participant's willingness to continue in the study arises during the conduct of the study, clinical investigators have a responsibility to inform the participant of the new information. As to the informed consent document itself, clinical investigators must assure that it not only complies with the content requirements set forth in 21 CFR part 50, but also that it complies with applicable state law requirements. For example, California requires, in addition to the informed consent document, that clinical investigators must provide all research participants with an Experimental Subject's Bill of Rights for signature.

The clinical investigator also has significant record-keeping and -reporting responsibilities. As discussed earlier, clinical investigators are responsible for controlling distribution of the study drug through the maintenance of adequate records identifying dates, quantity, and use by the research subjects. The PI and staff must create and maintain records to document receipt of the drug and will need to have appropriate storage facilities so the drug can be secured and not accidentally dispensed to a patient outside the study. During the study, the drug must be tracked so that records will accurately reflect how much of the drug was taken by the patient. Part of the study protocol may require questioning the subject about taking the drug. Any drug not taken by the patient should be returned to the PI. At the conclusion of the investigator's participation, unused study drug must be returned to the sponsor or disposed as directed by the sponsor.

In addition to study drug accountability records, the clinical investigator and staff must prepare and maintain adequate and accurate documentation reporting all observations and other data of significance for each research participant in the clinical study. Such documentation includes, but is not limited to, informed consent, CRFs, medical records, and laboratory results. The sponsor must collect CRFs at the conclusion of the study. However, the investigator must maintain other documentation for 2 years following the date of the application's approval, or if the application was not filed or there was no such approval, 2 years after the conclusion of the study and after FDA has been notified.

The clinical investigator should submit progress reports to the sponsor as specified in the investigational plan. In addition, the clinical investigator must report such adverse experiences to the sponsor that may reasonably be regarded as caused by, or probably caused by, the study drug. At the conclusion of the study, the investigator must issue a report to the sponsor discussing the investigator's participation in the study.

Finally, the clinical investigator has reporting responsibilities in relationship to the IRB or Board. The investigator must promptly report all changes in the research activity and all unanticipated problems involving risk to human subjects or others. Thus, the clinical investigator must provide the IRB with serious unexpected adverse experience information that occurs at the clinical investigator's site. The clinical investigator would also generally be expected to report to the IRB any adverse experience information the PI learns of that occurs at other sites in a multisite study. Changes in the study such as a change in protocol must be reported to, and approved by, the IRB before making the change unless the change is necessary to eliminate apparent immediate hazards to human subjects (13). The clinical investigator must also comply with other IRB-specific reporting requirements. These may include intermittent progress reports, continuing review reports, and study closeout reports. Failure to comply with IRB reporting requirements can and should result in termination or suspension of the IRB approval.

INSTITUTIONAL REVIEW BOARD

In the process of setting up the clinical study and arranging for manufacture of the drug, creation of the protocol, identification of the PI, and creation of the informed consent, it will be necessary for the sponsor, CRO, or PI to seek the services and oversight of an IRB. Under 21 CFR Part 56 of the agency's regulations, five subparts set out the requirements for IRBs. In 21 CFR §56.102 of the definitions section, the agency discusses what a clinical investigation is and defines an IRB. It notes that the primary purpose of such a review by a Board is to ensure the ethical quality of the research and the protection of the rights and welfare of the human subjects. The agency specifies the composition of the IRB membership under 21 CFR §56.107, and states that each IRB shall have at least five members with various backgrounds to evaluate different aspects of the proposed study. The Board reviews the protocol for the clinical study and the informed consent to determine whether the protocol is appropriate as to gathering clinical data and whether subjects are properly informed of the risks they are being asked to undertake as part of the clinical investigation.

In theory, the IRB has a direct working relationship with the PI, and in practice that is largely true. An often-overlooked fact is that the protocol and informed consent have been created by the sponsor or CRO who has been in contact with the

IRB and therefore the relationship between the PI and the IRB occurs because of the work of the sponsor/CRO. While the agency recognizes the relationship between the IRB and the PI, it often ignores the IRB's relationship with the CRO/sponsor. Usually, a good working relationship between all of the parties needs to exist to ensure that any information the IRB needs to review will be received. In addition to approving the study initially and looking at the informed consent, all of the serious, unexpected adverse events that the clinical site identifies are supposed to be immediately reported to the IRB.

Because the IRB has as its primary mandate the protection of the human subjects, it is necessary for the IRB to recognize when assumptions made in relationship to the safety of the study turn out not to be accurate and the risk–benefit ratio changes such that the informed consent is no longer valid. A case in point would be a clinical study that envisioned the likelihood of a serious adverse event as extremely rare but when the study is performed, the study has two patient adverse events, both of them life-threatening. Suddenly the informed consent appears to be no longer accurate and all of the study sites involved in the study need to be informed of the fact that the study needs to be immediately stopped until new information can be reviewed and evaluated to determine whether the clinical study can go forward. Clearly, the PI would be reporting the information to the IRB as required by the agency's regulation and the investigator's agreement with the IRB, but also to the sponsor, because the sponsor or CRO is equally concerned about the patients involved in the clinical study.

Like the clinical site, the IRB has a record-keeping and record-reporting requirement. First of all, it must document that it has reviewed the protocol and informed consent. In the minutes of the IRB meeting, to the extent there are issues discussed, the minutes should reflect that discussion. The IRB is also required to review, at least yearly, any studies that are continuing to be sure that nothing has changed in the specified period of time that would impact continued approval. The frequency of this continuing review is based on the study risks. To make sure the IRB fully understands the status of the study, it needs a report from the clinical site. To the extent the clinical site does not provide that report, the IRB may be forced to withdraw its approval. If it withdraws its approval from the site, it must notify FDA so that the agency is aware of the fact that the IRB of record no longer approves the clinical site.

To be sure that the IRB has proper procedures in place, FDA regulations require it to develop standard operating procedures. These standard operating procedures will outline the IRB meeting procedures; preparation of the minutes; how the minutes will be developed, reviewed, and stored; the procedure for notifying sites if the IRB has questions; methods for reviewing adverse events; methods of seeking continuing review and research change information from the clinical investigational sites; procedures for doing the continuing reviews; and procedures for withdrawing approval of the IRB in relationship to a clinical investigational site (14).

Because the FDA has recognized the need for the IRB in its regulations, and to the extent that it has created the entity within the context of the regulations, it will inspect the IRB to look at its method of reviewing clinical studies to determine whether or not the Board is meeting the agency's expectations. Failure to allow the FDA to inspect or to follow FDA's regulations could result in an FDA refusal to accept the studies approved by that IRB in support of an application. As with a clinical site, this will be, for the most part, a record review looking at the IRB's meeting minutes, correspondence with clinical sites, and whether the IRB has taken appropriate action in response to problems or issues that have arisen.

FDA OVERSIGHT/MONITORING

The FFDCA and its implementing regulations provide FDA with the authority to inspect sponsors, CRO, clinical investigators, and IRBs (15). Where FDA identifies violations of clinical research regulations, it has a number of statutory and regulatory remedies at its disposal, from letters requiring corrective action to criminal proceedings resulting in jail time and significant fines.

FDA inspections in the clinical research area are coordinated under the bioresearch monitoring program (BIMO), which is an agency-wide program coordinated by both the FDA Commissioner's Good Clinical Practice Program and the Office of Regulatory Affairs. Under BIMO, inspectional guidances are available to assist the FDA field investigators in their inspection of sponsors, monitors, CROs, investigators, and IRBs (16). In addition, each FDA center has its own bioresearch monitoring branch, which, in cooperation with BIMO, evaluates the results of inspectional investigations of sponsors, CROs, investigators, and IRBs, and reviews data submitted in support of an application. For drug studies, CDER bioresearch division, the Division of Scientific Investigation (DSI), is responsible for directing inspection requests to the field, conducting inspections with investigators from the appropriate field office, reviewing the inspection reports, assigning classifications to the inspection reports, and initiating appropriate regulatory action, as necessary.

Following the conclusion of an inspection, a field inspector may issue the site a form FDA-483, which lists inspectional observations that the field inspector believes rise to the level of a violation of clinical research requirements. In addition, the field inspector writes a much lengthier establishment inspection report and submits this to DSI for review. DSI then assigns a final classification to the report, which is used to determine whether regulatory action must be taken against the site. There are three possible classifications:

1. No Action Indicated (NAI) means that no objectionable conditions were found during the inspection. While NAI classifications may result in an FDA letter to the site noting the objectionable conditions, it will not rise to the level of a warning letter and no response is required from the site.
2. Voluntary Action Indicated (VAI) means that the inspection disclosed objectionable conditions that departed from the regulations. A VAI classification is more likely to result in an untitled FDA letter. Unless the written response to the FDA-483 has left no matter requiring a comment, a response to such an untitled letter is generally required.
3. Official Action Indicated (OAI) means that objectionable conditions or practices that represent serious departures from the regulations were discovered. In this case, the imposition of administrative/regulatory sanctions may be required. An OAI classification is much more likely to result in an FDA warning letter, and additional enforcement action if FDA deems appropriate.

FDA ACTIONS

FDA has a number of administrative and regulatory remedies at its disposal when it determines that a sponsor, CRO, investigator, or IRB is failing to act in accord with requirements under the FFDCA and its implementing regulations. An FDA warning letter can be issued, demanding immediate corrective action. If the violation is serious enough, criminal prosecution can be pursued by recommending the matter to the Department of Justice for violations of the FFDCA, its implementing regulations, and possibly violations under Title 18 of the U.S. Code (USC). In addition, several remedies are specific to the parties involved.

As to sponsors, FDA can impose a clinical hold, which either delays commencement of a clinical investigation or suspends an ongoing investigation. When a clinical hold is ordered, research participants cannot be enrolled in the study or given the study drug, and patients already in the study must be taken off the study drug unless FDA specifically permits continuation of the therapy for patient safety reasons. Among other factors, FDA can impose a clinical hold whenever human subjects are or would be exposed to an unreasonable and significant risk of illness or injury. The clinical hold can be complete or partial. If all investigations under an IND are subject to the clinical hold, it is deemed a "complete clinical hold." Whereas if only specific study sites in a multisite study are subject to the clinical hold, the hold is deemed partial. Serious sponsor or CRO monitoring failures could result in a complete hold. Investigator misconduct is more likely to result in a partial hold specific to that clinical investigator's research site. A study may only resume after FDA has notified the sponsor that the study can proceed, which will only occur after FDA is satisfied that the reason for the clinical hold no longer exists.

Sponsors can also be subject to an IND termination if FDA determines that the IND is deficient or the conduct of the study is deficient. Except where FDA concludes that an immediate and substantial danger to the health of individuals exists, it must first provide the sponsor with a proposal to terminate the study, and give the sponsor an opportunity to dispute the need to terminate. Termination is only pursued by FDA if the clinical hold procedures are insufficient to address the serious deficiencies identified by FDA.

If FDA determines that sponsor or CRO failures in their oversight or monitoring duties result in the submission of new drug applications containing false data, the agency could invoke the Application Integrity Policy (AIP). The drug AIP is based on a system of trust, in that FDA will accept the truthfulness and accuracy of the data presented in a new drug application unless FDA is given reason not to have such trust. When that trust is broken, and FDA subjects a sponsor to the AIP, it treats the data and information in all new drug applications submitted by the sponsor as suspect, and thus, FDA first assesses the validity of data and information contained in a drug application prior to conducting the substantive scientific review. In addition, if FDA investigations identify deficiencies in previously approved drug applications, FDA can proceed to withdraw drug approval, require new testing, and/or seek recalls of marketed products.

An FDA invocation of the AIP can be financially crippling to a company because it brings the drug approval process for any drug under review to a stop, and may affect the marketing of approved drugs. A recent case in point concerns a medical device firm. During a 3-month inspection of the firm, FDA determined that the firm had improperly substituted reread data for original data without notification to FDA in an application to support the efficacy of its antiadhesion gel. In issuing an AIP letter, FDA suspended review of three premarket approval submissions. Further, relaunch of the firm's only U.S. product was made contingent on submission and approval of an AIP corrective action plan. After the firm submitted a corrective action plan, FDA did not accept it until a year later. In light of the AIP and other FDA actions against the company, the firm was forced to file for chapter 11 bankruptcy.

Debarment is another enforcement option for FDA if a company or person has been convicted for misconduct related to the development or approval of a drug application (17). When a person or company is debarred, they are essentially barred from participating in the pharmaceutical industry. Debarred companies cannot submit, or assist in the submission of, an ANDA and debarred persons cannot provide services in any capacity to a person that has an approved or pending drug application. Each time a drug company applies for approval of a drug, it must submit to FDA a signed statement that no debarred persons worked on the application. Drug companies that use debarred persons can be subject to stiff civil penalties (18). As required by the FFDCA, FDA publishes a list of debarred persons on its Web site at www.fda.gov/ora/compliance_ref/debar/default.htm.

As a practical matter, FDA has never debarred a company, instead focusing its enforcement resources on debarring persons within a company who were convicted for conduct related to the development, approval, or regulation of a drug product. The statutory debarment provisions historically have been used to debar pharmaceutical industry personnel, particularly those connected with the generic drug industry. However, in recent years debarment of clinical investigators, as well as clinical research staff, has been more common. For example, a California doctor and three members of his research staff were debarred following criminal convictions associated with the fabrication of research data. The physician was president of a research company in California that, beginning in the 1990s, conducted over 200 studies for as many as 47 drug companies. FDA inspection of his research facility revealed extensive deficiencies, including the use of fictitious patients, fabrication of data by substituting laboratory specimens and manipulating laboratory instrumentation, and the prescription of prohibited medications to manipulate data.

Clinical investigator disqualification is another enforcement remedy that can be pursued by FDA if it has information that a clinical investigator has repeatedly or deliberately failed to comply with the requirements set forth in 21 CFR parts 312, 50, or 56, or has submitted to FDA or the sponsor false information in any required report (19). A disqualified investigator is ineligible to receive investigational drugs. When pursuing this remedy, FDA must provide the investigator with written notice of the basis for seeking disqualification and give the investigator an opportunity to respond in writing or, if requested by the investigator, at an informal hearing. If FDA does not accept the investigator's explanation, the investigator will be offered the opportunity to pursue an administrative hearing under 21 CFR part 16. At the conclusion of FDA's investigation, if it determines that disqualification is appropriate, it will notify the investigator and the sponsor of any investigation in which the investigator has been named as a participant that the investigator is not entitled to receive investigational drugs. FDA publishes a list of disqualified investigators on its Web site at: www.fda.gov/ora/compliance_ref/bimo/dis_res_assur.htm.

As to FDA actions against IRBs, FDA may limit an IRB's ability to continue to operate by withholding the IRBs authority to approve new studies, directing that no new subjects be added to ongoing studies subject to the IRB's review, terminating studies subject to the IRB's review, and notifying State and Federal regulatory parties and others with a direct interest in the matter about concerns with the IRB's operations. Such remedies must be presented in a letter to the IRB and to the parent institution, and a response describing corrective actions must be provided to

FDA within a specified period of time. While it has never pursued this regulatory enforcement option, if the IRB fails to provide FDA with an appropriate response letter and its corrective actions are insufficient, FDA can pursue disqualification proceedings. Such proceeding will be instituted in accordance with FDA's requirements for regulatory hearings under 21 CFR part 16. The IRB can then be disqualified if FDA determines that the IRB has refused or repeatedly failed to comply with any of the regulations set forth in 21 CFR part 56, and that this noncompliance adversely affects the rights or welfare of the human subjects in a clinical investigation. FDA will notify the IRB, the parent institution, and other affected parties, such as sponsors and clinical investigators, of the disqualification. In addition, it may publish the IRB disqualification in the *Federal Register*. FDA will not approve an IND for a clinical investigation that is under the review of the disqualified IRB, and it may refuse to accept data in support of a drug application from a clinical investigation that was subject to the disqualified IRB's jurisdiction.

OTHER OVERSITE BODIES

In addition to FDA-oversight, clinical studies may also be subject to oversight by the Department of Health and Human Services' (HHS) Office for Human Research Protections (OHRP), particularly if the studies are conducted at institutions that receive funding from the HHS. OHRP has compliance oversight authority over all institutions that conduct HHS-funded research. In order to participate in HHS-funded research, an institution must obtain an approved "Assurance" from the OHRP. The Assurance formalizes the institution's commitment to protect human subjects and generally contains a voluntary agreement that all research conducted at the site, regardless of funding, is subject to OHRP oversight and research regulations set forth at 45 CFR part 46. Thus, a drug study sponsored by a pharmaceutical company may be subject to OHRP oversight even if there is no government funding.

When OHRP initiates an investigation, it is usually in response to an allegation or indication of noncompliance. However, investigations can also occur in the absence of noncompliance. Generally, OHRP notifies the institution in writing of the investigation and provides it with an opportunity to respond. The investigation may occur completely by letter or telephone correspondence, or an on-site evaluation may be involved. At the conclusion of the investigation, no matter what the outcome, the OHRP issues a determination letter. Thus, even where full compliance is determined, the institution will receive a determination letter. If less than full compliance is found, OHRP's determination letter may cite remedies that can range from requiring improvements at the institutional site to withdrawal of the institution's Assurance. OHRP can also recommend debarment of the institution or individual investigators, rendering them ineligible to receive any government funding.

Sponsors and investigators conducting clinical research concerning recombinant DNA human gene transfer should also be aware of their responsibilities under the National Institutes of Health's Guidelines for Research Involving Recombinant DNA Molecules (NIH Guidelines) (20). The NIH Guidelines articulate standards for investigators and institutions to follow to ensure the safe handling and containment of recombinant DNA and products derived from recombinant DNA. They outline requirements for institutional oversight, including Institutional Biosafety Committees, and describe the procedures of the Recombinant DNA Advisory Committee.

Even where the study is privately funded, it may be subject to the NIH Guidelines if the site at which the research is conducted receives any NIH funding.

The sponsor, CRO, investigator, and IRB should also be aware of state laws and regulations concerning the conduct of clinical research. While most states exempt research that is subject to and in compliance with federal research requirements from state laws and regulations, several states have a number of clinical research requirements that exceed federal requirements. For example, California requires that all informed consent documents be signed by a witness. In addition, some states require state approval of research occurring with certain patient populations. Also, certain issues affecting informed consent are state specific. Age of consent varies from state to state ranging from 14 years in Alabama to 21 years in Puerto Rico. Where a patient is unable to provide informed consent due to mental or physical incapacity, legally authorized representatives must be utilized and it is imperative that the investigator understand the order of priority with regard to who can act as a legally authorized representative. Investigators must also comply with state medical record privacy requirements and sexually transmitted disease reporting requirements.

THE HEALTH INSURANCE PORTABILITY AND ACCOUNTABILITY ACT OF 1996

As to medical records privacy, it is important for the sponsor, CRO, clinical investigator, and IRB to be aware of privacy requirements under the Health Insurance Portability and Accountability Act of 1996 (HIPAA) (21). HIPAA was implemented to improve the efficiency and effectiveness of the health-care system by requiring HHS to adopt national standards for electronic health-care transactions. However, to assure the continued privacy of health information, HIPAA included a provision that required HHS to adopt federal privacy protections for individually identifiable health information. Regulations adopted by HHS, which became effective on April 14, 2003, require covered entities (i.e., health plans, health-care clearinghouses, and health-care providers who conduct certain financial and administrative health-care transactions electronically) to implement standards to protect and guard against the misuse of individually identifiable health information. Individually identifiable health information (protected health information) is health information that is collected from an individual patient that either specifically identifies the patient (e.g., name, address, social security number) or which could reasonably be used to identify an individual (e.g., gender and age information in connection with an unusual disease condition) (22).

Because filing for insurance reimbursement is the type of electronic transaction that triggers the applicability of HIPAA, most health-care providers are considered covered entities and thus subject to HIPAA requirements (23). For the purpose of research, if a clinical investigator is a covered entity, the clinical investigator must:

1. Provide all patients with a written notification of the office's privacy practices and the patient's privacy rights (while not required, clinical investigators are encouraged to obtain the signature of all patients acknowledging receipt of the privacy notice) (24),

2. Unless an IRB or privacy board waiver is approved, obtain written authorization from all research participants (i.e., a subcategory of patients) before disclosing information for research purposes (25), and
3. Have written agreements with all parties to whom it releases confidential information (Business Associates) that satisfactorily documents that the Business Associate will appropriately safeguard the protected health information (26).

Because it is possible that sponsors or IRBs may receive protected health information, it is likely that clinical investigators could require them to sign a Business Associate agreement. If the investigator learns that a Business Associate fails to comply with the written agreement, the investigator must take reasonable steps to cure the breach or end the violation. If such steps are unsuccessful, the clinical investigator must terminate the Business Associate contract, or if termination is not viable, report the problem to the HHS (27).

INTERNATIONAL GOOD CLINICAL PRACTICE

Going back a number of years, FDA had as a policy that all clinical investigations that were submitted in an NDA needed to be conducted on patients in the United States. Data from sites outside the United States were not considered acceptable. The concern was that patient populations were different, and differences in the use of the drug, diet, and other environmental factors were such that information obtained on subjects outside the United States might not be a valid comparison to the U.S. population. This approach to clinical research has been set aside and clinical data from all over the world is now used to obtain approval of drugs in the United States. While the data may come from Europe, Russia, China, South America, and Africa, the standards used in obtaining the data are the same as to the need for a protocol, informed consent, and proper record keeping. Much of the international agreement on standards is the result of most of the countries in the world establishing policies that are consistent with the clinical standards recognized in the United States. While it is clearly possible to conduct a study almost anywhere in the world and submit the data for approval to the U.S. FDA based on agreements with the clinical sites in the countries in which the studies are being performed, many countries are looking to the establishment of international standards.

The leading body in creating international clinical standards is the International Conference on Harmonization (ICH). ICH was organized in April 1990 and has as its sole and primary purpose the creation of international standards for the purpose of pharmaceutical research. The main bodies participating in the creation of ICH standards are the United States, the European Union, and Japan. In addition to these countries and their government delegates, ICH is heavily supported by the pharmaceutical industry [and in particular the Pharmaceutical Research and Manufacturers of America (PhRMA)] in the United States, the European Federation of Pharmaceutical Industries and Associations (EFPIA) in Europe, and the Japan Pharmaceutical Manufacturers Association (JMPA) in Japan. Further, the World Health Organization (WHO), the European Free Trade Area (EFTA), and Canada hold observer status in the ICH. The creation of ICH is a recognition of the fact that the pharmaceutical industry is an international business and that diseases and conditions being treated in the United States are not significantly different from those being treated in other parts of the world. Although clear differences in disease patterns exist (i.e., there are few tropical diseases in the United States), given the modern scale of human interaction through travel and commerce, the need for and use of pharmaceuticals is recognizably global. There is no practical reason to do the same clinical study on a Japanese population, a European population, and a U.S. population. If there are adequate clinical data to show that the drug works in the patient population for whom the drug can be prescribed, the quickest and most expeditious way of conducting the research will benefit the pharmaceutical industry, the governments, and the populations that they serve.

While only a small part of this chapter is devoted to international clinical research issues, the reader should understand that there has been an increasing demand for international harmonization of clinical research and drug development practices. Already, FDA has adopted a number of the ICH Guidelines as FDA Guidance documents, including the ICH Guideline for Good Clinical Practice. Thus, although we expect that FDA will maintain its deep involvement in the development of new international standards, we also expect that the future of clinical research will be largely driven by international standards and expectations, as opposed to national standards alone.

REFERENCES AND NOTES

1. There is a set of drugs that, in FDA's view, do not qualify as GRASE, but which continue to be marketed in the absence of an NDA or an ANDA as a result of an FDA enforcement discretion policy. See Compliance Policy Guide 7132 c.02. These drugs are part of FDA's Drug Efficacy Implementation (DESI) and its Prescription Drug Wrap-up (DESI II) programs, and FDA will take appropriate action in connection with these products as it determines their status.
2. DESI and DESI II. Because a number of drugs were marketed prior to 1960 without obtaining a New Drug Application approval, there were some 5000 drugs in the marketplace and FDA, until 2007, showed little interest in removing them from the market. However, in 2007, FDA adopted a policy that all drugs need either an approved application or to comply with the OTC monograph.
3. Federal Food, Drug, and Cosmetic Act (FFDCA) §§505(a) and 505(i), 21 USC §355 (2007). FDA, by regulation, has waived the requirement to submit an IND application for certain bioequivalence studies. See 21 CFR §320.31.
4. FFDCA §505(i), 21 USC §355 (2007).
5. Investigational New Drug Application, 21 CFR part 312 (2007).
6. 21 CFR §312.52 (2007).
7. See, Sanofi-Aventis U.S. LLC, FDA Warning Letter (Oct. 23, 2007) available at http://www.fda.gov/foi/warning_letters/s6551c.htm
8. 21 CFR §§312.57 and 312.62 (2007).
9. FDA Policy on Retention Samples, available at http://www.fda.gov/cder/ogd/retention_samples.htm (last updated March 8, 2001).
10. U.S. Department of Health & Human Services, et al., Guidance for Industry, Protecting the Rights, Safety, and Welfare of Study Subjects—Supervisory Responsibilities of Investigators, Draft Guidance (May 2007).
11. *Id.*, at section III(A)(1) (citing Good Clinical Practice Guidance, section 4.1.5).
12. *Id.*, at section III(B).
13. Institutional Review Boards, 21 CFR part 56 (2007).
14. 21 CFR part 50 (2007), see also, Guidance, at section III(A)(3).
15. FFDCA §§505(i) and 505(j), 21 USC §355 (2007).
16. Bioresearch Monitoring (BIMO) Compliance Program Guidance Manual available at http://www.fda.gov/ora/cpgm/default.htm#bimo (last updated Nov. 8, 2007).

17. FFDCA §306, 21 USC §335a (2007).
18. FFDCA §307, 21 USC §335b (2007).
19. 21 CFR §312.70 (2007).
20. National Institutes of Health, NIH Guidelines for Research Involving Recombinant DNA Molecules, available at http://www4.od.nih.gov/oba/rac/guidelines.html
21. Health Insurance Portability and Accountability Act of 1996, Pub L No. 104–191, 110 Stat 1936 (1996).
22. 45 CFR §164.501 (2007).
23. 45 CFR §§160.103 (defining covered entities), 164.500(a) (2007).
24. 45 CFR §164.520 (2007).
25. 45 CFR §164.512(i)(1) (2007).
26. 45 CFR §164.508(c)(3) (2007).
27. 45 CFR §164.504(e)(1) (2007).

10 Postapproval Marketing Practices Regarding Drug Safety and Pharmacovigilance

Robert P. Martin
RP Martin Consulting, Lebanon, P.A., U.S.A.

INTRODUCTION

Historically, the regulation of drugs in the United States has been driven by a concern for the safety of the drug product. From the Pure Food and Drug Act of 1906, the FD&C Act of 1938, and to the present day, drug safety has been the overriding concern. During the past century, drug regulation at the Food and Drug Administration (FDA) has evolved to a large extent in terms of statutory reforms. Past changes have more often than not been a response to new challenges to the understanding of drug safety. Although the FDA is highly respected as one of the world's premier regulatory bodies, recent events have called into question FDA's regulatory decision-making and oversight processes, and caused the public to question its ability to provide an acceptable level of drug safety.

Throughout the decades of the 70s, 80s, and 90s, the emphasis of drug safety shifted from the inherent toxicity of the drug substance to a focus on the quality of the product and the risk from manufacturing standards. More recently, drug safety has resurfaced in a new form. Acute toxicity is not the driving force. The new driver is long-term toxic effects and low-probability side effects that are taking over the headlines and driving the FDA to reexamine its role in the management of drug safety.

There is a new concern for drug safety, both in the FDA and in the Congress. The process of evaluating safety as part of a marketing application has come under scrutiny.A heightened emphasis on the safety of pharmaceutical products throughout the life cycle of the drug is placing more emphasis on the safety issues that become evident after a drug is FDA approved for sale. As Sandra Kweder, M.D., Deputy Director of the Office of New Drugs (OND) in the FDA's Center for Drug Evaluation and Research (CDER) stated in 2006, "No amount of study before marketing will ever reveal everything about a new drug's effectiveness or risks. This is why post-marketing surveillance is extremely important and serves to complement the pre-marketing assessment" (1).

The issue of postapproval drug safety is now a timely issue that involves not only the FDA but the public at large and as a result the Congress of the United States. With such powerful forces working on this issue with all the associated special interests attempting to shape the future of FDA regulation, it is not surprising that this controversial issue is receiving increased attention in the press. As this issue is playing out in the public forum, contradictory viewpoints present a confusing picture for the average person. This confusing and often contradictory image of the safety of drugs after approval has resulted in some key decisions by Congress and the FDA. It is only now that the future of regulation in this area appears to be taking more definitive shape.

THE HISTORY OF DRUG SAFETY EVALUATION

It is clear that the issue of drug safety requires a reevaluation and additional clarification. Since these more recent events associated with drug safety, the Congress, the FDA, and the press have spoken and written on the subject. It is also clear that the regulatory environment is in the process of change as a result of these events.

Historical Perspective for Drug Safety

Historically, the primary consideration of the FDA in approving a drug for sale has been the safety profile. The initial law governing drug safety was the Food, Drug and Cosmetic Act of 1938. This law resulted from the unintentional poisoning of patients, mostly children, given sulfanilamide elixir which later proved to be toxic (2).

This law was extended by the Kefauver-Harris Amendments of 1962—also passed as a result of a drug toxicity tragedy. In this case, the problem was the toxic effects of thalidomide that was taken by pregnant women, on the unborn fetus (3).

In each of these cases, Congress was driven to act based on presence of a well publicized tragedy. We may predict the future course of some drug regulations based on this history.

Recent Issues Concerning Drug Safety

The policy adopted by the FDA is based, not surprisingly, on an evaluation of benefit versus risk.A drug that treats a potentially life-threatening disease may be approved even with significant side effects where a drug treating a quality if life issue is not given the same latitude.

Drug safety is once again now in the headlines with the disclosure that safety data presented in marketing applications may not give an accurate picture of all of the safety concerns. More recent items include

- Clinical studies of Vioxx® indicate that there is an associated increased risk of heart attack and stroke (4,5).
- Antidepressants have been implicated in an increased risk of suicide in young people (6,7).
- Ketek®, an antibiotic indicated for the treatment of acute chronic bronchitis, acute bacterial sinusitis, and pneumonia, has been associated with rare cases of serious liver injury and liver failure (8,9).
- The safety of Avandia®, a drug used in the treatment of type 2 diabetes, was recently questioned. Safety data from controlled clinical trials indicate a potentially significant increase in the risk of heart attack and heart-related deaths (10,11).
- Recently, a popular news program reported the potential relationship between Trasylol®, a drug used for patients at high risk of bleeding, and kidney toxicity. This complication sometime resulted in kidney failure requiring dialysis and "a trend toward increased death in ... these patients" (12).

These examples have two things in common, i.e., they are all playing out in the popular press and the perceived risk was not evident at the time of FDA approval of the drug for sale.

For the most part, these safety issues affect a small percentage of the patient population and did not offer detection during early safety studies and clinical trials. It should be noted that during the course of drug development and FDA review and approval, many thousands of subjects are tested for any negative effects of the drug. After a drug is FDA approved, conceivably millions of patients will be treated with the drug, and safety issues that appear very infrequently may be revealed. On the other hand, safety issues and adverse events that appear postapproval of the drug, including additional clinical studies that are conducted postapproval, are to be reported to the FDA by the pharmaceutical manufacturer that has received approval to market the drug, i.e., called the drug sponsor. In this manner, drug safety issues can be written into the drug product labeling and promotional materials.

Logically, it is in the best interest of a pharmaceutical company to detect safety issues during development. Current methods, however, have limitations, and problems with the safety of a drug may not be uncovered during safety and clinical trials. Side effects with a low frequency of occurrence may only be detected after marketing of the drug. In part, some of the reasons for the failure to detect safety problems are a result of outdated tools used for toxicology and human safety testing (13).

There is, however, a strong regulatory concern behind drug safety issues. The FDA came under increased scrutiny and criticism as a result of their inability to detect and react to safety issues. At a congressional hearing, this criticism was summarized by Dr. David Graham, an FDA whistleblower. In his testimony, he stated, "Vioxx is a terrible tragedy and a profound regulatory failure. I would argue that the FDA, as currently configured, is incapable of protecting America against another Vioxx. We are virtually defenseless" (14). It was becoming clear that improvements in the technology of detecting drug safety problems would not be a sufficient solution, some fundamental changes within the FDA were necessary.

POSTAPPROVAL DRUG SAFETY BEFORE 2003

As expected, the FDA has encountered issues of drug safety before in the history of drug regulation. As a result, several programs were already in place when the more recent set of issues surfaced. The FDA realized that drug safety could not be completely defined by data submitted in a New Drug Application. The process of understanding the safety of a drug evolves over the life of the drug. Clearly, a mechanism for tracking and evaluating adverse reactions to medication was needed.

MedWatch Program

Reporting adverse drug reactions (ADRs) is an important component of postapproval drug safety. Initially, reporting of ADRs was accomplished through an informal network of clinical observations reported in professional journals. This system, sponsored by the American Medical Association, was the predecessor of an FDA system established in 1961 to report and track ADRs. In 1993, the then-FDA Commissioner David A. Kessler, M.D., citing confusion with the multiple forms, moved to consolidate them under a new program called MedWatch (15). (The agency also has a separate mandatory reporting system required by law for medical product manufacturers and certain health care facilities.)

The MedWatch program has four goals.

- To clarify what should and should not be reported to FDA.
- To increase awareness of serious reactions caused by drugs or medical devices.
- To make the reporting process easy.
- To give the health community regular feedback about product safety issues.

The FDA clarification contained in instructions for filing a MedWatch report is quoted as follows (16):

- **Death**—If an adverse reaction to a medical product is a suspected cause of a patient's death.
- **Life-threatening hazard**—If the patient was at risk of dying at the time of the adverse reaction or if it is suspected that continued use of a product would cause death (for example, pacemaker breakdown or failure of an intravenous (IV) pump that could cause excessive drug dosing).
- **Hospitalization**—If a patient is admitted or has a prolonged hospital stay because of a serious adverse reaction (for example, a serious allergic reaction to a product such as latex).
- **Disability**—If the adverse reaction caused a significant or permanent change in a patient's body function, physical activities, or quality of life (for example, strokes or nervous system disorders brought on by drug therapy).
- **Birth defects, miscarriage, stillbirth, or birth with disease**—If exposure to a medical product before conception or during pregnancy is suspected of causing an adverse outcome in the child (for example, malformation in the child caused by the acne drug Accutane, or isotretinoin).
- **Needs intervention to avoid permanent damage**—If the use of a medical product required medical or surgical treatment to prevent impairment (for example, burns from radiation equipment or breakage of a screw supporting a bone fracture).

To make a MedWatch report, a suspected association between the impairment and the drug is sufficient reason to make a report. Proof, such as a controlled study or a statistically significant finding, is not required.

While MedWatch is a valuable tool for surveillance of drug safety, there are limitations to this program. MedWatch is voluntary and relies on the vigilance of a health care provider or patient to fill out and file the MedWatch form. Also, under this program, the ability of the FDA to follow up on an indicated problem is limited.

Reporting Requirements for Marketed Drugs

If reporting of adverse reactions by health care providers and patients is voluntary, reporting of adverse reactions by drug manufactures is not voluntary (17). These requirements in the Code of Federal Regulations (CFR) categorize an ADR by the severity of the reaction.

"Adverse drug experience. Any adverse event associated with the use of a drug in humans, whether or not considered drug related, including the following: An adverse event occurring in the course of the use of a drug product in professional practice; an adverse event occurring from drug overdose whether accidental or intentional; an adverse event occurring from drug abuse; an adverse event occurring from drug withdrawal; and any failure of expected pharmacological action."

"Disability. A substantial disruption of a person's ability to conduct normal life functions."

"Life-threatening adverse drug experience. Any adverse drug experience that places the patient, in the view of the initial reporter, at immediate risk of death from the adverse drug experience as it occurred, i.e., it does not include an adverse drug experience that, had it occurred in a more severe form, might have caused death."

"Serious adverse drug experience. Any adverse drug experience occurring at any dose that results in any of the following outcomes: Death, a life-threatening adverse drug experience, inpatient hospitalization or prolongation of existing hospitalization, a persistent or significant disability/incapacity, or a congenital anomaly/birth defect. Important medical events that may not result in death, be life-threatening, or require hospitalization may be considered a serious adverse drug experience when, based upon appropriate medical judgment, they may jeopardize the patient or subject and may require medical or surgical intervention to prevent one of the outcomes listed in this definition. Examples of such medical events include allergic bronchospasm requiring intensive treatment in an emergency room or at home, blood dyscrasias or convulsions that do not result in inpatient hospitalization, or the development of drug dependency or drug abuse."

"Unexpected adverse drug experience. Any adverse drug experience that is not listed in the current labeling for the drug product. This includes events that may be symptomatically and pathophysiologically related to an event listed in the labeling, but differ from the event because of greater severity or specificity. For example, under this definition, hepatic necrosis would be unexpected (by virtue of greater severity) if the labeling only referred to elevated hepatic enzymes or hepatitis. Similarly, cerebral thromboembolism and cerebral vasculitis would be unexpected (by virtue of greater specificity) if the labeling only listed cerebral vascular accidents. 'Unexpected,' as used in this definition, refers to an adverse drug experience that has not been previously observed (i.e., included in the labeling) rather than from the perspective of such experience not being anticipated from the pharmacological properties of the pharmaceutical product."

All adverse drug experiences must be reported to the FDA. Under the rules of the CFR, reporting is required to be made by the "person" named on the label of the drug (NDA or ANDA applicant, manufacturer, packer, distributor). If the adverse reaction is serious, there is a 15-day time limit for reporting the adverse reaction.

It should be noted that there are some differences based on the regulatory status of the drug (i.e., postmarketing, clinical study, or biological). The reader should refer to the appropriate section of the CFR (21 CFR 310.305, 314.80, 314.98, and 600.80) for the section referring to their situation.

Reporting Requirements for Clinical Studies

Reporting of safety issues for a drug that is not yet FDA approved for sale is also required during clinical studies. This also applies to clinical studies conducted after a marketing application is approved. For clinical studies, reportable events have been defined as follows (18):

Adverse Event (or Adverse Experience): "Any untoward medical occurrence in a patient or clinical investigation subject administered a pharmaceutical product and which does not necessarily have to have a causal relationship with this treatment. An adverse event can therefore be any unfavorable and unintended sign (including an abnormal laboratory finding, for example), symptom, or disease temporally associated with the use of a medicinal product, whether or not considered related to the medicinal product."

ADR: "In the *pre-approval clinical experience* with a new medicinal product or its new usages, particularly as the therapeutic dose(s) may not be established: all noxious and unintended responses to a medicinal product related to any dose should be considered adverse drug reactions. The phrase 'responses to a medicinal product' means that a causal relationship between a medicinal product and an adverse event is at least a reasonable possibility..."

Unexpected ADR: "An adverse reaction, the nature or severity of which is not consistent with the applicable product information (e.g., Investigator's Brochure for an unapproved investigational medicinal product)..."

Serious Adverse Event or ADR: "During clinical investigations, adverse events may occur which, if suspected to be medicinal product-related (adverse drug reactions), might be significant enough to lead to important changes in the way the medicinal product is developed (e.g., change in dose, population, needed monitoring, consent forms)."

Organization Within the FDA

Having access to information about ADRs is not sufficient by itself; also, the agency must have the ability to manage and respond to these drug safety issues. To be effective in protecting the safety of pharmaceutical products, sufficient focus must be placed on these issues to provide for the needed actions. Sufficient focus is the degree of visibility that safety issues receive. In short, this is a fundamental issue of how the FDA is organized.

As of this writing, there are two offices within the FDA charged with the responsibility of evaluating drug safety. The evaluation of drug safety is divided based on the stage of the regulatory process. An unapproved new drug with a New Drug Application or a new indication for a marketed drug is the responsibility of the OND. A drug approved for sale becomes the responsibility of the Office of Surveillance and Epidemiology (OSE) formerly the Office of Drug Safety (ODS). Both offices are a part of the Center for Drug Evaluation and Research (CDER).

Office of New Drugs

The OND is responsible for evaluating both safety studies and clinical studies and determining the risk associated with approving the drug for sale. The OND has the authority for making decisions about whether or not a product will be approved for sale. OND is organized into divisions that represent clinical areas of expertise, such as oncology, endocrinology, psychiatry, and pulmonary medicine. Premarket safety studies are shared across divisions to provide the greatest expertise (19).

Until recent events focused the agency's attention on drug safety, efforts within the agency were designed to shorten the review time for approval to speed the benefits to patients. During the review process, the number of patients who would use a new drug is much fewer than the number of patients receiving the drug after approval.

After approval of a new drug, OND will review safety data when the drug is submitted for a new indication. However, after approval, safety is monitored by the OSE.

Office of Surveillance and Epidemiology

The purpose of the OSE is to evaluate the safety profiles of drugs throughout the life cycle of the drugs. Specifically, the OSE maintains for CDER a system of postmarketing surveillance and risk assessment programs to identify adverse events that did not appear during the drug development process. It is this office that receives and evaluates the MedWatch reports and the required reports from companies as described above.

The OSE staff handles a total, from each of these sources, of more than 250,000 reports annually. From these reports, drug safety issues are identified. To address these concerns, the OSE recommends actions, which may include

- updating drug labeling,
- providing more information to the community,
- implementing or revising a risk management program,
- on rare occasions, reevaluating approval or marketing decisions.

THE FDA RESPONSE TO THE EMERGING DRUG SAFETY ISSUES

Even though the FDA had, in place, programs to handle the new wave of adverse drug experiences, there was still a need to respond to the new public concern about drug safety. To address these newest safety concerns and in response to the mounting criticism, Dr. Lester M. Crawford, Acting FDA Commissioner, authorized the Center for Drug Evaluation and Research (CDER) to take the following measures (20):

- Sponsor an Institute of Medicine (IOM) Study of the Drug Safety System.
- Implement a program for adjudicating differences of professional opinion.
- Appoint Director, Office of Drug Safety.
- Conduct drug safety/risk management consultations.
- Publish risk management guidance.

The FDA response was emphasized a few months later in congressional testimony by Sandra L. Kweder, M.D., the Deputy Director, OND, and Janet Woodcock, M.D., the FDA's Acting Deputy Commissioner for Operations, before the U.S. Senate's Committee on Health, Education, Labor And Pensions (21).

Possibly the most significant and lasting outcome of these five steps was the IOM committee that was contracted to evaluate the effectiveness of the United States drug safety system with emphasis on the postmarket phase. The study report was described in congressional testimony in November 2006 (22) and published in 2007 (23). The report contained, in addition to the evaluation of the FDA's role in drug safety, recommendations intended to improve determination of side effects and measures to enhance the confidence of Americans in the safety and effectiveness of their drugs.

In her testimony before Congress, Sheila Burke, chair of the IOM committee stated.

> The FDA has an enormous and complex mission – both to make innovative new drugs available to patients as quickly as possible and to assess the long-term risks and benefits of these products once they are on the market. We found an imbalance in the regulatory attention and resources available before and after approval. Staff and resources devoted to preapproval functions are substantially greater. Regulatory authority that is well-defined and robust before approval diminishes after a drug is introduced to the market. Few high-quality studies are conducted after approval, and the data are generally quite limited. Many of the report's recommendations are intended to bring the strengths of the pre-approval process to the postapproval process, to ensure ongoing attention to medications' risks and benefits for as long as the products are in use (24).

FDA'S NEW DRUG SAFETY OVERSIGHT BOARD

On February 15, 2005, HHS Secretary Mike Leavitt and Acting FDA Commissioner Lester M. Crawford announced the creation of a new independent Drug Safety Oversight Board (DSB) to oversee the management of drug safety issues. The purpose of the DSB is to provide emerging information to health providers and patients about the risks and benefits of medicines (25).

This organizational change within the FDA was another step to improve the way the FDA manages drug safety information. The intention of this board is to provide focus on the management of the FDA's review and decision-making processes. The DSB will oversee the management of important drug safety issues within the Center for Drug Evaluation and Research (CDER).

The membership of the DSB is composed of representatives from the FDA and medical experts from other HHS agencies and government departments (e.g., Department of Veterans Affairs). Members are be appointed by the FDA Commissioner. The board also will consult with other medical experts and representatives of patient and consumer groups.

Functions and Goals

The DSB has been established to provide independent oversight and advice to the center director on the management of important drug safety issues and to manage the dissemination of certain safety information through FDA's Web site to healthcare professionals and patients (26).

FUNDING OF DRUG SAFETY

PDUFA Fees (Prescription Drug User Fee Act)

If it is true that the FDA will extend their review of drug safety to postapproval, it is also true that the FDA has shortened the review time for new drugs. Shortened review of an NDA is a direct result of the Prescription Drug User Fee Act. Originally enacted in 1992, this law allowed the FDA to charge a fee to a pharmaceutical company for the review of a marketing application by permitting the FDA to hire additional reviewers. The intended purpose was to speed the approval process of new drugs. The law was successful in that the average review time of an NDA fell from 22 to 14 months and the review time for fast-track drugs declined from 13 to 6 months (27). It is also true that this source of revenue has become a significant source of funding for the FDA.

PDUFA came with a "sundown" provision requiring Congress to evaluate the program and reauthorize the program after 5 years. In 1997, following the success of the previous 5 years, Congress reauthorized the program for an additional 5 years. With PDUFA II came additional goals designed to reduce drug development times.

In 2002, Congress reauthorized PDUFA for a third time. PDUFA III placed greater emphasis on ensuring that user fees provided a sound financial footing for FDA's new drug and biologic review process. PDUFA also gave the FDA authority to spend PDUFA income on risk management and drug safety activities during the approval process and during the first 2 to 3 years following drug approval. This new use for PDUFA funds allowed the FDA to collect, develop, and review safety information on drugs, including adverse event reports for up to 3 years after the date of approval. Although the changes to PDUFA stopped short of granting the FDA the additional power to require pharmaceutical companies to conduct additional safety studies, this change provided the foundation to future changes within the FDA to manage drug safety after approval of the drug for sale.

Following the enactment of PDUFA III, the FDA increased the risk assessment of newly approved drugs. From October 1, 2002, through December 31, 2004, FDA reviewed 63 risk management plans for drug and biologic products—28 for applications submitted after PDUFA III took effect (28). In addition, discussions with industry and the public were held to discuss risk management, and pharmacovigilance practices.

However, the ability to collect and analyze information on drug safety does not provide a clear mechanism to effectively manage drug safety issues. For example, a recent study by Berndt, et al. (29) of the National Bureau of Economic Research, found no significant differences in the rates of safety withdrawals for drugs approved before PDUFA compared to drugs approved during the PDUFA era.

> Given the recent safety concerns over the cyclooxygenase 2 (COX2) inhibitors rofecoxib (Vioxx®; Merck) and celecoxib (Celebrex; Pfizer), controversies concerning the issue of whether the FDA has been approving drugs too quickly and without adequate review have re-emerged ... A 2002 study conducted by the Government Accountability Office (GAO), formerly the General Accounting Office, analysed withdrawal rates prior to and during PDUFA up to 2002. The GAO found that 6 out of 193 (3.10%) NMEs [new molecular entities] approved from 1986 to 1992 (calendar year periods) were withdrawn for safety-related reasons. During the period 1993–2000 (calendar year periods), 9 out of 259 (3.47%) NMEs approved by the FDA were ultimately withdrawn.

The results of this study indicate that additional change is needed. In September 2007, the Prescription Drug User Fee Amendment of 2007 was signed into law (30) renewing the existing law for an additional 5 years. This updated PDUFA gives the FDA some new tools and powers to manage drug safety.

There are several changes to the previous acts. For example, FDA will increase the amount of user fees it collects to almost $400 million, up from approximately $300 million. The act expands the FDA authority over labeling and provides for a publicly available clinical trials database.

Perhaps the most significant change to PDUFA is a new provision to this legislation titled, "Enhanced Authorities Regarding Postmarket Safety of Drugs." Under this legislation, the FDA can require drug companies to perform postmarket safety studies and perform risk evaluation and mitigation for drugs exhibiting adverse effects. This is clearly an expansion of the FDA's authority and power to manage drug safety.

POSTMARKETING SAFETY STUDIES AND POSSIBLE FUTURE CHANGES TO THE FD&C ACT

In 2005, the FDA asked the Institute of Medicine (IOM) to evaluate the drug safety system (31). The IOM report was released on September 22, 2006 (32). Recommendations from this report form the basis of legislative action by the U.S. Congress. As of this writing, both the Senate (33) and the House of Representatives (34) have identical bills to amend the Food, Drug and Cosmetic Act. Both bills mandate the establishment of a Center for Postmarket Evaluation and Research for Drugs and Biologics within the FDA. The Director of the Center will report directly to the Commissioner of Food and Drugs. This new center will perform risk/benefit evaluations and will have the authority to require additional safety and effectiveness studies to be conducted. While the purpose of this proposed center is similar to the DSB, the authority to control issues of drug safety is, if enacted, greatly expanded.

CONCLUSIONS

The initial FD&C Act was passed because of concerns about the acute toxicity of drugs; specifically, the poisoning resulting from a toxic excipient. This was reinforced in the early 60s by the experience with thalidomide that proved toxic to the unborn fetus when used by pregnant woman. The establishment of safety and efficacy for pharmaceutical products have been the driving forces for the FDA to exist. This changed in the decades of the 70s, 80s, and 90s, where the priority of the FDA was on the risk to the public of manufacturing errors. With the current climate, the focus of the FDA has come full circle.

It is now clear that the ability of the FDA to manage the risk of the toxic effects of drugs will be enormously enhanced. The power of the FDA to require action from pharmaceutical manufacturers is greatly strengthened and assuming that the current bills before Congress are passed, this increase in power will be a permanent change. In addition, the results of clinical studies are no longer the private property of the pharmaceutical companies, as this data is to be provided to the FDA and also to the public and health care professionals in the form of product labeling and promotional materials.

These changes have been supported by the information that has become available during the life cycle of a product—from product development to clinical trials to marketed products—and people would agree that these changes will have a beneficial effect on the general population. All changes, whether positive or negative, carry with them unanticipated effects. While the changes within the FDA are now clear, the effects on the pharmaceutical industry caused by these changes are not easily apparent. It is only with the passage of time that the total effect of these new powers for the FDA will be known as relating to pharmaceutical companies and the consumer public.

REFERENCES

1. Meadows M. Keeping Up With Drug Safety Information. FDA Consumer magazine May–June 2006.
2. Ballentine C. Taste of Raspberries, Taste of Death, The 1937 Elixir Sulfanilamide Incident. FDA Consumer magazine June 1981.
3. Linda Bren. Frances Oldham Kelsey: FDA Medical Reviewer Leaves Her Mark on History. U.S. Food and Drug Administration. FDA Consumer magazine March–April 2001.
4. COX-2 Inhibitor Drug Review of adverse renal and arrhythmia risk, in JAMA 2006. Available at http://www.cox2drugreview.org/.
5. Armstrong D. How the New England Journal Missed Warning Signs on Vioxx®. Wall Street Journal May 15, 2006:A1. Available at http://online.wsj. com/article/SB114765430315252591.html.

6. Vedantam S. Antidepressants a Suicide Risk for Young Adults. Washington Post December 14, 2006:A16. Available at http://www.washingtonpost. com/wp-dyn/content/article/2006/12/13/AR2006121300452.html.
7. Elias M. Antidepressants and suicide. USA TODAY. Posted 1/21/2004 9:50PM, updated 1/25/2004 5:10 PM. Available at http://www.usatoday. com/news/health/2004–01–21-antidepressants-suicide-usat_x.htm.
8. Harris G.F.D.A. Warns of Liver Failure After Antibiotic. New York Times June 30, 2006. Available at http://www.nytimes. com/2006/06/30/health/30fda.html?_r = 1&oref = slogin.
9. FDA Completes Safety Assessment of Ketek® New Safety Information to be Added to Product Labeling. FDA News June 29, 2006. (This press release was corrected on April 11, 2007). Available at http://www.fda.gov/bbs/topics/NEWS/2006/NEW01401.html.
10. Harris G.F.D.A. Warns of Liver Failure After Antibiotic. New York Times June 30, 2006. Available at http://www.nytimes. com/2006/06/30/health/30fda.html?_r = 1&oref = slogin.
11. FDA Issues Safety Alert on Avandia®. FDA News May 21, 2007. Available at http://www.fda.gov/bbs/topics/NEWS/2007/NEW01636.html.
12. Pelley S. 60 Minutes, One Thousand Lives A Month, February 17, 2008.
13. Statement of Steven Galson, M.D., M.P.H., Acting Director, Center for Drug Evaluation and Research, Before the Committee on Government Reform, United States House of Representatives, May 5, 2005.
14. US PIRG (United States Public Interest Research Group). 2006. Drug Safety. [Online]. Available at http://uspirg.org/uspirg.asp?id2 = 17568&id3 = US& [accessed September 16, 2006].
15. Henkel J. MedWatch: FDA's 'Heads Up' on Medical Product Safety. FDA Consumer Magazine November-December 1998. Available at http://www.fda.gov/fdac/features/1998/698_med.html.
16. ibid
17. 21 CFR 310.305, 314.80, 314.98, and 600.80.
18. Guideline for Industry, Clinical Safety Data Management: Definitions and Standards for Expedited Reporting, ICH-E2A, March 1995.
19. Statement of Steven Galson, M.D, M.P.H., Acting Director, CEDER, before the Committee on Government Reform, US House of Representatives, May 5, 2005.
20. Crawford LM, FDA Acts to Strengthen the Safety Program for Marketed Drugs. November 5, 2004. Available at http://www.fda.gov/bbs/topics/news/2004/NEW01131.html.
21. Statement of Sandra L. Kweder, M.D., Deputy Director, Office Of New Drugs, and Janet Woodcock, M.D., Acting Deputy Commissioner For Operations, FDA, Dept. Of Health and Human Services, before the Committee On Health, Education, Labor And Pensions, U.S. Senate, March 1 & 3, 2005. Available at http://www.fda.gov/ola/listing.html.
22. Statement of Sheila P. Burke, Chair, Committee on Assessment of the U.S. Drug Safety System Board on Population Health and Public Health Practice, Institute of Medicine. The National Academies, Before the, Committee on Health, Education, Labor and Pensions, U.S. Senate, November 16, 2006. Available at http://www7.nationalacademies.org/ocga/testimony/Future_of_Drug_Safety.asp.
23. The Future of Drug Safety: Promoting and Protecting the Health of the Public. Committee on the Assessment of the US Drug Safety System. Baciu A, Stratton K, Burke SP., eds. National Academy of Sciences 2007. Available at http://www.nap.edu/catalog/11750.html.
24. Statement of Sheila P. Burke, Chair, Committee on Assessment of the U.S. Drug Safety System Board on Population Health and Public Health Practice, Institute of Medicine. The National Academies, Before the, Committee on Health, Education, Labor and Pensions, U.S. Senate, November 16, 2006. Available at http://www7.nationalacademies.org/ocga/testimony/Future_of_Drug_Safety.asp.
25. Manual of Policies and Procedures Center for Drug Evaluation and Research, MAPP 4151.3. Avalilable at http://www.fda.gov/cder/mapp/4151.3R.pdf.
26. ibid.

27. Brown D. Congress Seeks to Balance Drug Safety, Quick Approval. Washingtonpost.com July 5, 2007. Available at http://www.washingtonpost.com/wp-dyn/content/article/2007/07/04/AR2007070401712.html.
28. ibid (21)
29. Berndt, Ernst R, Gottschalk AHB, et al. Industry Funding of the FDA: Effects of PDUFA on Approval Times and Withdrawal Rates (PDF 412KB), Nature Reviews: Drug Discovery 2005; 4(7):545–554.
30. Food and Drug Administration Amendments Act of 2007, 110th Congress, Pub.L. No. 110–85, Sept. 27, 2007.
31. Statement of Andrew C. von Eschenback, M.D., Commissioner of the Food and Drug Administration, before the Committee on Oversight and Government Reform, US House of Representatives, May 1, 2007.
32. The Future of Drug Safety, Institute of Medicine, National Academies, Committee on the Assessment of the US Drug Safety System Board on Population Health and Public Health Practice, Baciu A, Stratton K, Burke SP, eds. 2007.
33. Food and Drug Administration Safety Act of 2007 (Introduced in Senate), S 468, 110th CONGRESS, 1st Session, January 31, 2007.
34. To amend the Federal Food, Drug, and Cosmetic Act with respect to drug safety, and for other purposes (Introduced in the House), HR 788, 110th CONGRESS, 1st Session, 1/31/2007.

11 Drugs Marketed Without FDA Approval

Jane Baluss and David Rosen
Foley & Lardner LLP, Washington, D.C., U.S.A.

INTRODUCTION

It often comes as a surprise to members of the American public, medical professionals, Congress, and even legal professionals that thousands of drug products now on the market have never been reviewed and approved as safe and effective by the U.S. Food and Drug Administration (FDA), notwithstanding the comprehensive review and approval systems laid out for both prescription and over-the-counter (OTC) drugs in the Food, Drug, and Cosmetic Act (FDCA or the Act) and the FDA's implementing regulations and regulatory programs (1). FDA estimated that there were "perhaps as many as several thousand" such drug products on the market in mid-2006, and other estimates over the years have been even higher. Indeed, the FDA has conceded that the exact number of such products is not and probably cannot be known precisely (2). Historically, the visibility of such products has flared when unapproved drug products have been the cause of high-profile safety risks (3), and subsided in periods when FDA has focused primarily on other issues such as implementing the major statutory amendments of 1962 and 1984 that put into place the current regulatory scheme for both prescription and OTC drugs. Since 2006, however, the FDA has made concerted efforts to bring both individual products and broad classes of marketed unapproved drugs under the NDA approval process, or to remove them from the market. This chapter will provide an overview of the history and current regulatory status of marketed unapproved drugs in the United States, and FDA's current policy for dealing with such products.

STATUTORY AND REGULATORY BACKGROUND

As the regulatory scheme has evolved under the FDCA, it is unlawful under section 505(a) of the act to market any new drug (4) without first obtaining an approved application in the form of either an NDA (which must be supported by extensive safety and efficacy data including reports of adequate and well-controlled clinical trials) or an ANDA (which must demonstrate that the product has the same active ingredient(s), indication(s), dosage form, dosage strength, and labeling as an NDA-approved reference drug product, and that the product is bioequivalent to and, therefore, therapeutically interchangeable with the reference drug) (5). OTC drugs likewise require an approved ANDA or NDA unless their marketing is otherwise permitted under the terms of an ongoing- or final OTC monograph proceeding, as discussed below. Marketed products that fail to satisfy applicable approval requirements are subjected to a range of FDA enforcement actions ranging from the relatively benign (i.e., the issuance of a warning letter) (6) to more serious consequences such as product seizures and/or litigation leading to civil or criminal fines and other penalties (7). In the vast majority of cases, products targeted for such actions by the FDA are either voluntarily removed from the market or brought into compliance by their manufacturers (8).

While this framework works straightforwardly for the great majority of current drug products, for various historic reasons a very large—and largely undeterminable—number of drug products are and long have been marketed without an approved NDA/ANDA or OTC monograph status. These are largely the result of several key historic developments.

To begin with, prior to the 1962 amendments, the FDCA required only that new drugs be approved as safe, a requirement which itself had only been in effect since the 1938 amendments to the act. Furthermore, by 1962 the market was rife with products that had never been approved even for safety, for various reasons. Most notably, once FDA had approved a given active ingredient or combination for one or more indications, for many years it was agency practice not to require additional NDAs for subsequent products having the same ingredient(s)/indication(s) (9). Other products were marketed without NDAs on the marketers' belief that they were not "new drugs" as defined in the FDCA, either because they were generally recognized as safe or were pre-1938 "grandfather" drugs under section 201(p) of the act. Still others were likely marketed in sheer ignorance or disregard of FDA requirements.

The 1962 amendments to the FDCA required for the first time that new drugs be approved for efficacy as well as safety, and required FDA to evaluate the effectiveness of drugs then on the market which had previously been approved only on the basis of safety, if at all. To accomplish this mandate, FDA created a program known as the Drug Efficacy Study Implementation (DESI). The DESI program was instituted in 1963 as the procedural mechanism for evaluating the status of marketed prescription drugs under the new efficacy requirement, and for regularizing their status by establishing additional approval requirements and schedules that companies had to meet in order to continue marketing products reviewed under the DESI program.

The DESI program was organized as multiple expert reviews and rulemaking proceedings based on therapeutic classes of drugs, some of which are still ongoing. In recognition of the large number of unapproved prescription drugs then on the market, all conclusions, requirements, and compliance policies emerging from the DESI proceeding for a given class of drugs were made applicable to all other "identical, related, or similar" (IROS) drug products. This policy is embodied in FDA regulations at 21 CFR §310.6. As defined in the regulation, the term "identical, related, or similar drug includes other brands, potencies, dosage forms, salts or esters of the same drug moiety as well as of any drug moiety related in chemical structure or known pharmacological properties" (10). Thus, at the completion of a DESI proceeding, it is expected that all affected drug products, including those that were marketed as identical, similar, or related products will either have approved NDAs or ANDAs, as appropriate, or will be withdrawn from the market. Given the impracticability of identifying all IROS products, the onus of determining that a given product is IROS to a DESI-reviewed drug product (and complying accordingly) was left entirely on drug marketers.

After the DESI program was well under way, FDA established a separate program, the OTC Drug Review, for reviewing and determining safety and effectiveness for OTC drugs. Like DESI, the OTC Review is organized according to therapeutic classes, each of which has been reviewed by an expert advisory panel. Each review proceeds through a series of administrative stages, culminating in the promulgation of an OTC monograph (in the form of a final regulation) (11). Once a final monograph becomes effective for a given therapeutic class or drugs, all OTC products having ingredients and/or indications covered by the monograph must either be marketed in compliance with the monograph, have an approved NDA or ANDA, or be withdrawn from the market. As with DESI, products subject to an ongoing review are permitted to enter and/or remain on the market until the review is completed and effective. Still other products, however, are marketed over-the-counter "outside" the monograph system and without an ANDA/NDA, and thus are unapproved new drugs.

FDA'S CURRENT POLICY

Over time, FDA has considered or adopted various policies for dealing with marketed unapproved drugs, including case-by-case enforcement actions (in which FDA has invariably prevailed) and periodic efforts to establish an "old drug monograph" system for therapeutic classes of products, similar to the OTC review monograph system (12). FDA's current policy is embodied in a "Guidance For FDA Staff and Industry" entitled "Marketed Unapproved Drugs – Compliance Policy Guide (June 2006) (the CPG)" (13). This policy supercedes an earlier (2003) version of the guidance, which in turn evolved from still earlier efforts to organize and prioritize enforcement of completed and ongoing DESI proceedings (14).

The CPG broadly affirms that, with the sole exception of products subject to an ongoing OTC review or DESI proceeding (discussed below), *all* marketed unapproved drugs are subject to FDA enforcement action at any time, and thus are marketed at the manufacturer's risk. Moreover, states the guidance,

> FDA is not required to, and generally does not intend to, give special notice that a drug product may be subject to enforcement action, unless FDA determines that notice is necessary or appropriate to protect the public health. The issuance of this guidance is intended to provide notice that any product that is being marketed illegally is subject to enforcement action at any time (15).

With respect to OTC and DESI drugs, the CPG reiterates FDA's long-standing policy that products subject to an ongoing OTC or DESI proceeding (including IROS products) may remain on the market during the pendency of the proceeding and any additional grace period specified in the proceeding. However, once the relevant DESI or OTC proceeding is complete and effective, all noncomplying products are considered to be unapproved new drugs subject to enforcement action at any time under the CPG (16).

Notwithstanding FDA's asserted authority to take action against marketed unapproved drugs at any time, the CPG also concedes the practical impossibility of ridding the market of such products at one fell swoop. Instead, FDA's policy is to "exercise enforcement discretion" (i.e., stay its hand) with respect to "the universe of unapproved, illegally marketed drugs in all categories" (17), while reserving its resources for products that pose the greatest risks to public safety, health, or the integrity of the regulatory process (18). Specifically, the policy outlines a hierarchy of potential risks that can cause particular products or product classes to be singled out for enforcement action, including the following:

- Drugs with potential safety risks;
- Drugs that lack evidence of effectiveness;
- "Health fraud drugs," i.e., products whose promotionally-claimed benefits are not adequately supported by scientific evidence (with priority to be given to products that present direct or indirect health hazards) (19);
- "Drugs that present direct challenges to the new drug approval and OTC drug monograph systems," e.g., unapproved products that compete directly with products sold in compliance with an approved ANDA/NDA or final OTC drug monograph (20);
- Drug products that also violate the act in other ways, e.g., unapproved products whose manufacture is found by FDA inspectors to violate current Good Manufacturing Processes (cGMP), FDA labeling requirements, or other regulatory requirements; and
- Drugs that are reformulated to evade FDA enforcement action; this category may apply in rare instances when a manufacturer attempts to avoid anticipated regulatory action by changing a product's formulation without otherwise bringing it into compliance.

Once FDA has determined that regulatory action is appropriate based on the above criteria, the form that action will take can vary, again depending on the level of perceived risk. In some circumstances, FDA will proceed by regulatory action against an individual product/manufacturer, e.g., when there are product-specific safety issues, or when the lack of required approval is discovered in the course of an inspection that reveals serious cGMP violations. Increasingly, however, FDA has chosen to act on a class-wide basis as discussed below. In such cases, the agency typically provides at least 1 year for affected manufacturers to obtain approval or remove their products from the market.

FDA ACTIONS UNDER THE CPG POLICY

FDA actions to bring unapproved marketed drugs into the drug approval system have accelerated markedly in the period from 2006 to early 2008, and there is every indication that this trend can be expected to continue barring major unforeseen regulatory developments. Following issuance of the revised CPG in mid-2006, FDA held an industry workshop in January 2007, reiterating the CPG principles and providing information on the NDA/ANDA process to encourage voluntary compliance. At the same time, FDA enforcement activities in connection with marketed unapproved drugs have greatly accelerated compared to earlier years. For example, FDA's Web site lists more than 25 selected enforcement actions involving a wide range of drug products and drug product classes (21). These include, among others, *Federal Register* notices announcing deadlines for obtaining approval of multiple products containing specified active ingredients, including injectable colchicine, hydrocodone, guaifenesin (single-ingredient and extended-release products only), and quinine sulfate, among others. In several such cases, FDA's class-wide administrative orders have followed on earlier developments such as company-specific warning letters or injunction actions, and/or the issuance of a first NDA for the class (often followed by pressure from the NDA sponsor for FDA to force other class members into compliance). Yet another source of potential pressure on continued marketing of unapproved new drugs is the prospect of denial of Medicaid coverage and/or Medicaid enforcement actions for fraudulent billing of such products (22).

CONCLUSION

Even though medical and legal professionals as well as the general public are often quite surprised when they learn that thousands of drug products currently on the market have never been reviewed and approved by the U.S. FDA as safe and effective,they should not be. FDA has acknowledged the existence of such products as a major enforcement priority, and has placed industry on notice that all marketed unapproved drugs are subject to FDA enforcement action at any time, and thus are marketed at the manufacturer's risk with the sole exception of products subject to an ongoing OTC review or DESI proceeding. Given limitations in resources, FDA has stated in the CPG, that higher enforcement priority will be given to products that pose potential safety risks, products that lack evidence of effectiveness, and fraudulently-promoted products. Notwithstanding FDA's efforts to encourage voluntary compliance, the process of eliminating unapproved products from the market has taken years thus far and will likely continue to be slow under the CPG. However, given the more recent safety concerns associated with a number of products that were marketed without FDA approval, e.g., carbinoxamine in pediatric patients and safety issues arising with injectable colchicine, among others, this category of products that are marketed without FDA approval has increasingly been the subject of stories in the medial and congressional interest. This trend is likely to continue until a regulatory scheme is developed and implemented to bring all such products marketed without an NDA into the new drug approval process.

REFERENCES

1. For example, a 2006 survey by Medical Marketing Research Inc. indicated that fully 91 percent of retail pharmacists believe that all medications available for dispensing with a doctor's prescription have been FDA-approved. Thompson Healthcare Company, Drug Formulary Review (Oct. 1, 2006).
2. FDA has generally attributed its inability to identify (count specific marketed unapproved drug products to limitations of the current Drug Registration and Listing System (DRLS). See, e.g. Letter from David W. Boyer, Acting Commissioner for Legislation, to The Honorable Edward J. Markey (Dec. 11 2006) at 6.
3. For example, one landmark in the evolution of the current policy was the 1984 "E-Ferol Incident," in which the use of an unapproved intravenous vitamin E product led to numerous serious adverse effects including infant deaths. Congressional reaction to this incident spurred FDA to review the status of unapproved marketed drugs and prioritize them for appropriate enforcement action, as well as to extending adverse event reporting requirements to all prescription drugs, not just products with approved NDAs/ANDAs.
4. The regulatory definition of "new drug" in section 201(p) of the act creates narrow exceptions for drugs that were "grandfathered" under the 1938 or 1962 amendments, as well as drugs that are considered "not new" because they are generally recognized by qualified experts as safe and effective (GRAS(E) based on a material time and extent of marketing history. FDA has historically applied such provisions very narrowly and its interpretations have been widely upheld by the courts. As a practical consequence, virtually any drug product that is marketed without an approved NDA/ANDA or under an applicable OTC drug monograph will be considered illegally marketed by the FDA.

5. See FDCA §§505(a) (prohibition against marketing of unapproved new drugs), *id.* 505(b) (NDA requirements), and 505(j) (ANDA requirements).
6. FDA uses warning letters to notify drug manufacturers of asserted regulatory violations and the risk of regulatory action without further warning if the manufacturer does not promptly come into compliance. Even in the absence of further regulatory action, the receipt of a warning letter is generally viewed as a serious matter.
7. It also should be noted that, apart from applicable approval requirements, all marketed drugs are subject to other regulatory requirements, including, e.g., compliance with current Good Manufacturing Practices, establishment registration, and drug listing requirements, as well as the obligation to report adverse events.
8. The total elapsed time from FDA's opening salvo, whatever form it takes, to the ultimate submission of an ANDA/NDA or market withdrawal is typically at least a year (by FDA policy, as noted below) and can take much longer, if it is to a manufacturer's perceived advantage to maximize sales by playing out the administrative process to the fullest extent possible (e.g., by filing citizen petitions, submitting extensive commentary, and data challenging FDA's scientific conclusions, requesting advisory committee review, appealing FDA decisions to higher administrative levels, and the like.
9. See 21 CFR §310.100 (withdrawing all prior opinion letters and other advice that particular drug products were "not new."
10. 21 CFR §310.6(b)(1).
11. Earlier stages include the publication of a "call for data," followed by publication and public commentary on the advisory panel's initial report and a "tentative final monograph" (technically a proposed rule) reflecting public comments and the FDA's views.
12. The alternative of an OTC (DESI-like monograph system for unapproved "old" drugs has been repeatedly considered and rejected by the FDA over the past five decades. In 2004, FDA submitted a report to Congress noting three prior considerations of this idea and reiterating its objections, including the impossibility of conducting class-wide reviews for prescription drugs with varying formulations and manufacturing specifications, and the impracticable time and resource demands of conducting such a review. The alternative urged by FDA was continued use of the current CPG approach (with modifications as reflected in the current Draft CPG). Reasons for preferring the CPG approach included greater flexibility for prioritizing regulatory actions and proceeding against either individual products or product classes, as well as significantly lower resource demands. FDA, Congressional Report on Feasibility and Cost of a New Monograph System for Marketed Unapproved Drugs, House Report 108–93 and Senate Report 108–97 (July 2004); see also "Generic Drug Monographs: Risks and Benefits," speech by Roger L. Williams, M.D. (May 1991).
13. Available at http://www.fda.gov/cder/guidance/6911fnl.pdf. The CPG is intended to supersede an existing and more detailed CPG, Compliance Policy Guide (CPG), section 440.100 "Marketed New Drugs Without Approved NDAs or ANDAs," and carries forward essentially the same principles in a more streamlined form. Although it has not been finalized by the FDA, the authors of this chapter think, it accurately reflects the approach that FDA would take to the products that are currently marketed without FDA approval. A CPG is a guidance document and is not legally binding on the agency or the industry. It represents the agency's best judgment and current thinking at the time. A company may deviate from the guidance and still be in compliance; however, a company who deviates from the guidance does so at its own risk. Moreover, since the guidance is not legally binding, FDA could take a position that is contrary to the statements that are presented in the guidance. Though were FDA to do so, it would have to clearly explain the basis for its change in policy.
14. This earlier version of the CPG is posted on FDA's Web site at http://www.fda.gov/ora/compliance_ref/cpg/cpgdrg/cpg440–100.html.
15. CPG at 4.
16. CPG at 9.
17. *Id.* at 2.

18. While this policy is straightforward with respect to products that are already on the market, it is important to note that there is at least some potential uncertainty as to whether it would also be applied to a never-before-marketed product that is "identical, related, or similar" to one or more marketed products. While the authors of this chapter believe that reading the policy to permit the introduction of a new product identical to one or more marketed unapproved products is arguably consistent with the policies' overall language and intent as well as FDA's general approach to the class-wide treatment of identical, related, and similar drug products in the DESI review, it is possible that FDA might take a different approach.
19. Direct health hazards are adverse health effects directly caused in patients as a result of using a drug product; indirect health risk refers to the likelihood that a patient will delay or discontinue appropriate alternative medical treatment in reliance on fraudulent claims.
20. More specifically, to encourage voluntary compliance with the drug approval system, as soon as any one drug in a general class of products obtains FDA approval, FDA intends to prioritize enforcement action against companies that market competing drugs in the same product class for enforcement if they fail to follow suit within a reasonable time (generally, 1 year).
21. For details, see http://www.fda.gov/cder/drug/unapproved_drugs/default.htm.
22. See, e.g., Letter from Sen. Chuck Grassley to FDA and the Centers for Medicare and Medicaid Services (Nov. 13, 2007) (noting reports of fraudulent billing for reimbursement of unapproved drug products).

12 FDA Regulation of Foreign Drug Imports: The Need for Improvement

Benjamin L. England

Benjamin L. England & Associates, LLC, FDAImports.com, Inc., Columbia, Maryland, U.S.A.

INTRODUCTION

FDA has become quite fond of saying that all regulated products are equally subject to all of the requirements of the FDCA irrespective of their source of origin. This is a true statement, whether the articles are (1) finished drugs or drug ingredients, (2) prescription or over-the-counter (OTC) products, (3) innovator or generic, (4) of any dosage or route of administration, or (5) drugs combined with other categories of products (e.g., drug–device combinations). With this as a first principle, one might reasonably be tempted to anticipate that FDA's regulatory regime and enforcement schema would reflect substantial international activities to ensure that foreign drug manufacturers comply with drug safety provisions of the Act. However, FDA's efforts to engage in regulatory oversight of foreign drug manufacturing and distribution have been reduced as a result of budget concerns and the difficulty of performing an audit outside the United States. For the most part FDA has focused its efforts on developing and issuing guidance documents that address requirements unrelated to product safety or quality.

There is little statutory or regulatory distinction between domestic- and foreign-sourced pharmaceuticals. The only meaningful distinction rests in the mandated frequencies of inspections. Foreign drug facilities are not subjected to the frequencies of inspections that apply to domestic facilities—simply because foreign facilities are remote and simply getting to the site to cross the threshold is so expensive. FDA is required to inspect domestic registered drug facilities every 2 years. See 21 USC §360(h). No similar statutory mandate exists for foreign drug manufacturers (1). That distinction aside, drug establishments must be registered with FDA irrespective of where they are located. Similarly, all such establishments must list the drugs they intend to distribute in the United States. However, foreign facilities may list drugs that are never shipped to the United States. When a foreign facility is registered with FDA and lists its drugs, FDA conducts virtually no evaluation of the data. Without a gatekeeper on the registration and listing data systems, the agency is able to say little more about the scope of its regulated foreign industry than identify the number of unique registrations and drug listings foreign entities submit. Consequently, FDA knows very little about the actual size of its foreign inventory, much less the adequacy of conditions in or drug processing occurring at these foreign facilities (2). This applies to virtually any and all drugs being exported to the United States. In this void of regulatory oversight, over the last decade and a half, FDA has routinely been assailed by congressional committees demanding more substantive regulation of drugs originating in foreign countries.

Given the rocky relationship between congressional oversight and FDA with regard to drug imports, it is worthwhile to consider some historical perspectives and review some case studies to lay the framework for evaluating the authorities FDA implements at the border.

A HISTORY OF PERFECT STORMS ADVERSE TO PUBLIC HEALTH

In the 1990s, the confluence of a few foreign FDA inspections of active pharmaceutical ingredient (API) manufacturers and domestic investigations of imported bulk drugs disclosed the existence of several significant bulk drug counterfeiting (3) operations. FDA inspectors, working in conjunction with U.S. Customs Service (4) special agents, uncovered a number of foreign sources of counterfeit bulk drugs shipping metric tons of counterfeit antibiotics, anticonvulsants, and other APIs into the United States. The primary (although not exclusive) sources for the counterfeit APIs were located in China.

These counterfeit APIs were sold through a series of multiple fine chemicals and API brokers in Hong Kong, followed by companies in Germany or Switzerland, to U.S. end users intending to use the APIs for finishing into new animal and human drug products. Although the transactions were funneled through Europe, the counterfeit product, for the most part, was shipped directly from China (sometimes through Hong Kong) to U.S. ports of entry.

Throughout that decade, FDA successfully prosecuted only one of these criminal enterprises. That case involved the importation of counterfeit antibiotics for use in the manufacture of animal drugs in the United States. The investigation, however, revealed that counterfeit bulk drugs almost certainly were used in the manufacture of human finished injectable drugs. The counterfeiters were able to take advantage of the lax oversight of FDA's registration and listing systems, its weak foreign and border inspection programs, and its inability to correlate data obtained from domestic drug manufacturer inspections with information available from its foreign inspections, drug master file (DMF) submission and review processes, and import data. These weaknesses were never corrected even after the conclusion of the criminal case. The U.S. drug supply remained vulnerable to these risks for a number of years, virtually unchecked since that case was closed.

In June 2000, and in response to a number of adverse events (including deaths) involving counterfeit bulk inactive ingredients in other countries, FDA was criticized for its failure to adequately manage the influx of imported APIs during a number of congressional hearings (5). In response to those hearings, the agency became more interested in the APIs entering the U.S. and their purported end users. In the meantime, the sheer volume of imported cargo under FDA jurisdiction had continued to skyrocket as more manufacturers (drug, device, food, and cosmetic alike) moved their processing operations off shore. The agency, however, shifted few new resources to its foreign drug and border inspection operations. Its data systems remained woefully inadequate and without meaningful integration. Over time, new adverse events involving foreign APIs (deaths and other serious drug reactions in the United States) continued to feed the congressional frenzy (and later that of the press) regarding FDA's inability to manage the risks associated with inadequate regulation of the foreign drug manufacturing industry.

In 2008, FDA's persistent difficulty to effectively regulate the foreign drug manufacturing industry and the continuing weaknesses in its information technology systems helped create the environment in which then developed the perfect storm. Sometime prior to 2004, a manufacturer of bulk heparin sodium

United States Pharmacopeia located in China had submitted a DMF to FDA's Center for Drug Evaluation and Research (CDER) for agency review. A major international finished heparin manufacturer operating in the United States agreed to begin sourcing some of its bulk heparin sodium from this Chinese source. When the finished heparin manufacturer submitted documents to the agency requesting permission to add the Chinese firm as an additional source for its heparin, some personnel at FDA, reportedly, confused the name of the Chinese manufacturer with that of another manufacturer in China which had been inspected by FDA. FDA, in fact, had never inspected the bulk heparin sodium manufacturer. FDA approved the bulk heparin supplier as an API source for the finished dosage manufacturer in 2004.

In January 2008, the finished dosage manufacturer began recalling lots of finished injectable heparin doses due to a spike in adverse events associated with the product, including a number of American deaths. The source of the bulk heparin used to make the finished product was identified by FDA to be uninspected Chinese heparin sodium manufacturer. FDA quickly conducted an inspection of the facility in February 2008, at the conclusion of which the agency issued an 11-item FDA-483 (6). As of the date of that inspection, FDA had still not determined the cause for the adverse events associated with the Chinese-sourced heparin sodium. The investigation continued for many months.

By March 5, 2008, FDA reported during a press conference that it had discovered a nonheparin component in the suspect heparin lots. The nonheparin component was present at concentrations ranging from 5% to 20% (7). According to FDA officials speaking on the record, the component was "heparin-like" but the agency had still not identified what the component was. The agency only knew it did not belong in the heparin sodium. By this date, even U.S. news reporters were piecing together the facts and suggesting (to the FDA during the press conference) that it appeared the product may be a "fake heparin." FDA, however, was unprepared at that point to commit that the "heparin-like", nonheparin component was even the cause for the adverse events. Eventually, FDA identified this "heparin-like" component as hypersulfated chondroitin sulfate, an ingredient used often as a dietary ingredient in dietary supplements.

By April 29, 2008, in testimony before the House Oversight and Investigations Subcommittee, FDA's Director of CDER, Dr. Janet Woodcock, explained that FDA had linked adverse heparin events to at least 12 different foreign (Chinese) bulk heparin manufacturers (8). It was again confirmed that the foreign heparin sodium API manufacturer had not been inspected by FDA prior to the February 2008 inspection. That inspection occurred after significant press and scrutiny respecting the adverse events and yet, still, FDA observed significant problems related to validation of the firm's methods, nearly any combination of which could have given rise to some contamination of the bulk heparin (9).

The preceding narrative, while troubling, helps to frame a discussion about FDA's import authorities related to foreign-made drugs. Therefore, it is at this stage we observe that FDA's foreign inspection process for drug manufacturers is primarily driven by the agency's new drug application (NDA) approval process and is primarily funded by the Prescription Drug User Fee Acts (PDUFA). When any foreign facility is identified as the manufacturer of a drug in an NDA, the agency goes through its assessment as to whether a foreign inspection should be scheduled. Ordinarily, FDA eventually schedules a foreign inspection in connection with the application to cover the specific drug or drug manufacturing process associated with the application. This foreign inspection is called a Pre-Approval Inspection (PAI). FDA does conduct some routine good manufacturing practices (GMPs) postmarketing surveillance inspections of foreign facilities. But these occur on an extremely limited basis, primarily, due to a prioritization of resources (10). These general rules of thumb regarding foreign drug inspections apply to finished drug manufacturers and for those foreign API manufacturers presented as API sources to FDA by finished dosage applicants.

As of September 2007, FDA reportedly could identify 3249 foreign drug establishments that, according to the agency's criteria, are subject to inspection ("should be inspected"). FDA has openly acknowledged that this number is only an estimate and that the agency has no idea how many actual foreign drug facilities have been exporting drugs to the United States. Out of this number, however, FDA officials noted that they had no evidence of any FDA inspection occurring at 2133 foreign establishments. China had the largest number of foreign establishments which should be inspected at 586 as of September 2007 (11).

CHANGING WORLDS: COMPOUNDING THE DIFFERENCES IN HOW FDA REGULATES IMPORTED AND DOMESTIC DRUGS

Foreign-sourced drugs, including APIs, must meet all the same safety, quality, and purity standards; labeling requirements; packaging standards; and manufacturing regulations that apply to domestically manufactured drugs. Drug establishment registration, drug listing, and the DMF submission requirements apply equally to both domestic and foreign APIs. FDA implementation of these requirements in the foreign industry is clearly inadequate. In the United States, this disparity has become more significant in relation to drug quality and patient safety as the "global economy" continues to evolve. As evidenced by FDA, Customs, and Census data, the number of foreign drug manufacturing facilities propagating APIs intended for the U.S. market has increased dramatically over the last 15 years. Much of this increase can be attributed to free trade agreements (FTAs); beginning with the North American Free Trade Agreement (NAFTA), which was ratified by Congress in 1993. But not all of the increase in foreign drug manufacturing must be attributed to FTAs. Economic growth and industrialization of large developing nations alone have contributed substantially to the growth of drug imports in the United States.

Over the last several decades, both the People's Republic of China and India have progressed dramatically in developing their capacities to manufacture drugs for export. These industries have advanced to the point where they represent the number one (China) and number two (India) countries with foreign drug facilities exporting drugs to the United States, even using FDA's own numbers (12). Because China's industrial expansion outpaced its development of a reliable internal regulatory infrastructure to manage its industries, most government oversight in China occurred at the local rather than the national level. In addition, China has moved millions of people from rural areas into the cities to promote economic and industrial growth (13). The central government is aware of the need to create jobs for those new city dwellers, and China is promoting manufacturing to keep them occupied and increase productivity. Although a decentralized local regulatory construct benefits entrepreneurship, new manufacturing development, and business growth, it also complicates the process of establishing and maintaining a national drug safety regime. Further, it limits the ability for the national government in China to monitor the industry's compliance to any national or international standards and it creates an environment rife with opportunities for corruption.

In India, there is far more commonality with U.S. drug manufacturing principles. In addition, the Indian drug regulatory authorities are more centralized promoting closer collaboration with FDA. But the same cannot be said with regard to labor regulation, environmental restrictions, and enforcement of criminal statutes. For various internal policy reasons, not explored here, drug research companies and other innovators enjoy weaker intellectual property protections in India than those enjoyed in the United States. This increases risks, from FDA's perspective, that normal economic arbitrage will attract to the U.S. consumer increasing quantities of unapproved foreign versions of FDA-approved pharmaceuticals.

Although only two countries are highlighted above, the economic realities of the international drug market simply compound FDA's challenges, whether considering the impact of European Union experiment, the increase in drug manufacturing in other Asian countries, the availability of drugs on the Internet, and the advance of the industry in most Latin American countries. The transshipment of drugs through third and fourth countries for further processing, repackaging, relabeling, and consolidation prior to arrival at a U.S. ports of entry further complicates FDA's ability to identify the supply chain and source for any particular API once it arrives. FDA's antiquated data systems, reliance upon drug registration and drug listing and inability to coordinate its domestic and foreign operations, persist.

The vast majority of FDA's drug resources are still, as of 2008, spent on domestic manufacturing. A surprisingly large percentage of foreign drug manufacturers, drug packers and repackers, drug labelers, and drug distributors are never inspected by FDA—never, over several decades of production. In contrast, domestic manufacturers of prescription and application drugs are inspected and reinspected by FDA about every two to 3 years. This glaring disparity is permitted by the FDCA and represents one of the only major statutory distinctions enabling FDA's lax regulatory oversight of foreign-sourced drugs and its far more vigorous domestic regime. With this as an initial backdrop we now explore current law and agency regulation and policy relating to the importation of APIs into the United States.

FDA'S IMPORT AUTHORITY

FDA's broadest regulatory enforcement authority is barely even regulatory. Foreign products entering the United States under the FDCA are reviewed by FDA under its "801" authority. See 21 USC §381(a) (section 801 of the FDCA). The agency has the authority under the statute to "refuse admission" to any article (e.g., a shipment of drugs) based upon the mere appearance of a violation of law. It is not necessary for FDA to establish the product that actually violates the law. Moreover, this appearance may arise by the "examination of [the product] or otherwise," enabling FDA to deny importation based upon some evidence other than what may have come from the shipment under review (14).

Irrespective of this broad authority, U.S. importers of APIs may import articles that would otherwise be subject to refusal if they are intended for further processing and export or for incorporation into another article under the FDCA's Import for Export (IFE) provisions. See 21 USC §§381(d)(3), (e) and 382 [FDCA §§801(d)(3), (e) and 802]. Under the IFE provisions, importers may bring into the U.S. drug components which would otherwise not be permitted entry, if the articles are intended for further manufacturing or incorporation into another article, and subsequently exported. Prior to the amendments of the Public Health Security and Bioterrorism Preparedness & Response Act of 2002 (the "Bioterrorism Act"), FDA had virtually no authority to prevent the importation of articles under the IFE provisions (15). In addition, the agency knew little about the articles being imported under the provision or the foreign entities shipping the products. The Bioterrorism Act amended the FDCA to grant FDA the authority to refuse admission to articles offered for import under the IFE provisions where the agency has "credible evidence or information" indicating the article is not for further processing or incorporation into another article and eventual exportation. See 21 USC §381(d)(3)(B). The Bioterrorism Act also increased the information that importers are required to provide to FDA upon importation under the IFE provisions, the records the importer must keep regarding the imported articles, and imposed a bond requirement sufficient to cover the imported articles while in the United States for IFE purposes.

The Bioterrorism Act also added declaration requirements for importers of drug shipments. Upon importation, importers, owners, or consignees of imported drug shipments must submit to FDA a statement that identifies the drug facility registration with respect to the article. If the importer fails to provide the statement, FDA is required to refuse admission to the drug. See 21 USC §381(o) [FDCA §801(o)]. The IFE refusal and the refusal related to the failure to provide the statement respecting registration of the foreign manufacturer is different from the traditional import refusal under section 381(a) [FDCA section 801(a)]. Under the subsection (a), refused articles must be destroyed if they are not exported within 90 days. No such requirement exists under subsections (d)(3)(B) or (o). Moreover, under subsection (o), the article may be admitted entry if the importer cures the defect (by providing the statement)—even after refusal. FDA will ordinarily not permit an importer to cure the defect once an article has been refused under subsection (a) unless the importer demonstrates the refusal was in error and convinces FDA to rescind the refusal of admission. On the other hand, if an article is refused for the importer's failure to submit the drug registration statement [under subsection (o)], the FDA is not permitted to release the shipment to the importer's, owner's, or consignee's custody pending a final disposition. FDA and Customs have never implemented this custody provision to date as all FDA-regulated imported products are imported under a basic importation bond authorizing release to the importer before FDA has been given an opportunity to review the articles' admissibility. FDA never issued any regulations governing either of these Bioterrorism Act amendments, but implements them solely through agency guidance documents.

FDA has promulgated only a few regulations over the last three decades addressing how it implements its import authorities over all, and even less related to drug imports. FDA's import regulations primarily focus upon the disposition of imported articles that are subject to an FDA notice of sampling (21 CFR 1.90); the issuance of a notice (providing an opportunity for a hearing) when articles "may be subject to refusal" (21 CFR 1.94); the procedures for reconditioning or relabeling imported product subject to refusal (but not yet refused) (21 CFR 1.95, 1.96 & 1.99); and the requirement that the importer, owner, or consignee post an importation bond (implemented under Customs law) prior to obtaining custody of the merchandise or manipulating it in any manner (21 CFR 1.97). FDA has issued even fewer regulations regarding the importation of drugs. New drugs, which are subject to an FDA investigational new drug (IND) application, may be imported provided the articles are consigned to the U.S. IND sponsor, or to a qualified investigator named in the IND, or to the domestic agent for the foreign sponsor. See 21 CFR 312.110(a). A new drug may be imported into the United States if it is subject to an approved NDA or an active IND, and bulk drug ingredients which, when further processed result in a finished new drug, may be imported subject to certain drug labeling exemption regulations (discussed later). See 21 CFR 314.410(a).

Everything else FDA does at the border is implemented by guidance, and not regulation. Most of the guidance FDA issues are in the form of:

- Chapter 9 of the *Regulatory Procedures Manual* (*RPM*) (16);
- Portions of the *Investigations Operations Manual* (*IOM*) (17);
- *Compliance Policy Guides* (*CPGs*) (18);
- *Compliance Program Guidance Manuals* (*CPGMs*) (19);
- Import Alerts (IAs) (20);
- Import Bulletins (IBs) (21); and
- Various unpublished procedures, policies, manuals, and training programs.

This administrative power, however, has its limits. Even though FDA only needs to find an apparent violation to refuse entry, the importer, owner, or consignee of the shipment (the person who takes possession of the shipment after entry) has the opportunity to provide to FDA some evidence overcoming the apparent violation. This evidence may be in the form of written or oral testimony regarding the shipment. It may consist of analytical data related to the shipment, copies of the labels affixed to the product containers, submission of registration or listing numbers, or presentation of evidence that a new drug approval or IND application is in existence with respect to the article.

Even though the amount of evidence FDA must amass to refuse admission to a shipment of drugs is very low, the remedy is also relatively mild (even if costly to smaller shippers and importers). Refused shipments may be exported (in lieu of destruction) out of the country. That is, FDA does not take possession, much less title to the goods (as in the case of civil seizure actions) (21 USC §334), the importer is not forbidden from importing drugs in the future (as may occur, for instance, in a civil injunction case) (21 USC §332), and nobody has to pay the government any money or suffer more severe criminal sanctions.

Because FDA has this broad authority at the border, and the agency's resources for regulating any of the industries under its purview has remained so limited in spite of the dramatic increase of imported shipments, FDA is inclined to find any violation it can to hold cargo and force the importer to demonstrate the article complies with U.S. requirements. The easiest violations for FDA to lodge are those that do not require the agency to expend inspectional resources, that is, failures of foreign drug manufacturers to register or list their drugs with FDA.

In the realm of APIs, this regulatory requirement is easy to meet—and so most drug manufacturers do so (22). As a result, FDA has developed other methods for charging a shipment that appears to violate the law. These new methods also do not require the agency to expend inspectional resources examining shipments.

DRUG LABELING EXEMPTIONS—IMPORT ALERT 66-66

As mentioned earlier, in June 2000 FDA was summoned before the Subcommittee on Oversight and Investigations of the Energy and Commerce Committee in the

U.S. House of Representatives to explain itself regarding its failures in the eyes of many representatives, to prevent the importation of counterfeit APIs and APIs that originated at foreign facilities which had never been inspected by FDA, had never been identified by a finished new drug manufacturer (in a NDA of any kind), had been found previously to have imported counterfeit APIs, or whose APIs had been the subject of numerous adverse events related to apparent manufacturing defects (23). In order to prepare some new program to address congressional concerns regarding the appropriateness of imported API shipments into the United States, the agency spent several months seeking a remedy to the problems. By October 2000, FDA personnel had trudged through hundreds (if not thousands) of records involving API shipments that had been imported into the United States over the previous months (and years). CDER compliance officials found a number of foreign API manufacturers which had exported APIs that were of the sort that they should have been referenced in a NDA, but FDA could not find an NDA referencing the foreign manufacturer (24).

As a result of this, FDA issued import alert 66–66 alleging that certain APIs from specific foreign companies appeared to be of the type of APIs that require the U.S. end user (finished dosage manufacturer) to have filed an approved NDA and to have come from foreign API manufacturers that have been subject to an FDA inspection (25). The general purpose of any import alert is to provide uniform guidance to agency import personnel throughout the United States regarding FDA's review of certain evidence related to specific product/manufacturer combinations and apparent violations FDA believes the reviewed evidence will support. A foreign manufacturer's placement on an import alert is equivalent to the near guarantee of an automatic detention of that manufacturer's shipments (26).

In this case, the APIs that fell within the ambit of import alert 66–66 included all those APIs that were of a type that would be used by the importer (or its customer) to produce finished drugs which would require submission of a NDA. See 21 USC §§321(p) and 355(a). Under the theory of the alert, imported APIs are incapable of bearing "adequate directions for use" as required by the FDCA because APIs are almost never used as they imported but are subject to some further processing prior to their administration. See 21 USC §352(f)(1). Congress recognized this reality for drug components and thus expressly authorized FDA to exempt certain "drugs" (such as components) from the "adequate directions for use" requirement. Under that statutory authority, FDA promulgated exemptions from this labeling requirement for kinds of many APIs. *Id.*; see also 21 CFR §§201.100 (prescription drugs for human drugs); 201.105 (veterinary drugs); 201.116 (drugs having commonly known directions); 201.117 (inactive ingredients); 201.119 (in vitro diagnostic products); 201.120 (prescription compounding); 201.122 (drugs for processing, repacking, or manufacturing); & 201.125 (drugs for use in teaching, law enforcement, research, and analysis).

The effect of the import alert was to shift the assessment regarding the applicability of a drug labeling exemption from the company where the API might be put into use in the United States (under the exemption) to the border review process. Thus, FDA began requiring U.S. importers of APIs to essentially prove that an exemption applied to any particular imported API shipment or FDA would automatically detain (and eventually refuse admission to) the API.

Since the October 2000 issuance of import alert 66–66, FDA has been detaining (and refusing admission to) importations of APIs coming from *any* foreign manufacturer unless some evidence is presented at the time of importation demonstrating a regulatory drug label exemption applies. In this regard, over time FDA expanded the applicability of the guidance contained in the import alert to *all* imported APIs, even though FDA never conducted the kind of review that it undertook to issue the alert initially and to add API/foreign manufacturer combinations to it. FDA's extension of the import alert guidance to all APIs was based upon *United States v. 9/1 kg Containers, More or Less, of an Article of Drug for Veterinary Use,* in which the United States Court of Appeals for the Third Circuit had ruled that a party claiming a drug labeling exemption bears the burden of proof that the exemption applies (27). Under FDA's theory, the agency presumes (at the point of importation) that the exemption does *not* apply and thus the guidance was extended to all imported APIs, not just those manufacturer/API combinations actually listed on the alert. Consequently, FDA deemed that all APIs "appear" to be misbranded because they lack adequate directions for use. See 21 USC §§352(f)(1) and 381(a)(3). To overcome the appearance of this violation, the importer is left with the burden of presenting the information cited in FDA's import alert 66–66 demonstrating the article enjoys the drug labeling exemption (28).

As a result of FDA's approach to imported APIs, the agency expanded the laborious review it conducted in the fall of 2000 (covering at least of a year's worth of imported API shipments) to initially populate import alert 66–66, to all APIs without any additional review of the particular APIs or foreign suppliers whatsoever. It did this, of course, by presumption and guidance and not by regulation. Although there is some logic to FDA's approach, the initial import alert never provided any guidance for any of the other drug labeling exemptions that could apply to any particular API importation (29). Consequently, FDA import officials were forced to learn about the other potential drug labeling exemptions when they detained, without physical examination, creating unexpected problems and delays for importers of legitimate API shipments.

Another result of FDA's approach is that APIs, which were well known to come from previously inspected foreign suppliers for use by an importer under an approved NDA or abbreviated new drug application (ANDA), were suddenly and unexpectedly undergoing the automatic detention process contemplated by the alert. This affected innovator and generic manufacturer alike so that foreign API facilities, owned and operated by (and at times operating under the same name as) the importer, could not gain access to their imported shipments for weeks or months at a time, while FDA field personnel struggled to understand and apply the extension of the new guidance. Finally, because FDA treats every shipment of such APIs as unique events, every shipment by one importer of the same API from the same previously inspected source was repeatedly detained by FDA as if it was the first importation subject to review under the guidance.

Over time, as the ramifications of FDA's expanded application of its published guidance became better understood, U.S. API importers began asking for clarity and uniformity regarding the documents necessary to import APIs into the United States FDA gave it; to such a degree that FDA compliance officers began detaining (and refusing) API shipments for the importer's failure to produce certain documents recommended in the new and evolving guidance *rather than* based upon evidence that the APIs appeared to violate the Act. In time, FDA compliance officers gained access to internal CDER data systems to assist them in determining whether foreign facilities were approved API sources for the specific

API/importer–manufacturer combinations; however, these data bases were notoriously incomplete and not up to date. Because the data in these databases were not initially collected to assist compliance officers at ports of entry to assess applicability with drug labeling exemptions, FDA compliance officers began detaining (and refusing) shipments because of errors in CDER's data bases—which errors were caused by FDA in entering the data into the systems or the agency's failure to keep the data up to date.

To add further insult to injury, some of the documents the agency demanded at entry to FDA compliance officers were copies of documents FDA had originally issued to the NDA or ANDA holder, for example, end user letters to NDA holders authorizing the holders to begin using a foreign API source for finishing in the United States. This development, at a minimum, begged the question whether the evidence being presented overcame anything. If, after all, FDA issued the document that overcame the evidence of the appearance of a violation, what evidence could FDA be relying upon to give rise to the apparent violation in the first place?

It remains to be seen what these "evidentiary" submissions required by FDA to overcome the appearance of these "adequate directions for use" violations will evolve into next. But this analysis demonstrates that FDA's compliance review for foreign-sourced APIs remains quite disparate from its oversight of the few remaining domestic API manufacturing sources. Moreover, it reveals how easily the agency converts statutory and regulatory requirements into administrative obstacles for industry resulting in the conversion of a statutory risk management concept (e.g., GMP requirements designed to ensure the safety and efficacy of drugs) into administrative compliance management (e.g., import-process administrative requirements designed to ensure the importer submits the right document). More to the point, though, it shows how FDA has so broadly defined the "appearance" standard in FDCA section 801(a) that it now means virtually anything FDA wants it to mean.

Legal Registration and Listing: Present and the Future

Prior to the enactment of the Food and Drug Administration Modernization Act of 1997 (FDAMA), FDA did not require foreign drug manufacturers to be registered with the agency. FDA did require foreign drug manufacturers to list those drugs intended for distribution in the United States, which resulted in a default registration process. See 21 USC §360(j). FDAMA amended the drug registration provision of the act to require the annual registration of virtually all drug manufacturers, foreign or domestic and FDA followed with the regulatory requirement. See 21 USC §360(i); 21 CFR Part 207. The next major statutory revisions to FDA's registration authority for foreign drug facilities came through the Bioterrorism Act (30). Then Congress enacted the Food and Drug Administration Amendments Act of 2007, which required all drug registrations and listing be provided in electronic format (31). Under the Bioterrorism Act, Congress mandated that foreign drug manufacturers to provide certain new specific information at the time of registration including:

- The name and place of business of the establishment,
- The name of a U.S. agent,
- The name of each U.S. importer of the manufacturer's drugs that is known to the manufacturer, and

- The name of each person who imports or offers for import the manufacturer's drugs into the United States.

See 21 USC §360(i)(1).

With these amendments, Congress began to lay the statutory framework for FDA to begin to identify (and potentially regulate) the international supply chain of drugs originating in foreign countries and, at the very least, to create some improved transparency of that supply chain to FDA. FDA first issued guidance regarding the new drug registration provisions, which resulted in little change for some time. Then in August 2006, FDA issued a proposed rule to expand its drug establishment registration regulations (32). FDA took its task of creating new drug registration regulations seriously. The proposed revisions had broad implications for foreign drug establishments and drug importers. These revisions were so broad that FDA found it necessary to reopen the comment period to the proposed rule in February 2007 to grant additional time for foreign drug manufacturers to review the proposed rule and provide comments to the agency (33).

Under the Proposed Registration Rule, the following observations are noteworthy:

- Under the current (2008) regulatory regime, foreign drug manufacturers may export to the United States a drug ingredient or drug product into a foreign trade zone (FTZ), even if the foreign drug manufacturer is not registered with the FDA or if the drug is not listed. In many circumstances, FDA-registered or non-registered manufacturing facilities in foreign countries use FTZs to stage drug shipments to other foreign countries. These articles may not be FDA approved or drug listed or may be from an unregistered manufacturing facility that is not subject to FDA GMPs. These shipments currently enter FTZs under an importation process that is entirely separate from FDA's import screening process. The facilities exporting such products to FTZs have been exempted from FDA's registration and listing requirements since Nov. 27, 2001. The Propose Rule would revoke this exemption entirely, thereby requiring all foreign facilities manufacturing, repacking, relabeling, or conducting drug product salvaging operations to register and list their drugs even if their drugs merely transit the United States through an FTZ.
- Under the current (2008) regulatory regime, foreign manufacturers may export to the United States a drug ingredient or drug product intended for further processing, packing, or labeling or intended for incorporation into another article and eventual export. See 21 USC 381(d)(3) ("Import for Export" or "IFE"). Similar to the FTZ scenario, facilities exporting such products have been exempted from FDA's registration and listing requirements since Nov. 27, 2001. IFE shipments are entered under a customs temporary import bond (TIB), permitting them to remain in the United States for up to 3 years (including all extensions) prior to exportation. Extensive record-keeping requirements reflecting the disposition (manufacture, exportation, or destruction) of drugs entered as IFE shipments are currently in place. The Proposed Rule would revoke this exemption entirely, thereby requiring all foreign facilities manufacturing, repacking, relabeling, or conducting drug product salvaging operations to register and list their drugs even if the drugs enter as an IFE shipment and are never intended for consumption (or use) in the United States.

- Under the current (2008) regulatory regime, a foreign manufacturer who is required to register and list its articles must submit information regarding the foreign manufacturer, its owners and operators, the activities which it conducts, and the drugs upon which such activities are conducted. The Proposed Rule would require foreign drug manufacturers to provide in their registrations the identity and contact information of U.S. importers known to them and for persons who import or offer for import their drugs into the United States. The former category of reported parties requires the person to be in the United States. No such distinction was made for in the proposed definition of "persons who import or offer for import," implying that foreign agents, brokers, or other entities who facilitate the importation of a foreign establishment's drugs into the United States must also be identified in that foreign establishment's registration. Although the Bioterrorism Act clearly requires foreign drug establishments to provide the names of their U.S. importers and the persons who offer their products for importation, the agency's definition is so broad that it requires identification of virtually every supply chain of a foreign drug that makes its way, eventually, to the U.S. market.
- The term "importer," under the proposed rule, includes a person in the United States, other than a consumer or patient using a drug, who is an owner, consignee, or recipient of a foreign establishment's drug, even if the person is not the initial owner, consignee, or recipient of the foreign establishment's drug. Under the proposed rule, therefore, foreign manufacturers must disclose in their FDA registrations the identity of third party (downstream purchasers) who import drugs manufactured by the foreign establishment even if the foreign manufacturer did not sell the drug to the importer.
- Any changes of all required information (including the identities and contact information of importers or third parties facilitating drug importation) must be updated in FDA's registration system. Because the "importer" and "persons who offer for import" definitions are so broad, any change in a foreign drug manufacturer supply chain would require an update be filed in FDA's registration system, creating a significant burden for foreign manufacturers.
- The new drug code (NDC) provisions in the proposed rule contemplate the development (and required management) of significant amounts of data about hundreds of thousands of entities not currently included in any FDA data record. This data must be cross-linked by the agency in order for FDA inspectors and compliance officers to be able to use it to create a drug establishment and listing inventory. In addition, companies not accustomed to providing registration and listing information will be required to do so for the first time under the proposed rule. Historically, data amendments supplied by industry to FDA for application, registration, or listing purposes are not current (or are keyed incorrectly) in FDA's own data systems. When FDA's field personnel evaluate information about imported drugs and compare that information against data in the FDA systems, the FDA official often views the discrepancy between the data sets as the "appearance of a violation" [under 21 USC §381(a)]. In these cases, an FDA compliance officer often detains the imported shipment, leaving the importer in the position of attempting to justify why *FDA's* data systems are incorrect. Such shipments are often refused admission. The importer is then forced to export the drugs, even though the articles do not violate the FDCA and there is no appearance of any such violation. With the addition of the new NDC requirements in

the proposed rule, the broad information relating to a "U.S. importer" or "persons who import or offer for import drugs" required in foreign establishment registrations and listings, and the revocation of the FTZ and IFE exemptions, it is foreseeable that FDA's data systems are not likely to be current resulting in even greater confusion at ports of entry.

The FDA relied upon Bioterrorism Act for its authority to make a number of the changes to the current drug registration and listing regime found in the proposed rule including:

- The revocation of the registration and listing exemptions for foreign establishments shipping their drugs into FTZs or under 21 USC §381(d)(3) (related to IFE shipments); and
- Requiring foreign establishments to include in their registrations and listing submissions the identity and contact information of known U.S. importers and persons who import or offer for import-specific drugs manufactured by the registering foreign establishments.

It is noteworthy that FDA recited other significant Bioterrorism Act provisions in the proposed rule, although these additional provisions were not directly implemented by the rule, such as:

- The requirement that drugs imported under 21 USC §381(d)(3)(A)(i)(III) (relating to IFE shipments) be accompanied by a certificate of analysis;
- The importer of any drug imported under 21 USC §381(d)(3)(A)(i)(I) (relating to IFE shipments) provides a statement to the FDA upon the drugs importation identifying virtually every person who was in possession of the drug back to the foreign manufacturer;
- The FDA's explicit authority to refuse admission to a drug imported under the IFE provisions where there is credible evidence that the drug is not intended for further processing or incorporation into another article and eventual exportation [21 USC §381(d)(3)(B)]; and
- The FDA's authority to refuse admission to any imported drugs (whether under the IFE provision, or any other provision) if the importer fails to provide a statement to FDA upon offering the drug for import identifying the registration of certain parties in the drug's foreign supply chain. See 21 USC §381(o). If refused under this authority, the FDA is prohibited from permitting the importer (owner, consignee, or designated recipient) from taking possession of the drug—requiring the refused drug be held at the port of entry.

The FDA did not proposed to implement these additional Bioterrorism Act authorities; however, it is likely that the agency would proceed toward such implementation once the registration and listing system is revised as proposed. The agency is already in the process of soliciting comments from industry regarding the electronic format of registration and listing data (34).

EVOLVING OBSTACLES (BARRIERS) TO FOREIGN-SOURCED APIS

FDA has never had the authority to charge a registration fee for drug establishments, in contrast to recent developments in FDA's medical device authority granting to the agency such authority for medical device establishment registration (35).

However, the numerous bills have been introduced in the U.S. House of Representatives and the U.S. Senate proposing the imposition of registration fees to be paid by foreign and domestic drug establishments as well as importation fees to be paid at the port of entry for every commercial invoice line that includes a pharmaceutical. For instance, in a bill entitled Food and Drug Administration Globalization Act of 2008 (FDAGA), FDA is granted the authority to require drug establishments to pay a fee to register with FDA. Under FDAGA, as it is currently proposed, FDA is permitted to set the fee amount. The agency is also required to collect a fee from commercial drug importers under FDAGA, as proposed. In conjunction with the newly proposed user fee authority, FDAGA also proposes to mandate FDA to conduct inspections of all registered facilities, without distinguishing between foreign and domestic establishments.

It is clear that between the congressional pressure FDA is receiving and the agency's own proposed regulations and administrative guidance documents, the importation of foreign-sourced drugs will come under far stricter scrutiny far more often. Even if this increased FDA scrutiny of foreign-sourced drugs does not occur in the foreign manufacturing facility or at the border, the administrative hurdles are increasing. With the breadth of authority granted to FDA under section 801 and FDA's apparent willingness to find ways to deem drugs misbranded (through the extension of the import alert process), foreign companies seeking to sell drugs in the United States, whether they be finished dosage or APIs, will find that the importation process has become more complicated and the pathway is less clear.

REFERENCES AND NOTES

1. FDA officials admitted to the Government Accountability Office during a review of the agency's foreign inspection program that FDA only inspects nonactive pharmaceutical ingredient manufacturers on a "for cause" basis. That is, the agency does not inspect drug excipient manufacturers even though all components of a drug fall within the definition of that term in the statute. See 21 USC §321(g)(1)(D).
2. See DRUG SAFETY, Preliminary Findings Suggest Weaknesses in FDA's Program for Inspecting Foreign Drug Manufacturers; Marcia Crosse, Director, Health Care (Government Accountability Office) in Testimony before the Subcommittee on Oversight and Investigations, Energy and Commerce Committee, U.S. House of Representatives, at 3 (http://www.gao.gov/new.items/d08224t.pdf). Nov. 1, 2007 (last viewed July 25, 2008). Note that this testimony does not prove that foreign-made drugs are unsafe. Rather, it demonstrates that FDA has little idea whether they are safe or not—except by evaluation of adverse event data which may rise above the radar, after it is too late for some.
3. The term "counterfeit drug" under the Food Drug and Cosmetic Act (FDCA) refers to a drug, or the container or labeling thereof, which falsely bears the name, imprint, mark, etc., of a company which is purported to be the manufacturer, packer, or distributor of the drug, but which company did not manufacture, pack, or distribute the drug. See 21 USC §321(g)(2).
4. The Office of Enforcement at the U.S. Customs Service is now the Immigration and Customs Enforcement (ICE), which is a part of the Bureau of Customs and Border Protection in the Department of Homeland Security.
5. See, e.g., Statement of Dennis E. Baker, FDA Associate Commissioner for Regulatory Affairs, before the Subcommittee on Oversight and Investigations, Energy and Commerce Committee, U.S. House of Representatives, at http://www.fda.gov/ola/2000/importeddrugs.html (June 8, 2000); see also, Statement of Jane E. Henney, FDA Commissioner, before the Subcommittee on Oversight and Investigations, Energy and

Commerce Committee, U.S. House of Representatives, at http://www.fda.gov/ola/2000/counterfeitdrugs.html (Oct. 3, 2000) (both last viewed July 27, 2008).
6. See Form FDA-483, FDA Inspectional Observations for FDA inspection of Changzhou SPL Company Ltd., Changzhou City, Jiangsu Province, China, at http://www.fda.gov/ora/frequent/483s/Changzhouspl_heparin_20080226_483.pdf (redacted) Feb. 26, 2008 (last viewed July 27, 2008).
7. See FDA Press Briefing by FDA Commissioner Dr. Andrew von Eschenbach and FDA CDER Director Dr. Janet Woodcock, at http://www.fda.gov/bbs/transcripts/2008/heparin_transcript_030508.pdf, March 5, 2008 (last viewed July 27, 2008).
8. See Statement of Dr. Janet Woodcock, FDA Center for Drug Evaluation and Research Director, before the Subcommittee on Oversight and Investigations, Energy and Commerce Committee, U.S. House of Representatives, at http://www.fda.gov/ola/2008/heparin042908.html (Apr. 29, 2008).
9. Dr. Woodcock maintained during her testimony (both written and oral) that had FDA inspected the firm in 2004 when the agency would ordinarily have inspected—but for the human error in assuming an inspection had already occurred—the agency still would have not discovered the contamination of the heparin and the deaths that resulted from it because it would have been nearly impossible to detect the contamination during any inspection. See *id.* This sheds an interesting light onto what the lead drug approval official at FDA thought at the time the agency was (or should be) doing during an inspection, that is finding evidence of contamination that could arise from a processing or validation deficiency in a manufacturing plant. On the one hand, FDA's good manufacturing practices (GMP) inspections are intended and designed to ensure that the facility is implementing GMPs in order to reduce the risk of placing on the U.S. market a drug that fails to meet the required strength, quality, and purity. See 21 USC §351(a)(2)(B); see also 21 CFR Parts 210 and 211. On the other hand, given the public, congressional, and governmental (U.S. and Chinese) scrutiny placed upon this particular inspection, there are few inspections this company would likely have been better prepared for. Yet FDA documented that the facility was clearly out of control in many significant respects. Consequently, a 2004 inspection might have prevented this facility from producing bulk heparin sodium contaminated with hypersulfated chondroitin sulfate. Further, if it were true that an inspection in 2004 could not have detected the contamination, one wonders why FDA inspected the facility in February 2008 before the agency knew what the contaminant even was.
10. There are those who argue, quite persuasively, that one of the political ramifications of PDUFA has been to render it far easier for appropriators to reduce the budgetary line items to FDA for its routine surveillance drug GMP inspections (which are funded from the agency's discretionary budget) because FDA inspections are already paid for by NDA applicants. There are two reasons this line of reasoning is persuasive. First, the PAI only applies to those articles subject to PDUFA and they are limited in scope to the specific drug (and manufacturing process) implicated by the application. Second, at the time of this writing, FDA lacks equivalent PDUFA authority to cover generic drug applications (abbreviated new drug applications). Thus, the impact of this lack of discretionary funding weighs more heavily on the generic drug industry.
11. The facts in this paragraph were derived from a GAO inquiry. See Crosse at 9–14, n. 2, *supra.*
12. In testimony before the Subcommittee, Dr. Janet Woodcock noted that in 2007 over 1000 foreign sites were referenced in abbreviated NDAs (for generic drugs) as the source of API for the finished products. "450 of those were in India, 407 of those were in China, for API manufacture of those generic drugs; and only 151 of them were in the United States." See Oral Testimony of Dr. Janet Woodcock, Directory, FDA CDER, at http://energycommerce.edgeboss.net/wmedia/energycommerce/subcommittee_on_oversight_and_investigations_hearing-42908.wvx (Apr. 29, 2008).
13. See, e.g., Berg, Nate, China's Rural-to-Urban Migration, The Economist, July 27, 2007.
14. The relevant portion of the statutory provision states: Secretary of the Treasury shall deliver to the Secretary of Health and Human Services, upon his request, samples of food,

drugs, devices, and cosmetics which are being imported or offered for import into the United States, giving notice thereof to the owner or consignee, who may appear before the Secretary of Health and Human Services and have the right to introduce testimony. The Secretary of Health and Human Services shall furnish to the Secretary of the Treasury a list of establishments registered pursuant to subsection (i) of section 510 [21 USC §360] and shall request that if any drugs or devices manufactured, prepared, propagated, compounded, or processed in an establishment not so registered are imported or offered for import into the United States, samples of such drugs or devices be delivered to the Secretary of Health and Human Services, with notice of such delivery to the owner or consignee, who may appear before the Secretary of Health and Human Services and have the right to introduce testimony. If it appears from the examination of such samples or otherwise that (1) such article has been manufactured, processed, or packed under insanitary conditions… or (2) such article is forbidden or restricted in sale in the country in which it was produced or from which it was exported, or (3) such article is adulterated, misbranded, or in violation of section 505 (21 USC §355), or prohibited from introduction or delivery for introduction into interstate commerce under section 301(ll) [21 USC §331(ll)], then such article shall be refused admission, except as provided in subsection (b) of this section. See 21 USC §381 (FDCA §801).

15. See Pub L No. 107–188 §322 (June 12, 2002).
16. http://www.fda.gov/ora/compliance_ref/rpm/chapter9/ch9.html
17. http://www.fda.gov/ora/inspect_ref/iom/
18. http://www.fda.gov/ora/compliance_ref/cpg/default.htm
19. http://www.fda.gov/ora/cpgm/default.htm
20. http://www.fda.gov/ora/fiars/ora_import_alerts.html
21. Import Bulletins are considered deliberative internal agency documents and are, therefore, not public.
22. APIs intended for further manufacturing are exempt from certain labeling requirements. See, e.g., 21 CFR §201.122.
23. See Baker testimony, n. 5, *supra.*
24. See Henney testimony, n. 5, *supra.*
25. See Import Alert 66–66, Detention Without Physical Examination of APIs that Appear to be Misbranded Under 502(f)(1) [21 USC §352(f)(1)] Because they Do Not Meet the Requirements for the Labeling Exemptions in 21 CFR 201.122, at http://www.fda.gov/ora/fiars/ora_import_ia6666.html (Oct. 3, 2000) (last updated Jan. 9, 2008) (last viewed July 27, 2008). Note the date of the issuance of this import alert corresponds to the date of testimony of FDA Commissioner Henney before the Subcommittee on Oversight & Investigations, Energy & Commerce Committee, U.S. House of Representatives.
26. See FDA Regulatory Procedures Manual, Chapter 9, Subchap. 9–6 "Detention Without Physical Examination", at http://www.fda.gov/ora/compliance_ref/rpm/chapter9/ch9–6.html (last viewed July 28, 2008).
27. 854 F2 d 173, 179 (7th Cir 1988).
28. See Import Alert 66–66, n. 25, *supra.*
29. *Id.*
30. See Pub L No. 107–188, §321 [amending 21 USC §360(i)].
31. See Pub L No. 110–85 [amending 21 USC §360(p)]. In a Federal Register notice of availability, FDA solicited comments and volunteer participation in a pilot electronic registration system. See Draft Guidance for Industry on Providing Regulatory Submissions in Electronic Format—Drug Registration and Listing; Availability, 73 Fed Reg 39964 (July 11, 2008).
32. See Requirements for Foreign and Domestic Establishment Registration and Listing for Human Drugs Including Drugs that are Regulated Under a Biologics License Application and Animal Drugs, 71 Fed Reg 51276 (Aug. 29, 2006).
33. See 72 Fed Reg 5944 (Feb. 8, 2007) (reopening comment period for FDA Proposed Rule regarding requirements for foreign and domestic establishment registration and listing for human drugs, see n. 31, *supra*).

34. See Draft Guidance on Drug Registration and Listing Electronic Formats, n. 31, *supra*.
35. See Medical Device User Fee Act of 2007 (MDUFMA), which established a new user fee for medical device establishments registering with the FDA under 21 USC §360. One bright spot in MDUFMA for foreign entities appeared. Under the renewal of the legislation (for fiscal years 2008–2012), foreign medical device companies are permitted to qualify as "small businesses" enabling them to enjoy reductions in certain user fees collected by FDA.

13 Active Pharmaceutical Ingredients

Max S. Lazar

FDA Regulatory Compliance Consulting, Surprise, Arizona, U.S.A.

INTRODUCTION

Active Pharmaceutical Ingredients (APIs) play an important role in the drug product industry. The most obvious contribution is that the API is the active ingredient that makes a drug product effective and provides the pharmacological activity of any drug product or dosage form.

Historically, many APIs used to produce drug products in the United States by the dosage form manufacturers were made in the United States either by contractors or by the owners of the drug product NDA or ANDA. However, an evolution has occurred which has caused a migration of API manufacturing to other parts of the globe. This migration may have occurred for one or more reasons. The movement could have been driven by a growing generic industry; low-cost labor and/or technology in India, China, or developing nations of the world; or other economically related reasons such as environmental and safety regulations which have been more costly to meet within the United States.

While the causes of production migration are constantly changing, the reality is that more APIs are imported into the United States (1) and Europe than ever before in recent history. This particular situation has been having a significant impact on regulators, especially the U.S. Food and Drug Administration.

The reduction in local manufacturing and the significant expansion of APIs manufactured overseas have severely strained the inspectional resources of the FDA and possibly other regulators around the world.

API SOURCING

APIs can be manufactured using a number of different methods and techniques.

1. Naturally derived APIs are usually extracted from natural sources and purified for use in drug products;
2. Chemically synthesized compounds;
3. Compounds derived from fermentation, isolated and purified;
4. Biotechnologically produced compounds; and
5. A combination of any of the above techniques.

As the world economy continues to grow, sourcing of APIs is not predicable. Development and manufacturing of an API can be performed by small technology firms that have evolved over the past 25 years. Many of these firms have either spun off from downsized companies or were formed by scientists and business people that left the original API firms during downsizing or optimization exercises conducted by the original holders of regulatory filing and licenses.

Producing an API can take significant investments in laboratory development and manufacturing facilities. As products are discovered during original research, firms are faced with the need to make fast economic decisions. Should the compound of interest be developed and initially manufactured by a development firm to avoid the high investment costs or should this work be performed within the discovery firm where complete control of information and resources can be totally managed?

Outsourcing of API development and/or manufacturing is not a simple decision. Time to market and development work will influence the long-term effect on the API quality and cost. Today, development of an API process is being influenced by factors that did not exist a few years ago. This industry has evolved from simply finding a good manufacturing process which is capable of producing an API that meets predetermined specifications of quality using a chemical, synthetic, biological, or fermentation route that is economically feasible. In the present day, new concepts and potential expectations are entering into the mix of concepts that need to be considered by companies developing and manufacturing new APIs.

Newly identified principles and techniques are being driven in part by some regulatory initiatives and international standard setting organizations. These include ISO 9000 Quality Standards; International Conference on Harmonization (ICH) Quality Activities; American Society for Quality (ASQ) as well as FDA Initiatives, for example, Risk Management, Quality by Design, Process Analytical Technology, HAACP (Hazard Analysis Critical Control Point); and other concepts are all being considered as possible applications to API development and manufacturing and controls.

APIs in the United States

APIs manufactured in or for use in the United States have long been expected to meet Good Manufacturing Practices (GMP). This GMP compliance expectation gains its origin in the U.S. Food Drug & Cosmetic (FD&C) Act. Unlike drug products which have regulations covering GMP (21 CFR Part 211), API has no regulations issued specifically for API GMP. However, application of GMP to API manufacturing has been a foundation of drug manufacturing and API producers used 21 CFR Part 211 as a guide in applying GMPs to API manufacturing until the issuance of Q7A (2) by the ICH in November 2000. Shortly after that date, this ICH guidance was adopted as guidance by the United States FDA for API GMP.

The U.S. FDA has performed inspections of API producers to assure their conformance with GMP practices and conformance with other regulatory filings such as NDAs or DMFs. Unlike most foreign countries, FDA also performed these inspections of foreign manufacturing sites even if the source of the materials was outside of the United States.

APIs that are incorporated into drug products covered by such filings as NDAs should follow the various guidances that are issued by the FDA. For example, the February 1987 "Guideline for Submitting Supporting Documentation in Drug Applications for the Manufacture of Drug Substances" (3) is a historical FDA document that still exists and addresses what documentation is expected by the FDA when filing API information. Newer guidances which cover FDA ICH work on the Common Technical Document (CTD) and the M4Q guidance covering quality issues which discuss Drug Substance Dossier information (4) should be referenced to assure that current information is properly provided when submitting

API-related information. It is interesting to note that FDA continues to use "Drug Substance" when referring to "API" in their current filing guidances. API continues to be a more common GMP-related term due to its use in FDA and ICH Q7A guidances.

API Sourcing in Other Countries

As the API industry has continued to expand in other areas of the world, other countries and regions have developed their own review and filing processes as well as compliance programs. For example, the European Union has strengthened its processes associated with APIs and now requires API GMP compliance within its directives. However, regulatory review and inspectional processes vary significantly. In some countries, APIs can gain regulatory approval simply by being published in an official compendium.

REGULATORY FOCUS AND INITIATIVES

While innovator firms would use their IND or NDA filings to provide needed information about APIs, other companies would more likely make use of Drug Master Files (DMFs), or their equivalent, to document the necessary information covering an API. The use of a DMF allows for the submission of confidential information without making this information available to the public or other commercial firms. However, references to DMFs need to be established in filings to allow the regulators to review the DMF documents.

DMFs should contain all of the expected and detailed information that the regulators need to complete an agency review process (5–8).

While impurities and impurity profiles are of great importance (9,10) during a regulatory filing review, physical attributes of an API also need to be addressed since such characteristics can affect drug products. Physical attributes can affect mixing and flow characteristics of the API during the processing of a drug product, which crystal structure and crystal characteristics can sometimes affect the bioavailability of the drug. DMF sponsors that need additional information about impurities beyond specific FDA guidances are referred to ICH Q3A by FDA (11).

Regulatory focus in the United States has been relatively stable for a number of years. However, the FDA initiative for the 21st century has certainly started to impact API at both the design and manufacturing stages of the API Life Cycle. As ICH continues its efforts to harmonize filing and quality-related practices, regulatory attention tends to migrate. As Process Analytical Technology gains greater recognition within the drug product industry, more online controls will tend to be used for all manufacturing sectors including API.

"Process Analytical Technology is:

- a system for designing, analyzing, and controlling manufacturing through timely measurements (i.e., during processing) of critical quality and performance attributes of raw and in-process materials and processes with the goal of ensuring final product quality" (12).

Online monitoring and controls are not new to API; however, as regulators accept such technology for drug products, its spillover application to API design and development is inevitable.

Other regulatory interest lies in another concept called Quality by Design. For API, it will ultimately redirect API development from compound structure and specifications to a more complex activity that will need to be determined during development, that is, the critical parameters and specifications associated with the API so that its use in a final dosage form can be assured of its quality and effectiveness.

Compendia and regulators now both express concerns and interest in the methods used for producing a reliable and reproducible API. Methods of production can and will affect potential impurity profiles and even physical characteristics which can affect a change in the performance of an API in a dosage form.

REGULATORY FILINGS

What is needed to get regulatory approval for drug products varies around the world. However, some form of:

1. New Drug Application(s) (NDA),
2. Abbreviated New Drug Application(s) (ANDA),
3. New Animal Drug Application(s) (NADA),
4. Dossiers (The term commonly used for the earlier terms inside the United States), and
5. Drug Master File(s) (DMF).

DMFs are commonly used as a way to provide confidential or proprietary information about an API to a regulatory agency such as the FDA. A DMF normally includes:

1. Information about manufacturing and control,
2. Facility and process information used to produce or quality control an API,
3. Synthesis descriptions or detailed process information, and
4. Manufacturer site location and facility/equipment usage.

The DMF is required to provide sufficient details for regulators such that the information can be used to either grant or deny approval of a drug-related filing.

In the United States, API process information is included in Drug Applications or DMFs. If an NDA holder does not include API details within the application itself, a DMF must be referenced for the FDA to start the review of a submitted DMF. When a DMF or Drug Master File is sent to FDA, no active review is undertaken by FDA until the DMF is referenced within other registration documents such as an NDA. Once referenced, the DMF will be considered during a review and approval process.

It is important that firms that reference a DMF should be sure that the company that issued the DMF has had a recent satisfactory GMP inspection. If that is not the case, FDA or other agencies from other countries may indeed request an inspection of the DMF initiator's facility. Until the API producer has passed a current GMP inspection, it is highly unlikely that the applicant that references that DMF will receive approval.

Application holders need to be sure that they understand and comply with current FDA expectations before they initiate any changes to their suppliers or processes used to manufacture or control the referenced API (13).

In spite of years of pressure upon the FDA, the agency has been very slow and reluctant to allow industry to implement changes to an API without prior review (14,15).

Current expectations for DMFs, New Drug Applications, or Dossiers around the world will continue to evolve. What is certain is that changes due to harmonization efforts will continue under ICH and compendia programs and these efforts will result in greater uniformity in requirements between countries or regions of the world.

Perhaps more importantly, the current and future growth of the generic drug industry worldwide will have a definite impact upon the API industry. The continuing expansion of producers; their country of origin; and due to technological growth, changes in synthetic or biological derivation of an API will all significantly impact API regulations from both a filing and on-site inspectional perspective.

The DMF

Since the DMF plays such an important role in the API approval process, we need to examine it more closely.

"A Drug Master File (DMF) is a submission to FDA of information concerning the chemistry, manufacturing, and controls (CMC) of a drug substance or a component of a drug product to permit the FDA to review this information in support of a third party's submission" (16). While there were originally five types of DMFs, there are currently only four that are active. FDA no longer requests a Type I DMF (that provided plant information) since plant information is easily obtained by investigators in the field.

We will focus on the Type II DMF that covers APIs and the CMC issues. According to FDA (16), of the more than 6000 active DMFs, almost 4000 are Type II. What is important to understand is that there is NO requirement in the United States for submitting a DMF to FDA. Submission of a DMF is usually done to permit review of third-party information during an NDA or ANDA review by the regulatory authorities responsible for approving drug applications. It is certainly the simplest way to provide this information in a confidential way to regulators in the United States. The DMF or an NDA will be the documents that contain the API or Drug Substance details that are reviewed by the regulatory agencies for approval. These details when in a DMF will contain information described later and are important to an approval decision from any regulatory agency. See Section "Filing Issues" of this chapter for additional details of what needs to be in a filing document whether it is a DMF or another filing.

Submission of a DMF does not mean FDA will ever review it. Such a review usually only occurs when it is referenced in other applications for drug product approval. Many over-the-counter products are not reviewed and therefore the API referenced in a DMF may never be examined under normal circumstances.

Applicants filing an NDA or ANDA will usually reference a DMF as the Authorized Party if they themselves do not produce the API. The company that submits the DMF usually is the producer of the API and will need to identify a U.S. representative for contact with the FDA. Historically, such a representative or agent was not an FDA requirement, but recent rules have now obligated foreign manufacturers to identify such a contact for the FDA.

Since API manufacturers may be producing APIs for several users, the DMF provides a way for multiple applicants to reference the same DMF while keeping proprietary information confidential.

For the convenience of the reader, references (5,16,17) included at the end of this chapter can be used to obtain detailed filing information.

The DMF should contain:

1. A cover letter and
2. The expected administrative and technical information.

Two copies should be submitted to the DMF Staff at FDA. Be sure to include a clear statement of commitment as discussed in the referenced guidances. Absence of such a statement will delay acceptance by FDA. Once accepted, the DMF is entered into the agency database and the holder or its agent should receive an acknowledgment letter.

The acknowledgement letter will provide the assigned number and will remind the holder to:

- Submit changes as amendments,
- Notify FDA of changes,
  - In holder name/address
  - Agent
- Submit Letter of Authorization for each customer authorized, and
- Submit an Annual Report.

Review of the DMF will only occur once it is referenced in an official application that contains the Letter of Authorization from the DMF Holder. Reviewing chemists must request the DMF from the FDA Central Document Room unlike an NDA, ANDA, or IND that goes directly to reviewing staff. Any deficiency in a DMF that is found during a review initiated by an application is communicated to the DMF holder.

An Agent for a foreign manufacturer is currently expected since it can facilitate and improve communication with companies not located in the United States.

For postapproval changes, the Bulk Actives Post Approval Changes (BACPAC) guidance should be followed as it is issued. Currently, BACPAC only exists for intermediates. Be sure to specify, where appropriate, the API starting material(s) (APISM) as defined in ICH Q7A since it has significant future impact on GMP operations of an API facility. This does not mean that a company does not need to provide chemistry information for materials in early stages of manufacturing. It just helps identify a GMP starting point in processes.

Importance of Impurities

Possibly the single most important and significant variable associated with the Active Pharmaceutical Ingredient's quality is impurities and the API Impurity Profile. Normally most regulatory bodies will focus on impurities and impurity profiles when examining filing information and data. Since the sources of the API and/or the synthetic or biological route for producing the API can and will all influence impurities, descriptions of the sources and or the routes of manufacturing will almost always be requested by regulatory agencies that are truly concerned about API purity and potential hazards resulting from the manufacturing process. The other significant source of potential impurities can come from degradation products caused by stability issues or storage conditions.

Regulators from around the world will continue to expand their requests for data to support a greater understanding of the API's impurity profile and the degradation products that could develop under storage or stress conditions.

COMPENDIA MONOGRAPHS FOR API

Government required or requested filings are only a part of the quality standards for APIs. While filings like an NDA contain quality specifications, compendia monographs can exist which actually add additional requirements to API specifications. Firms need to assure themselves that they meet not only Regulatory Agency filings but also compendia requirements if they exist for an API.

Monographs for many APIs exist in country or regional compendia around the world. The three most significant compendia include the United States Pharmacopeia, the European Pharmacopoeia, and the Japanese Pharmacopoeia. Use of APIs that meet compendia requirements are usually required to satisfy local use requirements in addition to what may be filed in individual NDAs or Dossiers.

In an international effort to gain greater uniformity, these three mentioned pharmacopoeia such as United States Pharmacopeia, European Pharmacopoeia, and Japanese Pharmacopoeia have established formal harmonization efforts to reduce the burden on manufacturers and drug product producers. However, it is very important to recognize that specifications established within a compendium can only be reliable and useable for a given API source or mode of manufacturing. Every firm must assure that the API being used in a drug product is indeed safe and free of objectionable impurities even when using official compendia requirements.

As API sources expand due to the availability of numerous producers, the critical quality criteria can be affected by subtle differences in the preparation of the API or its original source. It is the manufacturer's responsibility to assure the true quality of an API.

REGULATORY ISSUES

Regulatory Issues are composed of several different factors. These include GMP and Filing and Approval activities or actions.

Drug product and API producers must assure that a dossier and any other regulatory filings such as NDAs or ANDAs are correctly filed and accurate. While not every regulatory agency uses the actual filing documents during an on-site inspection, they can certainly refer to such filing documents when visiting a site. Any observed deviation from what is in filed documents describing an API process will certainly lead to regulatory and approval issues for the NDA holder and, in effect, the DMF submitter.

From a regulatory perspective, the scientific issues and data surrounding the manufacturing and control processes, drug safety, and efficacy of the API are always in question and must be addressed by applicants. Following those scientific issues, the regulatory course of action expects an accurate representation of the processes used to produce and control the manufacturing of the API. These descriptions form the basis for drug compliance and this establishes the foundation of procedures and activities that will need to be followed by applicants and their suppliers, agents, or employees.

The ICH has been working for a long time on a CTD, which will harmonize filing activities. The CTD describes the CMC or Chemistry, Manufacturing, and Control Section of these regulatory filings. API producers should take steps to assure that DMF and NDA/ANDA/Dossiers formatted with CTD information properly represent the API and its manufacturing and control.

Filing Issues

Filed API information should always include at a minimum:

1. The name of the compound;
2. The API structure and molecular weight;
3. A detailed full description of the synthesis, biological process, or extraction process used to produce the API;
4. Facility and Process description;
5. All Raw Materials, solvents, catalysts used;
6. Identify the APISM;
7. Impurities;
8. Impurity Profile;
9. Reprocessing Steps;
10. Water Quality identified;
11. The in-process and final product controls used to assure the quality of the API;
12. A Sample Batch Record;
13. The specifications for the API, intermediates and raw materials;
14. Identification of the manufacturer of the API, its supplier of key raw materials, intermediates, or other purchased materials;
15. Address of the manufacturer of the API and all purchased intermediate;
16. Stability data; and
17. Definition of the container/closure system.

Where an API is listed within a compendium, the API is expected to meet the specifications established for its attributes. This, in addition to any additional specifications established in a Regulatory Filing document, would also need to be satisfied by the manufacturers and users of APIs.

GMP Issues

All APIs used for the manufacturing of Drug Products are expected to be manufactured under GMP. Compliance with that expectation or requirement varies by country or region of the world. Historically, the United States has been a leader in establishing and inspecting for API GMP compliance. While there are individual countries that have also performed inspections on APIs, true enforcement of GMP on the API producers has been a rare occurrence. However, this situation has changed and it is much more common to see aggressive actions taken to enforce GMP principles upon API producers. It is no longer acceptable to only have published GMP expectations. Enforcement of these expectations has become an additional expectation.

Good Manufacturing Practices for API

Historically, API manufacturers were audited for GMP compliance using 21 CFR Part 211 which are the Drug Product GMP. However, these regulations were not written for APIs and were used as a guide when examining Bulk Pharmaceutical Chemicals (BPC) in the past. BPC was the term historically used before API was introduced late in the 20th century. The term BPC included both active and inactive ingredients used to produce drug products. The term API was designed to narrow the scope of application by addressing only active ingredients where the term is used.

In the United States, there are no regulations issued by the Food and Drug Administration that establish specific GMP requirements for APIs. The United States has adopted and agreed to the use of the ICH Q7A guidance as the GMP guide for API. This approach differs from some other parts of the world where the Q7A guidance has been incorporated into the region's directives, such as in the European Union. In this case, one may find that law may enhance the API GMP requirement in the European Union. However, one must realize that although no specific regulation exists in the United States, the FD&C Act which establishes the Food and Drug Law in the United States does specifically provide the force of law to API GMP.

When one examines the international agreement by the European Union, Japan, and the United States to adopt ICH Q7A as the API GMP, it is easy to understand the importance of the Q7A guidance to the world. The agreement is between the three largest producers and/or consumers of pharmaceuticals in the world. It therefore establishes the Q7A guidance as a de facto requirement worldwide.

Within Q7A there exists a Table 1 which defines at what point the requirements of Q7A should be applied. This table, reproduced later, is important since it helps identify when Q7A principles would start to apply and the degree of application that may be expected.

Identifying the point within an API process that the APISM is introduced is important to define for both the API producers and the API regulators. From Table 1, both the application of Q7A and the degree of application are influenced by the identification of the APISM. It is highly suggested that applicants identify their APISM in any applications. By defining the APISM, how Q7A is applied is clearer to all parties.

IMPORTANT ATTRIBUTES

What are the API attributes that are generally the greatest concern? Contamination, Impurity Profiles, and impurities present in the API usually gain the greatest attention followed by physical attributes and any API attribute that could affect the behavior of the API in the final dosage form. This area of concern can include bulk density and particle size and crystal structure and flow characteristics for solid dosage form uses. Practices used for reprocessing and mixing of lots can also raise concerns during compliance reviews.

As world harmonization activities continue to evolve, the ability to meet regulatory needs around the world will likely simplify. However, it is still likely that each country will continue to add local expectations to what is expected and these additional requests and expectation will continue to challenge the producers and users of API.

TABLE 1 Application of Q7A Guidance to API Manufacturing

Type of manufacturing	Application of this guidance to steps (shown in gray) used in this type of manufacturing				
Chemical manufacturing	Production of the APISM	Introduction of the APISM into process	Production of Intermediate(s)	Isolation and purification	Physical processing and packaging
API derived from animal sources	Collection of organ, fluid, or tissue	Cutting, mixing, and/or initial processing	Introduction of the API starting material into process	Isolation and purification	Physical processing and packaging
API extracted from plant sources	Collection of plant	Cutting and initial extraction(s)	Introduction of the APISM into process	Isolation and purification	Physical processing and packaging
Herbal extracts used as API	Collection of plants	Cutting and initial extraction		Further extraction	Physical processing and packaging
API consisting of comminuted or powdered herbs	Collection of plants and/or cultivation and harvesting	Cutting! comminuting			Physical processing and packaging
Biotechnology: Fermentation/ cell culture	Establish-ment of master cell bank and working cell bank	Maintenance of working cell bank	Cell culture and/or fermentation	Isolation and purification	Physical processing and packaging
"Classical" fermentation to produce an API	Establish-ment of cell bank	Maintenance of the cell bank	Introduction of the cells into fermentation	Isolation and purification	Physical processing and packaging

Source: ICH Q7A API GMP Guidance.
Note: Increasing GMP requirements.

CONCLUSIONS

API Impacting Guides, Laws, or Practices

Certainly, the single most influential document that impacts API worldwide is Q7A (2), the API GMP guidance issued originally by The International Conference on Harmonisation of Technical Requirements for Registration of Pharmaceuticals for Human Use (ICH). This document was then adopted by each of the three regions of the world that are voting members of ICH, namely, the European Union, Japan, and the United States.

Local laws or other legally required actions that cover APIs may have existed within single countries or regions; however, true enforcement of GMP upon APIs was in reality very weak. What has truly increased attention on enforcement occurred when countries crossed boundaries and demanded compliance with another country's requirements. As soon as that started to occur, there was a relatively rapid demand for greater enforcement by the local authorities.

Even compendia have increased their interest in GMP issues. Today, one can find references to GMP in various compendia and a recognition that materials listed as official articles are expected to be produced under recognized GMP conditions.

Governments and regulators tend to enhance enforcement activities and demands when bad or defective and/or unsafe materials are found either by accident or when the population is negatively impacted by the use of a particular material. Such negative experiences tend to highlight deficiencies within API manufacturing and/or control programs and certainly should be addressed by manufacturers or users of APIs.

Whether Q7A exists within a country or regions as law, directive, or guidance, its use and application are expected by pharmaceutical producers worldwide.

Impacts on API

As discussed, Q7A is likely the most influential document impacting API manufacturing and controls. Its application and influence upon API supplies, their quality, and reliability is significant. Q7A's legal status as a law, directive, or guidance is generally not of any significance except for enforcement or prosecution purposes. The true value of Q7A and its influence on API materials and their use is really driven by the manufacturers of drug products for direct consumer use and the regulators' application of Q7A around the world.

Manufacturers and regulators of drug products should and will expect that APIs be produced in compliance with GMP as defined in Q7A. Depending upon the country of use, GMP compliance of the API may be a legal requirement for the drug product producer, or it may be a regulatory responsibility of local government enforcement agencies. No matter what the local situation directs, it is ultimately the drug product producer that must assure that the active ingredients it uses are indeed in conformance with GMP.

Variation in compendia standards adds additional complexity in the use of monographed APIs. Due to differences in quality standards around the world, variations in the manufacturing process that may be utilized or weak process controls and poor manufacturing techniques can all contribute to significant variations in the ultimate quality and safety of an API.

Currently in the United States there are no regulations covering API GMP. API GMP is described in a guidance that was negotiated under ICH and issued as Q7A. Although this is a guidance and not regulation, GMP authority for FDA is gained from within the FD&C Act, which is the law in the United States. Whether API GMP is covered as a guidance or law around the world, API GMP remains an important requirement or expectation for APIs.

Compendia requirements can also vary from one country or region to another. It is also important to recognize that quality attributes of API are heavily dependent upon the method of manufacturing used to produce the API. Different synthetic routes, varying solvents, and varying purification techniques can all impact the quality attributes of the API. Therefore, manufacturers should be aware that simply performing compendia analysis and obtaining results that meet that compendia's requirements may not be sufficient evidence that the API is truly of good quality.

Economic, political, and cultural factors can also influence the true quality of an API. Care must be exercised to be sure that regulatory filings as well as manufacturing and controls used to produce an API meet international standards of GMP as well as conformance to the registered conditions stated in a dossier or NDA/ANDA. A DMF must represent accurate information about a manufacturer, its facilities, synthesis or biological process used, the purification process, and the analytical and biological controls that are to control the API quality.

Other Important Issues

The regulatory environment that exists within a country can have a significant impact upon the true quality of a finished API that can be used in a dosage form. In the United States, DMFs are not reviewed by the FDA until and unless they are referenced by a drug product applicant. It is only then, that U.S. regulators will examine a DMF. It is at that time that a request for a review of the GMP status of the firm that produces the API. API companies can expect to be examined for GMP compliance levels with Q7A being used as the GMP reference document, and they are likely to be reviewed to assure that the information that was filed in the dossiers or NDA/ANDA are indeed true and accurate. Sites that have never experienced an inspection will almost always be inspected prior to any approvals being granted to the drug product.

Manufacturing Operations

While simple revisions to manufacturing and control procedures are sometimes possible without prior approvals, producers and users of API must be sure that appropriate regulatory requirements are met for domestic and export uses of the API. In many cases, revisions to manufacturing and control uses for APIs require prior approvals from regulators, and always a notification to the drug product manufacturer.

Appropriate Change Control procedures and documentation systems must exist. Identification of the step at which an APISM enters a manufacturing process should always be noted for both GMP and Regulatory Filing purposes.

Raw materials, their acceptance criteria, and water quality should exist as predetermined quality attributes. Suppliers including the manufacturers' names and locations should be identified. API manufacturers should not contract or obtain materials without knowing the actual producers and their manufacturing and control locations.

While memoranda of understanding exist between many countries, they do not exist for every country or region. Memoranda of understanding can help reduce repetitive inspections, audits, and filing requests. However, API firms frequently find themselves being asked for information numerous times in order to satisfy local norms or practices that are not necessarily required in their own country, but in the importing country or region.

Final Thoughts

As the world economy grows, more companies from more countries are entering the supply chain for APIs. While the competition has many advantages such as economic growth, it also increases the complexity in obtaining quality products that can be assured to be in compliance with regulatory requirements and expectations.

Is the API made the way it is registered or filed? Is the API produced according to API GMP? Does the documentation exist that supports the answers to these and many other questions?

Can harmonization efforts truly reduce the negative impact of differing requirements? How and when will repetitive work be eliminated through effective harmonization efforts? Countries, their governments, and compendia are all working toward a truly harmonized environment for APIs. This effort will result in more efficient operations, controls, and reliable, quality API worldwide.

Indeed, APIs are the heart and soul of the drug industry. Without APIs, there is no drug industry as the API provides the active ingredient that produces the necessary medical benefit of any drug product.

REFERENCES AND NOTES

1. Various FDA presentations by Edwin Rivera, CDER, Office of Compliance.
2. International Conference on Harmonization, Guidance for Industry, Q7A Good Manufacturing Practice Guidance for Active Pharmaceutical Ingredients, November 2000.
3. Guidance for Submitting Supporting Documentation in Drug Applications for the Manufacture of Drug Substances; February 1987; Food and Drug Administration, Center for Drug Evaluation and Research, Office of Drug Evaluation I (HFD-100).
4. Guidance for Industry, M4Q: The CTD—Quality; August 2001; U.S. Department of Health and Human Services, Food and Drug Administration, Center for Drug Evaluation and Research (CDER).
5. EMEA Note for Guidance, European Drug Master File Procedure for Active Ingredients (III/5370/93).
6. Guideline for Drug Master Files, September 1989; Food and Drug Administration, Center for Drug Evaluation and Research, Office of Drug Evaluation I (HFD-100).
7. Guidance for Industry, Drug Master Files for Bulk Antibiotic Drug Substances, November 1999; U.S. Department of Health and Human Services, Food and Drug Administration, Center for Drug Evaluation and Research (CDER).
8. Guidance for Industry, ANDAs: Impurities in Drug Substances, November 1999; U.S. Department of Health and Human Services, Food and Drug Administration, Center for Drug Evaluation and Research (CDER).
9. Guidance for Industry, ANDAs: Impurities in Drug Substances, Draft Guidance, January 2005; U.S. Department of Health and Human Services, Food and Drug Administration, Center for Drug Evaluation and Research (CDER).
10. Guidance for Industry, NDAs: Impurities in New Drug Substances, February 2000; U.S. Department of Health and Human Services, Food and Drug Administration, Center for Drug Evaluation and Research (CDER).
11. Guidance for Industry, Impurities in New Drug Substances, January 1996; U.S. Department of Health and Human Services, Food and Drug Administration, Center for Drug Evaluation and Research (CDER). Reprint of ICH Q3 A Step 4 Document approved by ICH Steering Committee, March 1995.
12. Process Analytical Technology (PAT) Initiative; CDER Office of Pharmaceutical Science, U.S. Food and Drug Administration; web address: http://www.fda.gov/cder/OPS/PAT.htm, 2007.
13. Guidance for Industry, Changes to an Approved NDA or ANDA, Questions and Answers, January 2001; U.S. Department of Health and Human Services, Food and Drug Administration, Center for Drug Evaluation and Research (CDER).
14. Guidance for Industry, BACPAC I: Intermediates in Drug Substance Synthesis, Bulk Actives Postapproval Changes: Chemistry, Manufacturing, and Controls Documentation, February 2001; U.S. Department of Health and Human Services, Food and Drug

Administration, Center for Drug Evaluation and Research (CDER), Center for Veterinary Medicine (CVM).
15. Guidance for Industry, BACPAC I: Intermediates in Drug Substance Synthesis, Bulk Actives Postapproval Changes: Chemistry, Manufacturing, and Controls Documentation, June 1, 2006; U.S. Department of Health and Human Services, Food and Drug Administration, Center for Veterinary Medicine (CVM).
16. DMF Workshop, Arthur Shaw of FDA, March 25, 2002.
17. DMF Presentation, Arthur Shaw of FDA, October 26, 2003, revised for web posting June 20, 2006; FDA.gov Web site; web address: http://www.fda.gov/cder/Offices/ONDQA/presentations/shaw.pdf.

14 Obtaining Approval of New Drug Applications and Abbreviated New Drug Applications from a Chemistry, Manufacturing, and Controls Perspective

Dhiren N. Shah
Aventis Pharmaceuticals, Kansas City, Missouri, U.S.A.

INTRODUCTION

Chemistry, Manufacturing, and Controls (CMC) is a relatively small section (approximately 15–20%) of a typical new drug application (NDA), but it often becomes a reason for delay in the approval of NDA/biologics licensing applications (BLAs). For abbreviated new drug applications (ANDAs), however, the CMC section is significant (around 80–90%). This section also becomes quite important in the postapproval life-cycle management of the products. It should be noted that the CMC section is made up of three distinctly different but overlapping disciplines/sciences: synthetic/fermentation chemistry, analytical chemistry, and formulation chemistry. Also, the CMC section continuously changes with clinical phases. Typically during clinical phase 1 trials, the CMC section is quite small and contains laboratory-scale manufacturing experience for the drug substance and the drug products with quite simple analytical methodologies. During clinical phase 2 trials, the CMC section evolves to pilot-scale manufacturing of the drug substance and the drug products, and the specifications and analytical methodologies become more sophisticated. End of phase 2 (EOP2) usually becomes a pivotal point in the drug development since at this point decisions and major commitments are made to as to whether to go forward with the phase 3 clinical development and marketing authorization application (NDA/BLA). EOP2 means for the CMC section a major shift in planning and execution. The drug substance and drug product manufacture typically need to be moved to commercial site at a commercial scale, and the specifications and the analytical methodologies need to be upgraded and finalized. So, one can see that the CMC section is a "moving target." After the completion of clinical phase 3 studies, an NDA/BLA is submitted to the U.S. Food and Drug Administration (FDA) for review and approval. The CMC section of an NDA/BLA should contain all the relevant developmental information that bridges phase 1 through 3 leading up to the NDA/BLA submission.

This chapter will systematically analyze and describe the FDA organization, its various regulations and guidances, the industry process by which CMC information is generated and submitted, and various ways to compress timelines and secure timely approvals of NDA/BLAs and ANDAs. As this chapter is being written, it is expected that the CMC review and approval process for new chemical entities and possibly biotechnologically produced drugs and generic drugs at the FDA may undergo a paradigm change. However, the basic principles behind obtaining approval of NDAs/BLAs/ANDAs in a timely manner remain the same. It is anticipated that ICH Q8 (Development Pharmaceutics) and ICH Q9 (Risk Assessments) will reflect the paradigm shift at the agency.

CURRENT U.S. FDA ORGANIZATION

The U.S. FDA is one of the most important customers for pharmaceutical companies. In order to understand the review and approval process for the CMC section of NDAs and ANDAs, one should be familiar with the regulatory authority and the process in the United States. The U.S. FDA is an agency within the Department of Health and Human Services, and it regulates biologics, drugs, food, devices, and veterinary products. It is made up of eight centers/offices. The biologics such as vaccines and blood products are regulated by the Center for Biologics Evaluation and Research (CBER). The Center for Drug Evaluation and Research (CDER), which is the largest of the five centers in the FDA, regulates drugs that include NDAs and ANDAs. The devices are regulated by the Center for Device and Radiological Health (CDRH). Animal products are regulated by the Center for Veterinary Medicines (CVM). The Center for Food Safety and Applied Nutrition (CFSAN) regulates foods and nutritional products. The National Center for Toxicological Research (NCTR) regulates all types of toxicological research. The Office of the Commissioner (OC) and the Office of Regulatory Affairs (ORA) provide administrative and management support.

The CDER organization consists of therapeutic area–based review divisions. Each review division has the primary responsibility of reviewing submissions and provides an action that could involve approval, approvable, nonapproval, request for more information, etc. The review divisions are staffed by the division director, medical reviewers, pharmacologists, chemists, biostatisticians, bio-pharm reviewers, project manager staff, etc. The chemistry and bio-pharm reviewers report to the Office of Pharmaceutical Sciences (OPS). The Office of Generic Drugs (OGD) also reports to OPS. The OGD has two divisions of chemistry, each made up of five teams. This division of OGD is based on major therapeutic classes. As this chapter is being written, by the middle of 2005 the chemists from review divisions will be combined into one new drug chemistry group under the Office of New Drug Chemistry. The objective behind this change is consistency in reviews and better time management. This step is a predecessor to other CMC review and approval practices changes being planned at the agency.

Various regulations as published in the 21 Code of Federal Regulations (CFR), guidances and points to consider (PTC) published by FDA, the Manual of Practices and Procedures (MaPP) published by FDA, and guidelines published by the International Committee on Harmonization (ICH) are important documents that become the foundation of scientifically and regulatorily sound CMC submission documents.

FDA AND ICH CMC/QUALITY REGULATIONS AND GUIDANCES

FDA regulates new drugs as well as generic drugs under the Federal Food, Drug, and Cosmetic Act enacted by the U.S. Congress. The law, among other things, ensures that drugs and devices are safe and effective for their intended uses and all labeling used is truthful, accurate, informative, and not deceptive. Chapter 5 and specifically subchapter A of the act provides for Drugs and Devices. The interpretation of the act is provided in the CFR, which is published annually. There are 50 titles/sections in CFR, and title 21 specifically provides interpretation of the Federal Food, Drug, and Cosmetic Act. Typically the regulations are brief and often difficult to fully interpret for actual implementation. FDA issues guidances and PTCs, which provide further interpretation of the regulations. FDA also publishes MaPPs, which are approved detailed instructions to FDA reviewers in order to standardize reviews of submissions.

The reader is encouraged to make use of all FDA guidances and manuals. If properly used, they will ensure the quality of CMC submission, which should result in approval by FDA.

FDA'S QUALITY BY DESIGN AND PAT INITIATIVE AS PART OF CENTURY GOOD MANUFACTURING PRACTICES

FDA, in its latest initiative for the Twenty-First Century Good Manufacturing Practices has, among other things, two initiatives named Quality-by-Design (QbD) and process analytical technologies (PAT). PAT should not be considered as "infinite testing," but it is a part of the QbD. Both of these initiatives go to the basics of product development, whether it is for a new drug or a generic product. By employing basic principles of science-based drug substance and drug product development, one can achieve QbD. The whole idea behind QbD and PAT is to build quality into the drug product from the very beginning of the manufacturing process so that testing for quality at the end may not be that critical. For example, a thorough physical, chemical, and biological (as necessary) understanding of all the components of the dosage form and a complete analysis and knowledge of all the critical manufacturing processes should result in a product in which the quality is built in and there may be limited need for final testing for quality. Properly selected in-process testing and controls should provide the basis for QbD. PATs embrace the principles of QbD and include at-line, on-line, off-line, and in-line testing of in-process materials at critical stages of manufacturing. PAT provides for continuous manufacturing and real-time release of the product and the possibility of replacing the conventional validation batches. The reader is encouraged to read and follow FDA's draft guidance on PAT. One of the ways to successfully obtain approval of NDAs is to "retro-engineer" the drug substance and drug product. Once the sponsor identifies the final characteristics of the drug product to be marketed (dose, dosage type, shape, color, marking, packaging, etc.), a development and regulatory plan should be generated that will determine what kind of CMC information needs to be generated—and when—to secure an approval by the agency. Figure 1 summarizes the QbD and PAT initiatives. Aspects of QbD and PAT will be discussed later in this chapter.

SPONSOR COMPANY AND AGENCY PROCESSES TO SUCCESSFULLY DEVELOP THE CMC SECTION OF NDAs AND ANDAs BASED ON QBD AND ICH/FDA REGULATIONS

The activities at the sponsor company in regard to CMC development from pre-IND through various phases of INDs leading up to the NDA and, in the case of generic drugs, the process leading up to ANDA determine one's success or failure. The product one delivers to FDA is the CMC submission, and its scientific quality determines its successful approval by the agency.

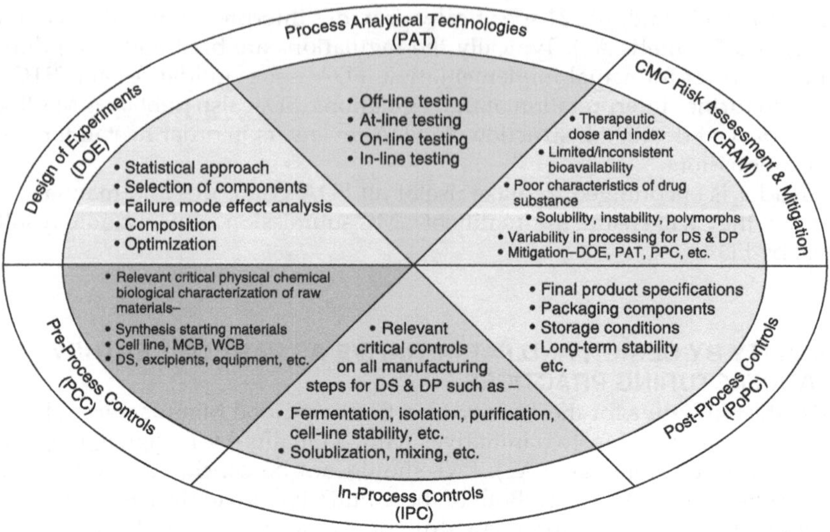

FIGURE 1 Quality-by-design and process analytical technologies initiatives.

Pre-IND Phase

In this very early phase of drug development some basic work is performed. Preliminary solubility in various solvents, stability, and other important structural elucidations and characterizations are typically determined, which become the basis for future development of the new molecular entity. Of course, limited work is done at this stage, since the failure rate for new molecular entities (NMEs) is quite high. The CMC information from this stage typically becomes the basis for development pharmaceutics, and as the drug development progresses, additional tests and information are carried out.

IND Phase 1

This phase is still an early phase of product development and a limited and necessary effort is typically made. Since CMC is a multifunctional section, it will be highly beneficial to put together multifunctional teams consisting of scientists from drug substance synthesis, formulation, analytical, regulatory, writing group, etc. This team of people becomes responsible and accountable for putting together the CMC section of the IND and following the new drug's progress through phases 2 and 3 and making sure an NDA is filed on a quality submission. In some instances, a sponsor may want to request a pre-IND meeting, which could be in the form of a teleconference, with the agency to seek advice and/or clarification. The agency requires that a briefing document be submitted by the sponsor at least 4 to 6 weeks prior to the meeting. The briefing document should contain relevant information on the drug substance and drug product and concise questions about which the sponsor seeks advice from the agency. FDA requires limited CMC information in a phase 1 IND. The main emphasis is on the safety of the volunteers and patients, and hence the sponsor is required to make a connection between preclinical material and the proposed clinical material from impurity and bioavailability points of view. (It is conceivable that the material used in the preclinical safety studies was not as bioavailable as the clinical material posing a safety risk to the patients.) Also, if the clinical material has any impurity with safety implications, the agency will want to know more about it. At the time of submitting an original IND, very limited stability information is required. A commitment to generate concurrent stability data during the course of a clinical trial and reporting the data in most cases should suffice. It is the sponsor's responsibility to make sure that the NME is stable in the dosage form when given to patients. During this early phase of clinical development, the analytical methods should be capable of determining the assay, impurities, etc., with specificity, accuracy, and precision. A formal validation of methods typically is not required at this early stage of development. Of course, as the drug development progresses, the analytical methods should be progressively validated so that they ensure strength, identity, purity, potency, and quality (SIPPQ) of the product. The sponsor must wait for a period of 30 days before initiating studies on human volunteers and patients. During this period, the agency determines whether the sponsor could proceed with proposed studies, and if it has any objection it will instruct the sponsor not to initiate the study (known as clinical hold) until the deficiencies are satisfactorily addressed. The agency has issued a guidance as to the format and the content of the CMC section of IND, and the reader is encouraged to read and apply it to fullest extent as possible.

IND Phases 2 and 3

IND phases 2 and 3 are pivotal and become the basis for successfully obtaining approval of NDAs, because under these phases critical CMC information that supports SIPPQ is generated, drug substance and drug product manufacturing are optimized, bioavailability of the drug product is established, and primary stability data for the drug substance and the drug product are generated. The multifunctional team plays a critical role in advancing the NME through phases 2 and 3 leading up to NDA submission. Based on input from the clinical studies through phase 2, the safe and effective dose of the drug is chosen and various QbD parameters for the drug substance and drug product are introduced in the product development. The agency requires that during phases 2 and 3 the sponsor inform the agency of any new patient safety–related information in the form of IND amendments. These amendments to the IND typically do not require a waiting period; however, if the new information is significantly different from the original and if it affects the safety of the patients in the clinical trials, then the agency may advise the sponsor not to implement the change. The usual changes to the CMC, such as optimization to synthesis/manufacture of the drug substance, analytical methods, the drug product, new stability data, etc., could be submitted in IND annual reports to the agency. The sponsor could take advantage of the IND amendments to update the agency on the progress in the CMC and identification of critical issues and proposed/planned solutions to the issues. During phase 2, typically, the drug substance and the drug product are produced in a large laboratory to pilot scale. At this phase, the drug substance synthesis/manufacturing, drug product formulation/process, analytical test methods, etc. are fine-tuned and the principles of QbD and PAT may be introduced and implemented. The EOP2 or the beginning of phase 3 becomes a pivotal point in the overall drug development process. At this point, the NME has shown a certain threshold for safety and desired efficacy and the drug development picks up the speed with which confirmation of clinical results from phases 1 and 2 are reached in a larger patient population in phase 3. The CMC has to match the increased clinical activity of phase 3 by gearing up all three disciplines: drug substance synthesis and manufacturing, drug product formulation and manufacturing, and analytical testing. Typically phase 3 clinical trials are conducted on many hundreds to thousands of patients, leading to marketing application. In this phase, the CMC section has to match the expanded clinical trials leading toward commercial distribution. In phase 3, the CMC section should focus on two important aspects of development: combining information and data from all three phases and bridging those with the future commercial product. FDA has issued a guidance for CMC information requirements for phases 2 and 3. The bridging study will be discussed in the next section.

Successful Bridging of Pre-IND, Phase 1, Phase 2, and Phase 3 with Commercial Product

One of the secrets of obtaining approval of NDAs and BLAs from a CMC perspective is successfully bridging the CMC information and data from preclinical through the three phases of IND and the commercial product. Bridging of critical information on SIPPQ starting from the preclinical phase leading up to commercial product is of utmost importance. Some important characteristics of the drug substance and the drug product are as follows:

Drug substance
Structural elucidation
Impurity/Related substances
Solubility
Critical relevant characteristics
Critical manufacturing information
Stability (RT and accelerated)
Drug product
Description
Degradation products
Dissolution

All relevant drug substance and drug product characterization information from all phases of development should be bridged to come up with a complete picture of strengths and weaknesses of the drug substance and the drug product. Key characteristics such as impurity profile, solubility of the drug substance, dissolution-friability balance (DFB) for SODF, accelerated/forced degradation to understand the mechanistic aspects of degradation, design of experiments, etc. should be bridged to get a complete picture of the drug product. The aforementioned information on the drug substance and the drug product from investigational phases is bridged to the planned commercial drug product. All of this bridging information, along with design of experimental data in which the boundaries of success and failures of all critical parameters (drug substance manufacturing processing parameters, formulation components, composition, processing equipment and parameters, in-process controls, specifications, etc.) are determined, become part of developmental pharmaceutics and should be included in an NDA. It should be emphasized that bridging in the form of evolution of analytical procedures starting from preclinical phase to phase 3 and commercial product testing should be thoroughly discussed in developmental pharmaceutics.

Developmental Pharmaceutics and Its Importance to CMC

As discussed earlier, Design of Experiments, QbD, PATs, bridging of all the phases of INDs, technology transfer, etc., become the basis for developmental pharmaceutics, which becomes the foundation of a good CMC section of NDAs and ANDAs. It provides an overview of the thoughts and rationale behind the product development and commercial product to the CMC reviewing staff at the agency and becomes an important tool in the review and approval process. The ICH CTD format also provides for a section for Development Pharmaceutics. ICH Q8 is on developmental pharmaceutics, and once this guidance (which is at early stages of its development at this time) is finalized, it should provide appropriate guidance to the industry.

Technology Transfer to Manufacturing

It is obvious that at the EOP3 clinical trials the most critical and important step is to make sure that the drug product is "manufacturable," because without it the new drug could not be commercialized. Over the past 30 years, major pharmaceutical and generic companies have often failed to produce commercial products immediately upon approval of NDAs/ANDAs because companies failed to perform timely technology transfer. Technology transfer involves transferring of information and experience from laboratory and pilot scales to a commercial level for the drug substance, drug product, and associated analytical testing procedures. All these become the basis for seamless and sound manufacturing of the new drug on a commercial scale.

Quality-by-Design and Process Analytical Technologies

As this chapter is being written, the OPS under CDER is in the process of redesigning and introducing a paradigm shift in the CMC reviews and compliance investigations. It is expected that by the end of 2005 the agency would have implemented the planned changes in CMC reviews and compliance investigations. The ICH through initiation of Q8 (Pharmaceutical Development) and Q9 (Risk Assessment) is also gearing up toward the same goal of OPS. Both ICH Q8 and Q9 will involve the concept of QbD. QbD, which encompasses PATs and embraces building quality in the process and product throughout the manufacturing process, may be summarized as follows:

QbD = preprocess controls (PPCs) + in-process controls (IPCs) + postprocess controls (POPCs)

PPCs: Preprocess controls (throughout the preclinical, the three phases of INDs, and for commercial production) such as thorough physical-chemical-biological characterization of the (1) drug substance and all its manufacturing/synthesis components and (2) excipients. The drug substance starting materials, its other components (catalysts, solvents, etc.), key and pivotal intermediates, etc., should be thoroughly characterized. The pharmacopoeias provide fairly good chemical characterization, but do not provide thorough functional physical characterization, and it is up to the sponsor to develop that characterization. The drug substance physical and chemical characterization is of critical importance to successful QbD. Some examples of PPCs are chemical purity of starting materials and intermediates, purification steps, drug substance particle size and specific surface area, density, excipient particle size and shape, density, etc.

IPCs: In-process controls are the heart of PATs. IPCs such as assay, purity, residual solvents, particle size, specific surface area, polymorphism, etc. are critical in the manufacturing of drug substance. For drug products, IPCs such as granulation endpoints, moisture level, content uniformity, etc. are critical. PATs could involve off-line, at-line, in-line, and on-line testing of in-process parameters for drug substance and drug product. Carefully and strategically chosen IPCs, if done in-line or on-line, may obviate final testing because of the large sample size.

PoPCs: Postprocess controls play an important role in QbD. Testing of final drug product per specifications, storage conditions, and long-term and accelerated stability studies are components of PoPCs.

Sponsor–FDA Meetings

FDA allows several kinds of meetings with sponsors in order to assist and gather information. Meetings such as pre-IND typically are clinical oriented. For CMC section, end of phase 2 and pre-NDA meetings are important for the CMC section of NDAs and BLAs. (FDA has issued a guidance on sponsor–FDA meetings.) The sponsor should submit a briefing document to the agency at least 6 weeks prior to the requested meeting, and the briefing document should contain relevant background information and questions on which the sponsor is seeking advice. The briefing document should not be voluminous. It should be a focused document that contains specific questions/issues. The sponsor can easily enhance its NDA/BLA/ANDA submissions by taking advantage of these meetings.

NDA Submissions

NDA submission on a new drug should follow the FDA and ICH guidance. From a technical regulatory perspective, if all the work is done properly as described in sections (a) through (h), the NDA submission should become fairly easy and result in approval in a timely manner. The submission should follow the FDA and ICH guidances, and, moreover, it should be reviewer friendly. The data should be presented in a clear-cut manner. One should remember that the product that the FDA sees from an applicant is the NDA/ANDA submission. The chemistry reviewers have a responsibility to make sure that the product they approve meets the regulatory requirements as prescribed in the CFR. Submissions to the FDA should be accurate and of high quality.

All submissions to the FDA must meet four important criteria in order to secure approval the first time:

1. Adherence to Regulations and Guidances—strict adherence to FDA CMC regulations and guidances for format and content, which include those ICH quality guidelines that have reached step 5. It is possible to adopt an approach other than that provided by the FDA guidances; however, it is the applicant's responsibility to secure approval on the alternative approach from the FDA reviewing staff (e.g., at EOP2 and/or Pre-NDA meeting). Careful and strategic implementation of guidance should be received from the reviewing staff at the FDA.
2. Introduction—submissions should have an introductory section that clearly provides the purpose, scope, and context of the submission that helps the reviewing team. This introduction should have a clear delineation of any agreement made prior to the submission. The introductory section should provide a

higher-level overview of the submission, which will lead into the next section, where the nuts and bolts of the submission are provided. This section should end with a summary of the submission.

3. Body of the submission—this part of a submission is of utmost importance since it provides the main basis for approval. The chemistry review staff has to provide a rationale for their action (approval, nonapproval, approvable, etc.) and a good introduction and summary aids them in making their decision. The information provided in submissions must be focused, relevant, precise, accurate, complete, and of quality. When it comes to quality of the submission, one should adopt the philosophy of "quality always." In this main body of the submission, one should pay special attention not to provide redundant and unrelated information, because it takes away from the reviewers' attention and wastes their precious time. The submission should have a logical flow of information and justified decisions based on scientific rationales. The logical flow of information and justified decisions along with clear objectives and findings that lead to clear conclusions provide a coherent submission. The main body of the submission should follow the time-tested organizational characteristics of a sound beginning, experimental details, organized results, discussion of results, and conclusions. Information should be provided with an appropriate combination of text, figures, tables, etc., which will provide a clear picture of the submission. The information should convey a clear message and conclusion and should follow the usual standards of quality (free of typographical and grammatical errors, clear legends, footnotes as necessary for clarity, etc.).
4. A summary and conclusion section should be provided, including any short- or long-term commitments (such as placing batch(es) of drug product on long-term stability and reporting the data to the agency at a later date, etc.).

ANDA Submissions

The ANDA submission on a generic drug should follow the FDA guidance. FDA has provided a clear-cut format and content guidance on the organization of an ANDA. Section VII of the guidance provides for detailed CMC requirements. The applicant should provide a statement on the components and composition of the product. This should be followed by information on raw materials (active ingredient and inactive ingredients), description of manufacturing facility, information on the outside/contract firms, manufacturing process and packaging instructions, in-process information, packaging material controls, controls for finished dosage form, analytical methods for the drug substance and drug product, stability of finished dosage form, and availability of samples. If the generic product is a parenteral product, the applicant must provide sterilization assurance information and data package. The earlier CMC section is somewhat similar to the NDA requirements, and if it follows the earlier recommendations, obtaining approval for an ANDA should be easy. The CMC section should be preceded by information on the bioavailability/bioequivalence of the dosage form in relation to the reference-listed drug.

Quick and Complete Response Team Approach to FDA Questions/Comments

Once an NDA or ANDA has been submitted by an applicant and filed (meaning accepted) by FDA, during and/or after the completion of the review, FDA might have questions/comments on the submission. The questions/comments may come verbally or in writing. In either case, it is very important for the applicant to respond to the questions/comments in a timely, thorough, and accurate fashion. Often applicants form a team [such as quick and complete response (QCR)] that develops complete and timely responses that aid the agency's review process. The QCR team, if properly organized, could play an important role in obtaining the approval of NDAs in a timely manner.

UNDERSTANDING THE CMC REVIEW PROCESS

The CMC review process at FDA is quite transparent. The agency publishes its most current Office of New Drug Chemistry (ONDC) organization chart and several MaPPs. The primary CMC review chemists review the submissions and share their reviews with the chemistry team leaders. Based on their reviews, they may issue information request letters. Alternatively, CMC reviews are further reviewed by CMC division directors and then ultimately by the director of ONDC. Once the reviews are finalized by the CMC reviewers and ONDC management, the review division director will issue appropriate letters (approval, nonapprovals, approvable, etc.). The CMC reviewers issue a review report, which includes their assessment and reasons for their recommendations. As stated earlier, the overall CMC review and approval processes may change in 2005 as a result of ICH Q8 and Q9. However, it should be remembered that the basics and fundamentals of CMC reviews (and compliance inspections) will focus on SIPPQ, which are surrogates of safety and efficacy of drugs. The OGD follows a similar review process. Of course, for ANDAs the final reviews stop at the OGD head level. The CMC reviewers have a legal responsibility to review and assess CMC submissions and to make sure that the submissions meet the law and regulations and the product meets the SIPPQ requirements. If for some reason a product is recalled because of SIPPQ, then the reviewing staff that approved the product is in part responsible. Thus, understanding the review process and the responsibility of the reviewing staff is important in obtaining approval of NDAs/BLAs.

As this chapter is being written, the OPS is planning for a paradigm change in the CMC reviews and compliance. The ICH through Q8 (Pharmaceutical Development) and Q9 (Risk Assessment) is also gearing up toward the same goal of OPS.

PROBLEMS AND CHALLENGES INVOLVED IN SECURING TIMELY APPROVALS AND POTENTIAL SOLUTIONS

Most delayed approvals are due to poor science contained in the submission and poor submission strategy. The poor science may be reflected in instability of the product or unacceptable levels of impurities or poor product bioavailability as measured by tablet dissolution, etc. A good product development plan based on the principles of QbD (see earlier) should result in an approvable submission. Judicial use of contacts with the agency and maximizing various FDA–sponsor meetings should avoid delays in the approvals of applications. Agency reviewers are available to assist the industry as long as it is done in a professional manner. The Agency is pushing for science-based regulations and review practices. Applicants should take advantage of this new paradigm to secure approvals in a timely manner. As described in section "NDA Submissions" earlier, the quality of submission is critical in securing approval of applications in a timely manner.

SUMMARY AND CONCLUSIONS

This chapter has offered some practical ways to develop a science-based, regulatory friendly application that should be approved at first submission. By focusing on the fundamental scientific principles and FDA and ICH guidances, it is quite feasible to obtain approval of NDAs and ANDAs. In order to obtain approval of NDAs/ANDAs in a timely manner, one should focus on four pillars: (1) development of CMC based on QbD/PAT, (2) application of FDA and ICH CMC regulations and guidances, (3) bridging of phases 1 through 3 to a successful NDA, and (4) preparing sound CMC scientific and regulatory submissions.

REFERENCES

1. Fed Reg, Vol. 69, No. 68, April 8, 2004, Code of Federal Regulations, Title 21, Part 314.70.
2. FDA, Center for Drug Evaluation and Research, "Changes to an Approved NDA or ANDA," Guidance Document (Apr. 2004).
3. FDA, Center for Drug Evaluation and Research, "Immediate Release Solid Oral Dosage Forms: Scale-up And Post-Approval Changes: Chemistry, Manufacturing and Controls; In Vitro Dissolution Testing; In Vivo Bioequivalence Documentation," Guidance Document (Nov. 1995).
4. FDA, Center for Drug Evaluation and Research, "Sterilization Process Validation in Applications for Human and Veterinary Drug Products," Guidance Document (Nov. 1994).
5. FDA, Center for Drug Evaluation and Research, "SUPAC-IR Questions and Answers," Guidance Document (Feb. 1997).
6. FDA, Center for Drug Evaluation and Research, "SUPAC-SS— Nonsterile Semisolid Dosage Forms; Scale-Up and Post-approval Changes: Chemistry, Manufacturing, and Controls; In Vitro Release Testing and In Vivo Bioequivalence Documentation," Guidance Document (June 1997).
7. FDA, Center for Drug Evaluation and Research, "Dissolution Testing of Immediate Release Solid Oral Dosage Forms," Guidance Document (Aug. 1997).
8. FDA, Center for Drug Evaluation and Research, "Extended Release Oral Dosage Forms: Development, Evaluation, and Application of In Vitro/In Vivo Correlations," Guidance Document (Sept. 1997).
9. FDA, Center for Drug Evaluation and Research, "SUPAC-MR: Modified Release Solid Oral Dosage Forms: Scale-Up and Post-approval Changes: Chemistry, Manufacturing, and Controls, In Vitro Dissolution Testing, and In Vivo Bioequivalence Documentation," Guidance Document (Oct. 1997).
10. FDA, Center for Drug Evaluation and Research, "PAC-ALTS: Postapproval Changes-Analytical Testing Laboratory Sites," Guidance Document (Apr. 1998).
11. FDA, Center for Drug Evaluation and Research, "Stability Testing of Drug Substances and Drug Products," Draft Guidance Document (June 1998).
12. FDA, Center for Drug Evaluation and Research, "Metered Dose Inhalers (MDI) and Dry Powder Inhalers (DPI) Drug Products: Chemistry, Manufacturing, and Controls Documentation," Draft Guidance Document (Nov. 1998).
13. FDA, Center for Drug Evaluation and Research, "SUPAC-SS: Nonsterile Semisolid Dosage Forms Manufacturing Equipment Addendum," Draft Guidance Document (Jan. 1999).
14. FDA, Center for Drug Evaluation and Research, "SUPAC IR/ MR: Immediate Release and Modified Release Solid Oral Dosage Forms, Manufacturing Equipment Addendum," Guidance Document (Feb. 1999).
15. FDA, Center for Drug Evaluation and Research, "Bioavailability and Bioequivalence Studies for Nasal Aerosols and Nasal Sprays for Local Action," Draft Guidance Document (June 1999).

16. FDA, Center for Drug Evaluation and Research, "Container Closure Systems for Packaging Human Drugs and Biologics," Guidance Document (July 1999).
17. FDA, Center for Drug Evaluation and Research, "NDAs: Impurities in Drug Substances," Guidance Document (Feb. 2000).
18. FDA, Center for Drug Evaluation and Research, "Analytical Procedures and Methods Validation: Chemistry, Manufacturing, and Controls Documentation," Draft Guidance Document (Aug. 2000).
19. FDA, Center for Drug Evaluation and Research, "Waiver of In Vivo Bioavailability and Bioequivalence Studies for Immediate Release Solid Oral Dosage Forms Based on a Biopharmaceutics Classification System," Guidance Document (Aug. 2000).
20. FDA, Center for Drug Evaluation and Research, "Changes to an Approved NDA or ANDA: Questions and Answers," Guidance Document (Jan. 2001).
21. FDA, Center for Drug Evaluation and Research, "BACPAC I: Intermediates in Drug Substance Synthesis: Bulk Actives Post-approval Changes: Chemistry, Manufacturing, and Controls Documentation," Guidance Document (Feb. 2001).
22. FDA, Center for Drug Evaluation and Research, "Statistical Approaches to Establishing Bioequivalence," Guidance Document (Feb. 2001).
23. FDA, Center for Drug Evaluation and Research, "Nasal Spray and Inhalation Solution, Suspension, and Spray Drug Products—Chemistry, Manufacturing, and Controls Documentation," Guidance Document (July 2002).
24. FDA, Center for Drug Evaluation and Research, "Comparability Protocols—Chemistry, Manufacturing, and Controls Information," Guidance Document (Feb. 2003).
25. FDA, Center for Drug Evaluation and Research, "Bioavailability and Bioequivalence Studies for Orally Administered Drug Products—General Considerations," Guidance Document (Mar. 2003).
26. FDA, Center for Drug Evaluation and Research, "Requests for Expedited Review of NDA Chemistry Supplements," Manual of Policies and Procedures MAPP 5310.3 (June 1999).
27. FDA, Center for Drug Evaluation and Research, "Drug Shortage Management," Manual of Policies and Procedures MAPP 4730.1 (Nov. 1995).
28. CFR, Title 21, Part 314.81(2). Other postmarketing reports—Annual Reports.
29. CFR, Title 21, Part 211.180. Current good manufacturing practice for finished pharmaceuticals—Records and Reports—General Requirements.
30. CFR, Title 21, Part 211.100. Current good manufacturing practice for finished pharmaceuticals—Production and Process Controls—Written procedures, deviations.
31. CFR, Title 21, Part 211.160(e). Current good manufacturing practice for finished pharmaceuticals—Laboratory Controls—General Requirements.
32. CFR, Title 21, Part 314.3(b). General Provisions—Definitions.
33. FDA, Center for Drug Evaluation and Research, "Format and Content for the CMC Section of an Annual Report," Guidance Document (Sept. 1994).
34. FDA, Center for Drug Evaluation and Research and Center for Biologics Evaluation and Research, "Formal Meetings with Sponsors and Applicants for PDUFA Products," Guidance Document (Feb. 2000).
35. CFR, Title 21, Part 314.50(a)5. Content and format of an application—cc Application form.
36. Pharmaceutical Research and Manufacturers of America, 2002 Industry Profile, PhRMA, Washington, DC, 2003.
37. DiMasi JA, Hansen RW, Grabowski HG. The price of innovation: new estimates of drug development costs. J Health Econ 2003; 22:151–185.
38. Grabowski H, Vernon J, DiMasi J. Returns on research and development for 1990s new drug introductions. Pharmacoeconomics 2002; 20(suppl 3):11–29.
39. FDA, Center for Drug Evaluation and Research. "A Framework for Innovative Pharmaceutical Manufacturing and Quality Assurance," Draft Guidance Document (Aug. 2003).
40. "GSK Announces FDA Approval of Their First PAT Submission," AAPS News Magazine (Apr. 2004): 10.
41. FDA, Center for Drug Evaluation and Research, "M2 eCTD: Electronic Common Technical Document Specifications," Guidance Document (Apr. 2003).

42. FDA, Center for Drug Evaluation and Research, ''M4 Organization of the CTD,'' Guidance Document (Aug. 2001).
43. FDA, Center for Drug Evaluation and Research, ''M4 The CTD Quality,'' Guidance Document (Aug. 2001).
44. FDA, Center for Drug Evaluation and Research, ''Providing Regulatory Submissions in Electronic Format—NDAs,'' Guidance Document (Jan. 1999).

15 Obtaining Approval of a Generic Drug, Pre-1984 to the Present

Loren Gelber
RRI Consulting Inc., Lake Wylie, South Carolina, U.S.A.

INTRODUCTION

In order to obtain approval of a generic drug product, a sponsor must submit an abbreviated new drug application (ANDA) to the FDA's Center for Drug Evaluation and Research (CDER) Office of Generic Drugs (OGD). The sponsor can be a drug company that intends to manufacture the generic drug itself and has performed the necessary research to obtain the data required for submission, which will be described in this chapter. Alternatively, the sponsor could be some individual or group that has done the research or obtained the rights to the research performed by others, even if the sponsor does not intend to manufacture the product itself. For simplicity in this chapter, we will refer to the sponsor as the applicant.

The goal of the applicant is to receive FDA approval of the proposed product with a rating that means that FDA considers the generic product bioequivalent to the brand-name drug product produced by an innovator company. If a generic product has such a rating, pharmacists may substitute that generic product for the brand product or one bioequivalent generic product for another. In FDA language, this innovator product is called the reference listed drug. Since the generic drug is "equivalent" to the brand, the former does not have to repeat the preclinical animal studies or the clinical human studies that were performed on the brand in order to prove that the brand product is both safe and effective.

In this chapter, we will cover several aspects of getting a generic drug product approved. There are a number of essential parts of this process. First the applicant must select a product to work on. Second, a formulation and manufacturing process for the generic drug product must be developed that show promise of producing a product that will be bioequivalent to the reference listed drug. Then one or more batches of the generic product must be manufactured. In most cases, one or more human bioequivalence trials (biostudies) must be performed on the product manufactured. Various chemical and physical tests must also be performed on this product. It must be demonstrated to be stable through its labeled expiration period. When sufficient information has been obtained, an ANDA is prepared and filed with the FDA.

We will discuss some general principles related to how to decide what product to pursue, how to develop a formulation, how to perform a biostudy, and how to prepare an ANDA. The information needed to submit the application will be considered in the ANDA preparation section. We will cover both the newer, common technical document (CTD) format, and the older format traditionally used by OGD and likely to be found if the reader encounters ANDAs submitted before 2008. We will end this chapter with a short discussion of applicant activities between submission of the ANDA and its approval.

Before we proceed to the substance of this chapter, a short review of the history of the FDA generic drug approval process is in order. For a detailed discussion of this history, the reader is referred to the Rosen chapter in the First Edition of this book (1).

Prior to 1984, generic drugs were available for new drugs approved between 1938 and 1962. FDA approved these drug products based on safety data—efficacy studies were not required at that time. In 1962, with the passage of the Kefauver–Harris Amendments, there were significant changes made and requirements added to the FD&C Act of 1938. One of those requirements was that efficacy studies were required for the FDA approval of new drugs. In order to justify the approval of new drugs approved between 1938 and 1962, FDA subsequently established the drug efficacy study program that required data to be submitted through clinical trials which would demonstrate efficacy. Information was also taken from the scientific literature to justify full approval of older products.

The drug efficacy study program review required that new drug products have sufficient data to demonstrate that they are effective. FDA suggested that these new and rather extensive programs would not be necessary for generic drugs—which were intended to be the same as brand-name (or new) drugs. Further, these brand-name drugs had by that time established a marketing history of safety and with published literature. In order to provide an appropriate generic drug approval process, FDA established what was referred to as a "paper" NDA. A generic drug application to FDA was then required to contain documentation that included safety and efficacy data available in the published literature along with an in vivo study that showed the generic drug product to be bioequivalent to the brand-name product. However, that process had limited value because of the lack of sufficient published literature.

The "paper" NDA process for FDA approval of generic drug products continued until 1984, when Congress passed the Hatch–Waxman Act, after lengthy discussion between the two sectors of the pharmaceutical industry—manufacturers of brand-name and generic drug products (2). The Waxman–Hatch Act provided a reasonable pathway for approval of generic versions of products approved by FDA after 1962.

DECIDE WHAT PRODUCT TO PRODUCE

With the earlier background and history established, the first step in obtaining approval of a generic drug is selecting the product to work on. Each generic drug product is declared by FDA to be equivalent to an innovator product that was originally approved via a full New Drug Application (NDA). Selection of the proper reference listed drug is critical to market success.

Depending on the strategy of the firm involved, one may choose the easy route or the hard route. The easy route is to work on a product for which there are already generic equivalents. One of the reasons this is the easy route is because there will be a body of information available from FDA and possibly also in the scientific literature about the product. This information can be very valuable during product development and biostudy testing. FDA will also be familiar with the product and what is required for it to be approved. The hard route is to work on a product for which there are no generic equivalents, usually because the product is still under patent or because it is difficult to formulate a product that is bioequivalent to the innovator product.

When considering which product to pursue, one of the first places to look for product information is the FDA *Orange Book* (3). Fortunately, this is available electronically on the FDA Web site: www.fda.gov. The address of the home page of the electronic *Orange Book* is http://www.fda.gov/cder/ob/default.htm. FDA also has another very useful electronic resource for information about drugs, called Drugs@FDA, http://www.accessdata.fda.gov/scripts/cder/drugsatfda/index.cfm. Using these resources, one can determine how many generic equivalents of a product are approved and the names of the holders of the approved applications. The patent numbers and expiration dates of all patents applicable to any NDA or ANDA, and listed by the owner of the brand drug application with the FDA, can be found in the electronic *Orange Book*. For many NDAs and a few ANDAs, the summary basis of approval document that indicates why FDA approved an application and describes the data on which the decision was based can be found at Drugs@FDA. Current and previous labeling can often be found at Drugs@FDA or at the NIH Daily Med website.

If generic equivalents already exist, the *Orange Book* and Drugs@FDA will indicate what their equivalence is to the innovator product. Two-letter codes are used for this purpose. If the first letter of the code is A, the product with this code is considered bioequivalent. The second letter of the code represents different situations. Product coded AA, AN, AO, AP, and AT do not require biostudies in order to be approved, because there is no evidence that they have any bioequivalence problems. These products are less expensive to pursue, but there are almost always many competitors for them. Products rated AB require biostudies that demonstrate bioequivalence of the applicant's product to the reference listed drug.

If the first letter of the code is B, the products are not bioequivalent to each other. FDA is in general unwilling to approve any new generic products with B ratings and is attempting to upgrade existing products with B ratings to AB status if possible. For further discussion of this rather complex topic, see the Preface to the *Orange Book*.

While the issue of pharmaceutical patents is covered in chapter 4, a discussion of practical aspects will be included in this chapter. The *Orange Book* listing of patent numbers is provided by the holder of the NDA for the innovator product. Patents lists were established by the Hatch–Waxman Act passed by Congress in 1984 (2). If an applicant has decided to submit an application for a product that has one or more patents listed in the *Orange Book*, the applicant needs to research the patents and decide whether it wants to, and can, challenge the validity of some or all of the patents, or develop a formulation that does not infringe on those patents that claim unique formulations. There are several ways in which an applicant can approach these patents and deal with, or certify, them in its application. A short discussion of the types of patent certifications appears later in this chapter.

One of the reasons that research is needed is that there are several different types of patents listed in the *Orange Book*. It is the opinion of this author that a patent covering the molecular structure of the drug can only rarely be successfully challenged by generic competitors. The original use for which the product was approved may be in the same patent or a different one. The applicant must usually wait for all of these patents to expire before it can receive final approval of an ANDA that refers to the reference listed drug included in the patent. It often seems to the layman that more than one patent is granted for the same purpose; this requires clarification from patent attorneys.

Patents for uses other than the one approved in the original NDA can be overcome by submitting, in the patent certification section of the ANDA, a statement that the generic drug application is not requesting approval for the other patented indication or indications. This statement is called a Section (viii) notice. In this case, all references to the patented indication or indications being certified must be removed from the proposed labeling included in the ANDA application.

Formulation patents require analysis by both chemists and attorneys, who are experts in pharmaceutical patents. Skilled formulators often devise products that are intended to "engineer around" restrictions created by formulation patents. In many cases, applications which certify that they do not infringe formulation patents result in litigation. The litigation outcome may hinge on the judge's interpretation of a few words in the patent being challenged. One must also consider the doctrine of equivalents, discussion of which is beyond the scope of this chapter.

To add to the complex situation described earlier, starting in the 1990s innovator firms began to list patents that have only a tenuous connection to the reference listed drug. These include patents for other crystal forms, isomers, and metabolites. Innovator firms maintained that they interpreted the Hatch–Waxman Act to require them to list any patent connected to the active ingredient in their product, even when the patent did not cover the final dosage form. This situation was somewhat corrected by the Greater Access to Affordable Pharmaceutical Act, which became law in 2003 (4). However, such "stretch" patents may still be encountered. See chapter 4 and a pharmaceutical patent attorney for more details.

When an ANDA contains a certification that a patent listed in the *Orange Book* is invalid or will not be infringed, there is a requirement that the ANDA applicant notify the patent holder of the filing of the ANDA and its certification. The applicant must also notify the holder to the approved NDA if different from the owner of the patent (5). There are rules for what needs to be in this notification and it is usually written by a pharmaceutical patent attorney. The applicant needs proof that the notifications were received by the required persons. That is the reason for notifications being submitted by Certified Mail, as required by FDA regulation.

In the majority of cases, the ANDA applicant will be sued for patent infringement if the application contains a certification that a patent is invalid or will not be infringed. If this occurs, FDA may not approve the ANDA for "30 months after the date of the receipt of the notice of certification by patent owner or by the exclusive licensee (or their representatives) unless the court has extended or reduced the period because of a failure of either the plaintiff or defendant to cooperate reasonably in expediting the action" (6). This provision is referred to as the 30-month stay.

One can see that filing an ANDA citing a reference listed drug that does not have any approved generic equivalents poses some risk. In an attempt to partially counterbalance this risk, the Hatch–Waxman Act provides 180-day exclusivity for the first applicant to file a substantially complete application containing the required biostudies and a Paragraph IV certification. The rules for this exclusivity have undergone a number of changes since the act was passed in 1984. The reader is referred to chapter 7 for further discussion of this complex subject.

In addition to the patents listed in the *Orange Book* at the time the ANDA is filed, the applicant must file a certification amendment if a new patent is listed in the *Orange Book* before the ANDA is approved. The owner of the patent may choose to initiate an infringement suit against the ANDA applicant based on this patent. In the past, a patent owner who sued based on these later patents would get a new 30-month stay; however, this potential for extensive blocking of ANDA approval has now been eliminated. Only one 30-month stay is permitted.

There are also economic considerations involved in deciding whether to file an ANDA citing a reference listed drug that does not have any approved generic equivalents. When patents for a reference listed drug with high sales are due to expire, many other firms are likely to prepare and submit ANDAs. If there is a potential for 180-day exclusivity, one or a few firms may make a great deal of money during this period. At the end of this exclusivity period, or if there are no other patents to challenge and thus no potential for exclusivity, many ANDAs will probably be approved on the same day. Having 13 or more manufacturers enter the market at the same time is quite possible and has happened more than once. In this case, competition is fierce and the sales pricing drops quickly. The product becomes a commodity, and the product may not be very profitable. The lower the sales units of the reference listed drug, the less likely this is to happen. These "niche" products can paradoxically produce much better profits than "blockbusters."

Another possible strategy is to submit a citizen's petition to FDA requesting approval of one of the permitted variations from a reference listed drug. One variation is an additional strength within those supported by the safety and efficacy data pertinent to the reference listed drug. This is also a complex area, discussion of which is beyond the scope of this chapter, and appropriate experts should be consulted.

As if this situation is not complicated enough, the Hatch–Waxman Act also granted various types of exclusivity to holders of NDAs. The most important type of exclusivity is new chemical entity (NCE) exclusivity, because FDA is not allowed to accept an ANDA citing a reference listed drug with NCE exclusivity in force (7). NCE exclusivity is awarded if the active moiety of the active ingredient in the new drug product has never before been approved in the United States. NCE exclusivity is not awarded if a different salt or ester of the active ingredient is already approved. NCE exclusivity is granted for 5 years from the date the NDA is approved.

There are several other types of exclusivity. For these, FDA may accept an ANDA but may not make its approval effective until the exclusivity expires. Orphan drug exclusivity is granted for 7 years. New indication, new combination, new dosing schedule, new dosage form, new ester or salt of the active ingredient, new chemical entity, new patient population, new route, and new strength exclusivities are granted for 3 years. For most of the exclusivities listed in the previous sentence, an applicant can carefully craft the submission not to include the matter subject to the exclusivity. However, occasionally the patent owner will sue and/or submit a citizen's petition to FDA, arguing that the exclusivity should apply to the ANDA so crafted.

A newer type of exclusivity is pediatric exclusivity. This is granted if the owner of an NDA obtains certain new information about the use of the product in children via new clinical trials. Pediatric exclusivity is an extension of an earlier patent or exclusivity for 6 additional months. It is usually granted shortly before the patent or exclusivity being extended expires. The prudent applicant involved in an ANDA for a product under patent or exclusivity checks the exclusivity listing in the *Orange Book* every month, when updates and supplements are listed.

DEVELOP A FORMULA

Once a firm has selected a candidate product to develop, the next step is to develop a formulation that can provide successful bioequivalence studies. The requirements for such studies are described in the next section of this chapter.

Patent issues aside, there are many techniques for developing a bioequivalent formulation. There are two commonly used approaches, that is, reverse engineering the reference listed drug to better understand its characteristics or building on a known formulation that for a similar product. These approaches can also be used together.

FDA regulations declare, "For certain drug products, the in vivo bioavailability or bioequivalence of the drug products may be self evident." These include liquid dosage forms that are true solutions, containing the same active and inactive ingredients in the same concentrations as the reference listed drug, and are used in parenteral, ophthalmic, or otic applications. Solution products administered by inhalation that contain the same active ingredients as the reference listed drug are also included. Topical and oral solutions (including elixirs, syrups, and tinctures) that contain the same active ingredients as the reference listed drug and do not contain any inactive ingredient that differs from those in the reference listed drug that may significantly affect drug absorption are also considered self-evidently equivalents. All of these products can be considered for a waiver that allows them to be approved without bioequivalence studies (8).

Parenteral products are required by FDA to include their qualitative and quantitative compositions in their labeling, so the formulator needs only to follow the labeling to make a product that FDA will accept. Ophthalmics or otics will list the concentration of any preservative present in the labeling and often the osmolality and/or pH, but other ingredients are listed only qualitatively.

In the reverse engineering approach, simple and sophisticated chemical and physical tests are applied to the reference drug product to determine its exact qualitative and quantitative composition. While listing of inactive ingredients in the labeling of solid dosage forms is technically voluntary, the author is not aware of any product that does not contain this list in its package insert. This can be helpful when trying to make an exact copy of a reference listed drug. However, there is a loophole. If the innovator claims that the reference listed drug contains ingredients that are trade secrets, these may be listed as "other ingredients."

In the late 1980s, just after the Hatch–Waxman Act passed, several firms tried to use reverse engineering to guide their formulators. It is interesting that solid dosage form products produced in this way failed bioequivalence studies more often than would be expected. As a result, formulators are more likely to use variations on known formulas. If the firm wishing to develop a generic drug already has a successful product that is similar, using a similar formulation for the new product is often a good starting point. Basic physical pharmacy textbooks and research articles in journals such as *Pharmaceutical Technology* can be good sources for basic formulas as well.

If the formulator chooses to be creative and use an original formulation, he or she must be aware of FDA's safety rules for generic drug formulations. FDA will not question the safety of an inactive ingredient if it has been used in an approved drug product and the level used in the proposed products is not higher than the highest level already approved for patient consumption via that route of administration. Since this information is generally part of the proprietary information in many applications, FDA published an Inactive Ingredient Guide, which may be accessed

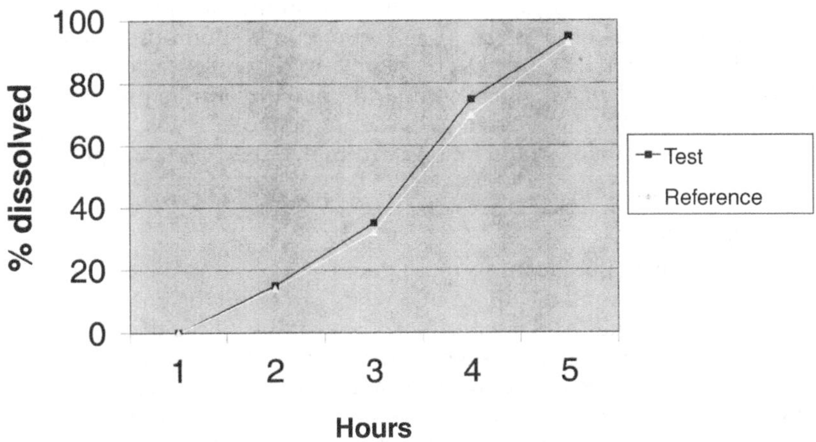

FIGURE 1 Graph of a typical comparative dissolution profile, obtained by measuring the dissolution of the proposed generic product and the reference listed drug every hour for 5 hours.

from the FDA Web site. While it is not always completely accurate, this guide is a valuable resource for formulators. OGD is now requiring excipient compatibility studies, which should be performed before the final formulation is selected. These requirements are part of the Quality by Design initiative. The author is aware of several generic product applications that were rejected by FDA but may have been acceptable if such studies had been performed.

How does the formulator know when he or she has developed a promising formulation? First, the product must be suitable for manufacture on a commercial scale. Extremely fragile (friable) tablets, ingredients that are very hard to blend uniformly, blends that do not flow well in manufacturing equipment, or processes that use toxic solvents are examples that the formulator must avoid. Second, one must obtain some information on the nature of the bioequivalence requirements. Then, if a biostudy (or two) is required, an in vitro test that can serve as a surrogate is highly desirable.

The most common surrogate for bioequivalence is the in vitro comparative dissolution profile for a solid dosage form. Typical results obtained for a comparative dissolution profile are shown in Figure 1, in which the generic drug is the test and the reference listed drug is the reference. A dissolution test measures the amount of drug that dissolves in a specific time, generally using diluents and apparatus defined in the United States Pharmacopeia (USP) (9). A dissolution profile is a group of measurements on the same dosage unit at various times. Comparative dissolution profiles compare the dissolution profiles of the average of 6 or 12 units of two different products or two different lots or two different versions of the same product.

OGD lists many FDA-approved dissolution tests on its Web site: http://www.accessdata.fda.gov/scripts/cder/dissolution/index.cfm. If a dissolution method exists in the USP or European Pharmocopeia (EP), or if a test approved for the reference listed drug can be obtained from FDA via a Freedom of Information request, then dissolution profiles using these conditions are a good place to start developing a predictive test. It is not unusual to find that different conditions are more predictive, in which case profiles under both sets of conditions must be included in the

ANDA, using 12 dosage units of each of the lots used in the bioequivalence trials. If there is no established dissolution test, FDA recommends submitting data using USP media at pH 1.2, 4.5, and 6.8 (10). FDA has defined a difference factor and a similarity factor that can be calculated when comparing two dissolution profiles (11).

Unfortunately, dissolution is not always predictive of bioavailability or bioequivalence. If it were, there would be no need to ever perform bioequivalence studies.

DO A BIOSTUDY OR TWO

Before considering even a pilot biostudy, those people involved in the design of the study protocol must evaluate all the information they can about the pharmacokinetics of the drug substance and the drug product. For example, if the drug substance has three characteristics—(*i*) the drug substance is highly soluble in water, (*ii*) biological membranes are likely to be highly permeable to the drug substance, and (*iii*) the dissolution of the drug product is high—then absorption of the product from the gut is unlikely to be the rate-limiting step in the distribution of the product throughout the body (12). If these conditions are met, any formulation that gives adequate dissolution should be bioequivalent to any other formulation.

While it is relatively easy to determine drug substance solubility and drug product dissolution, it is more difficult to determine membrane permeability. Methods for the latter exist and there are contractors who can do this for an applicant. Further discussion of these methods is beyond the scope of this chapter. If an applicant can determine permeability, a biostudy waiver can be requested in the ANDA. If the waiver is approved, the applicant does not need to conduct any biostudies. As of October 2007, few firms have been successful in obtaining such a waiver, usually because submitted permeability data is not adequate. If the drug substance is 100% bioavailable relative to a solution or if other information in the labeling of the reference listed drug makes it clear that membrane permeability is very high, this alone could be enough to demonstrate permeability for a waiver. In other cases, actual laboratory tests will be needed (13).

The standard design of a bioequivalence study is a two-way crossover, following an approved study protocol. The subjects are divided into two equal, randomly assigned groups. The first group receives the test product, while the second receives the reference product. Blood samples are taken at appropriate stated intervals and frozen for measurement of the concentration of drug in the sample. If there are important active metabolites, these will be measured as well. After a suitable time period following the first part of the study, called the washout period, the first group receives the reference product and the second group receives the test product. When all samples for each subject are collected, the analysis of each subject's samples from both periods is done sequentially, to minimize the effect of analytical variability. The results for each subject obtained during the two periods are compared.

In order to properly design a biostudy, one must have a good estimate of the expected time of maximum absorption t_{max} and the elimination half-life, $t_{1/2}$. The maximum time is needed to make sure that enough blood samples are taken before and after t_{max}. Since the blood levels change most rapidly near t_{max}, enough samples must be taken to ensure adequate data for estimation of the maximum blood concentration achieved, c_{max}. The elimination half-life is needed to decide how long to take blood samples in order to get a good measurement of the area under the blood concentration curve versus time, generally referred to as AUC. A good estimate of

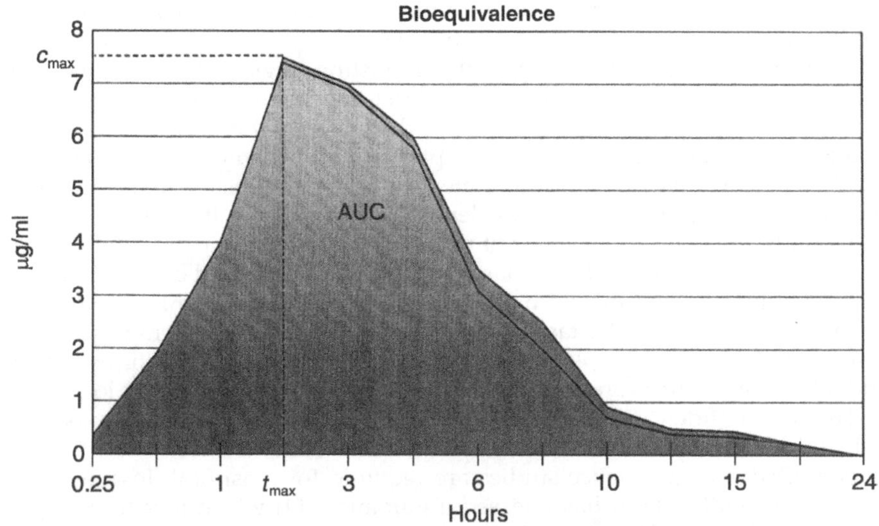

FIGURE 2 Graph illustrating the results of a typical biostudy. Drug level in blood is measured at various times, and the c_{max}, t_{max}, and AUC of the test and reference products obtained are compared.

c_{max} is also needed so that the method used to analyze the blood samples can be validated in the proper range. Figure 2 provides a graphic illustration of t_{max}, c_{max}, and AUC.

Values for t_{max} and t_{max} can sometimes be obtained from the labeling of the reference listed drug product and/or from the scientific literature. However, it is not infrequent for these values to differ from those obtained in the specific population to be used for the bioequivalence trials. Unless one has confidence in the data available, or if no data can be obtained, it is quite prudent to run a small pilot bioavailability study on the reference listed drug in about 4 subjects, representative of the population to be used for the bioequivalence studies.

Very few generic drug firms do their own biostudies, especially not the clinical portion, because it takes a very large product development program to keep an in-house biostudy clinic busy full time. Instead, these studies are done by separate firms called contract research organizations (CROs). At times the CRO may choose to perform the study needed to get an estimate of t_{max}, c_{max}, and $t_{1/2}$ in its subject population under its own auspices, rather than having a customer pay for it. Be forewarned, however, that this usually means that the CRO anticipates having many customers for its services involving this drug product.

Pilot bioequivalence studies are conducted on a small number of subjects. More subjects are used when the expected variability between subjects is higher. If an insufficient number of subjects are used, there is a large risk that the conclusions drawn from the results of the pilot study will not agree with the results of the full-sized study. The purpose of a pilot study is to obtain a relatively quick and inexpensive estimation of how close the bioavailability of the generic drug under development is to its reference listed drug.

It is advisable to perform a pilot biostudy for all but the simplest and most bioavailable products. It is imperative to perform a pilot study when there is any possibility that the dissolution profile does not reflect the actual bioavailability of the product and for all modified release products.

There are three types of biostudies, that is, fasting single dose, food effect single dose, and multiple dose steady state. At least one fasting single-dose study is required for every ANDA, except for products that are self-evidently bioequivalent, as discussed in the earlier section of this chapter, or product whose *Orange Book* rating is AA rather than AB. An AA rating means that the product is not regarded as having any actual or potential bioequivalence issues as long as it meets the appropriate dissolution specifications. Most, if not all, AA products that are solid dosage forms refer to reference listed drugs that were originally approved before 1984.

The standard to determine whether a biostudy passes is average bioequivalence. This means that, for the fasting single-dose biostudy, the average $c_{\max}$, the AUC measured to the last sample time, and the AUC extrapolated to infinity for the test and reference products are compared. These values are compared as log transforms. The 90% confidence interval (CI) of the ratio of the test to reference products for each of these three parameters must fall between 0.800 and 1.250.

Food effect bioequivalence studies are required for most oral dosage forms that require biostudies. FDA has released a guidance (14) which lists three types of immediate release oral products that are exempt from the requirement for food effect studies. The first is that products are exempt from the requirement for fasting studies based on solubility and permeability, as discussed earlier. The second is for a product for which the labeling of the reference listed drug requires that it be taken on an empty stomach. The third is for a product for which the labeling of the reference listed drug "does not make any statements about the effect of food on absorption or administration." Historically, the third reason has not, in many cases, been accepted by the OGD Division of Bioequivalence as a good reason for exempting a product from the requirements for a food effect bioequivalence trial.

There are additional complications in this area. For example, if the reference listed drug is labeled that it may be administered by sprinkling it on food, the generic applicant must demonstrate bioequivalence under these conditions in addition to all the other requirements.

The current guidance applies the same CI requirements to food effect studies that are applied to fasting studies. This was not true before 2002, and has increased the number of subjects used in food effect studies.

Multidose studies have been required for modified release products, but this is no longer the case. The FDA has determined that if a product is bioequivalent in a single dose fasting and a food effect study, it will be bioequivalent in a multidose study. Such studies are only required in special cases, the discussion of which is beyond the scope of this chapter.

Since transdermal products bypass the digestive system, their bioavailability and bioequivalence are measured without regard to food. Adhesion, skin irritation, and sensitization studies are also required for these products.

All of the above assumes that the level of the drug or its major active metabolites can be measured in plasma, serum, or urine. It also assumes that the drug product requires systemic absorption in order to be active. These assumptions are not true for topical, most nasal, and many inhalation products. For these products, a bioequivalence study with a clinical end point is almost always required. The end point must be one that can be clearly related to the function of the product under test. Its evaluation, especially if somewhat subjective, must be performed by a clinical team that is blinded to the identification of test versus reference products and well-qualified to evaluate the end point. Both active treatments, test and reference, must demonstrate superiority over vehicle and/or placebo. In most cases, bioequivalence studies with clinical end points do not differ greatly from the types of clinical trials used to demonstrate product efficacy. The reader is referred to chapter 9 for more details.

When an ANDA is submitted for multiple dosage strengths of the same product, it is usually not necessary to do all studies for each strength. Waivers from bioequivalence testing requirements are available for some strengths of a product line. FDA regulations permit waivers to be granted if the drug product for which the waiver is being requested meets three criteria. First, the drug product must be the same dosage form as the strength on which the biostudy or biostudies were performed. In other words, a tablet cannot be granted a waiver based on studies done on a capsule and vice versa. Second, the two strengths of the product must be proportionally similar in their active and inactive ingredient levels. Third, the product whose strength for which the waiver is being requested must meet appropriate in vitro dissolution requirements (15).

The General Considerations Guidance (10) gives three ways in which two strengths of a product can be proportionally similar. The first is when the ingredients are present in exactly the same proportions. In this case, a formulation for a 20-mg dosage form would contain exactly twice the amount of all ingredients as that for a 10-mg dosage form. When two products are formulated in this way, they are called "dose proportional." The second case is when two formulations differ from dose proportionality by no more than the amounts permitted by the postapproval changes guidances up to level II (16–17). The third case is limited to low-strength drugs. In this case, the total weight of the dosage unit stays the same, and the amount of one or more inactive ingredients is decreased by the same amount as the active ingredient is increased. The change in the amount of any inactive ingredient may not be more than that permitted by the postapproval changes guidances up to level II.

There are numerous additional details that must be controlled and rules that must be followed in order to achieve an acceptable set of biostudies for an ANDA submission. Before planning a biostudy, it is also necessary to check for a bioequivalence guidances on the FDA Web site that is specific to the product under consideration.

PREPARE A SUBMISSION

Since the First Edition of this chapter was prepared, OGD has transitioned from the older organization of an ANDA submission to the CTD format (18). The older organization of an ANDA was discussed in the earlier version of this chapter. It was formalized in a guidance dated February 1999 and was used for many years before that and is still being accepted by OGD as of the date this revised chapter is being prepared.

The CTD is a project of the International Committee on Harmonization (ICH) and applies to both NDAs and ANDAs. OGD strongly prefers that ANDAs be submitted in the CTD format. All of the information that was submitted in the older format, plus several newer items, are included in the CTD format. The discussion below will focus on the CTD format. However, the reader may well encounter older

ANDAs prepared in the earlier format. For this reason, differences between the formats will be pointed out as appropriate.

Cover Letter

The first page of every submission to an ANDA, whether it is an original submission, an amendment, a supplement, or other correspondence, must be a cover letter. This letter must make clear to FDA who is submitting the application and what they are submitting.

Regarding who is submitting the application, that is, the ANDA sponsor, the letterhead used for the cover letter and the signature of the applicant must match the corresponding fields in the FDA 356h form described later. All subsequent submissions must use the same letterhead and be from the same firm at the same address. If the name or address of the firm changes, FDA must be provided with adequate documentation. In a merger or sale, the agency wants documentation from both parties and a clear indication of who now owns the application.

The person whose signature is on the application cover letter and the 356h form will be the one to whom FDA will address all communications regarding the application, including telephone calls. It is most useful for this to be the employee who has the primary responsibility to prepare responses to FDA communications for this application. This is often the director of regulatory affairs. Be sure to provide phone and fax numbers so that FDA communications can be received expeditiously.

356h Form

The signed application form goes directly after the cover letter, in the first section of the application. An electronic form is available for download from the FDA Web site.

Fill in the Applicant Information section of the form to exactly match the information in the cover letter. If the firm submitting the application is located outside the United States, it is required that the firm appoint an agent with an office in the United States. The information about this agent should be placed in the appropriate box in this section. U.S. firms should leave this box either blank or fill it in as not applicable (N/A).

The first line of the product description section is left blank for an original ANDA submission. If a previously withdrawn application is being resubmitted, the number of the withdrawn application goes in this box. The generic name(s) of the product's active ingredient(s) are placed in the box marked Established Name. If a trade name has been chosen, this name goes in the Proprietary Name box. (Trade names require clearance from FDA in order to try to minimize the chances for errors due to similar names.)

The chemical name(s) of the product's active ingredient(s) are placed in the box marked Chemical/Biochemical/Blood Product Name. FDA usually prefers the official Chemical Abstracts name. For example, USP lists three names for ibuprofen in its active ingredient monograph:

Benzeneacetic acid, α-methyl-4-(2-methylpropyl), (±)
(±)-*p*-Isobutylhydratropic acid
(±)-2-(*p*-Isobutylphenyl)propionic acid [15687-27-1]

The third name is followed by a number in brackets. This is the Chemical Abstracts number, which can be used to search *Chemical Abstracts* for information about the compound, no matter which name is used in the publication. OGD has traditionally asked that the name before the Chemical Abstracts number in USP be the name used in the labeling and on the 356h form. If the active ingredient does not have a USP monograph, just use the chemical name in the reference listed drug labeling (RLD). OGD will tell you which name they prefer in their comments on your draft labeling.

Dosage form, strengths, and route of administration should be self-evident. The contents of the Indications for Use box should match the indication section of the labeling but may be paraphrased if it is too long to fit in this section. Be sure not to include any indications protected by exclusivity, unless you are requesting that your approval be made effective after the exclusivity expires. Refer to the *Orange Book* to be sure. If you include indications protected by a listed patent but not exclusivity, a patent certification regarding them will be required.

In the first box in the Application Information section, the box next to abbreviated new drug Application (ANDA, 21 CFR 314.94) should be checked. The next box is for NDAs only. In the next box, the trade name or brand name of the reference listed drug should be entered, as well as the name of the company that owns the approved application for this product. This entry should match the company listed in the *Orange Book* as owner of the application, regardless of who actually markets the product.

Since we are discussing a new ANDA submission, Original Application should be checked in the Type of Submission box. Partial submissions are not allowed for ANDAs, so the next box should be left blank. The box labeled If Supplement is also not applicable to original applications. The reason for submission is Original Application in this case. Proposed Marketing Status must be the same as that of the reference listed drug. Number of Volumes and Paper and/or Electronic should be self-evident.

For the last two sections on the first page of the 356h form, it is almost always necessary to attach one or more continuation sheets. In the Establishment Information section, the application must list all sites to be used to manufacture, package, and/or test both the bulk active pharmaceutical ingredient(s) and the finished product. Even an outside laboratory used to do one test must be listed here. The address, phone number, and name of a contact for FDA to call must be given. For firms in the United States that are required to be registered with FDA, the registration (CFN Central File Number or FEI Field Establishment Inventory number) number must be included. For firms that have Drug Master Files (DMFs), the DMF number must be provided. Finally for every firm listed, the applicant must state whether the firm is ready to be inspected or, if not, the date on which it will be ready.

A DMF is a separate submission made to FDA in which a firm other than the applicant can disclose information to the FDA that they do not want to disclose to the applicant because it is proprietary or a trade secret. FDA only reviews DMFs in connection with the review of an application; they are not independently reviewed.

Do not state that a firm is ready in the hope that it will be ready by the time FDA calls. It is not unheard of for the firm's District FDA Office to call to schedule a preapproval inspection shortly after the application is filed with FDA.

The last section of the first page of the 356h form is Cross References. For ANDAs, this is a list of all DMFs referenced throughout the application. In addition to the DMFs listed in the earlier section, packaging component suppliers and sometimes suppliers of inactive ingredients have DMFs. It is advisable to carefully review the assembled submission to ensure that all DMFs mentioned anywhere in the application are listed here. For every DMF mentioned, the holder of the DMF must send a letter to FDA for filing in the DMF, authorizing FDA to refer to the DMF on behalf of the ANDA applicant. A copy of each letter must be included in the appropriate section of the ANDA application.

The second page of the 356h form contains a list of various sections that might be included in an application. An initial ANDA submission normally contains item 2; labeling, items 4.A the chemistry section and 4.C the method validation package; item 6, the bioequivalence section; item 14, the patent certification section; item 16, the debarment certification; item 17, the field copy certification; and item 19, financial information for those who conducted the biostudies. Item 19 is normally provided by those who conduct the biostudies. These items do not appear in the application in the order they are listed on the 356h form.

Original ANDAs and NDAs are submitted in special covers available from the Government Printing Office. Make sure that the original 356h with the original signature, as well as the original of the cover letter, are placed in the archival copy of the ANDA; this is the copy that is submitted in the blue plastic covers and that contains all sections of the application. Also make sure that the address and telephone number on the second page match those on the first page.

Organization of Application

The current CTD format for ANDAs is organized into four modules. Module 1 is administrative, containing specific regulatory information required by FDA. Module 2 includes summaries of the important information in the succeeding modules. Module 3 is called the Quality module. It contains the information traditionally labeled Chemistry, Manufacturing and Controls (CMC). Module 4, Nonclinical Study Reports', is not applicable to ANDAs. Module 5 is called Clinical Study Reports and contains the biostudy reports. Each module will be discussed in some detail later. This discussion will be limited to the paper CTD; the electronic version will not be covered.

The Archival Copy goes in the blue plastic covers. It contains all modules. There are three other copies. The Chemistry copy goes in red paper covers. It contains modules 1, 2, and 3. The Bioequivalence copy goes in orange paper covers. It contains modules 1, 2, and 5. The Field copy goes in burgundy paper covers. It contains module 3, unless the firm has been told by their FDA District Office that other information should be included.

Module 1—Administrative

Module 1 contains the 356h form, the cover letter, a table of contents, a field certification, a debarment certification, financial certifications for those who conducted the biostudies, patent and exclusivity information and certifications, copies of all DMF authorization letters, a statement of the basis for the submission, a specific comparison between the generic drug proposed and its RLD, an environmental analysis, any requests for waivers of in vivo bioavailability studies, draft labeling, and the labeling of the RLD.

The 356h form and the cover letter were covered in the earlier sections. In the CTD numbering system, these are sections 1.1.2 and 1.2. The Table of Contents should be self-evident. It does not have its own number. The Field Copy

Certification states that a copy of module 3 has been sent to the appropriate FDA District Office simultaneously with the submission of the application to OGD. This copy should be sent to the District Office whose district includes the location of the applicant. This certification is numbered 1.3.2.

The Debarment Certification has two parts, each of which requires an original signature in the archival copy of the application. In the first part, the applicant certifies that they have not and will not use in any capacity any individual who has been declared debarred as specified in section 306(k)(1) and (3) of the Generic Drug Enforcement Act. A list of these individuals is maintained by FDA and can be found on the FDA Web site at http://www.fda.gov/ora/compliance_ref/debar/. The applicant must also certify that no one responsible for the development or submission of the ANDA has been convicted of a crime as defined by section 306(k)(1) and (3) within the last 5 years. Number these certifications 1.3.3.

As explained earlier, the contract research organization that performed the biostudies will provide the financial certifications for their staff. These need to be removed from the biostudy report and placed in module 1 and numbered 1.3.4.

The Patent and Exclusivity section used to be section III in the older ANDA format. It is section 1.3.5 of the CTD. If no patents for the RLD were ever listed in the *Orange Book* and the applicant is not aware that any other patents were ever filed, then the applicant should submit a Paragraph I certification. Suitable language would be "Paragraph I Certification: Company X (the applicant) certifies that patent information for product Y has not been submitted to FDA. In the opinion and to the best knowledge of (name of applicant), there are no patents that claim the listed drug referred to in this application or that claim a use of the listed drug."

If patents were listed in the *Orange Book* but they have all expired on the date the submission is sent to FDA, then a Paragraph II Certification is required. For example, "Paragraph II Certification: Company X (the applicant) certifies that all patents submitted to FDA for Product Y have expired." If there are patents still in force on the day of submission and the applicant does not intend to market the submitted product until they expire, a Paragraph III Certification is appropriate. Typical language would be "Paragraph III Certification: Company X (the applicant) certifies that Patent No. ZZZZZ will expire on QQ-QQ-QQQQ (date). Applicant requests that final approval of this application be made effective on that date."

Paragraph IV certifications are submitted when the applicant is challenging the patent or certifying that its product does not infringe on it. FDA regulations [21 CFR § 314.94(a)(12)(4)] give the language to be used: I, (name of applicant), certify that Patent N. ZZZZZ (is invalid, unenforceable, or will not be infringed by the manufacture, use or sale of) (name of proposed drug product) for which this application is submitted. Following the certification must be a statement that the applicant will comply with the requirements under section 314.95 (a) with respect to providing a notice to each owner of the patent or their representatives and to the holder of the approved application for the listed drug, and with the requirements under section 314.95 (c) with respect to the content of the notice. This notice as well as Section vii statements that the patents cover indications for which approval is not being sought is discussed in chapter 4.

The applicant must be sure to address any and all patents or exclusivity which is listed in the *Orange Book* for the RLD. An exclusivity statement must be included even if the RLD is not entitled to any exclusivity. For other types of exclusivity,

TABLE 1 Guide to Preparing Table for Section IV of an ANDA

	NDA holder's brand name of reference listed drug	Applicant's name of proposed generic drug
Conditions of use	e.g., Pain (exactly as in labeling)	e.g., Pain
Active ingredient(s)	Generic name of active(s)	Generic name of active(s)
Inactive ingredients (for products required to have the same inactive ingredients only, such as parenterals)	List all ingredients included in brand labeling	List all ingredients included in proposed product
Route of administration	Oral, parenteral, etc.	Oral, parenteral, etc.
Dosage form	Tablet, capsule, injection, ointment, etc.	Tablet, capsule, injection, ointment, etc.
Strength	X mg	X mg
Labeling	See section V	See section V

either request approval when the exclusivity expires or explain why the particular exclusivity is not applicable to the proposed product. For example, if the RLD has exclusivity for an indication which is not included in the labeling of the proposed product, it should be so stated.

The next part of module 1 is section 1.4.1, Letters of Authorization. This calls for copies of all DMF authorization letters. If the holder of the DMF is outside the United States, they are required to appoint a U.S. agent. A copy of the letter appointing this U.S. agent must also be included with each such DMF authorization letter.

The Basis for Submission, section 1.12.11 is either an RLD or a Citizen's Petition. If the basis is an RLD, the application should state that the basis is NDA number XX-XXX for product X. Use the name of the product exactly as it is stated in the *Orange Book*. If the basis for the submission is a Suitability Petition, for variations permitted by FDA law, the applicant must provide a copy of the approval letter for the Petition. If there is no RLD on the market, then a petition must be filed to have FDA declare that the RLD was not withdrawn for reasons of safety or efficacy. These petitions require legal advice.

The Comparison Between the Generic Drug and the RLD used to be section IV in the earlier format. It is now section 1.12.12. This comparison is usually submitted as a Table. Table 1 gives some guidance for preparing this item. With the exception of permitted variations in ingredients, the information for the RLD and for the proposed generic drug should be the same.

Environmental Analysis

The next section, 1.12.14, is titled Environmental Analysis. This was section XIX in the earlier format. For most ANDAs, this section is a claim of a categorical exclusion from the requirements to submit an environmental assessment because approval of the application will not increase the use of the active moiety. The applicant should refer to 21 CFR § 25.31(a) for details. A statement that the firm is in compliance with all federal, state, and local environmental laws is also needed. This section requires a signature, but it does not have to be original.

Section 1.12.15 is Request for Waiver of In-Vivo Bioavailability Studies. This is the place to request waivers from the biostudy requirements for those strengths that do not require such studies, as discussed.

Product Labeling

The last two sections in module 1 are for labeling. In the earlier format, labeling was section V. Section 1.14.1 includes four copies of the draft labeling for the proposed product, including insert, container labels, and any cartons. It also includes a side-by-side comparison of the proposed container labels and any carton labels with those of the RLD. In addition, all ANDAs submitted after June 8, 2004, have been required to include one electronic copy of the proposed insert labeling in Microsoft Word.

Section 1.14.3 is titled RLD. It includes the side-by-side comparison of the package and patient insert labeling with all differences highlighted and explained. It also includes one copy of each piece of labeling used by the RLD. Regarding the side-by-side comparison of the inserts, brand names in the reference labeling must always be changed to the generic name for the ANDA proposed labeling. It is not always easy to decide exactly how to do this, especially when the drug is a salt. There are two principles to keep in mind. First, the name of the product with its dosage form is used in the description of the product, in the Dosage and Administration section of the labeling, and in the How Supplied section. The second principle is that when the labeling is discussing the drug after it has been adsorbed into the circulation, any counterion is not included, since dissociation will have occurred when the drug enters the blood.

Module 2—Summaries

Module 2 is a new requirement; summaries were not required in the earlier format. These summaries are required for CMC and biostudy information, but not for microbiology as of November 2006. The proper way to prepare these summaries is to use the Question-based Review (QbR) format. The applicant should keep in mind that these are summaries and that the reviewer will use them to prepare the summary basis of approval. It is not appropriate to just reproduce all the information in the subsequent sections. Aspects of the discussion below are taken from the OGD presentations on Preparing a Quality Overall Summary for a Question-based Review ANDA (20), in November, 2006. There are also example summaries for IR tablets and ER capsules on the OGD Web site.

It must be emphasized that the applicant must check the summaries in module 2 very carefully against the information in modules 3 and 5. If the OGD reviewer finds any differences, the ANDA will be suspect and will be reviewed with extreme caution, taking a long time and producing many deficiency comments.

The first summary is for the chemistry of the drug substance(s), the active pharmaceutical ingredient(s) used in the dosage form. This is section 2.3.S and it has seven subsections.

Subsection 2.3.S.1 is General Information. The first question in this subsection is: What are the nomenclature, molecular structure, and molecular weight? The applicant should include the recommended international nonproprietary name, the compendial name if the substance is USP (often the same as the international nonproprietary name), any other nonproprietary names (such as those listed in USP and/or the Merck Index) and the CAS registry number. If the substance is chiral, be sure to include stereochemistry in the molecular structure.

The second question in subsection 2.3.S.1 is: What are the physicochemical properties, including physical description, pKa, polymorphism, aqueous solubility (as a function of pH), hygroscopicity, melting points, and partition coefficients? The

FDA wants all physicochemical properties listed, whether or not they are critical. If a property is left out, an explanation for the omission must be provided.

The next subsection, 2.3.S.2, is Manufacture. The first question is: Who manufactures the drug substance? The applicant should provide the name and address of each manufacturer. Make sure that the address is the actual manufacturing site, not the location of the firm's headquarters that does the paperwork. Also include all contractors used by the manufacturer and make clear the role and responsibility of each one. Include the DMF number and another copy of the letter of authorization provided in module 1. Make sure the letter includes the DMF number. The second question is: How do the manufacturing process and controls ensure consistent production of drug substance? In most cases, this information is in the DMF and the summary should state please refer to DMF XXX for this information.

Subsection 2.3.S.3 is Characterization. The first question is: How was the drug substance structure elucidated and characterized? Most of the information needed to answer this question will also be found in the DMF and should be referenced. However, the FDA says that the applicant should provide a discussion when certain properties, such as polymorphic form, particle size, solubility, pKa, or stereochemistry, are known to potentially affect drug product development, manufacture, and performance. The second question is: How were the potential impurities identified and characterized? A table of all known and unknown impurities in the drug substance is quite helpful in responding to this question. Identify known impurities by name and structure. Identify unknown impurities by relative retention time in the High Performance Liquid Chromatography (HPLC) test for impurities. Label each impurity as to whether it is a degradant or a process impurity. These can be distinguished by whether the level of the impurity has been seen to increase during stability testing.

The next subsection is 2.3.S.4, Drug Substance Specification. The first question is: What is the drug substance specification? A table giving the tests, specifications, analytical procedures, and results for the lot used to make the biostudy batch is most useful here. The second question is: Does it include all the critical attributes that affect the manufacturing and quality of the drug product? The answer to this question is based on the applicant's knowledge of the nature of the drug substance(s) and product. The third question is: For each test in the specification, is the analytical method suitable for its intended use and, if necessary, validated? Summary tables for the tests and validations are expected. The third question is: What is the justification for the acceptance criteria? Compendial and ICH specification references are appropriate. However, for parameters like particle size, there is often a connection made to the product development process and report, as discussed later.

Subsection 2.3.S.5 is Reference Standard. Its question is: How were the primary reference standards (RS) certified? If the firm used a USP standard, it should be so stated. If there is no USP standard, explain where the primary standard came from and how it was qualified. It should be emphasized that primary standards are the purest material available and that they are qualified with at least one additional qualitative and quantitative test, in addition to the tests in the drug substance specifications. If the firm uses in-house working standards, these should be listed and their qualification and testing be explained.

Container and Closure for Drug Substance is subsection 2.3.S.6. Provide a brief description of the container and closure in which the drug substance was received and then reference the DMF.

The last subsection for drug substance is 2.3.S.7, Stability. Its question is: What drug substance stability studies support the retest or expiration date and storage conditions for the drug substance? Here the applicant should state what retest or expiration date and storage conditions are being used for each active pharmaceutical ingredient (API). Since the actual testing is usually done by the API manufacturer, refer to the DMF.

We are now up to the second summary, which is for the drug product. The first subsection of this summary is numbered 2.3.P.1, Description and Composition, and its first question is: What are the components and composition of the final product? The second question is: What is the function of each excipient? The information required to answer the first question used to be Section VII in the earlier format, while the second question represents information that was not specifically addressed in the older format. This question is best answered with a table that shows each ingredient of the drug product, active, inactive, and those used in processing but not present in the final product. An example of the latter is water or solvent used in a wet granulation but removed during drying. Unless the ingredient does not appear in any official compendium give the grade, such as USP, National Formulary (NF), British Pharmacopeia (BP), European Pharmacopeia (EP), or Japanese Pharmacopeia (JP) for each. If there is no official standard, then state DMF holder standard, in-house standard, or the like. Typical functions of excipients are active ingredient, diluent, disintegrant, or lubricant. Include the amount present in each strength of the dosage form in a separate column. Do not include the amount per batch here, because it belongs in subsection 2.3.P.3.

The third question in this subsection is: Do excipients exceed the Inactive Ingredient Guide (IIG) limit for this route of administration? The IIG is the FDA Inactive Ingredient Guide which is published on the FDA Web site. Include a table to demonstrate that the answer to this question is no by comparing the highest amount of each ingredient present in the maximum daily dose to the IIG maximum daily dose information. If the answer to this question is not "no," the firm will have to prove safety to FDA. In some cases, the applicant can show that this ingredient is present in a product that was approved by FDA for this route of administration at or above the level used, which means it should be listed in the IIG but is not. If not, a long and arduous toxicology process will be required.

The last question in this subsection is: Do the differences between this formulation and the RLD present potential concerns with respect to therapeutic equivalence? For oral solid dosage forms, if the response to the earlier question is no and the product meets the bioequivalence standards, the answer to this question is no, and the application should simply state this. For all other dosage forms, a table comparing the RLD and the proposed product is needed and each difference needs to be explained and justified. It is advisable to make this table for solid oral dosage forms too.

The second drug product summary subsection is Pharmaceutical Development, 2.3.P.2. This section asks for new information that was not previously included in ANDAs. It has two sub-subsections. The first is, 2.3.P.2.1, Components of the Drug Product. The first question, 2.3.P.2.1.1, is: What properties or physical chemical characteristics of the drug substance affect drug product development, manufacture, or performance? OGD wants the ANDA applicant to identify which drug substance properties were studied and to summarize the findings of these studies. A typical example for solid oral dosage forms is active ingredient particle size. If the particle size is important to drug dissolution, the studies performed to establish the particle size range are summarized here. Question 2.3.P.2.1.2 is: What evidence supports compatibility between the excipients and the drug substance? OGD expects to see the results of various compatibility studies conducted under stress conditions summarized here.

The next sub-subsection is, 2.3.P.2.2, Drug Product. Its first question is: What attributes should the drug product possess? By this, FDA means what was the target product profile the formulator was trying to achieve? For example, an immediate release tablet might need rapid and complete dissolution to be bioequivalent to its RLD. It would also need acceptable content uniformity, stability, purity, and tablet characteristics such as friability. A pellet-filled controlled release capsule might need to have pellets of a given size, and dissolution performance as determined when developing the dissolution test and specification, as well as content uniformity, stability, and purity. A topical emulsion might need a controlled particle size, defined pH and viscosity, as well as acceptable homogeneity, stability, and purity.

The second, third, and fourth questions in this sub-subsection are: How was the drug product designed to have these attributes? Were alternative formulations or mechanisms investigated? How were excipients and their grades selected? The response to this question summarizes the thinking and experiments done by the formulators in order to achieve the target product profile in the proposed product.

The next sub-subsection in Pharmaceutical Development is 2.3.P.2.3, Manufacturing Process Development. It has four related questions: Why was the manufacturing process described in section 3.2.P.3 selected for this drug product? How are the manufacturing steps (and unit operations) related to drug product quality? How were the critical process parameters identified, monitored, and/or controlled? What is the scale-up experience with the unit operations in this process? This section may be optional for noncritical dosage forms and nonproblematic drug substances, such as oral solutions or immediate release dosage forms with highly stable active ingredients that exhibit good flow properties. Even when it is optional, it is advisable to include some justification for the proposed process, the in-process controls, and scale-up to commercial size. This is the applicant's chance to show OGD that the necessary work has been done and the product and process are well understood. An example of a study performed to justify an in-process parameter is a study of hardness versus dissolution for a tablet. At the time of submission, the applicant will probably only have scale-up experience with the proposed product from bench or experimental scale batches to the 100,000-dosage forms batch size used for the biobatch, that is, batch used for bioequivalence studies or batch whose information is to be submitted in the ANDA. However, if the applicant has other similar products, statements about experience in scaling these up might be useful.

The last sub-subsection in Pharmaceutical Development is 2.3.P.4., Container Closure System. It has one question: What specific container closure attributes are necessary to ensure product performance? The response to this question should include whether the container needs to be resistant to light transmission, how much moisture protection is needed, whether an inert atmosphere is needed and the like. For nonsolid forms, extractables, leachables, and migration of ink components from labeling need to be considered. For products with delivery devices, whether as simple as a dropper or as complex as a metered dose inhaler, delivery performance must be addressed.

The next subsection in the Drug Product Quality Overall Summary is 2.3.P.3., Manufacturing Process. Its first question is: Who manufactured the drug product? If all operations are performed in the same location, just give the name and address of the site, and state the regulatory status of its current good manufacturing practice (cGMP) certification and GDEA (Generic Drug Enforcement Act or debarment) certification. If more than one site is involved, a table should be provided for clarity. Be sure to explain the responsibility of each site. It might also be useful to state when the site was last inspected by FDA for cGMPs.

Question two for this subsection is: What are the unit operations in the drug product manufacturing process? Here OGD expects a detailed flow chart showing the unit operations, equipment, points of material entry into the process, and critical steps. There should also be a narrative summarizing the process through packaging, including the in-process controls. If the product uses a manufacturing process that the applicant suspects may be new to OGD, more detail should be provided. Do not include the actual master batch records; refer to their location in module 3.

The next question is: What is the reconciliation of the exhibit batch? OGD wants a summary of the accountability and yield of each submission batch throughout the manufacturing and packaging process. If the process has many unit operations, with a yield specification after each, a table is helpful. Explanations of deviations, investigations, or corrective actions taken because of low yield can be fully addressed in module 3.2. However, there are times when the existence of deviations in the manufacturing of an ANDA batch might mean that the process was not fully understood. In such a case, the applicant should consider correcting the problem and making a new batch.

The fourth and fifth questions are: Does the batch formula accurately reflect the drug product composition? If not, what are the differences and the justifications? The response to these questions is usually a table demonstrating that the unit composition, pivotal ANDA batch contents, and proposed commercial size batch contents are all proportional to each other. A table for each product potency is needed. Any overages used in manufacturing must be explained and justified. If the amount of active ingredient must be adjusted to account for active ingredient potency, as is done, for example, for certain antibiotics, this should be explained.

The next question is: What are the in-process tests and controls that ensure each step is successful? The answer should be a list or table giving the in-process tests, their acceptance criteria, the name or number of the analytical procedures, and the results for the ANDA batch(es). In many cases, the development of these tests and specifications will have been discussed in sub-subsection 2.3.P.2.3.

Scale-up planned from the size of the ANDA batch to the commercial batch size is covered in the last three questions of this subsection. Question seven asks: What is the difference in size between commercial scale and the exhibit batch? This question should be easy to answer by stating that the commercial batch will be n times the size of the exhibit batch. The number n should be no more than 10. Further scale-up should be delayed until some experience is gained at this size.

Question eight asks: Does the equipment use the same design and operating principles? This can be answered with a narrative or table comparing the equipment used for each unit operation in the development studies, ANDA batch, and planned commercial batch. The applicant can use the Scale Up and Post Approval Changes (SUPAC) manufacturing equipment addendum (17) to demonstrate that there is no difference in design and operating principles. Make sure that the equipment needed to manufacture the commercial batch is actually on site when the ANDA is submitted. If any equipment cited in an ANDA is not in place and qualified at the FDA preapproval inspection, the site will fail the inspection because it is not ready to manufacture the product.

The next-to-last question in this subsection is: In the proposed scale-up plan, what operating parameters will be adjusted to ensure that the product meets all in-process and final specifications? A frequent example of such a parameter is mixing time, which may be longer for larger mixers, depending on design and scalability. Other parameters are specific to the processes used. The last question asks: What evidence supports the plan to scale-up the process to commercial scale? OGD reviewers suggest using scale-up experience from development to pilot to ANDA batch size, prior experience with similar products and processes, and/or literature references including vendor scale-up factors. They remind applicants that in the absence of experience, or if difficulties are anticipated, no scale-up from ANDA to commercial size is always an option.

The next three subsections address analytical specifications. Subsection 2.3.P.4, Control of Excipients, has one question: What are the specifications for the inactive ingredients and are they suitable for their intended use? For USP or NF excipients that require no further testing beyond the compendial monograph, simply list the excipient and its manufacturer, and state that it complies with all USP or NF tests. If further testing has been shown to be required, list the tests, specifications, and results obtained on material used to make the ANDA batch(es). Noncompendial excipients and colors require a complete list of all tests, specifications, and results. If an ingredient of animal origin, such as gelatin, is used, reference the location of the information about steps taken to prevent Bovine Spongiform Encephalitis/Transmissible Spongiform Encephalitis. Novel excipients require details about manufacture, characterization and controls, or a reference to a DMF where this information may be located.

Subsection 2.3.P.5 is Control of Drug Product. Its first two questions ask: What is the drug product specification? Does it include all critical drug product attributes? All dosage forms are required to have tests for description, identification, assay, and degradation products. One specific identification test, such as the IR spectrum, or two nonspecific identification tests, such as retention time in HPLC, is necessary. Dissolution, uniformity of dosage units, water content, and microbial limits are among the other tests applicable to other dosage forms. The applicant should include a table of all tests used on the finished product, showing the specification, analytical procedure type, and results obtained on the ANDA batches. If the product is listed in USP, all USP tests should be included or their omission be explained. If there is a proposed monograph in USP Pharmacopeial Forum, its existence should be acknowledged and applicability to the proposed product be discussed. Degradation product limits should follow ICH rules and OGD guidance (21–24).

The next question for subsection 2.3.P.5 is: For each test in the specification, is the analytical method(s) suitable for its intended use and, if necessary, validated? OGD would like to see a summary of each method. For example, a table for an HPLC method would list the mobile phase, column, flow rate, temperature, detector, injection volume, run time, retention time, sample preparation concentration, and system suitability criteria. A summary table of the results of the method validation is also required. Such a summary might be a table of the results of specificity, linearity, precision, accuracy, and forced degradation tests. Compendial methods must be demonstrated to be stability indicating by using forced degradation tests as well as demonstrating that any known degradants do not interfere. This is required because different formulations may lead to different pathways of degradation. If the firm wants to use an in-house method when a compendial method exists, the two methods must be compared. It is acceptable for the two methods to be equivalent or for the in-house method to be superior.

The last question this subsection asks: What is the justification for the acceptance criteria? These may include compendial specifications, references to scientific literature and ICH/FDA guidance, results of the pharmaceutical development studies described in earlier subsections, or analytical data from batches produced.

The next subsection, Reference Standards or Materials, is 2.3.P.6. Its question is: How were the primary RSs certified? The response here is usually a reference to subsection 2.2.S.5, because the same RSs are usually used for drug product and drug substance. If there are any additional standards, provide the same information as that explained earlier for subsection 2.2.S.5.

Subsection 2.3.P.7 is next. It is entitled Container Closure System. Its first question asks: What container/closure system(s) is proposed for packaging and storage of the drug product? One or more tables, showing the container and closure sizes, material, and manufacturer for each package of each strength, are usually needed. Also include cap liners, desiccants, and other components of the primary package. Give a brief description of any carton or other secondary packaging.

The second question for this subsection is: Has the container closure system been qualified as safe for use with this dosage form? The response to this question is a list or table of the compendial and other appropriate tests that have been performed on the container and closure, their resins and colorants, or the system as a whole. Sections <87>, <88>, and <381> of USP are examples of tests for elastomeric closures. Sections <661> and <671> are applicable to many types of containers. 21 CFR § 174–186 deal with materials safe for food contact and may also be applicable to a drug product.

We have finally reached the last subsection of the Quality Overall Summary (QOS), Drug Product Stability, 2.3.P.8. Its first question is: What are the specifications for stability studies, including justification of acceptance criteria that differ from the drug product release specifications. A table of all stability specifications with their acceptance criteria and method types is used to respond to this question. Justify the absence of such tests as identification and content uniformity by stating that these attributes are not expected to change over time. If degradation has been observed during stability studies such that tighter limits are needed at release than those for the end of shelf life, an explanation is needed. The sample QOS on the FDA OGD Web site may provide further assistance.

The next question asks: What drug product stability studies support the proposed shelf-life and storage conditions? The response to this question should include a list or table of each batch that was placed into the stability testing program, the conditions used, and the packaging configurations involved. A summary table should also be provided for each parameter tested and whether any changes or trends were found. Indicate what expiration dating is being proposed and include the labeled storage conditions for the product.

The very last question is: What is the postapproval stability protocol? The storage conditions of the stability samples, their packaging configurations, testing intervals, and tests should be given. The minimum requirement is that the first three commercial batches, which will be used for the process validation, must be placed on room temperature stability testing and that at least one batch per year must be added to the stability testing program. The applicant must make a commitment to submit all stability data in the annual reports required for the ANDA and to handle any observed changes or degradation as per 21 CFR § 314.70(b) (1) (ii).

In addition to the long QOS described in the preceding paragraphs, module 2 must also contain a summary of the biostudies submitted in module 5. Number this section 2.7. OGD Division of Bioequivalence suggests that this summary be formatted similar to a bioequivalence review, to contain a table of contents, a submission summary, and an appendix. There are numerous tables, which are usually prepared by the CRO doing the biostudies. However, their accuracy is ultimately the applicant's responsibility, so it behooves those preparing the submission to check them carefully. They should be submitted on paper, in Microsoft Word, and as a pdf file made by Acrobat from the Microsoft Word file. Printing and scanning to make a pdf does not work, since too much resolution is lost.

The first section of the submission summary contains Drug Product Information. This includes the identity of the test and reference products, the reference product manufacturer, its NDA number, approval date, and approved indications. The next item is Pharmacokinetic and Pharmacodynamic (PK/PD) information. Information from the RLD labeling and/or scientific literature would be appropriate here. Often suitable information can be found in the introduction to the biostudy protocols. The next item, Contents of Submission, should list the title of each biostudy, dissolution profile, waiver request, and anything else relevant to bioequivalence submitted.

Pre-Study Bioanalytical Method Validation is the next item in the table of contents of a bioequivalence review. A table with the location of the biostudy reports (volume and page numbers), the analyte(s), internal standards, brief method description, limit of quantitation, average analyte recovery, standard curve concentrations, QC controls concentration, QC intraday precision range, QC intraday accuracy range, QC interday precision range, QC interday accuracy range, bench top stability, stock stability, processed stability, freeze thaw stability cycles, long-term storage stability in days, dilution integrity, selectivity, and a list of the CRO Standard Operating Procedures (SOPs) submitted in the report is requested.

A summary of the biostudies submitted is next. FDA requests a table that shows the study number, study objective, study design, number of subjects by gender, treatments (dose, dosage form, route, and product identity), c_{max}, t_{max}, AUC0-t, AUC∞, $t_{1/2}$, *Ke*, and study report location for each study. They also request a summary of the statistical analysis showing the test values, reference values, ratio, and 90% CIs for c_{max}, AUC0-t, and AUC∞.

The next item in the reviewers' summary is formulation. It is suggested that the same information in section 2.3.P.1 be provided here. This is followed by the in vitro dissolution profile information. Be sure to include the analytical method used or the applicant will receive a phone call asking for it, or perhaps even a deficiency. The last item in the summary is the waiver requests. Reproduce section 1.12.15, Request for Waiver of In-Vivo Bioavailability Studies.

Two additional tables are requested. The first is called Additional Study Information and contains the root mean square error for c_{max}, AUC0-t, and AUC∞, the number of subjects for which Kel and AUC∞ could be determined, the number of subjects with measurable drug concentrations at time 0 (predose), and whether the subjects were dosed as more than one group. The second table lists all study samples reanalyzed. This information includes the reason why the assay was repeated;

the number retested for each reason, test, and reference separately; and the number repeated expressed as a percentage of all samples.

There are also a number of tables in the appendix which document the reviewer's observations. Some or all of these may also be prepared by the CRO.

Module 3—Quality

Module 3 contains the details of, which used to be call the CMC, section of an ANDA. Similar to the summaries in module 2, it is divided into a section for the drug substance and a section for the drug product.

Section 3.2.S.1 is General Information (Drug Substance) and contains information about nomenclature, structure, and properties. Most, if not all, of this information is provided in section 2.3.S.1. This section may be reproduced and additional information, such as solubility, may be added.

The next section, 3.2.S.2, is called Manufacture (Drug Substance). This information is the same as that in section 2.3.S.2. The last drug substance section, 3.2.S.4, Control of Drug Substance, contains the testing specifications, sample spectra and chromatograms, and certificates of analysis for the drug substance manufacturer and the applicant. It also contains a statement that samples are available and will be submitted as soon as FDA requests them and instructs the applicant where to send them.

The first drug product section, 3.2.P.1, is Description and Composition of the Drug Product. This is the same information as in section 2.3.P.1. Pharmaceutical Development is section 3.2.P.2. The section contains a full report explaining the development of the formulation, manufacturing process, and container closure system. The information in section 2.3.P.2 is a summary of this report.

Section 3.2.P.3, Manufacture (Drug Product), comes next. Reproduce section 2.3.P.3 and add a full description of each firm, with its responsibility and functions. If outside contract laboratories are listed, make sure they are informed of what testing they might be required to do and that they have copies of any noncompendial methods. Each firm must provide a signed certification that they comply with all cGMP requirements for inclusion in this section.

The batch formulation (kg/batch), flow diagram of the process, and blank batch master records are part of section 3.2.P.3.2, Batch Formula (Drug Product). This section also requires a reprocessing statement. Reprocessing and rework procedures require prior approval from FDA. In general, OGD is reluctant to approve any such procedures, as they are taken as indication that the manufacturing process is not in control. The best reprocessing statement is that the applicant does not intend to perform any reprocess or rework in the course of manufacturing the product. The statement must also acknowledge that if any rework or reprocessing becomes required in the future, the applicant will submit a prior-approval supplement

The next section is 3.2.P.3.4, Controls of Critical Steps and Intermediates (Drug Product). All in-process controls should be given, with their specifications or acceptance criteria and a description of their test methods. After this section comes Process Validation and/or Evaluation (Drug Product), 3.2.3.P.5. Description, documentation, and results should be provided for any process evaluation or validation that has been conducted for the critical steps or assays used in the manufacturing process. Full-scale process validation is not required at the time of ANDA submission. It must be completed and approved by the manufacturer's Quality Unit before any product may be shipped. However, for sterile products microbiological sterilization validation and filter validation must be submitted in the ANDA.

Section 3.2.P.4, Control of Excipients, is next. The applicant should identify the manufacturers of all inactive ingredients used. A table would probably be the best way to do this. Subsection 3.2.P.4.1 is Specifications (Inactive Ingredients). Provide the specifications for each ingredient and the manufacturer's Certificate of Analysis here. For the next subsection, 2.4.P.4.2, Analytical Procedures (Inactive Ingredients), the applicant should state which excipients are subject to USP/NF specifications only. If there are any other tests, or noncompendial ingredients such as colors, the full text of those analytical methods belongs in this section. Subsection 3.2.P.4.3, Validation of Analytical Procedures (Inactive Ingredients), is usually not applicable for ANDAs, unless the applicant has developed a special test. Subsection 3.2.P.4.4, Justification of Specifications (Inactive Ingredients), contains the applicants Certificates of Analysis for each excipient lot used in an ANDA batch. If the applicant is using an excipient not in the IIG, results of pharmacology and toxicology studies belong in this section.

Controls of Drug Product, section 3.2.P.5, is the next section. Subsection 3.2.P.5.1 contains the drug product specifications. Subsection 3.2.P.5.2 contains the Analytical Procedures. Subsection 3.2.P.5.3 contains the Method Validation Report for the procedures in the earlier subsection. Following the Certificates of Analysis for the ANDA batch(es) are included in subsection 3.2.P.5.4, Batch Analysis. The next subsection, 3.2.P.5.5, is Characterization of Impurities. The applicant should place a list or table of all impurities expected or found in the drug product, with the identification of those that are known. It would be wise to relate these impurities to those observed in the drug substance(s). The last subsection, 3.2.P.5.6, is Justification of Specifications. The applicant can cite FDA Guidances, USP, ICH, or other relevant sources. If there is an impurity whose specification must be set above the ICH limits, the pharmacology and toxicology studies that support the higher specification belong in this subsection.

The next section is 3.2.P.7, Container Closure System. This used to be section XIII in the earlier format. The summary of the containers and closures from subsection 2.3.P.7 should be reproduced first. Next should be the specifications that the packager uses to accept each component and the test data for the lots used to package the ANDA batch(es). Then the applicant should include the engineering diagrams for each component which give the exact dimensions. These are available from the component manufacturer or supplier. Reports of compendial tests for the resins, colorants, components, and the system as a whole, such as water permeation, follow. The last item is a list of the name and address of the manufacturer of each component.

Stability, section 3.2.P.8, comes next. In the earlier format, this was section XVI. Include the Stability Testing Protocol and the proposed expiration dating period in subsection 3.2.P.8.1, Stability Summary and Conclusion; include the postapproval stability commitments from subsection 2.3.P.8 in subsection 3.2.P.8.2. The actual stability data reports go in subsection 3.2.P.8.3.

After all of the above, there is a section called 3.2.R, Regional Information. This section is for information required by FDA but not included in the CTD format. Subsection 3.2.R Drug Substance is used for the executed batch records for the API, which almost always is just a reference to the DMF. If the API is not a USP substance, include three copies of the Analytical Methods and their validation, for OGD to send to the laboratory that will test the samples. If there are any Comparability Protocols for the drug substance, discussion of which is beyond the scope of this chapter, they also go here.

Subsection 3.2.R Drug Product includes the executed batch records for each ANDA batch, including packaging records and reconciliations. FDA is also requesting information on components, including manufacturer information, function of contract facilities, and certificates of analysis, even though this information appears in other sections. Include three copies of the Analytical Methods and their validation, for OGD to send to the laboratory that will test the samples. If there are any Comparability Protocols for the drug product, discussion of which is beyond the scope of this chapter, they also go here.

Module 5—Clinical Study Reports

Module 5 is used for the biostudy reports. It should be kept in mind that the biostudy reviewer may not have access to the other modules, so certain information is repeated here. In the beginning of section 5.3.1, Bioavailability Study Reports, include the formulation tables. This is particularly important when submitting more than one strength and requesting a waiver from biostudy requirement for some of the strengths, as the reviewer will use this table to decide if the formulations meet the proportionally similar requirements. For parenterals, ophthalmics, otics, and topicals, also include a table comparing the formulation to that of the RLD. This is needed because the bioequivalence reviewer will decide if the proposed product meets the requirements for qualitative and for some products quantitative equivalence. This is referred to as Q1Q2 by the FDA.

Subsection 5.3.1.2, Comparative BA/BE Study Reports, is the location for the biostudy report(s) from the CRO. Subsection 5.3.1.3, In-Vitro-In-Vivo Correlation Study Reports, is the place for the comparative dissolution profile data, including mean, range, and standard deviation. This data is required for all solid dosage forms, suppositories, and oral suspensions. FDA is requesting that the validation of the analytical methods used for the biostudy be placed in subsection 5.3.2.4, Reports of Bioanalytical and Analytical Methods for Human Studies. All individual case report forms and individual subject lists go in subsection 5.3.7, Case Report Forms and Individual Patient Listing.

RESPONSE TO FDA COMMENTS

One to 3 months after the OGD receives the ANDA, the applicant can anticipate a letter indicating that the application has been accepted for filing and providing the ANDA number. If there is a relatively small matter preventing OGD from accepting the application, the usual procedure is for the Project Manager (PM) to call the person who signed the application and explain what is needed. A very quick response is required. If the application has a serious flaw, or if one does not respond quickly to the telephone call, the applicant will receive a refuse-to-file letter.

About 180 to 200 days after OGD receives the application, the applicant should anticipate receiving comment letters. Comments regarding the API, bioequivalence, drug product chemistry and labeling may be received separately or together. If the applicant has done a good job of preparing a consistent application in the CTD format, and if there are no difficult scientific issues involved, one might anticipate that the Division of Bioequivalence might have no comments other than informing the applicant of the official dissolution method and specifications, while the chemistry and labeling reviewers might require a Minor Amendment with information to respond to their concerns.

In OGD, each reviewer has a computer-generated work queue. New applications and Major Amendments go the bottom of the queue. Minor Amendments go after all other minors already in the queue but ahead of majors and new applications. As of this writing, OGD is short staffed and the difference in time between review of minor and major responses can be 6 months or more.

How an applicant responds to the FDA reviewer's observations is critical to how quickly the application can be approved. Read the comments very carefully. Make sure that your response addresses what the reviewer is asking for. Watch out for observations that require more than one item in their response. Include as much supporting data, as attachments or exhibits to your response, as is necessary to prove to the reviewer that your response is correct.

Sometimes the reviewer will ask for something that was already in the original submission. This should be less likely in the CTD format, but it is still possible. Politely point out in the response the section and page number where the information was located in the original application. It is a good idea to provide another copy as an attachment to the response for the reviewer's convenience.

APPROVAL

At this point, the applicant who has prepared a complete and consistent application and responded carefully and completely to all FDA requests for additional information can anticipate a speedy approval. As of this writing, the median time from submission to approval has varied from about 18 to 24 months. When you are close to approval, you may inquire with the OGD Program Manager assigned to your application as to the status of the approval package for your submission. This can help in planning scale-up, validation, and commercial marketing. The latter is, of course, the objective of the entire exercise, a commercial product that can produce profits for its sponsor.

REFERENCES AND NOTES

1. David L. Rosen. The pharmaceutical regulatory process. In: Berry, IR, ed. Drugs and the Pharmaceutical Sciences. Publisher: Informa Health Care, New York, 2005; 144:99–106.
2. The *Drug Price Competition and Patent Term Restoration Act of 1984*, United States Congress.
3. Approved Drug Products with Therapeutic Equivalence Evaluations. U.S. Food and Drug Administration, Published yearly and updated monthly.
4. The *Greater Access to Pharmaceuticals Act of 2003*, United States Congress.
5. United States Code of Federal Regulations (CFR). 21 CFR 314.95.
6. Food Drug and Cosmetic (FD&C) Act, United States Congress, section 505(2)(D)(ii).
7. United States Code of Federal Regulations (CFR). 21 CFR 314.90.
8. 21 CFR 320.22.
9. USP 30—NF 25, United States Pharmacopeial Convention,2007, section <711>.
10. Guidance for Industry; Bioavailability and Bioequivalence for Orally Administered Drug Products—General Considerations, U.S. Food and Drug Administration, March 2003.
11. Guidance for Industry; Dissolution Testing of Immediate Release Solid Oral Dosage Forms, U.S. Food and Drug Administration, August 1997.
12. Guidance for Industry; Waiver of the In Vivo Bioavailability and Bioequivalence Studies Based on a Biopharmaceutics Classification System, U.S. Food and Drug Administration, August 2000.

13. "Bioequivalence Review Issues," presentation by Dale Conner at the GPHA Fall Technical Conference, October 2007.
14. Guidance for Industry; Food-Effect Bioavailability and Fed Bioequivalence Studies, U.S. Food and Drug Administration, December 2002.
15. 21 CFR 320.22.
16. Guidance for Industry; Immediate Release Solid Oral Dosage Forms—Scale Up and Post Approval Changes; Chemistry, Manufacturing and Controls, In Vitro Dissolution Testing and In Vivo Bioequivalence Documentation (SUPAC-IR), U.S. Food and Drug Administration, November 1995.
17. Guidance for Industry; SUPAC-MR; Modified Release Solid Oral Dosage Forms—Scale and Post Approval Changes; Chemistry, Manufacturing and Controls, In Vitro Dissolution Testing and In Vivo Bioequivalence Documentation, U.S. Food and Drug Administration, October 1997.
18. Guidance for Industry; M4Q: The CTD—Quality, U.S. Food and Drug Administration, August 2001.
19. Guidance for Industry; SUPAC-IR/MR: Immediate Release and Modified Release Solid Oral Dosage Forms, Manufacturing Equipment Addendum CMC, Revision 1, U.S. Food and Drug Administration, January 1999.
20. FDA Office of Generic Drugs, Preparing a Quality Overall Summary for a Question-based Review ANDA, Rockville, MD, November 13, 2006.
21. Guidance for Industry; Q3A Impurities in New Drug Substances, U.S. Food and Drug Administration, February 2003.
22. Guidance for Industry; Q3B(R2) Impurities in New Drug Products, U.S. Food and Drug Administration, Revision 2, July 2006
23. Guidance for Industry; ANDAs: Impurities in Drug Products, Draft, Revision I, U.S. Food and Drug Administration, August 2005.
24. Guidance for Industry; ANDAs: Impurities in Drug Substances, U.S. Food and Drug Administration, November 1999.

16 New Developments in the Approval and Marketing of Nonprescription or OTC Drugs

William J. Mead

Consultant, Rowayton, Connecticut, U.S.A.

INTRODUCTION

"OTC" refers to an over-the-counter or nonprescription medicine. The term is now somewhat anachronistic since most drug products are easily available to consumers on a self-serve basis from in-store shelves as opposed to being handed over a counter as was the usual way years ago. The basic concept of OTCs, however, is that they are available without the necessity of obtaining a prescription from a health-care professional. This is advantageous to consumers since it yields ready access, convenience, and usually a cost saving, although OTCs tend not to be covered by health insurance plans.

OTC products are used for self-medication, which implies that the user must be able to diagnose the condition that requires treatment, must be able to make a prudent decision on the type of product required, and then must know the appropriate dosage and the proper way to use the product. Obviously, help in reaching self-medication decisions may be provided by a physician, a pharmacist, or other competent health-care personnel. Still, the labeling must be quite clear and understandable, the user needs to read and follow the directions, and to apply common sense and seek help if the condition being treated does not improve or worsens or unpleasant side effects occur. Some people believe that all OTCs are always mild and safe and therefore can be used indiscriminately, but this belief is false. Many OTCs were originally sold as prescription-only products and are in fact "serious" medicines.

Before the passage of the current Federal Food Drug and Cosmetic Act (FDCA) in 1938, there was no clear distinction between which drugs could or could not be sold without a prescription. Even after the FDCA came into being, this was not a distinct matter, and was decided by the Food and Drug Administration (FDA) on a case-by-case basis. However, the 1951 Durham–Humphrey amendments addressed the issue of drug *safety* in what is now § 503(b)(1) of the act, saying that a medication requires a prescription if it is one of certain habit-forming drugs, or is not safe for use except under competent professional supervision due to its toxicity, potential side effects, or method of use, or is specifically limited to prescription status by an approved new drug application (NDA). In other words, drugs were then by default *nonprescription* unless they fall under the specific conditions cited. Under these standards, it became largely up to the FDA to decide whether a drug should be classified as nonprescription or prescription only. This, in turn, resulted in much litigation between drug manufacturers and the FDA.

In 1962, the FDCA was further modified by the Kefauver–Harris Amendments, which for the first time required that all drugs on the U.S. market must demonstrate *effectiveness* as well as safety. This means that when a drug is properly used by consumers, the product will provide clinically significant relief of the type claimed for a significant portion of the persons using it. To comply with this new requirement meant that FDA had to consider all drugs being sold to determine whether or not they were truly effective. This meant that hundreds of thousands of existing drug products, prescription and nonprescription, had to be retroactively evaluated. This enormous undertaking caused the FDA to prioritize the order in which products would be studied. In 1968, FDA established a program for this, called the Drug Efficacy Study Implementation (DESI), to establish the effectiveness of the products originally marketed under NDAs between the passage of the 1938 FDCA and the 1962 amendments. This huge task was contracted to the National Academy of Sciences/National Research Council, to conduct the studies and make recommendations to FDA, after which FDA made the final decisions as to which products were and were not effective. Those deemed to be ineffective were ordered to be taken off the market. Many of the manufacturers of the products deemed to be ineffective disagreed with FDA, resulting in extensive litigation.

Most of the products in the DESI review were prescription drugs, but about 400 were OTCs which had approved NDAs. The DESI conclusions on these OTCs were published in the *Federal Register* of April 20, 1972.

THE OTC REVIEW PROCESS

The OTC Review process was established to evaluate the safety and effectiveness of all OTC drug products marketed in the United States *before* May 11, 1972 that were not covered by NDAs, and all OTC drug products covered only by "safety" NDAs that were marketed before the enactment of the 1962 amendments to the FDCA.

Since most of the then-existing OTC products on the market did not have NDAs, another approach needed to establish which were and which were not effective. Since it was impractical to attempt to study each of the estimated 250,000 existing OTC drugs one-by-one on a product-by-product basis, FDA decided instead to handle this by *class* or *category* (e. g., antacids, external analgesics, etc.). The goal was to establish *monographs* for each such therapeutic class, to determine which products had to be taken off the market due to being ineffective and also for future regulation of OTCs.

Eligibility for consideration of active ingredients to be included in this monograph system was determined by showing that they had been used in products for a "material extent" and for a "material time." Manufacturers who wished to have specific ingredients in the system were asked to submit data and information in a specific format, justifying consideration of them.

The first phase of the OTC drug review was conducted by advisory panels of experts such as clinicians, toxicologists, physicians, academicians, etc., each of whom had extensive experience with the class of products assigned to the panel on which they served. The panels also included persons that represented the interests of the consuming public. The panels reviewed the ingredients used for that category of products, the claims that should and should not be allowed, appropriate labeling, dosages, and warnings to be included in the labeling. Interested parties were invited to submit data and suggestions to the panels.

The ingredients were classified into three groups: Category I being generally recognized as safe and effective (GRASE), Category II *not* GRASE and therefore unacceptable, and Category III insufficient information available to allow making a decision. These classifications proved extremely useful in the decision-making process, although these terms are no longer used.

Each panel made recommendations to the FDA, and after consideration of the medical, toxicological, legal, and other issues, the panels' conclusions and recommendations were published in the *Federal Register* as an Advance Notice of Proposed Rulemaking (ANPR) to solicit public remarks and suggestions, and to stimulate discussion, following a process that is outlined in Part 330 of Title 21 of the *Code of Federal Regulations*. In each instance, FDA considered all of the information and comments received, and then published a Proposed Rule as a Tentative Final Monograph (TFM). Again, following the requirements of the Administrative Procedure Act, FDA digested and responded to the comments received, and published a Final Rule as a Final Monograph (FM). Although this has been in progress since the 1970s, the monographs for several categories of products still not have yet been finalized.

THE OTC MONOGRAPHS

Following the OTC Review process, there are now two separate regulatory pathways to legally marketing OTC drug products. One is following the appropriate monograph, and the second is having an NDA that yields preapproval for the product to be sold on a nonprescription basis. Neither establishes higher standards of safety and effectiveness than does the other.

Under Compliance Policy Guide 450.200, an OTC drug listed in subchapter 330 of Title 21 of the *Code of Federal Regulations* is generally recognized as safe and effective and is not misbranded *if* it meets each of the conditions listed in § 330.1, and also each of the conditions contained in the applicable FM. If an FM exists, but the product fails to fully comply with it, the product will be considered misbranded and subject to regulatory action. In other words, following the monograph regarding active ingredients, labeling, and other requirements is mandated. However, no filings nor approvals from FDA are required, other than that the producer must be registered and all drugs (including OTCs) in commercial distribution must be listed with the FDA on form FDA-2657 as required in 21 CFR 207.

There are provisions in the regulations for amending existing monographs, and also for creating new monographs.

In instances where an FM has not yet been published, a firm may continue to use ingredients that the expert panel has not recommended for inclusion in the final rule, provided that those ingredients do not pose a potential health hazard to consumers. However, there is an economic risk in doing so in that when the FM does appear, the ingredients may not be considered GRASE, which would require taking the product off the market.

FDA's OTC monograph system has worked well, and provides a straightforward way to legally bring OTC products to market. It has also worked well for sorting out and getting off the market products not considered GRASE. However, one disadvantage of the system is that it does not leave much room for innovation of exclusive new products. It is difficult to develop unique claims for what are essentially "me too" products, although some marketers have been successful through clever positioning of their OTC brands.

THE NDA APPROACH TO OTCs

The alternative to the use of the monograph system to legally introduce an OTC drug to the market involves getting an approved NDA. As opposed to the monographs, which are by categories, NDAs are product-specific individual licenses. This involves filing an application, which may require clinical studies. The NDA requirements are in 21 CFR 314. The approach differs product-by-product, requiring discussion with the FDA before starting. In some instances, FDA may first require an IND (Investigational New Drug) for human clinical studies as described in 21 CFR 312. Although an NDA may provide marketing exclusivity for a period of time, user fees may apply.

The FDCA provides three types of NDAs. The first is covered in § 505(b)(1), which requires full reports on safety and effectiveness, while the second type is in § 505(b)(2), in which safety and effectiveness where the testing was not done by the applicant but instead reference is made to the approval of another NDA or on data in the published literature. However, in both instances "full reports" of safety and effectiveness are required. The 505(b)(2) is a result of the Waxman–Hatch Amendments of the act in 1984, intended to encourage innovation (in the form of limited changes to the pioneer drug, such as a different dosage form or strength, or a different salt or polymorph of the active ingredient, or new indications for use) without requiring costly duplication of some clinical trials. The third type of NDA is the Abbreviated NDA or ANDA, covered in § 505(j) of the act, where the application is based on the product being identical to that of a previously approved NDA. An ANDA does not require new clinical studies, but does require proof of bioequivalence to the previously approved product (called the "reference listed drug" or RLD). This is the route used to obtain approval for most generic drugs.

THE SWITCH PROCESS

While it is possible to obtain an NDA to go directly OTC, and this is occasionally done, the most usual approach is to market a new product *first* as a prescription-only drug, then when the patent is about to expire or other business considerations come into play, apply to the FDA to switch the NDA to allow OTC sale of the product. This switch technique has been used extensively in recent years, so that products that were once prescription only can now be purchased over-the-counter without a prescription. The manufacturer must convince the FDA that the drug product is safe and effective for use by consumers without the assistance of a health-care professional. FDA usually refers switch applications to the Nonprescription Drugs Advisory Committee (NDAC) (and possibly also other advisory committees) for their opinion. FDA usually follows the advisory committee's recommendations, but they are not required to do so.

In theory, FDA can require a switch from prescription-only to OTC status, although this so-called "forced switch" mechanism is controversial.

GOOD MANUFACTURING PRACTICE

When the Kefauver–Harris Amendments to the FDCA were signed into law in 1962, a new section, § 501(A)(2)(b), was added, requiring all drug products to be made in accordance with *current good manufacturing practice*. It is from this wording that the term "GMP" evolved. The definition of this was not given, and it was at that time an entirely new concept, leaving it up to FDA to determine what was needed and to publish appropriate implementing regulations. FDA was less than sure just what Congress intended, so they sent representatives to meet with the various trade associations involved with the manufacture of drug products (including OTCs), to get their input. Shortly, thereafter, the first GMP regulations were published, stating broad requirements for *what* must be accomplished to be considered compliance with this requirement, but deliberately avoiding the specifics as to precisely how these goals should be met, leaving the "how to" points largely up to the discretion of each firm. These regulations have been revised several times in the intervening years, and in time, FDA expanded the GMP concept to foods, medical devices, and the other classes of products under their purview. The GMPs proved so useful that many other countries soon adopted similar systems, and even the World Health Organization has published international GMPs.

In the United States, the drug GMPs have the full force of law, and if not faithfully followed, the products made can be deemed to be adulterated and subject to regulatory actions such as recall, seizure, or even criminal charges brought against the firm and/or the responsible persons. Products made in other countries and exported for sale into the United States must also be made in compliance with the U.S. GMPs. Part of the approach to determining whether or not firms are in compliance with the GMP regulations is that FDA is empowered to, and does, send investigators into manufacturing facilities to conduct detailed inspections of the equipment, procedures, and operations.

FDA has made it clear that the GMP regulations apply to *all* drug products, both prescription and nonprescription. This is covered in Compliance Policy Guide 7132.10, entitled "CGMP Enforcement Policy— OTC vs. Rx Drugs."

COSMETICS VS. DRUGS

The determination of whether a given product is a cosmetic or a drug is often a gray area. The FDCA, in section 201(i) defines cosmetics as "Articles intended to be rubbed, poured, sprinkled, or sprayed on, or introduced into the human body . . . for cleansing, beautifying, promoting attractiveness, or altering the appearance." In general, to be considered as a cosmetic, a product should have no active ingredients.

Drugs, on the other hand, are defined in section 201(g)(1) as "(A) Articles intended for use in the diagnosis, cure, mitigation, treatment, or prevention of a disease . . . and (B) articles (other than food) intended to affect the structure or any function of the body. . . ."

There are some products that fall under *both* of these definitions. Examples include toothpaste that contains an active ingredient (e.g., fluoride) to help prevent caries and is therefore a drug, but it also cleanses the teeth and is therefore a cosmetic. Shampoos that merely clean the hair are cosmetics, but if they contain antidandruff ingredients, they are also drugs. Deodorants are cosmetics while antiperspirants are drugs. Cosmetics containing sunscreen ingredients are also drugs. Such products that meet both definitions must comply with the regulatory requirements for *both* cosmetics and drugs, and are subject to the GMP regulations. Moreover, the labeling requirements differ for cosmetics and drugs, and of course the drug portion would require either an approved NDA or be in compliance with the appropriate monograph.

The intended use of a product is an important factor in the decision of whether the product is a drug, a cosmetic, or both. This intended use may be inferred from the product labeling, promotional material, advertising, and other relevant information.

Cosmetics do not require premarket approval, and are not required to comply with the GMP regulations. Drug products must be made in FDA-registered facilities and must be listed with FDA, whereas these steps are not mandatory for cosmetics.

HOMEOPATHIC DRUGS

The practice of homeopathy is based on a concept developed in the late 1700s that disease symptoms can be relieved by using extremely small doses of substances that produce symptoms in healthy people. The dilutions are so great that some people question whether it is possible for the products to have any effect, and the suggestion has been made that any perceived benefit must come from the so-called "placebo effect" where patients not infrequently feel they get benefits from products that actually contain *no* active ingredient. However, the homeopathic drug market today is substantial and growing.

There is a publication containing standards for the source, composition, and preparation of homeopathic drugs. This publication, which is officially recognized in the FDCA, is the Homeopathic Pharmacopeia of the United States. This contains monographs of the ingredients used in homeopathic drugs, and for regulatory compliance products based on such ingredients must meet the standards of strength, quality, and purity set forth in the Homeopathic Pharmacopeia of the United States.

FDA's Compliance Policy Guide 7132.15 outlines the conditions under which homeopathic drugs may be marketed in the United States. There are both prescription and nonprescription homeopathic drugs.

DIETARY SUPPLEMENTS

Dietary supplements, as the name implies, are products intended to provide consumers with supplemental quantities of certain ingredients to help provide a healthy lifestyle. These products are regulated under the Dietary Supplement Health and Education Act of 1994, which is now incorporated into and is a part of the FDCA. By definition, a dietary supplement is a product that contains one or more dietary ingredients such as vitamins, minerals, herbs or other botanicals, amino acids, or other components of food, or combinations of these, used to supplement the diet.

The products are for ingestion (not topical), and are legally classified and regulated as foods, *not as* OTC drugs. They are usually in the physical form of tablets, capsules, softgels, powders, or liquids. There are separate GMPs for these products, that is, the manufacturers must follow these regulations as opposed to the drug GMPs. The labeling requirements also differ from those of OTC drugs.

It is estimated that about half of Americans use dietary supplements at least some of the time, so the sales are quite substantial and growing.

CHILD-RESISTANT AND TAMPER-EVIDENT PACKAGING

Some, but not all, OTC drug products are required to have child-resistant (CR) packaging under the Poison Prevention Packaging Act (PPPA), which was enacted in 1970. The purpose is to protect children from injury or illness from handling, using, or ingesting hazardous materials (including but not limited to specific OTC drugs). The PPPA is administered by the Consumer Product Safety Commission (CPSC), not by the FDA. The implementing regulations appear in Parts 1700 to 1750 of Title 16 of the *Code of Federal Regulations*. The PPPA does not specify what kinds of packaging are considered to be "child resistant," but the CPSC has a specific testing protocol which must be followed, which involves testing not only with small children to ensure they cannot get access to the product within a reasonable period of time, but also testing with adults to be certain that the packaging is not too difficult to use since if it is, there is a tendency for some adults to simply leave the package open which could put children at risk.

The CPSC regulations also allow packagers of products requiring CR packages to offer one single size or shelf keeping unit in a non-CR version for the convenience of elderly or handicapped individuals that might otherwise be inconvenienced by the child-resistant features.

Tamper-evident packaging is required for all OTC human drug products except dermatologics, dentifrices, insulin, and throat lozenges. This is covered in § 211.132 of the drug GMP regulations, and by Compliance Program Guide 7132a.17. This was originally called "tamper-proof" packaging, but it was soon discovered that nothing is truly tamper proof. The packaging must use an indicator or barrier to entry that is either distinctive by design or uses an identifying characteristic such as a pattern, name, registered trademark, logo, or picture, and a labeling statement on the container to alert consumers to the specific tamper-evident feature or features used.

MARKING SOLID DOSAGE FORMS

Part 206 of Title 21 of the *Code of Federal Regulations* requires all solid dosage forms (tablets, capsules, or similar drug products intended for oral use) to bear a distinctive identification number or symbol. This can be applied by imprinting, embossing or debossing, or engraving. Such marking, together with the product's size, shape, and color, permits the unique identification of the drug product and its manufacturer or distributor, whether prescription only or OTC.

NATIONAL UNIFORMITY

Over the years, some state lawmakers have attempted to establish standards for OTC drugs different from those established by the FDA. This could cause both confusion and unnecessary expense if it were to be allowed. Regulatory uniformity is clearly superior to having inconsistent regulations state-to-state. Consequently, it is now established that with certain minor exceptions, the states cannot have separate regulations for OTC medicines that differ from those of the FDA, that is, there is now national uniformity, which is in section 751 of the FDCA, added at the time that the FDA Modernization Act was passed.

LABELING OTC DRUG PRODUCTS

There are standard labeling requirements for OTC drug products, based on the "Drug Facts" format, intended to enhance consumers' understanding of OTC drug labels to help ensure safe and effective use of the products. This is described in detail in § 201.66, based on a Final Rule that was published in the *Federal Register* of March 17, 1999.

The Drug Facts box on product packaging aids consumers in selecting and correctly using OTC drug products by clearly listing important information in a standardized way. The headings within the box include the *active ingredient(s)* (the ingredient or ingredients that make the product work), the *purpose* (the type or category of the ingredient, such as an antacid or antihistamine), *use(s)* (the symptoms or illnesses for which the product should be used), *warnings* (cautions that need to be observed to avoid overdose, when a doctor or other health-care professional needs to be consulted, possible side effects, when to stop taking the product, etc.), *directions* (exactly how and when the product should be taken), *other information* (how to store the product, and any additional information required by the FDA), and *inactive ingredients* (a listing of excipients used in making the product, such as colors, fragrance, binders, etc., which is helpful to persons that may have a known allergy to certain ingredients).

In addition, the name and address of the manufacturer or distributor, a statement of net contents, a lot number, and an expiration date (if appropriate) will appear on the package.

ADVERTISING OTC DRUGS

In general, FDA regulates the advertising of prescription drugs, but the Federal Trade Commission (FTC) has the basic responsibility for OTC drug advertising. But, the two agencies do work in harmony together, and both are committed to prevent false or deceptive claims.

Section 5 of the FTC act gives FTC broad authority to prohibit unfair or deceptive acts or practices, while sections 12 through 15 prohibit the dissemination of misleading claims for drugs, foods, and cosmetics. FTC can and does issue cease and desist orders, and can seek civil penalties in the Federal courts for violation of their orders. The courts have held that advertisers are strictly liable for violations of the FTC act.

Much of OTC drug advertising controversies are handled in ways not directly involving the FTC. This is accomplished through the Council of Better Business Bureaus' National Advertising Division (NAD), which investigates complaints about the truthfulness of national advertisements, and works toward getting corrective action when needed. If an advertiser or challenger disagrees with NAD's findings, the decisions can be appealed to the National Advertising Review Board (NARB) for further review. The NAD/NARB process generally works well, with advertisers voluntarily agreeing to change or discontinue misleading advertisements. Thus, FTC usually gets involved in only major cases.

Since consumers get much of their information about OTC drug products through advertising, it is important that advertisers present their messages to the public in a fair and honest way.

The major trade associations strongly encourage their member companies to follow existing voluntary codes of advertising practices. The media tend to have their own codes of conduct, and often require proof of claims before running advertisements.

Both the FDA and the FTC are quite aware of the fact that much advertising and promotion is now done on the Internet. These agencies have programs for monitoring the Internet to take enforcement actions to minimize health fraud and improper marketing practices.

COMBINATION PRODUCTS

There are two separate and distinct meanings of the term "combination products" in connection with OTC drugs. The first refers to a product containing more than one active ingredient. Examples would include cough-cold products and topical first-aid antimicrobials products, both of which classes of products often have more than one active ingredient.

The second meaning refers to products composed of items regulated by different FDA centers, either when combined into a single product or sold as a kit containing two or more separate products of different regulatory categories. Examples of such combination products would include a drug and a device, a drug and a biological product, or a drug and a dietary supplement. FDA has an Office of Combination Products which oversees intercenter jurisdiction of such products as described in 21 CFR 3.7.

ADVERSE EVENT REPORTING

Drugs often produce more than one effect, the one wanted to treat the condition or disorder, and unwanted side effects. Side effects are usually mild and perhaps unpleasant, but in extreme instances may result in injury or death.

In 2006, the Dietary Supplement and Nonprescription Drug Consumer Protection Act was signed into law as an amendment to the FDCA, requiring the manufacturer, packer, or distributor whose name appears on the label of a nonprescription drug marketed in the United States without an NDA to submit to the FDA any report of a serious adverse event within 15 business days. This also requires keeping records of OTC adverse events for 6 years, whether or not the event was serious. The law allows FDA to inspect such records.

FDA's OFFICE OF NONPRESCRIPTION PRODUCTS

Until 2005 called the Division of Over-the-Counter Drug Products, the Office of Nonprescription Products (ONP) is the portion of FDA's Center for Drug Evaluation and Research that coordinates matters related to OTC drug products.

ONP has two divisions within it: the Division of Nonprescription Clinical Evaluation and the Division of Nonprescription Regulation Development. Division of Nonprescription Clinical Evaluation has the primary responsibility in the review management and oversight of INDs and NDAs for OTC products, while Division of Nonprescription Regulation Development is involved with the development of monographs through regulation, as part of the OTC drug review program. ONP reports to the director of the Office of New Drugs.

NONPRESCRIPTION DRUGS ADVISORY COMMITTEE

The NDAC is one of several advisory committees within FDA that give advice. While ONP and the FDA in general tend to follow such advice, they are not *required* to do so. Such committees operate in accordance with the Federal Advisory Committee Act and 21 CFR Part 14.

The committee addresses such issues as NDAs and supplements to them the OTC monographs, postapproval risk/benefit issues, prescription-to-OTC switches, and other such topics as related to OTCs. The expertise within the committee assists ONP in making timely and appropriate decisions.

Most, but not all, of their meetings are open to the public. Meeting notices are published in the *Federal Register* and on FDA's Web site. Members of the committee are selected by ONP and appointed by the FDA Commissioner, to serve 4 years as Special Government Employees. Members are usually preeminent scientists in their field, although some members are consumer representatives, and others are nominated by industry to nonvoting positions. Frequently the committee is also supplemented by consultants.

OTC TRADE ASSOCIATION

The leading trade association of manufacturers and marketers of OTC drug products is the Consumer Healthcare Products Association (CHPA), formerly known as the Nonprescription Drug Manufacturers Association and previous to that as the Proprietary Association. CHPA was founded in 1881 and maintains offices in Washington, DC. CHPA member companies represent over 90% of the retail sales of OTCs in the United States. CHPA sponsors meetings and seminars on topics related to manufacturing, quality assurance, and marketing of OTC drug products, and has voluntary codes and guidelines covering matters of interest to the member companies.

TRENDS IN OTC MEDICINES

There are currently more than 100,000 OTC products on the market. With the aging of the population, increasing interest in self-care, enhanced access to health-care information on the Internet, product innovations, continued switches from prescription-only to OTC, retail sales, and usage of OTC drug products will continue to grow in the years ahead.

Manufacturers of OTC drugs and their trade associations have been and will continue their efforts to inform consumers about the importance of always following label directions closely to achieve safety and efficacy from the products. Understanding product directions, what to do if the product is not working, and the ability to identify adverse effects together with what action needs to be taken when such effects occur are all crucial. Education and publicity on these aspects of self-treatment will be stressed. Similarly, efforts will continue toward educating parents about the potential abuse of OTC drug products (such as dextromethorphan-containing cough medicines) by teenagers. Due to the changing demographics in the United States, making such information available in Spanish will become more prevalent.

Self-medication is not limited to the United States, but is a global matter. Many of the manufacturers and marketers of OTC's offer their products in several countries. However, the regulatory environment and health-care systems vary country to country, making it difficult to internationalize brands. Efforts will continue toward harmonization, although this will be ongoing for many years.

There are OTC drug trade associations in many countries, and also international organizations coordinating their various efforts, including the Association of European Self-Medication Industry and the World Self-Medication Industry.

In some countries, there exists a *third* class of drug products, sometimes called a "pharmacy-only" medicine (POM), where certain nonprescription products are made physically inaccessible to consumers. To purchase such a product, the customer is required to obtain it from a pharmacist, and presumably would enter into discussion to guide the proper use of the product. This concept is periodically brought up for consideration in the United States by organizations representing retail pharmacists. However, this "third class" has been resisted by the OTC drug industry in general as negatively impacting access to nonprescription medicines. The industry strongly favors the current two-tiered system.

Although there is much interest in nanotechnology and its application in health-care products, some of which could be OTCs (including drug–cosmetics such as sunscreens), this is an area of product development that will advance.

REFERENCES AND NOTES

1. Draft Guidance for Industry on Postmarketing Adverse Event Reporting for Nonprescription Human Drug Products Marketed Without an Approved Application, 1997, Food and Drug Association, Center for Drug Evaluation and Research, Rockville, MD.
2. Soller, R. W. OTCness. Drug Inf J 1998; 32:555–560.
3. FDA, Is It a Cosmetic, a Drug, or Both? July 2002.
4. FDA, Guidance for Industry: National Uniformity for Nonprescription Drugs, April 1999.
5. FDA, Rulemaking History for Nonprescription Products: Drug Category List, http://fda.gov/cder/otcmonographd/rulemaking_index.htm. Accessed April 2008.
6. FDA, Frequently Asked Questions on the Regulatory Process of Over-the-Counter (OTC) Drugs, http://www.fda.gov/cder/about/smallbiz/OTC_FAQ.htm. Accessed April 2008.
7. U.S. Code, Federal Advisory Committee Act, Title 5, http://www.access.gpo.gov/uscode/title5a/5a_1_.html. Accessed April 2008.
8. FDA, Office of Nonprescription Products, http://www.fda.gov/cder/offices/otc/default.htm. Accessed April 2008.

17 Current Good Manufacturing Practice and the Drug Approval Process*

Ira R. Berry
International Regulatory Business Consultants, LLC, Freehold, New Jersey, U.S.A.

INTRODUCTION

Employment of* current good manufacturing practice (CGMP) and approval of a new drug application (NDA) are two pillars of federal law providing support of manufacturing quality for pharmaceutical drug products offered to American consumers in the U.S. marketplace. These requirements are established in the Federal Food, Drug and Cosmetic Act (FDCA). In this chapter, we will discuss these two requirements and how they interface with each other in the FDA programs designed to execute the mandates of the law.

The CGMP requirement focuses on manufacturing quality for the purpose of assuring that each pharmaceutical drug product is as safe as the law requires it to be and that it has the identity, strength, quality, and purity characteristics by which it is defined in large part. Under FDCA section 501(a) (2)(B), activities that amount to "manufacture, processing, packing, or holding" of a drug must be performed in conformance with this current good manufacturing practice. Very explicitly, the CGMP requirement applies to the methods used in performing the above regulated activities and to the facilities and the controls used for these activities in producing a drug.

Pharmaceutical drugs resulting from manufacturing methods, facilities, and controls that are not operated or administered in conformance with CGMP are considered to be adulterated. In essence, their manufacturing quality is not assured to a legally minimum level. They are in violation of the law, and they are subject to regulatory actions by the U.S. Food and Drug Administration (FDA).

Section 505(a) of FDCA prohibits in U.S. commerce any "new drug" unless that product is the subject of a properly filed application with FDA to place it in commerce, and an FDA approval of the application is effective. An NDA filed with FDA to meet the requirement to acquire approval may be disapproved if a number of conditions are not met. The full list can be found in sections 505 (d) (3) for NDAs and 505 (j) (4) for abbreviated new drug applications (ANDAs). Both sections contain the conditions for approval that the methods used in, and the facilities and controls used for, the manufacture are adequate to preserve its identity, strength, quality, and purity. It should be noted that this is essentially the same expression as the statement of the CGMP requirement. The CGMP requirement assures that legally acceptable product attributes result from manufacturing

* Author from the First Edition, Nicholas Buhay (Food and Drug Administration, Rockville, Maryland, U.S.A.), with an update by Ira R. Berry. This chapter was written by Mr. Buhay in his private capacity. No official support or endorsement by the Food and Drug Administration is intended or should be inferred.

operations; all manufacturing-related proposals in the application for the product must maintain these same attributes.

An NDA may not be approved if FDA finds the CGMP to be employed in its production is inadequate. FDA programs for assessment of conformance with the CGMP requirement use an approach that includes a number of variations in inspection action. The variations have been devised and put into use to satisfy a number of regulatory purposes as well as management efficiency purposes.

There is no such thing as virtual manufacturing of pharmaceutical drugs. They are real products fashioned in a real environment with real resources. It is a fundamental axiom of the regulatory scheme that this environment, both physical and operational, in large part determines the quality, identity, purity, and strength characteristics that have been established for drug products. Conditions and practices in this manufacturing venue are complex, involving many steps, sophisticated equipment, and many people. This complexity provides the potential or the occasion for variation or contamination that raises concern that the desired fundamental characteristics have been put into output products. An inspection operation directed at evaluating the ongoing conditions and practices in the site addresses this concern. Besides the concerns for manufacturing in an environment free from obvious conditions like insanitation, there are additional conditions and practices unique to the industry. Pharmaceutical drug manufacture is a part of the chemical industry; products are applied to the living individual. Most pharmaceutical manufacturing occurs in multiproduct facilities.

Manufacturing operations may create conditions resulting in cross-contamination. An example is chemical ingredient dust, generated by equipment operations. Many white powders are used to produce different products. Each may have a vastly different toxicity profile and treatment application. Wrong selection of materials and incorporation in a manufacturing process has occurred. Manufacturing processes are complex, employing many steps and ordered activities to realize the object product. Written procedures, preparation of records of actions, and training decrease or eliminate mistakes or variations that have an impact on product attributes. To ensure against manufacturing quality problems resulting from this situation, Congress has recognized the value and importance of inspection and established it as a required operation for the assessment of conformance with the CGMP requirement for manufacture of pharmaceuticals.

Periodic inspection of a pharmaceutical manufacturing factory is a specific requirement in the Food, Drug, and Cosmetic Act. Section 510(h) requires "every such establishment engaged in the manufacture, propagation, compounding or processing of a drug or drugs... shall be so inspected at least once in every... two-year period." Section 704 of the law discusses some purposes of the inspection and indicates both specific and general items of interest for the inspection. Those items include "processes, controls, facilities, equipment, finished and unfinished materials, containers, labeling and records and files."

Mandated periodic inspections are performed to assess the conformance of the factory site to the requirement for manufacture within current good manufacturing practice. The inspections are performed according to instructions provided by an FDA operating procedure called the Drug Manufacturing Inspections Compliance Program. This compliance program is one of a set of such programs established and maintained to allocate resources for, and to guide, the performance of investigative operations for compliance assessment in identified priority regulatory areas. The need for compliance programs is reviewed each year. Compliance programs may be established and retired in response to emerging developments in the regulated industry.

Because of the enduring priority of assurance against manufacturing error and of controlled manufacturing practice, the Drug Manufacturing Inspection Compliance Program has been and will continue to be a fixture in the overall drug regulatory program of the Center for Drug Evaluation and Research (CDER).

The outcomes of these inspections are available for use in the drug approval decision. Pharmaceutical factory sites found by the inspection to be in acceptable conformance with the CGMP requirement means that manufacturing methods, facilities, and controls are operated or administered satisfactorily in that site. This general conclusion may be applied to the case of a specific NDA pending approval, recalling that one of the approval requirements is that methods used in, and the facilities and controls used for, the manufacture are adequate to preserve its identity, strength, quality, and purity.

It is evident that some extrapolation is done in applying a CGMP inspection conformance assessment to an approval decision for an application. The inspection observes and assesses conditions and practices at a period in the past; a new drug application proposes future manufacture. The inspection evaluates manufacturing operations for products that are different from the product that is the subject of the application. The proposed product may involve for commercial production some manufacturing technology not yet in operation at the time of the CGMP inspection.

Judgments are made, indirect information is considered; a risk management approach is used. Similarities between the manufacturing experience in place and the proposed product manufacturing requirements, the complexity of the manufacturing process and the process controls, the CGMP compliance history of the factory site proposed, the physical and toxicologic properties of the materials that may be processed in a site, the completeness of information available supporting a factory site conformance with the CGMP requirement—all may be used to decide upon the use and extent of application of a CGMP inspection.

Where an existing report of CGMP inspection is judged insufficient for supporting an application approval decision, a special inspection will be scheduled. This is known as the preapproval inspection. As with CGMP conformance assessment inspections, performance of FDA preapproval inspections are organized in a compliance program. This program is called the Preapproval Inspections/Investigations Compliance Program. The program was established in August 1994, largely in response to the discovery that a number of applicant firms provided in NDAs to the FDA unreliable, misleading, and false information. In an investigation that spanned approximately 8 years, approxiamtely 20 companies and 75 individuals were prosecuted for various violations of requirements for submission of invalid, incomplete information related to NDAs. Such information is essentially worthless for the process of evaluating the safety and efficacy of a proposed new drug before it is introduced to the marketplace. The preapproval inspection (PAI) was designed to provide assurances that the data and information submitted in NDAs are reliable and that actual conditions and practices in a given manufacturing facility were adequate to incorporate the production of a new product.

Since FDA does not have the enough inspection resources to perform a PAI for every application received, risk management principles were incorporated into the program rules for selection of facilities for inspection. Considering the products,

PAIs are scheduled for applications proposing products with new chemical entities, with narrow therapeutic ranges, with the first generic version of a brand name product, and with generic versions of the most prescribed drug products. Considering producer firms, PAIs are scheduled when the application is the producer's first, and when the producer has a CGMP compliance history that has been inconsistent, trending down, or noncompliant. Any apparent discrepancy in an application may result in a PAI to investigate the matter thoroughly.

Data and information universally required to be included in an NDA document are trial manufacture of the proposed product and summarized results of various tests on samples from the trial manufacture. Trial manufacture may include one or more batches of the proposed product. Tests include those assessing conformance with the product specifications, those assessing the manufacturing process, and those assessing stability of the product in a container-closure presentation.

PAIs may be performed at any facility providing manufacturing or control services for, and associated data and information on, production of the proposed product. These facilities include not only the site where the dosage form is realized, but also at contract packagers and labelers, contract test laboratories, contract processors like sterilizers or micronizers, and at producers of the active pharmaceutical substance chemical and other ingredient chemicals.

A major objective of the PAI was to develop an assurance that application data and information are authentic and accurate. The PAI could include examination of any and all systems and records used to generate the data and information submitted to FDA. Trial manufacture is verified. Investigation of the industry has shown that trial manufacture was not done, that it was done on a much smaller scale than reported, or that it was done using different procedures than reported. The PAI will determine if resources were available at the time and place of the manufacture trial reported. The inspection will look for consistent and mutually supportive documentation of the manufacture. Reported test results are verified. The investigation of the industry has shown that reported tests were not done, the tests were not done on appropriate samples, or that results were not reported accurately. The PAI determines if test documentation supports the test results reported and if test methods had been developed, validated, and applied correctly. Application data and information from trial manufacture and tests are not all-inclusive; data showing support of the proposed product have been reported, while data not supporting the product have not been included in the application. The PAI inspection determines if development data not submitted was properly excluded. Reports of findings in a PAI are reported to the application review division.

PAI findings of data unreliability could cause review of the pending application to be suspended; findings of a pattern or practice of submission of unreliable data by an applicant could result in a broadscope evaluation of many, or even all, of the applicant's approved NDAs to determine if those also contained unreliable data. Suspension of review of any submission by the applicant could be put in place until the applicant has carried out an adequate corrective action-operating plan. Experience has shown that it can take years to clear up the concerns raised by an applicant's submission of unreliable data.

These regulatory procedures are implemented under FDA Compliance Policy Guide 7150.09 Fraud, Untrue Statements of Material Facts, Bribery and Illegal Gratuities published in the Federal Register on September 10, 1991. Also published with the policy was another document called "Points to Consider for Internal Reviews and Corrective Action Operating Plans." This document provides detailed discussion of elements of an adequate plan.

PAI findings may result in the withholding of approval of a pending application if the findings show that preapproval batches were not made in compliance with current good manufacturing practice or that noncompliance with CGMP may adversely impact the product that is the subject of the pending application. Drug product dosage form units resulting from trial manufacture using the proposed manufacturing procedure are those tested for data and information that will be used to determine if the product is safe and effective. The data and information could be difficult or impossible to interpret if the tests are made on units that are not uniform or that include an unknown contaminant. Manufacture in compliance with CGMP assures the quality, identity, purity, and strength in the products to be tested. Trial manufacturing performed in compliance with CGMP assures that the data and information used to evaluate the safety and efficacy of the proposed product are interpreted scientifically.

Likewise, PAI findings that indicate that CGMP would be incorrectly applied to the manufacture of the proposed product after approval would have to be resolved. Again, the approval of the application may be withheld until such resolution is achieved. Manufacture in compliance with CGMP assures quality, identity, purity, and strength in the products to be distributed to the marketplace after approval. Commercial manufacturing performed in compliance with CGMP assures that the untested units of products sold and used in the marketplace perform in an equivalent manner to the products tested and evaluated for approval.

The CGMP requirement provides support for the reduction of information required to be submitted to FDA in an NDA. From the earliest days of the use of the NDA for assuring the safety and efficacy of new drugs, there has been lively debate about the type and amount of data and information needed for FDA to agree with the applicant proposer that the product may be introduced to the marketplace for use by patients. FDA reviewers of applications have before them the need to decide on product questions that will impact the life and health of patients using them, beginning with the very first dosage unit sold. Having no other data and information except that before them in an application, an FDA reviewer is encouraged to be sure that all important attributes of the proposed product are supported. The producers of the proposed product have before them, as a matter of presence and experience, vast amounts of data and information about the conditions, practices, and resources used, available, or planned for the new product. With this as background, they are encouraged to interpret differently the needs for the collection, arrangement, and presentation of data and information they regard as routine or usual.

Reducing required data and information in applications has been part of an ongoing FDA process to make the application process and the review of applications as efficient as possible while maintaining the high level of public health protection the drug approval process provides. This process has included recognition of an existing CGMP requirement as adequate regulatory oversight of an issue being considered for an application requirement.

In October 1982, FDA proposed a significant revision to the regulations that govern the approval process.A major feature of that revision, finalized in February 1985, eliminated from applications substantial information about manufacturing practices that had been included in the September 1978 revision of the current good manufacturing practice regulations. It was recognized that the updated CGMP regulations set comprehensive standards for drug manufacturing conditions and practices that were enforced by required on-site inspections of manufacturing facilities. The CGMP regulations eliminated the need for application-by-application review of some drug manufacturing information.

The same revision eliminated NDA's record-keeping requirements for manufacturing and control data resulting from postapproval manufacturing of the application product. This was done because adequate record retention requirements are imposed on manufacturers of drug products under the CGMP regulations.

In April 1992, FDA published final regulations detailing requirements for ANDAs. During the regulation-writing process there had been a proposal for ANDA applicants to obtain samples and to retain them in their stability containers for all lots of a finished generic drug product. This proposal did not need to be accepted because manufacturers are already required to retain samples of each lot by existing CGMP regulations.

In March 1987, FDA published final regulations governing the submission and review of investigational new drug applications (INDs). That new regulation allowed a sponsor of a new drug under investigation to perform stability testing concurrently with clinical investigations of the product because concurrent testing was consistent with existing requirements for stability testing in the CGMP regulation. It was noted that permitting concurrent stability testing furthers the FDA objective of speeding up the drug development and approval process.

The application reduction program also includes a large effort in publishing guidance documents specifying the format and content of sections of applications and recommending types of data and information that will be useful in an efficient review of chemistry, manufacturing, and control issues. The latter guidances especially serve to inform the expression of CGMP requirements as they are applied to the manufacture of the application product or products using similar manufacturing processes. Most often the application requirement is the same as the CGMP requirement. Where they are different, the differences are usually in extent of use rather than in the nature of the compliance expected. An example would be that more frequent testing might be needed to meet a CGMP requirement than to meet the requirement for submission of data for the application.

Application guidances and CGMP guidances are developed using a process that includes cross-program participation. CGMP program representatives sit on work groups developing application guidance documents and attend application review coordinating committee meetings that monitor the development of guidance projects. Draft guidances are distributed to the CGMP program for review and comment at later stages of preparation. The development of CGMP guidances occurs with representatives of the application review program as participants.

The relationship between the GMP requirement and the application approval process continues to develop. In August 2002, FDA announced a formal management initiative to update the agency's approach to ensuring manufacturing quality. The initiative, titled "Pharmaceutical CGMPs for the 21st Century: A Risk-Based Approach," will examine closely the currency of both the CGMP program and the premarket review of chemistry and manufacturing issues. With a view toward the industry, goals identified include incorporation of modern concepts of risk management, quality systems, and advances in electronic technology into pharmaceutical manufacturing control. Specific attention will be given to fashioning a drug regulatory program that will encourage innovation in manufacturing to enhance efficiency and quality management. From the FDA view, coordination of the application review program with the CGMP inspection program is to be sought for effective, efficient, and consistent application of regulatory requirements. The 2-year CGMP initiative was concluded in September 2004.A full report of findings and goals is published on the FDA/Center for Drug Evaluation and Research Web site. Many of the goals provide for closer coordination of the CGMP program operations and application review activities.

Under certain conditions, FDCA permits exportation of unapproved drug products ordinarily requiring approval for interstate commerce. One of the conditions to allow unapproved products to be shipped out of the United States is that such products are manufactured, processed, packaged, and stored under conditions and practices substantially in conformance with the current good manufacturing practice requirement. This allows manufacture in U.S. factories of products that do not meet U.S. requirements for approval but meet a foreign country's requirements. Of course, they must be intended for use only in the identified foreign country. The CGMP provision provides basic protections against low-quality products being distributed from a U.S. base and assists foreign governments in establishing a level of acceptability for the products to be used in their country without conducting expensive regulatory programs and operations of their own.

Approval of an NDA does not insulate the product that is the subject of the application from the current good manufacturing practice requirement. When the NDA requirements were being established, some holders of applications had contended that the approval process and requirements made withdrawal of the application the exclusive method available to FDA for regulating application products. FDA rejected that contention and established a specific regulation explicitly stating the full applicability of the CGMP requirement to products that are the subject of NDAs. FDA explained that the approval process was a set of additional requirements on the new products in order to make a showing of safety and efficacy.

Thousands of drugs in U.S. commerce are not the subject of an NDA. These drugs are legally marketed because they are not "new drugs" under the law and so they are not required to have an approved application covering them. This includes many prescription drugs as well as the vast majority of over-the-counter products. While the application regulatory pillar for assurance of manufacturing quality is not available to the FDA oversight program, the CGMP requirement does apply. CGMP inspections are made to assess methods, facilities, and controls used to make these products to ensure that the consuming public gets the product attributes mandated for all drugs by the law. The CGMP requirement also provides protection against adverse conditions and practices in the distribution of drugs not required to be submitted for approval in NDAs.

In the FDA Modernization Act of 1997 (FDAMA), Congress again linked CGMP with NDAs in establishing certain procedures for the regulation of the quality of a special category of drugs and in establishing an exemption from the federal regulation of quality. Section 121 recognized the special characteristics of positron emission tomography (PET) drugs. This section directed FDA to establish special procedures for the approval of applications on PET drugs and directed the preparation of a special CGMP requirement for these drugs. The agency has prepared draft rules for meeting these directions and is now conducting a public debate of the proposed approaches. The resulting procedures and requirements will be closely coordinated as a result of their concurrent development.

A discussion of the regulation of the quality of pharmaceuticals in U.S. commerce would not be complete without a discussion of the approach and role of the official compendia.A compendium is a collection of products recognized, by the inclusion in the collection, as having medical value. Standards for each product are specified in monographs. The three compendia now recognized are the USP, the NF, and the Homeopathic Pharmacopoeia. Section 501(b) of FDCA provides that a compendium drug is adulterated if any sample is tested by the method specified, and the result falls outside the acceptance limits.

Standards for a new drug established in the FDA application review process enter the compendium monograph upon the product's acceptance into the compendium. In the application review process at FDA, standards for new generic drugs are closely coordinated with the existing standards in a compendium monograph. Compendia standards for nonapplication drugs, along with technical information on testing, are accepted as primary guidance in meeting many CGMP requirements, especially in testing procedures.

UPDATES AND CURRENT ISSUES

The basic requirements for a pharmaceutical manufacturer to comply with—as presented above in the First Edition chapter written by Mr. Buhay—remain in effect. However, in the past three years, there have been some basic updates to the practice of GMP and regulatory issues that have taken place. We can divide this subject into four categories.

First is the issue of the import of foreign manufactured pharmaceuticals—APIs and finished products. The issue is treated in a separate chapter in this book but let it suffice to mention two occurrences here. Heparin API, as included in a finished pharmaceutical product, has been reported to contain contaminants and on investigation has been shown to be incorporated into this finished product and being manufactured from a plant in China that was not inspected or approved by FDA. Thus, the regulatory system has failed with investigations pointing to the FDA and finished product and API manufacturers.

Also, as another example of this issue, questions have been raised regarding the FDA approved ANDAs of a prominent Indian company with manufacturing operations in India and the United States. These questions relate to GMP violations and data submitted in the approved ANDAs for product stability and bioequivalence. Investigations to discover the impact of these issues, and the assignable system failures, are being stimulated by the U.S. Congress.

The second category of these updates relates to the responsibilities of pharmaceutical manufacturers—of APIs and finished products—for outsourced materials. The sponsor of an NDA or ANDA is responsible to confirm that outsourced APIs or finished products are manufactured in compliance with GMP (1, 2). The outsourced manufacturers are responsible as well and are subject to FDA inspections that lead to satisfactory results. The point is that all pharmaceutical manufacturers are responsible to comply with GMP, and to monitor their suppliers; FDA's responsibility is to audit.

The third category that relates to the practice of GMP is risk management, which has been described in an FDA guidance (3). This guidance describes the suggested principles and process of quality risk management and the integration of quality risk management into industry and regulatory operations.

An example of risk management and risk assessment develops from the U.S. FDA CGMP regulations that stipulate the requirement to prevent product contamination by adequate separation, defined areas, and control systems in a multiproduct manufacturing facility (for dosage forms or APIs). By current standards, the FDA expects a manufacturer to conduct a process to evaluate the necessary controls, through careful analysis, to prevent product contamination through vectors such as facility, equipment, personnel, air handling, and any means deemed influential in risk analysis. The endpoint to this analysis is to evaluate how (material from) one product is possibly able to contaminate another product. Containment can be one consideration for separate or dedicated facility, equipment, equipment parts, and personnel. Cleaning procedures and cleaning validation is another consideration. There is not necessarily one answer to this question for any given compound. There is certainly regulatory support by having facilities with good physical separation and dedicated equipment parts, as practical and reasonable.

Another example of risk management is to monitor the production and cleaning operations and controls to confirm that the controls in use will prevent cross-contamination of products. For example, this can be done by testing wash samples after cleaning equipment and facilities.

The fourth category relating to the practice of GMP is updated principles of quality. FDA has published three FDA/ICH guidances (4–6) that elaborate upon the requirements for a quality system and product development. These guidances provide detail on the integration of quality system and risk management approaches into existing GMP programs. One guidance (4) describes a quality systems model that can accomplish this objective within existing GMP operations. It demonstrates that by developing a product under the principle of building quality into the product—or quality by design (QbD)—product quality will be maintained. Another guidance (5) relates the international scope of building an effective quality management system. The third guidance (6) describes the suggested program for product development and corresponding documentation for a regulatory submission.

Readers may refer to the reference section of this chapter for suggested readings in order to obtain details that are appropriate for their operations.

REFERENCES

1. FDA Guidance for Industry—Q7A Good Manufacturing Practice for Active Pharmaceutical Ingredients, U.S. Department of Health and Human Services (Aug. 2001).
2. 21 CFR 210 and 211, U.S. Government Printing Office (2008).
3. FDA/ICH Guidance for Industry—Q9 Quality Risk Management, U.S. Department of Health and Human Services (June 2006).
4. FDA Guidance for Industry—Quality Systems Approach to Pharmaceutical CGMP Regulations, U.S. Department of Health and Human Services (Sept. 2006).
5. ICH Draft Guidance—Pharmaceutical Quality System Q10, International Conference on Harmonization of Technical Requirements for Registration of Pharmaceuticals for Human Use (May 9, 2007).
6. FDA/ICH Guidance for Industry—Q8 Pharmaceutical Development, U.S. Department of Health and Human Services (May 2006).

18 The Influence of the USP on the Drug Approval Process

Edward M. Cohen
EMC Consulting Services, Newtown, Connecticut, U.S.A.

INTRODUCTION

The objective of this chapter is to provide the reader with an overview of the United States Pharmacopeia/National Formulary (USP/NF) and its formal and legal role in the Food and Drug Administration's (FDA) drug regulatory process in the United States (1). When considering the history of the USP and NF, once separate drug standards compendia originate from two different sectors of the health care delivery system, it is interesting to note in parallel the key milestones of U.S. Food and Drug Law History (2,3). The role of the USP (inception 1820) and NF (inception 1888) has always been to establish public standards for purity, quality, and strength for medicinal articles, and compounding information. The role of the FDA formally established in 1938, and all of its predecessor organizations, starting with the Bureau of Chemistry of the Department of Agriculture in 1862, has always been involved with the enforcement of purity and potency standards for drug materials, in addition to other stipulated regulatory responsibilities (2,3). The earliest recorded interface between the USP, as a private, nongovernmental drug standards-setting organization, and the federal government regarding enforcement of public standards for strength and purity of drugs occurred in 1848. Congress passed the Drug Importation Act in 1848 to prevent the importation of adulterated and spurious drugs and medicines into the United States. The U.S. Customs Service was empowered to test or have tested drugs and determine if they were inferior in strength and purity to the "standard established in the United States Pharmacopoeia, and therefore improper, unsafe, or dangerous to be used for medicinal purposes, the articles shall not pass the custom house" (4). Currently the USP/NF is recognized in Federal statutes as a drug standards setting body, which in turn mandates that all marketed medicinal articles in the United States, which are the subject of USP/NF monographs, must be fully compliant with all standards established in the monograph for the medicinal article. Noncompliance of the medicinal article with the USP/NF monograph standards makes the article adulterated. Marketing of adulterated articles is illegal and subjects the marketer to FDA compliance actions. While still the benchmark for quality and purity, the above comments regarding compliance of all compendial articles with monograph requirements, the FDA Office of New Drug Quality Assessment has recently issued guidance for new drug development submissions to FDA, MAPP 5310.7, "Acceptability of Standards from Alternative Compendia (BP/EP/JP)." The effective date for this document is November 3, 2007. The policy applies only to original NDA submissions. What the document offers NDA sponsors is the option of using standards from the alternative compendia provided that the rigor and acceptance criteria are equivalent to or better than USP/NF monograph requirements. This option applies to excipients, drug substances, or drug products. Further, if there is no USP/NF monograph in place but there is a BP/EP/JP monograph for the article(s) employed in the drug product submission, the NDA sponsor is authorized to employ the alternative compendial procedure provided that it is equivalent to or better than the corresponding procedures stipulated in USP general chapters. Full details for the new MAPP 5310.7 can be found on the FDA Web site [www.fda.gov/cder/map/5310.7R.pdf]. In addition to the formal monographs in USP/NF, there are sections termed General Notices and Requirements and General Chapters which contain information applicable to all drug substances, inactive ingredients (excipients), drug products, and all other official articles (5).

Finally, it should be noted that the USP was operated as a private, not for profit organization without any legal status until 1900 when the United States Pharmacopeial Convention (USPC) incorporated in the District of Columbia, with a formal constitution and bylaws. The USPC has a formal elected Board of Trustees that oversees the overall operations. Currently there is a staff of approximately 600 employees and a volunteer force of more than 1200 to support USP/NF activities. The volunteers represent practitioners from virtually all sectors of the health care delivery systems industry, globally. Volunteers participating in USP activities (including participation at the 5-year-cycle conventions of the USPC, the current USPC cycle is 2005–2010) include individuals representing accredited schools of medicine and pharmacy, state medical and pharmacy associations, national and international scientific and industry trade associations, consumer organizations, public interest groups, U.S. and international governmental and pharmacopeial agencies, and other sectors of health care delivery activities.A very descriptive overview of the current USP operations base can be found in the Mission and Preface, People/Committees and Convention Members sections of the USP (1,6). At this time, USP headquarters is located in Rockville, MD. Key operations units outside USA include

Europe/Middle East/Africa located in Basel, Switzerland
USP-India located in Hyderabad, India
USP-China located in Shanghai, China

Included in the "Mission and Preface" and "People" sections of the USP is a complete break out of the USP Council of Experts, Expert Committees, Information and Standards Development organization, and a listing of all USP products and services and relationships, as well as explanations on how the reference standards system works and the evolution of compendial changes.

BRIEF HISTORY OF THE USP AND NF

The USP traces its origin to 1820. American physicians in the post-Revolutionary War period were forced to depend on imported texts for information and counsel on the use, composition, and preparation of medicines. The need for a national pharmacopeia became apparent to key practicing physicians at the time.A number of independently developed formularies and pharmacopeias emerged, each servicing regional needs. Dr. Lyman Spalding took the lead and was instrumental in getting the medical establishment to recognize the need for a true national formulary. The process involved bringing together the major medical establishments at a national "convention" in Washington, D.C., in January of 1820 to work out the basis for a "national formulary." His vision, diligence, and leadership finally resulted in the compilation, preparation, and publication of the first USP on December 15, 1820, under the auspices of the convention (7). The first edition of USP bears on the title page the statement that the text was issued under the authority of the Medical Societies and Colleges. The pharmacopeia included a primary list of 221 drugs and a secondary list of 71 drugs. The so-called listing of drugs was referred to as the "materia medica," and represented what the medical experts of the time determined to be the critical medicines needed to treat the population. Primary objectives of the first USP were to provide the correct Latin and English name for a medicine and a description of the material. This point of "nomenclature" remains as a critical ongoing activity of USP, through the "United States Adopted Names" (USAN) Council and the "USP Dictionary of USAN and International Drug Names" (1). At the beginning of the USP process, there were no formal standards or quality specifications included in the compendia for the official articles. There were preparations sections that gave the reader recipes to prepare specific products. The scope of formulations types included solid, semisolid, and liquid dosage forms recognized at that time. The end result of the USP would be to help physicians across the country provide defined and standardized medicines to the public, without having to depend on importation of the articles from overseas. The listing of a medicinal article in the USP was akin to that named material being an "official" medicinal agent. As the USP continued to grow in stature and public recognition, from its inception in 1820, a revision process was put in place to assure that the compendia included the most currently recognized medicines. Further, that articles no longer in common use would be removed from compendial status. Augmentation of USP monographs with tests for identification and drug quality began in 1840 (4,7). As the USP continued on its path of growth and update, the practicing pharmacists of the time become organized into a national organization, the American Pharmaceutical Association (APhA) in 1852. Their primary concerns centered on dealing with the continuing problem of inferior quality medicinal articles coming into the United States from Europe. To attack this problem, the APhA established quality standards incorporated into "official monographs," to augment the USP. Further there were concerns about giving physicians the option to forego ready-made medications and write out prescriptions for such articles that could be compounded by practicing pharmacists. Many of the ready-made medicines were not included in the USP. Thus, the impetus to establish a formal compendia of "unofficial preparations." This activity came under the leadership of Charles Rice and Joseph Remington. The first National Formulary appeared in July 1888. The formal title of the compendium was the "National Formulary of Unofficial Preparations," published under the authority of the APhA. NF I contained only recipes for preparations, 435 recipes, covering all of the oral dosage forms recognized at that time. The theme of NF I was that it was not going to be only a repository for USP discards or a proving ground for novelties, but a source of reliable preparations.

As the USP and NF evolved independently, as compendia of medicinal agents, their formats and general content became quite similar. The APhA had established a laboratory in 1936 for conducting tests to establish adequate drug standards (8). Prior to that point in time, laboratory testing, incidental to the development of NF standards, was done voluntarily or supported by an APhA subsidy at outside laboratories. The USP did not have its own testing laboratory in place, but relied on outside laboratories. In 1962, an integrated Laboratory servicing the USP, NF, and

AMA, was put in place—the Drug Standards Laboratory. Key responsibilities of the laboratory were preparing and testing reference standards (9). The work of the laboratory advanced to investigations of analytical techniques. In 1975, the acquisition of the NF by the USP resulted in the combination of the USP and NF into one compendium, with two separate sections of entry for monographs. The Drug Standards Laboratory became the Drug Research and Testing Laboratory in 1978. The focal point for the laboratory was to qualify reference standards and establish standards for dissolution testing. Currently, USP maintains and operates two laboratories. One laboratory specializes in drug quality testing and the research and development of high quality reference standards. The second laboratory produces and packages those reference standards for distribution around the world. The laboratories are responsible for the validation of testing procedures developed to support the qualification and release of material to serve as USP reference standards. Currently a batch of material targeted to be a lot of a reference standard article is tested in two or more outside laboratories throughout the world plus the USP testing laboratory. Based on satisfactory testing results from the testing laboratories, the reference standards are released under the authority of the USP's Board of Trustees, on the recommendation of the USP Reference Standards Expert Committee, which approves selection and suitability of each lot (10). The USP laboratories also provide scientific support to the Expert Committees for the evaluation of analytical tests and methods proposed for inclusion in the USP.

Until 1906, there were no federal or state laws requiring adherence of medicinal articles being produced or sold in the United States, which were the subjects of USP and NF monographs, to meet the standards of the USP and NF. In 1906, the Federal Food and Drugs Act clearly and specifically acknowledged that drugs solid in interstate commerce, under names that are mentioned in the USP or NF monographs must comply with the listed standards of strength, quality, and purity for these drugs (4). Noncompliant articles would be considered as misbranded and subjected to the legal actions of the Bureau of Chemistry (part of the Department of Agriculture). Products sold under the compendial monograph name, which have differing quality attributes from those specified in the USP or NF monographs then, must declare on the product labeling the strength, purity, and quality of the article (4). In 1927, the Bureau of Chemistry was reorganized into two separate entities, one of which was the Food, Drug, and Insecticide Administration. In 1930, the unit was renamed as the Food and Drug Administration. The administrative control of the FDA was changed from the Department of Agriculture to the Federal Security Agency in 1940. In 1953, the Federal Security Agency became the Department of Health, Education, and Welfare. An excellent summary of the history of the FDA and all key milestones in the history of U.S. Food and Drug laws is provided in reference 2.

Continuing concerns about the shortfalls in the 1906 federal legislation regarding false therapeutic claims for patent medicines and food adulteration lead to efforts to revise the 1906 Food and Drugs Act. The revision efforts were accelerated by the deaths of more than 100 people in 1937 attributed to the ingestion of Massengill's Elixir of Sulfanilamide, which was formulated with highly toxic diethylene glycol. In June of 1938, Congress passed "The Federal Food, Drug, and Cosmetic Act" that now required manufacturers of drugs to submit a new drug application to the FDA, which included full reports of investigations made to show that such a drug is safe for use. The section of the law dealing with the New Drug

Application is section 505. There was no stipulation to require manufacturers to provide data to support the efficacy of new drugs or new formulations of already marketed drugs.A key element in the legislation was the retention of the recognition of the USP and NF as official public standards for medicines, including packaging and labeling requirements (11). Additionally, the new legislation extended control of the FDA to cosmetics and therapeutic devices.

In 1962, the Kefauver-Harris amendments to the 1938 Food, Drug, and Cosmetic Act (Drug Amendments) became U.S. legislation to further strengthen the role of the FDA in controlling prescription drugs, new drugs, and investigational drugs. The public standards role of the USP and NF was not materially affected by the legislation, except for the establishment of the antibiotic certification program. The compendial role in assigning official nomenclature to new drugs was not reduced (11). It is interesting to note that in the 1965 Medicare amendments to the Social Security Act regarding payments for, –"Medical and other health services, —, which cannot be self-administered and which are provided in a physician's office," such as drugs and biologics, must be included or approved for inclusion in the USP or NF (or in hospital formularies for administration in hospitals) to be eligible for Medicare coverage (12).

In 1994, the Dietary Supplement Health and Education Act, amendments to the Food, Drug, and Cosmetic Act, named the USP, NF, and the Homeopathic Pharmacopeia as official compendia for dietary supplements. If a USP/NF monograph exists for a dietary supplement, and the material in the marketplace represents that it meets "USP standards," it is considered as misbranded if it fails to comply with all monograph requirements. The program is voluntary and a dietary supplement that makes no assertion of compliance to USP cannot be held accountable to the monograph standards (12).

In 1997, the Food and Drug Administration Modernization Act (FDAMA) was passed, which included in sections 353 (a) and (c) the allowance for pharmacy compounding of drug products, outside the jurisdiction of the Food, Drug, and Cosmetic Act. The restriction on compounding in the FDAMA legislation was that compounding of drug products would not become an unregulated manufacturing sector. The role of the USP/NF in compounding matters is that compounded articles, which are the subject of USP/NF monographs must comply with all standards of the compendia (12). Currently, sections 353 (a) and (c) of the act has been ruled invalid by the U.S. Supreme Court regarding restrictions in the act to publicly advertise certain compounding services. Pharmacy compounding falls under the jurisdiction of State Boards of Pharmacy. There is no change with respect to requirements regarding compliance of compounded articles to USP monograph and general chapter standards dealing with compounding. FDA has recently issued warning letters to compounding pharmacies that sell and promote compounded menopause hormone therapy drugs for making claims for such products that are not supported by medical evidence.A detailed overview of FDA actions in this arena can be found on the FDA Web site, www.fda.gov/cder/pharmcomp/default.htm.

BRIEF OVERVIEW OF THE CURRENT CONTENTS OF THE USP/NF

The USP 31 and NF 26 (USP/NF 2008), combined in one publication, as three volumes, are actually two separate compendia. Each compendium consists of two primary sections, "General Notices and Requirements" and "Official Monographs."

Additionally, general chapters apply to both USP and NF monographs. The general chapters contain information that relates to testing procedures and practices and supporting information to aid in conducting the testing and interpretation of monograph information and requirements. Typically, each monograph will have specifications and test procedures relevant to the monograph article. Additionally, there will be references within each monograph to general chapter information for conducting certain tests as needed. As a prelude to the individual USP and NF sections of the publication, there is a general umbrella coverage of information that provides details about USP/NF terminology and clarification of practices under the banner of "General Notices and Requirements." Finally, in addition to the formal sections of the compendia identified as USP and NF, there is a section entitled "Dietary Supplements." This section contains monographs structured in similar fashion to the USP and NF monographs. Unlike the USP and NF sections there is no entry prior to the Dietary Supplements monographs of a "General Notices and Requirements" section. It should be noted that the Dietary Supplement section monographs can be considered as being included in the USP, but are distinguished from formal USP monographs.

Official Monographs

An official substance or article is defined in a USP or NF monograph and includes an active drug entity or drug substance, a recognized dietary supplement ingredient, a pharmaceutical formulation ingredient or excipient (or inactive ingredient), or a component of a finished device. An official preparation is a drug product that contains a drug substance or a dietary supplement ingredient. It is the finished or partially finished product or preparation containing one or more official substances intended for patient use.

There are a certain number of compounding monographs that provide detailed instructions for the preparation of the finished product. Currently, the USP section of the compendium has monographs which include virtually all of the above. The NF monograph section is principally devoted to pharmaceutical formulation ingredients or excipients. The NF also has some monographs for botanical articles, including some "compounding formulations." There is a monograph section between the NF and USP sections of the compendium dedicated to Dietary Supplements.

New monograph initiatives by USP are now in place regarding drug products which have been filed with the FDA but not yet approved, termed "Pending Standards," and drug products which are not intended for sale in the United States, but are legally marketed outside the United States, termed SALMOUS. The term SALMOUS stands for "Standards for Articles Legally Marketed Outside the United States." For both categories, the monograph development process will be executed online at the USP Web site and will not appear in either the Pharmacopoeial Forum (PF) (prior to formal authorization or approval of the monograph) or in the USP (post formal authorization or approval). Full details for this new sector of USP are on the USP Web site. Formal guidelines for processing these new categories of monographs from start to finish have been issued and are on the USP Web site. The focus for the SALMOUS monographs is for drugs targeted to treat "neglected diseases." For the pending standards, the focus is to be able to initiate the monograph process at the earliest possible stage during the drug approval process at FDA. As soon as FDA approval is reached, the monograph in principle is ready to become official. See the following Web sites for full details:

Pending Standards: www.usp.org/standards/pending/guidelines.html.
SALMOUS (International Standards): www.usp.org/standards/international/guidelines.html.

With respect to the content of a monograph, the formal terminology employed by USP is classified as follows:

Universal tests
- Description
- Identification
- Assay
- Impurities
- Organic, Inorganic, Residual Solvents

Specific Tests
- Physicochemical Characterization and Water Content

With respect to the categories of compendial articles, the following break out is now part of the USP culture:

Noncomplex Active Drug Substances and Drug Products
Biotechnology Derived Drug Substances and Drug Products
- Excipients
- Vaccines
- Blood and Blood Products
- Gene and Cell Therapy Products
- Dietary Supplement Ingredients and Products
- Compounding Substance/Preparations/Practice

Informational Sections of the USP/NF

General Notices and Requirements

Applies to all sections of the USP and NF.

General Chapters

These include general requirements for tests and assays for monograph articles. Included are sections dealing with specific chemical, microbiological, biological, physical tests, and a listing of all current USP reference standards. Currently, there are approximately 2000 reference standards sold by the USP covering drug substances, excipients, and dietary supplements. These reference standards are listed in each revision of USP and additions in the supplements. The general chapter listings start from <1> to less than <1000>. Individual monographs in the USP/NF can have specific general chapter references as part of the monograph testing protocol.

General Information Chapters

General Information Chapters are not currently mandated in any compendial monograph but do reflect good scientific practices, these practices/procedures are provided as supplemental information. The general information chapter listings start at <1000> and proceed upward. There is no scientific rationale for the order of chapters within the section or assignment of chapter numbers. Again one must regard these chapters as supplemental, nonbinding information, as is the case for general information chapters covering the USP and NF sections of the compendium.

As a prelude to the general chapters section in USP, there is an excellent overview of the breakout of how general chapters and general information chapters relate to the various categories of monographs in the USP. For the current USP 2008, this section is called "Guide to General Chapters" or "Chart Guide." What is provided to the reader is a break out of the terminology for the categories of official articles and defining which general chapters/general information chapters apply for the various categories of testing employed in the individual monographs.

Finally, the Chart Guide provides a clear overview of the testing categories that are required or incorporated into individual monographs.

Reagents, Indicators, and Solutions

Covers materials required for all monograph tests and assays

Reference Tables

Covers ancillary information that supplements the monograph content. Included within the Reference Tables are two very useful chapters about the monograph articles, "Description and Solubility" and "Solubilities."

Browsing these general information sectors of USP is valuable to assess the extraordinary scope and depth of the available information within USP. For example, there is one break out section in the beginning of the NF that categorizes the functionality of all USP and NF excipients (13).

Pharmacopeial Harmonization

A key USP initiative is the process of harmonization of monographs and general chapters with the European Pharmacopoeia (EP) and Japanese Pharmacopoeia. Under an umbrella organization called the Pharmacopeial Discussion Group (PDG) (formed in 1989), the USP, EP, and JP work to identify monograph or general chapter candidates for harmonization. The World Health Organization is present at PDG meetings as an observer. The PDG works in "harmony" with the International Conference on Harmonization of Technical Requirements (ICH), with the focus on compendial issues. The USP general information chapter <1196> Pharmacopeial Harmonization, provides a detailed explanation of the PDG process and the current metrics for the harmonization for excipients and general chapters. To date no active ingredients have been considered for harmonization. Advantages of harmonization relates to global use of an article and the need to have only one compendial standard for testing. The degree of harmonization can range from having "identical" monographs or general chapters in the USP/EP/JP to indicating which attributes are harmonized and which ones are not harmonized within the published text.

Revision Process for USP/NF

Both the USP and NF developed publication cycles for revisions, with interim revision announcements. The cycle times were 10 years then 5 years. In 1975 the USP and NF merged when the USP purchased the NF, and new title became the USP/NF. Starting in 2002, the USP/NF has become an annual publication with two formal supplements issued in the calendar year. For the current USP (USP 31/NF 26, 2008), the formal release date of the publication is November 1, 2008, with an official date of May 1, 2008, which will remain official until May 1, 2009, unless superceded by supplements, IRAs (Interim Revision Announcements), or revision bulletins (hard copy or online).

Supplement 1 will be published in February 2008 with an official date of August 2008. Supplement 2 will have a release date of June 1, 2008, with an official date of December 1, 2008. The updates of USP/NF is carried out with a publication termed "Pharmacopeial Forum" (PF). It is published on a bimonthly basis and is the manner in which the USP advises the public about changes that are being considered for both monograph and nonmonograph content of the USP/NF. Public comment is invited about all content in the PF and USP.A typical issue of the PF provides the reader with potential revisions (Pharmacopeial Previews), proposed revisions (In-Process Revisions), and adopted revisions (Interim Revision Announcement). Additionally, the PF encourages public involvement in the revision process and there is a section of the PF devoted to public comments called "Stimuli to the Revision Process." Instructions for public comment are provided in the PF (14). Finally each entry in PF that concerns a proposed change in USP/NF provides the reader with a guide for the future about the revision proposal. There are defined periods for public comment before a subsequent step occurs in the revision process. It is very important for readers of the PF to understand the cycle time for events so that changes that may be untoward or possibly "errata" must be intercepted by direct communication to the specified USP staff liaison person designated in the PF entry for the item in question. The "Interim Revision Announcement (IRA)" provides the reader with the date that the revision will become official.and identifies which subsequent publication of the USP will contain the official change. This could be either a future supplement or a future revision of USP. Currently, there is a 90-day period for public comment about IRAs. It is critical that USP Stakeholders be aware of all changes in dates of implementation for proposed revisions. As noted in sections above, the formal official date of the current USP is in fact May 1, 2008. There are critical changes underway at USP for key sections, such as General Notices and Requirements and the General Chapter on Residual Solvents, that have been involved in multiple periods of delayed implementation. For regulatory purposes, it is very important to be aware of delayed implementation actions by carefully monitoring the USP Web site and carefully reading the PF. USP has established periodic "press releases" such as a quarterly newsletter for updates of USP activities. Additionally, the bimonthly USP catalog is another very useful information pool about the status of reference standards and publication dates.

Formal and Informal Linkage of the USP and FDA

All official articles (active or inactive ingredients or preparations or drug products) dictate that the user must assure that the articles are fully compliant with all specified USP/NF monograph requirements and ancillary compendial requirements.

The submission of a drug application to the FDA that includes any article covered by a USP/NF monograph directly links the USP to the submission. The drug application sponsor must provide the FDA with data and information that demonstrate that the compendial articles or drug preparation included in the drug application is fully compliant with all compendial requirements.

Included in the information sections of the compendia are procedures for validation of compendial methods and the conduct of virtually all monograph test procedures. The concept of compliancy is that the article or preparation will maintain compliancy to the monograph requirements throughout the labeled expiry date or use period for the article or preparation.

Following satisfaction of the FDA drug product review branch with the drug application, the second tier of demonstration of compliance with all USP/NF requirements occurs during field inspections, at the sponsor's manufacturing site. Typically, this could be a preapproval inspection or a cGMP inspection. The drug application sponsor must be prepared to show the FDA that all USP/NF requirements were met from use of the appropriate USP reference standards (or qualified house standards), equipment qualification, and assay validation. It is very important to have complete understanding of the content of the general chapters" in USP and be prepared to explain any inconsistencies that may be in internal SOPs or control documents versus the USP content.

As noted above, USP monograph requirements are not release requirements but expected quality attributes through the defined expiry period for the product. This can only be confirmed by continued stability evaluation of the product.

Some typical issues that a drug application sponsor has to deal with are continued vigilance to respond to a monograph change(s) that may occur over time. Any change must be a catalyst to upgrade all procedures and documents affecting the drug article due to monograph or general chapter change(s). It is not uncommon that a drug application sponsor may be using alternate methods for the monograph article. Any monograph change dictates that a revalidation be implemented to demonstrate that the monograph change does not alter the comparability of the alternate method to the new monograph procedure. Evaluation of proposed monograph or general chapter changes must be made on a critical path to assure that appropriate comments are conveyed to USP in a timely manner to assure that inappropriate changes do not get to the final step of approval in the USP change process.

CURRENT ISSUES: USP INFORMATION VS. FDA REQUIREMENTS

The USP includes in the general chapters and general information topics that impact on compendial testing. Frequently, the same topics are the subject of FDA guidance or ICH guidelines. Updates occur and it is very important to always assess the currency of the information in the USP versus updated FDA guidance or ICH guidelines. Any inconsistencies or conflicts must be immediately conveyed to the USP. It is critical that stakeholders of USP products and services become cognizant of the USP change control processes. Who are the contact persons at USP for specific issues is something that should be defined and continually monitored. Participation and awareness of USP conferences and workshops can be a very important source of information about changes that USP may be considering that could impact a firm's understanding of USP defined procedures and practices. Updating internal controls and procedures and updating drug product applications based on USP changes is an eternal task that simply cannot be overlooked.

FUTURE ROLE OF THE USP IN THE DRUG REGULATORY PROCESS

As the USP continues to evolve with the introduction of new analytical technologies into general chapters, <1000>, and general information chapters, <1000>, such as Near-IR Spectrophotometry <1119>, the impact is to encourage USP stakeholders to consider using the newer technologies as a replacement for the current, and outmoded, USP monograph procedures. An interesting sidebar in using newer technologies is the fact that long standing specifications may have to change to reflect the accuracy and specificity of the technologies. This presents an interesting paradigm for FDA filed specifications for NDAs and ANDAs. Another interesting arena for USP is to consider what type of guidance to provide stakeholders on dealing with the global problem of counterfeiting and adulteration of drug products. Currently, the public standards provided by USP are totally focused on the purity and quality of the compendial articles. It is clear that dealing with issues of counterfeiting and adulteration will need a new focus. The FDA has been involved with counterfeiting and adulteration and there is need for greater involvement of the USP in these matters as it relates to upgrading public standards to try and deal with the issues.

There are two additional arenas for USP enhancements to public standards. One is to provide more flexibility in the execution of testing compendial articles to allow for minor differences in product characteristics, and not require specific multiple testing procedures in the monographs. Another arena is to enhance the use of performance/functionality testing of compendial articles.

The arena of Process Analytical Technology (PAT), which currently has a very strong endorsement by the FDA, dictates the need for USP to reengineer it's "mind set" about reference standards to support future drug product monographs which may have two tiers of testing. Tier 1 might be the traditional monograph portfolio of "Universal Tests" and "Specific Tests." As previously noted Universal Tests include description, identification, impurities, and assay. Specific tests include uniformity of dosage units, performance tests such as dissolution/drug release, pH, etc.

For PAT, process monitoring and control, where virtually every dosage unit can be expected to be within an acceptance boundary of critical quality attributes, end product testing may need to be totally redefined in Tier 2 testing requirements. What type of reference standards will be needed is currently unknown. With respect to USP monograph development, both the preparation of a new monograph and revision of an existing monograph, the USP has recently updated on its Web site "Submission Guidelines" for monograph development. The guideline goes across all types of articles, in the domain of "non-complex actives and excipients" and "complex actives" as well as the other monograph categories. For complete details see www.usp.org/USPNF/submiMonographs/subGuide.html

Heretofore, USP involvement in process development was very limited. With this new horizon of process monitoring/process control, a new era is upon the USP. The changing testing objectives will have a very important impact on regulatory submissions and routine quality control. PAT, at its ultimate refinement, is perceived to be an online/in-line continuous monitoring and control-based operation during routine manufacturing of a drug product (15,16). Every advance in process analytical chemistry and analytical technology introduced to the pharmaceutical industry will have an impact on compendial testing. In turn this will impact on regulatory filings.

Finally, one of the practices in place currently, aside from periodic meetings of USP Staff with FDA, which is a true attempt to link up USP and the Pharmaceutical Industry, with the presence and participation of the FDA, is the Prescription/Non-Prescription Stakeholder Forum. This brings together key players from all sectors of the industry, USP, and the FDA. Issues that have been identified, and in need of resolution, under the umbrella of the P/N-P Stakeholder Forum, lead to the formation of project teams. The role of the project team is to bring together the key factors associated with an issue and provide closure recommendations to the P/NP stakeholder forum, which in turn is provided to USP for follow-up. The FDA has input on all matters as a participant in the P/N-P stakeholder forum. All stakeholder forum meeting minutes are made public and available on the USP Web site. Further, the membership of every project team as well as key information generated by the project teams are also made available by USP.

The key point here is that FDA is right on top of all current USP issues identified by industry.

CONCLUSIONS

The USP/NF continues to serve the public health by providing public standards for pharmaceuticals and dietary supplements.By its current collaborative efforts on harmonization in concert with the EP and JP, the USP assures that monographs and general chapters have global recognition. Further, by continuing to upgrade the analytical technologies in the USP, the FDA will almost certainly continue to rely on the USP as an acceptable benchmark for the assessment of critical product quality attributes, suitable for regulatory submissions. The outreach activities of USP through the medium of the stakeholder forums further assures industry and the FDA that issues of concern can be brought to closure. For the future, we can envision that USP will play a role in dealing with global issues such as counterfeiting, and, providing pathways for industry employment of PAT with reduced dependence on standard analytical requirements for product release.

REFERENCES

1. Mission Statement and Preface. United States Pharmacopeia 31-National Formulary 26 [USP/NF 2008], The United States Pharmacopeial Convention, Rockville, MD, v–x.
2. Milestones in U.S. Food and Drug Law History. FDA, Backgrounder, http://www.cfsan.fda.gov/mileston.html.
3. Janssen W F. The Story of the Laws Behind the Labels, Part I 1906 Food and Drugs Act., Part II, 1938 The Federal Food, Drug, and Cosmetic Act., Part III, 1962 Drug Amendments, FDA Consumer, June 1981; available on FDA Web site; Part 1 = http://www.cfsan.fda.gov/lrd/history1.html, Part 2 = history1a, Part 3 = history1b.
4. Anderson L, Higby GJ. The spirit of voluntarism, a legacy of commitment and contribution, The United States Pharmacopeia 1820–1995, United States Pharmacopeial Convention, 1995:71, 6. www.ippsr.msu.edu/documents/forums/2006_may_perlstadt_history_of_fda.pdf.
5. General Notices and Requirements and General Chapters. USP 2008, 2008:1–31 and 33–374.
6. People/Committees, "People/Convention Members", USP 2008, 2008:xi–xxii.
7. Anderson L, Higby GJ. "The Spirit of Voluntarism." Board of Trustees, United States Pharmacopeial Convention. 1995:141–144, 155–156.
8. History of the National Formulary. The National Formulary, 10th edition (N.F. X), American Pharmaceutical Association, 1955:xxii–xxiii.
9. Anderson L, Higby GJ. "The Spirit of Voluntarism—", 1995:363–365. http://www.usp.org/aboutUSP/history.html?USP.
10. USP Catalog, September–October, 2008:19.

11. Anderson L, Higby GJ. The Spirit of Voluntarism— 1995:281, 357.
12. Valentino JG. USP Admissions Policy on Approving New Drugs for Inclusion in the United States Pharmacopeia (USP) is Presented. Pharmacopeial Forum November–December, 2000; 26(6):1519.
13. Excipients. USP 2008, 2008:1057–1061.
14. Pharmacopial Forum. USPC, Bimonthly Publication.
15. Hussain A. FDA's PAT & cGMP Initiative for the 21st Century: Status Update and Challenges to be Addressed. NJPhAST 2003 Symposium, Rutgers University, Piscataway, NJ, 2003.
16. Gary Ritchie. Topic 3, Process Analytical Technology: Near-IR. Analytical Methods and General USP Topics, Philadelphia, PA, 2003.
17. Mission Statement and Preface. United States Pharmacopeia 31/ National Formulary 26, (USP/NF 2008) 2008:ix.

19 Ways, Means, and Evolving Trends in the U.S. Registration of Drug Products from Foreign Countries*

Alberto Grignolo

PAREXEL International Corporation, Waltham, Massachusetts, U.S.A.

INTRODUCTION

There* is continuing interest in the development, U.S. Food and Drug Administration (FDA) approval, and importation of foreign drugs into the U.S. market—still the largest in the world. The existing FDA regulations continue to place significant challenges on both foreign and U.S. manufacturers, and are not expected to become more lenient in the foreseeable future. The drivers of FDA's position are as follows:

Drug Safety: FDA's appetite for approving drugs without "sufficient" safety information has been significantly diminished by safety-related withdrawals of approved drugs from the U.S. market; the degree of "data sufficiency" has become more of a moving target, as many companies have discovered in recent years.

Political Pressure: The U.S. Congress has expressed concern not only about drug safety, but also about perceived close ties between FDA and the pharmaceutical industry, and about a lack of industry transparency relating to the results of clinical trials.

The passage of the FDA Amendments Act of 2007 (FDAAA) reflected this congressional concern; while user fees were renewed (PDUFA IV), the new law gives FDA greater powers of enforcement with regard to drug safety surveillance after approval, and obligates pharmaceutical companies to publish the results (both negative and positive) of most clinical trials on a public Web site.

Critical Path: FDA's growing belief (at management levels, for the moment) that there must a better way to develop new drugs, and that scientists, regulators, and industry should find it by leveraging pharmacogenomics, adaptive trials, risk stratification, drug-diagnostic codevelopment, imaging endpoints, and more. Until then, drug development is viewed as "empirical" rather than "intelligent," and risk-benefit negotiations between industry and FDA are still characterized by a degree of arbitrariness.

Study Designs: Recent public (Advisory Committee) debates on noninferiority study designs for antibiotics reflect a discomfort within FDA about what

* A previous version of this chapter, published in 2005, was co-authored by Jill E. Kompa, Richard J. Schwen and David Skarinsky. A large majority of their contributions, which are gratefully acknowledged, is retained in this chapter. However, the author assumes full responsibility for its contents and can be contacted at Alberto.Grignolo@PAREXEL.com.

constitutes evidence of efficacy. No relaxation is envisioned in this matter or in the relevant regulations; companies expect to continue to have detailed negotiations with FDA on study designs, especially for Phase III development.

Foreign companies are subject to the same FDA scrutiny as U.S. companies, and are well-advised to appreciate these drivers and to work within them if they wish to be successful in the United States. The importation of foreign drugs needs to comply with regulations because FDA has become more enforcement-minded but with a twist; while in the past the agency cast a wide inspectional net, now FDA has reduced the frequency of inspections, but makes a visible and financially punitive example of those companies (foreign or domestic) that it catches in egregious violative behaviors. The agency is increasingly concerned about the GMP compliance in the manufacturing of Active Pharmaceutical Ingredients (APIs) used in the United States, a large percentage of which are imported (statement of FDA Commissioner Andrew C. von Eschenbach, before U.S. House of Representatives Committee on Energy and Commerce, Subcommittee on Oversight and Investigations, on FDA's Foreign Drug Inspection Program; Nov. 1, 2007) and may increase GMP foreign inspectional activity in the coming years.

An important factor driving foreign companies' interest in obtaining FDA approval is the desire to leverage foreign data and regulatory approvals to enter the U.S. market. The economics of pharmaceutical development have a significant impact on the strategy for global marketing approval of new drugs. This is particularly true when sponsors develop and register a drug in one country, and then seek marketing approval for the new drug product from regulatory bodies in a different country or region. However, although the drug development process may be similar in different regions, differences due to culture, medical practice, demographics, and other factors can impact how and how rapidly new drugs gain access to different markets. For instance, such differences could complicate the registration process when sponsors seek FDA registration of a pharmaceutical product for the U.S. market based on data gathered outside the United States. A thorough understanding of the issues involved and careful execution of the U.S. regulatory strategy can help make the process manageable.

This chapter addresses the following topics:

- FDA requirements for registration of foreign drugs, including criteria for acceptability of foreign data, as well as the impact of the International Conference on Harmonization (ICH) guidelines.
- Challenges facing foreign drugs, including chemistry, manufacturing, and control (CMC), clinical and nonclinical issues.
- Factors that can facilitate FDA approval of foreign drugs, including a comparison of the requirements for the New Drug Application (NDA) and the Common Technical Document (CTD).
- Practices and behaviors that increase the likelihood of FDA approval of foreign drugs, including especially communications with the FDA.

REGULATORY FRAMEWORK RELEVANT TO U.S. REGISTRATION OF FOREIGN DRUGS

Two regulatory entities have an impact on the issues surrounding U.S. registration of foreign drugs. The U.S. FDA plays the major role, as it sets the criteria for acceptance. Additionally, the International Conference on Harmonization (ICH), under the auspices of the six founding members representing the regulatory bodies and research-based industry in the European Union, Japan, and the United States, has addressed the issue with specific Guidelines and the CTD.

U.S. Food and Drug Administration

FDA regulations governing the approval to market a new drug are covered in the Code of Federal Regulations (CFR), Title 21, Part 314. The regulations do allow the approval of an NDA based solely on foreign clinical data, provided that the application meets three criteria outlined in 21 CFR 314.106.

The regulation states that "an application based solely on foreign clinical data meeting U.S. criteria for marketing approval may be approved if

1. "the foreign data are applicable to the U.S. population and U.S. medical practice;
2. "the studies have been performed by clinical investigators of recognized competence; and
3. "the data may be considered valid without the need for an on-site inspection or, if FDA considers such an inspection to be necessary, FDA is able to validate the data through an on-site inspection or other appropriate means. The FDA will apply this policy in a flexible manner according to the nature of the drug and the data being considered."

The regulation also encourages consultation between applicants and the FDA. It specifically suggests a "presubmission" meeting between applicants and agency officials when the sponsor intends to seek approval based solely on foreign data. For more about presubmission meetings, refer to "Communications with FDA" later in this chapter.

If the agency feels that the criteria listed above have been met, it may approve the product based on foreign studies. As Table 1 illustrates, the FDA has approved approximately 80 drugs based solely or predominantly on clinical data generated outside the United States.

International Conference on Harmonization

Recognizing the need to eliminate redundancies in research while supporting the sovereignty of the respective regulatory bodies, ICH has examined ways to help make clinical data collected in one region acceptable to the regulatory authority of another region. One outcome of this ongoing effort is the ICH guideline E5, "Ethnic Factors in the Acceptability of Foreign Clinical Data." Developed to facilitate registration of medicines within ICH regions, the guideline suggests a framework for evaluating the impact of a wide range of ethnic factors—genetic and physiologic, as well as cultural and environmental—on the safety and efficacy of the drug for which registration is being sought.

For sponsors of foreign drugs, ICH guideline E5 complements the FDA regulations. The ICH guideline notes that all data in the clinical section should meet the standards for study design and conduct, and should satisfy the regulatory requirements of the region in which the sponsor seeks approval. Once that has been accomplished, the sponsor must be able to extrapolate the study data to the population of the new region, in this case, the United States. If the sponsor or the regulatory agency is concerned that ethnic differences could have a significant impact on the safety or efficacy of the drug in the new population, additional data may be necessary.

TABLE 1 Drugs that have Received FDA Approval Based on non-U.S. Data

Acutect	Genotropin	Posicor
	Gonal-F	Pravachol
Albenza	Granisetron	
Ambisome	Halfan	Prograf
Anzemet	Haloperidol	Propafenone
Arimadex	Hycamtin	Prosynap
Betaxolol	Indium IN-111	Quinapril
Bravavir	Isosorbide mononitrate	Refluden
Buspirone	Lamictal	Rilutek
Calcitonin-Salmon	Lamivudine	Rivizor
Carboplatin	Levonorgestrel	Salmeterol
Cellcept	lutamide	Seroquel
Crixivan	Merrem	Stromectol
Cysteamine	Mesna	Strontium Chloride
Dalteparin	Metoprolol	Sumatriptan
Denavir	Mifepristone	Tacrine
Desogestrel/ethinyl estradiol	Myotrophin	Tacrolimus
Diazepam emulsion	Nafareline nasal solution	Tamoxifen citrate
Dinoprostone	Naropin	Thalidomide
Dostinex	Nefazodone	Ticlopidine
Dronabinol	Neufolie	Tranexamic acid
Enoxaparin	Nimodipine	Trovan
Exelon	Novantrone	Venlafaxine
Femara	Olsalazine	Vinorelbine
Finasteride	Omeprazole	Viramune
Follistim	Ondansetron	Zithromax
Gabapentin	Paclitaxel	Zoladex
	Plavix	

The core concept of ICH guideline E5 is the "bridging study." ICH defines the bridging study as "a study performed in the new region to provide pharmacodynamic or clinical data on efficacy, safety, dosage and dose regimen in the new region that will allow extrapolation of the foreign clinical data to the population in the new region. A bridging study for efficacy could provide additional pharmacokinetic information in the population of the new region. When no bridging study is needed to provide clinical data for efficacy, a pharmacokinetic study in the new region may be considered as a bridging study."

The concept assumes that the need for any new data is based on the drug's level of sensitivity to ethnic differences between the two regions. If the bridging study results in similar data in the new population, the original efficacy and safety data should be sufficient to support approval in the new region. In such cases, the sponsor should not need to replicate the original studies in the new population. On the other hand, if the bridging study fails, the sponsor would generally need to conduct a new efficacy and safety study in the population of the target region.

In writing guideline E5, ICH suggested that increasing experience with cross-regional acceptance would diminish the need for bridging studies. To date that has not been the case. Bridging studies have become much larger than ICH intended, and many fall outside the spirit of Guideline E5. ICH is in the process of reevaluating guideline E5 in order to make the guidance more practical and useful to sponsors.

The impact of guideline E5 on FDA approval of foreign drugs can be favorable to sponsors if FDA agrees that a bridging study can help satisfy the requirements for approval of a specific new drug, consistent with 21 CFR 314.106. Sponsors should discuss this possibility well in advance with FDA and determine if in fact the agency might require additional, larger phase III confirmatory trials conducted in the United States.

POTENTIAL OBSTACLES TO THE REGISTRATION OF FOREIGN DRUGS

Sponsors of foreign drugs face a number of challenges when attempting to persuade the FDA that a new drug is approvable. Most of these obstacles are inherent in the drug development process. They are not unique to foreign drugs; differences in culture, testing procedures, standard medical practices, demographics, and other factors can magnify the challenges. Sponsors must recognize the potential pitfalls and plan ahead in order to minimize the impact of ethnic factors on the approval of an NDA.

The issues that sponsors of foreign drugs must address fall into three broad categories—CMC, nonclinical, and clinical.

Chemistry, Manufacturing, and Controls Issues

The FDA requires the same CMC information for foreign drugs as it does for unapproved new domestic drugs. The amount of CMC information required varies, depending on the type of submission. Specific requirements are stipulated in the various FDA guidances relevant to Investigational New Drug (IND) applications, NDAs, Abbreviated New Drug Applications (ANDAs), etc.

All drug manufacturers must comply with current Good Manufacturing Practices (cGMPs) for finished pharmaceuticals, as specified in 21 CFR 211. Manufacturers must meet United States Pharmacopeia (USP) standards for the drug substance, its excipients, or the drug product, if available. If the substance is not listed in the USP, the sponsor may reference other pharmacopoeial standards, such as the British Pharmacopoeia (BP) or European Pharmacopoeia (EP). If no pharmacopoeial standards exist, the sponsor must provide a full characterization of the new ingredient in the NDA. As is true with all drugs, sponsors of foreign drugs should follow ICH quality guidelines regarding stability, validation of analytical procedures, acceptable levels of impurities, residual solvents, etc. In addition, sponsors should follow the new ICH guideline Q7 A—Good Manufacturing Practice Guide for Active Pharmaceutical Ingredients—given FDA's emerging concern about APIs that are sourced outside the United States.

Sponsors may submit information regarding the chemistry and manufacturing of drug substances, products, excipients, or packaging in a Drug Master File, which can be referenced in ongoing submissions to the FDA. A U.S.-based agent acting on behalf of the sponsor must submit foreign drug master files.

Importation procedures and related issues: Foreign sponsors must comply with the same requirements for establishment, registration, and product listing that apply to U.S.-based manufacturers. Foreign manufacturers must register with the FDA's Drug Listing Branch and have a drug establishment number assigned to them. Individual drug products to be imported must also be registered with this FDA branch. In order to import a foreign drug product through U.S. customs, the importer should provide relevant documentation. This might include an IND number, an approval letter if the drug is a marketed product, and proof that the product has been appropriately listed with the Drug Listing Branch. The import process is often best handled through an experienced import broker who can facilitate a positive outcome and avoid potential delays. Retrospectively, foreign drug establishments often cite delays in the import process as a common occurrence that they might have avoided, had they used an experienced broker.

Foreign manufacturers must also have a U.S. agent who resides in or maintains a physical place of business in the United States. The agent facilitates communication between the FDA and the foreign manufacturer. The FDA will contact the U.S. agent in regard to both facility and drug listing issues for the foreign-based manufacturer.

FDA inspections of foreign manufacturers: The FDA may inspect a foreign manufacturing site if, at any time, the agency determines that an inspection is warranted. Sometimes the initial act of registering an establishment with the Drug Listing Branch may prompt an inspection, particularly if the sponsor intends to import the listed drug in the very near future. The FDA is likely to consider an inspection if the facility has not been inspected previously.

If the FDA conducts an inspection and finds problems, the inspector will report his or her observations of the conditions and practices observed at the site on FDA Form 483. The firm is then required to respond to the FDA's findings and to indicate the corrective actions that they will take to resolve the issues. Depending on their nature and volume, the overall findings can be the basis of the FDA's determination as to whether the establishment is compliant with cGMPs. If the FDA does not consider a facility to be in compliance with cGMPs, it will not approve pending drug applications until the establishment resolves GMP-facility–related issues. If the findings are significant, the FDA will likely reinspect the facility to ensure adequate resolution of previous concerns.

Reinspection often takes time, and the additional lead time required for inspectors to travel to foreign sites can lead to approval delays. It is important to be aware that lack of inspection readiness on the part of the manufacturing site is a common reason why the FDA considers submissions to be nonapprovable.

Nonclinical Issues

FDA's nonclinical testing requirements for foreign drugs are identical to the requirements for unapproved new U.S. drugs. In all cases, the data must demonstrate safety for human subjects during clinical trials and for patients when the drug is marketed.

The efforts of the ICH have resulted in the harmonization of basic requirements for nonclinical study design; however, specific requirements for nonclinical studies can be very specific to each drug and indication. The ICH guideline M3, "Timing of Pre-clinical Studies in Relation to Clinical Trials," addresses general considerations in regard to when nonclinical studies are conducted in a "prototypical" drug development program. The guideline provides a point of reference, but it is not a substitute for communication with the FDA. Consultation with the FDA is appropriate at Pre-IND, End of phase II, and Pre-NDA conferences in order to clarify specific requirements on a case-by-case basis. However, the sponsor should not necessarily expect the FDA to provide guidance and direction spontaneously. Rather, it is the responsibility of the sponsor to design and propose the nonclinical testing program for FDA's concurrence and possible modification.

A proper toxicology program is designed with consideration for the following:

- known safety data on the drug (in vitro, animals, and humans),
- results of an early risk assessment identifying data gaps that need to be addressed,
- relevant FDA and ICH guidelines,
- proposed exposure and use/indication of the drug in man, whether in clinical trials or on the market,
- direct input from FDA, and
- sound toxicology advice.

In order for the foreign nonclinical data to be acceptable to the FDA, the testing must be conducted according to Good Laboratory Practices (GLPs, found in 21 C. F.R 58). The FDA may inspect the nonclinical testing facility, the nonclinical data, or both. The FDA is most likely to select for closer scrutiny of those studies that suggest potential and significant safety issues in humans. In these cases, the FDA tries to determine whether the study was designed and conducted properly, that is to say in accordance with GLPs. References and guidance for monitoring GLPs are available on the FDA Web site at www.fda.gov/ora/compliance_ref/bimo/glp/default.htm. The agency will also address the significance of the animal data in relation to humans. Although nonclinical investigational studies, such as dose-ranging or pilot studies, are technically exempt from the GLP requirement, safety (toxicology) studies—which are critical for safety assessment—certainly are not.

Serious concerns regarding the quality of the data can trigger a "for cause" inspection of the animal facility.

The drug substance and drug product, or formulation, tested in the nonclinical studies should be relevant to the product that the sponsor intends to market in the United States. This requirement is based on the need for the data from safety studies to be relevant to the risk assessment process, particularly if the product formulation or quality are different from that to be marketed in humans. Studies of such variants do not necessarily predict response in humans. This relevance is a critical factor in FDA's acceptance of foreign data.

As is usually the case in drug development, sequential "improvements" in the drug substance and/or drug product are made as the development program progresses from preclinical to clinical stages. The sponsor may need to repeat preclinical studies if the earlier studies were conducted with a product that the FDA considers significantly different from the clinical product.

While the final safety database should reflect known safety concerns that have been observed in either animals or humans throughout drug development, the actual timing of nonclinical studies should be linked to the drug's stage of development. The nonclinical testing should generate sufficient quantity and quality of data to allow for a reliable risk/benefit analysis prior to each clinical trial in a drug development program.

The sponsor should address the safety observations made in clinical trials and should work with nonclinical models addressing relevance to humans when appropriate. Dose relationship and reversibility of observed effects are normally required in order to allow for a proper risk assessment in humans. It is important that the sponsor conduct the nonclinical testing in a species whose absorption, distribution, metabolism, and excretion are relevant to humans.

As human data become available, the sponsor should reevaluate the selected nonclinical testing models in order to assure the program's relevance to humans. In reality, safety models and programs must be revised if the data collected indicate that different, more appropriate, studies are required to make an accurate risk assessment.

In recent years, FDA has developed a more generalized interest in assessing the potential of drugs to induce electrocardiographic changes (specifically QTc prolongation) that might lead to adverse cardiac events, including ventricular tachyarrhythmia and *torsade de pointes*. Sponsors are frequently required to conduct nonclinical studies demonstrating the presence or absence of QTc prolongation potential of new drugs; ICH has issued a safety guideline on this issue (S7B), reflecting a concern by all ICH partners. Sponsors should discuss with FDA in advance the need to conduct nonclinical studies to address this issue. ICH has also issued a companion clinical guideline (E14—The Clinical Evaluation of QT/QTc Interval Prolongation and Proarrhythmic Potential for Non-Antiarrhythmic Drugs) and sponsors are well advised to take it into account and to discuss with FDA the need to conduct clinical assessment of their investigational drugs to address the QTc prolongation potential issue in humans.

Clinical Issues

Regulatory bodies, such as the FDA, are cautious about basing registration solely on foreign data, due to the potential impact of ethnic differences on the product labeling and selection of dose and dose regimen. By planning to address intrinsic (i.e., genetic and physiologic) and extrinsic (i.e., cultural and environmental) ethnic differences throughout the drug development process, the sponsor of a foreign drug may save time, reduce the need to replicate studies, and build a stronger case for FDA acceptance, including nearly every aspect of clinical development from study design to patient issues, to investigator selection, to study conduct.

Investigator/site selection: For example, in order to evaluate the quality of foreign data, the FDA must feel comfortable with the selection of investigators and sites. Selecting academic or high-visibility centers of excellence and providing standardized investigator training can help address concerns about quality of data. However, the reputation of a center is not, in and of itself, an assurance that clinical trials conducted there are GCP-compliant or relevant to the U.S. population.

Selected investigators must be familiar with conducting controlled clinical trials according to Good Clinical Practice (GCP) guidelines; they must also understand the critical nature of timely safety reporting to support labeling. Selected sites should have sufficient research training and experience in conducting trials that may eventually be audited by the FDA. In case of an audit, documentation of adherence to GCPs and timely safety reporting may be a critical determinant of whether the data will be acceptable to FDA for purposes of NDA approval.

Qualified investigators and savvy sponsors need to be aware of the differences between local and cross-border standards of diagnosis and patient care. Standardization of diagnostic criteria and treatment measures prior to initiating a foreign study intended for U.S. registration helps minimize variability across sites and provides for validation of the criteria early in the development process. Linking those criteria and measures to analogous ones known to be acceptable in the United States may prove essential to ensuring acceptance of the trial data to the U.S. medical community and to FDA.

Control of investigational drug product and control over the conduct of the investigation are essential for U.S. registration. If the study is conducted under an IND, the FDA requires the investigator to sign FDA Form 1572, the *Statement of Investigator*. By signing this form, the investigator makes a legally binding commitment—under U.S. federal law and with federal penalties—to conduct the study according to the protocol, to personally conduct and supervise the investigation, to maintain study records and submit all materials to the Institutional Review Board (IRB) or local Ethics Committee (EC). No such commitment or enforcement mechanism exists for a non-IND study. Therefore, the sponsor must provide training and carefully document that the investigator has full control over the investigation and understands his or her ultimate responsibility for the quality of the outcome. It is important to realize that it is not necessary to conduct a foreign clinical trial under an IND for it to be acceptable to FDA, nor will its conduct under an IND make it "more acceptable" to FDA. The key success factors for clinical data acceptance are GCP compliance and relevance of the data to the appropriate U.S. patient population.

Ethics committee/Institutional Review Board selection: An FDA concern regarding some foreign studies is the lack of local control or inspection of studies by local ECs. It is important to be aware of how local ethical standards and review processes differ from the standards followed in the United States and how those differences may affect the credibility of the foreign data. For a successful submission of foreign data, it is critical to select sites governed by ECs with membership and rules of conduct that will be acceptable for U.S. registration. One obstacle that is common, particularly in developing countries, is inadequate or biased representation on the ECs. The EC should include sufficient representatives with the appropriate technical expertise and should provide objective evaluation by both the scientist and the patient advocate. It is also important to avoid the appearance of bias or conflict by excluding individuals from the voting process who might have a direct interest in the study, for example, the investigator or the discoverer of the drug.

Selection of sites with an EC that will be acceptable in case of an FDA audit may be a potential source of conflict for the sponsor. The sponsor must be careful to balance the needs and customs of the host country and the investigator who will conduct the study against the requirements of GCP.

Consent process: Inadequate study subject consent, as well as both overt and indirect coercion of patients to participate in the study, can undermine the acceptability of foreign data for U.S. registration. Providing choice of treatment and a comprehensible understanding of risk in the patient consent document is a critical test of adequate consent, governed by the Declaration of Helsinki and GCP guidelines. Lack of adequate consent can be problematic, particularly if the FDA finds that the study does not provide medically indicated treatment or conducts coercive trials in locations where sufficient medical care is not available. Additionally, local medical acceptability and cultural differences in patient beliefs may limit therapeutic choices and excessively expand what is acceptable, resulting in a biased, informed consent process that may preclude the use of foreign data to support a U.S. application.

Choice of comparator and dose: The relevance of foreign clinical data may also be judged by the choice of comparator, as well as relevant dose or dose range for both test and comparator drugs. Active comparators need to be chosen based on whether the drug, dose, and dosage are approved by the FDA. Demonstrating superiority or noninferiority versus an active comparator is only meaningful if the comparator, dose, and dosage are labeled in a previously approved U.S. marketing application based on established safety and efficacy trials.

The choice of dose and dosage of a drug in a pivotal trial that is used to support a U.S. application should also be carefully considered. Differences in local medical standards of practice, as well as cultural differences, often lead to different risk/benefit ratio considerations when selecting dose and dosage for marketing. For example, some foreign countries may favor a greater safety margin over additional effectiveness.

Concomitant medications and drug–drug interactions: Drug–drug interaction data from foreign studies may have limited utility in the United States. A wide range of factors may complicate the extrapolation of foreign data to support labeling for the U.S. population. These include cultural, economic, genetic, and ethnic differences. Genetic and ethnic difference may lead to differences in absorption, distribution, metabolism, and excretion. Limited availability of pharmaceutical products, cultural bias toward the use of homeopathic remedies, and the wide use of certain comedications, nutritional supplements, and/or herbal remedies in some locations may play a limiting role in the FDA's ability to consider drug–drug interaction data from foreign sources. In such circumstances, the sponsor and ultimately the FDA may determine that additional drug–drug interaction trials may be necessary to support U.S. labeling.

Contraception and reproductive toxicity: Local practice, economic conditions, levels of education and cultural differences often drive decisions regarding contraceptive methods. The FDA is particularly concerned with the safety of a test product for trial participants, as well as with defining an appropriate level of reproductive safety for labeling. The FDA requires any study to assure the safety of female and male patients and their offspring. In the United States, animal reproductive toxicity data—including gestation and effects on the various stages of fetal development—drive inclusion criteria for pivotal trials and labeling. Nonclinical reproductive toxicity data and the potential effect that such data may have on patient selection, the product safety profile and labeling, should be considered prior to initiating pivotal clinical trials.

Patient issues: Study treatment compliance, or lack thereof, can also be a barrier to acceptance of foreign data. In populations with low levels of education, it can be difficult to assure patient compliance and diary retention. Under-reporting adverse events may also be common due to cultural differences. In some cultures, for example, tolerance for higher degrees of pain or simple reverence for the physician may preclude complete and accurate patient reporting of adverse events. Incomplete reporting of adverse events leads to inadequate reporting of incidence for expected adverse events needed for U.S. labeling.

Study Design and Controls

When designing a study destined for eventual U.S. registration, it is helpful to begin with the intended labeling in mind. Pivotal trials should be designed prospectively. When studies are not conducted under an IND, little opportunity exists to obtain FDA input. In such cases, it is advisable to obtain external, expert consultations regarding regulatory strategy that incorporates consideration of the FDA's ability to label safety and activity claims. In the United States, labeling claims principally depend on data derived from two adequate and well-controlled pivotal trials. U.S. labeling claims often are

1. limited to the specific patient population studied,
2. limited to the route of administration, dose, and dosage used in the pivotal trial, and
3. limited to the prospectively stated objectives in the pivotal trials that proved to be statistically significant.

A number of common pitfalls in foreign trials may complicate U.S. approval. Outside the United States, medical experts, rather than statisticians, often define sample size based on clinical exposure–comfort levels rather than on statistical models that are the basis of appropriate sample size calculations used to test a hypothesis. Whenever possible, the sponsor should allow an expert U.S. statistical consultant to review the statistical analysis plans in advance of the study. Targeted review can help anticipate issues that may be raised by FDA statisticians.

When selecting active comparators or permissible concomitant treatment, sponsors should consider using drugs, doses, and dosages that are approved for marketing in the United States. It will be difficult for FDA to interpret safety data or to compare drug activity, if the agency is not familiar with the active comparator, dose, route of administration, or dose regimen.

Whenever ethically possible, the sponsor should consider placebo control, rather than active control, for pivotal trials. In the United States and the European Union, it is common for regulators and researchers to hold different opinions regarding the ethics of placebo control in clinical trials. Outside the United States, the use of retrospective historical controls and active comparators has been considered to be the more ethical approach. However, the FDA still considers placebo-controlled trials to be the "gold standard" for demonstrating and labeling safety and efficacy. The exception is in the case of specific life-threatening indications, such as those in the fields of oncology and infectious diseases.

In addition to the careful consideration of a control arm, complete blinding of treatment arms is critical to limit bias and gain acceptability of foreign data. One way to achieve complete blinding is through the use of a "jury of resemblance," which is a blinded group of individuals who help confirm the integrity of the blinding process. Such a jury will examine packaging and blinded product samples in order to identify matching homogenous versus heterogeneous treatment samples. Complete blinding is achieved if the jury cannot differentiate between the two blinded treatments.

Finally, in order to maximize chances for success and to support labeling efficacy for a particular subset population, it is preferable to stratify patients prospectively based on relevant endpoints. Such endpoints may be the diagnostic criteria, as well as the criteria to determine the severity of the disease and/or treatment. Prospective stratification assures appropriate balance of patients in the subset treatment arms and provides results that are easier to interpret. Compared to retrospective analyses conducted after the trial has been completed, prospective stratification is more likely to lead to successful identification of activity in a subset population. With retrospective analyses, low numbers in any one treatment arm may prevent achievement of the statistical power to detect a difference. Prospective stratification can be accomplished by using a telephone randomization system or a variety of site-specific randomization schemes that an expert statistician can design.

Endpoints

In addition to study design considerations, an appropriate choice of clinically relevant endpoints is key to help drive labeling and gain FDA acceptability of foreign data. Surrogate markers of activity, expert medical opinion and nonvalidated, nonstandardized endpoints (including genetic or nongenetic biomarkers) are often unacceptable to support labeling. A life-threatening condition or an orphan-drug indication might be an exception, but even in these cases, the sponsor has negotiated the strategy in advance with the FDA. Clinically relevant endpoints, such as disease activity, patient mobility, symptom control, or survival, are all preferable to endpoints, such as an obscure lab test result without a historical correlation in the clinic, that lack a clear clinical interpretation.

The sponsor should avoid choosing endpoints that lack cross-cultural applicability and validation. For example, food intake questionnaires or quality-of-life scales may contain questions that limit their use to support labeling when considered in a different cultural setting.

Even for studies with subjective endpoints that require ratings by the investigator or patient, the sponsor should provide adequate training and, whenever possible, define the limits of inter-rater variability. Inter-rater variability among a group of investigators can be assessed proactively by presenting patient case scenarios and having each investigator rate the symptoms or diagnoses based on a uniform patient case. Variability should be assessed. Raters whose results lie outside of the predefined acceptable range should be provided with additional training or excluded from trial participation.

Local Medical Practice, Therapeutic Differences, and Unmet Medical Needs

Considering variability in local medical practice is critical to understanding the relevance of the development program and the acceptability of foreign data in the United States. Variability may be based on differences in disease prevalence, diagnostics, test-ordering practices, prescribing practices, treatment options, treatment and medical care reimbursement and standard treatment guidelines. If differences are identified, the sponsor should address these differences prospectively by planning for culturally relevant locations for conducting trials or retrospectively via a bridging study.

Equally important are subtle cultural differences that may prevent a sponsor from identifying the maximal effective dose for U.S. registration. A physician's approach to adequate dosing may be culturally driven. For example, the standard of practice in Japan is often to identify a dose that is associated with fewer adverse drug reactions. In comparison, U.S. researchers might choose a dose based on maximal activity combined with an acceptable safety profile.

Additionally, unmet medical needs, that are often the target of pharmaceutical development plans, may differ from one region of the globe to another. Health needs are often defined by socioeconomic policy, levels of education, and cultural biases. Development plans and trial designs often incorporate local standards of practice, available therapy and accessible rescue drugs. These local realities may not apply and may preclude the foreign drug sponsor's ability to collect data that will be applicable for labeling in the U.S. environment.

For example, in Africa and certain parts of Southeast Asia, standard diagnoses and treatment guidelines may be limited by a variety of factors that include the patient's level of supplemental insurance and access to testing, as well as by his or her education and ability to read. In some areas of the world, the availability of alternative medicine and/or the reliance on traditional healers may play a role in defining medical need. Finally, in some regions, providing early access to study-associated medical care and investigational treatment may be more acceptable, and even expected. Prospective planning, a focus on cross-cultural acceptability and use of multinational advisory boards, may be the best way to design a single development program that has cross-cultural acceptability.

Collecting Foreign Clinical Data

Since 2000 the clinical trial enterprise has entered a new era of globalization, where pharmaceutical sponsors have increasingly turned to "nontraditional" countries (e.g., Russia, India, China) for recruitment of patients into clinical studies of investigational drugs. The drivers for this trend have been the high prevalence of available and suitable patients in those countries, and the generally much lower cost of conducting clinical trials there as compared to the ICH regions. As a consequence, it is expected that in the future FDA will receive NDAs that are increasingly supported by non-U.S. clinical data—adding further urgency to the need to ensure that these data will be acceptable to FDA. The usual criteria (21 CFR 314.106) will apply, but in order to meet them sponsors must ensure full GCP compliance in the "nontraditional" countries.

One issue for sponsors of foreign drugs to consider is whether to collect foreign clinical data under an IND prospectively. Clinical studies conducted outside the United States can be sponsored under an IND, but this is not an FDA requirement.

Two common and related misconceptions exist regarding foreign studies and INDs. Many sponsors believe that the FDA will give greater weight to studies that are conducted under an IND than to studies that are not. This is not true. Nor is it true that studies conducted under an IND are more compliant with GCPs than are non-IND studies. Another common misconception is that by conducting the study under an IND, the sponsor does not need to obtain local country approval to conduct the study.

Conducting a foreign study under an IND offers both benefits and drawbacks. Among the benefits is the fact that multinational studies and investigators are documented to the IND, which then becomes a "common archive" of study information. This approach allows the sponsor to conduct a single, global protocol for a multinational study, rather than conducting separate, though identical, protocols. Although studies conducted under an IND are not automatically more GCP compliant, such compliance is likely to be higher when investigators are aware that the FDA may inspect them. In point of fact, the FDA will audit investigator sites in pivotal studies regardless of country and regardless of whether the studies were conducted under an IND.

Conducting a foreign study under an IND can also have drawbacks. For one, some non-U.S. investigators may object to signing the FDA Form 1572. The concept of an FDA-mandated investigator statement may be unpalatable to them.

Another potential drawback to conducting a foreign study under an IND can occur if the FDA places the IND on hold. In that case, all IND studies underway in all countries must stop.

After weighing the pros and cons, the sponsor may decide not to conduct the foreign clinical studies under an IND. If that is the case, the studies must nevertheless conform to the regulations in 21 CFR 312.120, which describe the criteria for foreign studies not conducted under an IND.

a) In general, FDA accepts such studies provided they are well designed, well conducted, performed by qualified investigators, and conducted in accordance with ethical principles acceptable to the world community. Studies meeting these criteria may be utilized to support clinical investigations in the United States and/or marketing approval. Marketing approval of a new drug based solely on foreign clinical data is governed by Section 314.106.
b) Data submissions. A sponsor who wishes to rely on a foreign clinical study to support an IND or to support an application for marketing approval shall submit to FDA the following information:
   (1) a description of the investigator's qualifications;
   (2) a description of the research facilities;
   (3) a detailed summary of the protocol and results of the study and, should FDA request, case records maintained by the investigator or additional background data such as hospital or other institutional records;
   (4) a description of the drug substance and drug product used in the clinical study, if available; and
   (5) if the study is intended to support the effectiveness of a drug product, information showing that the study is adequate and well controlled under section 314.126.
c) Conformance with ethical principles.
   (1) Foreign clinical research is required to have been conducted in accordance with the ethical principles stated in the "Declaration of Helsinki" or the laws and regulations of the country in which the research was conducted, whichever represents the greater protection of the individual.
   (2) For each foreign clinical study submitted under this section, the sponsor shall explain how the research conformed to the ethical principles contained in the Declaration of Helsinki or the foreign country's standards, whichever were used. If the foreign country's standards were used, the sponsor shall explain in detail how those standards differ from the Declaration of Helsinki and how they offer greater protection.
   (3) When the research has been approved by an independent review committee, the sponsor shall submit to FDA documentation of such review and approval, including the names and qualifications of the members of the committee. In this regard, a "review committee" means a committee composed of scientists and, where practicable, individuals who are otherwise qualified (e.g., other health professionals or laymen). The investigator may not vote on any aspect of the review of his or her protocol by a review committee.

FDA Inspections of Foreign Clinical Investigators

As noted above, the FDA inspects selected foreign clinical investigator sites for studies considered pivotal for approval. Such FDA inspections of foreign clinical investigators have increased dramatically in recent years (Fig. 1) due to an increase in the number of sponsors who are submitting NDAs that contain pivotal foreign clinical data. In addition, some pivotal trials are so large, with 10,000 to 20,000 patients or more, that sufficient patients are not available for enrollment from the United States alone, therefore requiring the inclusion of foreign data.

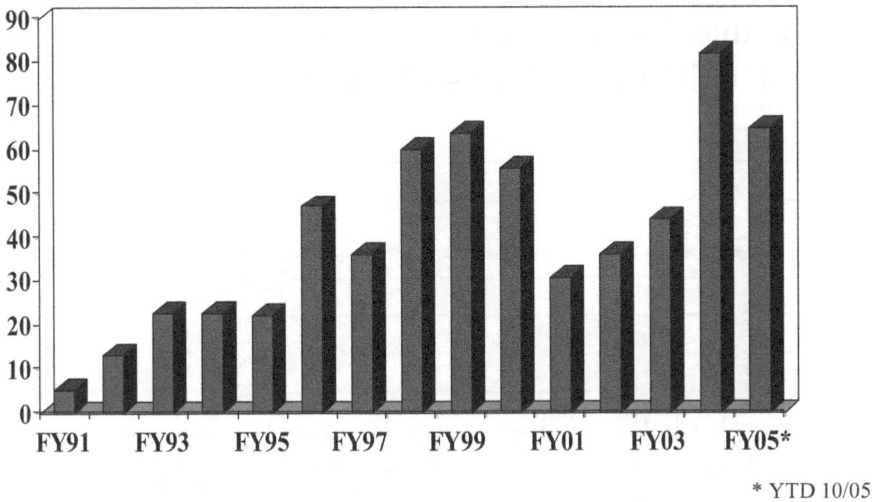

FIGURE 1 Total FDA inspections of foreign clinical investigators conducted annually from 1991 to 2005. *Source:* FDA.

FDA

The violations that lead FDA to reject foreign studies include nonavailability of source documentation, inadequate record-keeping, failure to follow the protocol, unreported concomitant therapy, and unavailability of patient diaries (A. El-Hage, FDA, Presentation at Drug Information Annual Meeting, 2002).

It is interesting to note that FDA inspections of clinical investigators uncover similar type and incidence of GCP violations at both U.S. and foreign sites (Fig. 2). These findings do not argue against the use of foreign sites, but do reinforce the message that it is in sponsors' best interest to promote and verify a high degree of GCP compliance at investigator sites, anywhere in the world, to protect their ability to use worldwide data for U.S. registration.

THE NEW DRUG APPLICATION AND THE COMMON TECHNICAL DOCUMENT

ICH has promulgated a common format for marketing approval applications in the United States, Europe, and Japan. This format is called the CTD. The CTD follows a logical and highly structured format (Fig. 3) designed to facilitate the preparation of marketing applications to multiple countries. Its common elements are intended to save time and labor by minimizing the need to reformat documentation or alter the sequence in which data is presented.

The CTD format is now compulsory in the European Union and Japan, and it has become common practice in the United States and Canada to use the CTD format for marketing applications.

In the United States, marketing applications submitted in the CTD format are still referred to as NDAs. As the FDA has received more applications in CTD format, reviewers have become familiar with using the format. Neither the FDA nor other agencies, such as the European Medicines Evaluation Agency (EMEA), report any significant difficulties in working with the new format. On the other hand,

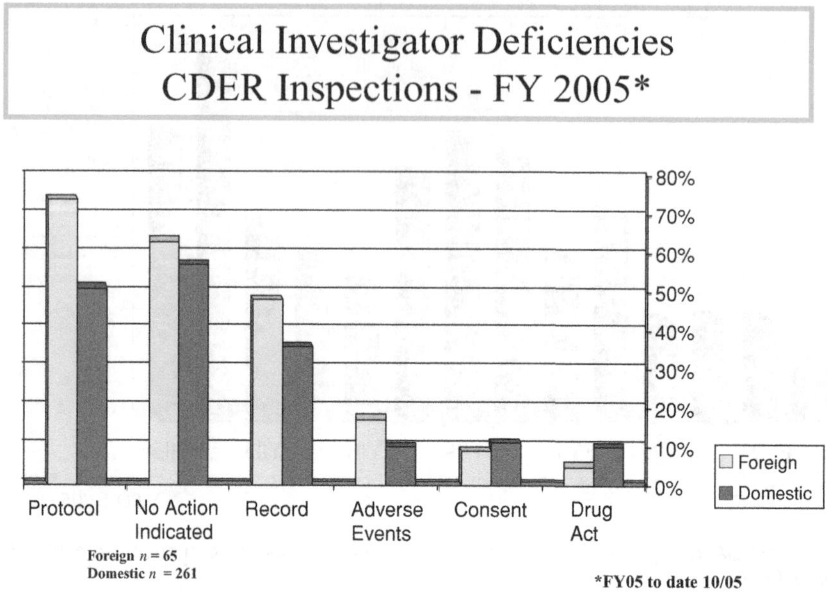

FIGURE 2 FDA Inspection of foreign and domestic clinical sites reveals most common GCP deficiencies. *Source:* FDA.

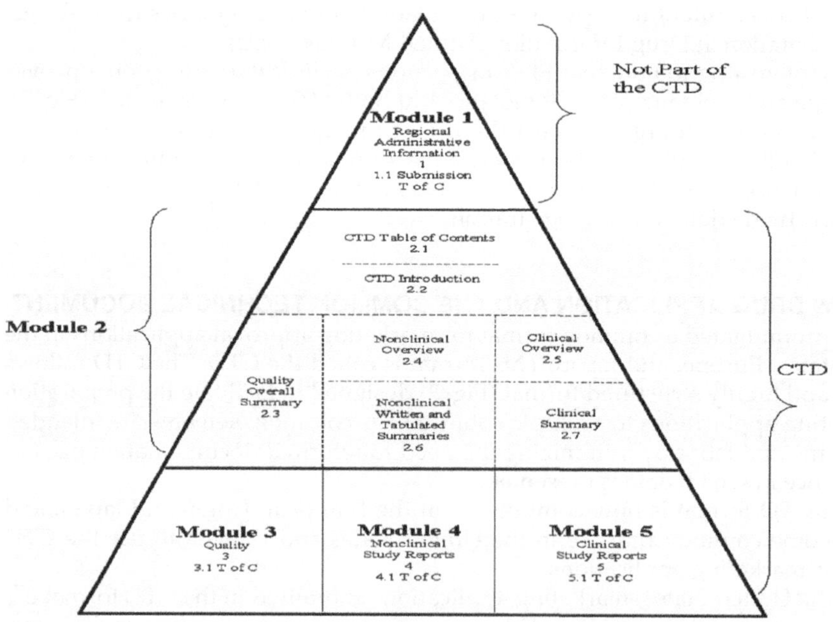

FIGURE 3 A diagrammatic representation of the ICH CTDs. Module I contains documents specific to each region, such as application forms and proposed labeling. The other modules are relatively common to all submissions.

some sponsors have experienced difficulty in determining where certain information, such as the Integrated Summary of Safety and Integrated Summary of Efficacy, should be placed within the CTD modules. Communications with the FDA at presubmission meetings (see below) can help resolve such issues.

The CTD benefits foreign drug development by streamlining the documentation process. Sponsors can submit documentation to the FDA and other authorities with relatively minor modifications to tailor the submission to local agency needs. This allows the sponsor to apply more focus on the document's scientific and medical content and less on its format. Ultimately, the need to submit a document that demonstrates quality, safety, and efficacy remains unchanged. Those requirements are driven by both FDA regulations and ICH guidelines.

FDA expectations regarding NDA and CTD submissions: The FDA has the same expectations for an NDA regardless of whether the data was collected in the United States or abroad. The submission must present a convincing, data-driven demonstration of quality, safety, and efficacy, and the data must be relevant to the U.S. patient population. In reality, however, the FDA may be more skeptical of data from "particular unnamed countries." When presented with extensive data from these regions, the FDA sends its inspectors to verify compliance with GCP, GLP, and GMP.

Whether the NDA is submitted to FDA in the traditional format or in CTD format, the FDA will look for the same standards, i.e.,

- clarity
- navigability
- reviewer friendliness
- completeness
- logical presentation
- data that enable FDA to make sound scientific and medical decisions, on the basis of the benefit–risk balance

COMMUNICATIONS WITH FDA

Effective communication with the FDA is of paramount importance in the drug development and approval process. For both foreign and U.S. sponsors, the FDA can be an "arm's-length partner" in drug development. The sponsor should keep the FDA informed of drug development plans and progress so that the agency can provide the best advice throughout the process and help the sponsor prevent costly errors. Foreign-based companies must be especially diligent about communicating with the FDA throughout the drug development process. Misunderstandings regarding the agency's expectations for the NDA can destroy a drug development program. The most significant concern is the potential that the foreign clinical data will have limited applicability to the U.S. patient population. If the FDA has concerns regarding limited applicability, the sponsor must be aware of these concerns early enough in the process to be able to take appropriate action, such as conducting studies in the United States rather than abroad.

Communicating with the FDA may differ from communicating with other agencies. Some methods of communication are more effective than others, and FDA has issued precise guidance (Formal Meetings With Sponsors and Applicants for PDUFA Products, http://www.fda.gov/cder/guidance/2125fnl.pdf) regarding communications and meetings with industry. As noted above, foreign companies that wish to communicate with FDA must do so through a U.S.-based agent.

Meetings with the FDA take place at several predetermined milestones in the drug development process.

Pre-IND Meetings

The purpose of the pre-IND meeting is to introduce the sponsor and the drug to the FDA. (The introduction may not be necessary if the sponsor is a well-known global pharmaceutical company.) Many FDA divisions will grant pre-IND meetings to sponsors, but some may be reluctant to do so, preferring to review a submitted IND and then provide comments to the sponsor. When granted, a pre-IND meeting can help a sponsor design additional nonclinical studies or refine the clinical protocol prior to submitting the IND; in turn, this level of communication and preparation can prevent the imposition of an IND Clinical Hold based on FDA concerns about safety. It is important to note, however, that holding a pre-IND meeting is no guarantee that the FDA will not issue an IND hold on the study.

In presenting the drug at the pre-IND meeting, the sponsor generally discusses the characterization of the drug and presents manufacturing and nonclinical data. The presentation should also address the proposed clinical investigational plan in relation to the desired final labeling (prescribing information). At this time, the company should identify any foreign clinical studies that it will sponsor and indicate whether they will be conducted under an IND. The sponsor should also present and discuss the initial clinical protocol.

In discussions during the pre-IND meeting, it may be possible to agree to the details of the initial clinical protocol. Critical issues will be identified; some may be resolved at the meeting. Examples of such issues include the inclusion and exclusion criteria, the use of concomitant medications or comparators that may not be approved drugs in the United States, or the use of patient populations that are underrepresented in the United States.

End of Phase II Meeting

This is by far the most important interaction between the sponsor and the FDA. Phase III of the drug development process represents the final path to the NDA. Phase III trials also require significant investment on the part of the sponsor. The End of phase II meeting gives the sponsor an opportunity to obtain the FDA's commitment on pivotal study designs and key endpoints. It allows the sponsor to make any necessary adjustments to the development plan regarding CMC, toxicology, and clinical or labeling claims. End of phase II meetings are especially critical for foreign sponsors because the meetings help identify "show-stopper issues" such as poor applicability of proposed phase III foreign studies to the U.S. patient population. This will help avoid large investments in misguided trials.

Several factors determine when it is most advantageous to hold End of phase II meetings. By the time the meeting is held, labeling claims should be reasonably well articulated and the apparent effective dose should have been established in phase II studies. The sponsor should be certain that the dose finding is sound, and the pharmacokinetics/pharmacodynamics (PK/PD) work is well advanced. The meeting should take place when the sponsor has designed the phase III program and is ready to present it to the FDA, and before the company makes the significant investments required for the phase III program, since agency recommendations may drive changes to the trial plans. In recent years, sponsors have been encouraged by FDA to submit their draft phase III clinical protocols to a new process known as Special Protocol Assessment (SPA; also available for stability study protocols and carcinogenicity study protocols. http://www.fda.gov/cder/guidance/3764fnl.PDF). The agency reviews the protocol and provides written detailed comments to the sponsor, in essence "committing" to not changing its mind later about the design.

Pre-NDA/BLA Meetings

Meetings with the FDA prior to submitting the NDA or the Biologics License Application (BLA) can be helpful. These conferences should be held when phase III studies near completion—usually about 6 months before the planned NDA submission date. One goal of these meetings is to uncover unresolved issues that might stand in the way of approval. Another goal is to identify those studies that are critical for approval and to ensure that they are adequate and well controlled to establish the drug's effectiveness and safety. In the case of a foreign drug, it is necessary to identify which of the critical studies for approval are foreign studies.

The meeting is held with the FDA division responsible for the drug's review. During the meeting, the sponsor should orient the reviewers to the technical content to be submitted in the NDA as well as the best formatting of the data. Proposed analyses and subanalyses of study data to be included in the application should also be discussed.

It is critical to understand the FDA's expectations for the NDA. As already noted, misinterpretations can derail a drug development program. Foreign sponsors may find it particularly helpful to discuss in advance the FDA's intentions to inspect the foreign studies so as to be able to alert investigators and prepare the clinical sites for FDA inspection.

Advisory Committee Meetings

Advisory Committee meetings may be advantageous to both the FDA and the sponsor. The FDA initiates these meetings, usually when the agency needs advice from the medical and patient communities before deciding on the approval of an NDA. These meetings provide an opportunity for the FDA to obtain the advice of medical experts regarding the approvability of the NDA. At the same time, advisory committee meetings enable the sponsor to present key findings of efficacy and safety to medical experts. The advisory committee includes outside experts in the appropriate medical specialty as well as consumer and patient representatives. The meetings are open to the public.

Advisory committee members are primarily interested in the quality and persuasiveness of the data presented and in the relevance of the data to the U.S. patient population.

At the end of the meeting, the advisory committee votes on recommending approval or disapproval of the NDA. Although the vote is nonbinding, the FDA usually follows the advisory committee's advice.

Although advisory committee meetings offer the sponsor an opportunity to make its case, they have several unique characteristics that can make them especially challenging for sponsors. These formal, structured meetings are governed by the Federal Advisory Committee Act of 1972, which governs all government advisory committees, and by regulations outlined in section 120 of the Food and

Drug Administration Modernization Act. Proceedings of these face-to-face meetings are recorded on audio- and videotape and the meetings themselves are webcast; written transcripts of each meeting are prepared and published on FDA's Web site. The meetings include sponsor and FDA presentations and committee discussions, all of which are open to the public, including financial analysts and competitors of the sponsor. The sponsor may present information that it considers to be trade secrets in a closed portion of the meeting. Personal information about clinical subjects may also be presented in the closed portion of the meeting.

As noted above, the committee's vote is not binding; however, the FDA rarely contradicts an advisory committee recommendation. As a result, committee recommendations carry great weight, not only with the FDA, but also with the financial community and the pharmaceutical industry at large. A negative committee vote can effectively devastate years of development work.

Considering the potential impact of the committee's recommendation for or against NDA approval, the sponsor must be prepared to make a persuasive presentation to the Advisory Committee members. A successful Advisory Committee meeting demands extensive preparation and infrastructure. Meetings may be scheduled as long as a year in advance and committee members must be provided with materials for review several weeks prior to the meeting. The sponsor's presenters, and any external parties presenting on the sponsor's behalf, should be excellent speakers who can clearly present the sponsor's case for approval. Presentations should be well rehearsed and supported with audiovisual aids to make the strongest positive impression possible.

The new FDAAA law requires the FDA to take any New Molecular Entity NDA to the appropriate advisory committee, or to explain in writing its decision to not do so. This may result in an increased frequency of advisory committee meetings and additional pressure on sponsors.

Labeling Meetings

Labeling meetings are held with the FDA after the sponsor has submitted the NDA. The purpose of labeling meetings is to reach agreement on the exact wording of the Package Insert for the pending application. The sponsor and the FDA may also discuss the need for any revisions to the label that might be required based on new safety information.

Reaching agreement on the exact wording for the label may require several rounds of negotiation. In contrast with most of the other FDA meetings, labeling meetings usually are teleconferences, rather than face-to-face sessions. Teleconferencing allows participants on both sides to take advantage of "muted caucusing" during the negotiation process. The foreign sponsor may wish to have its U.S. distributor participate in the negotiations regarding labeling language.

Much is at stake, because the final package insert wording will either facilitate or restrict the promotion and sale of the drug. Ideally, the labeling meeting results in package insert wording that satisfies both the sponsor and the FDA. Such agreement is a critical milestone toward the launch of a safe and effective product.

Labeling negotiations increasingly include, as a condition for NDA approval, a sponsor's commitment to conduct postapproval clinical studies to further establish the safety and/or efficacy of the approved drug after it is launched onto the market. The FDAAA law has given the agency increased powers to enforce these commitments and to conduct postmarketing surveillance of approved drugs.

Sponsors will no longer be able to "forget or ignore" such commitments after they are agreed and documented in the NDA approval letter.

SUMMARY AND CONCLUSIONS

In many ways, development of a foreign drug for approval in the U.S. market is similar to the development of U.S. drugs. Regardless of where the drug originates, or where data were collected, sponsors must meet the same requirements—adhere to recognized standards, protect patient rights, design studies that support labeling safety and efficacy claims, ensure the quality and integrity of the data, and submit a complete and clear marketing application. The differences that do exist among countries are due to geography, culture, medical practice, local preferences and practices, and level of comfort of regulatory agencies, such as FDA, with data collected in other countries and patient populations. To minimize the impact of these differences, and to reduce the need to conduct duplicate trials in multiple regions, companies that develop foreign drugs must plan carefully and communicate with FDA "early and often."

Foreign drug sponsors can facilitate the process of obtaining U.S. approval by communicating with the FDA appropriately and frequently. They should look after the details of development work conducted outside the United States to ensure that it is in line with FDA expectations and requirements. Finally, when sufficient data have been collected, the sponsor should make a solid case for approval.

Drug development is challenging for pharmaceutical companies everywhere. The "foreign" element may complicate the process somewhat, but it is not an insurmountable obstacle. Savvy planning and sound execution make obtaining U.S. approval rather manageable. Nonetheless, a diligent understanding of the external pressures which FDA faces from the Congress, the media, and the public is a must, and should guide foreign sponsors' decisions all along the drug development path.

20 Impact of Government Regulation on Prescription Drug Marketing and Promotion

Daniel Glassman and Gene Goldberg
Medimetriks Pharmaceuticals, Inc., Fairfield, New Jersey, U.S.A.

Barbara Spallitta
Reckitt Benckiser, Inc., Parsippany, New Jersey, U.S.A.

INTRODUCTION

The Food and Drug Administration (FDA) and the Federal Trade Commission (FTC) are the two governing U.S. regulatory agencies that affect the marketing and promotion of health-care industry products. The FDA primarily impacts the marketing and promotion practices of the prescription pharmaceutical, biological, medical device, and animal drug industries. The FTC primarily affects nonprescription/over-the-counter (OTC) pharmaceuticals, nutritional and cosmetic marketing, and promotional practices. A following chapter in this book will discuss the current responsibilities of the FTC and the health-care industries it regulates. Although, recent legislation not currently in effect, the Non-Prescription Drug Modernization Act (November 2007) has been proposed to allow FDA to regulate OTC drug advertising, this chapter will discuss the relationship of the FDA and the health-care industries it currently regulates, with a focus on prescription drug marketing and promotion.

Strengthened in the 1980s and 1990s, the formal legislation under which the FDA operates has not changed significantly since the early 1960s. However, the way in which the FDA, particularly the Division of Drug Marketing, Advertising and Communications (DDMAC) arm, interprets the legislation has resulted in a continuous broadening of power and involvement. In addition, the empirical judgment of the FDA/DDMAC reviewer regarding the regulated industries marketing and promotion has escalated geometrically over the last 10 years. References in the Food, Drug and Cosmetic Act (FD&C Act) to regulation of promotion are brief and vague. Indeed, such references are contained in a single paragraph. Most of the promotional policies of the FDA in recent years have not been made through a formal rule-making process with the force of law, via the Code of Federal Regulations (CFR), or publishing of rules and proposed rules in the *Federal Register*. Rather, the FDA generally has used informal methods, which have de facto force of law, to control promotion. These methods of communicating with the de facto force of law include issuance of policy statements and industry guidelines, warning letters and untitled letters, and speaking at industry conferences/educational meetings.

Biologic and medical device product promotional regulation has similarly developed, however, with less review and enforcement by their respective oversight centers. This is because these centers, the Center for Biologics Evaluation and Research (CBER) and the Center for Devices and Radiological Health (CDRH), have less staff and resources. For example, from 1997 to 2001, CBER issued two warning letters, while CDER/DDMAC issued 28 (1). CDER/DDMAC and CBER/OCBQ (Office of Compliance and Biologics Quality) intensified their efforts from 2001, issuing 26 warning letters from January 2005 through June 2006, with the great majority issued by CDER/DDMAC, of which, in 2004 alone, 13 involved direct-to-consumer (DTC) advertising (2,3). In 2007, DDMAC issued 10 warning letters for promotional materials.

The most significant promotional development affecting the FDA's involvement with industry, in recent years, is the growth of DTC advertising. DTC advertising expenditure by the pharmaceutical industry has increased from $12 million a year in 1995 to $4.1 billion a year in 2005 and is increasing more each year since then. Much of the FDA activity in recent years concerns the regulation of this increase in DTC. With few exceptions, virtually all the legislation and regulations were written at a time when print and personal/detailing promotions, primarily directed at physicians and other health-care providers, were exclusively employed by industry. The FDA has used these older positions as the basis of regulating the newer forms of electronic promotion, primarily directed at consumers/patients.

The most significant recent legislation related to marketing practices is the passage of the Prescription Drug Marketing Act (PDMA) and the subsequent Prescription Drug Amendments (PDA). These acts set guidance for distribution and accountability of trade, as well as sample sizes, of all prescription products from manufacturer through distribution to health-care professionals. These acts have been strictly enforced by the FDA and have required considerable documentation from companies, incurring significant industry costs to comply with the regulations.

EVOLUTION OF GOVERNMENT PRESCRIPTION DRUG, BIOLOGIC, MEDICAL DEVICE, AND ANIMAL DRUGS MARKETING AND PROMOTION REGULATIONS

Prior to 1900, the pharmaceutical industry was relatively small and fragmented. Prescription drugs, biologics, and medical devices did not exist, as we know them today. Expenses for marketing and advertising/promotion were rather modest. Products were generally produced, promoted, and sold with a minimum of regulation or scrutiny.

The pharmaceutical industry now spends billions of dollars in marketing and advertising/promotion activity currently estimated at approximately $7.2 billion on physician-directed promotion and another $18 billion on drug samples (4) and does so under rigid regulations established by the U.S. Food and Drug Administration (FDA). The industry of today is heavily regulated by FDA. This encompasses proof of the effectiveness and safety of products and the manner in which products are promoted and marketed.

To understand how this dramatic change in regulation has affected the health-care-related industry's overall marketing and promotional activities, it is important to review the evolution of the government's involvement regarding pharmaceutical products.

Prior to 1938

Only minor efforts were directed toward the classification, promotion, and marketing of medicines in the 1800s. The regulation of drug promotion started in 1905 when the American Medical Association (AMA), through the Council on Pharmacy and Chemistry, initiated a voluntary drug approval program. This program forced pharmaceutical companies to submit evidence to support their drug claims to the

AMA Council and outside experts for review in order to earn the right to advertise in AMA and related journals (5). This AMA program lasted until 1955.

In addition, in 1906 Congress passed the original Pure Food and Drug Act, which was designed to provide safe drugs to patients. However, it did not prevent false promotional claims for drugs. Also at that time, the Center for Drug Evaluation and Research (CDER) began as a one-man operation. The force of the 1906 act was challenged when the government seized a large quantity of a product promoted to fight cancer. The government found the product to be "a worthless product that bore false therapeutic claims on its label." Upon trial in 1910, the judge ruled against the government, finding that claims made for effectiveness were outside the Pure Food and Drugs Act. This triggered action that prompted Congress to enact the Shirley Amendment in 1912, which prohibited the labeling of medicines with false therapeutic claims. However, the Amendment also required the government to prove that claims were false and fraudulent before they could act. In 1916, the government established the existing Division of Drugs as the office responsible for the investigation of false and fraudulent drug claims.

Throughout the following years, it was repeatedly demonstrated that the original 1906 Pure Food and Drug Act and the Shirley Amendment were obsolete and ineffective for the regulation of promotional claims. The major weakness of the legislation was the lack of authority of the government agencies to stop distribution of unsafe products. Since the law did not require drug safety, the government's Office of Drug Control could only issue warnings. It was restricted from seizing product.

1938 Through 1961

Two significant drug safety events in the mid-1930s, leading to the deaths of more than 100 people, focused national attention on the shortcomings of the regulatory system at the time. As a result, in 1938, Congress passed and President Franklin Roosevelt signed the new broad-based Federal FD&C Act into law. This act required that new drugs be tested for safety prior to marketing and that new drugs have adequate labeling for safe use. At that time, all drug advertising regulations were assigned to the FTC (6,7).

During the next 20 years, the strength and scope of the FDA was substantially increased due to safety problems related to a variety of drugs tested, produced, and prescribed in the United States. Drug safety and related promotion had become a major issue for FDA. In 1951, the Durham–Humphrey Amendment established the legally defined difference between prescription and nonprescription drugs. The amendment specifically stated that dangerous drugs, defined by several parameters, could not be dispensed without a prescription, as indicated by the prescription legend: "Caution: Federal law prohibits dispensing without prescription" (8).

The year 1960 marked dramatic steps designed to further strengthen and expand FDA's powers. Senate hearings on strengthening the drug provisions of the 1938 act were chaired in June 1960 by Senator Estes Kefauver, who had an established reputation as a crime investigator. During the course of the Senate pharmaceutical hearings, the FDA received a request from a pharmaceutical company for the approval, via a new drug application (NDA), of the sedative drug thalidomide, which was found to have caused birth defects in thousands of babies in Western Europe. Although pressure had been exerted by the U.S. manufacturer hoping to introduce the product, FDA Medical Officer Dr. Frances Kelsey refused to allow the NDA to be approved because of insufficient safety documentation, thus avoiding what would have been a substantial tragedy in the United States. This striking event gave impetus to Senator Kefauver to submit a bill tightening the regulation of all drugs in the United States, which was approved and signed into law (9).

1962 Through 1979

In October, 1962, President Kennedy signed the Kefauver–Harris Amendments. Basically, the 1962 Kefauver–Harris Amendments to the original 1938 Federal FD&C Act required drug manufacturers to prove that their products were both effective and safe prior to marketing and required that all antibiotics had to be certified. Most importantly from the perspective of promotional regulation, FDA was given control over all prescription drug advertising. In addition, the act provided for informed consent by subjects recruited for clinical investigation studies. Moreover, the FDA had to be provided with full information concerning clinical trials.

Although the various divisions of FDA were becoming more comprehensive and sophisticated in nature, concern about the safety of America's drug supply continued. This concern would lead to greater FDA oversight of drug marketing and advertising/promotion.

To further comply with the 1962 act, the FDA contacted the National Academy of Science/National Research Council (NAS/NRC) to evaluate drugs approved between 1938 and 1962 for efficacy claims. The Drug Efficacy Study Implementation (DESI) that resulted evaluated over 3000 separate drugs and over 16,000 therapeutic claims. The last report was submitted in 1969, but then the contract was extended. The initial report of the task force was completed in 1970 and contained a provision for the development of an Abbreviated New Drug Application (ANDA) that allowed companies to bring to market additional products or change existing labeling of prior reviewed products (10).

Pressure from the FDA on drug marketing and advertising/promotion escalated in the 1970s. In the early 1970s, the FDA started two new forums in order to increase drug communication with the public. One result was the production of the FDA Bulletin (1971) by the Bureau of Drugs, which alerted physicians and pharmacists to changes in drug use and labeling requirements (11). The other result was the National Drug Experience Reporting System (1971), which allowed FDA to collect expanded data on drug adverse reactions, drug abuse, and drug interactions and provided a mechanism for FDA to take the lead in creating and maintaining the system for health professionals. The production/publication of the FDA Bulletin became a very powerful tool for enforcing findings of the FDA. Virtually, it allowed FDA interpretation of legislation to become de facto regulation through the publishing of that interpretation.

1980 Through 1989

As a result of the earlier NAS/NRC review of drugs approved prior to 1962, in 1984, final action was taken for over 90% of the drugs originally studied. Of the 3443 products studied, 2225 were found to be effective, 1051 were found not effective, and 167 were pending (12). As time elapses, a number of products that have never been reviewed have come to light. This unfulfilled FDA responsibility continues to be viewed as a constant weak point by congressional and public advocate critics alike.

In the 1980s, in order to render its operations more efficient, the FDA made a number of changes, one of which was the change of the Division of Drug Advertising to that of the Division of Drug Advertising and Labeling in order to increase the public's assurance of pharmaceutical promotional adherence to approved drug safety and efficacy.

By this time, drug advertising in professional journals and direct mail and promotion through pharmaceutical sales representatives were well-accepted practices. However, the first DTC television advertising of prescription drugs occurred in 1983, via Boots Pharmaceuticals, which encountered resistance from FDA. FDA took action because of concern that the consumer could not possibly read the long list of side effects flashing across the screen. This was promptly addressed (13) via an accurate but simplified listing of potential side effects. This area of electronic promotion would play a central role in FDA/industry interaction through the 1980s and the early part of the 2000s.

Also, in 1983, the Orphan Drug Act was passed, offering means to market and promote drugs for rare diseases. In addition, in 1984, the Drug Price Competition and Patent Term Restoration Act gave FDA the authority to accept ANDAs for generic versions of post 1962 drugs. This was the start of the rapid growth of the generic industry, as we know it today.

In October 1987, the established FDA Center for Drugs and Biologics was divided and the Center for Drug Evaluation and Research (CDER) and the Center for Biologics Evaluation and Research (CBER) were formed. These two centers are at the core of pharmaceutical and biologic product marketing and promotional regulation to this day.

The Prescription Drug Marketing Act (PDMA) was signed into law in 1988. This was a key piece of legislation that protected the consumer, through safeguards in the drug distribution system, from counterfeit, expired, or adulterated drugs. The PDMA of 1988 soon became the basis for further laws and regulations in the 1990s that heavily impacted industry's marketing, specifically the use and distribution of samples.

1990 Through 2007

With the fast growing use of generics and the race for the first to generic market entry, in the early 1990s came what is known as the FDA/generic industry scandal. Five FDA reviewers were convicted for unlawful contacts with the regulated generic industry. Moreover, several generic industry executives were convicted of falsifying documentation. As a result of the publicity, Congress passed the Generic Drug Enforcement Act in 1992. This act provided for significant penalties for illegal acts related to ANDA approvals.

The passage of the PDA of 1992 expanded upon the earlier PDMA law regarding drug distribution control. PDA established rules to control the use of drug samples and sample coupons. It made the selling, purchasing or trading of drug coupons, trade, or sample products illegal. This law made product accountability mandatory and required drug manufacturers to account for and maintain documentation of drug distribution.

PDMA of 1988 and PDA of 1992 were very far-reaching regulations that required great amounts of detailed documentation and cost for industry to comply. PDMA/PDA literally changed the way industry handled distribution of trade products and samples, documenting and verifying each step of movement from the manufacture of the product through the pharmacy or doctor's office. Through the 1990s and every year through 2006, with the exception of 2005, the FDA and industry tried to come together to define a way to best implement the acts. Finally, during 2006, various guidelines regarding product distribution were issued by the FDA, including Compliance Policy Guide, Donation of Samples to Free Clinics, and PDMA Requirements: Questions and Answers.

Also, in 1992, as a result of a bottleneck in new product NDA review procedures within the FDA, the Prescription Drug User Fee Act (PDUFA) was passed. This is a unique piece of legislation that requires industry to make payment to the FDA to increase staff to review applications. Specifically, PDUFA requires drug and biologic producers to pay an annual company fee, and a product fee to the FDA for their evaluation of submissions such as New Drug Applications (NDAs) and supplements. Following the passage of this legislation, the number of new drug approvals increased significantly.

In 1997, the Food and Drug Administration Modernization Act (FDAMA) became law. This legislation permitted, with certain limitations, drug, biologic, and device manufacturers to disseminate information concerning safety, effectiveness, or benefits of a use that are not described in the approved labeling. This is the basis of extensive and strictly controlled "off-labeling" marketing efforts that have been frequently used since implementation of FDAMA. This will be discussed, more fully, in following sections of this chapter.

Under pressure from the FDA, AMA, and public advocates, as well as the general public, in 2002, the Pharmaceutical Research and Manufacturers of America (PhRMA) adopted a new marketing code to govern the pharmaceutical industry's relationship with physicians and other health-care professionals. Although not law or federal regulation, the PhRMA code soon took on the cloak of law. PhRMA is the largest association representing leading innovator (brand name) pharmaceutical companies. PhRMA members invested $55.2 billion in research and development in 2006, up from $30 billion in 2001. The PhRMA code defines that interaction between company sales representatives, as well as all other company agents, and health-care providers is strictly for the benefit of the patient, and for providing scientific information. It also spells out that "gifts" to health-care professionals must be of educational nature, patient related, and modest in price ($100 or less). In addition, no grants, scholarships, consulting contracts, subsidies, support, or educational or practice related items, be offered to health-care professionals in exchange for prescribing products (14,15). This voluntary industry code has been very effective. Adherence is the rule and it continues as an industry standard today.

Using PDUFA of 1992 as a model for financing and a catalyst for FDA/DDMAC staff increase, in 2007, the FDA began promoting the need for legislation to require industry to pay a fee to be used to significantly increase DDMAC staff to monitor and review DTC promotion. This underscores both the growth of DTC promotion and the broadening of FDA/DDMAC involvement in DTC promotion. Indeed, an entirely new section, Direct to Consumer Review Group II, had been added to DDMAC between November 2006 and March 2007.

Prescription Drug Promotion Today

With continued and constant scrutiny, the landscape of prescription drug advertising and promotion continue to evolve in an abyss of regulation and law, influenced by the government, as well as the industry and individuals. Laws such as the Federal FD&C Act enacted by the FDA; Fraud and Abuse (Anti-kickback) Statutes, Medicaid Rebate Statutes and False Claims Act monitored by the Office of the Inspector General (OIG) and Department of Justice (DOJ); the Lanham Act which prohibits false advertising; various State Statutes (regarding consumer protection, drug marketing/pricing, aggregate spending, etc.) monitored by individual State Attorney Generals or individual citizens; and product liability, privacy laws and the Health Insurance Portability and Accountability Act (HIPAA) for individuals—all do, and have, the ability to affect advertising and promotion of prescription medicines either exclusively or inclusively. And with an estimated 3500 promotional pieces anticipated for review in 2007, DDMAC and industry both have a considerable promotional chasm to navigate.

FDA ORGANIZATION

To understand how FDA regulates pharmaceutical, biologic, medical device, and animal drug marketing and promotion, it is important to first understand how FDA is organized.

It is within the Office of the FDA Commissioner that FDA policies are established. The various centers within the FDA set the policies applicable to the products they regulate. Figure 1 illustrates the five FDA centers that regulate specific marketing and promotional areas of health-related products:

1. Center for Drug Evaluation and Research (CDER): prescription drugs, as well as significant input for nonprescription drugs (OTC) and biologics.
2. Center for Biologics Evaluation and Research (CBER): biologics, including vaccines and blood tissue products.
3. Center for Devices and Radiological Health (CDRH): medical devices and radiological equipment.
4. Center for Food Safety and Applied Nutrition (CFSAN): foods, food additives, and cosmetics.
5. Center for Veterinary Medicine (CVM): animal health products.

Each center monitors marketing and promotion in several ways, namely:

1. Review of product materials submitted by companies.
2. Review of medical journals, trade publications, medical exhibits, electronic media, and publicly available documents that are issued by various firms.
3. Review of complaints received from competitors, or others about marketing or scientific-related practices geared toward health-care professionals, as well as DTC promotion used by companies.
4. Review of materials supplied by the product review divisions.
5. Monitoring and surveillance of promotional materials including internet sites, recently approved and high risk materials.

CDER is the focal point of FDA's regulation of pharmaceutical drugs, and therefore, the focus of this chapter.

Center for Drug Evaluation and Research

CDER represents the largest staff center within the FDA that regulates marketing and promotion. CDER includes over 1500 people, who are headquartered in about a half-dozen office buildings. Drug reviews have become very complex and challenging as the sophistication of drug design and manufacturing increases.

CDER is responsible for the overall regulation of pharmaceutical and biologic products, while the DDMAC is responsible for overseeing all labeling and promotional activities. Figure 2 illustrates the manner in which DDMAC is organized.

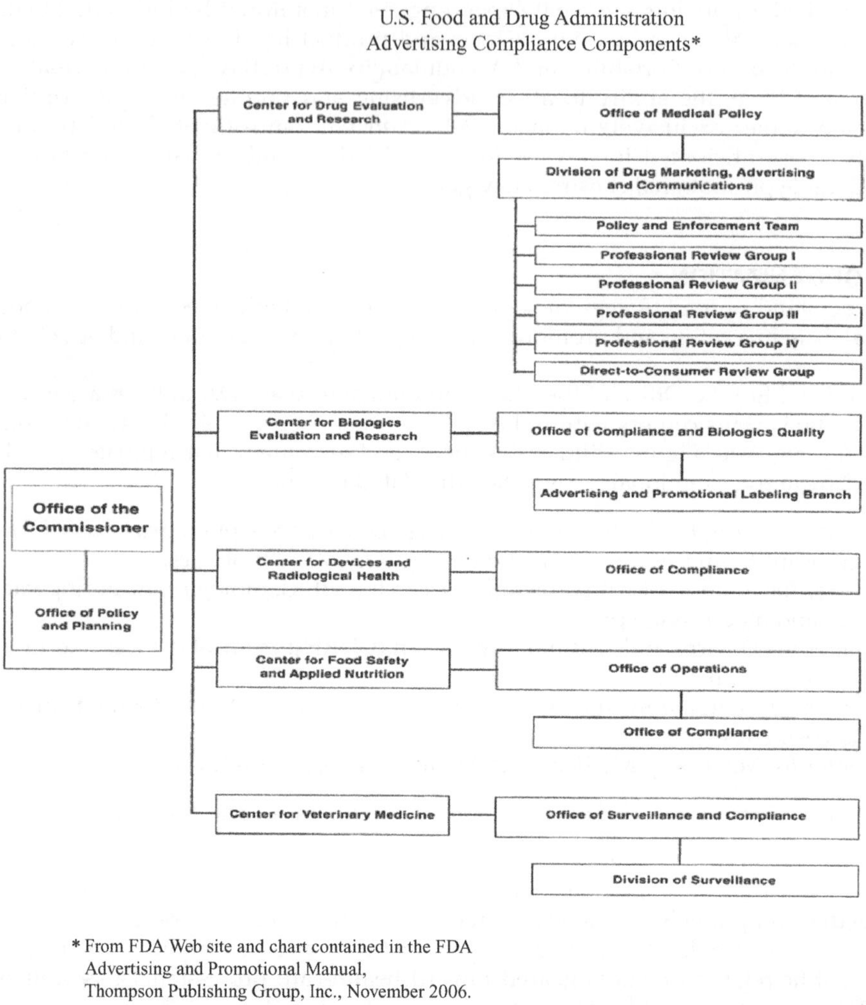

FIGURE 1 FDA centers that regulate specific marketing and promotional areas of health-related products.

DDMAC reviewers have the responsibility for reviewing prescription drug and biologic advertising and promotional labeling to make certain that the materials are not false or misleading and ensuring clear and unambiguous communication. The general regulatory requirements are the same basic practices established more than 10 years ago. At that time, industry and FDA's interpretation of the rules were relatively narrow. However, in the last decade or so, these basic rules have become only a starting point. Intense documentation and verification, including the strength and publication of source data, placement of elements within promotion, use of artwork, and presentation of models, are now being evaluated by DDMAC reviewers, often subjectively and empirically. In addition, the

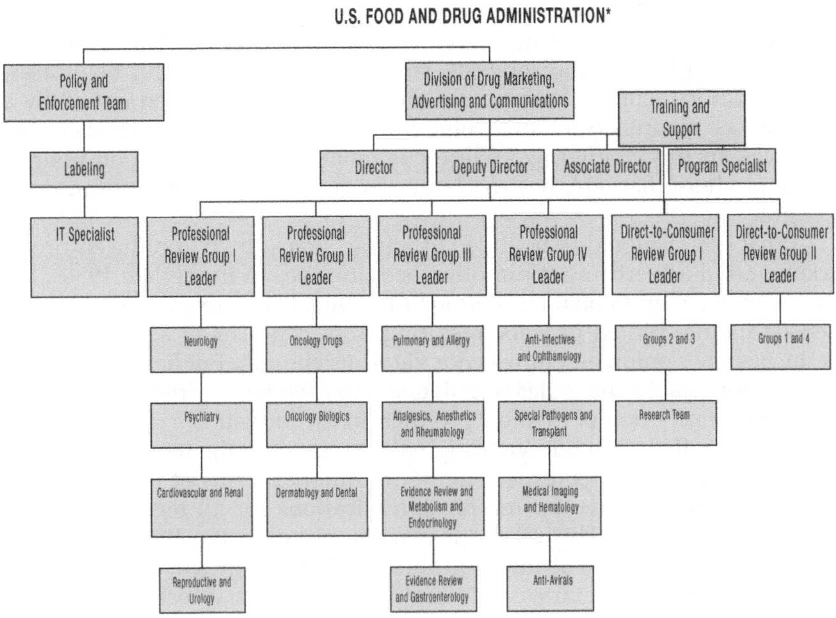

* From FDA Web site and chart contained in the FDA Advertising and Promotional Manual, Thompson Publishing Group, Inc., March 2007.

FIGURE 2 DDMAC organization as of March 2007.

acceptance of "fair balance" has shifted from the inclusion of prescribing information (PI)/package insert and reference to its placement in the promotional piece, to a listing of risks/disclaimers/qualifiers to all positive statements, and with equal weight. In short, DDMAC reviewers use broad individual judgment in evaluating marketing and promotional practices to determine what constitutes a violation and what degree of corrective action is warranted.

The staff of DDMAC monitors drug marketing and promotion from a variety of sources. They have the power to identify violative and incorrect practices and implement corrective action directly with the companies concerned (16). Members of the DDMAC staff regularly consult with CDER and CBER medical reviewers regarding specific product labeling issues and claims and also coordinate with the review divisions when companies request preclearance of product launch materials for newly approved drugs as well as for established brands. Other DDMAC responsibilities include conducting research on marketing, advertising, and labeling activities.

In 2003, the review and monitoring function for some biologic products was also assigned to DDMAC. This is a result of the transfer of regulation of therapeutic biologic products from CBER to CDER.

MARKETING AND PROMOTION REGULATIONS

Although the FDA regulates the marketing and promotion of prescription medicines, biological products, restricted devices, and prescription animal products, the focus of FDA's enforcement of advertising and labeling laws has centered on prescription drugs. This is primarily because it has been actively regulating in this area the longest—since 1962. However, the FDA also has a broad regulatory scope to encompass virtually any information issued by a medical products manufacturer of drugs, biologics, veterinary medicines, or medical devices. In this chapter, we will focus more on the prescription pharmaceutical sector, where the FDA has the largest segment of its staff, by far, devoted to oversight.

What is considered to be the FDA's true "crackdown" on the enforcement of marketing and advertising/promotion activities began in the late 1980s. This was not a result of congressional legislation but, rather, FDA's expansion of its authority based on its interpreted powers, resulting from concerns of a number of sources that the agency's enforcement was not vigorous enough. Public sentiment was that FDA was not establishing rules (regulations) to keep pace with the new methods of advertising/promotion of medical products in the industry.

This so-called "crackdown" originally focused on the marketing and promotion of prescription drugs (especially nontraditional forms of promotion) and has now been shown to have far-reaching implications for all medical product marketing and promotion. This crackdown really began in the 1960s and accelerated in the 1980s, a result of a string of groundbreaking, aggressive Health, Education and Welfare (HEW) secretaries and FDA commissioners, directors, and executives, including Joseph Califano, Robert Temple, Peter Rheinstein, Carl Peck, and Janet Woodcock, to name only a few. This aggressive approach resulted in many years of antagonism between FDA, pharmaceutical companies, and representatives of the pharmaceutical industry associations, including the Pharmaceutical Manufacturers Association (PMA), later renamed the Pharmaceutical Research and Manufactures of America (PhRMA). PhRMA was led for many years by the powerful association leader C. Joseph Stetler (Executive Vice President and General Council from 1963 to 1965 and President from 1965 to 1979 and 1984 to 1985).

In recent years, relations between the FDA and the industries it regulates have become increasingly cooperative, with industry less combative and more accepting of control and compliance. It is true that various companies continue to follow legal strategies to uphold their position and opposition to specific FDA regulatory action. However, overall, the industry has quietly complied with the expanding FDA regulatory interpretation of its authority.

FDA's AUTHORITY OVER MARKETING AND PROMOTION

The authority for FDA's regulations emanates from the Federal FD&C Act of 1962, which established FDA's control over the marketing and promotion of prescription drugs, and was the basis for regulation of restricted medical devices, prescription veterinary medicine, and biological products. With the passage of the Medical Device Amendments in 1976, FDA also received jurisdiction over the regulation of promotion for "restricted" devices. The regulations are enforceable through the imposition or recommendation of the FDA to seek civil or criminal sanctions against violators.

The FD&C Act is vague and general. It does not define advertising, promotion, or marketing. However, the FDA has defined these areas in the broadest terms possible. This is the basis on which their influence/power has grown.

It should be noted that FDA's regulations on drug promotion were written at the time in which journal advertising, direct mail, and "detailing" were the most common ways in which prescription drugs were promoted to the medical profession. As the years progressed, manufacturers' press releases, medical symposia and other medical education programs, electronic advertising, direct-to-consumer (DTC) advertising, therapeutic monographs, dinner meetings, and verbal communications between physicians and company staff or consultant representatives, as well as other modes of promotion, were added to the traditional forms of product promotion (17).

Much has changed regarding the FDA's regulation of prescription medicine marketing and promotion. As delineated earlier, after years of initial combat between the industry and the FDA expansion of regulatory power and after years of experience with the FDA, companies and industry representatives have become reluctant to challenge FDA jurisdiction. The expanded role of informal rules that FDA applies to various product communication mechanisms has made it difficult to predict what the FDA will deem as acceptable.

The FDA can use a number of enforcement tools when they perceive a violation, depending on the seriousness of the perceived violation. This is routinely a judgment call initiated by an individual reviewer. Although since 2001 FDA's warning and untitled letters to the pharmaceutical industry must first be cleared with the FDA chief counsel, the type of enforcement tool issued may be based on the track record of an individual company and the past trouble that company caused the FDA. Primary enforcement tools used by the FDA include:

1. Notices of violation (NOVs)/untitled letters: least serious action, advising a company of a violation of a routine nature that is expected to be remedied, does not greatly impact public health.
2. Warning letter: stating violations, but not in need of action of the DOJ, requiring reply within 15 days. Warning letters often require the company to immediately cease the use of the action or material in violation, destroy the material, issue a "Dear Doctor/Healthcare Professional" letter, or take other corrective action.
3. Seizures and injunctions: civil action, usually to seize a product, initiated by the FDA and brought by a federal court through a U.S. Attorney. This is a rarely invoked procedure. However, the threat is there and is used to "stimulate" negotiation between the FDA and the company. This action can and is used to control marketing of products that are in violation of regulations.
4. Criminal prosecution: the most serious action FDA can take against a company or individual(s). The FDA must present its charges to the DOJ in order to prosecute.

It should be underscored that although members of the FDA are not law officers, their warning and regulatory letters to companies have almost the same effect as issued laws. Moreover, the number of warning letters issued by DDMAC has risen recently, from an average of 5 a year to 16 for the first 10 months in 2006. The most common violations resulting in DDMAC's issuance of a warning letter for promotional materials are for omission of, or inadequate presentation of risk information; unsubstantiated safety or efficacy claims; or comparative claims not supported by substantial evidence.

EXTERNAL PRESSURES ON FDA REGULATION FOR MARKETING AND PROMOTION

A new intensity of regulatory enforcement, in the late 1980s, was due to the fact that the FDA staff recognized that new methods of communicating product information were becoming prevalent and were being extensively and intensely utilized by pharmaceutical companies. Also, concern had been expressed by external observers about the FDA's level of enforcement of misleading advertisements by the drug industry. This new FDA initiative coincided with increased external pressures on FDA to increase its activities in regulating the marketing and advertising/promotion not only of prescription drugs but also for other medicinal products.

In 1990, FDA's activities were further intensified by the arrival of Dr. David A. Kessler as the new Commissioner. He increased the staff in CDER, as well as other centers, and "began the process of setting forth written guidelines for certain marketing and advertising/promotional activities" (18).

Congress, the Department of Health and Human Services (HHS), competitor complaints, consumer advocacy groups, and public opinion are a constant source of external pressure for tighter regulation. As demonstrated in a recent Harris Poll, reported in 2007, 71% of adults surveyed believe it is "very important or highly important" that marketed drugs remain under close review by the FDA and drug companies. Only 9% said such review is only "somewhat or not very important" (19).

COMPLAINTS BY COMPETITORS

Two methods are primarily used by FDA to identify potential company violations in marketing and promotion practices. The first is through FDA's monitoring activities, which, with significant additions in staff, have increased substantially. The second method of FDA scrutiny involves complaints received from competitive firms who monitor the activities of their competition, including marketing and promotion. In fact, for years, competitive complaints formed the basis of half of the regulatory actions taken by DDMAC within CDER. In addition, pressures on FDA can emanate from Congress, OIG, public press, and others, including health-care professionals.

IMPACT OF THE U.S. CONGRESS

A significant and continuing influence over FDA policies and enforcement activities is exerted by the U.S. Congress (i.e., via Senators and members of the House of Representatives), who, periodically, send letters to FDA (receiving priority attention), hold congressional hearings with FDA officials invited to testify, conduct staff investigations, and issue subsequent reports.

A major focus of these congressional issues is the amount of money that the pharmaceutical industry spends on marketing, including marketing and advertising/promotion (20). This is a continual area of contention between Congress and the pharmaceutical industry.

INSPECTOR GENERAL OF THE HHS

The Office of Inspector General (OIG) operates as a politically independent office that conducts investigations, frequently as the result of a complaint or external request concerning what are deemed to be illegal activities. Reports by the OIG are considered significant because of their presumed objectivity and are thus regarded as credible. As a result, OIG reports usually result in publicity with resultant pressure on FDA to take some form of regulatory action.

During the period from 1981 through 1992, OIG focused strongly on FDA regulatory matters, such as the "generic drug scandal," prescription drug advertising, and gifts or payments by firms to physicians. The OIG report noted that many of the gifts to physicians are regarded under the AMA Guidelines on Gifts to Physicians as inappropriate.

This led to the recommendation that FDA should finalize guidelines that defined what was considered to be promotional activity, including gifts, and what was considered scientific exchange. The recommendation was issued in the November 27, 1992 publication concerning proposed policy on scientific exchange and continuing medical education.

IMPACT OF CONSUMER ADVOCACY GROUPS

Consumer advocacy groups provide an important source of external pressure on the FDA in a number of areas. The most prominent consumer advocacy group is the Public Citizen's Health Research Group (HRG), founded by Ralph Nader in 1971 and headed by Dr. Sidney Wolfe. HRG has a special interest in pharmaceutical marketing and advertising/promotion and is known for its opposition to certain marketing and advertising/promotion practices.

Although the HRG has no policy paper or quantifying data on the subject, it claims, as an empirical observation, that the medical products industries spend too much on marketing and advertising/promotion and that much of this marketing and advertising/promotion is misleading. Therefore, HRG, relying heavily on the media, attempts to pressure FDA to monitor the marketplace more closely and to take more aggressive enforcement actions (21).

HRG and other advocacy groups, such as Commercial Alert and National Woman's Health Network, have enjoyed significant success in their endeavors to pressure Congress and the FDA to action. To offset these influences, the Washington Legal Foundation (WLF) has been very successful in ensuring that First Amendment rights are protected in industries' and scientific educators' right to present factual information and findings, within or outside FDA-approved labeling.

AUTHORITY OF THE FTC OVER MARKETING AND PROMOTION OF FDA-REGULATED PRODUCTS

A relationship pertaining to the regulation of product promotion that is often confusing is the interaction of FDA and the FTC: "Under the Federal Food, Drug, and Cosmetic Act (FD&C), the FDA regulates the safety, efficacy, functionality (when appropriate) and labeling of foods (except meat and poultry), prescription and over-the-counter drugs, biologics, veterinary medicine, cosmetics, and prescription and non-restricted medical devices" (22).

In 1938, the FTC received the authority from Congress to regulate the advertising of foods, drugs, and cosmetics. In 1962, this authority was altered by Congress to give FDA jurisdiction over most aspects of the advertising/promotion of prescription drugs but not OTC drugs. Moreover, over the years, FDA has adopted a very broad interpretation of marketing and promotion. While advertising is commonly considered to be paid advertising, FDA considers promotion to apply to any materials issued by or on behalf of a company or any event that is sponsored by or on behalf of a company that mentions one or more products.

Because of their complex working relationship over the regulation of labeling and advertising/promotion of identical products, FDA and FTC entered into what is known as the Memorandum of Understanding (MoU) in 1971, which established the working relationship and division of responsibility between FDA and FTC. As a result of this understanding, FDA and the FTC work closely on many issues that involve promotion. FDA retains full responsibility for all aspects of prescription drug labeling and promotion and the labeling of OTC products, whose advertising the FTC regulates. But with the introduction of the proposed Non-Prescription Drug Modernization Act of 2007, OTC drug advertising may eventually be regulated, to some extent, by the FDA.

FDA REGULATION OF MARKETING AND PROMOTION OF PRESCRIPTION DRUGS: BASIC REGULATIONS AND POLICIES

CDER is responsible for most of the regulations and broad policies that apply to the marketing and advertising/promotion of FDA-regulated products, with the marketing and advertising/promotion of prescription medicinal products being the most carefully monitored product communications. Within CDER, DDMAC is responsible for these regulatory activities.

FDA subjects to regulation any advertising or promotional materials issued by a drug company for a specific product. The following general requirements apply to prescription drug marketing and advertising/promotion:

1. There should be no claims made for a product other than those that are FDA approved and are included in the product's labeling.
2. There must be "fair balance"* in the product's advertising and promotion so that the physician, other health-care professionals, or consumers will have a clear understanding of the product risks as well as benefits.
3. When a journal advertisement contains both the name of the drug and its indications, it must also include an abbreviated summary of the package insert.† This requirement applies to any advertisement that is direct-to-consumer, as well as directed to health-care professionals. Concerning electronic advertising, there must be a provision for easy access to the product package insert by the health-care professionals and consumers.

* This is an evolved interpretation by FDA and refers to FDA's requirement that risks associated with the product's use should be clearly identified, relative to the product's benefits for the patient.

† The product package insert contains all of the essential information about the product, including, but not limited to: pharmacology, clinical studies, indications and usage, ingredients, contraindications, warnings, precautions, dosage and administration.

4. It is illegal to make safety or efficacy claims for a product prior to its approval.
5. "The fact that an advertisement or promotional item may be completely accurate in terms of information is not an adequate defense if any of the specific rules are violated" (23).
6. The product must be accurately represented in the advertisement, even in its graphics.
7. When FDA finds an advertisement or promotional piece in violation, the corrective measures it will use will vary as to the potential impact on public health.
8. Relative to company-sponsored meetings that mention specific products, FDA then regards every aspect of the meeting as within its jurisdiction, such as the location of the meeting, those attending it, who is speaking and what is said, and the relationship that exists between the company and the organization that conducts the meeting.

FDA DEFINITIONS OF LABEL, LABELING, MISBRANDING, AND ADVERTISEMENTS/PROMOTION

Although the Federal FD&C Act does not define "advertising," "promotion," or "marketing," FDA has chosen to define those terms in the broadest sense possible. This is especially true of "promotion," which FDA considers to be any materials that are issued on behalf of a company or any event that is sponsored by or on behalf of a company that mentions one or more products. The key to these regulations begins with labeling and extends through policies on the advertisement and promotion of drugs.

According to the FD&C Act, a label is defined as a display of written, printed, or graphic material upon the immediate container of any article. Any word, statement, or other information that also appears on the label shall not be considered as in compliance unless such word, statement, or other information also appears on the outside wrapper (if there is any) of the retail package of such article, or is easily legible through the outside wrapper or container (24).

FDA has interpreted labeling to include brochures, booklets, mailing pieces, detailing pieces, file cards, bulletins, calendars, price lists, catalogs, house organs, letters, motion picture films, videos, CDs, sound recordings, exhibits, literature, reprints, and similar pieces of printed, audio, or visual matter description of a drug and references published for use by medical practitioners, pharmacists, or nurses, containing drug information supplied by the manufacturer, packer, or distributor which are disseminated by or on behalf of its manufacturer, packer, or distributor (25). In recent years, this has been extended to include DTC advertising, investor press releases, and other public or investor relations programs mentioning a drug product, as well as other electronic/web/computer interactive materials.

Misbranding of a product is considered when the labeling or advertising/promotion is alleged to be misleading. To determine this status, FDA takes into account the representations made (or suggested) by the statement, word, design, device, or any combination of the aforementioned. The FDA also considers the extent to which the labeling or the advertising/promotion fails to reveal facts that are material in light of such representations or material with respect to the consequences that could result from the use of the article to which the labeling or advertising/promotion relates under the conditions of use prescribed in the labeling and advertising/promotion or under such conditions of use as are customary or usual.

CONTENT AND FORMAT REQUIREMENT FOR PRESCRIPTION DRUG PI

FDA has recently implemented new content and format for label requirements that will affect all new and recently approved prescription drugs to make it easier for health-care professionals to access, read, and use PI. These changes have been implemented to enhance ease of use and comprehension of the PI. Most notably, the new format will include a "highlights" section and a "Table of Contents." The "highlights" will contain the information that the health-care professional most frequently refers to and considers the most important. The "Table of Contents" includes section numbers for quick reference to various sections of the PI. In addition to the new content and format of the PI, sections of the PI will also be reorganized to allow easier access to the more commonly used/critical sections.

GENERAL FDA POLICIES FOR PROMOTING DRUGS

FDA has made it clear to pharmaceutical firms that all advertising and promotional materials to be used for specific regulated categories, such as prescription drugs, must be submitted to FDA routinely at the time of first use. The materials concerned include advertisements, detailing pieces, product brochures, price lists, audio–visual materials, and all other materials that fall into the category of advertising or promotional labeling. These requirements apply to the standard forms of marketing and advertising/promotion including electronic advertising.

When these submissions occur, the firm must complete form FDA 2253, entitled "Transmittal of Advertisements and Promotional Labeling for Drugs and Biologics for Human Use." The name, title, and signature of the submitting official must be included on form FDA 2253. All such materials must be submitted to CDER's DDMAC. In order to expedite the review process, companies are required to submit referenced materials with all promotional materials in which the references are cited. DDMAC has issued notice of violation letters when firms "batch" several promotions for collective submission after some or all of the materials have been disseminated since submission to DDMAC is required upon dissemination of promotional materials.

PRECLEARANCE OF PROMOTIONAL LAUNCH MATERIALS

Normally, the routine submission of promotional materials is not required in advance of use. This applies to all health-care professional and direct-to-consumer advertising. However, FDA does specify that if information on the product is not widely known, if the medicine may cause fatalities or serious danger to patients, or if the company has been notified by CDER of a need to publicize such information and has not yet satisfactorily complied, then FDA requires prior approval of the promotion. In addition, there are two other situations in which preclearance of marketing and promotional materials is required or strongly advisable, namely:

1. When it is believed that there has been a serious or repeated violation of FDA regulations by the firm.
2. When a major new product is being introduced, the FDA generally requests that the initial marketing and advertising/promotional materials be submitted voluntarily.

ITEMS FOR PRECLEARANCE

Although submission of prelaunch materials to DDMAC is strictly on a voluntary basis, the FDA encourages companies to seek advisory comments on core materials that are representative of the launch campaign. Core materials include the primary detail aid, the primary journal advertisement, introductory letters, and press releases. FDA also requests that submissions for advisory comments be accompanied by hard copies of all references annotated and highlighted that support the claims of the promotional materials. If core materials are submitted to DDMAC for advisory comments before labeling is final, DDMAC will consult with the responsible review divisions to ascertain product status. If critical matters or concerns, such as safety or efficacy issues are identified, DDMAC will not review core materials. "All core materials that are submitted to DDMAC for advisory comments should be submitted in triplicate, with a cover letter specifically stating that advisory comments are being requested." It is permissible to call DDMAC to advise that materials are being submitted for advisory comments and to inquire about the current time queue. Even though DDMAC reviews preclearance materials on a first-in/first-out basis, it is helpful if the request for expedited review of core materials includes a prioritized list of the order in which the materials are needed. The length of time that a review takes is dependent upon many factors, including, but not limited to, the complexity of the promotional materials submitted, the quality of the submission, the staffing in the review division, and the overall status of the product review/approval process. In the event that DDMAC is unable to provide advisory comments in an expeditious manner, a company may decide to withdraw its request for advisory comments and disseminate promotional materials. In such instances, DDMAC should be notified immediately and materials should be submitted on form FDA 2253 upon dissemination.

FAIR BALANCE

Every advertisement must meet FDA's "Fair Balance" requirements (26), which mean that FDA has mandated, through administrative authority, that interpretative risks associated with a product must be clearly identified to offset the product's benefits. This applies to all promotional materials, including advertisements (printed and electronic), detail aids, and public relations materials.

In April 1994, CDER indicated that fair balance applies equally to the content and the format of promotional materials. It will consider both the representations that are made for the product and the extent to which the labeling or promotion fails to reveal "material" facts about potential consequences resulting from the product's use. In other words, the benefits of the product must be in balance with the risks associated with its use.

A company's compliance with this FDA fair balance provision varies depending on the nature (type) of promotional material. It also seems to ebb and flow in the extent of risk balance needed. However, the day of the inclusion of the product package insert or the brief product summary to meet the requirements of fair balance is long gone. Fair balance now requires the promotion to include risk information and qualifiers to effectiveness claims or study data to be in prominence and readability that is comparable to the effectiveness-related information that is presented. DDMAC has made it clear that risk information that is placed within the footnotes and not in the body of the text of a promotional piece does not meet the requirements for fair balance if the benefit information is included in the main body of a promotional piece. In short, fair balance, as interpreted by FDA/DDMAC, requires substantial qualification and presentation of risk and substantial, well-established, evidence of safety and effectiveness.

The following are examples of violations in which a promotional piece may be false or misleading or fair balance may not be sufficient to preclude agency notification:

1. Claims made comparing the product with another product without specific proof.
2. Making claims that the product is safer or more effective than the labeling indicates.
3. Misrepresenting a study or other information pertaining to the clinical data as it pertains to the product.
4. Using product graphics in a misleading manner.
5. Using a study that is badly (poorly) designed.
6. Misrepresenting the statistical data.
7. Misusing the graphics for the promotional material.
8. Misrepresenting what is accepted as the product's mechanism of action.
9. Failing to provide a balanced emphasis of product warnings, precautions, side effects, and contraindications.
10. When appearing on multiple pages, failing to clarify where the product's fair balance statement appears.
11. In the case of a multiple page advertisement, failing to refer readers to the product's fair balance statement if located on a different or multiple page(s).

Black Box Warning Promotion

Drugs that are considered by the FDA to be associated with a major risk or hazard, even when the drug is used as directed, must contain a black box warning within the package insert. Such warnings are highlighted by a black box outline and appear at the beginning of the full PI and in summary form at the beginning of the highlights section of the package insert when applicable. Black box warnings contain the most significant warnings and/or contraindications associated with the drug. Because of the risks associated with these types of drugs, additional regulations are applicable for promotion. For instance, reminder ads, that call attention to the name of a drug but do not make any drug claims, are not permitted for drugs that contain black box warnings, or for drugs in the preapproval stage that may potentially include black box warnings. It is imperative that all relevant information contained within a black box warning is included to fairly balance any promotional materials.

BRIEF SUMMARY OF PRODUCT INFORMATION

When FDA required product information (PI) for all promotional material, the practical matter of cost to include the full PI in journal advertising became an issue. Journal advertising space is sold by the page. The need to add a one-, two-, or three-page PI to a one-page promotional message obviously would double, triple, or quadruple the cost of promoting a product by advertising in medical journals. Therefore, a practical solution was agreed upon. FDA found that the labeling contained in a journal advertisement would be in compliance if it contained an abbreviated product information summary. This usually could be contained in a column or a page encompassing a true (correct) statement, or brief summary of information that relates to the product's side effects, warnings, precautions, contraindications, and adverse reactions from the approved product package insert (27).

Wrap-Around Advertisements

DDMAC further clarified in April 1994 that "wrap-around" advertisements, those presenting advertising copy in the front of a publication with the brief summary in the back, were not in compliance with brief summary requirements. It stated that the brief summary must appear adjacent to the advertisement (28) and that an advertisement appearing in the front of a publication with the brief summary in the back of the publication that is separated by the entire contents of the publication is not compliant.

Electronic Advertisements

The preceding requirements also apply to electronic advertisements. Such advertisements, as well as commercials, must include warnings, precautions, major side effects, and contraindications in either the audio or the audio and video portions of the presentation. A number of company violations have occurred in the establishment of rules for electronic advertisements. The companies concerned were issued a violation warning with a complete explanation of the extent to which FDA considered that the matter of fair balance was violated. The companies concerned then complied with the FDA's request to change or modify the advertisement/commercial.

Reference to the Product Generic Name

In the 1960s, FDA regulated that the generic name of each product must be referenced in advertising/promotion for brand-name drugs. The generic name must be cited, for example, the first time, or with the most prominent placement, on each page each time the brand name is featured. Also, the type size of the generic name, except where there are combinations of active ingredients, must be at least half the type size of the brand name and must have prominence comparable to the brand name. Many in the industry consider this matter to be more political than regulatory, especially in light of the efforts that have and are continuing to be made to drive physician prescriptions and pharmacy dispensing to the usage of generic versus trademark drugs.

Reminder and Other Advertisements Exempt from the Brief Summary Requirement

FDA has indicated that some advertisements—generally, prelaunch and reminder ads—are exempt from the brief summary requirement. These ads are designed to call attention to the drug but do not include the product indications, dosage recommendations, or any beneficial claims. However, it should be noted that these ads are not permitted for products that carry, or may be anticipated to carry, a black box warning, which is imposed by FDA to highlight a particular major health issue related to the use of a product.

Reminder advertisements in the past were commonly used for a product with a well-established brand name. FDA restrictions today limit the use of reminder promotion. Note that ads for generic drugs that include representations of the bioequivalence of the products as compared to the brand-name products are not considered reminder ads and must contain prescription disclosure information. Advertisements that focus exclusively on price are technically reminder ads and thus exempt from brief summary requirements.

Help-seeking advertisements are designed to inform the consumer of the symptoms of a particular condition, encouraging the consumer to see a health-care professional in order to discuss appropriate treatment options. This type of promotion is exempt from the brief summary requirement. However, such ads must not refer to a particular prescription product, imply that the product is the preferred treatment for the condition featured, or discuss any unique properties of the drug that allow for its identification.

Bulk-sale drugs are exempt from carrying the brief summary if they are intended to be processed, manufactured, labeled, or repackaged in substantial quantities. They also must not contain any claims of safety or efficacy.

Drugs sold to pharmacists for compounding are also exempt from the brief summary requirement as long as they make no safety or efficacy claims.

PROMOTION OF PRESCRIPTION DRUGS FOUND LESS THAN EFFECTIVE IN THE "DRUG EFFICACY STUDY"

A major effort to require that all drugs be proven not only safe (as required under the 1938 law) but also effective was put into action when Congress in 1962 amended the FD&C Act to this effect. Based on this amendment, FDA decided that all drugs approved between 1938 and 1962 on the basis of safety alone should be evaluated on the basis of efficacy claims.

This massive study was initially performed by panels of experts under the aegis of the NAS/NRC. It became known as the "Drug Efficacy Study," which placed indications for all reviewed drugs into one of the following six categories:

1. Effective
2. Probably effective
3. Possibly effective
4. Ineffective
5. Ineffective as a fixed combination
6. Effective but

As a result of this extensive review, hundreds of older medicine formulations were removed from the marketplace. Additionally, claims that were unproven were eliminated from drug labeling.

The FDA regulations provide for disclosure in both the label and promotion of the status of those drugs and indications that were found to be less than fully effective. The labeling for those drugs with indications found to be less than fully effective should carry a box statement as to this fact. Because there are relatively few medicines remaining with "probably effective or possibly effective" indications, this section of the regulations is seldom applied.

FDA ISSUES CONCERNING COMPANY EFFORTS TO PROMOTE PRESCRIPTION DRUGS

There is a substantial number of issues concerning the FDA regulations for company advertising/promotion of prescription products, including company efforts regarding comparative advertising, price advertising, promotion of unapproved product indications, advertising for investigational and orphan products, and promoting to formularies. In order to understand these issues, each will be reviewed separately.

Comparative Advertising/Promotion and Claims of Superiority

In general, FDA tends to discourage company marketing and advertising/promotion that compares specific products or makes claim of superiority of one product to another. However, in April 1994 CDER released a statement that set standards for claims that "represent, suggest or imply that their product's safety or effectiveness is comparable or superior to that of a competing product or products" (29). But, with this proviso appeared the statement that such claims were then considered to be subject to the same standards of review as for efficacy and safety claims in a product's approved labeling.

A company that makes such claims must support them with substantial evidence or substantial clinical experience that supports the claims presented. CDER further stipulated that such a comparison must be derived from a well-controlled study that compares the products, head to head. The CDER statement indicated that effectiveness claims should be based on at least two adequate, well-controlled studies. Safety claims normally require direct comparisons between the products being compared. Also, there should be statistical clinical therapeutic significance between the products in the comparison.

Another significant guideline in CDER's statement is that both drugs being compared must have been approved for at least the same indications being compared and that the dosage regimens being compared must be consistent with the dosage recommendations in the approved labeling and in the same part of the dose range.

Before the claim can be used in company advertising/promotion, CDER recommends, but does not require, that the studies be reviewed by its medical reviewers. Therefore, CDER indicated that the data also could be submitted upon dissemination of the advertising/promotional claim. The matter of comparative advertising/promotion has thus been made quite clear from the FDA's regulatory perspective.

Price Advertising/Promotion

This is an area of product advertising/promotion that is not always well understood. Thus, the FDA has certain rules that set the conditions for a company using this marketing approach, namely:

1. That the only purpose of the promotion is to advertise price.
2. That the promotion states nothing about the product's safety or efficacy.

3. That both the brand and generic names of the drug be contained in the promotion, as well as, the dosage strength for each ingredient.
4. That the promotion explains the charge for a specific product, strength, dosage form, and quantity.
5. That all product charges are included in the promoted price.

This type of promotion also may include other information, such as the identification of professional services provided by the pharmacy or pharmaceutical company, as long as it is not false or misleading.

If some pharmaceutical manufacturers advertise nationally that their drugs are less expensive than competing or similar products, but no specific price is indicated, the promotion is not considered to be traditional price advertising.

Promotion of Unapproved Product Indications and Off-Label Claims

Unapproved product indications and off-label claims are two areas of intense FDA scrutiny. The main concern of the FDA regarding marketing and promotion is the application of traditional and nontraditional promotion and/or scientific dissemination of unapproved off-label claims for marketed drugs. It is the agency's contention that such promotion has the greatest potential to damage public health because it encourages patients to seek, and doctors to prescribe, products for indications and modes of actions that have not been approved by FDA. Another major concern to FDA is the promotion of products during the preapproval stage. This is a period during which opinions are being formed by clinicians as to the potential range of usefulness (i.e., the indication(s), mode of actions, safety, and effectiveness) for the product being evaluated.

Once the product is approved, it becomes difficult for physicians to limit their prescribing of the product only for approved indications, risks, effectiveness, or mode of action if, in fact, they are aware that the drug is useful for other purposes or has other effects due to the preapproval promotion for the product.

Therefore, the FDA has indicated that an unapproved product or use can be promoted at independent scientific symposia and scientific exhibits. But the materials developed from the symposia may not be used in preapproval promotion campaigns. After approval, these unapproved claims can be made only within a tightly defined set of circumstances, under the umbrella of scientific information disseminated through set criteria (see section "Educational and Scientific Events" of this chapter).

Two Types of Permitted Preapproval Promotion

Safety and efficacy claims are not allowed for a drug during FDA review, or prior to FDA approval, of an indication. And, although preapproval promotion is generally not permitted, there are two exceptions to the regulations that allow institutional or coming soon promotion. Institutional promotional materials identify a drug company and state that the company is conducting research in a specific therapeutic area, but do not identify the drug. Coming soon promotional materials announce the name of a new drug, but do not include any representations regarding the intended use, safety, or efficacy of the drug. Coming soon promotional materials cannot be used for a drug that will include or is likely to include a black box warning. A company that chooses to use either institutional or coming soon promotion must choose one type of promotion only. A company cannot use both types of promotion for the same drug.

Although regulations do not allow safety, efficacy, or mode of action claims for a drug prior to approval, scientific exchange is allowed. Scientific exhibits can include information about unapproved drugs as long as exhibits are clearly separate from commercial areas, staffed only by scientists or medical personnel, and free of commercial materials.

Advertising for Investigational Products

FDA "specifically prohibits any claims of safety or efficacy for the product being researched, or any claims that the product is equivalent or superior to another—such claims would violate FDA regulations concerning promotion of investigational drugs" (30). An FDA policy on the subject explains that Institutional Review Boards (IRBs) are responsible for reviewing how research subjects are selected. It also indicates that the clinical investigators may use advertising to attract research subjects, but an IRB should approve such advertising. FDA considers the IRB review to be necessary in order to ensure that the request for participants is not misleading to subjects, especially in those circumstances in which a study will involve persons with acute or severe physical or mental illness or persons who are economically or educationally disadvantaged.

Orphan Drug Act 1983

The Orphan Drug Act was passed by Congress in 1983 to stimulate development of drugs for rare diseases. The act provides for grants for research, marketing exclusivity for 7 years to the first sponsor to obtain FDA product approval, and FDA assistance including development incentives for research and marketing of drugs for serious rare diseases or conditions that affect fewer than 200,000 people. Among other incentives, such as tax benefits, FDA also provides firms with recommendations on studies required to obtain product approval and encourages sponsors to make orphan drugs available for treatment on an "open protocol" basis prior to final FDA approval for marketing. The act was passed in an effort to attract firms to develop and manufacture products that may have or may appear to have limited profitability.

Promoting to Formularies

Due to the industry's increasing promotion to managed care groups, hospitals, and formularies, FDA presented a guidance regarding the promotion of products to drug formularies. FDA indicated that it considers all formulary informational material or kits to be promotional. As such, the formulary informational kits are considered by FDA to be any materials prepared for review by pharmaceutic and therapeutic committees, etc., that review a regulated product and are prepared for, and disseminated to hospitals, managed health-care organizations, buying groups, and other institutions. However, formulary informational material kits are exempt from the FDA submission requirement if they are prepared in response to unsolicited requests for information. In addition, "Under the FDA Modernization Act of 1997, pharmacoeconomic information provided to a formulary committee will not be considered false or misleading if the information 'directly relates to' an approved indication for the drug and is based on competent and reliable scientific evidence" (31).

In 2000, The Academy of Managed Care Pharmacy (AMCP) format for formulary submissions was established. AMCP urges plans to formally request standardized dossiers from drug companies. Such requests for an AMCP dossier made by a plan must be strictly on an unsolicited basis. AMCP recommends that all dossiers include detailed information regarding a drug's efficacy and safety, overall economic value relative to alternative therapies, published and unpublished studies, data on off-label indications, drug's place in therapy, related disease management strategies, and economic model to provide evidence of value. The AMCP may only be disseminated after product approval and must be compliant with FDA standards: provided upon a truly unsolicited request and not prompted, information must not be false or misleading; response must be specific to requestor, pharmacoeconomic models must be transparent, and model assumptions must be clearly stated. Companies must assure that the dossier is not promotional, must refrain from taking any proactive steps that may be construed as marketing and/or promotion, cannot prepare identical dossiers with the intent of soliciting plans or informing plans of the availability of a dossier, and must assure that dossier is provided peer to peer.

DIRECT-TO-CONSUMER ADVERTISING

Direct-to-consumer (DTC) advertising has had an immense impact on the increased sales of prescription drugs. Many consider DTC advertising to be a prime mover in increasing the volume of drugs used in the United States. In a study conducted by the National Institute for Health Care Management, it was reported that the increases in sales for the 50 drugs that were most heavily advertised to consumers accounted for almost half of the multibillion-dollar increase in drug spending (32). DTC advertising seems almost like the genie that regulatory groups find a need to contain.

FDA has been opposed to DTC advertising of prescription drugs since inception, but DTC advertising remains legal as long as it fully complies with all of the FDA regulations applicable to prescription drug advertising and any relevant laws or regulations enforced by other federal authorities, such as the FTC. According to FDA, DTC advertising consists of any materials that are intended by the manufacturer to be seen or used by a consumer, including traditional product print and electronic advertisements, computer e-mails or Web sites, videotapes, cassettes, pamphlets, brochures, and other printed materials.

Because of FDA's earlier negative attitude toward DTC advertising, it was not expected that this promotional medium would thrive. However, the future of DTC advertising was changed in 1982 when FDA Commissioner Albert Hull Hayes, Jr. predicted that this country "may be on the brink of the exponential growth ... of direct-to-consumer promotion of prescription products" (33).

After seeking a voluntary moratorium on DTC advertising in 1983, the moratorium was lifted by FDA in 1985. Although it did not encourage DTC advertising, FDA permitted such advertising as long as it met all the provisions of the labeling and advertising requirements.

Of interest is the fact that the initial results from an FDA 2002 consumer survey, released at the April 2002 DTC National Conference in Boston, appear to justify continued FDA support for DTC advertising. Eighty-one percent of the consumers surveyed by FDA indicated that they had seen a drug advertisement in the past

3 months (34). Even former FDA Commissioner David Kessler, who spent years at the FDA rejecting staff requests that he allow regulations to be changed to permit DTC advertising, admitted that he was wrong in adhering to that position (35).

However, U.S. physicians continue to indicate that they do not like DTC advertising by pharmaceutical companies. More than 46% of the physicians surveyed stated that DTC advertising negatively affects their impression of the drug companies that sponsor the promotion. Contrary to these findings, the sixth biennial Scott-Levin Pharmaceutical Company Image 2002 study showed that DTC-promoting companies enjoy high esteem by physicians (36). DTC advertising controversy continues to this date, particularly for the DTC promotions that highlight a condition or therapy and encourage patients to seek physician treatment.

FDA POLICY ON DTC ADVERTISING

The following general guidelines for DTC advertising are delineated by FDA:

1. DTC advertisements that meet the requirements of reminder and/or help-seeking promotions can be sponsored by pharmaceutical companies. But such advertisements should be designed to be educational rather than promotional and deliver the basic message to "see your doctor."
2. Advertisements that mention specific products are allowed, but must meet every condition that applies to prescription drug advertising directed at physicians. This includes the appearance of information that is contained in the product package insert. A fair balance of product information is required.
3. DTC advertisements that have been defined to include materials, such as product brochures, that may also be regarded as labeling may be voluntarily submitted to FDA for clearance in advance of their use.
4. Although FDA may initially clear a DTC advertisement voluntarily submitted by a firm, the agency may later take regulatory action following the advertisement's appearance if it considers it to be misleading in some manner.
5. DTC advertisements or other promotional materials must not indicate that only physicians can prescribe prescription drugs, because there are many instances in which nurse practitioners or physician assistants may also prescribe such drugs.
6. The FDA, whose officers continue to object to DTC advertising in principle, expresses concern over broadcast DTC advertisements. Those broadcast advertisements that include a major statement of the drug's critical risk information, present all of the product's indications and contraindications in consumer-friendly language, and are not false or misleading may fulfill the FDA's adequate provision requirements (37).

The FDA guidance outlines adequate methods of information dissemination, namely:

1. A toll-free telephone number. This should provide the consumer with several options, such as the full package insert mailed to them, or read to them over the telephone, or the full package labeling sent via e-mail or accessible via the Internet. Each method should provide requested information to the consumer in a timely manner.
2. Reference to a print advertisement or brochures that are publicly available.

3. A statement that indicates that physicians and/or pharmacists may serve as another source of information.
4. An Internet Web site address that directs consumers to the approved package labeling.

The FDA mechanisms described earlier will satisfy the adequate information provision requirement, but pharmaceutical companies may use an alternative approach if it satisfies the regulatory requirements. However, regardless of the preceding, consumer groups and members of Congress continually criticize the use of DTC promotion and legislation is being proposed to curb or eliminate the promotional practice.

Additionally, with the continued wake of criticism against industry for DTC advertisements, PhRMA adopted a voluntary set of guiding principles for DTC advertising, with which the great majority of the industry members comply. The guiding principles uphold the standards required by the FDA: to be accurate and not misleading, to make claims only when supported by substantial evidence, to reflect balance between risks and benefits, and to be consistent with the FDA-approved labeling.

Since it has been well established that DTC communications about prescription drugs serve the public health by increasing awareness about disease; educating patients about treatment options; motivating patients to contact their physicians and engage in a dialogue about health concerns; increasing the likelihood that patients will receive appropriate care for conditions that are frequently underdiagnosed and undertreated; and encouraging compliance with prescription drug treatment regimens, and to demonstrate PhRMA's commitment to serve as valuable contributors to public health, a number of voluntary guiding principles were established. PhRMA Guiding Principles, in part, state the following:

- To responsibly educate the consumer about the medicine and the condition for which it may be prescribed.
- Clearly indicate that the medicine is a prescription drug.
- Foster responsible communications between patients and health-care professionals.
- Companies should:
  - Spend an appropriate amount of time to educate health-care professionals about a new medicine or a new therapeutic indication before commencing the first DTC campaign,
  - Continue to responsibly alter or discontinue a DTC advertising campaign should new and reliable information indicate a serious previously unknown safety risk, and
  - Submit all new DTC television advertisements to the FDA before releasing for broadcast.
- Advertising should include information about the availability of other options such as diet and lifestyle changes where appropriate for the advertised condition.
- DTC television advertising that identifies a product by name should clearly state the conditions for which the medicine is approved and the major risks associated with the medicine.
- Advertising should be designed to achieve a balanced presentation of both the benefits and the risks associated with the medicine.

- Advertising should respect the seriousness of the health conditions and the medicines being advertised.
- Advertisements should be targeted to avoid audiences that are not age appropriate for the messages.
- Companies are encouraged to:
  - Promote health and disease awareness and
  - Include information, where feasible, about help for the uninsured or underinsured (38).

PRESCRIPTION DRUG USER FEE ACT (IV)

The PDUFA (IV) was to establish a separate user fee program for DDMAC review of DTC television advertisements. With the impetus of Congress and consumers concerned about DTC advertisements that overstate benefits but do not fully convey risks, PDUFA was to help fund expeditious review of DTC television advertisements for prescription drugs. Timely FDA advisory comments on DTC television advertisements would increase incentives for voluntary submission, which would lead to better quality advertisements.

Approximately $6.25 million were to be collected annually, from the pharmaceutical industry, which would fund 27 Full Time Staff reviewers. User fees would only be paid by firms that submitted DTC TV advertisements for advisory comments. Currently, there are approximately 30 firms that seek advisory comments on DTC prescription drug advertisements for television. However, the DTC television advertisement user fee program was abandoned in January 2008, before inception, since the necessary user fees for the program were not provided in advance by firms as required.

ADVERTISING ON THE INTERNET

The growth of consumer interest in health-care information on the Internet has been phenomenal. Even a few years ago, some 70 million Americans searched the web for information on such subjects as diseases, nutrition, pharmaceuticals, and related topics, and this use is still growing (39). Now consumers can obtain more information from the Internet about drugs than they can get from their health-care providers. As a result, pharmaceutical companies have substantially increased their use of the Internet as a vehicle for marketing to consumers and the medical profession.

The interest of physicians for health information on the Internet seems to be moving hand-in-hand with that of consumers who view their physicians as the most valuable source of this information. A recent study indicated that physician demand for e-detailing is significant and growing: "Eighty-one percent of the physicians surveyed think it's a good idea to have access to this type of information when and where it is convenient" (40). It must also be pointed out that many companies provide physician monetary honorariums for the time spent by physicians during e-detailing.

Because of the extremely rapid growth of consumer and physician interest in health information on the Internet and the growing use of this vehicle for marketing promotion by the pharmaceutical industry, DDMAC has been designated to serve as an agency-wide working group to draft policy on marketing and advertising/

promotion on the Internet (41). Thus, FDA intends to issue a document that provides the drug companies with this guidance in the near future.

NON-TRADITIONAL PROMOTION—FDA POLICIES

For many years, pharmaceutical firms advertised and promoted their products primarily through journal advertising, direct mail, detailing by sales representatives, sampling, and hospital exhibits. However, due to the advent of newer communication technologies, an increased level of consumers of health care, and greater competition within the industry, many new ways to promote products have been adopted (42). These newer methods of product promotion include medical symposia, public relations techniques, greater use of single-sponsor publications, an increased use of electronic media, and responses to unsolicited requests for information. As a result, FDA has adapted existing, traditional policies to cover these new communications vehicles.

Such FDA policies on nontraditional promotion are not written in a single document but, rather, are learned and understood by the regulated industry through various methods, such as warning letters, policy announcements, the issuance of guidance documents, or by similar means. Fairness in dealing with these issues has been reflective of the FDA policy. These policies are briefly explored later.

Educational and Scientific Events

FDA's final guidance on industry-sponsored scientific and educational activities was issued in December 1997. This applies to all communications about or regarding FDA-regulated medical products, including prescription medicines, made by, or on behalf of the company. Essentially, this FDA policy states that all such activities that are controlled or substantially influenced by a company must meet all of the traditional FDA requirements for marketing and promotional labeling, including full disclosure and fair balance (43).

What has concerned the FDA about company-sponsored activities is that the companies may influence the content of educational programs by being involved in the selection of speakers and/or direct the content of the activities. FDA also indicated that it would focus intense scrutiny on any discussion of unapproved uses/claims involving marketed products.

DDMAC had previously stated that materials developed from symposia could not be used in preapproval promotion campaigns. However, DDMAC has stated that in conducting scientific exhibits, information about unapproved drugs and drug claims can be displayed in an area that is clearly separated from the commercial exhibit area; is staffed by scientific personnel only; and has no commercial materials for distribution.

DDMAC indicated that pharmaceutical companies might disseminate scientific reprints about an approved product as long as its focus is on FDA-approved labeling which is published in a reputable peer-review journal. In all instances, the companies must use promotional information in the reference text that is consistent with the product's approved labeling.

Essentially, if a product communication is made either by or on behalf of a company, all FDA promotional and advertising regulations apply except for the following exclusions:

- Response to an unsolicited medical request from a health care practitioner that is not prompted in any manner by the company or any representative of the company. Note that a response to an unsolicited request may contain information that is not included in the approved labeling if the information provided is a direct response to the unsolicited request.
- Dissemination of a peer-reviewed scientific journal reprint that includes unapproved uses of an FDA-approved drug to health-care professionals is allowed in accord with section 401 of the FDAMA.

Thus, FDA's Guidance on Industry Support of Scientific and Educational Activities "ISSEA Guidance" established recommendations to help evaluate independence of activities regarding industry-sponsored scientific and educational activities in order to adhere to compliance of guidance. The guidance addresses issues such as:

1. Control of program content;
2. Selection process of organizing firm, presenters, and moderators;
3. Disclosures regarding funding for program(s);
4. Disclosures regarding unapproved uses of product(s) presented;
5. Disclosures of relationship between company and firm organizing program, presenters, and/or moderators;
6. Educational tone of program;
7. Organizing firms standards of independence, objectivity, scientific rigor, and balance; and
8. Promotional tone or component of program, including, but not limited to audience selection, dissemination of materials, bias in manner, or presentation.

An independent scientific or educational activity that is independent (free of the influence) of the company and is not promotional adheres to the guidance. A company may provide a grant to support an educational activity even if the activity refers to an unapproved product or an unapproved use of a product as long as the activity is both nonpromotional and free of the company's influence. As is the case for peer reviewed scientific journal reprints of unapproved product uses, the FDA tightly regulates and monitors information disseminated from scientific and educational sources.

Public Relations Materials

FDA considers product-specific public relations materials as labeling if they are included in press releases, kits, or backgrounders and used by the media. FDA thus requires that all such materials be fairly balanced, containing both the benefits and indications of the product and a fair representation of the risks associated with the product's use.

FDA has no formal requirement that public relations material for drugs be submitted to the agency for preclearance. However, if a new drug which may have a significant impact on public health is about to be approved by FDA, the agency often requests the materials for preclearance. If the pharmaceutical firm submits the materials, but decides to ignore the agency's comments on the materials, it does so at its own risk.

When a company plans to make a major public announcement about a drug, it is usually a good idea for the company to provide the press materials to the FDA

Office of Public Affairs and to the appropriate office within CDER for preclearance (44).

Although there is no formal policy that requires public relations materials to be submitted to DDMAC, FDA does expect product-specific public relations materials to be submitted at time of first use.

Drug Sampling

The use of samples as an effective part of the marketing/promotion effort has become a point of contention in recent years and deserves each company's close attention relative to effective promotion versus violations of intended use in promotion. The distribution of prescription drug samples to health-care professionals by company sales representatives, through the mail, or via a common carrier is enforced by the Prescription Drug Marketing Act of 1987 (PDMA).

Under PDMA, health-care practitioners must request samples in writing and include the name, address, professional designation, and signature of the practitioner who makes the request. The identity and quantity of the samples requested must also be provided, in addition to the name of the manufacturer and the date requested (45). This law was passed in order to correct alleged abuses such as diverting the samples into channels where the samples could be sold. FDA has indicated that decades of sampling abuses have resulted in the sale of misbranded, expired, and adulterated pharmaceutical products to consumers.

The matter of sample abuse in promotion had become such an urgent issue to the FDA that in the October 3, 2002, issue of the *Federal Register*, the Office of the Inspector General (OIG), Department of Health and Human Services stated, in part: "The provision of drug samples is a widespread industry practice that can benefit patients, but can also be an area of potential risk to the pharmaceutical manufacturer. PDMA, The Prescription Drug Marketing Act of 1987 governs the distribution of samples and forbids their sale. A drug sample . . . is intended to promote the sale of the drug" (46).

A case in point was the situation in which the FDA's Office of Criminal Investigation and other law enforcement agencies charged a former pharmaceutical sales representative with "failing to comply with federal regulations governing distribution of free drug samples to physicians. The sales representative allegedly provided samples of a steroid product used in the treatment of prostate cancer to urologists who had not provided a written request for the samples as required by law. Apparently, the sales representative was instructed by the district manager and other company officials to use the samples as a tool to help obtain sales of the drug" (47).

This issue is so critical that all drug manufacturers have been urged by their trade associations to closely follow PDMA requirements including maintaining all documentation that is required. The PhRMA, in the July 1, 2002, New Marketing Code indicated that product samples should be provided for patient use in accordance with the Prescription Drug Marketing Act. It is quite clear to marketing executives that product samples are designed as an integral part of promotion to physicians, to be used as "starters" for patients being treated. The industry is in full agreement that abusive uses of product samples should never be tolerated.

However, the current distribution of samples, as mandated by FDA, has substantially increased sampling costs as part of the marketing budget for promoting each product. And yet there do not appear to be any controls on how the physicians (who request samples) actually use the product samples. It is likely that sample distribution by pharmaceutical companies and sample dispensing to patients by doctors will be clearly monitored and new laws/guidelines to previous abuses will be passed.

The PDMA states that it is illegal to sell, trade, or profit from prescription drug samples. Federal and state laws regulate and establish civil and criminal penalties for violations of the PDMA. Penalties for violations may apply to individual Sales Representatives as well as pharmaceutical companies. An authorized distributor of drug samples must establish, maintain, and adhere to written policies and procedures that delineate the administrative systems for distributing drug samples, including, but not limited to the following: reconciliation of requests and receipts; conducting annual physical inventories; implementing a sample distribution security and audit system; and identifying and monitoring a significant loss of drug samples. The PDMA mandates the storage, handling, and record-keeping requirements for distribution of prescription drug samples and mandates verification with the appropriate state authority that the practitioner has a current license or is authorized to prescribe the sampled drug. Additional requirements for controlled drug samples must also be adhered to. Additionally, the regulations also provide for a reward for information leading to the institution of a criminal proceeding against, and conviction of, a person for the purchase, sale, or trade of a drug sample. A person who provides information that leads to a successful criminal prosecution may be entitled to one-half of the criminal fine imposed and collected for such a violation, but not more than $125,000.

One section within the PDMA established the "Pedigree" requirement for prescription drugs. A drug pedigree is a statement of origin that identifies each prior sale, purchase, or trade of a drug including the date of the transactions and the names and the addresses of the parties involved. Under the pedigree requirement, each person who is engaged in the wholesale distribution of a prescription drug into interstate commerce, who is not the manufacturer or authorized distributor of record for that drug, must provide to the person who receives that drug, a pedigree for that drug. This requirement was established to maintain a clear and accurate record of the movement of drugs and to prevent illegal diversion and unauthorized prescription drug transactions.

Single-Sponsor Publications

"Because the FDA regulates only materials sponsored by FDA-regulated companies, there is a question about whether or not publications by independent publishers can be regulated, regardless of company influence" (48).

There has been much controversy and misunderstanding concerning single-sponsor publications financed by pharmaceutical firms because these publications often involve parties, such as organizations that sponsor continuing medical education programs, or medical journals that publish these documents as supplements.

Single-sponsor publications, including product monographs, are closely monitored by CDER because there is the potential that such publications can be clearly influenced by companies that want to promote unapproved product indications. In general, FDA regards the publication as labeling, and thus the publication must accurately portray the uses of the drug referenced and provide the traditional fair balance. In other words, FDA believes that simply because a medical journal or other commercial publication is involved in a single-sponsor publication, the sponsoring company is not relieved of regulatory responsibility.

Company Representatives: Drug Detailing Activities

This is the most predominant form of promotion for most companies and one that is always under the scrutiny of FDA. FDA considers all of the materials utilized by drug sales representatives as subject to the advertising/promotion regulations. Therefore, during a product's preapproval stage, sales representatives may not provide physicians with materials about product indications or information that is not yet approved.

Often the question arises as to whether or not drug sales representatives are permitted to provide physicians with published clinical studies that appear in peer-reviewed medical journals. The FDA's position is that if it concerns an approved indication for the product, it can be provided to the medical profession. However, if an unapproved product indication or use/claim is discussed in the article (i.e., for a marketed product or during the preapproved stage), the article may not be given to physicians. An exception to this position would be the instance in which the physician requests (via a truly unsolicited request, not prompted by the sales representative) the article from the representative. It may then be provided, but FDA prefers that such requests be handled by the medical department of the company.

Verbal statements made by sales representatives to physicians about their products are also subject to FDA regulation but are virtually impossible for the FDA to monitor. However, a physician or other health-care practitioner may notify the agency about inappropriate statements or misrepresentations made by a sales representative, although enforcement action by the FDA against a drug company in this area has not yet occurred.

Exhibits

Exhibits for drugs at medical meetings and conventions have become an increasingly popular part of the product's/company's overall promotion efforts. Thus, FDA considers all such materials used at these medical meetings to be subject to all of the marketing and advertising/promotion regulations for prescription drugs. Even the text of materials that are displayed at exhibits must meet FDA advertising/promotion regulations.

Because of FDA oversight, pharmaceutical companies need to pay as close attention to exhibit materials as they do to other regulated materials, such as print advertisements. Exhibits that present drugs during the preapproval stage will be considered violative by FDA if the materials mention a specific product indication. The same would apply to an exhibit that mentioned an unapproved indication or use/claim for an approved drug.

The pharmaceutical industry also has been reminded by FDA that all text for program books used at professional meetings must meet pharmaceutical advertising regulations for full disclosure if the company descriptions contain information about the drug's indications or usage.

Responding to Requests for Information

Generally, DDMAC has assured the industry that their individual, nonpromotional responses to unsolicited requests for information will not be considered promotional labeling if each firm maintains documentation concerning the nature of the requests and shows no pattern that suggests that these requests were solicited or prompted by the sponsor (i.e., the firm). DDMAC further notes that the use of toll-free telephone numbers disclosed in promotional labeling or advertising, which invite or somehow prompt requests for information, are considered to be forms of solicitation and thus are subject to all advertising and labeling requirements.

FDA Policies for Broadcast Media

The informal FDA policy regarding the use of broadcast media in promotion is provided as issuance of guidance to the industry. If changes in broadcast advertising are required, FDA notifies the companies directly by letter and, subsequently, releases the changes required to the trade press.

When it was decided that all video news releases (VNRs) should be routinely submitted to FDA at the time of first use, this change in policy was communicated directly in a letter to all holders of approved New Drug Applications (NDAs) and Abbreviated New Drug Applications (ANDAs). This information was also provided to the trade press for dissemination.

FDA Criteria for Advertising Electronically

Policies were developed by FDA, over a number of years, concerning physician-directed television advertising that is product specific. Such advertising must include the major risk statement and include access to the full PI. A toll-free telephone number, Web site address, and/or current nationwide publications are often referenced to alert viewers to the availability of additional patient information or the full PI. In addition, FDA requires that the product's generic name must be used in the advertisement and that fair balance must be included in the body of the advertisement, including major product warnings, precautions, side effects, adverse reactions, and contraindications.

Further, for products that are required to carry special warnings (i.e., black box warnings), information must be provided in the audio portion of the advertisement. The FDA was concerned that physicians not receive confusing or contradictory messages in any video broadcast advertisements that might obscure or undermine important product warning information (49).

FDA Policy on Video News Releases

Health-related stories on television are among the most compelling subjects for TV viewers and, as such, are attractive to pharmaceutical companies via VNRs. VNRs can be used by TV stations in a manner that makes them seem to be original segments produced by the TV stations. A variant, called a "B-roll," is a video that contains raw footage that may include various segments of the manufacturing process, interviews with industry executives, health-care professionals or patients, animations, or other information related to a pharmaceutical product or the industry. These segments are distributed to news agencies that then create a finished news segment, in whole or part, based on the VNR submitted by the company.

Though specific rules for VNRs have not been set forth, FDA did issue a letter to all holders of NDAs and ANDAs that they submit the following information to the news outlet when the VNR is product oriented:

1. The VNR source or sponsor should be made clear to the TV station.
2. All product information or references should be within the approved labeling for the product.

3. When a specific product is mentioned, there should be "fair balance." In other words, the major warnings, precautions, contraindications, adverse reactions, and side effects related to the product should be included.
4. A product package insert should accompany the VNR. If the VNR is sent by satellite, a scroll of the package insert should be included.
5. For a product that is the subject of an NDA or ANDA, the VNR should be submitted to CDER when it is initially issued or disseminated. This includes accompanying information issued at the same time, that is, letters, scripts, press releases, and package inserts (50).

Although there has been some controversy over the use of VNRs, "Pharmaceutical companies . . . have become enamored with the VNR because it allows them to circumvent the usual restrictions concerning the use of television advertising to promote their prescription products directly to the consumer" (51). However, FDA has treated VNRs the same as it treats written press releases. The VNR is treated as labeling when specific products are mentioned and thus requires fair balance, discussing not just the product benefits but also the major risks of the drug.

Infomercials

Infomercials are extended advertisements used on commercial and cable television. They may appear in the format of an entertainment or television show and have not been commonly used to promote prescription medicines to consumers.

Although the FDA does not have a specific written policy on infomercials, they are regarded as advertisements that are subject to established advertising and labeling regulations. To the extent that an infomercial mentions a drug or treatment, it must meet all disclosure and fair balance requirements.

Radio–Television Media Tours and the Use of Celebrities

When a pharmaceutical firm sponsors a radio–television interview tour, FDA considers any product-specific content of the interview to be subject to regulations. This applies even if the spokesperson concerned is not employed by the pharmaceutical firm. FDA has been especially concerned when celebrities appear on such tours. Currently, there are no FDA regulations prohibiting either the use of celebrities to endorse prescription drugs or the use of radio–TV tours with paid spokespeople. However, it is interesting to note that one recent industry study showed that drug advertisements using celebrities are more memorable, but do not motivate patients to seek treatment.

FDA believes that firms that hire spokespersons, or use their employees in this role, must train them to keep their promotional statements in line with the product's approved labeling or to provide the perspective necessary to assure fair balance for the product.

Guidelines for Advertising to Physicians on Radio

FDA does not object to advertising prescription drugs on the radio, as long as the product advertisements contain clear information about the product's warnings, precautions, side effects, and contraindications and provide a balanced presentation of the benefits as well as the risks of the drugs promoted.

Telephone Advertising

Communications by telephone that discuss prescription medicines are considered by FDA to be subject to the same requirements as broadcast advertising. Those pharmaceutical firms that decide to disseminate product information to health-care professionals or consumers via a toll-free telephone number must include a major statement that provides information about product side effects, warnings, precautions, and contraindications before the listener can branch off to other segments of the telephone presentation. The full package insert should be readily available either to be read over the telephone, sent via mail, e-mail, or provided by a link via the Internet. Each method should provide the requested information in a timely manner. Just as with all prescription medicine advertisements, copies of the telephone recordings and scripts must be submitted to DDMAC at the time of initial use.

CHANGING IMPACT OF FDA CONTROLS

Although the FDA was charged with the responsibility to regulate drug promotion throughout the years, it began to exert strong enforcement of the regulations in the late 1980s. FDA had become extremely concerned about the level of misleading promotion. This level of concern has focused on what the FDA considers exaggerations of claims, especially newly issued claims.

For example, a pharmaceutical corporation was warned by DDMAC concerning its cholesterol-lowering product DTC advertisement that appeared in major magazines and mistakenly suggested that this product lacked the side effects of other products of the same class. DDMAC stated a concern about a "continuing pattern and practice of violative behavior." The company pulled the misleading advertisement. Several other pharmaceutical companies have been forced to correct promotions considered to be misleading by DDMAC (52).

Increased pressure continues on FDA from external groups, as well as individuals, while the U.S. Congress has and continues to exert significant pressure on the FDA to strictly enforce marketing and advertising/promotion regulations.

Of added significance, the Office of Inspector General (OIG), in a HHS draft guidance published in the October 3, 2002, *Federal Register* (53), indicated that drug companies should expect prosecution or other action if they do not change some of the ways that they market prescription drugs, including the giving of gifts, grants, and scholarships to physicians and health-care providers in exchange for help in promoting their products. The OIG went to the extent of strongly recommending that pharmaceutical manufacturers should designate a compliance officer to serve as the point person to oversee these compliance activities.

Throughout all of its regulating activities over the years, FDA has expressed concern that there should always be a fair balance in a company's claims for the efficacy of its products and its indication and the potential adverse reactions associated with each product's usage. This applies to all promotional materials.

It has appeared that the FDA would like to increase its regulatory authority, but potential future trends may put some limits on its ambitions in this regard.

POSSIBLE FUTURE FDA REGULATORY ACTIVITIES

It is doubtful that many would challenge the benefits associated with FDA's efforts over the years to determine that drug manufacturers, in their efforts to market and promote their products, present to the health profession and the consumer a fair balance as to the efficacy and risks of their respective products. FDA controls and surveillance in this area have increased year after year, and the overall impact of FDA on drug companies' marketing and advertising/promotion activities will continue in the future. However, recent events have begun to slow the overall regulatory efforts of the FDA relative to drug marketing and advertising/promotion activities.

In November 2001, the Bush administration's new leadership in the HHS released an unprecedented directive that the FDA's "warning" and "untitled" letters to the pharmaceutical industry must first be cleared with the new FDA chief counsel, Daniel E. Troy. This was implemented because there were so many people and offices that could issue warning letters that they had lost their overall desired impact on the industry (54).

Much concern had been raised that the directive would have a chilling effect on the FDA's "watchdog" activities. The HHS, however, indicated that it was expecting the FDA, as a result of the directive, to set forth priorities and enforce those priorities with a much-improved effectiveness for their "Warning Letters."

Another development that has truly shaken the FDA is the Supreme Court Ruling in *Western States v. Shalala*, which endorsed the lower courts' criticisms of the FDA culture. Basically, it said that the FDA's DDMAC "... had no business, even with encouragement from the FDA Modernization Act of 1997, trying to curb the free speech of compounding pharmacists advertising their services" (55). Several legal decisions have indicated that the FDA has been too accustomed to getting its own way in challenging hundreds of industry advertisements and other promotional pieces and has not paid enough deference to the First Amendment.

Cognizant of these decisions, FDA has begun to seek input from the public as to how it should balance statutory responsibilities with First Amendment obligations. Some of the input sought included whether certain promotional speeches about medicines is inherently misleading unless it complies with FDA requirements, whether FDA's current DTC advertising policy is consistent with the effects of such advertisements or leads to overprescribing, whether product disclaimers should have the same type size as claims, and whether off-label promotions undermine the approval authority of the FDA. Meanwhile, FDA's "old guard" started to argue, internally, that the Supreme Court decision threatened its control over what is said about product effectiveness, thus allowing broadened product claims.

However, a positive move by FDA has already taken place. CDER released an article entitled "Think It Through: A Guide to Managing the Benefits and Risks of Medicines," which reminds consumers of the benefits and risks associated with different drugs and provides helpful tips designed to minimize the potential risk of drug use (56).

FDA is quite concerned that its authority will be undermined "... if unapproved products can be promoted, or new uses of approved products can be promoted without FDA approval" because FDA believes that neither consumers nor physicians can properly evaluate information about the extremely complex products that it regulates (57). However, the courts have ruled that, if a drug is lawfully marketed following its initial approval, physicians can legally prescribe products for off-label uses if they have access to the information on those uses. How this matter will ultimately be resolved is not at all clear.

Also, it is unclear what course of action will be taken on drug importation from foreign countries. After a hot debate in past years, concerning the value/need for consumers to receive drugs via foreign markets, in recent years, the debate has cooled. Both in Congress and throughout the general public, the progress made through Medicare/Part D, improved generics and the debate on medical case and insurance coverage has overshadowed the discussion and call for information reform. Indeed, in a presidential election year, there is virtually no dialog concerning this issue. There is, however, a stronger call for federal negotiation of drug prices as well as increasing the FDA approval process and efficiency. These are factors that could affect industry's future marketing of products that are overseen by the FDA.

Another big factor affecting marketing is the status and future of prescription tracking market research. This provides individual doctor prescribing habit profiles, by doctor and number of prescriptions written by that doctor for all specific brands and generics. Virtually all drug companies use these data heavily, which are gathered and provided by several service organizations. These data are used to direct and focus promotional activity, including sales representative detailing and sampling, to those doctors that represent the highest potential for prescriptions, leading to sales.

Physician profiling based on prescription activity has been used for years. In general, physicians know about it and accept its use. However, a growing objection from consumer groups has led to increasing concern from Congress and state legislations regarding the practice. Thus far, New Hampshire has taken the boldest steps, passing state law limiting drug company access to doctors' prescribing habits. This legislation is currently being challenged in the courts.

If the New Hampshire law is upheld and other states follow suit, it will have a significant impact on the marketing and promotion of pharmaceuticals in the future.

DTC promotion will continue to be attacked by consumer groups and Congress. The national headlined exposures of early 2008, concerning several heavily DTC promoted cholesterol-lowering drugs, brought fuel to the fire calling for DTC limitation or elimination. Various congressional leaders have called for action ranging from removal of DTC promotion for all prescription products to not allowing DTC promotion during the first 2 to 3 years postmarketing approval. It is likely that some form of legislation will be passed to "reduce the risk to the public" attributed to DTC promotion, as well as, "reduce the cost of over $4 billion per year," that it adds to drug pricing. Where this new attention to DTC promotion ends up will greatly affect marketing and promotion, as well as, FDA action.

FDA must follow the mood of the courts and Congress, but the pharmaceutical industry has lost some of its luster due to pricing disclosures, industry related scandals, and the general public disenchantment with overall corporate ethics. FDA may relax its regulatory activities, but should some health accidents occur due to the decision of the courts, the regulatory pendulum will, undoubtedly, swing further in the agency's direction. Only time will tell if regulatory changes will occur and the degree to which FDA's regulatory controls of drug marketing and advertising/promotion will be altered.

REFERENCES AND NOTES

1. FDA Advertising and Marketing Promotional Manual, July 2002:15
2. DDMAC Watch: The Year in Review, Washington Legal Foundation 29 (Aug. 2006).
3. Arnold Matthew, DTC Report, Medical Marketing & Media, December 2006.

4. St. Petersburg Times, Doctor Combats Pull of Drug Reps, December 27, 2007.
5. Chronology of Drug Regulation in the United States: US FDA, Center for Drug Evaluation and Research's, www.fda.gov/CDER/about/history.htm. 2002:1.
6. Ibid, p. 4.
7. Patrick W. Know Your Government—The Food and Drug Administration, Chelsea House Publishers, 1988:16.
8. A Brief History of the Center for Drug Evaluation and Research, www.fda.gov/cder/about/history/Histext.htm, p. 5.
9. Ibid, p. 7.
10. Ibid, p. 8.
11. Ibid, p. 10.
12. Ibid, p. 8.
13. Ibid, p. 12.
14. About PhRMA, www.phrma.org/about_phrma/, p. 1.
15. PhRMA Adopts New Marketing Code, www.phrma.org/phrma_adopts_new_marketing_code.
16. FDA Advertising and Marketing Promotion Manual, October 1999:21.
17. FDA Advertising and Marketing Promotion Manual, October 1993:15.
18. FDA Advertising and Marketing Promotion Manual, March 1997:23.
19. Dickerson J. People Want Drug Oversight. Washington Insider, Medical Marketing & Media, February 2007.
20. FDA Advertising and Marketing Promotion Manual, March 1997:25.
21. Ibid, p. 29.
22. FDA Advertising and Marketing Promotion Manual, May 1993:39.
23. Ibid, p. 7.
24. Ibid, p. 7.
25. Ibid, pp. 7–8.
26. FDA Advertising and Marketing Promotion Manual, May 1997:17.
27. FDA Advertising and Marketing Promotion Manual, September 1997:19.
28. Ibid, pp. 19–20.
29. FDA Advertising and Marketing Promotion Manual, August 1994:33.
30. FDA Advertising and Marketing Promotion Manual, August 1997:35.
31. FDA Advertising and Marketing Promotion Manual, March 1998:39.
32. Liebman M. Drug Industry is a Winner, Medical Marketing & Media, January 2002:50.
33. FDA Advertising and Marketing Promotion Manual, November 1997:46.
34. Dickinson J. DTC Report—FDA Survey Data Supports DTC, June 2002:32.
35. Ibid, p. 32.
36. Dickinson J. DTC Report—Physicians Turned Off by DTC ad, Medical Marketing & Media, September 2002:40.
37. FDA Advertising and Marketing Promotion Manual, November 1997:48.
38. PhRMA Guiding Principles: Direct to Consumer Advertisements About Prescription Medicines, November 2005.
39. Mack J. You have a brochure on the web. Now what? Pharma Exec Suppl, March 2000:16–18.
40. Dickinson J. DTC report—E-detailing gaining acceptance among physicians, Medical Marketing & Media, September 2002:10.
41. FDA Advertising and Marketing Promotion Manual, March 1998:40.
42. Ibid, p. 55.
43. Ibid, pp. 55–56.
44. FDA Advertising and Marketing Promotion Manual, December 1996:59.
45. Ibid, pp. 62–63.
46. Fed Reg, Vol. 67, No. 192, October 3, 2002, Notices, 62063.
47. FDA charges TAP sales rep., Medical Marketing & Media, September 2002, p
48. FDA Advertising and Marketing Promotion Manual, December 1996:61.
49. FDA Advertising and Marketing Promotion Manual, November 1996:72.
50. Ibid, p. 73.

51. Ibid, p. 74.
52. Liebman M. Industry update—FDA keeps up the pressure, issues repeat ad warnings, Medical Marketing & Media, October 2002:18.
53. Fed Reg, Vol. 67, No. 192, October 3, 2002, Notices, 62063.
54. Dickinson J. As I see it—Bush reviews FDA letters to industry, Medical Marketing & Media, January 2002:14.
55. Dickinson J. As I See It—Supreme Court trims DDMAC's, Medical Marketing & Media, July 2002:14.
56. FDA advises on drug benefits, risks, Medical Marketing & Media, October 2002:32.
57. Castagnoli W. Rx marketing regulations hang on first amendment debate, Medical Marketing & Media, September 2002:88.

21 CMC Postapproval Regulatory Affairs: Constantly Managing Change

Leo J. Lucisano and Kevin A. Miller
GlaxoSmithKline, Research Triangle Park, North Carolina, U.S.A.

Lorien Armour
Armour CMC Regulatory Consulting, LLC, Durham, North Carolina, U.S.A.

INTRODUCTION

You arrive at work this morning feeling refreshed and unburdened. Last night was the first time in the last 6 months that you had a full and restful sleep. Late yesterday afternoon, you finally received the approval letter for the new drug application (NDA) for your company's projected blockbuster product, and you are savoring the moment. You casually saunter to the break room for your morning cup of coffee, take a few minutes to celebrate with your coworkers, and return to your office, expecting a light day by recent standards. As you wait for your computer to boot up so you can catch up on the seemingly infinite backlog of e-mail, the phone rings. You note on the caller ID display that it is the marketing director for the new product. "She's probably calling to congratulate me on the approval letter," you speculate as you reach for the receiver. The tone of her greeting immediately tells you otherwise. New market research data just arrived on her desk that morning indicating that patients preferred a blister package compared to a plastic bottle. She wants to know if a submission is required for a blister package and, if so, how long it will take for preparation and approval. She indicates that time is of the essence to maximize market penetration, as a competitor's product is anticipated to be approved imminently. While speaking with the marketing director, you receive an urgent message from your administrative assistant to call the vice president of manufacturing as soon as possible. You tell the marketing director that you will research the regulatory implications of the proposed packaging change and will call her back with an answer as soon as possible.

You phone the vice president of manufacturing, and he tells you that content uniformity failures have been encountered during process validation of the commercial batch size for the new product. To correct the problem, it appears that the blending speed and time for the bulk powder need to be modified. He wants to know if the changes have any regulatory implications and comments that any production downtime will almost certainly delay the launch. You advise that you will research the regulatory implications of the proposed manufacturing change and will call him back with an answer as soon as possible. "Well, so much for the light day," you think to yourself as you hang up the phone. What will you do?

While the above scenario is fictitious, it is an accurate depiction of the dynamic world of Chemistry, Manufacturing, and Controls (CMC) (referred to by the authors as "constantly managing change") Postapproval Regulatory Affairs. This chapter provides an overview of the scope of CMC postapproval regulatory affairs, the recent U.S. history of CMC postapproval regulations and their current status, the different types of regulatory submissions to file CMC changes, and the relationship of Current Good Manufacturing Practice (cGMPs) regulations to CMC postapproval activities. Measurements of performance are suggested to gauge the effectiveness of the CMC postapproval regulatory function, and commentary is provided regarding the development of professionals in this field. The chapter concludes with a discussion of the forces affecting the future of this expanding arena of regulatory oversight.

CMC POSTAPPROVAL REGULATORY AFFAIRS OVERVIEW

CMC regulatory affairs is concerned with the technical characteristics of a drug molecule and the dosage form used for its administration. The regulatory affairs professional is responsible for assuring that sufficient CMC knowledge is accumulated about the molecule to permit evaluation by the U.S. Food and Drug Administration (FDA) through the product life cycle. Table 1 depicts a typical list of CMC information required for evaluation.

In the preapproval phase of the product life cycle, CMC information is initially provided to FDA through an investigational new drug application (IND). Depending on the outcome of clinical trials conducted under the IND, an NDA may be filed with an additional level of CMC information that may result in approval of the drug product and its commercialization. The CMC section of the NDA establishes the approved conditions for manufacturing and testing the drug substance and its dosage form(s). In the postapproval phase, the regulatory affairs professional is responsible for managing changes to these conditions.

Table 2 compares the different environments encountered during the two phases of the product life cycle. Prior to approval of the NDA, the CMC regulatory professional interacts primarily with a research and development (R&D) team that is dedicated to developing the body of information required to gain FDA approval of the drug product. The sequence of steps from the application of the IND to NDA approval takes several years, and the process is well defined. Various initiatives supported by FDA, such as the International Conference on Harmonization, provide a clear road map regarding the CMC information and data that need to be accumulated to adequately characterize a new drug product and its active ingredient. (Refer to www.ich.org for additional information.)

Following the approval of the NDA, the CMC regulatory professional interacts primarily with marketing and manufacturing, whose priority is to maximize

TABLE 1 CMC Database for a New Drug Application

Drug substance	Drug product
Physicochemical properties	Components and composition
Synthetic process	Manufacturers
Controls for starting materials, reagents, etc.	Method of manufacturing and packaging
Process controls for intermediates	Specifications and analytical methods
Specifications and analytical methods	
List of impurities	Stability information
Stability and life to retest	

the commercial potential and return on the investment of the drug product. These drivers may result in a stream of requested changes to the originally approved CMC conditions in the NDA. Unlike R&D, the productivity of the manufacturing environment is measured in weeks and months, and multiple changes to the drug substance and/or drug product often need to be evaluated and implemented in a parallel time frame. Additionally, the approval of an NDA often results in a number of CMC postapproval commitments that must be fulfilled, including the statutory requirement to file Annual Reports. The regulatory professional supporting these CMC postapproval activities must be diligent in providing regulatory oversight and strategies that ensure that CMC changes are implemented in a reasonable time frame while adhering to appropriate regulations.

CMC POSTAPPROVAL REGULATIONS AND GUIDANCE

In order to make CMC changes to the conditions of approval in the NDA, the drug manufacturer must file the changes with FDA through one of the various types of postapproval submissions described later. An appropriate level of information and data must be included in the submission to demonstrate that the changes do not adversely affect the quality attributes of the drug substance and/or drug product.

Prior to 1997, the regulation governing CMC changes to an approved NDA was 21 CFR 314.70 (Supplements and Other Changes to an Approved Application) (1). This statute was established in February 1985 as part of a comprehensive effort to improve the NDA and postapproval application process. It defined three reporting categories for postapproval changes: (*i*) prior approval supplement, (*ii*) changes being effected (CBE) supplement, and (*iii*) Annual Report.

In practice, the provisions in the original version of 21 CFR 314.70 were vague, and the interpretation and review of CMC changes by different review divisions within FDA were inconsistent. The situation led to increasing criticism by the pharmaceutical industry that the postapproval regulations stifled changes in the manufacturing environment.

On November 21, 1997, the Food and Drug Modernization Act was signed into law by the President. Section 116 of the act required that 21 CFR 314.70 be revised to streamline the regulatory process for CMC postapproval changes. Two years later 21 CFR 314.70 expired without an updated version in place. As a result, FDA issued an interim guidance document, Guidance for Industry: Changes to an

TABLE 2 Comparison of CMC Regulatory Environments

	Preapproval	Postapproval
Type of submissions	INDs and NDAs	Supplemental NDAs Annual Reports CMC Commitments
Internal customer	R&D	Manufacturing
Customer priority	Supporting INDs and NDAs	Manufacturing product
Time lines	Months and years	Weeks and months
Format of submission	Well defined	Less defined
Reference base of information	Being developed as part of the NDA	Approved conditions in NDA

Approved NDA or ANDA (CANA), that has been the current reference for determining the appropriate regulatory submission for CMC postapproval changes (2). In April 2004, the revised 21 CFR 314.70 rule was published, and the CANA Guidance was updated accordingly. The final rule became effective on June 22, 2004.

The revised rule and both versions of the CANA Guidance retained the same reporting categories identified in the original rule but expanded the CBE supplement into two types, CBE-30 and CBE-0. They also linked the submission reporting category to the potential for a change to have an adverse effect on the identity, strength, quality, purity, or potency of a product as it relates to the safety or effectiveness of the product. By establishing this link, the revised rule and CANA Guidance integrated the quality and regulatory perspectives in evaluating CMC changes.

The revised rule and CANA Guidance provide recommended filing categories for changes to the following: (*i*) components and composition, (*ii*) manufacturing sites, (*iii*) manufacturing process, (*iv*) specifications, (*v*) packaging, (*vi*) labeling, (*vii*) miscellaneous changes, and (*viii*) multiple related changes. However, neither defines the information and data required in the application. Recommendations regarding the appropriate information and data package required to assess the impact of CMC changes are contained within the battery of guidance documents issued by FDA in recent years. The content of information and data packages may also be dependent upon historical precedence with a particular drug substance and/or drug product. Figure 1 depicts a spectrum of guidance documents that the CMC postapproval regulatory professional can consult in determining the appropriate submission category and supporting data and information package to appropriately assess and file changes.

FDA issued the first guidance document in 1995 that specifically addressed CMC postapproval changes, namely, the Guidance for Industry; Immediate Release Solid Oral Dosage Forms; Scale-Up And Post-Approval Changes, Chemistry, Manufacturing and Controls; In Vitro Dissolution Testing; and In Vivo Bioequivalence Documentation (3) (commonly known as the SUPAC-IR Guidance). Since that time the FDA's Center for Drug Evaluation and Research (CDER) has issued more than 20 additional guidance documents in draft and final form (4–23). They range from covering changes to specific dosage forms to addressing relevant scientific and technical topics in assessing change (e. g., equipment design and dissolution testing). Many concepts and the vocabulary introduced in these postapproval documents have now been embedded into the NDA process. Examples include the terminology associated with the design and operating principles of manufacturing equipment, as well as the various approaches to demonstrating dissolution similarity when changes are made to the drug product.

CMC POSTAPPROVAL REGULATORY SUBMISSIONS

Table 3 lists the types of CMC postapproval submissions addressed in the revised rule and CANA Guidance.

Prior Approval Supplement

A Prior Approval Supplement is required for a CMC change that has a substantial (major) potential to have an adverse effect on the identity, strength, quality, purity, or potency of the product as they may relate to its safety or effectiveness. Its title is self-defined, meaning that FDA must approve the change before drug product

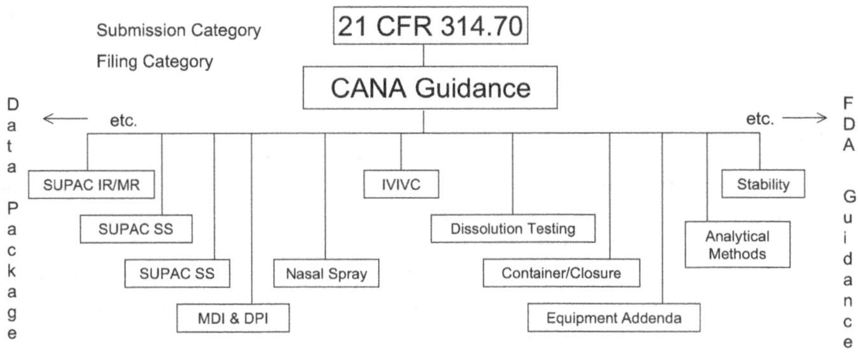

FIGURE 1 Regulations and guidance affecting CMC postapproval changes.

incorporating the change can be distributed for patient consumption. Occasionally, a Prior Approval Supplement may need to be approved as soon as possible in the interest of the public health (e. g., drug shortage) or if a delay in implementation will cause extraordinary hardship on the drug manufacturer (24,25). When these situations arise, the applicant can request an Expedited Review of the supplement. The supplement should be clearly labeled Prior Approval Supplement—Expedited Review Requested, and a justification for the request should be provided in the accompanying cover letter (24).

Changes Being Effected Supplement

A CBE supplement is required for a CMC change that has a moderate potential to adversely affect the drug product as it relates to its safety or effectiveness. The 1999 CANA Guidance provided for two types of CBE supplements: (*i*) Supplement–Changes Being Effected in 30 Days (CBE-30) and (*ii*) Supplement–Changes Being Effected (CBE-0). The revised 21 CFR 314.70 rule and CANA Guidance have retained these filing categories.

A CBE-30 Supplement requires that an applicant wait at least 30 days following receipt of the submission by FDA before distributing product incorporating the change. This waiting period permits FDA to conduct a cursory review of the supplement to assess if the proposed change has been filed in the proper reporting category and is supported by a sufficient data package to justify its implementation (1,2). Unlike a CBE-30 Supplement, a CBE-0 Supplement does not require a

TABLE 3 Types of CMC Post-Approval Submissions

Submission type	Potential impact on product quality	Implementation
Prior Approval Supplement	Major (substantial)	After approval of submission
CBE supplement--30 day	Moderate	30 days after FDA receipt of submission
CBE supplement—0 day	Moderate	Immediately upon FDA receipt of submission
Annual Report	Minor (low)	Immediately—filed yearly within 60 days of anniversary date of NDA approval

waiting period. Drug substance/product incorporating this category of change can be distributed immediately following receipt of the submission by FDA.

Annual Report

The Annual Report is a periodic, postmarketing submission required by 21 CFR 314.81(2) (other postmarketing reports) (26). From a CMC perspective its purpose is twofold: it provides a reporting mechanism for changes that are considered to have minimal potential to adversely affect the drug product, and it serves as a conduit for providing updates to nonsupplemental postapproval commitments (e. g., stability updates). Unlike changes requiring supplemental applications, annual reportable changes are filed after implementation has already taken place and do not undergo a formal review and approval process. However, FDA has the authority to disagree with a change filed in the Annual Report and require the submission of a supplemental application if the Annual Report filing category is deemed inappropriate for the change or additional information is requested to support the change.

Impact of Revised 21 CFR 314.70 Rule and CANA Guidance

The Food and Drug Modernization Act in 1997 was intended to streamline the regulatory process, and the revised 21 CFR 314.70 rule and CANA Guidance that emerged has accomplished this objective in several areas of CMC changes. For example, a move to a different manufacturing site for a drug substance intermediate can now be reported in an Annual Report, whereas earlier it required the submission of a Prior Approval Supplement.

However, the revised rule and guidance also increased the regulatory burden for other types of changes. For example, a change in a packaging component that controls the dose delivered to the patient (e. g., the valve of a metered dose inhaler) now requires a Prior Approval Supplement, whereas under the original 21 CFR 314.70 rule it was possible to file this change in an Annual Report.

The revised rule and CANA Guidance (Section IV, Assessment of the Effects of the Change) also require that the effects of any CMC changes be assessed by the holder of the application regardless of the submission category required to report the change. Assessment includes evaluation of the postchange product to assure that the changes do not negatively affect the quality attributes of the drug product. This may require additional testing beyond that required by the specifications approved in the NDA. If an assessment concludes that the change has an adverse impact and the applicant still desires to implement the change, then the applicant must file a Prior Approval Supplement for the change, regardless of the recommended filing category for the change being considered.

cGMPs AND CMC POSTAPPROVAL REGULATORY AFFAIRS

The earlier sections described the various submission mechanisms and information requirements for supporting CMC postapproval changes. However, the submission process is not conducted in isolation. Many complementary activities occur before, during, and after the submission to comply with cGMPs, and these activities are described later.

Change Control

Change control is required by 21 CFR 211.180(e) (General Requirements) and entails proper review, assessment, implementation, and adherence to written procedures for making CMC changes (27). A drug manufacturer's change control process is frequently scrutinized by FDA during inspections and is often the subject of objectionable citations in inspection reports. An effective change control system is the foundation for successful management of CMC postapproval changes.

In providing the appropriate regulatory perspective to a change control request from manufacturing, four steps are conducted by the CMC postapproval regulatory affairs professional:

1. Define the change: This may require several iterations of discussion with the manufacturing site in order to understand the change(s) being proposed. For example, a change request may specify that the site is considering a batch size change. This type of change may require related changes to equipment and process. The full extent of the changes must be understood in order to provide comprehensive regulatory advice.
2. Establish the regulatory basis for the change: Once the true extent of the changes is elucidated, the change scenario needs to be evaluated against the context of the approved conditions in the NDA file and current FDA guidance. A small increase in batch size for an immediate-release solid dosage form, with no additional changes, is categorized as an annual report change in section VII.D.1 of the CANA Guidance. If multiple changes are required to attain the increase in scale, section XII (Multiple Related Changes) of the Guidance requires that the filing category be defined for each individual change and the most restrictive filing category applied. If the increase in scale requires adopting equipment of different design and operating principles, a Prior Approval Supplement would be required to implement the sum of the changes.
3. Determine the data and information required to assess and implement the change: This information can be obtained from the various guidance documents issued by FDA that address specific dosage forms and regulatory topics, as well as prior experience with FDA in implementing related changes. In the earlier example, the SUPAC-IR Guidance would provide the information and data package required to support the changes in scale and equipment (3). The guidance document on dissolution testing addresses the considerations in developing and evaluating comparative dissolution profiles to assess the impact of the changes on the release profile of the drug product (7).
4. Provide the appropriate regulatory advice: Once the earlier steps have been completed, a recommendation should be prepared that integrates the regulatory, quality, and commercial aspects surrounding the proposed change(s) to the drug product. It may be as straightforward as communicating the required regulatory submission and the associated data package, or it may require that the change not be progressed at this time due to mitigating circumstances. In the example of the batch size increase, the regulatory affairs professional might be aware that an alternate supplier of the drug substance is being considered. Consequently, it may be prudent to advise the manufacturing site to delay the evaluation of the batch size increase and equipment change for the drug product until a supply of the alternate source of the drug substance is available for concomitant evaluation.

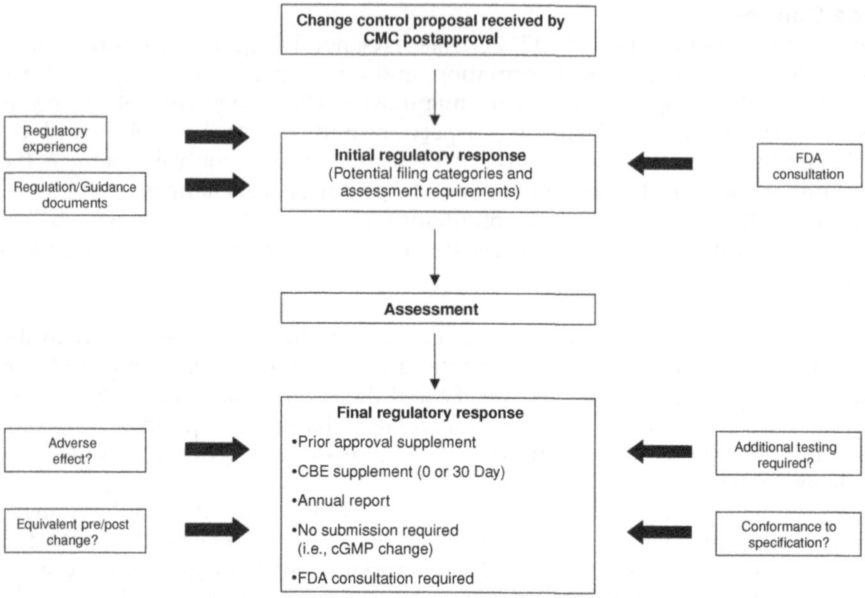

FIGURE 2 CMC regulatory change control—two-stage process.

Occasionally, the filing category cannot be defined until the information and data package required for the submission has been provided for assessment. In this case a two-stage response may be required from the regulatory affairs professional. The initial response describes the submission requirements, regardless of filing category, and includes a statement that the reporting category will be determined when the data and information package has been assembled and assessed. Upon completion of the assessment, a second (final) response is provided confirming the appropriate filing category for the proposed change. A flow diagram of a two-stage regulatory response is provided in Figure 2.

Validation

Postapproval CMC changes that pertain to the manufacturing process or analytical method of a drug substance or drug product may have validation implications. cGMPs (21 CFR 211.100 and 211.160) require that manufacturing processes and analytical methods be appropriately validated (28,29). The implementation requirements of a CMC change may include revalidation of the manufacturing process or analytical method, even if the change does not require a submission. Regardless of whether a submission is required, validation documentation should be available for FDA inspection purposes to support the implemented change.

FDA Inspections

FDA periodically inspects manufacturing and testing facilities for adherence to cGMPs, and inspections may require involvement by the CMC postapproval regulatory professional depending on their purpose. In a general inspection, questions about the regulatory advice provided in a change control proposal may arise, and the regulatory professional must be prepared to respond accordingly. Other inspections may be the direct result of a CMC postapproval submission, in which case the regulatory representative is likely to be a member of the core inspection team or possibly even the inspection team leader. In either case, the regulatory affairs professional must be thoroughly knowledgeable of relevant regulations and submission information, as well as the systems and processes used by the manufacturing site for managing CMC changes. This overview is required to interact effectively with FDA inspectors and facilitate a successful outcome of the inspection.

PERFORMANCE MEASURES FOR CMC POSTAPPROVAL REGULATORY AFFAIRS

The manufacturing environment that is the primary internal customer of the CMC postapproval regulatory affairs professional is monitored by various measurements such as the number of recalls, batch rejects, cost of goods, and utilization of manufacturing capacity. Similarly, a number of performance measures can be used to gauge the activities within CMC postapproval regulatory affairs.

PDUFA Goals and First-Time Approvals of sNDAs

The Prescription Drug User Fee Act of 1992 (PDUFA), which was most recently reauthorized in 2007, defined FDA review targets for manufacturing supplements. Table 4 provides the action dates for supplements reviewed in the fiscal years 2008–2012. These goals are intended for FDA's Office of Pharmaceutical Sciences and provide a level of predictability regarding the timing of feedback and the acceptability of changes filed through supplemental new drug applications (sNDAs). After the review is completed, either an approval letter is issued indicating the supplement is approved or a complete response letter is issued informing applicants or changes that must be made before the supplement can be approved (30). If a complete response letter is issued subsequent to the implementation of a change filed through a CBE or CBE-30 Supplement, generally the manufacturer can continue to distribute the postchange product while addressing the deficiencies unless FDA specifically objects (1,2,19).

While the PDUFA Goals establish guidelines for timely review, a regulatory affairs group is in the business of obtaining approvals, and goals should be set with respect to achieving approval of sNDAs within the PDUFA time frame. A low percentage of first-time approvals is an indication that the sNDAs being filed do not provide a sound regulatory justification for the changes or that an insufficient information and data package is provided to support the changes. It may also signal a poor rapport with the particular FDA reviewer within the Office of Pharmaceutical Sciences that may need to be addressed.

TABLE 4 FDA Review Goals for Manufacturing Supplements

Supplement category	PDUFA goal fiscal years 2008–2012[a]
Prior Approval Supplement	90% reviewed and acted upon within 4 mo
CBE supplement—30 Day	90% reviewed and acted upon within 6 mo
CBE supplement—0 Day	90% reviewed and acted upon within 6 mo

[a]PDUFA of 1992, reauthorized most recently in 2007, provided FDA additional resources for accelerated drug evaluation without compromising review quality.

Submission of Annual Reports

Section 21 CFR 314.81(2) requires that Annual Reports be submitted within 60 days of the anniversary date of the approval of the NDA (26). A CMC postapproval group should strive to collaborate with the manufacturing sites to compile and submit the CMC section of the Annual Reports on time. A consistent trend of providing late Annual Reports or ones that are lacking in sufficient detail may affect the agency's review of related supplemental applications.

CMC Commitments

Both NDAs and supplemental applications are often approved with commitments to provide additional data once the manufacturer has gained a greater level of experience with the drug product and related changes. The postapproval CMC function needs to monitor these commitments and assure that the firm appropriately fulfills its obligations according to the deadline specified by the FDA or proposed by the drug manufacturer.

Continuity of Supply

Situations sometimes arise that may prevent the manufacture of the drug product according to the approved conditions of an NDA. For example, an accident at a packaging site may prevent it from continuing operations, or a supplier of a key component (e. g., drug substance or packaging material) may no longer be able to maintain inventory.

In these situations, the CMC postapproval regulatory affairs professional may be able to negotiate a strategy with the appropriate branch of FDA to quickly restore supply. For example, the Division of Post-Marketing Evaluation may grant Expedited Review of a Prior Approval Supplement for an alternate supplier of the drug substance if the currently approved supplier can no longer manufacture the drug substance. Successful negotiations under these circumstances reflect active engagement by the CMC postapproval regulatory affairs professional.

NDA Conformance

Site inspections conducted by FDA may result in observations of nonconformance to the approved conditions in the NDA. The firm's quality organization may also conduct internal audits to verify site practice and correct conditions of nonconformance to the NDA. These instances typically point to a lapse in communication between the manufacturing site and the CMC regulatory affairs function. A useful measurement of the adequacy of the change control process is to track the number of NDA nonconformance observations resulting from these external and internal audits.

Due Diligence (Divestments)

Pharmaceutical companies seeking to purchase an established product conduct a due diligence exercise prior to purchase to assess the status of the CMC aspects of the NDA file. The buyer seeks to verify that all commitments to the FDA have been met and that there are no regulatory deficiencies that may result in nonconformance or jeopardize supply following the sale. For example, the analytical testing of an older product may not meet current standards such that it may be viewed as a regulatory risk. A product that is well managed by the CMC postapproval

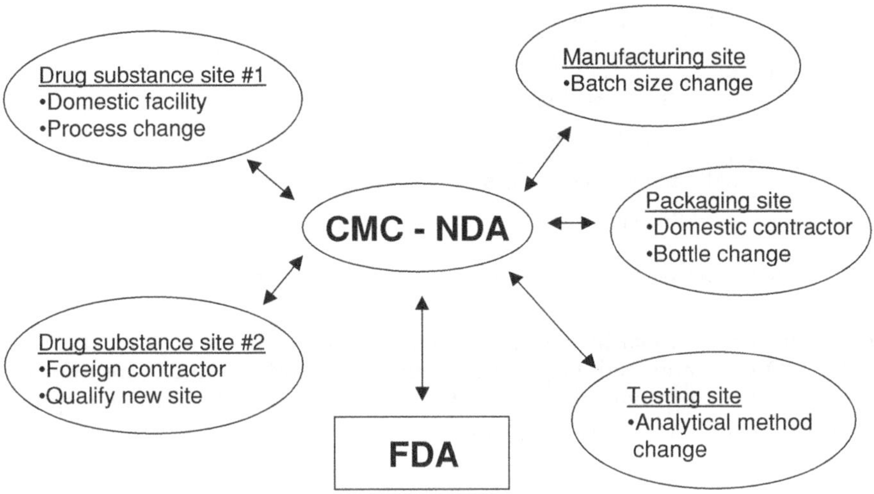

FIGURE 3 Change control in a global supply chain.

regulatory function should facilitate the current application holder's efforts to divest the drug product.

Regulatory Strategies and Cost Savings

In a complex supply chain in which multiple sites supply either the drug substance or the drug product, CMC regulatory affairs may be the only department that has a comprehensive overview of the various changes affecting the NDA. Figure 3 illustrates the number of changes that may be simultaneously affecting a drug product and its active pharmaceutical ingredient in a global supply chain. From this vantage point, the regulatory affairs professional has the opportunity and bears the responsibility to recommend that various changes be assessed concurrently or staged in a reasonable manner. The data required to support CMC postapproval changes often cost tens, sometimes hundreds of thousands of dollars, and it may be possible to evaluate several changes in an integrated set of experiments (e. g., reducing the number of stability studies to evaluate multiple changes through a matrix approach).

DEVELOPMENT OF THE CMC POSTAPPROVAL REGULATORY AFFAIRS PROFESSIONAL

The competencies required for effectively supporting the CMC postapproval regulatory arena differ somewhat from the CMC preapproval arena due to differences in customer base and the types of submissions that are filed to the FDA. Figure 4 depicts the steps associated with the development of a postapproval regulatory affairs professional. These steps are described in greater detail later.

Change Control

Change control is fundamental to CMC postapproval regulatory affairs and is the area in which new personnel should start in order to develop a sound foundation in the field. Addressing change control inquiries from the manufacturing sites requires

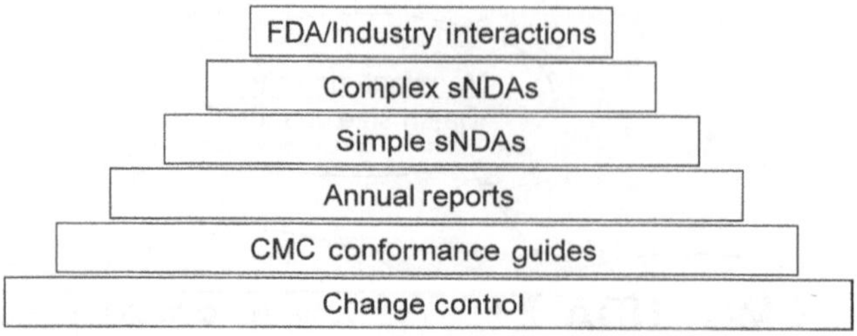

FIGURE 4 Career development in CMC postapproval regulatory affairs.

the regulatory professional to evaluate the change, research the drug product history in the NDA file, and read the pertinent regulations and guidance. This information must then be interpreted and articulated in a succinct, clearly written response to the customer at the manufacturing site.

CMC Conformance Guides

CMC Conformance Guides are a distillation of the conditions approved in the NDA for the drug product and its active ingredient(s). Table 5 is a representative table of contents of a CMC Conformance Guide for a tablet formulation. Compiling a CMC Conformance Guide for a product that has been marketed for several years requires researching the entire NDA file to establish the currently approved CMC conditions. Developing and maintaining CMC Conformance Guides is a worthwhile activity for the regulatory affairs professional. The guides provide a reference tool for both regulatory affairs and the manufacturing sites in determining the regulatory ramifications of proposed changes.

Annual Reports

The compilation of Annual Reports is the next appropriate step for the CMC postapproval regulatory affairs professional. It requires a review of the data and information provided by the manufacturing sites to support the filed changes with a cross-check to the change control advice provided earlier for those changes.

Annual Reports also contain an updated stability profile of the drug substance/product that requires a critical review by the CMC postapproval regulatory affairs professional. The data reported need to be consistent with approved stability protocols and support the approved retest date/shelf life for the drug substance/product while being reported in a format consistent with current FDA guidance (31). Fulfilling this responsibility may require the CMC postapproval regulatory affairs professional to have several iterations of discussion with the manufacturing sites involved with the Annual Report.

Simple sNDAs

Understanding the process and obligations associated with filing the CMC Section of the Annual Report leads to the ability of the postapproval CMC regulatory affairs professional to compile and submit sNDAs. Working on submissions that address a single change (e. g., change in analytical testing site) and progressing to submissions that combine multiple changes (e. g., change in manufacturing site coupled with changes in packaging and testing) is a logical progression. Starting with the less complex type of CMC submission allows the maturing professional to gain an understanding of the review and approval process for sNDAs. Filing a supplemental NDA requires the postapproval regulatory affairs professional to understand the responsibilities associated with being a "responsible agent" for the NDA holder and to begin interacting with FDA personnel, such as project managers and members of the CMC review team.

TABLE 5 Contents for CMC Conformance Guide for Tablet Formulation

I. Product description
  A. Name, dose form
  B. NDA numbers
  C. List of approved pack configurations with NDC codes
  D. Outstanding commitments
  E. Approval date
II. Drug product
  A. Components
  B. Composition
  C. Specifications and analytical methods for inactive components
    1. Inactive components included in the USP/NF
    2. Inactive components not included in the USP/NF
    3. Quality control of inactive components
  D. Manufacturers
    1. Name and address of manufacturer(s), packager(s), tester(s), and what part is done by each
    2. List of DMF references (if any)
  E. Method of manufacture and packaging
    1. Description of the manufacturing process
    2. In-process controls
    3. Reprocessing/Rework operations
    4. Container–Closure system
      a. Bulk product container
      b. Bottles
      c. Child-resistant closures
      d. Blister pack
  F. Specifications and analytical methods
    1. Sampling plan (if any)
    2. Specifications
    3. Description of analytical methods and any alternates
  G. Stability information
    1. Stability protocols
    2. Storage conditions and expiration dating
    3. Other
      a. Commitment for ongoing studies
      b. List of batches for continued monitoring (if applicable)
      c. Analytical methods used during stability studies
III. Index of approved changes
IV. History of changes

Complex sNDAs

With time and experience, the regulatory affairs professional can support very complex supplemental NDAs, such as those requiring a biostudy or biowaiver to gain approval of CMC changes. Examples include reformulation of a drug product or a manufacturing site change associated with a modified-release solid oral dosage form. These complex sNDAs often require meetings with FDA in which the regulatory affairs professional needs to submit a formal meeting request with an accompanying Information Package. The Information Package outlines the issues that need to be resolved and the supporting data that are the basis for discussion at the meeting (32). The regulatory affairs professional is expected to chair the meeting with FDA and to appropriately prepare the project team and direct the dialogue during the meeting to achieve the desired outcome.

FDA/Industry Interactions

After gaining proficiency with complex sNDAs and chairing meetings with FDA, the CMC postapproval regulatory affairs professional likely has achieved the experience, confidence level, and stature to participate in FDA/industry interactions. Activities include giving presentations at professional meetings or assisting in workshops that address CMC regulatory issues. It typically takes several years to progress to this level of development.

THE CMC POSTAPPROVAL REGULATORY PROFESSIONAL AS THE "RESPONSIBLE AGENT"

All regulatory submissions are accompanied by FDA Form 356h signed by the regulatory affairs professional acting as a "responsible agent" for the drug manufacturer (33). The form includes a number of certification statements that define the scope of responsibility associated with this role. They require that the regulatory professional attest to the veracity of the information provided in the supplement and assure that the application complies with all applicable laws and regulations, including adherence to cGMPs. It also includes a reminder that it is a criminal offense to willfully provide fraudulent information.

The role of acting as a responsible agent is what differentiates the CMC regulatory affairs professional from other functional groups involved with compiling and submitting a postapproval application. Although the regulatory affairs professional does not generate the data and information included in a CMC submission, specific measures need to be taken to assure the authenticity of its contents.

Such steps may include reviewing source documentation housed at the manufacturing site, which may not be included in the application. Examples include internal technical reports, supplier specifications, and batch records. The regulatory affairs professional may also conduct a submission audit at the site as a double check prior to submission. These measures provide the necessary checks and balances to assure that the regulatory affairs professional fulfills the associated requisite obligations of the responsible agent while at the same time becoming familiar with the systems utilized by the site to evaluate and support manufacturing changes.

FUTURE OF CMC POSTAPPROVAL REGULATORY AFFAIRS

The SUPAC-IR Guidance issued in November 1995 was the first guidance document that specifically addressed CMC postapproval changes, and it marked the beginning of a transformation in the level of sophistication in this regulatory arena (3). It provided a scientific basis for the evaluation of changes to an approved product and introduced a new vocabulary with which to discuss these changes.

The publication of the SUPAC-IR Guidance coincided with a trend toward consolidation of the pharmaceutical industry that spurred a number of mergers and acquisitions. This often resulted in an overabundance of desired manufacturing capacity for an acquiring or postmerger firm requiring the closure of a number of manufacturing sites. Drug substance/product transfers require active management by the CMC postapproval regulatory affairs function and increase the importance of this role in supporting the manufacturing environment.

A number of business and regulatory drivers will likely continue to increase the complexity and demand for specialized CMC postapproval regulatory affairs support. Developing a new medicine takes 10–15 years and was estimated in 2001 to cost approximately $800 million (34–36). Consequently, time lines are constantly being shortened in the NDA preapproval phase to reduce the time to market. These pressures may result in nonoptimized manufacturing processes or analytical specifications that require postapproval modification. Advances in manufacturing experience and technology provide opportunities to reduce production costs and increase profitability, while consumer preference is ever dynamic and satisfying this need will require continual changes in product presentation to maintain market share.

The regulatory environment also continues to evolve, and several ongoing initiatives will present new challenges for CMC postapproval regulatory affairs:

Pharmaceutical cGMPs for the 21st Century: A Risk-Based Approach

In August, 2002 FDA launched a new initiative entitled Pharmaceutical cGMPs for the 21st Century: A Risk-Based Approach to enhance and modernize the regulation of pharmaceutical manufacturing and product quality (37). The concept is intended to encourage the pharmaceutical industry to adopt modern technological advances and risk-based quality management techniques that focus on critical areas, also known as Quality by Design (QbD). Principles of QbD include process and product knowledge, application of process analytical technologies, and the use of risk assessment and management tools (38,39).

FDA recognizes that the current postapproval regulations reflect a prescriptive approach to regulating manufacturing changes and do not incorporate the risk-based and QbD approaches. FDA is considering revising 21 CFR 314.70, which may provide for regulatory flexibility based on a manufacturer's application of QbD principles. The revised 21 CFR 314.70 may also retain aspects of the current regulations to allow applicants to continue working within the current regulatory structure (40). While current regulations may not incorporate QbD principles, the International Conference on Harmonisation of Technical Requirements for Registration of Pharmaceuticals for Human Use (ICH) has published guidelines that describe tools and approaches for implementation of QbD. These include ICH Q8 Pharmaceutical Development, ICH Q9 Risk Management, and ICH Q10 Pharmaceutical Quality System (41–43).

As part of the cGMPs for the 21st Century initiative, CDER's Office of New Drug Chemistry reorganized in November 2005 to form the Office of New Drug Quality Assessment, which has dedicated pre- and postmarketing groups (44). The

Office of New Drug Quality Assessment launched a new risk-based pharmaceutical quality assessment system intended to facilitate innovation and continuous improvement throughout the product life cycle, provide regulatory flexibility for postapproval changes and streamline the submission and review processes (45).

Globalization of the Regulatory Environment

The efforts invested in the International Conference on Harmonization and the Common Technical Dossier (CTD) continue to make progress in defining global standards for the content and format of regulatory submissions (46–48). Although these advances will initially have their greatest impact on new applications (INDs and NDAs), they will establish a new reference upon which to evaluate and file the changes made after product approval.

Electronic Submissions

FDA has been accepting electronic submissions for a number of years. Effective from January 1, 2008, all electronic submissions to FDA's CDER for INDs, NDAs, Annual Reports, and other documents are required to be in electronic CTD (eCTD) format (49,50); however, paper submissions are still accepted. This poses a challenge to the CMC postapproval regulatory affairs professional to integrate the requirements for eCTD publishing into the manufacturing environment and to reformat existing NDA regulatory files to comply with current specifications for postapproval submissions.

CONCLUSION

Recall that at the beginning of this chapter, the fictional CMC postapproval regulatory affairs professional faced a day of unexpected changes that required urgent attention. Continuing this story, the regulatory affairs professional had to review the CMC section of the NDA files, consult FDA guidance documents, interact with various functional groups within the company, and potentially contact the FDA to address the change scenarios posed by marketing and manufacturing. As the day concluded, the regulatory affairs professional was able to offer a variety of regulatory strategies and time lines to assure timely supply of the drug product and address marketing preferences within the boundaries of the approved conditions of the NDA and current FDA regulations and guidance. Such is a typical day in the career of the CMC postapproval regulatory affairs professional—constantly managing change.

REFERENCES AND NOTES

1. Fed Reg, Vol. 69, No. 68, April 8, 2004, Code of Federal Regulations, Title 21, Part 314.70.
2. FDA, Center for Drug Evaluation and Research, Changes to an Approved NDA or ANDA, Guidance Document (Apr. 2004).
3. FDA, Center for Drug Evaluation and Research, Immediate Release Solid Oral Dosage Forms: Scale-Up And Post-approval Changes: Chemistry, Manufacturing and Controls; In Vitro Dissolution Testing; In Vivo Bioequivalence Documentation, Guidance Document (Nov. 1995).
4. FDA, Center for Drug Evaluation and Research, Sterilization Process Validation in Applications for Human and Veterinary Drug Products, Guidance Document (Nov. 1994).

5. FDA, Center for Drug Evaluation and Research, SUPAC-IR Questions and Answers, Guidance Document (Feb. 1997).
6. FDA, Center for Drug Evaluation and Research, SUPAC-SS—Nonsterile Semisolid Dosage Forms; Scale-Up and Post-approval Changes: Chemistry, Manufacturing, and Controls; In Vitro Release Testing and In Vivo Bioequivalence Documentation, Guidance Document (June 1997).
7. FDA, Center for Drug Evaluation and Research, Dissolution Testing of Immediate Release Solid Oral Dosage Forms, Guidance Document (Aug. 1997).
8. FDA, Center for Drug Evaluation and Research, Extended Release Oral Dosage Forms: Development, Evaluation, and Application of In Vitro/In Vivo Correlations, Guidance Document (Sept. 1997).
9. FDA, Center for Drug Evaluation and Research, SUPAC-MR: Modified Release Solid Oral Dosage Forms: Scale-Up and Post-approval Changes: Chemistry, Manufacturing, and Controls, In Vitro Dissolution Testing, and In Vivo Bioequivalence Documentation, Guidance Document (Oct. 1997).
10. FDA, Center for Drug Evaluation and Research, PAC-ALTS: Post-approval Changes-Analytical Testing Laboratory Sites, Guidance Document (Apr. 1998).
11. FDA, Center for Drug Evaluation and Research, Metered Dose Inhalers (MDI) and Dry Powder Inhalers (DPI) Drug Products: Chemistry, Manufacturing, and Controls Documentation, Draft Guidance Document (Nov. 1998).
12. FDA, Center for Drug Evaluation and Research, SUPAC-SS: Nonsterile Semisolid Dosage Forms Manufacturing Equipment Addendum, Draft Guidance Document (Jan. 1999).
13. FDA, Center for Drug Evaluation and Research, SUPAC IR/ MR: Immediate Release and Modified Release Solid Oral Dosage Forms, Manufacturing Equipment Addendum, Guidance Document (Feb. 1999).
14. FDA, Center for Drug Evaluation and Research, Bioavailability and Bioequivalence Studies for Nasal Aerosols and Nasal Sprays for Local Action, Draft Guidance Document (June 1999).
15. FDA, Center for Drug Evaluation and Research, Container Closure Systems for Packaging Human Drugs and Biologics, Guidance Document (July 1999).
16. FDA, Center for Drug Evaluation and Research, NDAs: Impurities in Drug Substances, Guidance Document (Feb. 2000).
17. FDA, Center for Drug Evaluation and Research, Analytical Procedures and Methods Validation: Chemistry, Manufacturing, and Controls Documentation Draft Guidance Document (Aug. 2000).
18. FDA, Center for Drug Evaluation and Research, Waiver of In Vivo Bioavailability and Bioequivalence Studies for Immediate Release Solid Oral Dosage Forms Based on a Biopharmaceutics Classification System, Guidance Document (Aug. 2000).
19. FDA, Center for Drug Evaluation and Research, Changes to an Approved NDA or ANDA: Questions and Answers, Guidance Document (Jan. 2001).
20. FDA, Center for Drug Evaluation and Research, Statistical Approaches to Establishing Bioequivalence, Guidance Document (Feb. 2001).
21. FDA, Center for Drug Evaluation and Research, Nasal Spray and Inhalation Solution, Suspension, and Spray Drug Products—Chemistry, Manufacturing, and Controls Documentation, Guidance Document (July 2002).
22. FDA, Center for Drug Evaluation and Research, Comparability Protocols—Chemistry, Manufacturing, and Controls Information, Draft Guidance Document (Feb. 2003).
23. FDA, Center for Drug Evaluation and Research, Bioavailability and Bioequivalence Studies for Orally Administered Drug Products—General Considerations, Guidance Document (Mar. 2003).
24. FDA, Center for Drug Evaluation and Research, Requests for Expedited Review of NDA Chemistry Supplements, Manual of Policies and Procedures MAPP 5310.3 (June 1999).
25. FDA, Center for Drug Evaluation and Research, Drug Shortage Management, Manual of Policies and Procedures MAPP 4730.1 (Nov. 1995).

26. CFR, Title 21, Part 314.81(2). Other postmarketing reports—Annual Reports.
27. CFR, Title 21, Part 211.180. Current good manufacturing practice for finished pharmaceuticals—Records and Reports—General Requirements.
28. CFR, Title 21, Part 211.100. Current good manufacturing practice for finished pharmaceuticals— Production and Process Controls—Written procedures, deviations.
29. CFR, Title 21, Part 211.160(e). Current good manufacturing practice for finished pharmaceuticals—Laboratory Controls—General requirements.
30. CFR, Title 21, Part 314.3(b). General Provisions—Definitions.
31. FDA, Center for Drug Evaluation and Research, Format and Content for the CMC Section of an Annual Report, Guidance Document (Sept. 1994).
32. FDA, Center for Drug Evaluation and Research and Center for Biologics Evaluation and Research, Formal Meetings with Sponsors and Applicants for PDUFA Products, Guidance Document (Feb. 2000).
33. CFR, Title 21, Part 314.50(a)5. Content and format of an application—Application form.
34. Pharmaceutical Research and Manufacturers of America,2002 Industry Profile, PhRMA, Washington, DC, 2003.
35. DiMasi JA, Hansen RW, Grabowski HG. The Price of Innovation: New Estimates of Drug Development Costs. Health Econ 2003; 22:151–185.
36. Grabowski H, Vernon J, DiMasi J. Returns on Research and Development for 1990s New Drug Introductions. Pharmacoeconomics 2002 20(suppl. 3):11–29.
37. FDA, Pharmaceutical cGMPs for the 21st Century—A Risk-Based Approach Final Report (Sept. 2004).
38. International Conference on Harmonisation, Pharmaceutical Development Annex to Q8 (Draft Consensus Guideline), (Nov. 1, 2007).
39. FDA, Center for Drug Evaluation and Research, PAT—A Framework for Innovative Pharmaceutical Development, Manufacturing and Quality Assurance, Guidance Document (Sept. 2004).
40. Fed Reg, Vol. 72, No. 3, January 5, 2007, Notices Supplements and Other Changes to an Approved Application; Public Meeting, Docket No. 2006N-0525.
41. International Conference on Harmonisation, Pharmaceutical Development Q8, (Nov. 10, 2005).
42. International Conference on Harmonisation, Quality Risk Management Q9, (Nov. 9, 2005).
43. International Conference on Harmonisation, Pharmaceutical Quality System Q10, (May 9, 2007).
44. FDA, ONDC's New Risk-Based Pharmaceutical Quality Assessment System, http://www.fda.gov/cder/gmp/gmp2004/ONDC_reorg.pdf (accessed Feb. 2008).
45. Fed Reg, Submission of Chemistry, Manufacturing, and Controls Information in a New Drug Application Under the New Pharmaceutical Quality Assessment System; Notice of Pilot Program, Vol. 70, No. 134, July 14, 2005, 40719, Docket No. 2005N-0262.
46. FDA, Center for Drug Evaluation and Research, M2 eCTD: Electronic Common Technical Document Specifications, Guidance Document (April 2003).
47. FDA, Center for Drug Evaluation and Research, M4 Organization of the CTD, Guidance Document (Aug. 2001).
48. FDA, Center for Drug Evaluation and Research, M4 The CTD—Quality, Guidance Document (Aug. 2001).
49. Memorandum 33 to Public Docket No. 92S-0251 http://www.fda.gov/ohrms/dockets/dockets/92s0251/92s0251.htm accessed Feb. (2008).
50. FDA, Center for Drug Evaluation and Research and Center for Biologics Evaluation and Research, Providing Regulatory Submissions in Electronic Format—Human Pharmaceutical Product Applications and Related Submissions Using the eCTD Specifications, Guidance Document (Apr. 2006).

22 Living with 21 CFR Part 11 Compliance

Richard L. Burcham
BPI Technologies, Corp., Irving, Texas, U.S.A.

INTRODUCTION TO FDA 21 CFR PART 11

Introduction

This chapter provides to manufacturers, contract research organizations (CROs), data management centers, clinical investigators, and institutional review boards, recommendations regarding the use of computerized systems in regulated industries. The computerized system applies to records in electronic form that are used to create, modify, maintain, archive, retrieve, or transmit data required to be maintained or submitted to the FDA.

Because the source data are necessary for the reconstruction and evaluation to determine the safety of food and color additives and safety and effectiveness of new human and animal drugs, and medical devices, this is intended to assist in ensuring confidence in the reliability, quality, and integrity of electronic source data and source documentation (i.e., electronic records).

This guidance supersedes the guidance of the same name dated April 1999, and supplements the guidance for industry on *Part 11, Electronic Records; Electronic Signatures—Scope and Application* and the agency's international harmonization efforts when applying these guidances to source data. FDA's guidance documents do not establish legally enforceable responsibilities. Instead, guidances describe the agency's current thinking on a topic and should be viewed only as recommendations, unless specific regulatory or statutory requirements are cited. The use of the word *should* in agency guidances means that something is suggested or recommended, but not required.

What is 21 CFR Part 11 and What Is It Not

21 CFR Part 11 is FDA's ruling on the requirements for the acceptability of records recorded and signed electronically. It covers nearly everything that is created and stored in an electronic form, and it applies to all businesses regulated by the FDA—not just pharmaceuticals.

Part 11 was first introduced in 1997 and is part of FDA's attempt to modernize the regulation and compliance of industries under their auspices. It is widely viewed by FDA as an opportunity for industry to improve business processes as opposed to just another regulatory burden.

These regulations, which apply to all FDA program areas, are intended to permit the widest possible use of electronic technology, compatible with FDA's responsibility to promote and protect public health. The use of electronic records as well as their submission to FDA is voluntary.

In short, 21 CFR Part 11 is not a mandate to replace paper or manual record-keeping systems. If a record is not generated or stored electronically, the ruling does not cover it. What is more, Part 11 is not just another IT exercise, and is not solvable with vendor-supplied software alone. Compliance also requires planning, resource, and process change.

Compliance with Part 11 will require investment in time and capital. It is estimated that the worldwide cost of compliance will range from $1billion to $5 billion. The wide range is further evidence that the FDA must strive for clearer definition of the principles and practices of Part 11.

Do not make the mistake of assuming that this is another unenforceable government regulation. The FDA is very serious about implementation and compliance, and sends out warning letters examples of which can be found on the FDA Web site. These letters are considered as public information.

Background

There is an increasing use of computerized systems to generate and maintain source data and source documentation. Such electronic source data and source documentation must meet the same fundamental elements of data quality (e.g., attributable, legible, contemporaneous, original, and accurate) that are expected of paper records and must comply with all applicable statutory and regulatory requirements. FDA's acceptance of data for decision-making purposes depends on FDA's ability to verify the quality and integrity of the data during FDA on-site inspections and audits.

In 1991, members of the pharmaceutical industry met with the agency to determine how they could accommodate paperless record systems under the current good manufacturing practice regulations in parts 210 and 211 (21 CFR Parts 210 and 211). FDA created a Task Force on Electronic Identification/Signatures to develop a uniform approach by which the agency could accept electronic signatures and records in all program areas. In a February 24, 1992, report, a task force subgroup, the Electronic Identification/Signature Working Group, recommended publication of an advance notice of proposed rulemaking to obtain public comment on the issues involved.

FDA received 49 comments on the proposed rule. Those commenting represented a broad spectrum of interested parties: human and veterinary pharmaceutical companies as well as biological products, medical device, and food interest groups, including 11 trade associations, 25 manufacturers, and 1 Federal agency (2).

In March 1997, FDA issued 21 CFR Part 11, which provides criteria for acceptance by FDA, under certain circumstances, of electronic records, electronic signatures, and handwritten signatures executed to electronic records as equivalent to paper records and handwritten signatures executed on paper.

Highlights of the Final Rule

The final rule provides criteria under which FDA will consider electronic records to be equivalent to paper records, and electronic signatures equivalent to traditional handwritten signatures. Part 11 (21 CFR Part 11) applies to any paper records required by statute or agency regulations and supersedes any existing paper record requirements by providing that electronic records may be used in lieu of paper records. Electronic signatures which meet the requirements of the rule will be considered to be equivalent to full handwritten signatures, initials, and other general signings required by agency regulations (2).

Section 11.2 provides that records may be maintained in electronic form and electronic signatures may be used in lieu of traditional signatures. Records and signatures submitted to the agency may be presented in an electronic form provided the requirements of part 11 are met and the records have been identified in a public docket as the type of submission the agency accepts in an electronic form. Unless records are identified in this docket as appropriate for electronic submission, only paper records will be regarded as official submissions.

Section 11.3 defines terms used in part 11, including the terms: biometrics, closed system, open system, digital signature, electronic record, electronic signature, and handwritten signature.

Section 11.10 describes controls for closed systems, systems to which access is controlled by persons responsible for the content of electronic records on that system. These controls include measures designed to ensure the integrity of system operations and information stored in the system. Such measures include (1) validation; (2) the ability to generate accurate and complete copies of records; (3) archival protection of records; (4) use of computer-generated, time-stamped audit trails; (5) use of appropriate controls over systems documentation; and (6) a determination that persons who develop, maintain, or use electronic records and signature systems have the education, training, and experience to perform their assigned tasks.

Section 11.10 also addresses the security of closed systems and requires that (1) system access be limited to authorized individuals; (2) operational system checks be used to enforce permitted sequencing of steps and events as appropriate; (3) authority checks be used to ensure that only authorized individuals can use the system, electronically sign a record, access the operation or computer system input or output device, alter a record, or perform operations; (4) device (e.g., terminal) checks be used to determine the validity of the source of data input or operation instruction; and (5) written policies be established and adhered to holding individuals accountable and responsible for actions initiated under their electronic signatures, so as to deter record and signature falsification.

Those who use computerized systems must determine that individuals (e.g., employees, contractors) who develop, maintain, or use computerized systems have the education, training, and experience necessary to perform their assigned tasks [21 CFR 11.10(i)]. Training should be provided to individuals in the specific operations with regard to computerized systems that they are to perform. Training should be conducted by qualified individuals on a continuing basis, as needed, to ensure familiarity with the computerized system and with any changes to the system during the course of the study. The FDA recommends that computer education, training, and experience be documented.

Section 11.30 sets forth controls for open systems, including the controls required for closed systems in § 11.10 and additional measures such as document encryption and use of appropriate digital signature standards to ensure record authenticity, integrity, and confidentiality.

Section 11.50 requires signature manifestations to contain information associated with the signing of electronic records. This information must include the printed name of the signer, the date and time when the signature was executed, and the meaning (such as review, approval, responsibility, and authorship) associated with the signature. In addition, this information is subject to the same controls as for electronic records and must be included in any human readable forms of the electronic record (such as electronic display or printout).

Under § 11.70, electronic signatures and handwritten signatures executed to electronic records must be linked to their respective records so that signatures cannot be excised, copied, or otherwise transferred to falsify an electronic record by ordinary means. Under the general requirements for electronic signatures, at § 11.100, each electronic signature must be unique to one individual and must not be reused by, or reassigned to, anyone else. Before an organization establishes, assigns, certifies, or otherwise sanctions an individual's electronic signature, the organization shall verify the identity of the individual.

Since Part 11 does not require that electronic records be signed using electronic signatures, e-records may be signed with handwritten signatures that are applied to electronic records or handwritten signatures that are applied to a piece of paper. If the handwritten signature is applied to a piece of paper, it must link to the electronic record. The FDA will publish guidance on how to achieve this link in the future, but for now it is suggested that you include in the paper as much information as possible to accurately identify the unique electronic record (e.g., at least file name, size in bytes, creation date, and a hash or checksum value.) However, the master record is still the electronic record. Thus, signing a printout of an electronic record does not exempt the electronic record from Part 11 compliance.

Section 11.200 provides that electronic signatures not based on biometrics must employ at least two distinct identification components such as an identification code and password. In addition, when an individual executes a series of signings during a single period of controlled system access, the first signing must be executed using all electronic signature components and the subsequent signings must be executed using at least one component designed to be used only by that individual. When an individual executes one or more signings not performed during a single period of controlled system access, each signing must be executed using all of the electronic signature components.

Electronic signatures not based on biometrics are also required to be used only by their genuine owners and administered and executed to ensure that attempted use of an individual's electronic signature by anyone else requires the collaboration of two or more individuals. This would make it more difficult for anyone to forge an electronic signature. Electronic signatures based upon biometrics must be designed to ensure that such signatures cannot be used by anyone other than the genuine owners.

Under § 11.300, electronic signatures based upon use of identification codes in combination with passwords must employ controls to ensure security and integrity. The controls must include the following provisions: (*i*) The uniqueness of each combined identification code and password must be maintained in such a way that no two individuals have the same combination of identification code and password; (*ii*) persons using identification codes and/or passwords must ensure that they are periodically recalled or revised; (*iii*) loss management procedures must be followed to deauthorize lost, stolen, missing, or otherwise potentially compromised tokens, cards, and other devices that bear or generate identification codes or password information; (*iv*) transaction safeguards must be used to prevent unauthorized use of passwords and/or identification codes, and to detect and report any attempt to misuse such codes; (*v*) devices that bear or generate identification codes or password information, such as tokens or cards, must be tested initially and periodically to ensure that they function properly and have not been altered in an unauthorized manner.

Goals and Expectations

The FDA has released a new Part 11 guidance on electronic copies that outlines seven key principles and practices that the agency advises industry to follow—and its inspectors to scrutinize:

1. Electronic copies of e-records provided to the FDA should be accurate and complete, but they do not necessarily have to be in the same file format and in the same media as the original e-records.
2. The process of making an electronic copy of an e-record in a file format that differs from the original should be validated.
3. Copies of hyperlinked records incorporated by reference should be included with the electronic copy of the electronic record.
4. Electronic copies of database queries should be included with electronic copies of electronic records when appropriate.
5. Electronic copies of electronic records should include, or be appended with, an authentication value.
6. Electronic copies of electronic records should be in a file format and on media that enable the FDA to read and process record data.
7. If the original electronic records were signed electronically, electronic copies of the original electronic records should have electronic signatures that are capable of being authenticated.

The FDA has done this to prevent and detect data falsification in order to ensure that electronic records are reliable. The purpose is to enable data reconstruction that can be checked and verified. Confidence in the data integrity is foremost. As a result, records must be under control of the company, not the individuals. (1)

Implications for Regulated Businesses

FDA recognizes that it will take time for existing systems to attain compliance. This is a major undertaking for regulated industries because all systems generating GxP records are covered in the ruling. For noncompliance situations, FDA will consider the following factors when deciding appropriate corrective action.

- Extent of deviations
- Impact on product quality and data integrity
- Timeliness of planned corrective measures
- Compliance history of establishment

The extent of remediation will be determined by FDA on a case-by-case basis and may include

- acceptance of corrective action plan,
- delay of product approval, and
- halt product shipments.

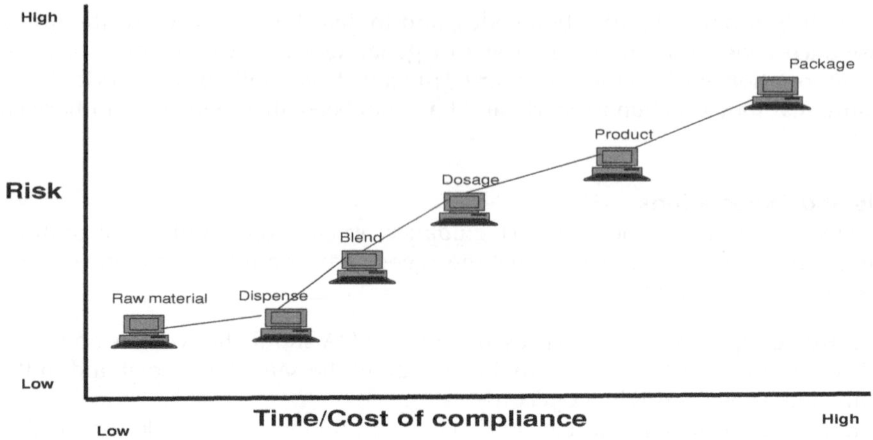

FIGURE 1 Risk escalation. *Source*: From Ref. 4.

FDA warning letters (a. k.a Form 483) relative to electronic records are actively being issued today. Many cite computer systems validation (CSV) and security, and a growing number cite Part 11 specifically. These warning letters, of course, are and will continue to be public record! They can be accessed at www.fda.gov/foi/warning.htm.

PhRMA's response to Part 11 guidance asks for more time or a phased approach over 5 to 10 years. It also requests prioritized remediation based on risk and availability of compliant software. Unfortunately, FDA disagrees strongly and will continue to aggressively issue warnings.

The risk grows at each stage of the process where computer systems are used to manage the production process for regulated industries. An illustration of this for process manufacturing is shown in Figure 1.

Given the potential for escalating risk, most companies are scrambling to hire expertise to get systems running in the short run. In the long run, they are developing in-house expertise. Companies must change their processes and learn to "think" like a regulator while keeping in mind that compliance is a continuous process. What's more, companies must demonstrate to the FDA that they have control over all changes.

UNDERSTANDING THE PART 11 RULING

Archiving Data and Part 11 Compliance

As discussed earlier, Subpart B of Part 11 is broken down into three major sections.

1. 11.10 Controls for Closed Systems
2. 11.50 Signature Manifestations
3. 11.70 Signature/Record Linking

Each of these sections will be discussed in detail but first a few common definitions are needed.

Definitions

There are several terms used in the Part 11 ruling that need to be defined and understood in order to interpret compliance requirements. Interpretation of Part 11 centers on the following terms.

Definition—Electronic Record (ER)

"Any combination of text, graphics, data, audio, pictorial or other information representation in digital form that is created, modified, maintained, archived, retrieved, or distributed by a computer system." (2)

Definition—Electronic Signature (ES)

"A computer data compilation of any symbol or series of symbols, executed, adopted, or authorized by an individual to be the legally binding equivalent of the individual's handwritten signature."(2)

Definition—Biometrics and Digital Signatures

Biometrics

"A method of verifying an individual's identity based on the individual's physical feature(s) or repeatable action(s) where those features and/or actions are both unique to that individual and measurable."(2)

Digital Signature

"An electronic method of signing electronic records based on cryptographic techniques of authentication that enables the verification of the identity of the signer and the integrity of the electronic record."(2)

Definition—Closed System

"An environment in which system access is controlled by persons who are responsible for the content of the electronic records on the system."(2)

Definition—Open System

"An environment in which system access is not controlled by persons who are responsible for the content of the electronic records on the system."(2)

Definition—Hybrid System

A "Hybrid System" is defined as an environment consisting of both electronic and paper-based records (Frequently Characterized by Handwritten Signatures Executed on Paper). A very common example of a Hybrid System is one in which the system user generates an electronic record using a computer-based system (e-batch records, analytical instruments, etc.) and then is require to sign that record as per the Predicate Rules (GLP, GMP, and GCP). However, the system does not have an electronic signature option, so the user has to print out the report and sign the paper copy. Now he has an electronic record and a paper/handwritten signature. The "system" has an electronic and a paper component, hence the term, hybrid.

Understanding Section 11.10 Controls for Closed Systems

According to the ruling "Persons who use closed systems to create, modify, maintain, or transmit electronic records shall employ procedures and controls designed to ensure the authenticity, integrity, and, when appropriate, the confidentiality of electronic records, and to ensure that the signer cannot readily repudiate the signed record as not genuine."

Section 11.10 goes on to define what types of controls need to be in place for closed loop systems.

a. Systems must be validated.
b. Copies of records must be provided to the FDA.
c. Protection of records must be done throughout the retention period.
d. Limited access to the electronic records must exist.
e. All audit trails must be recorded.
f. There must be operational system checks.
g. Controls must be in place for user authority.
h. Device source controls must be in use.
i. Users must be trained on requirements.
j. Policies must exist for electronic signatures.
k. There must be controlled access to documentation.

The closed loop system must have the ability to generate and complete copies of records in both human readable and electronic form. What's more, it must be suitable for inspection, review, and copying by the agency. Records must be protected to enable their accurate and ready retrieval throughout the records retention period.

The agency agrees that providing exact copies of electronic records in the strictest meaning of the word "true" may not always be feasible. FDA, nonetheless, believes that it is vital that copies of electronic records provided to the agency be accurate and complete. Accordingly, in 11.10(b) the original language "true" has been replaced with "accurate and complete." The agency expects that this revision should obviate the potential problems noted in the draft comments. The revision should also reduce the costs of providing copies by making clear that firms need not maintain obsolete equipment in order to make copies that are "true" with respect to format and computer system.

How we store data is just as important as the information it contains. As an example, consider the 1986 BBC Doomsday Project. Text, pictures, documents, video, audio, etc. were all recorded on "state of the art" laser disks. One would expect that this would pass FDA Part 11 compliance. Unfortunately, 21 years later these electronic records are now "unreadable." What's more, who has a laser disk reader? The lesson learned is that organizations must look forward as much as possible when deciding on how they are going to manage electronic records. Obviously, the ability to perform migration as technology changes is a fundamental requirement (3).

The question arises as to just how long of a lifetime does the FDA expect an electronic record to have? Relative to regulatory compliance, is the time frame equal to the lifetime of the product + X years? Or is it the statue of limitations on intellectual property: 17 years, legal-statute of limitations? These are issues that still need to be clearly defined.

Also clouding the lifetime issue is the fact that there are many different types of electronic data. So, should the lifetime be different for each data type? Again, no clear answer. Included among the many different types of electronic data are:

Common data types	Rich data types
1. Images	1. Chemical structures/reactions
a. JPEG	a. MOL
b. GIF	b. SDF
c. TIF	c. PDB
d. Etc.	d. Etc.
2. ASCII text	2. Instrument applications
a. CSV	a. Vendor equipment specific
b. Etc.	
3. Web pages	3. Office applications
a. HTML	a. Documents
b. ASP	b. Spreadsheets
c. PHP	c. PDF
d. DHTML	d. Presentations
	e. Etc.

In particular, rich data types present an archiving problem because storage formats are often proprietary. Consequently, data is only accessible via specialized software applications and may be platform specific including proprietary operating systems, databases, and software versions. There are also concerns with application integration. That is, is it practical and/or possible to broadly distribute specialized applications software for accessing the data? Lastly, rich data types have more finite lifetimes than common data types—for example, will the specialized applications still be available, supported, and operational throughout the lifetime of the data?

Fortunately, FDA realizes that it must provide guidance on these issues. In a September 5, 2002, statement, FDA provided additional guidance for maintenance of electronic records. FDA defined two acceptable practices:

1. "Time Capsule" Approach
   a. Preserve exact computing environment hardware and software.
   b. FDA admits that this is only viable as a short-term solution.
2. "Data Migration" Approach
   a. Translate and migrate data forward as computer technology changes.
   b. Viable long-term strategy
   c. In the migration approach, the new computer system should enable organizations to search, sort, and process information in the migrated electronic record at least at the same level as what could be attained in the old system (even though) the new system may employ different hardware and software.

Another major requirement of section 11.10 relates to "Security and Authentication." Section 11.10 requires limited system access to authorized individuals only. Authority checks must be used to ensure that only authorized individuals can use the system, electronically sign a record, access the operation or computer system input or output device, alter a record, or perform the operation at hand. All individuals must have a unique identifier for access, creation, and modification of electronic records.

Many individual data systems already have security capabilities. However, organizations must keep in mind that data archive systems are generally independent of other systems and there likely will be a need to integrate multiple authentication mechanisms. An example would be the need to integrate Oracle/database, MS, Networking, MS Active Directory PKI, and LDAP.

A common misconception about archives and audit trails is that a compliant system can make noncompliant instruments and applications compliant by adding security and audit trail capabilities to the process. The reality is that archiving systems can only audit trail changes made to *their own data.* What's more, archiving systems cannot track/approve specific changes made to rich data types with native applications. Reprocessing, method alteration, and data manipulations are key considerations.

FDA's guidance on archives and audit trails is to use secure, computer-generated, and time-stamped audit trails to independently record the date and time of operator entries and actions that create, modify, or delete electronic records. In short, record changes shall not obscure previously recorded information. Moreover, audit trail documentation shall be retained for a period of at least as long as that required for the subject electronic records and shall be available for agency review and copying.

Understanding Sections 11.50, Signature Manifestations, and 11.70, Signature/Record Linking

Section 11.50 provides guidance on signed electronic records in that such records must clearly indicate:

1. the printed name of the signer,
2. the date and time when the signature was executed, and
3. the meaning (such as review, approval, responsibility, or authorship).

The above items are subject to the same controls as for electronic records. Furthermore, Part 11.70 requires that electronic signatures and handwritten signatures executed to electronic records shall be linked to their respective electronic records to ensure that the signatures cannot be excised, copied, or otherwise transferred to falsify an electronic record by ordinary means.

According to FDA, compliance can be ensured with "Closed Loop" systems where signatures and data can be linked via specific implementations. Unfortunately, current implementations are generally proprietary and there is a lack of industry standards in this area. Also, migration will be difficult with large volume of data. However, this *is* where we are today.

ACHIEVING COMPLIANCE—COMPLIANCE ENABLING TECHNOLOGIES

Compliance and Flexibility

Electronic records and/or signatures must meet several conditions in order to be acceptable as an alternative to a paper record or handwritten signature. These conditions are necessary to permit the agency to protect and promote the public health. For example, FDA must retain the ability to audit records to detect unauthorized modifications, to detect simple errors, and to deter falsification.

Whereas there are many scientific techniques to show changes in paper records (e.g., analysis of the paper, signs of erasures, and handwriting analysis), these methods do not apply to electronic records. For electronic records and submissions to have the same integrity as paper records, they must be developed, maintained, and used under circumstances that make it difficult for them to be inappropriately modified. Without these assurances, FDA's objective of enabling electronic records and signatures to have standing equal to paper records and handwritten signatures, and to satisfy the requirements of existing statutes and regulations, cannot be met.

Within these constraints, FDA has attempted to select alternatives that provide as much flexibility as practicable without endangering the integrity of the electronic records. The agency decided not to make the required extent and stringency of controls dependent on the type of record or transactions, so that firms can decide for themselves what level of controls are worthwhile in each case.

For example, FDA chose to give firms maximum flexibility in determining: (*i*) The circumstances under which management would have to be notified of security problems, (*ii*) the means by which firms achieve the required link between an electronic signature and an electronic record, (*iii*) the circumstances under which extra security and authentication measures are warranted in open systems, (*iv*) when to use operational system checks to ensure proper event sequencing, and (*v*) when to use terminal checks to ensure that data and instructions originate from a valid source.

As a rule of thumb, for records required to be maintained but not submitted to the agency, persons may use electronic records in lieu of paper records or electronic signatures in lieu of traditional signatures, in whole or in part, provided that the requirements of Part 11 are met.

For records submitted to the agency, persons may use electronic records in lieu of paper records or electronic signatures in lieu of traditional signatures, in whole or in part, provided that:

1. The requirements of Part 11 are met, and
2. The document or parts of a document to be submitted have been identified in public docket no. 92 S—0251 as being the type of submission the agency accepts in electronic form. This docket will identify specifically what types of documents or parts of documents are acceptable for submission in electronic form without paper records and the agency receiving unit(s) (e.g., specific center, office, division, branch) to which such submissions may be made. Documents to agency receiving unit(s) not specified in the public docket will not be considered as official if they are submitted in electronic form; paper forms of such documents will be considered as official and must accompany any electronic records. Persons are expected to consult with the intended agency receiving unit for details on how (e.g., method of transmission, media, file formats, and technical protocols) and whether to proceed with the electronic submission (2).

STANDARD OPERATING PROCEDURES

Standard operating procedures (SOPs) and documentation pertinent to the use of a computerized system should be made available for use by appropriate study personnel at the clinical site or remotely and for inspection by FDA. The SOPs should include, but are not limited to, the following processes:

- System setup/installation (including the description and specific use of software, hardware, and physical environment and the relationship);

- System operating manual;
- Validation and functionality testing;
- Data collection and handling (including data archiving, audit trails, and risk assessment);
- System maintenance (including system decommissioning);
- System security measures;
- Change control;
- Data backup, recovery, and contingency plans;
- Alternative recording methods (in the case of system unavailability);
- Computer user training; and
- Roles and responsibilities of sponsors, clinical sites, and other parties with respect to the use of computerized systems in the clinical trials.

STRATEGIES FOR IMPLEMENTATION

We have discussed the rules and guidelines of the Part 11 ruling but the question is: How do organizations comply? Most technologies, as mentioned earlier, are proprietary, nonglobal, and lack universal standards to be an effective means for Part 11 compliance.

However, XML or extensible markup language is one exception in that industry and government worldwide as a means of compliance have embraced it.

What Is XML and What Is the Role of Extensible Markup Language?

XML is a standardized representation for data content. It is used for text, instrumentation data, and application integration. What's more, it is not proprietary and was developed and is supported by the W3 C, a nonprofit consortium. There are several standards developed by the W3 C that relate to XML including schema definition, style sheet and transformation, and search capabilities—all of which make it easier to comply with Part 11.

Extensible Markup Language is global in scope and according to a recent survey; over 95% of Life Sciences executives responding said that they are currently planning to deploy XML as part of their R&D strategy. Nearly all said that they expect to be employing XML by 2010 (Fig. 2) (4).

What's more, XML has the support of FDA and according to Software Quality Assurance (SQA) Computer Validation Initiative Committee (CVIC) meeting 6/10/97 with Paul Motise (FDA): "The problem of system obsolescence can be solved by careful migration from one electronic file format and platform to another. E-commerce and e-government are moving toward, not away from, common e-record formats that are interoperable on many different platforms. Consider the rise of XML, for example."

Extensible Markup Language can be used to represent any type of data and it is specifically designed for strong typing of rich data—thereby solving some of the rich data problems discussed earlier in this chapter. Furthermore, XML is platform independent, which simplifies distribution and forward migration to avoid obsolescence. XML is extensible; a requirement to support future data types; and it is a public domain standard. Perhaps most importantly, it allows data models to be made available to anyone, but be "closed" to interpretation—a key Part 11 requirement.

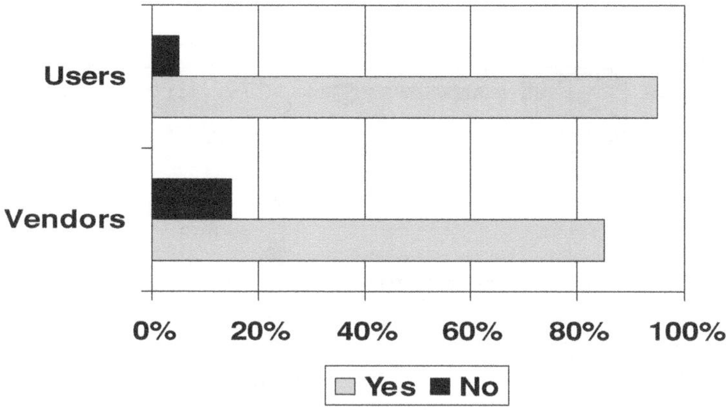

FIGURE 2 XML in life sciences. *Source*: "XML in the Life Sciences", 2007 BPI Research Center.

Extensible Markup Language can satisfy electronic data collection requirements of Part 11 as well. XML schemas exist for all instrument data types, and different archiving systems may be implemented for different data types such as:

1. analytical and laboratory instruments,
2. chemical structures/reactions,
3. clinical trials/studies, and
4. documents.

Application integration, internal or external to your organization, can be accomplished through the exchange of data and transaction instructions as XML. This has wide industry support in Life Sciences as well as with application vendors. Practically, everyone and everything is involved with web services making application integration, for the purposes of Part 11 compliance, both feasible and achievable. (3)

All of the major application and database vendors are committed to XML and web support including IBM, Hewlett-Packard, Sun Microsystems, Oracle, Microsoft, SAP, etc. The languages supported include Java, C, C++, Python, Perl, and Microsoft languages (VB, C#, etc.) Supporting platforms include NET, J2EE, Apache, Zope, etc; and operating systems include Unix (Solaris, Linux, etc.), Windows, MacOS X, etc.

In short, companies have a wide selection of technologies utilizing XML with which to achieve ongoing Part 11 compliance.

Example of Part 11 Compliance

Discussed later is an example of how Part 11 compliance can be achieved even when two separate companies are working together on a common project but with different systems and technologies. In this example, a CRO is collaborating with a pharmaceutical company to research a new product (4).

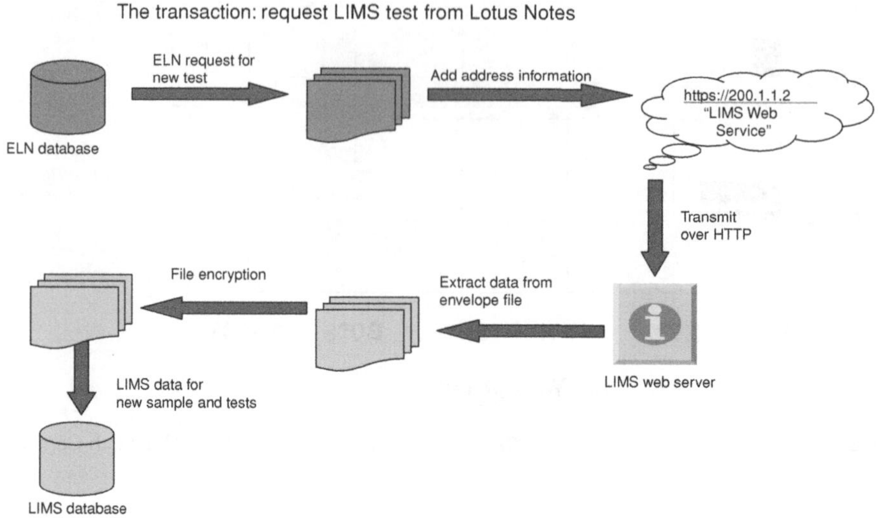

FIGURE 3 Example from Part 11 compliance.

Assumptions:

1. A CRO based in the United Kingdom is working on a research project with a pharmaceutical company in the United States.
2. The CRO uses Lotus Notes ELN authoring application.
3. The pharmaceutical company uses Thermo LabSystems Nautilus LIMS and eRecordManager.
4. The companies worked separately over the web to develop system interfaces.

Transaction process:

Step 1: ELN user at CRO in the United Kingdom logs in and creates a sample request in the LIMS of the Pharmaceutical Company—this is done directly from the ELN and the user has no awareness that the request was sent to the LIMS.

Step 2: LIMS user logs in, sees the request, and processes the sample request—Analysis results are entered directly into LIMS, and eRM automatically captures the chromatogram. The LIMS user has no idea that the sample request came from the CRO's ELN.

Step 3: The ELN user at the CRO refreshes his screen/page and the analysis results and chromatogram automatically appears—The chromatogram can be zoomed using an XML enabled plug-in and data are pulled from LIMS and eRM systems using XML.

The set of transactions is illustrated in Figure 3.

The only thing that needs to be added to this set of transactions for Part 11 compliance is electronic signatures—that is, the electronic record criteria of Part 11 has been satisfied. There are two criterions that must be added to the electronic record of this transaction in order to be compliant with electronic signatures.

1. Identifying information for the individual and date/time.
2. Connective links to the information that was signed.

Implementation of the first criterion requires authentication of the individual. This can be satisfied in a variety of ways including passwords and digital codes of identification and the printed name of the signer; the date and time that the signature was executed and the meaning such as review, approval, responsibility, or authorship.

Implementation of the second criterion requires encrypting hash calculation of data and signature; requires strong encryption algorithm (i.e., SHA); and, at a minimum, it requires a private digital key. Public/private key mechanisms can also be used.

The technologies available for electronic signatures are largely application specific in that many Part 11 applications have internal signature-data linking. However, the proprietary nature of these applications makes forward migration of data & signature difficult, if not impossible. There are also commercial packages available including Verisign, Entrust, ValiCert, Microsoft (Passport), and Liberty Alliance. However, perhaps the best solution for all of the reasons previously discussed is to use the public domain—that is, XML Signature Encryption.

The final step to make the above example Part 11 compliant is archiving the transaction. Archiving systems must be implemented as "closed" systems. By this FDA guidance calls for:

- Record validity must not be challenged.
- Inseparability of data, audit trail, e-signatures, etc.
- Must be maintained when moving from application-specific implementations to more open technologies (e.g., XML Signature).

With respect to infrastructure, the FDA's focus is on "system security," not on "application" security. Specifically, they are interested in whether or not the records are stored so that only the "system" has access—no back doors, and, that tampering can be detected.

BENEFITS OF 21 CFR PART 11 TO ORGANIZATIONS

Because the Part 11 affects such a broad range of industries, no data currently exist to estimate precisely the total number of entities that will potentially benefit from the rule, but the number is substantial. For example, within the medical devices industry alone, the Small Business Administration estimates that over 3221 firms are small businesses (i.e., have fewer than 500 employees). Small Business Administration also estimates that 504 pharmaceutical firms are small businesses with fewer than 500 employees. Of the approximately 2204 registered blood and plasma establishments that are neither government owned nor part of the American Red Cross, most are nonprofit establishments that are not nationally dominant and thus may be small entities as defined by the Regulatory Flexibility Act (2).

Not all submissions to FDA will immediately be acceptable electronically, even if the submission and the electronic record conform to the criteria set forth in this rule. A particular required submission will be acceptable in electronic form only after it has been identified to this effect in public docket 92 S–0251. (The agency unit that can receive that electronic submission will also be identified in the docket.)

Thus, although all entities subject to FDA regulations are potentially affected by this rule, the rule will actually only benefit those that (*i*) are required to submit records or other documents that have been identified in the public docket as acceptable if submitted electronically, and (*ii*) choose this method of submission, instead of traditional paper record submissions. The potential range of submissions includes such records as new drug applications, medical device premarket notifications, food additive petitions, and medicated feed applications. FDA will consider these and all other required submissions as candidates for optional electronic format.

Although the benefits of making electronic submissions to FDA will be phased in over time, as the agency accepts more submissions in electronic form, firms can, upon the rule's effective date, immediately benefit from using electronic records/signatures for records they are required to keep, but not submit to FDA. Such records include, but are not limited to, pharmaceutical and medical device batch production records, complaint records, and food processing records.

What's more, as stated earlier in this chapter, the activities regulated by this rule are voluntary—no entity is required by this rule to maintain or submit records electronically if it does not wish to do so. Presumably, no firm (or other regulated entity) will implement electronic record keeping unless the benefits to that firm are expected to exceed any costs (including capital and maintenance costs). Thus, the industry will incur no net costs as a result of this rule.

Ultimately, the rule will permit regulated industry and FDA to operate with greater flexibility, in ways that will improve both the efficiency and the speed of industry's operations and the regulatory process. At the same time, it ensures that individuals will assign the same level of importance to affixing an electronic signature, and the records to which that signature attests, as they currently do to a handwritten signature.

Benefits and Costs

Compliance is just one of the benefits. Some of the other perceived and actual benefits experienced by life sciences companies include: (2,4)

- better quality control,
- cost reduction associated with reduced product loss,
- dramatically simplifies the management processes required for compliance,
- able to search and find records in a fraction of the time,
- minimized compliance-related headcount,
- always prepared for FDA inspections,
- minimized human error,
- reductions in entry errors,
- implements a solution quickly without disrupting the organization,
- improved ability to analyze trends and problems,
- improved data integrity and accountability controls,
- increased speed of information exchange,
- reduced cost for storage and control of records,
- faster and more efficient FDA reviews and approvals of FDA-regulated product,
- reductions in system vulnerability and abuse,
- lower regulatory or compliance-driven costs,
- shorten validation time,
- reduces the costly time delays associated with lengthy approval cycles,

- reduction in costs related to record retention,
- and more.

There may be some small organizations that currently submit records on paper, but archive records electronically. These entities will need to ensure that their existing electronic systems conform to the requirements for electronic record keeping described in this rule. Once they have done so, however, they may also take advantage of all the other benefits of electronic record keeping. Therefore, no individual small entity is expected to experience direct costs that exceed benefits as a result of this rule.

Furthermore, because almost all of the rule's provisions reflect contemporary security measures and controls that respondents to the advance notice of proposed rulemaking identified, most firms should have to make few, if any, modifications to their systems.

For entities that do choose electronic record keeping, the magnitude of the costs associated with doing so will depend on several factors, such as the level of appropriate computer hardware and software already in place in a given firm, the types of conforming technologies selected, and the size and dispersion of the firm. For example, biometric signature technologies may be more expensive than nonbiometric technologies; firms that choose the former technology may encounter relatively higher costs. Large, geographically dispersed firms may need some institutional security procedures that smaller firms, with fewer persons in more geographically concentrated areas, may not need.

Firms that require wholesale technology replacements in order to adopt electronic record/signature technology may face much higher costs than those that require only minor modifications (e.g., because they already have similar technology for internal security and quality control purposes). Among the firms that must undertake major changes to implement electronic record keeping, costs will be lower for those able to undertake these changes simultaneously with other planned computer and security upgrades. New firms entering the market may have a slight advantage in implementing technologies that conform to this rule, because the technologies and associated procedures can be put in place as part of the general start-up.

There is an additional cost often overlooked that will be incurred as part of compliance—professional skills. If a firm elects electronic record keeping and submissions, it must take steps to ensure that all persons involved in developing, maintaining, and using electronic records and electronic signature systems have the education, training, and experience to perform the tasks involved.

The level of training and experience that will be required depends on the tasks that the person performs. For example, an individual whose sole involvement with electronic records is infrequent might only need sufficient training to understand and use the required procedures. On the other hand, an individual involved in developing an electronic record system for a firm wishing to convert from a paper record-keeping system would probably need more education or training in computer systems and software design and implementation. In addition, FDA expects that such a person would also have specific on-the-job training and experience related to the particular type of records kept by that firm.

The relevant education, training, and experience of each individual involved in developing, maintaining, or using electronic records/submissions must be documented. However, no specific examinations or credentials for these individuals are required by the rule.

COMPUTER SYSTEMS VALIDATION

CSV Overview

FDA-regulated companies are very familiar with a variety of validation processes ranging from full process and facilities validation to that of qualifying individual utilities, equipment, instruments, and everything in between. When it comes to 21 CFR Part 11 and CSV, however, regulated companies are purchasing configurable electronic quality management systems from software manufacturers that may have little or no experience with validation. This is especially important since the vendor is responsible for managing the ongoing development and maintenance of the system.

The use of vendor-supplied "off-the-shelf" configurable software offers many challenges to validation, including supplier audits. A knowledgeable and "validation-ready" supplier can make the process much easier and faster. To this extent, regulated companies must continually educate themselves about validation of computer systems for electronic documentation management as applied in 21 CFR Part 11. FDA's expectations for Part 11 compliance and validation of computer systems were seen initially in the FDA 483 s and warning letters issued during inspections.

Now we are operating within the new FDA enforcement discretion under the September 2003 Guidance for Industry; Part 11, Electronic Records; Electronic Signatures—Scope and Application.

This chapter will provide an overview of CSV and what FDA is requiring companies to do to become and remain compliant.

Validation Realities

FDA's interpretation of 21 CFR Part 11 for inspections of computer systems and computer validation has been refocused through the Scope and Application to emphasize predicate regulation record requirements and shift the emphasis to documented risk assessment of each company's particular circumstances. Compliance will remain a part of routine FDA inspections based on predicate regulations, including validation.

Software development methodologies, standards, and guidelines have been available for 30 to 40 years. There is no excuse for developers of configurable "off-the-shelf" software not to be capable of validation and 21 CFR Part 11 compliance. FDA has emphasized that software/engineering principles can be applied to, and are an integral part of, the system development life cycle (SDLC). Software and system development and testing are part of the SDLC.

Software and computer system life cycle principles in a GxP setting should be supported by a corporate CSV policy with supporting global SOPs for the SDLC, Validation, Supplier Assessment and Audits, Change Control, and Revalidation—along with local SOPs for specific systems.

Corporate CSV policy should be in place and empower a CSV Committee and a Systems QA Planning process.

Verification answers the question: "Was the product built right?" and Validation answers the question: "Was the right product built right?"

Current FDA Expectations—21 CFR Part 11 and Validation

21 CFR Part 11 was developed to set standards for systems containing electronic records and electronic signatures. Inherent in 21 CFR Part 11 compliance is validation of the system used within its current operating environment.

Under the 2003 Guidance for Industry; Part 11, Electronic Records; Electronic Signatures—Scope and Application, "Persons must still comply with all applicable predicate rule requirements for validation [e.g., 21 CFR 820.70(i)]."

Also, "We recommend that you base your approach on a justified and documented risk assessment and a determination of the potential of the system to affect product quality and safety and record integrity."

Finally, "For further guidance on validation of computerized systems, see FDA's Guidance for Industry and FDA Staff CDRH "General Principles of Software Validation" and industry guidance such as the "GAMP4 Guide for Validation of Automated Systems" (6).

FDA In-house Training and Industry Education

Training for Investigators has expanded since the promulgation of 21 CFR Part 11, focused on evaluation of CSV. Martin Browning provided input into the design of the training program prior to his retirement from FDA and conducted the training through his company, EduQuest, Inc., including Janis Halverson, a former FDA expert on CSV. The primary purpose of the course was to provide FDA personnel (across all program areas) with a greater knowledge of computer system development and validation so as to provide a more consistent and thorough approach to investigation of these systems.

FDA insists that computer systems must be validated through a development life cycle containing strict guidelines with concept, user and functional requirements and design phases, followed by the implementation and testing with qualification protocols.

Since the promulgation of 21 CFR Part 11, extensive education and training programs on software/system development and validation have been promoted in the FDA industry. Initially, Martin Browning provided the FDA compliance training to industry audiences. Now online training through FDA's Virtual University is available. International Society for Pharmaceutical Engineering's (ISPE) Good Automated Manufacturing Practice (GAMP) offers education and training (see www. ispe.org). In addition, professional organizations such as PDA and IVT offer courses along with other organizations and consultants in the field.

GAMP: The "V" Model Framework for Specification, Design, and Testing, using IQ/OQ/PQ Qualifications

Basic FDA requirements for CSV include Installation Qualification (IQ), Operational Qualification (OQ), and Performance Qualification (PQ). The "V-Model" diagram shown in Figure 4 is one of the most commonly used methods for representing the "basic" framework for specification, design, and build qualification. This methodology particularly lays emphasis on creating and maintaining a Master Validation Plan, documenting the entire process, while generating system

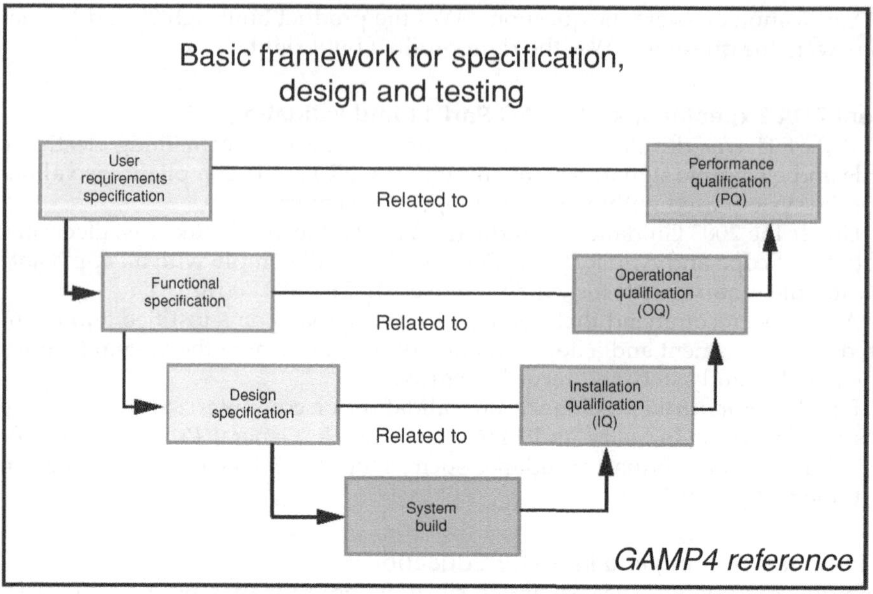

FIGURE 4 GAMP4 V-Model for validation of automated systems.

requirements, design specifications, executing IQ/OQ/PQ qualifications, and maintaining the software after it has been validated.

The "V-Model" was taken from the ISPE's GAMP4 Guide for Validation of Automated Systems, used widely in Pharmaceutical and Medical Device Manufacturing.

GAMP4 is the most widely used, internationally accepted, guideline for validation of computer systems. The GAMP4 guide is now produced by ISPE and its GAMP forum, a technical subcommittee of ISPE. Sion Wyn, GAMP founder, was part of the FDA Part 11 workgroup that developed the 2003 Guidance for Industry; Part 11, Electronic Records; Electronic Signatures—Scope and Application. It referenced industry guidance such as the "GAMP4 Guide for Validation of Automated Systems."

Paul D'Eramo, Executive Director for Worldwide Quality Policy and Compliance Management at Johnson & Johnson, and former FDA investigator, presented the "V-Model" at the ISPE annual meeting in November 2000 in his Part 11 Implementation Strategies presentation. Johnson & Johnson is utilizing the GAMP methodology as an integral part of their computer validation guidelines in their Part 11 compliance program. (For more detailed information and how to obtain a copy of the GAMP4 guide, visit: http://www.gamp.org.)

GAMP4 defines categories of software and the guidance for the CSV approach, as shown in Figure 5. "Off-the-shelf" document control systems fall in category 4—Configurable Software Packages. GAMP4 guide for validation includes a supplier audit and validation of the application and any custom code. The validation of the application is focused on specifications tied to IQ/OQ/PQ qualifications.

Category	*Type of software*	*Validation approach*
1	Operating systems	Record version
2	Standard instruments	Record configuration
3	Standard software packages	Validate application
4	Configurable software packages	Audit supplier, validate application, and any customer code
5	Customer systems	Audit supplier and validate complete system

FIGURE 5 Validation approach for software systems.

In order for FDA to consider configurable software systems to be validated, the following steps in the system life cycle must be followed and documented. All these important elements of validation are presented in the GAMP4 guide in performing "full-cycle" validation services.

- Validation Master Plan
- Risk Management Plan*
- User Requirements Specifications
- Vendor Assessment/Audit, Qualification and Acceptance
- Functional Description and Specification
- Design Specifications
- System Installation Qualification
- System Operational Qualification
- System Performance Qualification
- Validation Summary Report
- System SOPs and Training
- Maintenance, Continuous Monitoring, Change Control, and Corrective and Preventive Action (CAPA)
- Security Measures

Risk-Based Assessment and Risk Management Plans

As both FDA and industry have discovered over the past few years, "a one size fits all" interpretation of regulations, such as 21 CFR Part 11, is not feasible. The agency has decided to put the onus of regulatory interpretation on the organizations that it regulates. This will allow and obligate companies to use a professional "science-based" approach with documented justification through risk management plans.

* The Risk Management Process has been defined through the GAMP4 Appendix M3 and through the FDA-referenced ISO 14971:2000 (Application of Risk Management to Medical Devices) standard

FDA-regulated organizations must now justify their course of action based on their interpretation of the regulations as well as any risk associated with those actions. This has been discussed in the earlier GAMP section and in the guidance document itself (2003 Guidance for Industry; Part 11, Electronic Records; Electronic Signatures—Scope and Application). There are various recommendations for using a documented justification to determine the need and/or extent of implementing certain Part 11 controls or performing certain regulatory activities. At the core of such justification would typically be some form of risk-based assessment with the purpose of targeting potential risks that may adversely affect operations and to document the strategies used to manage or avoid those risks. Documentation may include a formal Risk Management Plan that would detail the risk assessment and the risk mitigation activities during system implementation and IQ/OQ/PQ testing. In regard to Part 11, where predicate rule requirements do not exist, a risk-based assessment may be used to determine the following:

- The critical risk factors
- The need for validation and the extent of testing required
- The need to implement audit trails (or an equivalent control) in the system and the form the audit will take
- The strategy for maintaining records integrity and reliability throughout their record retention period

Risk assessment methodologies are well defined and typically involve identifying hazards and risk scenarios and the consequences of those adverse events. The next step is to classify and prioritize those risks using a number of risk factors. Business and GXP "Impact" is the most critical factor. The factors often used to assess are:

Impact—The severity of the negative impact that will accompany an adverse event. This can be expressed on any scale deemed appropriate (high–low).

Likelihood/Probability—The likelihood of an adverse event occurring. This can be measured on a relative scale such as across a time period or number of operations. (high–low, 1–5)

Detection—The likelihood that a negative condition will be detected before the negative impact occurs.

The purpose of the GAMP4 Guide Appendix M3 is to describe a simple risk assessment process that may be applied to systems to enable targeting of the validation efforts to those areas and functions that most require it.

The following Figures 6(A) and 6(B) represent simple, graphical methods for assessing risk, which have been adapted from that found in the GAMP4 guide. There are many other acceptable methods for performing such assessments including FMEA (Failure Mode and Effects Analysis), FMECA (**Failure Mode, Effects, and Criticality Analysis)**, FTA (**Fault Tree Analysis)**, HAZOP (**Hazard and Operability Analysis**), and HACCP (**Hazard Analysis and Critical Control Point)** analysis.

Risk factors are generally rated on a scale of low, medium, or high, although a wider scale can be used to achieve a finer granularity in classifying and prioritizing the likelihood of risks. There we use a scale of 1 to 5. Once the risk factors are

Business/GxP impact	Risk likelihood: Low (1)	Low (2) to medium	Medium (3)	Medium (4) to high	High (5)
Low	L1	L2	L3	L4	L5
Medium	M1	M2	M3	M4	M5
High	H1	H2	H3	H4	H5

FIGURE 6(A) Risk assessment chart.

Risk classification	Probability of detection: High	Medium	Low
Low	L	L	M
Medium	L	M	H
High	M	H	H

FIGURE 6(B) Risk assessment chart.

determined, the impact and likelihood factors can be cross-referenced as in Figure 3 to achieve a risk classification. A final risk priority can then be determined by cross-referencing the results from Figure 3 with the detection factor in the 2003 Part 11 Guidance—Scope and Application, references ISO 14971:2000, Medical Devices—Application of Risk Management to Medical Devices as a standard for risk methodology. The schematic representation of the risk management process is shown in Figure 7.

The final risk classifications and priorities can be used to make decisions on the need for/extent of validation, the need for/extent of audit trail implementation, and the strategy for record retention. For electronic document management system applications, the risk classification is sufficient.

In determining the need for validation, the risk assessment should generally involve reviewing, at a high level, the major functionalities and usage of the system and the potential health and business risks posed by adverse events based on those functions.

For justifying the extent of validation to be performed, the risk assessment will be similar to the one for identifying the need for validation. The key difference is that this assessment will be much more detailed and includes "digging down" into the subfunctions and user requirements and identifying the potential health and business risks posed by adverse events associated with those functions.

To establish the need for and extent of audit trail functionality required by a system, the risk assessment should generally involve reviewing the potential health and business risks posed by both accidental and intentional adverse events associated with the traceability of and data integrity of the records. To determine the strategy for record retention, the risk assessment should generally involve reviewing the potential health and business risks posed by a loss in value of the records over time.

Consider an automated electronic document management system as a risk assessment example. It is used to store and revise documents; it maintains a database of all documents. Persons in different job descriptions can generate and automatically reference documents. In quality and production systems, the quality management documents include numerous predicate rule documents, such as Master Batch Records, Product Specifications, Test Methods, SOPs, Training Records, and CAPA forms.

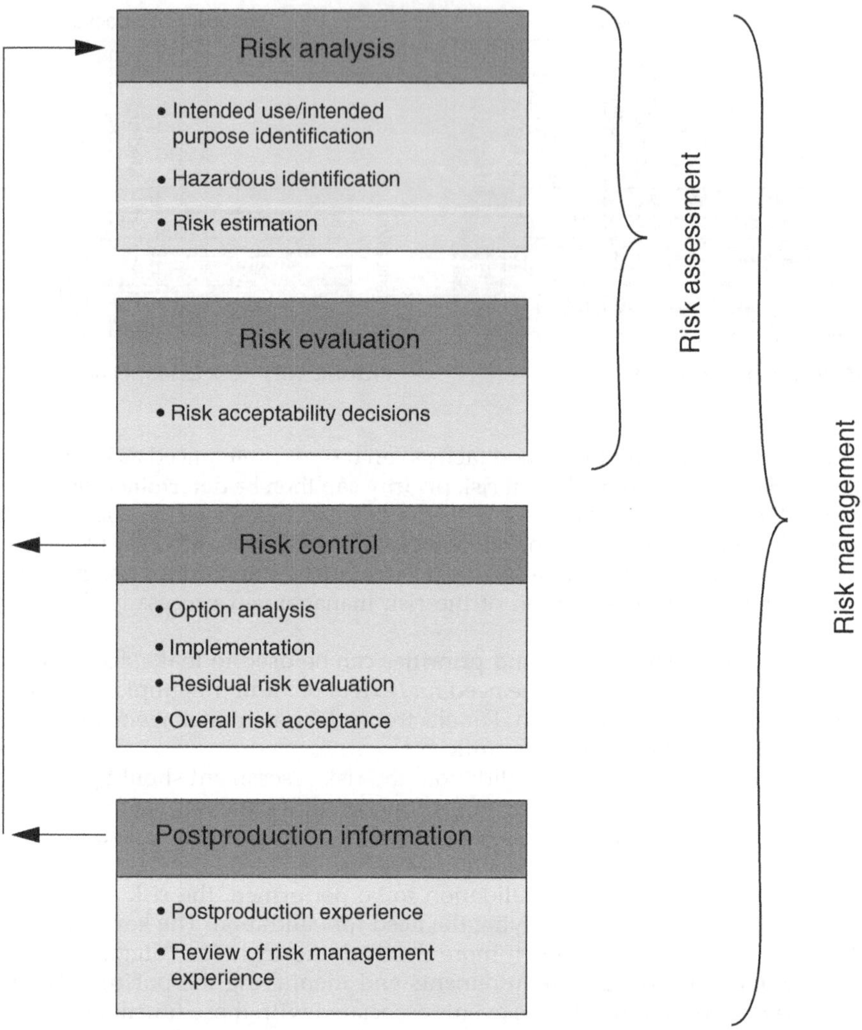

FIGURE 7 Risk management process.

In an FDA-regulated industry, the system is subject to validation requirements. Validation is pertinent under the 21 CFR 820.70(i) reference.

One company that deploys this system is a small biotech pharmaceutical company. Performing risk assessment early and quickly identified that the failure of this system could lead to serious implications, for regulatory risk (inability to demonstrate the necessary control of documents required by 21 CFR 210/211/820), and more importantly, that insufficient control could possibly result in compromise of regulatory documentation and/or the adulteration of the drug. Thus, the "full cycle" of validation with IQ/OQ/PQ was undertaken, as delineated in the GAMP section.

PROBLEMS AND CHALLENGES

The life science industry is under ever-increasing pressure to adhere to FDA rules for process compliancy. Without this critical compliance, these companies are unable to bring products to market and are subject to financial, civil, and potentially criminal sanctions.

With the increasing competition in the market for new products/drugs and the decreases in available staff, and it's clear why these companies need to look to effective methods for ensuring compliance with government policy and procedure while decreasing time-to-market and increasing competitiveness.

The following issues may impact a company in its compliance efforts:

- Improve productivity while reducing product liability.
- Maintain superior-quality performance while conforming to regulatory requirements.
- Protect the integrity of data records.
- Understand what is required for 21 CFR Part 11.
- Spend time and money trying to comply with every process.
- Expensive consulting and customization services.
- Inconvenient Part 11 policies and procedures.

All of these are significant challenges. However, the implementation of a management system helps an organization achieve continuous performance improvement.

REFERENCES AND NOTES

1. Guidance for Industry Part 11, Electronic Records; Electronic Signatures—Scope and Application August 2003.
2. Fed Reg, Department of Health and Human Services, 21 CFR Part 11.
3. Institute of Validation Technology, **Electronic Records and Signatures: The FDA Perspective.**
4. BPI Research Centre, Validation, Compliance and Beyond Updated November 2007.
    - XML in the life sciences, Sillico Research Limited, 2001.

Index

For Product Safety Concerns and Information please contact our
EU representative GPSR@taylorandfrancis.com Taylor & Francis
Verlag GmbH, Kaufingerstraße 24, 80331 München, Germany